CAMBRIDGE
Phrasal Verbs
Dictionary

CAMBRIDGE UNIVERSITY PRESS
Cambridge, New York, Melbourne, Madrid, Cape Town, Singapore, São Paulo

Cambridge University Press
The Edinburgh Building, Cambridge CB2 2RU, UK

http://www.cambridge.org
Information on this title: www.cambridge.org/9780521677707

First published 1997
Second edition 2006

Printed in Italy by Grafica Veneta S.p.A.

A catalogue record for this publication is available from the British Library

ISBN-13 978-0-521-86038-3 hardback
ISBN-10 0-521-86038-5 hardback

ISBN-13 978-0-521-67770-7 paperback
ISBN-10 0-521-67770-X paperback

9510

Cambridge Phrasal Verbs Dictionary

Academic Consultant
Professor Michael McCarthy

Senior Commissioning Editor
Elizabeth Walter

Theme pages and exercises
Julie Moore

Editorial Contributor
Virginia Klein

Illustrations
David Shenton

Previous edition:
Project manager
Glennis Pye

Lexicographers
Stephen Curtis, Ann Kennedy, Kerry Maxwell, Clea McEnery,
Elaine McGregor, Susannah Wintersgill, Kate Woodford

American English Consultant
Carol-June Cassidy

Australian English Consultant
Barbara Gassman

Editorial Contributors
Annetta Butterworth, Dominic Gurney, Lucy Hollingworth,
Geraldine Mark, Jane Reeves

Contents

Introduction

Phrasal verbs are a very important part of the English language. Not only are they used in spoken and informal English, but they are also a common part of written and even formal English.

However, phrasal verbs can seem difficult to learn. Often it is impossible to guess their meanings from the verb and the particle. It can also be difficult to know how to use them in sentences, especially knowing where to put the object. Why can we say '*He got over the shock.*' but not '*He got the shock over.*' ?

The Cambridge Phrasal Verbs Dictionary helps learners of English to understand phrasal verbs and use them in a way that is natural and appropriate. Meanings are explained clearly and simply, and examples show how they are used in context. There is also clear information about how formal or informal phrasal verbs are, as well as common grammar patterns and collocation.

At the end of the dictionary, there are topic pages, which show ways of using phrasal verbs to talk about particular subjects, e.g. health and illness, technology or travel. There are also photocopiable worksheets to use either in class or for studying alone.

Often a native speaker of English would be more likely to use a phrasal verb than a single (often more formal) verb. You can lose marks in exams for failing to use phrasal verbs when they are appropriate, so this dictionary helps in two ways. Firstly, the most common phrasal verbs are printed on blue boxes, to show you that they are important to learn. Secondly, at the back of the book you can find a list of single verbs that have a very common phrasal verb equivalent.

We hope you enjoy using the *Cambridge Phrasal Verbs Dictionary*. You can contact us or look at our other dictionaries on our website at: dictionary.cambridge.org.

How to use this dictionary

Using phrasal verbs in sentences

This dictionary shows you everything you need to know about they syntax of phrasal verbs. This means things like whether they can be separated, and where you can put the object of the verb.

> This phrasal verb is intransitive. It does not take an object.

drift off drifts, drifting, drifted

drift off

to gradually start to sleep • *As Tim started telling her about his holiday for the third time, she closed her eyes and drifted off.*

> This phrasal verb is transitive. The object can be placed after the phrasal verb or between the two parts of the phrasal verb.

flag down flags, flagging, flagged

flag down sth or **flag** sth **down**

to make a vehicle stop by waving at the driver • *A police officer flagged the car down.* • *We tried to flag down a taxi but they were all full.*

> This phrasal verb is transitive. The object can only be placed after the phrasal verb.

see to sees, seeing, saw, seen

see to sth/sb

to deal with something that needs doing or to help someone who needs your help • *The cats need feeding twice a day, but Paula's seeing to that.* • *Would you like any help or are you being seen to?*

> Brackets show that this phrasal verb can be transitive or intransitive.

build up builds, building, built

build up (sth) or **build** (sth) **up**

to increase in amount, size, or strength, or to make something increase in amount, size, or strength • *There were big delays as traffic built up on the roads into the city.*

> This phrasal verb is always followed by an object or by the –ing form of another verb.

see about sees, seeing, saw, seen

see about sth/doing sth

to deal with something, or to arrange for something to be done • *It's getting late – I'd better see about dinner.* • *You should see about getting your hair cut.*

This phrasal verb is always followed by the infinitive form of another verb.

bend over backwards bends, bending, bent

bend over backwards to do sth
to try extremely hard to do something to help or please someone • *She would always bend over backwards to help anyone in trouble.*

This phrasal verb is always used in the passive form.

sandwich between

be sandwiched between sb/sth (always passive) informal
to be in a small space in the middle of two people or things • *Kim was sandwiched between her brothers in the back of the car.*

This phrasal verb is always used in the reflexive form.

fend for fends, fending, fended

fend for yourself (always reflexive)
to take care of yourself without needing help from other people • *She's 83 years old and still fends for herself.*

This phrasal verb is always used in continuous tenses.

die for

be dying for sth (always in continuous tenses) informal
to want something very much, especially food or drink • *Put the kettle on – I'm dying for a cup of coffee.* • *I'm dying for a cigarette.*

X

Grammar patterns

If a grammar note refers to the whole entry it is shown at the beginning of the entry.

Common grammar patterns are also shown next to examples which show them in context.

keep on at keeps, keeping, kept

keep on at sb (never in continuous tenses)
to talk to someone about something many times, usually because you want to complain about something they have done or not done • *I wish she wouldn't keep on at me, it's not my fault.* • (often + **about**) *He keeps on at me about the kind of clothes I wear.* • (sometimes + to do sth) *The boss keeps on at me to sort out the filing system.*

Nouns and adjectives

Nouns and adjectives formed from phrasal verbs are shown after the phrasal verbs they come from.

grow up grows, growing, grew, grown

grow up
1 to gradually change from being a child to being an adult • *She grew up in New Zealand.* • *What do you want to be when you grow up?* • *Learning to take disappointments is all part of growing up.*

grown-up n [C]
a child's word for an adult • *Daddy, why are all the grown-ups laughing?*

grown-up adj
fully developed as an adult, or behaving or appearing like an adult • *The couple, married for 32 years, had four grown-up children.* • *I hadn't seen her for three years and she suddenly looked so grown-up.*

Phrases and collocation

Some phrasal verbs are also used as part of a fixed expression. These are shown in heavy type in the example, and explained in brackets after the example.

get along gets, getting, got
(*American pp* **also gotten**)

get along
1 if two or more people get along, they like each other and are friendly to each other • *Vicky and Ellen seem to be getting along much better these days.* • (often + **with**) *I really don't get along with my sister's husband.* • *We've been getting along like a house on fire.* (= very well)

Common collocations are also shown in heavy type in the example sentences.

go ahead goes, going, went, gone

go ahead
1 to start to do something • *The preparations are complete but we can't go ahead without government money.* • (often + **with**) *We're going ahead with the offer unless we're told we can't proceed.*

go-ahead n (U)
permission for something to start • *The government has given the go-ahead for a multi-billion pound road-building project.* • *We've got to get the go-ahead from our director before we take on more people.*

Frequency

The most common idioms are shown on blue boxes. It is worth trying to learn these idioms.

deal with deals, dealing, dealt

deal with sth
1 to take action in order to achieve something, or in order to solve a problem • *I haven't got time to reply to this letter. Could you deal with it? Emergency services claim they do not have the resources to deal with a major disaster.*

Abbreviations

adj	adjective		*pt*	past tense
n	noun		*pp*	past participle
adv	adverb		esp.	especially
prep	preposition		e.g.	for example
[C]	a noun that can be used in the plural		sth	something
			sb	someone
[U]	a noun that does not have a plural form and cannot be used with *a* or *one*		swh	somewhere
[singular]	a noun that does not have a plural form and can be used with *a* or *the*			
[plural]	a noun that can only be used in the plural form			

Regional labels

British   this phrasal verb is only used in British English

mainly British   this phrasal verb is mainly used in British English

American   this phrasal verb is only used in American English

mainly American   this phrasal verb is mainly used in American English

Australian   this phrasal verb is only used in Australian English

Register labels

informal   phrasal verbs which are used with friends or family or people you know in relaxed situations

formal   phrasal verbs which are used in a serious or polite way, for example in business documents, serious newspapers and books, lectures, news broadcasts etc

slang   phrasal verbs which are used in an informal or not very polite way, often between members of a particular social group

old-fashioned   phrasal verbs which are still used but sound old-fashioned

taboo   phrasal verbs which are likely to offend people and are not used in formal situations

humorous   phrasal verbs which are intended to make people laugh

literary   phrasal verbs which are mainly used in literature

old-use   phrasal verbs which were used before the 20th century but are now rare

abide by   <small>abides, abiding, abided</small>

abide by sth

to accept or obey an agreement, rule, or decision ● *Staff who refused to abide by the new rules were fired.* ● *We are quite willing to abide by their decision, whatever it may be.*

abound in/with   <small>abounds, abounding, abounded</small>

abound in/with sth *formal*

to contain a lot of something ● *Its forest and plains abound with deer and elk.* ● *His later novels abound in plots and schemes.*

accede to   <small>accedes, acceding, acceded</small>

accede to sth *formal*

1 to agree to something that someone has asked for [e.g. request, demand], often after disagreeing with it ● *The government finally acceded to the nationalists' demand for independence.*

2 if someone accedes to the throne or to power, they become king or queen, or they take a position of power ● *The diaries were written in 1837 when Queen Victoria acceded to the throne.* (= became queen) ● *Traidenis acceded to power in 1270 and ruled Lithuania for twelve years.*

accord with   <small>accords, according, accorded</small>

accord with sth *formal*

to be the same as something, or to agree with something ● *His version of events does not accord with the witness's statements.*

account for   <small>accounts, accounting, accounted</small>

account for sth

1 to explain the reason for something or the cause of something ● *Can you account for your absence last Friday?* ● *She was unable to account for over $5000.* (= she could not explain where the money was) ● *'Have you seen that awful dress she's wearing?' 'Yes, I know, **there's no accounting for taste**, is there?!'* (= you cannot explain why some people like the things that you do not like)

2 to form a particular amount of something ● *Students account for about 50% of our customers.*

account for sb

to explain where someone is, especially someone who is lost ● *The army made no attempt to account for the missing men.*

ace out   <small>aces, acing, aced</small>

ace out sb or **ace** sb **out** *American informal*

to defeat someone ● *We were aced out by a rival agency.*

ache for   <small>aches, aching, ached</small>

ache for sb/sth

to want someone or something very much ● *He lay awake, his whole body aching for sleep.* ● *After only two weeks apart she was aching for him.*

act out   <small>acts, acting, acted</small>

act out sth or **act** sth **out**

1 to perform the actions and speech of a situation or story ● *The children were told to act out a verse of their favourite poem.*

2 to express your thoughts or emotions by using words or actions to represent them ● *In therapy sessions children are encouraged to act out their aggressions and talk about their fears.* ● *Playing another character allows you to act out your repressed desires.*

act up   <small>acts, acting, acted</small>

act up

1 *slightly informal* if part of your body or a machine acts up, it stops working properly ● *If my knee starts acting up, I might have to give tomorrow's walk a miss.* ● *My car has been acting up again – I must get someone to have a look at it.*

2 if someone, especially a child, acts up, they behave badly ● *As soon as one of the kids starts acting up, the others follow.*

3 *British* to do a more important job than you usually do for a limited period ● *Junior staff are frequently required to act up but they don't get paid extra.*

add up   adds, adding, added

add up (sth) or **add** (sth) **up**

to calculate the total of two or more numbers • *If you add those four figures up, it comes to over £500.* • *Kids who only ever use calculators to do sums quickly forget how to add up in their heads.*

add up (never in continuous tenses) *slightly informal*

1 to increase and become a large number or amount • *If you put a few pounds away each week, it's surprising how quickly it adds up.* • *You may only be eating a hundred calories here and a hundred calories there, but **it all adds up**.*

2 to be a reasonable or likely explanation for something • (often negative) *So why would she accept a job offering less money and fewer prospects; it just doesn't add up.*

add up to   adds, adding, added

add up to sth

1 to become a particular amount • *The various building programmes add up to several thousand new homes.*

2 to have a particular result or effect • *Trains are frequently cancelled and always late, all of which adds up to a lot of frustration for the passenger.* • *Whether such proposals add up to any real help for the poor remains to be seen.*

adhere to   adheres, adhering, adhered

adhere to sth *formal*

to obey a rule or principle • *Companies failing to adhere strictly to safety guidelines are penalised.*

adjourn to   adjourns, adjourning, adjourned

adjourn to swh *humorous*

to finish something and go to a different place, usually for a drink and some food • *Shall we adjourn to the sitting room for coffee?*

agree with   agrees, agreeing, agreed

agree with sb *slightly old-fashioned*

if new situations or conditions agree with you, they are right for you and make you feel happy • *The sea air seemed to agree with him – he looked fitter than he had in a long time.* • *It's good to see you looking so well – motherhood obviously agrees with you.*

not agree with sb (always negative; never in continuous tenses)

if a type of food or drink does not agree with you, it makes you feel slightly ill • *I tend to avoid onions – they don't agree with me.*

aim at   aims, aiming, aimed

aim at sth/doing sth

to intend to achieve something, or to be intended to achieve something • *We're aiming at a 50% increase in production.* • *This is the latest in a series of talks aimed at settling the conflict.*

aim sth **at** sb

to intend something to influence someone, or to be noticed or bought by someone • (usually passive) *Roughly half of the magazines bought in Britain are aimed exclusively at women.* • *I don't think his remarks were aimed at anyone in particular.*

allow for   allows, allowing, allowed

allow for sth

to consider or include something when you are making plans or judging a situation • *The whole journey should take just over five hours – that's allowing for delays.* • *Even allowing for exaggeration, these reports of human suffering are an appalling tale.*

allow of   allows, allowing, allowed

allow of sth *formal*

to accept that something is possible or correct • *The old woman was too full of energy to allow of their walking slowly on her account.*

allude to   alludes, alluding, alluded

allude to sth/sb *slightly formal*

to mention something or someone in an indirect way • *She mentioned some trouble that she'd had at home and I guessed she was alluding to her son.* • *So what is the dark secret alluded to in the title of Wellbrock's latest novel?*

amount to   amounts, amounted

amount to sth (never in continuous tenses)

1 to become a particular amount • *The cost of treating heart disease and cancer amounts to 100 billion dollars a year.*

2 to be the same as something, or to have the same effect as something ● *He gave what amounted to an apology on behalf of his company.* ● *It remains to be seen whether his threats amount to anything more than tough talk.*

3 to be or become very good or important ● (usually negative) *The changes in the department did not amount to much.* ● *If you don't work hard in school, you'll never amount to anything.*

angle for   angles, angling, angled

angle for sth
to try to get something without asking for it in a direct way ● *I suspect she's angling for promotion.* ● *He's been angling for an invitation all week.*

announce against   announces, announcing, announced

announce against sb/sth *American*
to say publicly that you do not support a particular politician or political party ● *Many show business people have announced against the Republican candidate.*

announce for   announces, announcing, announced

announce for sth *American*
to say publicly that you are going to try to be elected for a particular political position ● *He surprised the whole nation by announcing for the Presidency.*

announce for sb/sth *American*
to say publicly that you support a particular politician or political party ● *The union announced for the Democratic candidate.*

answer back   answers, answering, answered

answer (sb) **back**
if someone, especially a child, answers back or answers someone back, they reply rudely to someone they should be polite to ● *Don't you dare answer me back, young lady!* ● *What shocks me about Terry's kids is the way they answer back.*

answer for   answers, answering, answered

answer for sth
to be responsible for something bad, or to be punished for something bad ● *If the government decides to send all these men off to war, they will have a lot of deaths to answer for.* ● *Do you think parents should have to answer for their children's behaviour?* ● *This was a perfectly happy office till Phil took over – he's **got a lot to answer for**.* (= everything is his fault)

answer for sb/sth
if you say that you can answer for someone or for a quality that they have, you mean that you know from experience that they can be trusted, or that they have that quality ● *I can answer for Tanya because I used to work with her but I've no idea what the other candidates are like.* ● *Just from those three months of working together I can answer for her professionalism.*

answer to   answers, answering, answered

answer to sb *slightly formal*
if you answer to someone in a higher position, they are the person you have to explain your actions or decisions to ● *We were living in a police state, where the police answered to no one.*

ante up   antes, anteing, anted

ante up (sth) *American*
to pay an amount of money ● *Each person is being asked to ante up $12 to cover expenses.*

appertain to   appertains, appertaining, appertained

appertain to sth *formal*
to be about or connected to something ● *She enjoyed the privileges appertaining to the office of chairman.*

arrive at   arrives, arriving, arrived

arrive at sth
to achieve an agreement or decision, especially after thinking about it or discussing it for a long time ● *We discussed the matter at length but failed to arrive at a decision.* ● *It is hoped that after this round of talks they will be able to arrive at an agreement.*

arse about/around · arses, arsing, arsed

arse about/around *British & Australian slang*
to waste time doing silly or unimportant things ● *I wish he'd stop arsing around and help me clear up this mess.*

ascribe to · ascribes, ascribing, ascribed

ascribe sth **to** sth *formal*
to believe or say that something is caused by something else ● *If this had been the first time such a disaster had occurred, it could have been ascribed to misfortune.* ● *He ascribes his phenomenal success to being in the right place at the right time.*

ascribe sth **to** sb/sth *formal*
to believe that someone or something has a particular quality ● *It seems strange that she can ascribe such callousness to her own son.* ● *People often ascribe different values to the same word.*

ascribe sth **to** sb *formal*
to believe that something was said, written, or created by a particular person ● *Most experts have ascribed the drawing to Michelangelo.*

ask after · asks, asking, asked

ask after sb/sth
to ask for information about someone, especially about their health ● *Graham's been asking after you again.* ● *Julia asked after your health.*

ask around · asks, asking, asked

ask around
to ask several people in order to try to get information or help ● *I'll ask around at work and see if anyone can babysit.*

ask for · asks, asking, asked

couldn't ask for sb/sth (always negative)
if you say that you couldn't ask for someone or something better, you mean that that person or thing is the best of their kind ● *She's great to work for – I really couldn't ask for a better boss.*

ask for sb
to say that you would like to speak to someone or see someone ● *A young man was here earlier, asking for Rebecca.*

be asking for sth (always in continuous tenses) *informal*
to behave stupidly in a way that is likely to cause problems for you ● *Drinking and driving is just asking for trouble.* ● *Coming into work late almost every morning – he was really asking for it!*

ask in · asks, asking, asked

ask in sb or **ask** sb **in**
to invite someone to come into a building or room, especially your home ● *I didn't want to leave him on the doorstep so I asked him in.* ● (often + **for**) *I'd ask you in for a coffee but I have to be up early in the morning.*

ask out · asks, asking, asked

ask out sb or **ask** sb **out**
to invite someone to come with you to a place such as the cinema or a restaurant, especially as a way of starting a romantic relationship ● *There's some girl in the office he fancies but he's too scared to ask her out.* ● (sometimes + **for**) *She phoned him to ask him out for a drink.*

ask over/round · asks, asking, asked

ask sb **over/round**
to invite someone to come to your house ● *I've asked Adrian and David over to dinner next Saturday.* ● (often + **for**) *I thought we might ask Nicky and Steve round for drinks one night.*

aspire to · aspires, aspiring, aspired

aspire to sth
to have a strong desire to achieve or pos-

sess something ● *Unlike so many men, he has never aspired to a position of power.*

associate with   associates, associating, associated

associate sb/sth **with** sb/sth
to connect someone or something in your mind with someone or something else ● *Patience isn't a virtue I normally associate with Clare.* ● *Why do men always associate enjoying themselves with drinking loads of beer?* ● *It's interesting how different styles of dress can be associated with different types of music.*

be associated with sth (always passive)
if problems or dangers are associated with a particular thing or action, they are caused by it ● *The cancer risks associated with smoking are well publicized.* ● *Tackling the problems associated with inflation is not going to be an easy task.*

associate with sb
to spend time with a group of people, especially people who are disapproved of ● *Tim's mother has always disapproved of the sort of people that he associates with.*

atone for   atones, atoning, atoned

atone for sth *formal*
to do something in order to show that you are sorry for doing something bad and that you want to improve the situation ● *Why should the new generation feel they have to atone for the country's past?*

attend to   attends, attending, attended

attend to sb/sth
1 *formal* to deal with a situation or problem ● *I've got to go into the office. I have one or two matters to attend to.*
2 to help or care for someone or something ● *The doctors tried to attend to those with the worst injuries first.* ● *As a child you always assume that your parents are there to attend to your needs.*

attest to   attests, attesting, attested

attest to sth *formal*
to prove that something is true ● *A national poll conducted last week attests to her popularity.*

attribute to   attributes, attributing, attributed

attribute sth **to** sth *slightly formal*

to believe or say that something is the result of something else ● *He attributes his lack of self-confidence to a troubled childhood.* ● *She attributes her success to having a good team of people working for her.*

attribute sth **to** sb/sth *slightly formal*
to believe that someone or something has a particular quality ● *I would never attribute such a lack of judgement to you.*

attribute sth **to** sb *slightly formal*
to say that something was said, written, or created by a particular person ● (usually passive) *The poem was originally attributed to a little-known Welsh author.* ● *Both statements were attributed to the minister in the press.*

auction off   auctions, auctioning, auctioned

auction off sth or **auction** sth **off**
to sell something, especially buildings or furniture, at an auction (= a public sale where things are sold to the person who offers the most money) ● *Conally's house and belongings were auctioned off to repay his business debts.*

avail of   avails, availing, availed

avail yourself **of** sth (always reflexive) *formal*
to take the opportunity to use something, often in order to improve your situation ● *As an employee I thought I might avail myself of the opportunity to buy cheap shares in the company.*

average out   averages, averaging, averaged

average out sth or **average** sth **out**
to calculate the average of a set of numbers ● *When I average out what I spend on clothes it comes to about £150 a month.*

average out
to be equal in amount or number ● *In the end the highs and lows of life tend to average out.*

average out at   averages, averaging, averaged

average out at sth
to have as the average number ● *My time off work this year averages out at two days a week.*

B

back away   <small>backs, backing, backed</small>

back away

1 to move backwards away from someone or something, usually because you are afraid • *She saw that he had a gun and backed away.*

2 to show that you do not support a plan or idea any more and that you do not want to be connected with it • (usually + **from**) *The government has backed away from plans to increase taxes.*

back down   <small>backs, backing, backed</small>

back down

to admit that you are wrong or that you have been defeated, often because you are forced to • *You could tell by the look on his face that nothing would make him back down.* • (often + **on**) *Local residents have forced the council to back down on its plans to demolish the library.*

back off   <small>backs, backing, backed</small>

back off

1 to move backwards away from someone or something, usually because you are afraid • *I saw his knife and backed off.*

2 *slightly informal* to stop being involved in a situation, especially in order to allow other people to deal with it themselves • (often an order) *Just back off and let us do this on our own, will you?* • *I thought I'd better back off and leave her to make her mind up.*

3 *mainly American* to stop supporting something that you used to support, or to not continue with a plan • (usually + **from**) *The president seems to have backed off from his 'no new taxes' promise.*

back onto   <small>backs, backing, backed</small>

back onto sth

if a building backs onto something, its back faces that thing • *They've got a beautiful house that backs onto the beach.*

back out   <small>backs, backing, backed</small>

back out

to decide not to do something that you were going to do or that you had agreed to do • (often + **of**) *They backed out of the deal at the last minute.* • *She's signed the contract so she can't back out now.*

back up   <small>backs, backing, backed</small>

back up sb or **back** sb **up**

1 to say that someone is telling the truth • *Will you back me up if I say that he wasn't here?* • (often + **on**) *I know you're telling the truth so I'll back you up on that.*

2 to support or help someone • (often + **in**) *My family backed me up in my fight for compensation.*
  back-up *n* [U] • *Our engineers will provide technical back-up.*

3 if a musician backs up another musician, they play music or sing with them • *Can you back me up on piano?*
  back-up *adj* (always before noun) *American & Australian* • *She's a back-up singer for Whitney Houston.*

back up sth or **back** sth **up**

to prove that something is true • *Her findings have been backed up by recent studies.*

back up (sth) or **back** (sth) **up**

1 to drive a car backwards • *Back up a little more so there's room for another car in front.*

2 to make a copy of computer information so that you do not lose it • (often + **on/onto**) *I back up all my files onto floppy disks.* • *Make sure you back up every night.*
  back-up *n* [C] • *Always make a back-up of your files.* • (used as *adj*) *Where are those back-up tapes?*

back up

1 if traffic backs up, the vehicles have to wait in a long line because there are too many of them • *Traffic is starting to back up on both lanes of the motorway.*

2 if a drain, toilet or sink backs up, it becomes blocked and does not let water flow away through it • *One of the ladies' toilets is backing up – could you phone the plumber?*

back up or **back** sb **up**

to move or step backwards, or to make someone move or step backwards a certain distance ● *Could you all back up a bit please, so that I can open the door?*

bag up   bags, bagging, bagged

bag up sth or **bag** sth **up**
  to put something into bags ● *We bagged up the vegetables to put in the freezer.*

bail out   bails, bailing, bailed

bail out sb or **bail** sb **out**
  to pay an amount of money to a law court so that a person who has been accused of a crime can be released until their trial ● *His wife refused to bail him out.*

bail out sb/sth or **bail** sb/sth **out**
  to help a person or organization by giving them money ● *She keeps running up huge debts and then asking her friends to bail her out.*

bail out *American*
  to stop supporting or being involved with someone or something ● *My advice to you is to bail out now before there's trouble.* ● (often + **on**) *A lot of Bob's friends bailed out on him when he got into trouble.*

bail/bale out   bails, bailing, bailed

bail out (sth) or **bail** (sth) **out** *British, American & Australian*

bale out (sth) or **bale** (sth) **out** *British & Australian*
  to remove water from something [e.g. boat] because it is sinking or flooded ● *It had rained all night and we had to bail the boat out in the morning.* ● *As the water poured in, he frantically bailed out.*

bail out *American*

bale out *British & Australian*
  to jump out of an aircraft because it is going to have an accident ● *The pilot had managed to bail out safely.*

bail up   bails, bailing, bailed

bail up sb or **bail** sb **up**
1 *Australian* to make someone late, usually by talking to them for too long ● *I'm sorry I'm late – your neighbour bailed me up at the gate for half an hour.*
2 *Australian* to threaten someone with a gun and steal money from them ● *The prisoner bailed up the guard, took his wallet, and fled.*

balance out/up   balances, balancing, balanced

balance out/up (sth) or **balance** (sth) **out/up**
  to be equal in amount or value, or to make things equal in amount or value ● *We'd better ask a few men to the party to balance up the numbers.* ● *I spend a lot one month and not so much the next and in the end it balances out.*

bale out   bales, baling, baled
  see **bail/bale out**

balk/baulk at   balks, balking, balked

balk at sth/doing sth *British, American & Australian*

baulk at sth/doing sth *British & Australian*
  to not want to do something or let something happen ● *I balked at the prospect of four hours on a train in his company.* ● *I think that most people would baulk at spending so much on a meal.*

balls up   ballses, ballsing, ballsed

balls up sth or **balls** sth **up** *British & Australian informal*
  to spoil something by doing it badly ● *I ballsed up the second interview completely.*
  balls-up n [C] *British & Australian informal* ● *She made a right balls-up of the arrangements.*

band together   bands, banding, banded

band together
  if people band together, they make a group in order to be able to do something better ● (often + **to do** sth) *Shoppers in the neigh-*

bourhood are banding together to make bulk orders.

bandage up bandages, bandaging, bandaged

~~bandage up~~ sb/sth or ~~bandage~~ sb/sth **up**

to put a long, narrow piece of cloth around a part of the body that is injured • *One of his arms, resting outside the bed, was bandaged up.* • *When Alison cut her leg, the school nurse bandaged her up and sent her home.*

bandy about/around bandies, bandying, bandied

bandy about/around sth or **bandy** sth **about/around**

to mention a word or number often when you are talking, especially in order to impress the person you are talking to • (usually passive) *A lot of phrases are bandied about and I wonder if anyone really knows what they mean.*

bang about/around bangs, banging, banged

bang about/around

to move around a place, making a lot of noise • (often + **in**) *I could hear him banging about in the kitchen.*

bang away at bangs, banging, banged

bang away at sth *informal*

to work hard at something • *Tom's been banging away at his homework all evening.*

bang down bangs, banging, banged

bang down sth or **bang** sth **down**

to put something down with force, often because you are angry • (often + **on**) *'Five dollars,' he said, banging the glass down on the counter.*

bang into bangs, banging, banged

bang into sth

to knock against something, usually by accident • *I couldn't see where I was going and I kept on banging into things.*

bang on bangs, banging, banged

bang on *British informal*

to talk about something for a long time, especially in a way that is boring to other people • (often in continuous tenses; usu-ally + **about**) *He's always banging on about how much better life is outside of London.*

bang out bangs, banging, banged

bang out sth or **bang** sth **out**

1 *slightly informal* to play a tune on the piano loudly • *She banged out some well known songs on the old piano.*
2 *informal* to write something quickly on a computer or typewriter • *Reporters in the newsroom sat at their computers, banging out stories for the next day.*

bang up bangs, banging, banged

bang up sb or **bang** sb **up** *British informal*

to put someone in prison • (usually passive) *He was banged up for 16 years for a murder that he didn't commit.*

bang up sb/sth or **bang** sb/sth **up** *American informal*

to badly damage something or to hurt someone • *She's afraid to tell him she's banged up his car.* • *Mike got banged up in a bar brawl.*

banged-up *adj* old and damaged • *a banged-up old truck*

bank on banks, banking, banked

bank on sth

to depend on something happening • *I hope to be there but don't bank on it.* • *She's banking on getting a pay increase this year.*

bargain for/on bargains, bargaining, bargained

bargain for/on sth

to expect something to happen and be prepared for it • (usually negative) *Neither pilot had bargained for the hazards of the land that they were flying over.* • *She hadn't bargained on the house being sold so quickly.* • *The strength of the opposition was rather **more than she'd bargained for**.* (= more than she had expected)

barge in/into barges, barging, barged

barge in

barge into swh

to walk into a room quickly and without being asked to enter it • (often + **on**) *I certainly wasn't about to go barging in on them uninvited.* • *You don't just go* *barging into someone's bedroom without knocking.*

barge in

barge into sth

to interrupt what someone is saying, or to get involved in something even though you have not been asked to ● *Sorry to barge in, but did I hear you say that you were driving into town?*

bark out   barks, barking, barked

bark out sth or **bark** sth **out**

to shout something [e.g. order] ● *The officers expect you to act the moment they bark out the orders.*

base on/upon   bases, basing, based

base sth **on/upon** sth

if you base something on particular facts or ideas, you use those facts or ideas to develop that thing ● (usually passive) *The film is based on a short story by Thomas Mann.* ● *Their predictions were based on a survey of 19 local companies.*

bash about   bashes, bashing, bashed

bash sth/sb **about** *British & Australian slightly informal*

to treat something or someone in a rough way ● *If you bash it about like that, it won't last very long.* ● *At school he always got bashed about by the bigger kids.*

bash in   bashes, bashing, bashed

bash in sth or **bash** sth **in** *informal*

to break or damage something by hitting it hard many times ● *Someone had bashed in the side window of the car and taken the stereo system.*

bash on   bashed, bashing, bashed

bash on *informal*

to continue doing something that is difficult, boring, or that takes a long time ● (often + **with**) *Oh well, that's enough chatting. I suppose I'd better bash on with this essay.*

bash up   bashes, bashing, bashed

bash up sb/sth or **bash** sb/sth **up** *informal*

to hurt or damage someone or something by hitting them hard ● *He got bashed up in a fight.* ● *Someone had gone and bashed his car up while he wasn't there.*

bask in   basks, basking, basked

bask in sth

to enjoy the way other people admire you ● *She smiled complacently, basking in their admiration.*

bat around   bats, batting, batted

bat around sth or **bat** sth **around** *slightly informal*

to talk about a plan or idea and to discuss different ways of dealing with it ● *We batted around various proposals but didn't come to a decision.*

bat out   bats, batting, batted

bat out sth or **bat** sth **out** *American informal*

to write something quickly and without taking much care ● *Ruth batted out a few lines to use in her talk.*

batten down   battens, battening, battened

batten down (sth) or **batten** (sth) **down**

to fasten parts of a ship or building [e.g. hatch, window] in order to prevent damage from strong winds ● *Before the storm hit, we had battened down the windows.* ● *Everyone on the coast is battening down for Hurricane Lily.*

batten on/upon   battens, battening, battened

batten on/upon sb *literary*

to live well by using someone else's money ● *He's spent these last five years battening on some rich aunt of his.*

batter down   batters, battering, battered

batter down sth or **batter** sth **down**

to hit a door or wall hard until it falls down ● *They came in the night and battered down his front door.*

baulk at   baulks, baulking, baulked

see **balk/baulk at**

bawl out   bawls, bawling, bawled

bawl out sth or **bawl** sth **out** *informal*

to shout or sing in a loud, unpleasant voice ● *Someone from the crowd bawled out his name.*

bawl out sb or **bawl** sb **out** *American &*
Australian informal
to tell someone angrily that something
that they have done is wrong ● (often +
for) *His boss had bawled him out twice*
that week for being late.

bear down   bears, bearing, bore, borne

bear down
1 *American* to do something in a very determined way, especially while playing
sport ● *The pitcher bore down and struck*
out the next two batters.
2 if a woman who is giving birth bears
down, she uses a lot of effort to push the
baby out ● *When the woman's time comes,*
her partner holds her while she bears
down.

bear down on   bears, bearing, bore, borne

bear down on sb/sth *slightly formal*
to move quickly towards someone or
something in a threatening or determined way ● *A large bus was bearing*
down on them at high speed. ● *The striker*
found a gap in the defence and bore down
on the goal.

bear on/upon   bears, bearing, bore, borne

bear on/upon sth *formal*
to be directly connected to something, or
to influence something ● *A number of*
court cases that bear on women's rights
will be coming up soon.

bear out   bears, bearing, bore, borne

bear out sth/sb or **bear** sth/sb **out**
to prove that something that someone has
said or written [e.g. claim, theory] is true,
or to say that someone is telling the truth
● *The facts do not bear out the government's*
claims. ● *If you tell him what happened*
I shall certainly bear you out.

bear up   bears, bearing, bore, borne

bear up
to deal with a very sad or difficult situation in a brave and determined way
● (often in continuous tenses) *'How is she*
doing since the funeral?' 'Oh, she's bearing
up.' ● (sometimes + **under**) *Many soldiers*
have trouble bearing up under the strain
of battle.

bear upon

see **bear on/upon**

bear with   bears, bearing, bore, borne

bear with sb
to be patient and wait while someone
does something ● *If you'll just bear with*
me for a moment, I'll find you a copy of the
drawings.

beat down   beats, beating, beat, beaten

beat down
1 if the sun beats down, it shines strongly
and makes the air very hot ● (often + **on**)
A blazing Mediterranean sun beats down
on the café tables. ● *The sun beat down*
over the desert.
2 if the rain beats down, it comes down in
large amounts with force ● *The rain beat*
down all day and kept them inside.

beat down sb/sth or **beat** sb/sth
down
to force someone to reduce the price of
something ● (often + **to**) *The dealer was*
asking £5000 for the car, but I managed to
beat him down to £4600. ● *High prices were*
beaten down by a flood of imports.

beat off   beats, beating, beat, beaten

beat off sb/sth or **beat** sb/sth **off**
to succeed in defeating someone who is
trying to attack or in some way oppose
you ● *She beat off an attacker with an um-*
brella. ● (often + **from**) *The advertising*
agency beat off competition from several
leading companies.

beat off (sb) or **beat** (sb) **off** *American*
taboo
to rub or touch the sexual organs in order
to get or give sexual pleasure ● *Some guy*
was beating off in the john next to me.

beat out   beats, beating, beat, beaten

beat out sth or **beat** sth **out**
1 if a drum beats out a rhythm, or you beat
out a rhythm on a drum, the drum makes
a repeated pattern of sound ● *The drums*
beat out their hypnotic rhythms. ● *He beat*
out a simple rhythm on a drum.
2 to stop a fire from burning by hitting it
with something ● *We managed to beat out*
the fire with a blanket.

beat out sb or **beat** sb **out** *American*
to defeat someone or do better than them

in a competition, sport or in business • *Their company beat out five other competitors for the contract.*

beat out of   beats, beating, beat, beaten

beat sth **out of** sb

to make someone say things they do not want to by hitting them hard until they talk • *Malloy claimed that his statements to the police had been beaten out of him.*

beat up   beats, beating, beat, beaten

beat up sb or **beat** sb **up**

to hurt someone badly by hitting or kicking them again and again • *He claims he was beaten up by police.* • *Four soldiers dragged him out of his car and beat him up.*

beat up on   beats, beating, beat, beaten

beat up on sb

1 *American informal* to attack someone physically, especially someone who is weaker • *City gangs are roaming the streets beating up on anyone they see alone.*

2 *American informal* to criticize someone severely or blame them for something • (often reflexive) *Stop beating up on yourself – it wasn't your fault.* • *Why does the coach always beat up on Tim? He's the best pitcher on the team.*

beaver away   beavers, beavering, beavered

beaver away *informal*

to work hard at something for a long time, especially something you are writing • (often + **at**) *Lucy has been beavering away at her studies all afternoon.*

become of   becomes, became, become

become of sb/sth (always used in questions; never in continuous tenses)

if you ask what became of someone or something, you want to know where they are and what happened to them • *Whatever became of that parcel you sent?* • *What will become of her children if she is sent to prison?*

bed down   beds, bedding, bedded

bed down

1 (always + *adv/prep*) to lie down in order to go to sleep somewhere, especially somewhere different from where you usu-

ally sleep • *He bedded down for the night in a doorway.*

2 *British & Australian* if something new [e.g. process, organization] beds down, it starts to work well because it has existed for long enough • *The new system had not bedded down in the way he had hoped.*

bed out   beds, bedding, bedded

bed out sth or **bed** sth **out**

to move young plants from inside and plant them in the ground outside • *May is the time to bed out geraniums.*

beef up   beefs, beefing, beefed

beef up sth or **beef** sth **up** *informal*

to make something stronger or more important • *You could beef up your image with a new hairstyle.* • *They want to employ young graduates to beef up their sales force.*

beefed-up *adj* (always before noun) • *a beefed-up version of the original computer program*

beg off   begs, begging, begged

beg off (sth/doing sth)

to say that you cannot do something that you are expected to do • *It was no surprise to me that she'd begged off again.*

begin with   begins, beginning, began, begun

begin (sth) **with** (sth)

to begin something in a particular way, or to be the way in which something begins • *He always began his classes with a prayer.* • *There were six of us to begin with and then two left.* • *The essay begins with a section on religion.*

believe in   believes, believing, believed

believe in sth (never in continuous tenses)

1 to be sure that something [e.g. God, ghosts] exists, or that something is true • *She doesn't believe in God.* • *They believe in astrology and let it rule their lives completely.*

2 to think that something is effective and right • *Sue believes in capital punishment for terrorists.* • *They did not believe in living together before marriage.*

believe in sb

to trust someone because you think that

they can do something well, or that they are a good person ● *It is important to believe in your doctor.* ● (sometimes reflexive) *Gradually, since her divorce, she's starting to believe in herself again.*

belly out   bellies, bellying, bellied

belly (sth) **out**
to become round and full of air, or to make something round and full of air ● *The sail bellied out in the wind and soon the boat was gathering speed.*

belly up to   bellies, bellying, bellied

belly up to sb/sth *American informal*
to move close to someone or something [e.g. bar, table] ● *He bellied up to the bar for a drink.*

belong to   belongs, belonging, belonged

belong to sb

1 to be someone's property ● *Who does this book belong to?* ● *The house belonged to her father but it's hers now.*
2 to be someone's responsibility, or to be the result of someone's action ● *The job of arresting the man must belong to the police.* ● *All the credit for the project's success belonged to Tom.*

belong to sth

1 to be a member of a group or organization ● *I think she belongs to some kind of dance group.* ● *Seaweed belongs to a group of plants known as algae.*
2 to be connected with a particular thing, time, or place ● *Her novels belong to the European tradition.* ● *She seemed to belong to a different age with her strange ways.* ● *Does this belt belong to your trousers?*

belt into   belts, belting, belted

belt into sb *Australian*
to hit someone quickly and using a lot of force ● *I didn't say a word, he just started to belt into me for no reason.*

belt into sth *Australian*
to begin to do something quickly and with a lot of effort ● *When he's got a job to do, he just belts into it.*

belt out   belts, belting, belted

belt out sth or **belt** sth **out** *informal*
to sing or to play a musical instrument very loudly ● *The band was belting out all the old favourites.*

belt up   belts, belting, belted

belt up! (always an order) *British & Australian informal*
something that you say angrily to someone in order to tell them to be quiet ● *Just belt up, would you! I'm trying to concentrate.*

belt up *British & Australian informal*
to fasten the belt that stops you from falling out of your seat in a car or plane ● (usually an order) *Belt up in the back, kids!*

belt up sb or **belt** sb **up** *Australian slang*
to hit someone ● *Sam's got a black eye – he got belted up by his father for telling lies.*

bend down   bends, bending, bent

bend down
to move the top part of your body towards the ground ● (often + to do sth) *Simon bent down to tie his shoelaces.* ● *Bend down as you go through the door, or you'll hit your head.*

bend over   bends, bending, bent

bend over (sth)
to move the top part of your body nearer to the ground or over something ● *Joseph was bending over the fire, staring into the*

flames. ● *He was bending over trying to tie his shoelaces.*

bend over backwards   bends, bending, bent

bend over backwards to do sth
to try extremely hard to do something to help or please someone ● *She would always bend over backwards to help anyone in trouble.*

bet on   bets, betting, bet or betted

bet on sth
to expect something to happen or to expect someone to do something, especially when this is what you want or need ● (often negative) *It'd be great if they invited us, but don't bet on it.* ● *He was betting on making enough money from the sale of his house to pay off all his debts.*

bid on   bids, bidding, bid

bid on sth
to make an offer to do work or provide a service at a particular price, and to compete against other people for the work ● *Their company lost the opportunity to bid on White House travel business.*

bill as   bills, billing, billed

bill sb/sth **as** sb/sth
to describe someone or something in a particular way in order to advertise them ● *The travel offer was billed as 'a chance to taste the romance of France'.* ● *They billed her as 'the woman with rubber bones'.*

bind over   binds, binding, bound

bind over sb or **bind** sb **over** *formal*
to tell someone that they are not allowed to do something by law and that they will be punished if they do ● (usually passive + to do sth) *She was **bound over to keep the peace** (= ordered not to cause trouble) for a year.*

bind to   binds, binding, bound

bind sb **to** sth *formal*
to make someone obey an agreement, promise, or idea ● (usually passive) *Unfortunately we are bound to the original contract and cannot change now.* ● *His sister had been bound to secrecy.* (= made to promise not to tell anyone anything)

bind up in/with

be bound up in/with sth/sb (always passive)

1 *slightly formal* to be closely connected with someone or something ● *Their identity was bound up with their language and culture.*

2 *mainly British & Australian* to be so involved with something or someone that you cannot do anything else ● *She was so utterly bound up in herself that she remained unaware of the people around her.*

bite back   bites, biting, bit, bitten

bite back sth or **bite** sth **back** (never passive)
to stop yourself from saying something that shows your real feelings or thoughts ● *He turned red and bit back an angry response.*

bite back
to do something bad to someone because they have done something bad to you ● *They bit back with some equally damaging criticism of their opponents.*

bite into   bites, biting, bit, bitten

bite into sth

1 to press so hard against someone's skin that it hurts them ● *The rope was wrapped around her hand and bit into her flesh.* ● *The cold began to bite into my bones.*

2 to remove part of something ● *Her job was demanding and began to bite into her free time.*

black out   blacks, blacking, blacked

black out
to suddenly become unconscious ● *He blacked out so he remembers very little.*
blackout n [C] ● *He suffers from blackouts and isn't allowed to drive.*

black out sth or **black** sth **out**

1 to make a place dark, especially by covering or switching off all the lights ● *The entire city was blacked out.*
blackout n [C] ● *The city's constant blackouts mean the streets are often unlit in the evenings.*

blackout n [singular] a period of time during a war when no lights can be shown so that they will not be seen by the enemy ● *She remembered the blitz and **the black-out** bringing people together during the war.* ● (used as *adj*) *black-out curtains*

2　to cover a piece of writing in order to stop anyone from reading it ● *Names of the victims and their details had been blacked out in the report.*

blackout *n* [C] ● *a news blackout on the police investigation*

blank out　blanks, blanking, blanked

blank out sth or **blank** sth **out**

1　to cover a piece of information [e.g. name] so that it cannot be read ● *Many of the key names in the report had been blanked out.*

2　to stop yourself from thinking about something unpleasant because it upsets you ● *He claims not to remember anything about his mother's death – I think he just blanked it all out.*

3　to destroy electrical systems that are used for sending messages ● *The explosion has blanked out all radio and communications equipment.*

blank out

American informal if you blank out, or if your mind blanks out, you stop thinking clearly and stop noticing what is happening around you ● *As he walked along the busy street his mind suddenly blanked out.* ● *I don't remember anything more after that point – I think I just blanked out.*

blanket with　blankets, blanketing, blanketed

be blanketed with sth (always passive) to be covered with something ● *The graveyard was blanketed with snow.*

blanket sth **with** sth *mainly American* to advertise or supply something to a lot of people at the same time over a wide area ● *These companies blanket the state with direct-mail promises of easy money.*

blast away　blasts, blasting, blasted

blast away

to fire a gun again and again ● (often + **at**) *The navy's guns blasted away at enemy units on shore.*

blast off　blasts, blasting, blasted

blast off

if a rocket blasts off, it leaves the ground to go into space ● *The space shuttle is due*

to blast off at 2 o'clock.

blast-off *n* [U] ● *The satellite was ready for blast-off at 14.15 hours.*

blast out　blasts, blasting, blasted

blast out (sth) or **blast** (sth) **out**

to produce a lot of noise, especially loud music ● *A car drew up at the traffic lights, dance music blasting out from its radio.*

blend in/into　blends, blending, blended

blend in

blend into sth

if something or someone blends in, they look or seem the same as the things or people around them and so you do not notice them ● *Some butterflies blend in with their surroundings to confuse their enemy.* ● *By day, these sounds blend into the sound of the traffic.*

block in　blocks, blocking, blocked

block in sb/sth or **block** sb/sth **in**

to put a car or other vehicle so close to another vehicle that it cannot drive away ● *A van had parked behind me and blocked me in.*

block in sth or **block** sth **in**

1　*mainly American* to fill a space on a piece of paper by writing or drawing in it ● *He carefully blocked in the areas of shadow in the drawing.* ● *Activities were blocked in on the calendar for the next few weeks.*

2　*American* to draw the main shape of an object, or to write the main points of a plan ● *The architect has blocked in a few cars and trees around the building.*

block off　blocks, blocking, blocked

block off sth or **block** sth **off**

to put something across the entrance to something [esp. road] in order to stop people from going into it ● *All the roads out of town were blocked off by the police.*

block out　blocks, blocking, blocked

block out sth or **block** sth **out**

1　to stop something [esp. light] from coming into a place ● *Unfortunately, there's a tree near the window which blocks out the light.*

2　to stop yourself from thinking about something unpleasant because it upsets you ● *The whole experience was so painful that I just tried to block it out.*

3 *American* to draw the main shape of an object, or to write the main points of a plan ● *Kay blocked out my essay for me.*

block up   blocks, blocking, blocked

block up sth or **block** sth **up**
to fill a narrow space with something so that nothing can move through that space ● *Dead leaves had blocked the drains up.* ● *You don't want cars and coaches blocking up the street.*
blocked-up adj ● *My nose gets really blocked-up at night and I can't breathe through it.*

blot out   blots, blotting, blotted

blot out sth or **blot** sth **out**
1 if smoke or a cloud blots out the sun, it covers it and prevents it from being seen ● *Smoke from the burning oilfields had formed a black cloud that blotted out the sun.*
2 to stop yourself from thinking about something unpleasant because it upsets you ● *Perhaps there are some memories so bad that you have to blot them out.*

blow apart   blows, blowing, blew, blown

blow sth **apart** or **blow apart** sth
1 if a bomb, explosion or violent event blows something apart, it destroys it ● (often passive) *The chemicals caught fire and the whole building blew apart.*
2 to destroy an idea, claim or hope by showing clearly that it is untrue or impossible ● *This new discovery blew apart scientific ideas about how life began.*

blow away   blows, blowing, blew, blown

blow away (sth) or **blow** (sth) **away**
if something blows away, or if the wind blows something away, that thing moves from its usual place because the wind blows it ● *You'd better put something on top of the tablecloth before it blows away.*

blow away sb or **blow** sb **away**
1 *American slang* to kill someone by shooting them with a gun ● *He just gets his shotgun out and blows the guy away.*
2 *American informal* to defeat someone completely, especially in a sports competition ● *She blew away the other swimmers to win her race.*
3 *American informal* to surprise or please someone a lot ● *When I first read that*

book it blew me away – *it was just so extraordinary.*

blow down   blows, blowing, blew, blown

blow down (sth) or **blow** (sth) **down**
if something blows down, or if the wind blows something down, that thing falls to the ground because the wind blows it ● *Two huge trees had been blown down in the storm* ● *Our fence blew down last week.*

blow in   blows, blowing, blew, blown

blow in *mainly American & Australian informal*
to arrive somewhere when you are not expected ● (often + **from**) *My cousin just blew in from Florida for a three-day visit.*

blow off   blows, blowing, blew, blown

blow (sth) **off** (sth)
if something blows off, or if the wind or an explosion blows something off, it is removed from its position by the wind or the explosion ● *The shed roof blew off in the storm.* ● *A sudden gust of wind blew her hat off.* ● *The explosion blew the door off its hinges.*

blow off sth or **blow** sth **off**
1 if a bomb or gun blows off part of someone's body, it removes it ● (usually passive) *His right leg was blown off by a landmine.*
2 *American slang* to decide not to do something that you were going to do ● *We decided to blow off the movie and went dancing instead.*

blow off sb/sth or **blow** sb/sth **off**
American slang
to treat someone or something as if they are not important ● *He would have been selected as a finalist if he hadn't blown off the interview.* ● *He said he'd help out but she blew him off.*

blow off *British slang, humorous*
to allow gas to escape from your bottom, especially loudly ● *He's always blowing off!*

blow out   blows, blowing, blew, blown

blow out (sth) or **blow** (sth) **out**
if a flame or fire blows out, or if you blow it out, it stops burning because the wind has blown it or because you have blown it

• *She blew out the candles on her birthday cake.*

blow out sth or **blow** sth **out**

if an explosion blows out something [e.g. windows], it is so strong that that thing falls out • *The windows of the church had been blown out in the blast.*

blow out

if a car tyre blows out, it suddenly bursts • *It's a good thing you weren't going any faster when your tyre blew out.*

blow-out *n* [C] *informal* • *We hadn't driven far when we had a blow-out.*

blow itself **out** (always reflexive)

if a storm blows itself out, it becomes weaker and then stops • *After a few hours the storm blew itself out.*

blow out sb or **blow** sb **out**

1 *British informal* to disappoint someone by not meeting them or not doing something that you had arranged to do with them • *You're not going to blow me out like you did last time are you?*

2 *American slang* to easily defeat someone in a competition • *Cincinnati blew out the Browns 44-29.*

blow-out *n* [C] *American slang* • (usually singular) *Last night's game wasn't just a victory, it was a blow-out.*

blow over blows, blowing, blew, blown

blow over (sth) or **blow** (sth) **over**

if something blows over, or if the wind blows something over, that thing falls to the ground • *Their tents had blown over during the night.* • *The wind was so strong it blew the fence over.*

blow over

1 if a storm blows over, it becomes less strong and then ends • *The storm had blown over by the evening.*

2 if an unpleasant situation [e.g. argument] blows over, it gradually becomes less important and is then forgotten • *Like most arguments, after a few days it just blew over.* • *I think the government hoped that the whole affair would blow over, but it didn't.*

blow up blows, blowing, blew, blown

blow up (sth/sb) or **blow** (sth/sb) **up**

to destroy something or kill someone with a bomb, or to be destroyed or killed

with a bomb • *They threatened to blow up the airliner if their demands were not met.* • *He drove over a land mine and his jeep blew up.* • *The man threatened to blow himself up rather than surrender.*

blow up sth or **blow** sth **up**

1 to fill something [e.g. balloon, tyre] with air • *He blew his tyres up using the pressure pump.* • *I spent the morning blowing up balloons for Joe's party.*

blow-up *adj* (always before noun) • *I got one of those blow-up travel pillows.*

2 to make a large copy of a photograph • *The police had blown up a photograph of the riot to show more detail.*

blow-up *n* [C] • *Was that the original photo or a blow-up?*

3 to make something seem much worse or much better than it really is • *The problem had been **blown up out of all proportion**.*

blow up

1 if a problem or difficult situation blows up, it suddenly happens or starts to exist • *Another row blew up this week over the proposed rise in school fees.* • *Everything seemed perfect until all this trouble with my relatives blew up.*

2 *informal* to suddenly become very angry • (often + **at**) *She blew up at me and started calling me all these names.*

blow-up *n* [singular] *informal* • *After his blow-up with Lila, he needed a walk.*

3 if a storm blows up, it starts • *They could hear a tremendous storm blowing up as they sat in the tent.*

blow up sb or **blow** sb **up** *Australian informal*

to speak to someone in a very angry way because they have done something wrong • *Ted was two hours late home from the party and his father really blew him up.*

bluff out bluffs, bluffing, bluffed

bluff out sth/sb or **bluff** sth/sb **out** *American informal*

to lie or pretend in order to deceive someone • *The boy was caught stealing the money, but he still tried **to bluff it out**.* (= to pretend he did not take it) • *We managed to bluff the doorman out and got into the building.*

blunder about/around   blunders, blundering, blundered

blunder about/around

to move in an awkward way, usually because you cannot see where you are going • (often + **in**) *I blundered about in the darkness trying to find a light.*

blunder into   blunders, blundering, blundered

blunder into swh/sth

to arrive in a place or get into a difficult situation by accident, usually because you have made a stupid mistake • *An American spy plane had blundered into Siberian airspace.* • *The two countries might have blundered into nuclear war.*

blurt out   blurts, blurting, blurted

blurt out sth or **blurt** sth **out**

to say something suddenly and without thinking, especially because you are excited or nervous • *Just before he left to board his plane she suddenly blurted out, 'I love you!'*

board out   boards, boarding, boarded

board out sth or **board** sth **out** *mainly British & Australian*

to arrange for an animal that lives with you to be taken care of in a place away from home • *We always board our cats out when we go away.*

board up   boards, boarding, boarded

board up sth or **board** sth **up**

to cover a window or door with pieces of wood • *Stores on the main street were boarding up their windows in case of riots.*

bob up   bobs, bobbing, bobbed

bob up

1 to float to the surface after being under water • *He threw a bottle into the river and watched it bob up a moment later.*

2 to suddenly appear, usually from behind something • *Suddenly a head bobbed up from behind the hedge.*

bog down   bogs, bogging, bogged

be bogged down (always passive)

to become so involved in something that you cannot do anything else • (often + **in**) *Try to look at the article as a whole and not get too bogged down in the details.*

bog down (sth) or **bog** (sth) **down** *American*

if an activity bogs down, or if something bogs down an activity, it is prevented from making progress • (often + **in**) *The discussion gradually bogged down in questions about voting procedures.* • *The extra paperwork will bog down the whole project.*

bog in/into   bogs, bogging, bogged

bog in *Australian informal*

bog into sth *Australian informal*

to start to eat in an enthusiastic way • *I put the food down on the table and they all bogged into it as if they hadn't eaten for a week.*

bog off

Bog off! (always an order) *British & Australian informal*

something slightly rude that you say in order to tell someone to go away immediately • *Oh, tell him to bog off!*

boil down   boils, boiling, boiled

boil down (sth) or **boil** (sth) **down**

if food or liquid boils down, or if you boil it down, it reduces in amount after boiling • *After ten minutes on a high heat the liquid boils down.*

boil down sth or **boil** sth **down**

to reduce something, especially a piece of writing, until only the most important parts are left • *I've boiled down the report for discussion in the meeting.*

boil down to   boils, boiling, boiled

boil down to sth (never in continuous tenses) *slightly informal*

if a situation or problem boils down to a particular thing, that is the main reason for it • *The whole housing shortage problem boils down to one thing: money.* • *What it boils down to is that you just don't trust me.*

boil over   boils, boiling, boiled

boil over

1 if a liquid that is being heated boils over, it flows over the side of the pan • *Take the milk off the heat before it boils over.*

2 if a difficult situation or bad emotion boils over, it cannot be controlled any more and people fight or argue • *Finally, her frustration and anger boiled over and*

she lashed out at him. ● (often + **into**) *Disputes in the region have boiled over into two wars.*

boil up boils, boiling, boiled

boil up sth or **boil** sth **up** *mainly British & Australian*
to heat liquid or food in a pan until it boils ● *Just add a spoonful of coffee to the water and boil it all up with a little sugar.*

boil up *literary*
if a bad emotion [e.g. anger] boils up, it becomes very strong and is difficult to control ● (often + **in**) *Anger suddenly boiled up in him.*

bolt down bolts, bolting, bolted

bolt down sth or **bolt** sth **down** *informal*
to eat food very quickly ● *If you bolt your dinner down like that you'll get indigestion!*

bomb out bombs, bombing, bombed

be bombed out (always passive)
if a building is bombed out it is completely destroyed by a bomb ● *Many of the city's buildings had been bombed out in the war.*

bomb out *mainly American & Australian informal*
to fail ● (often + **of**) *Tracy bombed out of the tennis match in straight sets.* ● (often + **in**) *I bombed out in my final exams.*

bombard with bombards, bombarding, bombarded

bombard sb **with** sth
to direct a lot of something [e.g. questions, letters] at one person ● *The kids bombarded the teacher with questions.* ● *In prison, he had been bombarded with visits from psychologists.*

bone up bones, boning, boned

bone up *informal*
to learn as much as you can about something ● (often + **on**) *She's boning up on her history for an exam tomorrow.* ● (sometimes + **for**) *He was boning up for the written part of the driving test.*

book in/into books, booking, booked

book in *mainly British & Australian*

book into sth *mainly British & Australian*
to say that you have arrived when you get to a hotel ● *After booking into our hotel we went for a stroll around the city.* ● *I've booked in at the Castle Hotel for the night.*

book in (sb/sth) or **book** (sb/sth) **in** *mainly British & Australian*

book (sb/sth) **into** sth *mainly British & Australian*
to arrange to go somewhere, or to arrange for someone or something to go somewhere, especially a hotel ● *Book him in at the Central if it's possible.* ● *I've booked into the most expensive hotel there.* ● *I must remember to book the car into the garage for a service.*

book up

be booked up (always passive)
if an event, person, or place is booked up, they have no space or time available for someone ● *The hotel's conference rooms are booked up two years in advance.* ● *The dentist is booked up today, could you manage later in the week?* ● *I'd love to come, but I'm completely booked up this week.*

boom out booms, booming, boomed

boom out (sth) (never passive)
to speak in a loud voice, or to make a loud noise ● *'What's your name?' the man boomed out as he approached.* ● *A Beatles' song came booming out of a nearby radio.*

boomerang on boomerangs, boomeranging, boomeranged

boomerang on sb
if someone's action boomerangs on them, it affects them instead of the person it was supposed to affect ● *His joke had boomeranged on him and Cathy was furious.*

boot out boots, booting, booted

boot out sb or **boot** sb **out** *informal*
to make someone leave a place or job ● *The military regime booted out all foreign journalists.* ● (often + **of**) *He was booted out of the company after a financial scandal.*

boot up   boots, booting, booted

boot up (sth) or **boot** (sth) **up**
if a computer boots up, or if someone boots a computer up, it is turned on so that it is ready to use ● *You'll need to boot up the computer before you can start work.* ● *The system boots up automatically every morning.*

border on   borders, bordering, bordered

border on sth
1 if one country borders on another country, it is next to it ● *Swaziland borders on South Africa and Mozambique.*
2 if something, especially a quality or feeling, borders on another more extreme thing, it is almost that thing ● *He treated the women with an indifference that bordered on contempt.* ● *She possesses a self-confidence that borders on arrogance.*

bore into   bores, boring, bored

bore into sb
if someone's eyes bore into you, they look at you very hard and make you feel nervous ● *He's got this cold stare that seems to bore into you.*

boss about/around   bosses, bossing, bossed

boss about/around sb or **boss** sb **about/around**
to tell someone what they should do all the time ● *Did you notice the way he bosses his wife around?*

botch up

botch up   botches, botching, botched

botch up sth or **botch** sth **up** *informal*
to spoil a piece of work by doing it badly ● *He was trying to mend that table but he's gone and botched it up.*
botch-up n [C] *mainly British & Australian informal* ● *They **made a botch-up** of painting the hall and we're going to have to redo it.*

bottle out   bottles, bottling, bottled

bottle out *British informal*
to suddenly decide not to do something because you are afraid ● *She was going to do a parachute jump but bottled out at the last minute.*

bottle up   bottles, bottling, bottled

bottle up sth or **bottle** sth **up** *informal*
1 to not allow yourself to show or talk about your feelings, especially feelings of anger and sadness ● *A lot of men bottle things up instead of talking about how they feel.* ● *Feelings that had been bottled up for years suddenly came flooding out.*
2 *mainly American & Australian* to prevent something from being moved from one place to another ● *Nato tried to bottle up the Soviet fleet in the Black Sea.* ● *Their money is bottled up in Poland because of the tight monetary controls.*

bottom out   bottoms, bottoming, bottomed

bottom out
if a situation, level, or rate that is getting worse bottoms out, it reaches the lowest point and remains at that level or amount, usually before improving ● *The sharp fall in house prices has finally bottomed out.* ● *Unemployment will continue to rise until the recession bottoms out.*

bounce around   bounces, bouncing, bounced

bounce around sth or **bounce** sth **around** *mainly American informal*
to discuss ideas with other people ● *They bounced a few ideas around and eventually came up with a solution.*

bounce back   bounces, bouncing, bounced

bounce back
to start to be successful again after a

period of failure ● (often + **from**) *They are sure to bounce back from last week's defeat.*

bounce into · bounces, bouncing, bounced

bounce sb **into** sth/doing sth
to make someone do something so quickly that they do not have time to think carefully about it ● (usually passive) *The party chairman firmly stated that they would not be bounced into an early election by recent opinion polls.*

bounce off · bounces, bouncing, bounced

bounce sth **off** sb *informal*
to tell someone about an idea or plan in order to find out what they think of it ● *The two researchers were constantly bouncing ideas off each other.* ● *Bounce those suggestions off Marge and see what she thinks.*

bow down · bows, bowing, bowed

bow down to sb
to obey someone and show them respect ● *He expects me to bow down to him and do everything he tells me.*

bow out · bows, bowing, bowed

bow out
to leave a job or stop doing an activity, usually after a long time ● (often + **of**) *After a succession of defeats and disappointments he decided to bow out of politics.* ● *He **bowed out gracefully** (= to leave his job so that other people respect him) at the age of 71.*

bow to · bows, bowing, bowed

bow to sth/sb
to do what someone else wants you to do ● *The government refuses to bow to public pressure.*

bowl over · bowls, bowling, bowled

bowl over sb or **bowl** sb **over**
1 to surprise or please someone a lot ● (usually passive) *When we first visited Crete we were just bowled over by its beauty.* ● *I was bowled over by him – I'd never met anyone so devastatingly attractive.*
2 to make someone fall to the ground by knocking them ● *An old man had been bowled over by the crowd.*

box in · boxes, boxing, boxed

box in sb/sth or **box** sb/sth **in**
to move so close to someone or something, especially a vehicle, that they cannot move ● (usually passive) *When I returned I found that my car had been boxed in.* ● *He was running well until the final lap when he was boxed in by the Italian.*

box in sb or **box** sb **in**
to prevent someone from doing what they want to do ● (usually passive) *She did not want to send her son to a school where he would be boxed in by so many rules and regulations.*
boxed-in *adj* (always after verb) ● *I think he feels boxed-in at work and wants greater independence.*

box up · boxes, boxing, boxed

box up sth or **box** sth **up**
to put something in a box, usually in order to move or send it from one place to another ● *I need to get all this stuff boxed up and sent off as soon as possible.*

brace up · braces, bracing, braced

brace up *old-fashioned*
to feel more hopeful about a situation ● (usually an order) *Brace up, the journey is almost over!*

branch off · branches, branching, branched

branch off
1 to leave a main road by turning onto a smaller road ● (often + **from**) *We branched off from the main route and went through the countryside.*
2 if a road or path branches off, it goes in another direction ● *We noticed a path which branched off to the east.* ● (often + **from**) *A number of smaller roads branch off from the main one.*
3 to start talking about something different from what you were talking about before ● (often + **into**) *The discussion branched off into a debate about abortion.*

branch out · branches, branching, branched

branch out
to start to do something different from what you usually do, especially in your job ● (often + **into**) *The clothes manufacturer recently branched out into children's*

wear. • (sometimes + **from**) *It's possible to branch out from computing to jobs in banking, accountancy and so on.* • *Mr Robertson and his friends decided to **branch out on their own** and start a new company.*

brave out braves, braving, braved

brave out sth or **brave** sth **out** *mainly British & Australian*
to deal bravely with a difficult or unpleasant situation • *The weather looked stormy as we put up the tent, but we decided to **brave it out.***

brazen out brazens, brazening, brazened

brazen out sth or **brazen** sth **out**
to act confidently and show no embarrassment for something bad that you have done • *You can either admit that you were wrong and apologise or you could just **brazen it out.***

break away breaks, breaking, broke, broken

break away
1 to leave or escape from someone who is holding you • *Two police officers tried to restrain him, but he broke away and ran into a nearby house.*
2 to stop being part of a group because you disagree with them or because you do not want to be controlled by them • *A group of National Party members broke away in 1982, protesting against the reforms.* • (often + **from**) *At the age of 19, she broke away from her family and moved to New York.* • (sometimes + to do sth) *A group of employees broke away to set up a rival company.*
  breakaway *n* [C] • (usually singular) *The breakaway of the football club has come as a great shock to many people.*
  breakaway *adj* (always before noun) • *The new president has asked for international recognition for his breakaway republic.*
3 to be different or to do something in a different way from what is usual or expected • (usually + **from**) *Her photographs of the male body break away from conventional images.* • *She broke away from the traditional role of wife and mother and became a journalist.*

break down breaks, breaking, broke, broken

break down
1 if a machine or vehicle breaks down, it stops working • *His car broke down on the way to work.* • *The washing machine's broken down so I have to wash all our clothes by hand.* • *I broke down* (= my car stopped working) *just before I got to the bridge.*
  broken-down *adj* (always before noun) • *The shed was full of broken-down machinery and rusty tools.*
2 if a discussion, system, or relationship breaks down, it fails because of a disagreement or problem • *Talks between the two countries broke down when the two sides failed to reach an agreement.* • *One in three marriages in Britain breaks down and ends in divorce.*
  breakdown *n* [C] • (usually singular) *The president has expressed deep disappointment at the breakdown of peace talks.*
3 to be unable to control your feelings and to start to cry • *When I told her the news, she broke down.*
4 to become mentally or physically ill because of an unpleasant experience • *Two days after the death of his wife he broke down and needed to seek medical help.*
  breakdown *n* [C] • (usually singular) *He's going to have another breakdown if he carries on working like this.* • *I think she's heading for a **nervous breakdown**.* (= going to become mentally ill)

break down sth or **break** sth **down**
1 to hit a door or wall hard until it falls down • *No-one would answer so they broke the door down.*
2 to divide information or a piece of work into smaller parts so that it is easier to understand or deal with • (often + **into**) *The project has been broken down into sections for different teams to work on.* • *We can break down the results of the survey by age and gender.*
  breakdown *n* [C] • (usually singular) *Have you asked for a breakdown of your exam marks?*
3 to change someone's ideas or feelings about something because you think they are wrong • *Many women are concerned with breaking down the prejudice they still face at work.* • *The company's resistance to*

change is gradually being broken down.

breakdown n [C] • (usually singular) *Education plays an important role in the breakdown of racial prejudice.*

break down (sth) or **break** (sth) **down**
if a substance breaks down, or if something breaks it down, it separates into the simple chemical substances from which it is formed • *The damaged liver may lose its ability to break down chemicals in the body.* • (sometimes + **into**) *During digestion, the protein foods we eat are broken down into amino acids.*

breakdown n [singular] • *The enzyme causes the breakdown of food in the stomach.*

Break it down! (always an order) *Australian informal*
something that you say in order to tell someone to stop being angry or too excited • *Just break it down!*

break for   breaks, breaking, broke, broken

break for sth *American informal*
to move quickly and suddenly towards something • *They got out of the car in heavy rain and broke for the door of the house.* • **Break for it** (= run away) – *the police are coming!*

break in   breaks, breaking, broke, broken
break in

1 to get into a building or car by using force, usually in order to steal something • *They broke in through the kitchen window.*

break-in n [C] • *Two expensive paintings were stolen during the break-in.*

2 to use someone else's computer without permission in order to find out or change information • *Use a password to prevent anyone from breaking in.*

break in sth or **break** sth **in**

1 to wear something new [esp. shoes] for short periods of time in order to make them comfortable • *I'm just wearing these boots around the house to break them in.* • *He's breaking in a new baseball mitt.*

2 if you break in a young or wild horse, you train it to behave well • *He had spent*

months breaking this horse in.

3 *American* to drive a vehicle carefully and slowly for a short time when it is new, so that you do not damage its engine • *She can't drive fast as she's still breaking the car in.*

break in (sth)
to start talking when someone else is talking so that they cannot continue what they were saying • *'Tom,' Maggie broke in anxiously. 'Do we have to leave tomorrow?'* • (often + **on**) *I'm sorry to break in on you like this, but there's an urgent call for you, Jenny.*

break in sb or **break** sb **in** *informal*
to make someone become used to a new job or activity • *She was worried about starting a new job but her boss broke her in gently.*

break in on   breaks, breaking, broke, broken

break in on sth/sb
if you break in on someone or on what they are doing, you stop them from continuing by suddenly entering the room they are in • *I don't want to break in on their meeting.*

break into   breaks, breaking, broke, broken

break into sth

1 to get into a building or car by using force, usually in order to steal something • *My car's been broken into twice this month.*

2 to use someone else's computer without permission in order to find out or change information • *He broke into their computer system and stole some top secret records.*

3 to start to use an amount of money or food that you have been saving • *You can always break into your savings if you're short of cash.* • *Our food supply ran out after five days and we had to break into our emergency rations.*

4 to open a container of food or drink in order to start eating or drinking what is in it • *Next time, could you use the cheese that's open before you go breaking into a new packet?*

5 *British & Australian* to use paper money to

buy something because you do not have enough coins to pay for it ● *Could you lend me 50p – otherwise I'll have to break into a £10 note to pay my bus fare.*

6 to become involved in a type of business or activity that is difficult to become involved in ● *American banks are starting to break into the British finance market.* ● *The job provides good experience for people who want to break into charity work.*

7 to suddenly start to do something ● *The audience broke into cheers as the band came on stage.* ● *I told him that a letter from the bank had just arrived and he broke into a sweat.* (= started sweating) ● *Without warning, she had broken into a run and he thought he would never catch up.*

break off breaks, breaking, broke, broken

break off (sth) or break (sth) off
1 to stop doing something ● *We are breaking off our broadcast to make an urgent announcement.* ● (sometimes + **from**) *She broke off from reading and looked up at him.*
2 if discussions between two groups of people break off, or if someone breaks them off, they end suddenly, before they have been completed ● *Talks between protesters and government officials broke off yesterday.* ● *They broke off talks and there now seems little hope of a settlement.*

break off
to suddenly stop speaking ● *I broke off in the middle of speaking and now I can't remember what I was saying.*

break off sth or break sth off
to end a relationship ● *She broke off their engagement after discovering that he was having an affair.* ● (often + **with**) *In 1950 they broke off diplomatic ties with Britain.*

break off with breaks, breaking, broke, broken

break off with sb
to end a romantic relationship with someone ● *She broke off with Philip to start a relationship with Jamie.*

break out breaks, breaking, broke, broken

break out
1 to escape from prison ● (often + **of**) *They broke out of the prison camp by digging a tunnel.*
 break-out n [C] ● *The prison governor resigned after a series of break-outs.*
2 if something dangerous and unpleasant [e.g. war, disease, fire] breaks out, it suddenly starts ● *Two men were injured when a fight broke out in the bar.* ● *He had wisely left the country just before war broke out.* ● *The fire broke out on the 19th floor of the 30-storey building.*
 outbreak n [C] ● (often + **of**) *They're investigating an outbreak of food poisoning at a fast food restaurant.*
3 if peace breaks out, a peaceful period starts ● *At last it seems that peace has broken out in the region.*
4 if noise made by a group of people [e.g. applause, laughter] breaks out, it begins suddenly ● *Thunderous applause broke out as she walked on stage.*
5 if sweat (= watery liquid) or spots break out, they suddenly appear on your skin ● (often + **on**) *Perspiration broke out on her forehead.*
6 to do something different from what you usually do in order to make your situation or way of living better or more exciting ● *Each of them wanted a chance to break out, to dare to be different and to find themselves.* ● (often + **of**) *Every once in a while it's good to break out of your routine.*

break out sth

to say something suddenly, often because you are angry or excited ● *'The idiot!' broke out Mr Gomez.*

break out sth or **break** sth **out** *American*

to separate one type of information from a large collection of facts ● *I'd like you to break out the sales figures for regions 4 and 6.*

break out in/into breaks, breaking, broke, broken

break out in/into sth

if you break out in something [e.g. sweat, spots, rash], it suddenly appears on your skin ● *I broke out in a huge red rash the day before the party.* ● *When I saw the knife I **broke out in a cold sweat.*** (= I sweated a lot because I was afraid)

break through breaks, breaking, broke, broken

break through sth

1 to move through something that is intended to hold you back ● *The prison riot ended when 140 officers succeeded in breaking through a barricade.*

2 to become higher in number or quantity than something [e.g. target, level] ● *Sales of their new video have now broken through the 10 million level.*

3 to succeed in dealing with a problem or difficult situation ● *Part of my job as a teacher is to break through the apathy that stops these kids from achieving anything.* ● *With this campaign we're hoping to break through people's prejudices.*

breakthrough n [C] an important discovery or success that helps you achieve or deal with something ● *Her big breakthrough came when her novel was made into a tv drama.* ● (often + in) *Scientists have **made a** major **breakthrough** in the treatment of cancer.*

break through (sth)

if the suns breaks through or breaks through the clouds, it starts to appear from behind the clouds ● *By midday the sun had started to break through.* ● *The sun's just starting to break through the clouds.*

break up breaks, breaking, broke, broken

break up

1 if a marriage breaks up, or if two people who have a romantic relationship break up, their marriage or relationship ends ● *He started drinking heavily after his marriage broke up.* ● *I didn't know that Jenny and Mike had broken up.* ● (often + with) *It's now three years since she broke up with her boyfriend.*

break-up n [C] ● (often + of) *She associated the house with the break-up of her marriage.* ● (sometimes + with) *The bad news came during his breakup with a longtime girlfriend.*

2 *British & Australian* if schools or universities, or the people who study or work in them break up, classes end and the holidays start ● (often + for) *When do we break up for the summer holidays?*

break up (sth) or **break** (sth) **up**

1 to break into many pieces, or to break something into many pieces ● *We had to break the old fireplace up before we could move it from the house.*

break-up n [C] ● *It was feared that the break-up of the oil tanker would result in further pollution.*

2 to divide into several parts, or to divide something into several parts ● (often + into) *After she had finished her talk we broke up into smaller groups.* ● *The government wanted state farms to be broken up into small holdings.*

break-up n [singular] ● (often + into) *A complete break-up into independent nation states would cause many economic problems.*

3 if an occasion when people meet [e.g. meeting, party] breaks up, or if someone breaks it up, it ends and people start to leave ● *The meeting broke up at ten to three.* ● *I don't want to break up the party, but I have to go now.*

4 if a group of people who work or live together breaks up, or if someone or something breaks it up, they separate and stop working or living together ● *War can often break up families.* ● *After four years the band decided to break up.*

break-up n [C] ● (often + of) *The break-up of the pop group came as no surprise.*

5 if a fight breaks up, or if someone breaks it up, the people in it stop fighting or are made to stop fighting ● *The fight broke up when the police arrived.* ● *Just **break it up**, you two!* ● *They decided to break up*

the demonstration before it became too violent.

break up sth or **break** sth **up**

1 if an event breaks up a period of time, it makes it more interesting by being different to what you are doing for the rest of the time ● *A day on my own can seem quite long so I usually go out for a walk just to break it up.*

2 if you break up something that is all the same colour, you add a different colour to make it more interesting ● *I might put a red scarf with that black suit just to break it up.*

break (sb) **up** *American & Australian informal*

to laugh a lot, or to make someone laugh a lot ● *That show was so funny, it really broke me up.* ● *The kids break up whenever she starts speaking French.*

---

break with breaks, breaking, broke, broken

break with sth/sb

to leave an organization or end a relationship with someone, usually because you do not feel happy with it any more ● *The argument caused him to break with his brother.* ● *Gates broke with the party over their changes in education policy.*

break with sth

to stop doing things in the way that they were done in the past and do them completely differently ● *American film producers are being encouraged to break with tradition and look abroad for new actors.* ● *Artists should have the courage to break with established ideas.*

---

breathe in breathes, breathing, breathed

breathe in (sth) or **breathe** (sth) **in**

to take air or a substance [e.g. gas, smoke] into your lungs through your nose or mouth ● *Count to six as you breathe in, three as you breathe out.* ● *Think of all the chemicals you breathe in when you cycle to work.* ● *She leaned over to breathe in the scent of the roses.*

---

breathe out breathes, breathing, breathed

breathe out (sth) or **breathe** (sth) **out**

to make the air or other substances in your lungs come out through your nose or mouth ● *He breathed out slowly and tried to stay calm.* ● *You breathe in oxygen and breathe out carbon dioxide.*

---

breeze in/into breezes, breezing, breezed

breeze in

breeze into swh

to walk into a building or room quickly and confidently, without seeming worried or nervous about anything ● *He breezes in every morning, always happy and smiling.* ● *He just breezed into the office as if yesterday's argument had never happened.*

---

breeze into breezes, breezing, breezed

breeze into sth

to get an important and well-paid job, quickly and easily ● *He left Cambridge in '78 and breezed into a top banking job.*

---

breeze through breezes, breezing, breezed

breeze through sth *slightly informal*

to succeed in something [e.g. exam] very easily ● *The exam won't be a problem for her – she'll just breeze through it.* ● *I had breezed through school and assumed that university would be just as easy.*

---

brew up brews, brewing, brewed

brew up sth *British, American & Australian informal*

brew up *British & Australian informal*

to make a drink [e.g. tea, coffee], usually in a pot ● *You sit there and I'll brew up a nice cup of tea for you.* ● *I'm brewing up if you'd like a cuppa.*

brew up sth or **brew** sth **up**

to do or plan something that will cause trouble ● *I don't know what you're brewing up, but I don't want any part of it.*

brew up

if a difficult situation brews up, it starts to develop ● (usually in continuous tenses) *A nasty row is brewing up over the meeting between the two countries.*

---

brick in/up bricks, bricking, bricked

brick in/up sth or **brick** sth **in/up**

to fill a space [e.g. window, door] with bricks ● *We weren't using the fireplace so we decided to brick it in.* ● *The windows of the local army office have been bricked up, I notice.*

brighten up brightens, brightening, brightened

brighten up sth or **brighten** sth **up**
to make somewhere more attractive, often by adding colours ● *I thought yellow walls might brighten the place up a bit.* ● *A few plants will brighten up any office at very little expense.*

brighten up
1 if the weather brightens up, the sky becomes lighter and the sun starts to shine ● *If the weather brightens up this afternoon we could go for a walk.*
2 to suddenly look or feel happier ● *As soon as she heard that you were coming she brightened up.*

brim over brims, brimming, brimmed

brim over
if a container for liquid [e.g. glass] brims over, some of the liquid in it flows out because it is too full ● (usually in continuous tenses) *She filled the jug with cream until it was brimming over.*

brim over with brims, brimming, brimmed

brim over with sth
to feel or show a lot of a good emotion or good quality ● *I remember him brimming over with joy at the birth of his first son.* ● *Even in her nineties she brims over with energy.*

brim with brims, brimming, brimmed

brim with sth
1 to be or to become very full of something ● *As she was telling me her eyes brimmed with tears.*
2 to have or show a lot of a good emotion or good quality ● (often in continuous tenses) *She remembered him as an energetic man who was brimming with self-confidence.*

bring about brings, bringing, brought

bring about sth or **bring** sth **about**
to make something happen ● *We are hoping to bring about major changes in the way this company is organized.* ● *Jealousy in a relationship is often brought about by a lack of trust.*

bring along brings, bringing, brought

bring along sb/sth or **bring** sb/sth **along**
to bring someone or something somewhere ● *Bring your friend along if you like.* ● *I asked everyone to bring along something to eat.*

bring along sb or **bring** sb **along** *mainly American*
to help someone to improve their skills ● *The team's manager has a special ability for bringing new players along.*

bring around/round brings, bringing, brought

bring sb **around/round**
1 to make someone who is unconscious become conscious again ● *I tried slapping her face to bring her round.*
2 to persuade someone to agree with you or to do what you want them to do ● *At first she didn't want to take on any more staff, but I eventually managed to bring her around.* ● (often + **to**) *He hasn't yet managed to bring the others round to his way of thinking.*

bring around/round sb/sth or **bring** sb/sth **around/round** *mainly British & Australian*
to bring someone or something somewhere, especially to someone's house ● *Ann brought her new baby round this afternoon.*

bring around/round to brings, bringing, brought

bring sb/sth **around/round to** sth
to make someone start talking about what you want them to talk about ● *She managed to bring him around to the question of price.* ● *I gently tried to bring the discussion round to the subject of his divorce.*

bring back brings, bringing, brought

bring back sth or **bring** sth **back**
1 to make someone remember or think about something from the past ● *We talked about our time together in Edinburgh and it really brought back memories.* ● *I spent a couple of hours looking at my old holiday photos and it brought it all back.* (= it made me remember events from the past)

2 to start to do or use something that used be done or used in the past • *Trams have recently been brought back in Manchester.* • *They're always campaigning to bring back the death penalty.*

bring back sb or **bring** sb **back**

1 to give someone their previous job or position • *He resigned his post in 1987 but was brought back by the new administration.*

2 to make someone live again after they have died • *Margaret was dead and no amount of grieving would bring her back.* • *His heart stopped beating during the operation and the doctors tried to **bring him back to life** but they were too late.*

bring back to   brings, bringing, brought

bring sb **back to** sth
to make someone start talking about a particular subject again • *This talk of holidays brings me back to my original question, which was what are we doing this summer?*

bring before   brings, bringing, brought

bring sb **before** sb/sth
to make someone go to a place where a judge or official group will hear what they have been accused of doing and make a decision about it • (often passive) *He has been brought before the court twice on similar charges.*

bring sth **before** sb/sth
to arrange for a situation or problem to be discussed and considered formally by particular group or person • *The developers will bring their scheme before the planning committee next week.*

bring down   brings, bringing, brought

bring down sb or **bring** sb **down**
to cause people in positions of power [e.g. government, president] to lose their position • *The current crisis threatens to bring down the government.*

bring down sth or **bring** sth **down**

1 to reduce the amount, rate, or level of something • *The government is trying to bring down inflation.* • *Her doctor's told her she needs to relax more to bring her blood pressure down.*

2 to shoot at an aircraft, bird, or animal and make it fall to the ground • *Enemy*

fire brought down two fighter planes during the raid.

bring down on/upon   brings, bringing, brought

bring down sth **on/upon** sb or **bring** sth **down on/upon** sb *formal*
to make someone feel an unpleasant emotion [e.g. envy, hate] towards you • *Her obvious talent and natural beauty have brought the envy of many other actresses down on her.*

bring forth   brings, bringing, brought

bring forth sth

1 *formal* to produce something, or to make something happen • *The guilty verdict has brought forth sharp criticism from women's groups.*

2 *old-fashioned* to take something from the place where it is kept or hidden and let people see it • *He put his hand in his pocket and brought forth a small notebook.*

bring forth sb *old-fashioned*
to give birth to a baby • *Six months ago, his wife had finally brought forth a son and heir.*

bring forward   brings, bringing, brought

bring forward sth or **bring** sth **forward**

1 to change the date or time of an event so that it happens earlier than planned • *The book's publication date has been brought forward.* • (sometimes + **to**) *We've brought forward the date of the wedding to May 21st.*

2 to suggest a subject or problem so that it can be formally discussed or considered • *The reforms are part of a series of anti-terrorist measures being brought forward by the government.*

bring in   brings, bringing, brought

bring in sth or **bring** sth **in**

1 to earn or make a particular amount of money • *Neither film brought in any money at the box office.* • *She left college and went to work because her father thought it was time she brought some money in.*

2 if a government or organization brings in something new [e.g. law, rule], they make it exist for the first time • *The government will bring in legislation to restrict the sale of guns.*

3 to include a particular subject or piece of information, especially in writing • *If you bring in a few references to other authors it makes an essay more impressive.*

bring in sb or **bring** sb **in**

to ask someone with the necessary skills or knowledge to help you deal with something • *Management consultants have been brought in to make the company more profitable.* • *They brought in a team of experts to advise them.* • (often + **on**) *I'd like to bring Alex in on that project.*

bring in sb/sth or **bring** sb/sth **in**

if something, for example a company, brings people or business in, it attracts people, often encouraging them to buy products or services • *It is hoped that the company's attractive new premises will bring in some business.* • *He convinced the channel that the show could bring in a new, younger audience.*

bring into brings, bringing, brought

bring sb/sth **into** sth

to talk about someone or something in a conversation • *I don't really want to bring price into the discussion just now.*

bring off brings, bringing, brought

bring off sth or **bring** sth **off** *slightly informal*

to succeed in doing something difficult • *It's a really difficult part to act but I think she brought it off.* (= she succeeded) • *If he brings off the deal he'll be a wealthy man.*

bring on brings, bringing, brought

bring on sth or **bring** sth **on**

to make something unpleasant start • *Headaches are often brought on by stress.* • *This depression of his – what do you think brought it on?* • *Many companies have failed because of the problems brought on by the recession.*

bring on sb or **bring** sb **on** *mainly British & Australian*

to help someone to improve their skills • *Alice's sessions at nursery school have really brought her on.* • *The college golf scholarships are excellent at bringing on*

talented young players.

bring on/upon brings, bringing, brought

bring sth **on/upon** sb

to cause trouble for someone • *He felt deep regret for the shame he had brought upon his family.* • (often reflexive) *I don't have any sympathy for her – she's brought it all on herself.*

bring out brings, bringing, brought

bring out sth or **bring** sth **out**

1 to produce something to sell to the public • *In 1931, the company brought out a new, smaller car.* • *Haynes, like many photographers, has brought out his own book.*

2 to make a particular quality more noticeable • *Somehow the lemon brings out the flavour of the fish.* • (often + **in**) *Something about fishing brings out the hunter in us.* • *A crisis can bring out the best in someone.* (= show a person's best qualities) • *Something about him just brings out the worst in me.* (= makes me behave badly)

bring out sb or **bring** sb **out**

to make a shy person happier and more confident • *Having a girlfriend seems to have brought him out.* • *Being away at college has really brought her out of herself.* (= made her more confident with other people)

bring out in brings, bringing, brought

bring sb **out in** sth *British & Australian slightly informal*

if something, for example food, brings you out in something [e.g. spots, rash], it causes them to appear on your skin • *Fatty food generally brings me out in spots.* • *Certain washing-powders bring her out in a rash.*

bring over to brings, bringing, brought

bring sb **over to** sth

to persuade someone to agree with you • *She hasn't been able to bring her sister over to her point of view.*

bring round

see **bring around/round**

bring round to

see **bring around/round to**

bring to   brings, bringing, brought

bring sb **to**
to make someone who is unconscious become conscious again ● *Sam collapsed and at first no one could bring him to.*

bring together   brings, bringing, brought

bring together sb or **bring** sb **together**
to cause people to be friendly with each other, especially people who have argued with each other or who would not usually be friendly with each other ● *Everyone hoped that the wedding would bring the two families together.* ● *The disaster brought the community closer together.*

bring up   brings, bringing, brought

bring up sb or **bring** sb **up**
to look after a child and educate them until they are old enough to look after themselves ● *She decided she'd rather bring her children up in the countryside.* ● *I was brought up by my grandmother.* ● (sometimes + to do sth) *We'll bring them up to respect other people.* ● (sometimes + **as**) *They're bringing their son up as a Catholic.*

bring up sth or **bring** sth **up**
1 to start to talk about a particular subject ● *There are several points I'd like to bring up at the meeting tomorrow.*
2 to vomit something ● *He suddenly went white and brought up his breakfast all over the kitchen floor.*

bring upon
see **bring on/upon**

bristle with   bristles, bristling, bristled

bristle with sth *informal*
to have a large amount of something or to be full of something ● *It was a Saturday afternoon and the town was bristling with people.* ● *The helicopters hovered above them bristling with machine guns.*

broaden out   broadens, broadening, broadened

broaden out (sth)
to begin to include more, or to make something do this ● *I thought we might broaden out the discussion to include health issues.*

broaden out
to become wider ● *The track broadens out and becomes a path at this point.*

brush aside   brushes, brushing, brushed

brush aside sb/sth or **brush** sb/sth **aside**
to refuse to listen to what someone says, or to refuse to think about something seriously ● *The president continually brushed aside his critics during the eighteen-month campaign.* ● *He just brushed aside any objections to the proposal.*

brush by   brushes, brushing, brushed

brush by sb
to walk quickly past someone, touching them slightly as you pass them ● *She brushed by me in the corridor but we didn't speak.*

brush down/off   brushes, brushing, brushed

brush down/off sb/sth or **brush** sb/sth **down/off**
to remove dust, dirt etc. from someone or something by using your hands or a brush ● *He stood up, brushed himself down and got back on his bike.* ● *You'd better brush the chair off before you sit down.*

brush off   brushes, brushing, brushed

brush off sb/sth or **brush** sb/sth **off**
to refuse to listen to what someone says, or to refuse to think about something seriously ● *I tried to say I was sorry but she just brushed me off.* ● *He brushed off the allegations, claiming that they were 'complete nonsense'.*

brush-off n [singular] *slightly informal*
behaviour that shows that you do not want to be friendly with someone any more ● *I tried being friendly with him but he gave me the brush-off.*

brush up (on)   brushes, brushing, brushed

brush up (on) sth
to practise and improve your skills or your knowledge of something that you learned in the past but have partly forgotten ● *He was hoping to brush up on his Italian before our trip.* ● *Paul's challenged me to a game of tennis so I thought I'd better brush up on my technique.*

bubble over bubbles, bubbling, bubbled
bubble over
to be very excited and enthusiastic ● (usually + **with**) *None of them was exactly bubbling over with enthusiasm for the project.*

bucket down buckets, bucketing, buckets
bucket down *British informal*
to rain very heavily ● *Look at those dark clouds – it's going to bucket down in a minute.*

buckle down buckles, buckling, buckled
buckle down
to start working hard ● (usually + **to**) *It's about time he buckled down to some serious work.*

buckle up buckles, buckling, buckled
buckle up *American informal*
to fasten the belt that stops you from falling out of your seat in a car or plane ● *You'd better buckle up, it's going to be a bumpy ride.*

buddy up to buddies, buddying, buddied
buddy up to sb *American informal*
to try to make friends with someone ● *I saw her buddying up to the boys in the school cafeteria.*

budge up budges, budging, budged
budge up *British informal*
to move along on a seat in order to make more space ● (often an order) *Budge up, and then Sarah can sit here with us.*

bug off
Bug off! (always an order) *American informal*
something that you say in order to tell someone to go away, usually because they are annoying you ● *Bug off, I'm trying to work.*

bug out bugs, bugging, bugged
bug out
American informal if someone's eyes bug out they open very wide, usually because that person is very surprised or pleased ● *When Sally saw the gown her eyes just bugged out.*

bugger about/around buggers, buggering, buggered
bugger about/around *British & Australian informal*
to waste time doing silly, unimportant things ● *He's spent half the morning buggering about on his computer.*

bugger sb **about/around** *British & Australian informal*
to treat someone badly by wasting their time or causing them problems ● *He's changed the date three or four times and I'm fed up of being buggered around.*

bugger off buggers, buggering, buggered
Bugger off! (always an order) *British & Australian slang*
something that you say in order to tell someone to go away, usually because you are angry with them ● *Oh bugger off! I'm not in the mood.*

bugger off *British & Australian informal*
to leave quickly or suddenly ● *Everyone else had buggered off home and I was the only one in the office.*

bugger up buggers, buggering, buggered
bugger up sth or **bugger** sth **up** *British & Australian informal*
to spoil something or do something badly ● *He was messing with the central heating and I think he's gone and buggered it up.*

build around builds, building, built
build sth **around** sth
to base something on something else ● *It's a mistake to build your life around your work.* ● *The whole film is built around such an improbable storyline.*

build in/into builds, building, built
build in sth or **build** sth **in**
build sth **into** sth
1 to include something as a part of a plan, system, or agreement ● *I've been exercising for so long now that it's built into my daily routine* ● *If you want kids to study hard you have to build in a few incentives.*
   built-in *adj* (always before noun) ● *We've opted for a monthly savings plan with built-in life insurance.*
2 to make something so that it fits into part

of a wall or room • *The cupboards in the kitchen are all built in.* • *We're having shelves built into the wall over the bed.*

built-in *adj* (always before noun) • *a stereo with built-in speakers*

build on   builds, building, built

build on sth

to use a success or achievement as a base from which to achieve more success • *Once your company has established a good reputation you've got something to build on.* • *We had a certain amount of success in the European championships and we hope to build on that success.*

build up   builds, building, built

build up (sth) or **build** (sth) **up**

to increase in amount, size, or strength, or to make something increase in amount, size, or strength • *There were big delays as traffic built up on the roads into the city.* • *She needs something to build up her confidence again.*

build-up *n* [singular] • *These last six months have seen a pronounced military build-up in the region.* • *A rise in the earth's temperature is supposed to be caused by the build-up of polluting gases.*

build up sth or **build** sth **up**

1 to develop and improve something • *He'd spent the last ten years building up his printing business.* • *She's concentrating on building up her career.* • *Like a lot of countries in this region, they're struggling to build up their economy.*

2 to gradually make or create something • *Police are slowly building up a profile of the killer.* • *Personal relationships built up over a year will be lost when we move.*

build up sb/sth or **build** sb/sth **up**

to praise someone or something and say that they are very important or special • *The media builds people up, only to knock them down again.* • *They'd built the programme up so much that when it was finally shown it was a disappointment.*

build-up *n* [singular] • *The guy presenting the show gave me such a build-up it was almost embarrassing.*

build up sb or **build** sb **up** (never passive)

to make someone healthier and stronger after an illness, especially by making

sure that they eat a lot • *Come on, have some food – we've got to build you up.*

build up to   builds, building, built

build up to sth

to gradually prepare yourself for a particular occasion or event • *You can't start by running long distances – you've got to build up to it in stages.*

build-up *n* [singular] • (usually + **to**) *He got a lot of media coverage in the build-up to the elections.*

bulk out/up   bulks, bulking, bulked

bulk out/up sth or **bulk** sth **out/up** *informal*

to make something bigger by adding something to it • (often + **with**) *You can bulk out the salad with potatoes or pasta.* • *I added some statistics to my report to bulk it up a little.*

bulk up   bulks, bulking, bulked

bulk up (sth) or **bulk** (sth) **up** mainly American

to gain weight, or to increase the size of something • *He was told to bulk up if he wanted to become a heavyweight boxer.* • *Dan is going to the gym every day to bulk up his muscles for football.*

bum about/around/round   bums, bumming, bummed

bum about/around/round *informal*

to spend time being lazy and doing very little • *He spent most of last year just bumming around.*

bum about/around/round swh *informal*

to travel around with no plans and little money • *I spent last summer bumming around Europe with some friends.*

bum off   bums, bumming, bummed

bum sth **off** sb

to get something from someone without paying for it, or to borrow a small amount of money from someone • *If you're leaving now can I bum a lift off you?* • *He's always bumming money off me for cigarettes.*

bum out   bums, bumming, bummed

bum out sb or **bum** sb **out** American *informal*

to upset or annoy someone • *These reports are really beginning to bum me out.*

bum round

see **bum about/around/round**

bump along   <small>bumps, bumping, bumped</small>

bump along

if a process or system bumps along, it continues even though there are problems • *The property market bumped along until Friday when there was a sudden fall.*

bump into   <small>bumps, bumping, bumped</small>

bump into sb

to meet someone you know when you have not planned to meet them • *I bumped into Mark when I was out shopping this afternoon.*

bump off   <small>bumps, bumping, bumped</small>

bump off sb or **bump** sb **off** *informal*

to kill someone • *He plays the hit-man who's hired to bump off the main character's wife.*

bump up   <small>bumps, bumping, bumped</small>

bump up sth or **bump** sth **up** *informal*

to increase the size or amount of something [e.g. price] by a large amount • (sometimes + **to**) *Leather seats will bump up the price of the car to $15,995.* • (sometimes + **by**) *Our landlord has just bumped the rent up by £50.*

bump up sb or **bump** sb **up** *American informal*

to move someone to a better or higher position • (often + **to**) *They've bumped Greg up to supervisor.* • *She was bumped up to first class on her flight home.*

bunch up   <small>bunches, bunching, bunched</small>

bunch up (sth/sb) or **bunch** (sth/sb) **up**

to move close together so that you make a tight group • (usually passive) *We were all bunched up at the back of the room.*

bunch up (sth) or **bunch** (sth) **up**

if material bunches up, or if someone bunches it up, it moves into tight folds • *My shirt's all bunched up at the back.*

bundle off   <small>bundles, bundling, bundled</small>

bundle off sb or **bundle** sb **off**

to quickly send someone somewhere, especially a child • (often + **to**) *I was wrapped in a thick coat and bundled off to school.*

bundle up   <small>bundles, bundling, bundled</small>

bundle up (sb) or **bundle** (sb) **up**

to put warm clothes or coverings on yourself or someone else • *Bundle up well before you go out in the snow.* • (often + **in**) *The children were bundled up in blankets for the journey.*

bundle up sth or **bundle** sth **up**

to gather or tie a group of things together • *I bundled up some old clothes and gave them to a charity shop.*

bung up   <small>bungs, bunging, bunged</small>

bung up sth or **bung** sth **up**

to cause something to be blocked so that it does not work properly • *I don't like to put paper down the toilet in case I bung it up again.*

bunged-up *adj slightly informal* • *I've got a cold and I'm all bunged-up.* (= my nose is blocked) • *a bunged-up nose*

bunk down   <small>bunks, bunking, bunked</small>

bunk down (always + *adv/prep*)

to lie down to sleep somewhere, especially not in a bed • *I can't offer you a bed but you're welcome to bunk down on the sofa.*

bunk off   <small>bunks, bunking, bunked</small>

bunk off (sth) *British informal*

to stay away from school or work or to leave school or work early, especially without permission • *If we bunk off early, we could do some shopping.* • *I remember bunking off school when I was a kid.*

buoy up   <small>buoys, buoying, buoyed</small>

buoy up sb or **buoy** sb **up**

to make someone feel happier or more confident about a situation • *We buoyed each other up, saying 'This is going to work'.*

buoy up sth or **buoy** sth **up**

to support something and help to make it more successful • *Information technology will buoy up the nation's economy.*

burn down   <small>burns, burning, burnt or burned</small>

burn down (sth) or **burn** (sth) **down**

to destroy something, especially a building, by fire, or to be destroyed by fire • *They came back to find that their house had burnt down.* • *Dozens of people were hurt and a police station was burned down.*

burn off   burns, burning, burnt or burned

burn off sth or **burn** sth **off**
to remove something by burning it ● *Up to 40 oil wells have been set alight to burn off the lethal gases.*

burn off/up   burns, burning, burnt or burned

burn off/up sth or **burn** sth **off/up**
to use or get rid of energy or something which provides energy [e.g. calories, fat], by doing a lot of physical exercise ● *Aerobics certainly burns off a lot of calories.* ● *Do you think you burn off much fat in the gym?* ● *Research shows that fat people actually burn up energy faster than thin ones.*

burn out   burns, burning, burnt or burned

burn out or **burn** itself **out**
1 if a fire burns out, or if it burns itself out, it stops burning because nothing remains that can burn ● *I left the fire to burn out.* ● *The blaze spread from shop to shop until it burned itself out.*
   burnt-out *adj* ● *We drove past burnt-out buildings and boarded windows.* ● *Burnt-out cars litter the street.*
2 if an illness, problem, or emotion burns out or burns itself out, you gradually stop feeling it or suffering from it ● *Generally speaking, the disease burns out within a couple of years.* ● *The international community chose to wait until the conflict burnt itself out.*

burn out sb or **burn** sb **out**
to make someone leave their home by burning it ● (often + **of**) *Hundreds of families have been burnt out of their homes.*

burn out (sth) or **burn** (sth) **out**
if a piece of machinery or electrical equipment burns out, or if someone or something burns it out, it stops working because it has become too hot or has been used too much ● *I turned on a switch but the light had burnt out.* ● *Large voltage swings can cause electric motors to burn out.* ● *Terrorists had planted devices designed to burn out signal cables in rail lines.*

burn out or **burn** yourself **out** *informal*
to have to stop working because you have become ill or very tired from working too hard ● *If he carries on working as hard as this he'll burn out before the exams.* ● *You've got to keep up a steady rate of progress but you don't want to burn yourself out.*

burnt-out *adj informal* ● *By the time we'd finished the project I was completely burnt-out.*

burnout *n* [U] ● *Teaching has a high rate of professional burnout.*

burn out
to suddenly lose the ability to be creative or think of new ideas ● *His critics were saying that he'd burnt out and that he'd made all his best films.*

burn up   burns, burning, burnt or burned

burn up sth or **burn** sth **up**
if an engine burns up fuel, it uses a lot of fuel to work ● *A car this size burns up a lot of fuel.*

burn sb **up** *American informal*
to make someone very angry ● *He'd made some remark about incompetent women that really burned me up.*

be burning up (always in continuous tenses) *informal*
to have a fever ● *I've just felt his forehead – he's really burning up.*

burn up (sth) or **burn** (sth) **up**
to destroy something completely, or to be destroyed completely by burning or very strong heat ● *The spacecraft finally burned up in the atmosphere of Venus.* ● *It was proposed that the nuclear power station be used to burn up nuclear weapons waste.*

burst in   bursts, bursting, burst

burst in
to enter a room suddenly and without warning, interrupting the people who are in it ● (often + **on**) *Masked gunmen burst in on the meeting, killing 15 people.* ● *The door was flung open and Oliver suddenly burst in.*

burst into   bursts, bursting, burst

burst into swh
to enter a room suddenly and without warning, interrupting the people who are

in it ● *The police had burst into her flat in Lambeth, South London, with a search warrant.*

burst into sth

to suddenly start to make a noise, especially to start crying, laughing or singing ● *I told her what he'd said and she **burst into laughter**.* ● *He looked as if he was on the point of **bursting into tears**.* ● *The whole room seemed to **burst into song**.*

burst out   bursts, bursting, burst

burst out sth

1 to suddenly say something loudly ● *'Don't go!' he burst out.* ● *In the middle of the service my nephew suddenly burst out 'That man's got a dress on.'*

2 if you burst out laughing or crying, you suddenly start to laugh or cry ● *He took one look at her in her new hat and burst out laughing.* ● *He looked as if he was about to burst out crying.*

outburst *n* [C] a sudden, strong expression of feeling, especially anger ● *The outbursts of temper increased as he got older.*

burst with

be bursting with sth (always in continuous tenses)

to have a lot of something ● *She's a woman in her prime, bursting with energy and humour.* ● *They're not exactly bursting with enthusiasm for the project.*

bury away

be buried away (always passive; always + *adv/prep*)

if something is buried away somewhere, it is in a place that is difficult to find ● (often + **in**) *I found the article buried away in the business section of the newspaper.* ● *She found the letter buried away at the back of a drawer.*

bury in   buries, burying, buried

bury yourself **in** sth (always reflexive)

to give all your attention and time to something, especially work ● *Partly to forget about his troubles, he buried himself in his studies.*

bust out   busts, busting, bust
American pt & pp also **busted**

bust out

1 *mainly American informal* to escape from

somewhere, especially prison ● (often + **of**) *He busted out of the county jail.*

2 *American informal* to do something different from what you usually do in order to make your situation or way of living better or more exciting ● (often + **of**) *The dancers seemed to enjoy busting out of the stricter forms of classical ballet.*

bust out sth *American*

if you bust out laughing, you suddenly start to laugh or cry ● *She took one look at him and busted out laughing.*

bust up   busts, busting, bust
American pt & pp also **busted**

bust up *mainly American informal*

to end a relationship after an angry argument ● *Her parents bust up when she was small.* ● (often + **with**) *She'd bust up with Carlo and had nowhere to stay.*

bust-up *n* [C] *informal* an angry argument ● (often + **with**) *Jane had a big bust-up with Roger in the middle of the meeting.* the end of a relationship ● *Two marriages in five are likely to end in a bust-up.*

bust up sth or bust sth up

1 *American informal* to cause a lot of damage somewhere [e.g. room, building] breaking things inside it ● *He went crazy and started to bust up the apartment.*

2 to prevent an event, especially a meeting, from continuing ● *He'd been part of a gathering that the police had bust up.*

3 *mainly American* to break a large company or other organization into smaller parts ● *Busting up large telecommunication companies should lead to lower phone bills.*

bust-up *n* [C] *American* ● *It's a huge global company in need of a bust-up.* ● (used as *adj*) *The Directors have a bust-up plan ready and waiting.*

bustle about/around   bustles, bustling, bustled

bustle about/around (swh)

to move around quickly in a busy way, doing a lot of different things ● *Gina bustled around the room, tidying things away.* ● *I could hear her bustling around in the kitchen making dinner.*

butt in   butts, butting, butted

butt in

1 to rudely add a remark to someone else's conversation or speech, often stopping them from continuing what they were saying ● *He kept butting in all the way through her speech.* ● (often + **on**) *It irritates me the way she butts in on other people's conversations.*

2 *American & Australian informal* to become involved when you are not wanted in a situation that is connected with other people ● *His mother is always butting in instead of letting us make our own plans.* ● *The manager warned the other players that his decisions were final and not to butt in.*

butt out   butts, butting, butted

butt out *informal*
to stop involving yourself with situations connected with other people ● *This is between Lou Ann and me so why don't you just butt out!*

butter up   butters, buttering, buttered

butter up sb or **butter** sb **up** *informal*
to be very nice to someone so that they will do what you want them to do ● *All these compliments – I know you're only trying to butter me up!*

button down   buttons, buttoning, buttoned

button down sth or **button** sth **down** *American informal*
to think about or state something in an exact way ● *Before you argue with him, button down the specific points you want to make.*

button up   buttons, buttoning, buttoned

button up sth or **button** sth **up**
to fasten a piece of clothing by putting buttons through holes ● *Come on, Hettie, button up your coat.*
buttoned-up *adj American* having a very formal appearance or way of behaving ● *The American lawyers were more open, less buttoned-up than their British counterparts.*

buy in   buys, buying, bought

buy in sth or **buy** sth **in** *British & Australian*
to buy a lot of something [e.g. food, drink], usually for a special occasion ● *They'd bought in all this wine for the party and scarcely anyone showed up.*

buy into   buys, buying, bought

buy into sth

1 to buy a part of a company or organization ● *It was rumoured that McDowell was trying to buy into the newspaper business.*

2 *informal* to accept completely a belief or set of beliefs and be very influenced by them ● *I never did buy into the idea that earning lots of money will bring you happiness.*

buy off   buys, buying, bought

buy off sb or **buy** sb **off**
to pay someone money so that they do not cause you any trouble ● (often + **with**) *Strikers were bought off with big wage settlements.*

buy out   buys, buying, bought

buy out sb/sth or **buy** sb/sth **out**
to buy part of a company or building that belonged to someone else so that you own all of it ● *He bought out his partner for £3 million.* ● *They had a joint mortgage but Clare was able to buy John out.*
buyout *n* [C] the buying of a company, especially by the people who previously managed it or worked for it ● *Rumours of a sale or **management buyout** for Phibro never die.*

buy out of   buys, buying, bought

buy sb **out of** sth *British & Australian*
if you buy someone out of the armed forces, you pay money so that they can leave earlier than they had previously agreed to ● (often reflexive) *Whittingham was a soldier until he bought himself out of the army for £450.* ● *He started to play for the club after they bought him out of the army for £700.*

buy up   buys, buying, bought

buy up sth or **buy** sth **up**
to quickly buy a lot of something, often all that is available ● *Most of the land in the area has been bought up by property*

developers. ● *In Hawaii, Japanese investors have bought up nearly half of the resort hotels.*

buzz about/around/round · buzzes, buzzing, buzzed

buzz about/around/round (swh)
to move around a place quickly and with energy ● *Reporters were buzzing around trying to get the full story.* ● *We spent the afternoon buzzing about town on our bikes.*

buzz off · buzzes, buzzing, buzzed

buzz off *informal*
to leave a place ● *I've got some stuff to do at home so I'm going to buzz off now.*

Buzz off! (always an order) *informal*
something that you say in order to tell someone to go away ● *Look, I'm busy so just buzz off, would you!*

buzz round

see **buzz about/around/round**

call around calls, calling, called

call around *mainly American*
to telephone several people, often in order to find out information • *I'll call around and see if anyone's free on Saturday.*

call away calls, calling, called

call away sb or **call** sb **away**
to ask someone to stop what they are doing in order to go somewhere else • (usually passive) *Paul wasn't at the meeting. He was called away on urgent business, apparently.*

call back calls, calling, called

call back (sb) or **call** (sb) **back** (never passive)
to telephone someone for the second time or to telephone someone who rang you earlier • *'I'm sorry but Mr Lewis is in a meeting at the moment. Can you call back later?'* • *Jill wasn't there when I called so I'll call her back tomorrow.* • *I'm running out of change. Do you think you could call me back?*

call-back *n* [singular] *British & Australian* a device in a telephone which automatically calls a number which was busy when you tried to call it • *We have automatic call-back on our phone.* • (used as *adj*) *a call-back facility*

callback *n* [C] *American* a telephone call that someone makes to you to answer a call that you made to them earlier • *I phoned the store this morning and am expecting a callback.*

call back *mainly British & Australian*
to go back to a place in order to visit someone or collect something that you were unable to visit or collect earlier • (often + *adv/prep*) *If you call back in half an hour he should be here.* • *Is it alright if I call back this afternoon to pick up those books?*

call by calls, calling, called

call by *British & Australian informal*
to visit someone for a short time, usually when you are going somewhere else • *I just thought I'd call by on my way into town.*

call down calls, calling, called

call down sth or **call** sth **down** (never passive) *literary*
to pray that something unpleasant will happen to someone, or to make something unpleasant happen to someone • *He feared that such an act would call down the wrath of God.*

call for calls, calling, called

call for sth
1 to need or deserve a particular action or quality • *It's the sort of work that calls for a high level of concentration.* • *It's not every day a good friend tells you she's getting married. This calls for a celebration!*

2 to say that you think a particular thing should be done, usually in order to change or improve a situation • *Some critics have called for an independent investigation into the affair.* • *The report calls for a minimum wage.*

call for sb *mainly British & Australian*
to visit a place in order to collect someone • *How about if I call for you around eight o'clock?*

call forth calls, calling, called

call forth sth or **call** sth **forth** *formal*
to make something exist or happen • *His remarks called forth a storm of protest.*

call in calls, calling, called

call in
1 *British & Australian* to visit a place or person for a short time, usually while you are going somewhere else • (usually + *adv/prep*) *I'll call in on my way home.* • *Do you mind if we just call in at the supermarket?* • *I might call in on Mira while I'm in town.* • *Call in for a coffee and a chat some time.*

2 to telephone your place of work, usually to explain why you are not there • *I'd better call in and tell them I'm going to be late.* • *Melanie called in sick this morning.* (= telephoned to say that she was ill

and could not come to work)

3 to telephone a radio or television programme in order to give your opinion or to ask for advice ● *It's one of those programmes where viewers call in to talk about their problems.*

call-in *n* [C] *mainly American* ● *I was listening to a radio call-in.* ● (used as *adj*) *We heard him interviewed on a radio call-in show.*

call in sb *or* **call** sb **in**

to ask someone to come to help in a difficult situation ● (often + to do sth) *British detectives were called in to conduct a fresh inquiry.* ● *The police called him in for questioning.*

call in sth *or* **call** sth **in** *British*

if a company calls in a product, it asks people to return the product because there might be something wrong with it ● *They've had to call in some of the latest models to check the brakes.*

call off sth *or* **call** sth **off**

1 to decide that a planned event or activity will not happen, especially because it is no longer possible or useful ● *The match had to be called off because of the freezing weather.* ● *The wedding was planned for June and they've just called the whole thing off.*

2 to decide to stop an activity that has already started ● *Police have called off the search for the missing child until dawn tomorrow.*

call off sb/sth *or* **call** sb/sth **off** *slightly formal*

to order a dog or person to stop attacking someone or something ● *I shouted at him to call his dog off but he just ignored me.*

call on sb

1 to visit someone for a short time ● *I'd like to call on Isobel while I'm in London.*

2 *American* to ask a person in a group of people to answer a question or to give their opinion about something ● *She was afraid the teacher would call on her and she wouldn't know the answer.*

call on/upon sb to do sth *formal*

to officially ask someone to do something ● (usually passive) *The army is in a state of readiness in case it should be called upon to launch an offensive.*

call on/upon sth *formal*

to use something, especially a quality that you have, in order to achieve something ● *She would have to call on all her strength if she was to survive the next few months.*

call out (sth) *or* **call** (sth) **out**

to say something in a loud voice, especially in order to get someone's attention ● *Someone in the crowd called out his name, but he couldn't see who.* ● (often + to) *I called out to him but he didn't hear me.* ● *I think I heard him call out in the night.*

call out sb *or* **call** sb **out**

1 to ask a skilled person or organization to come to help you ● *A hundred firefighters were called out to the blaze which took 90 minutes to contain.* ● (sometimes + to do sth) *I had to call the doctor out in the middle of the night to have a look at her.*

call-out *n* [C] *British* ● *If your washing machine breaks down, a call-out can easily cost more than £100.* ● (used as *adj*) *The call-out charge alone will cost you £30.*

2 to order workers to strike (= to refuse to work because of an argument with an employer) ● *After a series of unsuccessful talks, the miners were called out.*

call out for sth *American*

to telephone a place in order to arrange for something, especially food, to be brought to you ● *I don't want to cook tonight. Should I call out for a pizza?*

call over sb *or* **call** sb **over** *British & Australian*

to ask someone to come to where you are, usually in order to speak to them or to show them something ● *She called me over to where she was sitting.* ● (sometimes + to do sth) *He was amazed* at what he saw and called the others over to look.

call over
to visit someone who lives near to you for a short time • *I'll call over later this afternoon.*

call round   calls, calling, called

call round *British & Australian*
to visit someone who lives near to you for a short time • (sometimes + **for**) *You should call round for a drink some time.* • (sometimes + to do sth) *She called round this afternoon to collect the plates for the party.*

call up   calls, calling, called

call up (sb) or **call** (sb) **up** (never passive) *mainly American*
to telephone someone • *Why don't you call me up at home?* • *You can call up and leave a message if I'm out.*

call up sb or **call** sb **up**
1 to order someone to join the army, navy, or airforce • (usually passive) *He was called up a month after the war started.*
   call-up *n* [U] • *Students are applying for education courses to avoid the call-up.*
2 to ask someone to join something, especially a sports team • (usually passive) *He's been called up to play for England.*
   call-up *n* [singular] • *Carlton received his call-up to the Scottish side yesterday.*

call up sth or **call** sth **up**
1 to find and show information on a computer screen • *Can you call up last year's sales figures on Janice's computer?*
2 if something calls up a memory or an idea, it makes you remember or think about it • *The temple called up images of ancient Egypt.*

call upon
see **call on/upon**

calm down   calms, calming, calmed

calm down (sb) or **calm** (sb) **down**
to stop feeling upset, angry, or excited, or to make someone stop feeling this way • (often an order) *Calm down. There's no point worrying about it now.* • *She was so annoyed – it took me half an hour to calm her down.* • (sometimes reflexive) *I tried to calm myself down with a glass of wine.*

calm down (sth) or **calm** (sth) **down**
if a situation calms down, or if you calm it down, it becomes more peaceful • *They went through a period of arguing a lot but things seem to have calmed down recently.* • *I managed to calm the situation down by talking to them.*

camp out   camps, camping, camped

camp out
1 to sleep outside in a tent (= shelter made of cloth) • *The kids love camping out in the garden.*
   campout *n* [C] *American* • *The kids like having campouts in the backyard in summer.*
2 to stay and sleep in a place for a short time because you cannot stay where you usually do • *Tom and Barbara camped out at our place for a couple of days until their house was ready.*

camp up   camps, camping, camped

camp it up *informal*
to speak and move in an exaggerated and sometimes funny way that is intended to be noticed by others • *The best thing in the whole show was Steven Dykes, camping it up as the prince.*

cancel out   cancels, cancelling, cancelled

cancel out sth or **cancel** sth **out**
if one thing cancels out another thing, the first thing has the opposite effect of the second thing and there is therefore no change in the situation • *The cost of staying there just one night cancelled out any savings we had made by sleeping on the*

train. • *The negative and positive sides of the argument seem to cancel each other out.*

capitalize on capitalizes, capitalized, capitalizing

capitalize on sth
to use a situation in order to achieve something good for yourself • *Of course the opposition intend to capitalize on the government's lack of popularity.*

care for cares, caring, cared

care for sb
1 to look after someone who is too young, too old, or too ill to look after themselves • *Very little support is given to people who care for their elderly relatives.*
2 *old-fashioned* to love someone in a romantic way • *You know I care for you, Julia.*

care for sth (always used in questions) *formal*
to want something • *Would you care for a glass of wine?*

not care for sth/sb (always negative) *formal*
to not like something or someone • *Your father thought she was nice but Camille and I didn't care for her.*

carry away

be carried away (always passive)
to be so excited about something that you do not control what you say or do and you forget about everything else • *I got a bit carried away when I was dancing and got up on the table.*

carry forward carries, carrying, carried

carry forward sth or **carry** sth **forward**
1 to include an amount of money in a later set of calculations • *Some businesses tried to avoid tax by carrying forward losses from earlier years.*
2 to copy a total from the bottom of one page to the top of another page so that other numbers can be added to it • *$4000 is the figure carried forward from the previous page.*
3 to help something to progress • *He had found the man who could carry the company forward when he retired.*

carry off carries, carrying, carried

carry off sth or **carry** sth **off** (never passive)
1 to succeed in doing or achieving something difficult • *It's not an easy part to act but I thought he carried it off brilliantly.* • *I wouldn't dare wear anything so outrageous but somehow Dil manages to carry it off.*
2 to win a prize • *Davies, as predicted, carried off the award for Best Female actress.*
3 to take something somewhere, especially without permission • *Thieves broke into the shop and carried off jewellery worth thousands of pounds.*

carry off sb or **carry** sb **off** *literary*
if a disease carries someone off, it causes their death • *Hunger and cold carried off many of the children in the camp.*

carry on carries, carrying, carried

carry on *mainly British & Australian*
1 to continue doing something • *I'll just carry on till I've got it finished.* • (often + doing sth) *If he carries on drinking like that he's going to have a problem.* • (often + **with**) *Shall I just carry on with the painting?*
2 to do the things that you usually do, especially when you are in an unpleasant situation • *Three days ago my wife tells me she's got another man. I just can't carry on as if nothing's happened! • If it weren't for you, Michael, I just don't think I could carry on. • In the remote mountain villages life carries on as normal, even during the fighting.*
3 to behave in an excited and uncontrolled way • *The children have been carrying on all day.*

carry-on *n* [C] *old-fashioned* a situation in which people get very angry or excited about something that is not important • *There was a right old carry-on over who should accept the award.*
4 *old-fashioned* to have a sexual relationship with someone who is not your usual partner • (usually + **with**) *And all that time her husband had been carrying on with Olga Jones next door!*

carry on sth or **carry** sth **on** *mainly British & Australian*
to continue doing something that someone else started • *She's going to carry on*

the family tradition and become a lawyer.
• *He died six years ago but a team of scientists carry on his work in a laboratory in Switzerland.*

carry out   carries, carrying, carried

carry out sth or **carry** sth **out**

1 to do or complete something, especially something important • *A survey of ten schools in the area will be carried out next year.*

2 if you carry out something that you said you would do, or that you have been told to do [e.g. instructions, order, threat], you do it • *No one actually thought that the kidnappers would carry out their threat.* • *He claimed that he was blameless because he was merely carrying out instructions.*

carry over   carries, carrying, carried

carry over sth or **carry** sth **over**
to use something or do something at a later time than planned • (often + **to**) *The performance has had to be carried over to next week.* • *How much holiday can you carry over from one year to the next?*

carry over (sth) or **carry** (sth) **over**
if something from one situation carries over, or is carried over into another situation, it is allowed to exist in or affect the other situation • (often + **into**) *Inevitably, problems at work are carried over into your private life.* • *Military culture involves drinking heavily and this carries over into civilian life.*

carry-over n [singular] something that continues to exist from a previous time • (usually + **from**) *Black polo-neck sweaters are a carry-over from the 1960's.*

carry through   carries, carrying, carried

carry through sth or **carry** sth **through**
to complete something successfully • *It will almost certainly be the next decade before this package of reforms is carried through.*

carry sb **through** (sth) (never passive)
to help someone to be able to deal with a difficult situation • *It was my faith that carried me through.* • *Determination alone will carry you through the bad times.*

cart off   carts, carting, carted

cart off sb or **cart** sb **off**
to take someone away, usually to prison
• *Opponents of the government were simply carted off to prison.*

carve out   carves, carving, carved

carve out sth or **carve** sth **out** (never passive)
to successfully create or obtain a work position [e.g. career, niche] by working for it • *She's carved out a nice little career for herself as a daytime chat-show hostess.* • *Over the last five years they've carved out a very profitable niche in the computer industry.*

carve up   carves, carving, carved

carve up sth or **carve** sth **up**
1 to cut cooked meat into pieces • *She carved up the chicken.*
2 to divide something, especially land, into smaller parts • *Prussia was abolished and most of its territory carved up between Poland and the Soviet Union.*
   carve-up n [singular] *British & Australian* • *Managers have promised that there will be no carve-up of the business.*

carve up sb or **carve** sb **up**
British informal to drive past someone in a car, then suddenly move in front of them so that you are too close to them • *Some idiot carved me up and I had to brake suddenly.*

cash in   cashes, cashing, cashed

cash in sth or **cash** sth **in**
to exchange a financial arrangement that you have paid for [e.g. shares, bonds] for the money itself • *She cashed in her savings bonds to raise money to buy the car.*

cash in on   cashes, cashing, cashed

cash in on sth
to make money from an event or situation, or to get some other advantage from it, often in an unfair way • *Should the families of criminals be allowed to cash in on their crimes by selling stories to the papers?* • *Anti-road protesters are hoping to cash in on growing public support.*

cash up   cashes, cashing, cashed

cash up *British & Australian*
to count all the money taken by a shop or business at the end of the day • *The gunman broke in just as she was cashing up.*

cast about/around/round   casts, casting, cast

cast about/around/round
1 *slightly formal* to look around you to try to find something • (usually + **for**) *He was casting around for something to use as a weapon.*
2 *slightly formal* to try very hard to think of something • (usually + **for**) *She cast around in her mind for an excuse.*

cast aside   casts, casting, cast

cast aside sth/sb or **cast** sth/sb **aside** *formal*
to get rid of something or someone, or to ignore something or someone because you do not need them or like them any more • *That's when I was seeing Jamie – before I was cast aside in favour of the gorgeous Italian.* • *Some of his toys he plays with for months, others are cast aside after a couple of weeks.*

cast aside sth or **cast** sth **aside** *formal*
if you cast aside bad feelings [e.g. doubts, inhibitions, prejudices], you get rid of them • *Cast aside your prejudices for a moment and keep an open mind.*

cast away

be cast away (always passive)
to be on an island with no other people after swimming from a ship that is sinking • (usually + **on**) *If I were cast away on a desert island, I think it's chocolate that I'd miss most.*
castaway *n* [C] • *Have you seen that film where he plays a castaway?*

cast down   casts, casting, cast

cast down sth or **cast** sth **down** *literary*
to look down, especially because you are ashamed or shy • (usually passive) *She stood before them with eyes cast down.*
downcast *adj* • *Tears formed in his downcast eyes.*

be cast down (always passive) *literary*
to be very sad and without hope • *He seemed very cast down by the situation.*

downcast *adj* • *She left the house feeling downcast.*

cast off   casts, casting, cast

cast off sth or **cast** sth **off** *literary*
to suddenly get rid of something bad or something that has been preventing progress • *She was impatient to cast off the restraints of formality.*
cast-offs *n* (plural) things, usually clothes, which have been given to someone else because the first owner cannot use them any more • *My sister always had new clothes, while I had to make do with her cast-offs.*

cast off sth or **cast** sth **off** *formal*
to take off clothes very quickly • *He cast off his jacket and plunged into the water.*

cast off
to untie a boat from the place it is fastened to so that it can sail away • *She started up the engine, cast off and sailed away.*

cast off (sth)
in knitting, to use a special type of stitch to remove it from the needle and form the edge of an item you are making • *At the beginning of the next row, cast off three stitches.*

cast on   casts, casting, cast

cast on sth
in knitting, to use a special type of stitch to start the item you are making • *First I'll show you how to cast on.*

cast out   casts, casting, cast

cast out sb or **cast** sb **out** *slightly formal*
to make someone leave a place, or to refuse to accept someone as part of a group because you are angry with them or do not like them • (usually passive) *Sometimes she felt cast out by her family.* • *He was cast out of his home at the age of fourteen.*
outcast *n* [C] • *People treat you like a social outcast if you don't have a television.*

cast round
see **cast about/around/round**

cast up   casts, casting, cast

cast up sth or **cast** sth **up**
if the sea casts something up, it carries that thing onto the beach • (usually pas-

sive + **on**) *Their bodies were cast up on the beach.*

catch at   catches, catching, caught

catch at sth

to pull something quickly, or to try to get hold of something, especially someone's hand or a piece of clothing • *In great excitement, he caught at my sleeve and tried to pull me back.* • *As we walked, thorns caught at our clothes.*

catch on   catches, catching, caught

catch on

1 to become popular • *The practice of taking cold showers is unlikely to catch on in Britain.* • (often + **with**) *The movie did not catch on with black audiences.*

2 *slightly informal* to understand something, especially after a long time • *They sold the fake jewellery for years before anyone caught on.* • (often + **to**) *The audience soon catches on to the fact that he is only joking.*

catch out   catches, catching, caught

catch out sb or **catch** sb **out**

1 to trick someone so that they make a mistake • *Some of the exam questions seemed designed to catch you out.* • (sometimes + **on**) *You can't catch them out on American history.* (= they know everything about it)

2 to discover that someone is lying or doing something wrong • (often + **in**) *He caught her out in a lie about her past.*

3 *British & Australian* to put someone in a difficult situation because of something which they did not expect or plan for • *Thousands of drivers were caught out by the sudden snowstorms.*

catch up   catches, catching, caught

catch up *British, American & Australian*

catch up sb or **catch** sb **up** *British & Australian*

1 to reach someone in front of you by going faster than them • (often + **with**) *He caught up with the other runners on the last lap.* • *You go on ahead, and I'll catch you up later.*

2 to reach the same quality or standard as someone or something else • (often + **with**) *My piano playing's improved, but I've got a long way to go before I catch up with my sister.* • *Children who come to our classes without basic reading skills often find it hard to catch up.*

catch up *British, American & Australian*

catch up sb or **catch** sb **up** *American*

to learn the newest facts about something • (usually + **on**) *I'll phone you tonight to catch up on all the gossip.* • *I'll catch you up on the details later.*

catch up in

be caught up in sth (always passive)

1 to be involved in a situation, often when you do not want to be • *I found myself caught up in an expensive legal battle.* • *Thousands of innocent civilians were caught up in the invasion.*

2 to become involved in an activity or situation which prevents you from moving or making progress • *I got caught up in heavy traffic on the way home.*

catch up on/with   catches, catching, caught

catch up on/with sth

to do something you did not have time to do earlier • *I'm hoping to catch up on some sleep.* • *I need a couple of days in the office to catch up with my paperwork.*

catch up with   catches, catching, caught

catch up with sb

1 if something that you have done [e.g. crime, lies] or something that has been happening to you [e.g. stress] catches up with you, it starts to cause problems for you • *The pressures of supporting a big family are beginning to catch up with him.*

2 if someone in authority [e.g. police, tax officials] catches up with you, they discover that you have been doing something wrong and often punish you for it • *They had been selling stolen cars for years before the police caught up with them.*

3 to meet someone you know, after not seeing them for a period of time • *I caught up with him in Singapore a few years later.* • *I'll catch up with you later!* (= I'll see you later today)

catch up with sth

to try to understand or learn something new • *I'm trying to catch up with all this new technology.*

cater for caters, catering, catered

cater for sb/sth

to provide all the things that people need or want in a particular situation ● *Our travel advice centre caters for the independent traveller.* ● *Large classes cannot cater for the needs of all the pupils in them.*

cater to caters, catering, catered

cater to sb/sth

to try to provide what people want or need, especially something that is unusual or that some people think is wrong ● *This form of nationalism caters to the worst elements of racism in our society.* ● *Music shows that cater to older audiences tend to be more traditional.*

cave in caves, caving, caved

cave in (sth) or **cave** (sth) **in**

if a ceiling, roof, or other structure caves in, or if something caves it in, it suddenly breaks up and falls inward ● *The explosion caused the roof of the building to cave in.* ● *He'd had a blow to the head which had caved his skull in.*

cave in

to agree to something that you were against before, after someone has persuaded you or threatened you ● (often + **to**) *The government are insistent that they will not cave in to the strikers' demands.*

centre/center around/round centres, centring, centred/centers, centering, centered

centre (sth) **around/round** sth *British & Australian*

center (sth) **around/round** sth *American*

if an activity or discussion centres around something, or if it is centred around something, that is the main or most important part of it ● *Much of the discussion centred around the reduction of pollution.* ● *My social life is centred round one or two pubs.*

centre/center on centres, centring, centred/centers, centering, centered

centre (sth) **on** sth *British & Australian*

center (sth) **on** sth *American*

to give a lot of attention to one particular activity, situation, or idea ● *The main action of the play centres on a young woman and her older lover.* ● *Most architectural debate is still centred on controversial buildings.*

centre/center round

see **centre/center around/round**

chain up chains, chaining, chained

chain up sb/sth or **chain** sb/sth **up**

to fasten a person, animal, or object with chains so they cannot escape or be stolen ● *She left the dogs chained up in the yard.* ● *My bike was chained up outside the house.*

chalk up chalks, chalking, chalked

chalk up sth or **chalk** sth **up**

to achieve something successful [e.g. victory, points, profit] ● *British companies last year chalked up their highest profits in 25 years.* ● *He's chalked up ten goals this season.*

chalk up to chalks, chalking, chalked

chalk up sth **to** sth or **chalk** sth **up to** sth *mainly American & Australian*

to think that a problem or bad experience is caused by something else ● *The company chalked up their deficit to problems in manufacturing.* ● *If a relationship breaks up you just have to **chalk it up to experience*** (= accept failure and learn from the experience)

chance on/upon chances, chancing, chanced

chance on/upon sb/sth

to meet someone or find something when you do not expect to ● *I wasn't actually looking for the photo – I just chanced on it in a drawer.* ● *She'd chanced on an old teacher of hers in a shop.*

change around/round changes, changing, changed

change around/round sth or **change** sth **around/round**

to move objects such as furniture into different positions, or to change the appearance of a room by moving furniture into different positions ● *Why don't you change the furniture around so the bookcase is near the door?* ● *I'm going to change my bedroom round and put the bed next to the window.*

change down   changes, changing, changed

change down *British & Australian*
to put a vehicle into a lower gear (= part of a machine that controls the speed of a vehicle), usually in order to go slower • *You should really change down to go round a corner.* • (often + **into**) *Change down into second.*

change into   changes, changing, changed

change (sth/sb) **into** (sth/sb)
to change and become a different thing or person, or to make someone or something do this • *Read me the story about the caterpillar that changed into a butterfly.*

change over   changes, changing, changed

change over
to stop using or having one thing and start using or having something else instead • (often + **from**) *We've just changed over from gas central heating to electric.* • (often + **to**) *He's old enough to remember when Britain changed over to decimal money.*
    changeover *n* [C] • (often + **to**) *The changeover to the new taxation system has caused a lot of problems.*

change over/round   changes, changing, changed

change over/round
if two people change over, each one starts to do what the other one was doing before, or each one moves to where the other one was standing or sitting before • *Tell me when you get tired of scrubbing the floor, and we'll change over.* • *If you don't like where you're sitting, why don't we change over?*

change round

see **change around/round** or **change over/round**

change up   changes, changing, changed

change up *British & Australian*
to put a vehicle into a higher gear (= part of a machine that controls the speed of a vehicle), usually in order to go faster • *Listen to the noise of the engine to decide*

when to change up. • (often + **into**) *I'd just changed up into fourth gear when I had to brake suddenly.*

charge up   charges, charging, charged

charge up sth or **charge** sth **up**
if you charge up a piece of electrical equipment, you put electricity into it • *The heating works off solar batteries which you can charge up when it is sunny.*

chase down   chases, chasing, chased

chase down sb/sth or **chase** sb/sth **down** *American slightly informal*
to try hard to get something [e.g. information] or someone that you want or need for a particular purpose • *The FBI are chasing down information in a number of states in new enquiries.* • *Relatives were chased down by journalists after the trial.*

chase off   chases, chasing, chased

chase off sb/sth or **chase** sb/sth **off**
to run after a person or animal in a threatening way to make them go away • *We used to chant insults outside his house until he'd come out and chase us off.*

chase up   chases, chasing, chased

chase up sb or **chase** sb **up** *mainly British & Australian slightly informal*
to ask someone to do something that they said they would do but that they have not done yet • *Adrian still hasn't paid his rent – you're going to have to chase him up.* • (often + **about**) *I must chase up the store about that fabric they've ordered for me.*

chase up sth or **chase** sth **up** *mainly British & Australian slightly informal*
to try to get something that belongs to you or that you need, or to try to discover more information about something • *Her job is to chase up loans which people haven't repaid.* • *I think the story about her previous marriage is worth chasing up.*

chat up   chats, chatting, chatted

chat up sb or **chat** sb **up**
1 *British & Australian informal* to talk to someone in a way that shows them that you are sexually attracted to them and to try to make them attracted to you • *He spent all evening trying to chat Jane up.*
    chat-up *adj* (always before noun) *Brit-*

ish & Australian informal • *Her favourite*
chat-up line (= remark that she uses to
start a conversation with someone she is
attracted to) *is to ask someone what they
want to drink.*

2 *mainly American* to talk to someone in a
friendly way, especially in order to persuade them to give you something or do
something for you • *Why don't you chat
your Mother up and see if we can borrow
her car?*

cheat on　cheats, cheating, cheated

cheat on sb *informal*

to behave in a dishonest way towards
your husband, wife, or usual sexual partner by having a sexual relationship with
someone else • *She decided to leave her
husband when she found out he'd been
cheating on her.*

check in　checks, checking, checked

check in

to show your ticket at an airport so that
you can be told where you are sitting and
so that your bags can be put on the aircraft • *When I flew to New York, I was told
to check in two hours before my flight.*

check-in *n* [U] the time at which you
have to check in • *Check-in is at 9 a.m.
and the flight departs at 10.30 a.m.*

check-in *n* [C] the place in an airport
where you check in • *When we got to the
check-in, there were already long queues of
people.* • (used as *adj*) *The woman at the
check-in desk asked if I wanted a smoking
or a non-smoking seat.*

check in/into　checks, checking, checked

check in
check into sth

to arrive at a hotel and say who you are
so that you can be given a key for your
room • *After I had checked in, I had a
shower and then unpacked my suitcase.*
• *He checked into a cheap hotel near the
station.*

check into　checks, checking, checked

check into sth

to try to get more information about
something in order to discover the true
facts about it • *The police, foolishly,
hadn't bothered checking into the man's
background.*

check off　checks, checking, checked

check off sth or **check** sth **off**

to look at each item on a list, or to write
something next to each item on a list, in
order to make sure that everything or
everyone on it is correct, present, or has
been dealt with • *She told the children to
get on the coach after checking off their
names on a list.*

check out　checks, checking, checked

check out

1 to leave a hotel after paying and giving
back the key of your room • (often + **of**)
*We checked out of the motel early the next
morning.*

check-out *n* [U] *mainly American &
Australian* the time by which you must
check out of a hotel • *Check-out is 11
o'clock.* • (used as *adj*) *I think check-out
time is 12 noon.*

2 if information checks out, it is shown to
be true or correct • *None of the information he gave me checked out.*

3 *American slang* to die • *Can you believe
Don just checked out like that?*

check out sth/sb or **check** sth/sb **out**

1 to examine something, or to get information about something or someone, to
make sure that what you have been told
about them is true, or that they are safe
or suitable, or to see what is wrong with
them • *He hired private investigators to
check out his future business partner.*
• *Safety inspectors checked the hotel out
before giving it a licence.* • *She took her*

car into the garage to have the rattling noise checked out.

2 *informal* to look at a person or object, or to go to a place because you are interested to see what they are like ● *Why don't we check out that new bar in the town centre?* ● *Wow! Check him out – he's gorgeous!*

check out sb or **check** sb **out** *American*
if someone working in a large shop checks you out, they calculate how much you have to pay and take the money from you ● *Bring your cart round to the next aisle and I'll check you out there.*

checkout *n* [C] the place where you pay for things in a big shop ● *I had to wait 15 minutes at the check-out.*

check out (sth) or **check** (sth) **out** *American*
to pay for things you buy in a big shop ● *It took me nearly an hour to check out, the store was so busy.* ● *I had checked out the milk before I noticed the container was leaking.*

check out sth or **check** sth **out** *American*
to borrow something [e.g. book, video] from a library (= place that lends people books) after an employee has recorded that you have taken it ● *You can check out these books at the main desk.*

check over   checks, checking, checked

check over sth/sb or **check** sth/sb **over**
to examine something or someone to make sure that they are correct, healthy, or working correctly ● *She sent an early copy of her novel to her publisher so that he could check it over.* ● *Get yourself checked over by a doctor before you take up squash.*

check up   checks, checking, checked

check up
to make certain that you have the correct facts about something ● *When I checked up at the library, I found out that the land had been sold by the council.*

check up on   checks, checking, checked

check up on sb
to discover what someone is doing in order to be certain that they are doing what they should be doing or what they

said they would do ● *My mum checks up on me most evenings to see that I've done my homework.* ● *Inspectors checked up on the company and discovered that it had not been paying enough tax.*

cheer on   cheers, cheering, cheered

cheer on sb or **cheer** sb **on**
to shout encouraging words at someone, especially a person or team in a race or competition ● *Swedish supporters crowded into the tennis centre to cheer their players on.* ● *He managed to do the jump at the third attempt, cheered on by a crowd of 25,000.*

cheer up   cheers, cheering, cheered

cheer up (sb) or **cheer** (sb) **up**
if someone cheers up, or if someone or something cheers them up, they start to feel happier ● *We sent some flowers to the hospital to cheer her up.* ● (often an order) *Come on, cheer up! Things aren't so bad.* ● (often reflexive) *She bought a skirt to cheer herself up a bit.*

chew on   chews, chewing, chewed

chew on sth *informal*
to think carefully about something, or to discuss something in detail ● *Surrogate mothers have given the media a new moral issue to chew on.* ● *Why don't you just chew on it for a while before making your decision?*

chew out   chews, chewing, chewed

chew out sb or **chew** sb **out** *American & Australian informal*
to tell someone angrily that they have done something wrong ● *The coach chewed the team out for quitting practice early.*

chew over   chews, chewing, chewed

chew over sth or **chew** sth **over** *slightly informal*
to think carefully about something, or to discuss something in detail ● *They've been chewing the problem over since last week.* ● *We meet every now and then to chew over the past.*

chew up   chews, chewing, chewed

chew up sth or **chew** sth **up**
1 if a machine chews up something that you put into it, it damages or destroys it

• *Your tape recorder has just chewed up my favourite cassette.* • *My washing machine has started to chew up my clothes.*

2 to chew something until it is completely soft, broken, or has lots of holes in it • *The dog chewed up the living room carpet while we were out.* • *Do you think you could stop your baby chewing up all the magazines?*

chicken out chickens, chickening, chickened

chicken out *informal*

to decide not to do something you had planned to do because you are too frightened • *I was going to tell him what I thought of him at the meeting, but I chickened out.*

chill out chills, chilling, chilled

chill out *informal*

to relax completely, or not allow things to upset you • (usually an order) *Sit down, have a drink and chill out, girl!* • *We spent the whole week chilling out in the country.*

chime in chimes, chiming, chimed

chime in (sth)

to suddenly say something in a conversation, in order to agree with what has been said or to give an opinion • *'I agree 100%,' Martin chimed in.* • (often + **with**) *She chimed in with another argument against the move.* • *Bob chimed in to challenge my views on marriage.*

chime in with chimes, chiming, chimed

chime in with sth

if one statement or fact chimes in with another, they agree with each other, or if an action chimes in with a situation, it is suitable for that situation • *What you've just told me chimes in with what I heard yesterday.* • *The president's interest in domestic issues chimes in with the voters' concerns about their jobs.*

chip away at chips, chipping, chipped

chip away at sth

to gradually reduce something, or to gradually make something less effective • *Her constant criticisms chipped away at my self-confidence.* • *Inflation has steadily chipped away at our savings.*

chip in chips, chipping, chipped

chip in (sth) or **chip** (sth) **in** *slightly informal*

to give an amount of money, especially when a group of people are giving money to pay for something together • *We all chipped in so that we could afford a really special present.*

chip in *mainly British & Australian slightly informal*

to interrupt a conversation in order to say something • *I tried to explain things to Jenny but Jane kept chipping in.* • (sometimes + **with**) *While I was talking John chipped in with a comment about one of the slides.*

chivvy along/up chivvies, chivvying, chivvied

chivvy along/up sb/sth or **chivvy** sb/sth **along/up** *informal*

to try to make someone do something more quickly, or to try to make something happen more quickly • *He kept stopping to rest so I had to chivvy him up a bit.*

choke back/down chokes, choking, choked

choke back/down sth or **choke** sth **back/down**

to force yourself not to show your feelings, or to stop yourself from saying something • *'John has had an accident,' said Jane, choking back the tears.* • *She had to choke down an overpowering urge to tell them she didn't want the job anyway.*

choke down chokes, choking, choked

choke down sth or **choke** sth **down**

to eat or drink something with difficulty, especially when you are ill, upset, or do not like what you are eating or drinking • *He managed to choke down the raw fish.*

choke off chokes, choking, choked

choke off sth or **choke** sth **off**

to stop something happening, or to stop a supply of something • *Higher interest rates could choke off an improvement in the housing market.* • *The wire choked off his oxygen supply.*

choke up   chokes, choking, choked

choke up

1 to become unable to speak, usually because you are starting to cry ● *She can't talk about her mother without choking up.* ● **choked up** *adj* (always after verb) ● *I'm sorry, I'm feeling a little choked up at the moment.*

2 *American informal* to become nervous and fail to compete well in a sport or fail to perform well in public ● *Sandy choked up as soon as she got on the court and was easily beaten.* ● *He sounded great at rehearsal, but just choked up in the show.*

choke up sth or **choke** sth **up**
to block an area so that it is difficult for something to move through it ● *The chimney was choked up with crumbled bricks and rubbish.* ● *Heavy traffic choked up the city centre every weekend before Christmas.*

choose up   chooses, choosing, chose, chosen

choose up (sth) *American*
if people, especially children, choose up, or choose up teams, they divide themselves into teams to play a game ● *Let the captains choose up so we can play ball.* ● *There were just enough of us to choose up sides for a game.*

chop down   chops, chopping, chopped

chop down sth or **chop** sth **down**
to cut through a tree or a group of trees so that they fall to the ground ● *They decided to chop the elm tree down because it was too close to the house.* ● *Workmen chopped down the pine forest in order to clear the land for building.*

chop up   chops, chopping, chopped

chop up sth or **chop** sth **up**
to cut something, especially food, into small pieces ● *Chop up the onion and fry in oil.*

chow down   chows, chowing, chowed

chow down *American slang*
to eat a lot of food ● *The bikers pulled up in front of the diner ready to chow down.*

chuck away/out   chucks, chucking, chucked

chuck away/out sth or **chuck** sth **away/out** *informal*
to get rid of something that you do not want or need any more ● *It's time you chucked out those old newspapers.*

chuck in   chucks, chucking, chucked

chuck in sth or **chuck** sth **in**
British & Australian informal to add something [e.g. suggestion, remark] to a conversation or a piece of writing ● *The shareholders chucked in a few surprise recommendations at the annual outing.*

chuck in/up   chucks, chucking, chucked

chuck in/up sth or **chuck** sth **in/up** (never passive)
to stop doing an activity, especially a job or a course, and to leave the place where you were doing it ● *He chucked in his job to travel round the world.* ● *She chucked up her art class half way through the term.*

chuck out   chucks, chucking, chucked

chuck out sb or **chuck** sb **out** *informal*
to force someone to leave a place ● *He had been chucked out of school for taking drugs.* ● *Several kids were chucked out of the dance after a fight broke out.* ● (used as *adj*) *They were in the pub from the end of work until **chucking out time**.* (= the time it closed)

chuck up   chucks, chucking, chucked

chuck up (sth) (never passive) *informal*
to vomit ● *Oh no! The cat's just chucked up all over the kitchen floor.* ● *She chucked up her dinner.*

chum up   chums, chumming, chummed

chum up *British & Australian old-fashioned, informal*
to become friends with someone ● (often + **with**) *Alice chummed up with Jenny and they often walked to school together.* ● *The boys chummed up while on holiday.*

churn out   churns, churning, churned

churn out sth or **churn** sth **out**
to produce large amounts of something, especially something of low quality ● *The factory churns out thousands of pairs of shoes every week.*

churn up churns, churning, churned

churn up sth or **churn** sth **up**
1 to damage the surface of something [e.g. mud, road] by moving it around violently • *Heavy vehicles had churned up the mud on the road, making it impassable.*
2 to cause a strong reaction or serious problems • *Each new book about the actress churns up a frenzy of interest.* • *Plans to develop the area have been churned up by political issues.*

churn up sb or **churn** sb **up**
to make someone angry or very upset • *Seeing children who are seriously ill always churns me up.*

clam up clams, clamming, clammed

clam up *informal*
to become silent or to refuse to speak about something, usually because you are shy or afraid • *It's difficult to get proper information because everyone clams up the moment they realise the police are involved.*

clamp down clamps, clamping, clamped

clamp down
if someone in authority clamps down, they do something in order to stop or limit a particular activity • (usually + **on**) *Local residents have pleaded with police to clamp down on street crime.*

clamp-down n [C] • (usually singular + **on**) *a government clamp-down on public spending*

clap out claps, clapping, clapped

clap out sth or **clap** sth **out**
to hit your hands together in order to make a rhythm that is the same as the rhythm in a piece of music • *Try to clap out the rhythm as you listen to the song.*

claw back claws, clawing, clawed

claw back sth or **claw** sth **back** *mainly British & Australian*
to work very hard in order to get back something that you had before • *The airline is beginning to claw back some of the business it lost after the bomb scare.* • *By the end of the match, Holdsworth had clawed two goals back for Newcastle United.*

clean down cleans, cleaning, cleaned

clean down sth or **clean** sth **down**
mainly British & Australian
to clean something completely, especially something with a flat surface • *It's a good idea to clean down the woodwork before you paint it.*

clean out cleans, cleaning, cleaned

clean out sth or **clean** sth **out**
1 to clean the inside of something • *I wish I could find the time to clean these cupboards out.* • *One of his jobs was cleaning out the bird cages.* • *She carefully cleaned out the cut on his cheek.*

clean-out n [singular] *British & Australian* • *Let's have a good clean-out in the kitchen.*
2 to steal everything from a place • *She returned home to find her flat had been cleaned out by burglars.*

clean out sb or **clean** sb **out**
informal if someone cleans you out, they take or use all the money you have, or if something expensive cleans you out, you spend all the money you have on it • *Buying our new house has completely cleaned us out.* • *She threatened to clean him out if he tried to divorce her.*

clean up cleans, cleaning, cleaned

clean up (sth/sb) or **clean** (sth/sb) **up**
to make something or someone clean and tidy • *We'll go out as soon as I've cleaned up the kitchen.* • *We'll need to clean up before we can leave the building.* • *She'd spilt some coffee and was cleaning it up just as John walked in.*

clean-up n [C] • *It's time you gave your bedroom a good clean-up.* • (used as adj) *A clean-up operation had been under way at the works since early Monday.*

clean up sth or **clean** sth **up**
to make something more acceptable by getting rid of things that are dishonest or morally bad • *Some people think that television should be cleaned up.* • *The new mayor had promised to close down late-night bars and generally clean up the town.*

cleanup adj (always before noun) • *a cleanup campaign aimed at corruption in businesses*

clean up (sth) or **clean** (sth) **up**

to win a lot of money ● *We cleaned up at the roulette table last night.* ● *I hear he cleaned up a small fortune in the lottery.*

clean up after   cleans, cleaning, cleaned

clean up after sb

to remove dirt or problems that someone else has made ● *I'm fed up with cleaning up after you all the time.*

clear away   clears, clearing, cleared

clear sth **away** or **clear away** sth

to make a place tidy by removing things from it or putting them where they should be ● *She hadn't even cleared away the breakfast dishes when I got home.*

clear away (sb) or **clear** (sb) **away** *American*

to leave or to make someone leave a place ● *A crowd had gathered around the injured and had to be cleared away by the police.* ● *Clear away from there – it's dangerous!*

clear off   clears, clearing, cleared

clear off *mainly British informal*

to leave a place quickly ● (often an order) *Clear off and leave me alone!* ● *The press cleared off when they saw the police arriving.*

clear out   clears, clearing, cleared

clear out sth or **clear** sth **out**

to make a place tidy by removing things that are unwanted ● *They spent the weekend clearing out the attic.*

clear-out *n* [C] *British & Australian* ● *We need to give the garage a good clear-out.*

clear out *informal*

to leave a place ● *When he returned he was glad to find that the squatters had cleared out.* ● (often + **of**) *My landlord's given me a week to clear out of my flat.*

clear up   clears, clearing, cleared

clear up (sth) or **clear** (sth) **up**

to make a place tidy and clean, especially by putting things where they usually belong ● *We'll have to clear up before my parents come home.* ● *Can you clear up that mess in the kitchen before you go out?*

clear up sth or **clear** sth **up**

1 to give or find an explanation for some-

thing, or to deal with a problem or disagreement ● *I hope that clears up the situation for you, but please ask if there's anything else you'd like to know.* ● *Before we sign the contract there are a few points that we should clear up.*

2 if an illness clears up, or if medicine clears an illness up, the illness goes away ● *After several days the infection started to clear up.* ● *I'll give you something which should clear that up very quickly.*

clear up

if the weather clears up, it improves ● *I hope the weather clears up before we have to leave.*

clear up after   clears, clearing, cleared

clear up after sb

to make things clean and tidy after someone has made them dirty or untidy ● *You really shouldn't expect your mother to clear up after you all day.*

cleave to   cleaves, cleaving, cleaved

cleave to sth

1 to stick or hold firmly onto something ● *The ancient ivy cleaved to the ruined castle walls.*

2 to continue to believe strongly in something ● *People in the remote mountain villages still cleave to their old traditions.*

cleave to sb *literary*

to stay firmly with or close to someone ● *Cleave to your master in obedience and loyal service.*

climb down   climbs, climbing, climbed

climb down

British & Australian to admit that you are wrong ● *He chose to climb down in the face of pressure.* ● (sometimes + **on**) *She would never climb down on what she regards as an issue of principle.*

climb-down *n* [C] *British & Australian* ● *The fact that she agreed to talk to him at all represented a climb-down.* ● (sometimes + **on**) *The statement signalled a climb-down on his earlier decision.*

clock in/on   clocks, clocking, clocked

clock in/on

to record the time you arrive at work, usually on a machine with a clock ● *We're supposed to clock in by 10 o'clock at the latest.* • *What time did you clock on this morning?*

clock off/out   clocks, clocking, clocked

clock off/out

to record the time you leave work, usually on a machine with a clock • *Don't forget to clock out as you leave the building.* • *Have you clocked off for lunch?*

clock on

see **clock in/on**

clock up   clocks, clocking, clocked

clock up sth or **clock** sth **up** *mainly British & Australian informal*

to win or achieve a large number of similar things • *In 1986 the company clocked up total sales of $38.2 million.* • *Several of these planes have already clocked up around 21,000 flying hours.*

clog up   clogs, clogging, clogged

clog up (sth) or **clog** (sth) **up**

if something [e.g. road, pipe] clogs up, or if something clogs it up, it becomes blocked and nothing in it is able to move • *If they decide to build this new business park, the roads in the area will clog up.* • (often + **with**) *This disease causes the lungs to clog up with a thick substance.*

close down   closes, closing, closed

close down (sth) or **close** (sth) **down**

if a business or organization closes down, or if someone or something closes it down, it stops doing business • *Many of the city's leading restaurants close down for the whole of August.* • *I don't understand why we can't keep the park and close down that ugly factory.*

close in   closes, closing, closed

close in

1 if people close in, they gradually get nearer to someone and surround them in order to stop them escaping • *The enemy were fast closing in.* • (often + **on**) *The police gradually closed in on the man, and this time he knew he wouldn't get away.*

2 if bad weather closes in, it gets nearer • *Storm clouds began to close in and so they turned for home.*

3 if the nights or days close in, the length of time when it is light gets shorter • (often in continuous tenses) *My granny hates it*

every autumn when the nights start closing in.

close off   closes, closing, closed

close off sth or **close** sth **off**

to put something across the entrance to something [e.g. road, building, area] in order to stop people entering it • *We used to get a lot of pleasure from walking in those hills until they were closed off.* • (sometimes + **to**) *It is our aim to close off areas of the city centre to traffic.*

close on   closes, closing, closed

close on sb/sth

to get nearer to a person or animal, especially in a race • *She screamed encouragement as the horse she had chosen began to close on the leader.*

close out   closes, closing, closed

close out sth or **close** sth **out**

1 *informal* to make something end quickly, especially a sports match • *Agassi closed out the match by hitting a powerful serve that his opponent couldn't reach.* • *The president closed out the interview with a one-line joke.*

2 *American* to arrange to stop having or using something • *He closed out his checking account and transferred the money to another bank.*

3 *American* if a shop closes out something, it sells it cheaply in order to try to get rid of it • *They are closing out winter jackets and there are some good buys.*

close out sth/sb or **close** sth/sb **out** *mainly American*

to ignore someone or something, or to decide not to allow someone to be part of a group or activity • *I hate the way she closes me out when she's worried.* • *Some countries close out foreign competition.*

close out *American*

if a shop closes out, it sells everything at cheap prices before closing the business • *Business has been bad for months and we may have to close out.* • *Is there anything you want at the sports store – they're closing out.*

close-out *n* [C] *American* • *I bought this skirt at a close-out.* • (used as *adj*) *close-out merchandise*

close up closes, closing, closed

close up (sth) or **close** (sth) **up**
1 to close a building [esp. shop] for a period of time • *As we were closing up for the night, a woman came running into the shop, screaming and shouting* • *I wanted so much to close my home up and go travelling.*
2 if an opening [e.g. wound] closes up, or if you close it up, the sides of it start to join together again • *The wound will take about three weeks to close up completely.* • *The flower's white and purple petals close up at night.*

close up (sb) or **close** (sb) **up**
if people close up, or if you close them up, they move closer together • *They closed up to prevent anyone reaching him.*

cloud over clouds, clouding, clouded

cloud over
1 if the sky clouds over, it becomes covered with clouds • *We watched as the sky clouded over, waiting for the rain to come.*
2 if someone's face clouds over, they suddenly look unhappy or worried • *Steve's shining, happy morning face suddenly clouded over.*

clown about/around clowns, clowning, clowned

clown about/around
to behave in a silly way • *They were clowning around and seemed not to notice me come in.*

club together clubs, clubbing, clubbed

club together *mainly British & Australian*
if a group of people club together, they share the cost of something between them • (often + to do sth) *We all clubbed together to buy her a wedding present.*

clue in/up clues, clueing, clued

clue in sb or **clue** sb **in** *American informal*

clue up sb or **clue** sb **up** *British informal*
to tell someone something new or something that they need to know in order to do something • (often + **on**) *Let's meet for lunch and you can clue me in on what's been happening.*

clued-in *adj American informal*

clued-up *adj British informal* • *Clued-up travellers know not to buy anything from these unofficial market traders.*

clutch at clutches, clutching, clutched

clutch at sth
to try to get hold of something and hold it tightly • *She clutched at the rope to try to stop herself from falling.*

coast along coasts, coasting, coasted

coast along
to do only the things that you have to do without trying to go faster or be more successful • *She already knew enough to pass the exam, so she just coasted along in class.* • (sometimes + **on**) *The company is coasting along nicely on its exports to African countries.*

cobble together cobbles, cobbling, cobbled

cobble together sth or **cobble** sth **together**
to make something quickly and not very carefully • *I didn't have much food in but I managed to cobble something together which everyone said was delicious.* • *It was obvious to all that his statement had been hastily cobbled together.*

cock up cocks, cocking, cocked

cock up (sth) or **cock** (sth) **up** *British & Australian slang*
to spoil something by making a mistake or by doing something stupid • *He had one very simple job to do and he managed to cock it up totally.*
cock-up *n* [C] *British & Australian slang* • *We're being watched by an audience of millions so I don't want any cock-ups.*

colour/color in colours, colouring, coloured/colors, coloring, colored

colour in sth or **colour** sth **in** *British & Australian*

color in sth or **color** sth **in** *American & Australian*
to fill an area with colour using paint, coloured pencils etc. • *She coloured in all the squares and triangles on the page of her book.* • (sometimes + **in**) *She coloured the squares in in red and the triangles in in blue.*

colour/color up   colours, colouring, coloured/colors, coloring, colored

colour up *British & Australian*

color up *American*
to become red in the face because you feel embarrassed or angry • *He's so shy, a girl only has to talk to him and he colours up.*

comb out   combs, combing, combed

comb out sth or **comb** sth **out**
if you comb out your hair, you make it tidy by combing it • *She sat in front of the mirror, combing out her long brown hair.*

come about   comes, coming, came, come

come about
when you say how or why something comes about, especially something which is not planned, you explain how or why it happens • *The company director admitted that he had no idea how the mistakes came about.* • *The discovery came about while scientists were working on a different project.*

come across   comes, coming, came, come

come across sth/sb (never passive)
to discover something by chance, or to meet someone by chance • *While she was tidying up the living room, she came across her old photograph album.* • *I came across an old school friend of mine when I was travelling in Canada.*

come across
1 to behave in a way which makes people believe that you have a particular characteristic • (usually + **as**) *The hero in the film comes across as slightly crazy.* • *Helen came across as being an extremely intelligent woman.* • *I thought Paul Glover came across well in the interview.* • *We were told that Sue would be ideal for the job, but she came across badly when we talked to her.*
2 if an idea or an emotion comes across in writing, film, music, or when someone is speaking, it is expressed clearly and people understand it or notice it • *Her ideas came across with great force in the article.* • *His bitterness comes across in much of his poetry.*

come across with   comes, coming, came

come across with sth *British informal*
to produce or provide something that someone wants or needs • *Steve's Dad won't come across with the money he needs to buy a car.*

come after   comes, coming, came, come

come after sb
to chase someone, or to search for someone, often in order to punish them • *He saw us picking his apples and he came after us with a stick.*

come along   comes, coming, came, come

come along
1 to arrive at a place • *We needed someone who knew about first aid, and Claire came along at just the right moment.* • *We're going to the party now, and Jane and Chris are coming along later.* • *I waited 25 minutes for a bus and then three came along at the same time.*
2 to go somewhere with someone • *I'm going to the Monet exhibition this afternoon – why don't you come along?*
3 (never in continuous tenses) to start to exist, happen, or be available • *Can you imagine what life was like before electricity came along?* • *We had to change our lifestyle once our first child came along.* • *Since Tom left school, he has been doing any odd jobs that come along.* • *I think she's the best crime writer to come along since P.D. James.*

Come along! (always an order)
mainly British & Australian old-fashioned
something that you say in order to tell someone to do something more quickly or with more effort • *Come along, Andy, you've spent over an hour in the bathroom!* • *Come along, Ellen! You can go faster than that!*

be coming along (always in continuous tenses)
if you ask or explain how an activity or a person learning a new skill is coming along, you ask or explain what progress they are making, and if a person or activity is coming along, it is making good progress • *How's your thesis coming along?* • *Jason's coming along well on drums.*

5 if a regular event comes around, it happens at its usual time • *The annual flower festival is coming around again this month.*

6 if a letter or document comes around, it is sent to a group of people • *A memo came around telling us about arrangements for the Christmas lunch.*

come at   comes, coming, came, come

come at sb (never passive)

1 to move towards someone in order to attack them • (often + **with**) *He came at her with a knife.*

2 if a lot of questions or pieces of information come at you, you are asked them or given them very quickly, in a way that is confusing or difficult to deal with • *Questions were coming at her so fast that she didn't have time to think about what she was saying.*

come at sth (never passive; always + adv/prep)

to think about something in a particular way • *Let's come at the problem from a different angle, because this approach has got us nowhere.*

come apart   comes, coming, came, come

come apart

if something comes apart, it separates into pieces • *I picked up the book and it came apart in my hands.*

come around/round   comes, coming, came, come

come around/round

1 to visit someone at their house • *'Have you seen Adrian recently?' 'Yes, he came round last week.'* • (sometimes + **for**) *Why don't you come round for dinner next Saturday?* • (sometimes + to do sth) *Halfway through the party, a neighbour came around to complain about the noise.*

2 to move around a group of people in order to talk to them, give them something, or take something from them • (often + **with**) *After the performance, one of the performers came around with a collection box.* • *A waitress came round with snacks and drinks.*

3 to agree to a plan or idea that you were against, or to stop having a bad opinion about something, after thinking about it for a long time or being persuaded by other people that it is good • *I know Debbie doesn't like the idea of you borrowing her car, but she'll soon come round.* • (often + **to**) *I spent several hours telling him what a good project it was, and he finally came around to the idea.* • *I'm sure she'll **come around to our way of thinking**.* (= agree with us)

4 to become conscious again • *I stayed next to Kathy all night because I wanted to be there when she came around.*

come away   comes, coming, came, come

come away

if something comes away from something else, it becomes separated from it • (often + **from**) *The paper has started to come away from the wall because it's so damp.* • *I just opened the drawer as usual and the handle **came away in my hand**.*

come away with   comes, coming, came

come away with sth

to leave a situation or place with a particular feeling or idea that stays with you • *I came away with the impression that they were hiding something important from me.*

come back   comes, coming, came, come

come back

1 to return to a place • *I'll come back and pick you up around 8.00.* • *It's strange coming back to the place where you used to live.* • (often + **from**) *I've just come back from the dentist's.*

2 if something, for example a piece of clothing or hairstyle, comes back, it becomes fashionable again after being unfashion-

able for a period of time • *Padded shoulders are coming back.* • (often + **in**) *Those 50's style dresses are coming back in.* • (often + **into**) *Long hair on men seems to be coming back into fashion.*

comeback *n* [C] • *Ripped jeans are **making a comeback** apparently.* (= are fashionable again) • *After nearly ten years without public performances he is **staging a comeback*** (= giving a performance he hopes will make him popular again) *in New York.*

3 to start to happen again • *I thought I'd got rid of my cough but it seems to have come back again.* • *Those old doubts have come back again.*

4 if something comes back to you, you remember it • (usually + **to**) *I'm trying to remember his name – it'll come back to me when I'm not thinking about it.* • *She used to drive around in an old black car – **it's all coming back to me now**.*

5 *mainly American & Australian* to reply angrily or humorously • (often + **with**) *He came back with some insult or other and walked off.*

comeback *n* [C] *mainly American & Australian* • *I wish I'd been able to think of a good comeback.*

come back to   comes, coming, came, come

come back to sth
to start talking about a particular subject again • *I'd like to come back to what Rachel was saying.*

come before   comes, coming, came, come

come before sb/sth
to be discussed or judged by a person or group in authority [e.g. judge, court of law, committee] • *Their complaints are due to come before the Committee for a public hearing.* • *Rubenfeld's case will come before the court on Friday.*

come between   comes, coming, came, come

come between sb
if an argument or other problem comes between two or more people, it spoils their relationship • *Don't let one little quarrel come between you!*

come between sb/sth and sth
to stop someone getting, achieving, or doing something • *He won't let anything come between him and his Saturday morning golf.*

come by   comes, coming, came, come

come by sth
to get something, especially something unusual • *So how did you manage to come by this job?* • *I'd like to know how he came by that black eye.* • *Accurate statistics are hard to come by.*

come by (swh) *mainly American & Australian*
to visit a person or place for a short time, often when you are going somewhere else • *You should come by some time after work – it would be good to have a chance to talk.* • *I'll come by the office one day this week and give you my report.*

come down   comes, coming, came, come

come down
1 if something comes down, it breaks and falls to the ground • *A lot of trees came down in the storm.* • *If you put any more books on that shelf the whole thing's going to come down.*

2 if an aircraft comes down, it falls out of the sky • *The plane came down over the Atlantic, killing all hundred and eighty passengers.*

3 if a story or tradition comes down, it is passed from older people to younger people so that it continues • *The story came down from the early pioneer days of the country.*

4 if a statement or order comes down, it is given by someone in authority to other people who need to know about it • *Word came down that we were expected to work later.*

5 if a price or level comes down, it becomes lower • *Property prices have come down dramatically over the last few months.* • *Strawberries usually come down* (= get cheaper) *at this time of year.*

6 if you come down when you are suggesting a price for something, you suggest or agree to a lower price • *He's asking £300 for the piano, but he might be prepared to come down a bit.*

7 (always + *adv/prep*) to decide, and usually to state publicly, that you support or

oppose something • *The minister came down in favour of a reformed prison system.* • *The White House has come down on the side of military action.* • *The author comes down against private pensions in this article.*

8 *informal* to stop feeling the excitement caused by a drug or by a very enjoyable experience • *She likes the high she gets from drugs – it's coming down afterwards that's the problem.* • *The whole weekend was so wonderful that I haven't really come down yet.*

comedown *n* [singular] • *A Monday at work is a bit of a comedown after such a brilliant weekend.*

9 *British formal* to leave university at the end of a course, especially Oxford or Cambridge University • (often + **from**) *He came down from Oxford in '63 and started working for a bank.*

come down on   comes, coming, came, come

come down on sb

to punish or criticize someone very strongly • *They're coming down heavily on people for not paying parking fines.* • *The police are coming down hard on offenders.* • *If he is rude in class again, the headmaster will come down on him like a ton of bricks.* (= punish him severely)

come down to   comes, coming, came, come

come down to sth

if a situation or decision comes down to something, that is the thing that will influence it most • *It depends on whether you want children or a career – because that's what it comes down to.* • *It all comes down to money in the end.* • *When it comes down to it* (= the basic truth is) *you can't trust anyone.* • *If it comes down to it* (= if we really need to) *we'll have to cancel the whole event.*

come down with   comes, coming, came, come

come down with sth *slightly informal*
to become ill, usually with a disease that is not very serious • *I think I'm coming down with a cold – I've been coughing all day.*

come forth   comes, coming, came, come

come forth *formal*

to be provided or to appear • *She applied for jobs with several foreign companies and an offer to work overseas soon came forth.* • (sometimes + **from**) *The original proposal came forth from the commission in October 1994.*

forthcoming *adj* (always after verb) if money, help, or information is forthcoming, it is given to you • (usually negative) *The theatre has been informed that further government funds will not be forthcoming.* • *I wrote to the council about the new parking scheme, but no answer was forthcoming.*

forthcoming *adj* (always before noun) a forthcoming event, action, or product is one which will happen or become available soon • *The Senator has decided not to stand again in the forthcoming elections.* • *An extract from Martin Amis's forthcoming novel will be published in the newspaper this Sunday.*

come forth with   comes, coming, came, come

come forth with sth

mainly American formal to make a suggestion or an offer, or to give someone information • *There is a reward of $20,000 for anyone who comes forth with information about the crime.* • *She criticized the committee for failing to come forth with any concrete proposals.*

forthcoming *adj* (always after verb) if someone is forthcoming when you ask them about something, they are willing to give you a lot of information about it • (often + **about**) *She wouldn't say much about her latest film, and she was even less forthcoming about her love life.*

come forward   comes, coming, came, come

come forward

to offer to do something, especially to help someone or to give information to someone in authority • *300 donors have come forward in response to a request for people to give blood.* • (sometimes + **with**) *The police are asking members of the public to come forward with information.* • *The company is unlikely to come forward with a higher offer in the next 48 hours.*

• (sometimes + to do sth) *Several patients have come forward to support allegations of abuse at the hospital.*

come from   comes, came, come

come from swh (never in continuous tenses)

1 if someone comes from a particular place, they were born there and lived there when they were a child • *'Where do you come from?'* • *Manuela comes from Bologna.*

2 if something comes from a particular place, that is where it is made or exists • *This wine comes from a small vineyard near Bergerac.*

come from sth (never in continuous tenses)
to be from a particular source or origin • *The term 'aqueduct' comes from the Latin words 'aqua', meaning water, and 'ducere', meaning to convey.* • *Although he came from a poor background, Smith went on to become a millionaire.*

come in   comes, coming, came, come

come in

1 if someone comes in when you are in a room or building, they enter that room or building • (often an order) *She knocked on the door and a voice from inside shouted 'Come in!'*

2 if a train, bus, ship, or aircraft comes in, it arrives at the place it is travelling to • *Has the 8.05 train from Edinburgh come in yet?*

incoming *adj* (always before noun) an incoming aircraft or weapon [e.g. missile] is one which has reached or almost reached the place it is travelling to • *Passengers on incoming flights must collect their luggage before they pass through customs.* • *This new defence system can track and destroy incoming short-range missiles.*

3 to arrive at the place where you live or work • *I was so tired, I didn't even hear James come in last night.* • *I'll come in early tomorrow to finish that off.*

4 to do some work for a company or in someone's house • (often + to do sth) *We've got an electrician coming in to fix the lights tomorrow.*

5 if news, a result, a letter, or a telephone call comes in, it is received • *Reports are coming in of a plane crash off Long Island.* • *We stayed up all night watching the election results come in.* • *Hundreds of letters have come in complaining about the programme.*

incoming *adj* (always before noun) • *I have a special tray for incoming mail on my desk.* • *This phone is for incoming calls only.*

6 if something comes in, it arrives at a shop or place of work and becomes available to buy or to use • (usually + *adv/prep*) *You can't buy Seville oranges all year round – they usually come in just after Christmas.*

7 (always + *adv/prep*) if you describe how someone in a race or competition comes in, you describe how quickly they finish the race or competition • *Smith finished the course in 2 minutes 50 seconds, and the next competitor came in 5 seconds later.* • *The Christian Democrats came in third with 12.3% of the vote.*

8 (always + *adv/prep*) if you describe how the result of an activity, especially a business deal, comes in, you describe how successful it is, especially how much it cost or how much profit you made • *The project came in £150, 000 under budget.* • *The results came in slightly better than we expected.*

9 if work comes in, a company is asked to do it • *Despite the recession, new business is coming in steadily.*

10 if the tide (= the regular change in the level of the sea) comes in, the sea comes nearer the beach or coast • *As we walked back along the beach, the tide was coming in fast.*

incoming *adj* (always before noun) • *The wreckage of the boat was washed onto the beach by the incoming tide.*

11 if you describe how someone comes in when you are discussing a plan, you describe how they will be involved in it • *We need someone to drive us to the airport, and that's where Bob comes in.*

12 to start speaking during a discussion • *Do you mind if I come in here and tell you about the arrangements for this afternoon?* • (often + **on**) *I'd like to come in on that point.* • (sometimes + **with**) *Steve came in with a suggestion about how we could improve the system.*

13 to be useful for something ● *Those old blankets will come in when the weather gets colder.* ● *Helen's mechanical know-how* **came in handy** *when our car broke down last night.*

14 to become involved in something which a group of people are planning ● *(often + on) It'll cost you £500 if you want to come in on the deal.* ● *(sometimes + with) Do you want to come in with us to buy Sheila's present?*

come in for   comes, coming, came, come

come in for sth *(never passive)*
  if someone comes in for criticism or praise, they are criticized or praised for something they have done ● *The minister has come in for a lot of criticism over his handling of the affair.* ● *Our department came in for particular praise in the report.*

come into   comes, coming, came, come

come into swh
  if someone comes into the room or building that you are in, they enter that room or building ● *Would you ask Ms Hudson to come into my office please.*

come into sth
1 to arrive at the place where you work ● *She's been coming into the office every weekend.*
2 to get money from someone who has died ● *I came into a lot of money on my aunt's death.* ● *He will* **come into a fortune** *on his twenty-first birthday.*
3 to begin to exist or happen, or to begin to be fashionable ● *The new rules will come into force in April.* ● *Most staff will need retraining when the changes come into effect next year.*

come into it
  if you say that a particular emotion or quality [e.g. pride, love, luck] comes into it when you are describing a situation, you mean that it influences the situation ● *(usually negative) I've decided to move to Vancouver because of my career, not because Jay lives there – love doesn't come into it.* ● *Christina got the job because of her skills and experience, but a certain amount of luck did come into it as well.*

come of   comes, coming, came, come

come of sth
  to happen as the result of an event or situation ● *Did anything come of your meeting with Peter?* ● *She shouldn't keep meeting him. No good can come of it.*

come off   comes, coming, came, come

come off
1 to happen successfully or as planned ● *(often negative) Using children in the movie was a gamble that didn't quite come off.*
2 to happen ● *The planned football game never came off.*
3 (always + adv/prep) to be in a good or bad position because of a fight or an argument ● *She usually comes off best in an argument.* ● *Teachers came off badly in the pay negotiations.*
4 (always + adv/prep) *American* to behave in a way which makes other people think that you have a particular characteristic ● *(usually + as) He comes off as a snob when you first meet him.* ● *I think he came off well* (= seemed to have the right characteristics) *in the interview.*

come off sth
1 to stop using medicine or drugs ● *I've got a book on how to come off tranquillizers safely.*
2 *American informal* to have recently completed a period of time when something very successful or very difficult happened ● *The dollar has just come off a period of strength.* ● *He just rejoined the team after coming off knee surgery.*

Come off it! *informal*
  something that you say in order to tell someone that you do not believe them or that you disagree with them ● *Ask him to cook the meal? Come off it, he can hardly boil an egg!*

come on   comes, coming, came, come

Come on!
1 something that you say to someone in order to encourage them to do something you want them to do, especially to hurry up, to try harder, or to tell you something ● *Come on, we'll be late if you don't hurry up!* ● *Come on! Push as hard as you can!* ● *Come on, Jilly, you can tell me. I won't say anything to anyone.*
2 something that you say in order to tell someone that you do not believe them or that you disagree with them or are angry

with them • *Oh, come on Teresa, you made the same excuse last week!*

come on

1 if something [e.g. lights, heating] or a supply of something [e.g. water, electricity] comes on, it starts working • *What time does the heating come on?*

2 if a radio or television programme comes on, it starts being broadcast • *The football comes on after the news.*

3 to improve a skill, or to make progress • *With better teaching, they should come on a lot.* • *How's your new novel coming on?* • *Since moving to America, his tennis has come on in leaps and bounds.* (= improved very quickly)

4 if an illness, a feeling, or a mood comes on, it starts • *Arthritis tends to come on gradually in elderly people.* • *I've got a headache coming on.*

5 if a season or period of time is coming on, it is getting near • *With winter coming on, I thought I'd buy a new coat.*

6 to appear in a play, film, or television or radio programme • *There was great applause when the Russian ballerina came on.*

7 *British informal* if a woman comes on, she starts her monthly period (= the flow of blood from her womb) • *I came on a bit late this month.*

8 *British & Australian literary* if rain comes on, it starts • *The rain came on during the afternoon.*

come on (sth)

to start speaking on the telephone • *My father came on and begged me to come home.* • *When John came on the line, I hung up.*

come on sth *American & Australian informal*

to behave in a way that makes other people think that you have a particular characteristic • (sometimes + **as**) *She comes on as a real hothead.* • *He comes on real stupid – but don't be fooled.*

come on to sb *informal*

to show someone that you are sexually attracted to them • *I get guys coming on to me all the time.*

come-on *n* [C] • *He interpreted my smile as a come-on.*

come out

1 to leave a room, building, or covered place • *You're not allowed in there. Come out immediately!* • (often + **of**) *The train began to pick up speed as it came out of the tunnel.*

2 to go somewhere with someone for a social event • *I can't come out tonight because I've still got work to do.* • *Do you want to come out for a drink sometime?*

3 if dirt or colour comes out of something, especially clothing or cloth, it disappears or becomes less strong after being in water • *Do you think this red wine stain will come out of the carpet?* • *I've used a chestnut colour in my hair, which should come out after about six washes.*

4 if someone who has been in prison or hospital comes out, they leave • *He was sentenced to 25 years in prison. He'll be an old man when he comes out.* • *My mother's coming out of hospital tomorrow.*

5 if something that is published [e.g. book, newspaper], a musical recording [e.g. single, album], or a film comes out, it becomes available for people to buy or see it • *He bought REM's new album on the day it came out.* • *The dictionary has just come out on CD-ROM.*

6 if the truth about something comes out, it becomes known publicly after it has been kept secret • *She is confident that the truth will come out during the trial.* • *During our conversation, it came out that he was not as rich as we had thought.*

7 (always + *adv/prep*) if you describe how something or someone comes out at the end of a process or activity, you describe what condition they are in or what they have achieved • *How did your chocolate cake come out?* • *Gina's sketch of the house came out really well.* • *We came out much better than the other companies in the report.* (= the report said we were better)

8 if results or information come out, they are given to people • *When are your exam results coming out?* • *Next month's sales figures are due to come out on April 4th.*

9 if a characteristic of a thing or a person comes out during an activity or a process, you realise that it exists • *Once the project was underway, problems with the software began to come out.* • *I had always thought* *of Tom as a calm person, but his bad temper came out when we started working together.*

10 if the sun, the moon, or a star comes out, it appears in the sky ● *The sun came out in the afternoon.*

11 if flowers or plants come out, the flowers grow and open ● *It was late March, and the daffodils in my garden were beginning to come out.*

12 if a photograph or an image in a photograph comes out, the picture can be seen clearly ● *My photos of the party didn't come out because the room was too dark.* ● *Alice's red dress comes out really well in this photo.*

13 if something you say comes out in a particular way, you say it in that way ● *I didn't mean to insult you – it just came out like that.* ● *When I tried to tell her I loved her it just came out all wrong.*

14 (always + *adv/prep*) to state publicly that you support or oppose an issue ● *The opposition* **came out** *strongly* **in favour of** *capital punishment.* ● *The committee* **came out against** *any change to the rules.*

15 to tell people that you are homosexual ● *He joined the Gay Society after he came out.* ● (sometimes + **to**) *Louise still hasn't come out to her parents.*

16 *British* if workers come out, they stop working because of a disagreement with their employers ● *300 factory workers have come out to protest over planned job losses.* ● *The union has threatened that postal workers will* **come out on strike** *unless an agreement is reached.*

17 *old-fashioned* if a young woman comes out, she starts going to parties and social events of upper-class society ● *Helena was married just eight months after she came out.*

coming-out *n* [singular] *old-fashioned* ● *Penelope's parents decided to hold a party to celebrate their daughter's coming out.* ● (used as *adj*) *She met her future husband at a coming-out dance.*

come out in   comes, coming, came, come

come out in sth

if you come out in a skin disease [esp. spots, rash], it appears on your skin ● *I think Jenny must have measles because she's come out in spots.* ● *This face cream has made my skin come out in a rash.*

come out of   comes, coming, came, come

come out of sth

1 if something comes out of a process or an event, it is one of the results ● *Kate's suggestion was the only good idea to come out of the discussion.* ● *It is difficult to see what will come out of these peace talks, because neither side is willing to compromise.*

2 to stop being in a particular state [e.g. recession, retirement] ● *The economy is expected to come out of recession within six months.* ● *She was persuaded to come out of retirement* (= to start working again) *and become the managing director of the new company.*

come out of swh

to start or to be made in a particular place ● *He is responsible for some of the funniest travel writing to come out of America.*

come out with   comes, coming, came, come

come out with sth

1 to say something suddenly ● *Clare does come out with some strange ideas sometimes.* ● *I asked one innocent question and he came out with a stream of abuse!* ● *She came straight out with it and accused him of cheating.*

2 to make a new product available for people to buy ● *Microsoft has just come out with a new version of the software.*

come over   comes, coming, came, come

come over

1 if someone comes over, they move towards you, usually in order to speak to you ● *As I walked into the room, Tim came over to greet me.*

2 to travel from another country to the country that you are in now, especially across the sea ● (often + **from**) *I've come over from the States on business.* ● (often + **to**) *Thousands of foreign tourists come over to London each year to do their Christmas shopping.*

3 to visit someone at their house ● *Do you want to come over after work?* ● *Why don't you come over and see me next time you're in Manchester?*

4 to leave a group or an organization and join a competing one ● (often + **to**) *This*

latest victory for the rebels might encourage government troops to **come over** *to their side.* • (sometimes + **from**) *Two of the most promising members of the party have come over from Labour.*

5 if an idea or an emotion comes over in writing, film, music, or when someone is speaking, it is expressed clearly • *Do you think his ideas about freedom* **come over** *in the film?* • *Her message* **came over loud and clear** (= I understood exactly what she meant) – *I would lose my job if I was late again.* • *The music came over with such intensity, I found myself in tears.*

6 (always + *adv/prep*) to behave in a way which makes other people think that you have a particular characteristic • (usually + **as**) *I spent an hour talking to Henry about steam trains – he comes over as a real enthusiast.* • *She's a very intelligent woman, but she didn't come over very well on that TV programme.*

come over sb

if a feeling comes over you, you suddenly experience it • *A great sense of calm came over me when I realised that I was no longer responsible for the situation.* • *You're not usually so rude – what's come over you?*

come over sth *British & Australian slightly informal*

if you come over in a particular way [e.g. faint, dizzy, sleepy], you start to feel that way • *Ben came over all shy when he met Nicola for the first time.* • *I'm going to have to sit down – I've come over rather faint.*

come round

see **come around/round**

come through   comes, coming, came, come

come through

1 if a message, a telephone call, or a document comes through, you receive it • *Have your exam results* **come through** *yet?* • *My visa hasn't* **come through** *yet and we're leaving for Australia next week.*

2 if an idea or emotion comes through in writing, film, music, or when someone is speaking, other people can notice it • *When you speak in public you mustn't let your nervousness* **come through**. • *Her*

bitterness always **comes through** *in her poetry.*

3 to move from one room to another • *Would the next patient like to* **come through**?

4 to do or provide something important when it is needed or wanted • (often + **for**) *When I had no job and no home, these people really* **came through** *for me.*

come through (sth)

to manage to get to the end of a difficult situation • *It was a miracle that he* **came through** *that car crash.* • *She* **came through** *the exam with flying colours.* (= she was very successful in the exam)

come through with   comes, coming, came, come

come through with sth (never passive)

to provide something [e.g. money, information], especially when someone is expecting it or hoping for it • *She wanted to buy the house but wasn't sure whether her father would* **come through with** *the money for the deposit.* • *Our London office finally* **came through with** *the necessary legal documents.*

come to   comes, coming, came, come

come to

to become conscious again • *All I could remember when I* **came to** *was my mother's anxious face.*

come to sth

1 to be a particular total when amounts or numbers are added together • *That* **comes to** *£25, please.*

2 to reach a particular state or situation • *He won't* **come to** *any harm* (= be in any danger) *so long as his Dad is there.* • *The war had just* **come to** *an end.* • *If it comes to a fight, I'll be there with you.* • *We worked really hard on the plans, but they never* **came to** *anything.* (= did not succeed)

3 if you come to a decision or a conclusion (= opinion), you make a decision about something, or you decide what you think about something • *It was several weeks before she* **came to** *a decision.* • *I've thought about what happened for a long time, and I've* **come to the conclusion that** *it must have been an accident.*

come to sb (never passive)

if a thought or idea comes to you, you suddenly remember it or start to think about it ● *I can't remember his name, hang on, it'll come to me in a minute.* ● *The idea of starting her own business came to her in the bath.*

come together   comes, coming, came

come together

to start working well as a complete thing or process, after some time or effort ● *The project is starting to come together now, but at first it was rather chaotic.*

come under   comes, coming, came, come

come under sth

1 if something or someone comes under a particular action by other people [e.g. attack, criticism, scrutiny, review, pressure], that thing is done to them ● *Dupont's proposal has come under fire* (= has been criticized) *from others within the party.* ● *The government has come under increasing pressure to deal with rising unemployment.* ● *Several management decisions have recently come under scrutiny.* ● *A 10-year trade agreement between the two countries is now due to come under review.*

2 to be controlled or dealt with by a particular authority ● *His case came under the jurisdiction of the criminal court.* ● *Playground guidelines come under the Department of Health and Safety.*

3 if a piece of information comes under a particular part of a list, book, or collection of things, you can find it in that part ● *I think 'swimming pools' usually come under 'leisure centres' in the telephone directory.*

come up   comes, coming, came, come

come up

1 to move towards someone or something so that you are near them or next to them ● *After the concert, several members of the audience came up and congratulated her.* ● (often + **to**) *As we came up to the border, we could see a crowd of people waiting to cross.*

2 if a subject [e.g. issue, name] comes up in a conversation, it is discussed or mentioned ● *The issue of safety came up twice*

during the meeting. ● *We were discussing who would be suitable for the job, and your name came up.*

3 if a job or opportunity comes up, it becomes available ● *A job has come up in the sales department. Are you interested in applying?* ● *When the opportunity to run a major film studio came up, she took it immediately.*

4 if a problem or difficult situation comes up, it happens when you do not expect it ● *I'm sorry I couldn't go with you last night, but something came up.* ● *You can phone Steve if a problem comes up with your computer.*

5 if a question or a subject comes up in an exam, that question is asked or questions about that subject are asked in the exam ● *Did any questions on phrasal verbs come up in your English exam?*

6 if a legal case comes up, it is considered by a judge ● *The case is due to come up at Nottingham Crown Court on February 1st.*

7 if information comes up on a computer screen, it appears there ● (often + **on**) *She pressed 'enter' on her computer and the text came up on screen.* ● *He entered the information they had on the killer into the computer and the names of two possible suspects came up.*

8 if a number comes up in a competition, it is one of the winning numbers ● *Three of my numbers came up in last week's lottery and I won £10.*

9 to become more successful in your job, or to achieve a better position in society ● *He's just been made an advertising executive – he's really **coming up in the world**.*

up-and-coming *adj* (always before noun) showing skill or producing good results at an early stage and likely to be more successful in the future ● *The lead role in the film is played by an up-and-coming young Scottish actor.*

10 if the sun or moon comes up, it moves up into the sky ● *She awoke just as the sun was coming up.*

11 if the lights come up in a cinema or theatre, they become brighter after the film or performance has finished ● *The actors took a final bow before the lights came up.*

12 if a seed or a plant comes up, it grows and appears above the ground ● *It was late*

February, and snowdrops were just coming up in my garden.

13(always + *adv/prep*) to be in a particular state at the end of a process, activity, or period of time • *I've spent two hours polishing the table, and it's come up beautifully.*

be coming up (always in continuous tenses)

if an event is coming up, it will happen soon • *Christmas is coming up shortly and I still haven't bought all my presents.* • *Coming up in the second half of the programme: a competition to win tickets for the Madonna concert.*

coming up!

something that someone serving food or drink [e.g. waiter, waitress] says to tell you that the food or drink you have ordered will be ready soon • *'I'd like a hamburger and fries, please.' 'Coming right up, sir!'*

come up against   comes, coming, came, come

come up against sth/sb (never passive)

to have to deal with a difficult situation or someone who disagrees with you or tries to stop you doing what you want to do • *When she started her career, she came up against racism and prejudice.* • *In the campaign to stop the road being built, they have come up against the council and local businesses.*

come up against sb (never passive)

to have to compete against someone who will be difficult to beat • *If he reaches the semi-finals, he will come up against the Australian champion, Greg Martin.*

come up for   comes, coming, came, come

come up for sth

1 to become available for a particular purpose • *That house you like in Victoria Park has just come up for sale.*

2 if a subject comes up for something [e.g. discussion, debate], it will be discussed or a decision will be made about it at an official meeting • *This issue will come up for discussion at next week's meeting.*

3 to reach the time when something should be dealt with, usually in an official way • *Your contract will come up for renewal in August.* • *The senator comes up for*

reelection in November.

come up on

be coming up on sth (always in continuous tenses) *American*

to be almost a particular time or age • *It's coming up on 11 o'clock so stay tuned for the news.* • *I can't believe it's coming up on Thanksgiving already.*

come up to   comes, coming, came, come

come up to sth (never passive)

to reach an acceptable or expected standard • (usually negative) *This essay doesn't come up to your usual standards.* • *If his work doesn't come up to scratch* (= reach the standard we expect), *we'll have to get someone else to do it.*

be coming up to sth (always in continuous tenses; never passive)

to be almost a particular time or age • *It was just coming up to 5 o'clock and he was getting rather hungry.* • *'How old are you, Helen?' 'I'm coming up to fifteen.'*

come up with   comes, coming, came, come

come up with sth (never passive)

1 to think of or to suggest a plan or idea, a solution to a problem, or an answer to a question • *A team of advertisers is hard at work trying to come up with a slogan for the product.* • *Experts have failed to come up with an explanation of why the explosion happened.*

2 to get or produce something which someone needs or which they have asked you for • *Each member of the expedition needs to come up with £3,000 to fund their trip.* • *We need someone to create a new software program. Can Bob come up with the goods?* (= create what we want)

come upon   comes, coming, came, come

come upon sb/sth *formal*

to meet someone or to find something when you do not expect to • *On my way home, I came upon Connie returning from the market.* • *During his research, he came upon a case of a woman who was allergic to water.*

come upon sb *formal*

if something unpleasant [e.g. punishment] comes upon you, it happens to you • *She knew that a heavy punishment would come upon her if she returned home late.*

condole with   condoles, condoling, condoled

condole with sb *old-fashioned*

to tell someone that you feel sorry for them, especially because one of their friends or relatives has died ● (sometimes + **on**) *He went round to condole with Mrs Emerson on the loss of her beloved husband.*

cone off   cones, coning, coned

cone off sth or **cone** sth **off** *British*

to prevent traffic from using a road by putting special objects that are shaped like cones on it ● (usually passive) *The southbound lane was coned off because of roadworks.*

confide in   confides, confiding, confided

confide in sb

to tell someone things that you keep secret from other people ● *He didn't trust his brother enough to confide in him.*

conform to   conforms, conforming, conformed

conform to/with sth

1 to obey a rule or to reach the necessary standard in something ● *Always check that the pram you intend to buy conforms to the official safety standards.*
2 to be similar to something that is traditional or normal ● *The book doesn't conform to most people's idea of a detective novel.*

conjure up   conjures, conjuring, conjured

conjure up sth or **conjure** sth **up**

to make something [e.g. picture, image, memory] appear in someone's mind ● *The word 'Alps' conjures up images of snow and blue skies.* ● *She writes from experience, conjuring up a sleazy world of clubs and drugs.* ● *The smell of polish conjures up memories of school days.*

conjure up sth/sb or **conjure** sth/sb **up**

to quickly create or achieve something very difficult ● *How am I meant to conjure up a meal for six with nothing in the fridge?* ● *If I could just conjure up the perfect boyfriend for you, I would.*

conk out   conks, conking, conked

conk out *informal*

1 if a vehicle or machine conks out, it suddenly stops working, often because it is old ● *My car's so old that one of these days it's just going to conk out.* ● *I think the washing-machine has finally conked out.*
2 to die ● *The neighbour's dog is so old and sick he looks like he could conk out any minute.*
3 to go to sleep very quickly, or to suddenly become unconscious ● *One minute he was standing there, and the next minute, he just conked out!* ● *I nearly conked off in the meeting, I was so tired.*

connect up   connects, connecting, connected

connect up sth or **connect** sth **up**

to join something [e.g. telephone, computer] to the main supply of power or to the main system ● *We've just moved into the house and the telephone hasn't been connected up yet.* ● (often + **to**) *Has the cooker been connected up to the gas?*

connive at/in   connive, conniving, connived

connive at/in sth *formal*

to allow something bad to happen or continue even though you know it should be stopped ● *The government connive at the problem because they know it would be too costly to solve it.* ● *She had little patience with women who connived in the oppression of their sisters.*

consign to   consigns, consigning, consigned

consign sth/sb **to** sth *formal*

to get rid of something or someone, or to forget about something or someone ● *I have no intention of consigning my elderly mother to some awful institution.* ● *Is anyone interested in this article before I consign it to the dustbin?*

consist in   consists, consisting, consisted

consist in sth (never in continuous tenses) *formal*

to have something as a major and necessary part or quality ● *The beauty of air travel consists in its speed and ease.*

consist of   consists, consisted

consist of sth (never in continuous tenses)

> to be formed from two or more things
> • *The team consists of four Americans and two Europeans.* • *It's a simple dish to prepare, consisting mainly of rice and vegetables.*

contend with   contends, contending, contended

contend with sth

> to have to deal with a difficult or unpleasant situation • *Teachers have to contend with a growing use of drugs in schools.* • *Both teams had to contend with icy rain and a strong wind during the match.*

contract in/into   contracts, contracting, contracted

contract in mainly British

contract into sth mainly British

> to formally agree to become involved in an activity or system • *The health scheme was begun six months ago, and 2000 people have already contracted in.*

contract out   contracts, contracting, contracted

contract out sth

> to formally arrange for other people to do a job which you are responsible for • (often + **to**) *We have decided to contract out the cleaning and maintenance of the offices to a private firm.*

contract out mainly British

> to formally state that you do not want to be involved in an activity or system any more • (often + **of**) *Five years ago, she decided to contract out of her pension scheme.*

contribute to   contributes, contributing, contributed

contribute to sth

> to be one of the causes of an event or situation • *Pollutants in the air contribute to a wide range of heart and lung diseases.* • *Falling sales in the American market contributed to the company's collapse.*

cook up   cooks, cooking, cooked

cook up sth or **cook** sth **up**

> 1 to make a meal quickly • *While I was hav-*

ing a bath, Pete cooked up a large pot of vegetable soup.

> 2 *informal* to invent something, especially in a dishonest or very imaginative way • *He cooked up a plan to set fire to his garage and then claim £15,000 from the insurance company.* • *Her mother asked her if she'd been in the pub, so she had to cook up a story about working late in the library.*

cool down/off   cools, cooling, cooled

cool down/off (sb/sth) or **cool** (sb/sth) **down/off**

> 1 to become cooler, or to make someone or something cooler • *She waited until her coffee had cooled down before taking a sip.* • *We went for a swim to cool off.* • *He put his feet in a bucket of ice to cool them down.*

> 2 to become calmer, or to make someone or something become calmer • *Just leave her to cool off and then talk to her.* • *The trial was delayed by six months to allow racial tensions in the city to cool down.* • *They threw him in jail for a few days to cool him off.*

cool down/off (sth) or **cool** (sth) **down/off**

> to stop developing or increasing, or to make something stop developing or increasing • *Trade among the European partners cooled off in 1990.* • *Higher tax should cool down the stock market.*

coop up   coops, cooping, cooped

coop up sb/sth or **coop** sb/sth **up**

> to keep a person or animal in a small area • (usually passive) *I felt in need of a holiday in the sun after being cooped up inside all winter.* • (often + **in**) *Many of the prisoners were cooped up in tiny cells for 23 hours a day.*

cop off   cops, copping, copped

cop off British informal

> to meet someone who you think is attractive and start a sexual relationship with them • (often + **with**) *Who did you cop off with last night, Sarah?*

cop out   cops, copping, copped

cop out informal

> to avoid doing something that you should do or that you have promised to do because you are frightened, shy, or you

think it is too difficult ● *I was meant to be going bungee jumping with Mark, but I copped out at the last minute.*

cop-out *n* [C] *informal* ● *Saying it's a problem of money is a complete cop-out really.*

copy down   copies, copying, copied

copy down sth or **copy** sth **down**

to write on a piece of paper something that someone has said or written so that you can remember it ● *He sat through the lecture, busily copying down her words.* ● *She told her students to copy down the essay titles she had written on the board.*

copy in   copies, copying, copied

copy sb **in** or **copy in** sb

to send someone a copy of a letter or email that you are sending to another person ● *When you reply to her, don't forget to copy me in.*

copy out   copies, copying, copied

copy out sth or **copy** sth **out**

if you copy out a piece of writing, you write it again on a piece of paper ● *She carefully copied out two verses of the poem.*

cordon off   cordons, cordoning, cordoned

cordon off sth or **cordon** sth **off**

if people in authority [e.g. police] cordon off an area, they put something around it in order to stop people from entering it ● *Police had cordoned off the city centre.* ● *The area was cordoned off while fire fighters tried to keep the blaze under control.*

cosy up to   cosies, cosying, cosied

cosy up to sb

to be friendly to someone, especially when you think you could benefit from becoming their friend ● *They accused the Prime Minister of cosying up to the US President.*

cotton on   cottons, cottoning, cottoned

cotton on *informal*

to begin to understand a situation or fact ● *I didn't know he was the spy and it took me a while to cotton on.* ● (often + **to**) *I'd only just cottoned on to the fact that they were having a relationship.*

cotton to   cottons, cottoning, cottoned

cotton to sb/sth *American informal*

to like or approve of someone or something when you first meet, experience, or think about them ● *I didn't really cotton to him.*

couch in

be couched in (always passive)

to be expressed in a particular way or style of language ● *Like all agreements it's couched in incomprehensible legal terminology.*

cough up   coughs, coughing, coughed

cough up sth or **cough** sth **up**

to bring a substance [e.g. blood, phlegm] into your mouth from your lungs or throat by coughing ● *She'd started coughing up blood and was understandably worried.*

cough up (sth) or **cough** (sth) **up** *informal*

to provide money for something, especially when you are not very willing to do this ● *I've already had to cough up £200 for his bike.* ● *It's your turn to buy the drinks – come on, cough up!*

count against   counts, counting, counted

count against sb/sth

to make someone or something more likely to fail ● *She has the qualifications for the job but her age will probably count against her.*

count among   counts, counting, counted

count (sb/sth) **among** sth

to be included as part of a group, or to include someone or something as a part of a group ● *I've known her for years but I wouldn't count her among my closest friends.* ● *It's a film that he counts among his personal favourites.* ● *They will count among some of the country's finest works of art.*

count down   counts, counting, counted

count down (sth) or **count** (sth) **down**

to wait excitedly and sometimes impatiently for an important event to happen ● (often + **to**) *The press is already counting down to what they believe will be the* *wedding of the century.* • *'So, are you looking forward to leaving work?' 'Oh, I'm just counting down the days.'*

countdown *n* [C] the period just before an important event in which everyone is waiting for the event to begin • (often + **to**) *As the countdown to a full-scale ground war continues, troops gather in the east.* • *The countdown to the election has already begun.*

count for   counts, counting, counted

count for sth

if something, for example an achievement or quality, counts for something, it is important or valuable • *Experience is certainly important but qualifications still count for something.* • *My opinion doesn't count for anything around here.*

count in   counts, counting, counted

count in sb or **count** sb **in** *informal*

to include someone in an activity • *You can count me in for the ice-skating trip on Wednesday.*

count off   counts, counting, counted

count off *American*

if people in a group count off, they each say their number loudly when it is their turn • *The soldiers counted off in tens.*

count off sb/sth or **count** sb/sth **off** *American*

to count or name the people or things in a group, in order to see if they are all present, or which ones are present • *Before the bus leaves the driver will have to count off the children.* • *He liked to count off the places he still remembered in the city.*

count on/upon   counts, counting, counted

count on/upon sb

to have confidence in someone because you know that they will do what you want • *You can always count on Martin in a crisis.* • (often + to do sth) *You can usually count on Patrick to keep the conversation going.*

count on/upon sth

to expect something to happen and make plans which depend on this thing happening • *I was counting on that extra bit of income to pay for the course.* • *I'm counting on getting away by 4:30.* • *Sorry I'm late, I*

didn't count on being held up in the traffic

count out   counts, counting, counted

count out sb or **count** sb **out** *informal*

to not include someone in an activity • *If you're going swimming before ten o'clock tomorrow morning you can count me out!*

count out sth or **count** sth **out**

to count coins or notes as you put them into a pile • *She counted out $100 in $20 bills and handed it over.*

count towards   counts, counting, counted

count towards sth

to be part of what is needed in order to complete something or achieve something • *The work that you do during the year counts towards your final degree.*

count up   counts, counting, counted

count up sth/sb or **count** sth/sb **up**

to add together all the things or people in a group • *Have you counted up how many people are coming on Saturday?*

count upon

see **count on/upon**

couple with

be coupled with (always passive)

if one thing is coupled with another thing, they exist or happen together and therefore have a particular effect or result • *It was her charm, coupled with her extraordinary energy, that made her so good at the job.* • *High interest rates, coupled with high inflation, are major deterrents to investment.*

cover for   covers, covering, covered

cover for sb

1 to do the job that someone would usually do, while they are not there • *Could you cover for me while I pop out for a few minutes?*

2 to tell a lie or give an excuse for someone so that they avoid problems or punishment • *When I was late for work, Lucy covered for me by telling the boss I was in the toilet.*

cover over   covers, covering, covered

cover over sth or **cover** sth **over**

to cover the top of something in order to hide or protect it • (often + **with**) *We* *planted the seeds in the trench and covered them over with earth.*

cover up   covers, covering, covered

cover up sth/sb or **cover** sth/sb **up**

to cover something or someone in order to hide or protect them ● *We used the painting to cover up a damp patch on the wall.* ● *Make sure you're well covered up* (= wearing enough clothes to keep your body warm) *if you're going out in this weather.* ● (sometimes + **with**) *We laid him on the sofa and covered him up with a warm blanket.*

cover up (sth) or **cover** (sth) **up**

to stop people from discovering the truth about something bad ● *They had attempted to cover up their own mistakes by accusing junior officials of incompetence.* ● (sometimes + **for**) *The police think he won't answer questions not because he's guilty, but because he's covering up for someone else* (= to protect someone else).
cover-up *n* [C] ● *There had obviously been a police cover-up.*

cozy up to   cozies, cozying, cozied

cozy up to sb *American informal*

to try to become friendly with someone, especially because you want them to like you or help you ● *Look at her, cozying up to the director. It makes me sick.*

crack down   cracks, cracking, cracked

crack down

if someone in authority [e.g. police, government] cracks down, they start treating people much more strictly in order to try to stop them from doing things they should not do ● (usually + **on**) *The police are cracking down on drug traffickers.* ● *The parents are demanding that teachers should crack down on bad behaviour in the classroom.*
crackdown *n* [C] ● (usually + **on**) *a crackdown on tax-dodgers*

crack on   cracks, cracking, cracked

crack on *British informal*

to continue what you are doing with energy and enthusiasm ● *Let's crack on now and try to finish by six o'clock.*

crack up   cracks, cracking, cracked

crack (sb) **up** *informal*

to suddenly laugh a lot, or to make someone suddenly laugh a lot ● *They cracked up when they saw me in that hat.* ● *There's something about that guy's face that simply cracks me up.*

crack up *informal*

to become mentally ill and be unable to continue your normal life and work ● *When someone becomes neurotic about pens and paper clips, it's a sure sign they're cracking up.*

crack up (sth) or **crack** (sth) **up** *American informal*

if a vehicle cracks up, or if someone cracks it up, it hits another vehicle, building, tree etc. and is badly damaged ● *The truck cracked up at the intersection when it hit a van going through a stop light.* ● *Zach cracked up a car while blind drunk.*
crack-up *n* [C] *American informal* ● (usually singular) *There was a bad car crack-up on the freeway.*

cram in/into   crams, cramming, crammed

cram in sth or **cram** sth **in**

cram sth **into** sth

to push a lot of things into a very small space so that the space becomes very full ● *You can't cram any more clothes into that suitcase.* ● *The book is only sixty pages long, we can't cram any more information in.*

cram in
cram into swh

if a lot of people or animals cram in or cram into a place, they all go into it even though it is too small for all of them and becomes very full • *Hundreds of people crammed into the church for the memorial service.*

crank out   cranks, cranking, cranked

crank out sth or **crank** sth **out** *mainly American informal*

to produce a lot of something quickly, especially without thinking about what you are doing • *She cranks out, on average, 23 new novels a year.*

crank up   cranks, cranking, cranked

crank up sth or **crank** sth **up**

1 to make something [e.g. engine] work by turning a handle • *He gets up first thing in the morning to crank up the generator so that there's enough hot water.*

2 to increase or improve something • *Clare used the remote to crank up the volume on the TV.* • *The author cranks up the tension to provide an exciting finish to the novel.* • *The company are cranking up their technical research.*

crap on   crap, crapping, crapped

crap on *offensive*

to talk for a long time in a boring way • (usually + **about**) *I had to listen to Mikey crapping on about his music collection.*

crash out   crashes, crashing, crashed

crash out *informal*

to go to sleep suddenly because you are very tired • (often + *adv/prep*) *When I get home after a full day's work, I often just crash out in front of the TV.*

crawl with

be crawling with sb/sth (always in continuous tenses)

if a place is crawling with people or insects, it is full of them or covered with them • *The kitchen was just crawling with ants.* • *In the summer this place is crawling with tourists.*

cream off   creams, creaming, creamed

cream off sb or **cream** sb **off**

to separate the cleverest or most skillful people from a group and treat them differ-ently • *Their policy is to cream off the brightest children and place them in special schools.* • *The best of the troops are creamed off for elite units.*

cream off sth or **cream** sth **off** *informal*

to take some of a supply of money, especially in order to use it for yourself • *During his 12 years as dictator he has creamed off 5% of the country's oil revenues.* • *The government has creamed off large profits from the electricity supply industry.*

crease up   creases, creasing, creased

crease (sb) **up** *British & Australian informal*

to laugh a lot or to make someone laugh a lot • *It's something about his manner – he just creases me up.* • *I took one look at him and creased up with laughter.*

credit with   credits, crediting, credited

credit sb **with** sth

to believe that someone has a particular quality • *You might at least credit me with some intelligence.*

creep in/into   creeps, creeping, crept

creep in
creep into sth

1 to gradually start to be noticeable or felt • *It was later in the relationship that the doubts started to creep in.* • *She used to sound very American but a few British phrases are starting to creep in.* • *A note of irritation had crept into his voice.*

2 if mistakes creep in or creep into a piece of text, they are included despite efforts not to include them • *A few mistakes always creep in during the editing process.* • *One or two typing errors had crept into the report.*

creep over   creeps, creeping, crept

creep over sb *literary*

if a bad feeling [e.g. unease, tiredness] creeps over someone, they gradually start to feel it • *A vague feeling of unease crept over her.*

creep up on   creeps, creeping, crept

creep up on sb

1 to move closer to someone, usually from behind, without being seen by them • *He*

followed her down a dark alley and crept up on her. • *Don't creep up on me like that – you made me jump!*

2 if a feeling or state creeps up on someone, they start to experience it so gradually that they are not aware of it • *You don't even realise that you're getting older – it just creeps up on you.* • *The worst thing about stress is how it creeps up on people.*

3 if a date or an event creeps up on someone, it seems to come or happen sooner than they were expecting • *Somehow the deadline crept up on me.*

crop up   crops, cropping, cropped

crop up

1 if a problem crops up, it suddenly happens, often when it is not expected • *We tend to deal with problems as they crop up.* • *If anything crops up and you can't come on Thursday, just ring me.*

2 if something, especially a word, crops up, it appears, often in something that you read, hear, or see • (often + *adv/prep*) *Her name kept cropping up in conversation.*

cross off   crosses, crossing, crossed

cross off sth or **cross** sth **off** (sth)

to remove a word [e.g. name] from a list by drawing a line through it • *When you've read the article cross your name off.* • *Well we've bought the drink for the party so I can cross that off the list.*

cross out   crosses, crossing, crossed

cross out sth or **cross** sth **out**

to draw a line through something that you have written, usually because it is wrong • *If you make a mistake just cross it out neatly.*

crossings out *n* (plural) mainly British & Australian • *It was the usual letter from Tony – full of crossings out and spelling mistakes.*

cross over   crosses, crossing, crossed

cross over (sth) mainly British & Australian

to walk from one side of the road to the other • *Look both ways before you cross over.* • *I crossed over the road near the traffic lights.*

cross over

1 to start to support a different, often opposing, person or group • (often + **to**)

During this period a lot of French socialists crossed over to the communists.

2 if a musician or other performer crosses over, they change from one style of music or performance to another, or they combine the two styles • (often + **to**) *They used to play a lot of dance music but they've recently crossed over to jazz.*

crossover *adj* (always before noun) • *They're one of a number of dance-rock crossover bands.* (= combining these two styles of music)

cross up   crosses, crossing, crossed

cross up sb or **cross** sb **up** American informal

to confuse or deceive someone • *The pitcher crossed up the batter with a curveball.* • *Trust me – I wouldn't cross you up.*

crowd around/round   crowds, crowding, crowded

crowd around/round (sth/sb)

if a group of people crowd around or crowd around something or someone, they surround something or someone, standing very close to them • *We all crowded around the television screen.* • *As soon as he appeared, reporters crowded round.*

crowd in/into   crowds, crowding, crowded

crowd in

crowd (sb) **into** swh

to enter a place in large numbers, filling it completely, or to make people do this • *Do we need a bigger room or can we all crowd in here?* • *Demonstrators were crowded into a small hall.* • *More than 1500 people crowded into St James' church for the service.*

crowd out   crowds, crowding, crowded

crowd out sth/sb or **crowd** sth/sb **out**

to prevent something or someone from succeeding or existing by being much more successful than them or by being present in much larger numbers • *There are worries that all these big nationwide companies will crowd out local firms.* • *Younger students are actually being crowded out by mature students.*

crowd round

see **crowd around/round**

crumple up crumples, crumpling, crumpled

crumple up sth or **crumple** sth **up**
to crush something, especially a piece of paper, into a ball ● *She crumpled up the letter and threw it in the bin.*

cry off cries, crying, cried

cry off *British & Australian informal*
to decide not to do something that you have arranged to do ● *Now, if I say we'll be there you're not going to cry off at the last minute, are you?*

cry out cries, crying, cried

cry out (sth) (never passive)
to shout or make a loud noise because you are in pain or very afraid ● (often + **in**) *She cried out in pain.* ● *I heard him cry out in the middle of the night.* ● *He fell to his knees and cried out 'I'm so scared. Oh God, I'm so scared.'*

cry out against cries, crying, cried

cry out against sth
to complain strongly about something that you disapprove of ● *Civil rights groups are crying out against the new laws.*

outcry n [C] a public expression of anger or disapproval ● *His imprisonment caused a public outcry.* ● *The executions have sparked an international outcry.*

cry out for

be crying out for sth (always in continuous tenses) *informal*
if one thing is crying out for another thing, it needs it very urgently ● *The country's crying out for a change of government.* ● *These bare walls are just crying out for a spot of colour.*

cuddle up cuddles, cuddling, cuddled

cuddle up
to sit or lie very close to someone in an affectionate way ● (often + **to**) *I got under the duvet and cuddled up to Steve to get warm.*

cull from culls, culling, culled

cull sth **from** sth
to collect something, especially information, from various places ● *The book contains a number of quotes culled from various interviews over the years.*

culminate in culminates, culminating, culminated

culminate in sth
if an event or series of events culminates in something, it ends with it, often having developed until it reaches this point ● *They'd had a series of arguments which culminated in Matt leaving the company.* ● *The celebrations culminated in a magnificent firework display at midnight.*

curl up curls, curling, curled

curl up
1 to lie or sit with your back curved and your knees close to your stomach ● *I left her curled up on the sofa with a book.* ● *He watched the cat as she lay down in front of the fire and curled up into a ball.* ● *I was so embarrassed – I just wanted to **curl up and die**.*
2 if something flat, for example paper or a leaf, curls up, its edges bend upwards towards its centre ● *I'd left the book open in the sun and its pages had started to curl up.* ● (used as *adj*) *The sandwich consisted of a curled-up lettuce leaf between two pieces of stale bread.*

curse with

be cursed with (always passive)
to have something that is a disadvantage to you or that other people think is very unpleasant ● *My brother is cursed with very smelly feet.*

cuss out cusses, cussing, cussed

cuss sb **out** *American informal*
to shout angrily at someone using offensive words ● *When I told the passenger his flight was delayed, he started cussing me out.*

cut across cuts, cutting, cut

cut across sth
1 to go from one side of an area to the other instead of going round it, in order to get somewhere quickly ● *If we cut across this field it'll save time.*
2 if a problem or subject cuts across different groups of people, all of those groups are affected by it or interested in it ● *Support for environmental issues cuts across traditional party lines.* ● *Sport has a way of cutting across social or racial differences.*

cut back   cuts, cutting, cut

cut back (sth) or **cut** (sth) **back**

to reduce the amount of money that is being spent on something • *When companies are cutting back, the first people to lose their jobs are temporary staff.* • *The government is committed to cutting back its defence budget.* • (often + **on**) *We're having to cut back on investment this year.*
cutback *n* [C] • (often + **in**) *Cutbacks in public spending are expected in the next budget.*

cut back sth or **cut** sth **back**

to cut or remove some of the branches of a plant in order to help it grow more strongly • *The roses need to be cut right back at this time of year.*

cut back *mainly American*

to eat, drink or use less of a particular thing, usually in order to improve your health • (usually + **on**) *He's trying to cut back on fat in his diet.* • *You smoke far too much. You should cut back.*

cut down   cuts, cutting, cut

cut down sth or **cut** sth **down**

1 if you cut down a tree or bush, you make it fall to the ground by cutting it near the bottom • *The new owners cut down the apple trees and built a bigger garage.*
2 to reduce the amount, number, length or size of something • *They've cut her hours down at work so she doesn't have much money.* • *If an article is too long for the space allocated, you have to cut it down.*

cut down

to eat or drink less of a particular thing, usually in order to improve your health • (often + **on**) *I'm trying to cut down on the amount of sugar I eat.* • *I don't drink so much alcohol these days – in fact I've really cut down.*

cut down sb or **cut** sb **down** *literary*

to kill someone, especially with a gun • *One of the victims tried to escape over the wall but was cut down by automatic fire.*

cut in   cuts, cutting, cut

cut in

1 if a motor or a piece of equipment cuts in, it starts working automatically • *If the pressure drops below the safety level, the pump will cut in.*

2 to suddenly drive in front of someone, not leaving enough space between the two vehicles • *A car suddenly cut in right in front of us and I had to slam on the brakes.*
3 to interrupt two people who are dancing in order to dance with one of them • *'Can I cut in?' he asked, looking at Alice.*

cut in (sth)

to interrupt what someone is saying by saying something yourself • *Anna suddenly cut in and asked who was paying for the tickets.* • (sometimes + **on**) *I'm sorry to cut in on your conversation like this.*

cut in sb or **cut** sb **in** *informal*

to let someone take part in something [e.g. game, business] or to let someone have a share in the money that is got from something • *If we cut Mike in, we'll have to split the profit between five of us.* • (sometimes + **on**) *Let's talk to Ann – she may want to be cut in on the business and she'd be a good partner.*

cut in/into   cuts, cutting, cut

cut in sth or **cut** sth **in**

cut sth **into** sth

American to mix fat and flour together by cutting the fat until it combines with the flour • *After sifting the flour, cut the lard in.*

cut off   cuts, cutting, cut

cut off sth or **cut** sth **off**

to stop providing something [e.g. aid, electricity, supplies] • *The U.S. threatened to cut off military aid.* • *Water and electricity supplies have been cut off and there's very little food.*
cutoff *n* [singular] *American* • *A cutoff of military assistance would mean certain death for thousands.* • *The engine has an automatic cutoff.* (= device to stop it working) • (used as *adj*) *Where's the cutoff valve for the heating system?*

cut off sb/sth or **cut** sb/sth **off**

1 to prevent people from reaching a place or leaving a place • (usually passive) *All the roads were blocked by snow so the whole village was cut off.* • *We often get cut off in the winter.*
2 *American* to suddenly drive in front of another vehicle in a dangerous way • *Some idiot cut me off at the light.* • *Did you see*

that guy? He just cut off the car in front of us.

cut off sb or **cut** sb **off**

1 to stop talking to someone because you do not want to be friendly with them any more ● *Her family didn't approve of the match so they cut her off.* ● (sometimes reflexive) *He's completely cut himself off from his family.*

2 to stop the supply of something such as electricity, gas or water ● *We'd better pay that electricity bill before they cut us off.* ● *If you get cut off you have to pay loads of money to get re-connected.*

3 to stop someone speaking by interrupting them ● *She cut me off in mid-sentence.*

4 *American informal* to stop serving someone alcoholic drinks in a bar because they have already drunk too much alcohol ● *So you're telling me I've had too much to drink and you're cutting me off, right?*

5 to stop people from continuing a telephone conversation by breaking the telephone connection ● (usually passive) *I don't know what happened then – somehow we got cut off.*

6 to not allow someone to receive your money or property, especially when you die ● *His father so disapproved of his lifestyle that he cut him off without a penny.*

be cut off (always passive)

1 to be a long way from other places and people ● (often + **from**) *We're a bit cut off from other people here living, so far from the town.*

2 if someone is cut off, they are not able to see many other people ● (often + **from**) *Cut off from friends and family, prisoners often suffer from acute loneliness.* ● (used as adj) *I think I'd feel very cut-off if I were on my own in the house all day.*

---

cut out   cuts, cutting, cut

cut out sth or **cut** sth **out**

1 to remove something by cutting, especially something made of paper or cloth ● (often + **of**) *She had a picture of him that she'd cut out of a magazine.*

cutout *n* [C] ● *There was a large cardboard cutout* (= shape cut from cardboard) *of the star outside the cinema.*

2 to cut a shape from a piece of paper or

cloth ● *Fold the paper in two and cut out a semi-circle.*

3 to remove part of a piece of writing ● *She cut out the offending paragraph before she delivered her speech.* ● (often + **of**) *Two long speeches have been cut out of the first act.*

4 to stop eating or drinking something, usually in order to improve your health ● *I still eat fish and chicken but I've cut out red meat altogether.*

5 if something cuts out the light, it stops the light from coming into a place ● *The trees have grown so tall that they're cutting out the light.*

cut out

1 if an engine, machine, or piece of equipment cuts out, it suddenly stops working ● *I don't know what's wrong with this car – the engine keeps cutting out.*

cutout *n* [C] a device that automatically stops something working if there is a problem ● *There's a cut-out that switches off the machine automatically if it gets overloaded.*

2 *mainly American* to make a sudden sideways movement out of a line of traffic ● *The car in front of us cut out with no warning and began weaving through the traffic.*

3 *American informal* to leave suddenly ● *I have to cut out – see you later guys.*

cut out sb or **cut** sb **out**

to not let someone share something ● *We can sell direct to the customer and cut out the middleman.* ● (sometimes + **of**) *They cut me out of the conversation completely.* ● *Her father cut her out of his will.* (= did not leave her anything when he died)

Cut it out! (always an order) *informal* something that you say to tell someone to stop doing something annoying ● *Cut it out, you two! The last thing I want to hear is you guys arguing!*

be cut out to do sth (always passive)

to have the right qualities for something, especially a job ● (usually negative) *Sometimes I don't think I'm cut out to be a teacher.*

---

cut out for

be cut out for sth (always passive)

to have the right qualities for something, especially a job ● (usually negative) *I'm not sure you're cut out for the army.*

cut through   cuts, cutting, cut

cut through sth

1   to go across an area or place instead of around it, in order to get somewhere more quickly ● *I cut through the park to get to the shops.*

2   to move quickly and smoothly through something, especially water ● *The slim yacht cut through the sea.* ● *He cut through United's defence to score.*

3   if you cut through something that usually causes problems [e.g. bureaucracy, red tape], you quickly deal with it so that it does not cause problems for you ● *I wish there was some way we could cut through all this bureaucracy.*

cut up   cuts, cutting, cut

cut up sth or **cut** sth **up**

to cut something, for example food, into small pieces ● *He eats what we adults eat but I cut it up for him.*

be cut up (always passive)

1   *slightly informal* to be very upset about something ● (often + **about**) *He seemed pretty cut up about his grandmother dying.*

2   *slightly informal* to be injured by being cut in several places ● *He was badly cut up in a fight.* ● *What have you been doing? Your hands are all cut up.*

cut up *American informal*
to behave in a noisy, silly way, especially to try to make people laugh ● *The kids cut up as soon as the teacher left the classroom.*

cutup *n* [C] *American informal* a person who jokes a lot or behaves in a silly way, especially to get attention ● *Fox acts the part of the loud-mouthed cutup in the family.*

cut up sb or **cut** sb **up**

1   *American informal* to criticize someone in a very unpleasant way ● *She seems to cut up most of the people she works with.*

2   *British* to suddenly drive in front of another vehicle in a dangerous way ● *He cut me up and I had to brake suddenly.*

dab at · dabs, dabbing, dabbed

dab at sth

to touch something, especially your face, several times with quick, light movements • *She dabbed at her eyes as if she was crying.*

dabble in/with · dabbles, dabbling, dabbled

dabble in/with sth

to become involved in a particular activity for a short period of time and not in a very serious way • *He dabbled in advertising before starting a career in magazine publishing.* • *I dabble with photography but just as a hobby.*

dally with · dallies, dallying, dallied

dally with sth

to think about something [e.g. idea], but not in a serious way • *She dallied with the idea of starting her own business but she never made any serious plans.*

dally with sb *old-fashioned*

to have a short and not very serious romantic relationship with someone • *He had dallied with one or two of the local women in the village.*

dam up · dams, damming, dammed

dam up sth or **dam** sth **up**

to build a wall across a river in order to stop the water from flowing • *The river was dammed up and a reservoir built.*

damp/dampen down · damps, damping, damped/dampens, dampening, dampened

damp/dampen down sth or **damp/ dampen** sth **down**

1 to make a fire burn more slowly by covering it so that it gets less air • *He threw leaves on in an attempt to damp down the flames.*

2 if you damp down a part of your body that is swollen (= bigger than usual because of disease), you put something on it to make it smaller and less sore • *Nasal sprays can help to damp down any inflammation in the nose.*

3 to make a strong feeling [e.g. anger] be felt less strongly • *The murder has roused anger in the community which may not be easily damped down.*

4 to make a surface slightly wet • *On hot days you should damp down your greenhouse to lower the temperature.*

dash off · dashes, dashing, dashed

dash off sth or **dash** sth **off**

to write or draw something [e.g. letter, book] very quickly and without trying very hard • *His latest novel, already a bestseller, was dashed off in under three weeks.*

dash off *informal*

to leave a place quickly • *I'm going to have to dash off – I've got a doctor's appointment at four.* • *You dashed off after the show and I didn't get a chance to speak to you.*

date back · dates, dating, dated

date back (always + *adv/prep*)

to have existed since a particular time • *The oldest part of the building dates back to the early 16th century.* • *There had been an amazing discovery of human remains dating back nearly two million years.*

dawn on/upon · dawns, dawning, dawned

dawn on/upon sb

if a fact dawns on you, you realize or understand something after a period of time when you did not realize or understand it • *Then **it dawned on** me that my exams were only 2 weeks away.* • *It was when I saw them talking at Michelle's party that the truth suddenly dawned on me.*

deal in · deals, dealing, dealt

deal in sth

1 to buy and sell particular goods as a business • *She used to sell modern art but now she deals in antiques.* • *He made most of his money by dealing in drugs.*

2 *informal* to be involved with a particular type of thing • *As a journalist, she's used*

to dealing in hard facts.

deal in/into   deals, dealing, dealt

deal sb **in**

deal sb **into** sth

to give someone cards so that they can play in a game of cards ● *We're playing poker Kerrie, should I deal you in?*

deal out   deals, dealing, dealt

deal out sth or **deal** sth **out**

1 to give playing cards to each player in a game ● *Who's going to deal out the cards, then?*

2 to give a punishment to someone ● *The same punishment was dealt out to everyone who was caught stealing.*

deal with   deals, dealing, dealt

deal with sth

1 to take action in order to achieve something, or in order to solve a problem ● *I haven't got time to reply to this letter. Could you deal with it? ● Emergency services claim they do not have the resources to deal with a major disaster.*

2 if something [e.g. book, film, article] deals with a particular subject or idea, it is about that subject or idea ● *His latest novel deals with the relationship between a man and his son. ● The second part of this document deals with staff training.*

deal with sb/sth

to do business with a person or organization ● *We have been dealing with this firm for over ten years. ● He was the first Soviet leader to deal constructively with western governments.*

deal with sb

1 to meet or talk to someone as part of your work ● *As a family doctor, she deals with 20 to 30 patients a day. ● He mainly deals with children who have emotional problems.*

2 *informal* to punish someone for doing something wrong ● *The group said it would deal with any of its members who were selling drugs. ● Go to your room and I'll deal with you later!*

decide on/upon   decides, deciding, decided

decide on/upon sth/sb

to choose something or someone after thinking carefully ● *Have you decided on*

a name for the baby? ● We've decided on a beige carpet for the dining-room.

deck out   decks, decking, decked

deck out sth or **deck** sth **out**

to decorate somewhere, especially a room or street, for a special occasion ● (usually passive + **with**) *The streets leading into town were decked out with flags and banners.*

deck out sb or **deck** sb **out**

to put on fashionable or colourful clothes for a special occasion ● (usually reflexive) *He'd decked himself out in a dark suit and a bright yellow tie. ● The women were all decked out in summer dresses and hats.*

declare against   declares, declaring, declared

declare against sth/sb *formal*

to publicly state that you disagree with something or someone or that you do not support something or someone ● *The health minister has declared against the new bill.*

declare for   declares, declaring, declared

declare for sth/sb *formal*

to publicly state that you support something or someone ● *The king abdicated after the national referendum declared for a republic.*

defer to   defers, deferring, deferred

defer to sb/sth *formal*

to accept someone else's opinion because they know more than you or are more important than you ● *I tend to defer to Guy on financial matters – he's much better informed than I am. ● I defer to your judgment.*

delight in   delights, delighting, delighted

delight in sth/doing sth *slightly formal*

to get a lot of pleasure from something, especially something unpleasant ● *As a nation we delight in scandal about the famous. ● He seems to delight in telling everyone about the mistakes I make.*

deliver of   delivers, delivering, delivered

be delivered of sb (always passive) *formal*

if a woman is delivered of a baby, she gives birth to a baby ● *The Princess was delivered of a healthy baby girl at 9 o'clock this morning.*

deliver yourself **of** sth (always reflexive) *formal*

to express something • *He delivered himself of a bitter attack on his opponent.*

deliver on   delivers, delivering, delivered

deliver on sth

to do what you promised or agreed to do • (usually negative) *He was accused of failing to deliver on his promise to make life better for the people.*

deliver over/up   delivers, delivering, delivered

deliver over/up sth/sb or **deliver** sth/sb **over/up** *formal*

to give something or someone to a person in authority • (often + **to**) *They were forced to deliver up their passports to the border control.* • *The two thieves were delivered over to the sheriff.*

delve into   delves, delving, delved

delve into sth

to examine something carefully in order to discover more information about someone or something • *I don't like to delve too deeply into his past.* • *It must be terrible to have journalists delving into your private life all the time.*

depart from   departs, departing, departed

depart from sth *formal*

to be different from the usual or expected way of doing or thinking about something • *The film departs from almost every cinematic convention.*

depend on/upon   depends, depending, depended

depend on/upon sth/sb

1 to need the help or support of something or someone in order to survive or continue as before • *The city's economy depends largely on the car industry.* • (sometimes + to do sth) *People depend on their lungs to breathe.* • (sometimes + **for**) *She depended on her family for support during the trial.*

2 (never in continuous tenses) if something depends on a particular situation, condition, or person, it is influenced by

them or cannot change without them • (often + question word) *The cost of your flight depends on what time of year you go.* • *I might go this evening – it depends on whether I can leave work early.* • *A house in this area will cost between £60,000 and £80,000, depending on its size and condition.*

depend on/upon sb/sth

to trust someone or something and know that they will help you or do what you want or expect them to do • *It's so hard to find a reliable hairdresser who you can depend on.* • (sometimes + to do sth) *I don't feel I can depend on him to do anything.*

deprive of   deprives, depriving, deprived

deprive sb/sth **of** sth

to take something important away from someone or something • *The new law will deprive religious minorities of their right to vote.* • *No one can function properly if they're deprived of adequate sleep.*

derive from   derives, deriving, derived

derive from sth

to come from something • *The name of the cave, Fingal's Cave, derives from the legendary Irish figure, Fin MacCool.* • *Pollutants like these derive mainly from the combustion of fuel in car engines.*

descend from   descends, descending, descended

descend from sth

to have developed from something which existed in the past • *According to the theory of evolution, human beings descended from apes.*

be descended from sb (always passive)

to be related to someone who lived a long time ago • *Her father is descended from the Greek royal family.*

descend into   descends, descending, descended

descend into sth

if a situation descends into a particular state, it becomes worse • *The demonstration, which began peacefully, rapidly descended into a riot.*

descend on/upon   descends, descending, descended

descend on/upon swh/sb

if a group of people descends on a place or person, they arrive, especially without warning or without being invited ● *A crowd of press photographers descended on the hotel.* ● *My sister and her family descended on us last Saturday.*

descend on/upon sb

if a feeling, especially a bad feeling, descends on a group of people, they begin to feel it ● *A feeling of despair descended on us as we realised that we were lost.*

descend to   descends, descending, descended

descend to sth/doing sth

to behave badly in a way that other people would not expect you to ● *I never imagined he would descend to stealing.* ● *You should never descend to that sort of behaviour.*

descend upon

see **descend on/upon**

despair of   despairs, despairing, despaired

despair of sth/sb or **despair of** doing sth *formal*

to feel that there is no hope that a situation will improve or that someone will do what they should ● *I despair of my son – he just refuses to do any homework.* ● *I'd been 18 months without work and I'd begun to despair of ever finding a job.*

detract from   detracts, detracting, detracted

detract from sth

to make something seem less good than it really is or than it was thought to be ● *The recent scandal has further detracted from the company's reputation.* ● *She does have a big nose but it in no way detracts from her overall prettiness.*

devolve on/upon   devolves, devolving, devolved

devolve on/upon sb *formal*

if property or money devolves on someone, they receive it when the person who owns it dies ● *When James Allen died, the estate devolved on his nephew.*

devolve (sth) **on/upon** sb/sth *formal*

to give power or the responsibility for something to a person or organization at a lower level ● *The Home Secretary has devolved the task upon junior ministers.*

devolve to   devolves, devolving, devolved

devolve (sth) **to** sb/sth *formal*

to give power or the responsibility for something to a person or organization at a lower level ● *The new bill will devolve some power to local government.*

devolve upon

see **devolve on/upon**

devote to   devotes, devoting, devoted

devote sth **to** sth/doing sth

to use all of something, for example your life or your time, for a particular purpose ● *He resigned from his job to devote more time to his family.* ● *She never married but devoted her life to writing and speaking about women's rights.* ● *Two whole pages of the newspaper were devoted to the news of the royal divorce.*

devote yourself **to** sth/doing sth (always reflexive)

to spend all your time or energy doing something that you think is important ● *He retired in 1814 to devote himself to social reforms.*

dial in/into   dials, dialling, dialled   (*American & Australian* also **dials, dialing, dialed**)

dial in

dial into sth

to connect one computer to another by using a modem (= electronic device which lets one computer send information to another through telephone wires) ● *I tried to dial in to download the file but the line was busy.*

dial out   dials, dialing, dialled   (*American & Australian* also **dials, dialing, dialed**)

dial out

to use a telephone in order to call someone in another building ● *Can you dial out from this phone or is it for internal calls only?*

dictate to   dictates, dictating, dictated

dictate to sb

to tell someone what to do, often in a way that annoys them • *I will not be dictated to by some idiot in the personnel department.*

diddle around   diddles, diddling, diddled

diddle around *American & Australian informal*

to waste time doing unimportant things • *She's been diddling around all morning.*

diddle with   diddles, diddling, diddled

diddle with sth *American informal*

to use your hands in a series of small movements in order to try to do something • *Lisa diddled with the tape recorder waiting for Tom to speak.*

die away   dies, dying, died

die away

if something, especially a sound, dies away, it gradually becomes less strong or clear and then stops • *I listened till the echo of Jackson's footsteps died away.*

die back   dies, dying, died

die back

if a plant dies back, the parts that are above the ground die although its roots are alive • *The fuschia always dies back in the winter.*

die down   dies, dying, died

die down

if something, especially noise or excitement, dies down, it gradually becomes less loud or strong until it stops • *When the applause had died down he started to speak.* • *Eventually the fuss will die down and everything will return to normal.*

die for

be dying for sth (always in continuous tenses) *informal*

to want something very much, especially food or drink • *Put the kettle on – I'm dying for a cup of coffee.* • *I'm dying for a cigarette.*

die off   dies, dying, died

die off

if a group of people, animals, or plants dies off, all of that group dies over a

period of time • *The ground and climate isn't right for growing grass so after a few years it dies off.*

die out   dies, dying, died

die out

to become more and more rare and then disappear completely • *Dinosaurs died out 65 million years ago.* • *Many of the customs of village life have died out over the years.*

dig in   digs, digging, dug

dig in sth or **dig** sth **in**

to mix a substance into earth by digging • *The soil was very poor so I dug in a big pile of compost.*

dig in or **dig** yourself **in**

if soldiers dig in, they dig holes in the ground that they can hide in to protect themselves • *We received orders that we were to move to the hills and dig in.* • *His troops had five months to dig themselves in before the war started.*

dig in *informal*

1 to start eating food • (often an order) *The food's on the table so dig in before it gets cold.*

2 *American* to begin to do something in a determined way • *They dug in immediately so as not to waste any more time.*

dig into   digs, digging, dug

dig into sth

1 to put your hand in something [esp. pocket, bag] in order to try to find something • *He dug into his pocket and pulled out a few coins.*

2 to use part of a supply of something that you have been saving, especially money • *The Taylors have had to dig into their savings to pay for the legal fees.*

3 to start eating food • *I watched him dig into an enormous plateful of food.*

4 *American* to start to do something in a determined way • *He sat down at his desk and dug into the work that had piled up while he had been away.*

dig sth **into** sth

to mix a substance into the earth by digging • *Dig plenty of compost into the soil.*

dig into sth or **dig** yourself **into** sth

if soldiers dig into something, they dig holes in the ground that they can hide in to protect themselves ● *They had dug into fixed positions around the area.*

dig out   digs, digging, dug

dig out sth or **dig** sth **out**
1 *slightly informal* to find something that you have not seen or used for a long time ● *I'm sure I have a map of Prague – I'll try and dig it out tonight.* ● (often + **of**) *We were looking at some old school photographs I'd dug out of a drawer.*
2 *slightly informal* to discover information about a person or a situation after a lot of searching ● *I had to dig out information for my dissertation from old manuscripts.*

dig over   digs, digging, dug

dig over sth or **dig** sth **over**
to dig an area of earth in order to improve the condition of the soil ● *I spent the afternoon digging over the flowerbed so that I could plant some bulbs.*

dig up   digs, digging, dug

dig up sth or **dig** sth **up**
1 to dig holes in or destroy the ground or a floor ● *They're digging up the road outside our house.* ● *When we moved in we had to dig up the cellar floor and replace it.*
2 to discover new facts about a person or situation after a lot of searching ● *They've recently dug up some new evidence which suggests that he was innocent.* ● *The press are always digging up scandalous facts about people's pasts.*

din into   dins, dinning, dinned

din sth **into** sb *British & Australian old-fashioned*
to force someone to believe in a particular idea or remember a particular thing by repeating it to them again and again ● (usually passive) *It was dinned into us at school that we must always be organized.*

dine off/on   dines, dining, dined

dine off/on sth
to eat a particular type of food as a meal, especially expensive food ● *We dined off smoked salmon and drank champagne.*

dine out   dines, dining, dined

dine out *slightly formal*
to eat your evening meal in a restaurant ● *We're dining out on Friday with some*

friends of David's.

dine out on   dines, dining, dined

dine out on sth *mainly British & Australian humorous*
to often entertain people during meals by telling them about something special that happened to you ● *Christine was once invited to the palace – in fact she's dined out on it ever since.*

dip in/into   dips, dipping, dipped

dip sth **in** (sth)
dip sth **into** sth
to quickly put something into liquid and take it out again ● *He dipped his brush in the paint.* ● *There's some bread for dipping into your soup.*

dip into   dips, dipping, dipped

dip into sth
1 to read small parts of a book or magazine ● *It's the sort of book you can dip into every now and again.*
2 to spend part of a supply of money that you have been keeping or saving ● *I've had to dip into my savings to pay for the repairs.*
3 to put your hand in a container and remove one of the things from inside it ● *She had a box of chocolates beside her that she kept dipping into.*

disabuse of   disabuses, disabusing, disabused

disabuse sb **of** sth *formal*
to persuade someone that something that they believe is not true ● *He said he thought that all women liked babies but I soon disabused him of that notion.*

disagree with   disagrees, disagreed

disagree with sb (never in continuous tenses)
if a type of food disagrees with you, it makes you feel slightly ill or uncomfortable ● *I tend to avoid coconut as it disagrees with me.* ● *I must have eaten something that disagrees with me – my stomach really hurts.*

dish out   dishes, dishing, dished

dish out sth or **dish** sth **out**
1 to serve food to people, usually by putting it onto plates ● *Maurice, could you dish the potatoes out for me, please?*

2 *informal* to give or say things to people without much care, control or thought • *He was on TV last night, dishing out prizes at some award ceremony.* • (sometimes + **to**) *Doctors have been criticized for dishing out drugs to patients who don't need them.* • *It's the sort of criticism that the press routinely dishes out to the stars.* • *He **can dish it out** but he **can't take it**!* (= he often criticizes people but does not like to be criticized)

dish up   dishes, dishing, dished

dish up sth or **dish** sth **up**

1 to put all the food for a meal onto plates, ready to be eaten • *She dished up the most delicious meal for us.*

2 *slightly informal* to offer or produce something, often in a careless way • *Film critics seem to applaud anything this young director dishes up.*

dish up *British & Australian*
to put all the food for a meal onto plates, ready to be eaten • *If you want to sit at the table, I'm ready to dish up.*

dispense with   dispenses, dispensing, dispensed

dispense with sth/sb *formal*
to stop using something or someone, or to get rid of something or someone, often because you do not need them • *Nobody would suggest that companies dispense with interviews altogether.* • *New drugs may dispense with the need for injections altogether.* • *The newspaper began to lose readers when it dispensed with one of its most popular writers.*

dispose of   disposes, disposing, disposed

dispose of sth

1 *slightly formal* to throw something away • *Nuclear waste is often disposed of under the sea.* • *The court heard how Mellor had disposed of his victims' bodies in rivers and lakes.*

2 *formal* to deal with something successfully • *That's disposed of items one and two on the agenda so let's move onto number three.* • *A case which goes to trial will naturally take longer to dispose of.*

3 *formal* to sell something valuable [e.g. assets, property, shares] • *The bank disposed of its shares at just the right time.*

dispose of sb/sth *slightly humorous*
to kill a person or animal • *When the time came to dispose of the pig, he found himself unable to do it.*

dispose of sb
to defeat someone • *Within fifty minutes, the nineteen year-old German had disposed of the ex-champion.*

dissociate from   dissociates, dissociating, dissociated

dissociate sb/sth **from** sb/sth
to consider two things or people as separate and not related to each other • *I can't dissociate the man from his political opinions.*

dissociate yourself **from** sb/sth
(always reflexive)
to say or show that you are not connected to something or someone because you think that thing or person is bad • *Most party members are keen to dissociate themselves from the extremists.* • *The writer has publicly dissociated himself from the film of his book.*

dissolve into   dissolves, dissolving, dissolved

dissolve into sth

1 to develop into a bad state or situation • *There are fears that the present conflict might dissolve into full-scale civil war.*

2 if you dissolve into tears or laughter, you suddenly start to cry or laugh • *She saw his photograph on the wall and dissolved into tears.* • *We dissolved into fits of giggles just like silly schoolgirls.*

dive in/into   dives, diving, dived   (*American pt and pp* also **dove**)

dive in

dive into sth

1 to start doing something suddenly and energetically, often without stopping to think • *When neighbouring countries are having a war you can't just dive in.* • *Unfortunately, I had dived into the discussion without being fully informed.*

2 to start eating • *The food's on the table and there's plenty, so dive in everyone.*

dive into   dives, diving, dived   (*American pt and pp* also **dove**)

dive into sth
to quickly put your hand in something

[e.g. pocket, bag] to get something out of it ● *I dived into my trouser pocket and – thank goodness – found the key.*

divest of divests, divesting, divested

divest yourself **of** sth (always reflexive) *formal*

to remove something that you are wearing or carrying ● *He divested himself of his cloak and hat and proceeded to the drawing room.*

divest sb/sth **of** sth *formal*

to get rid of something that you have had for a long time, especially something bad ● (usually reflexive) *It is very difficult to divest yourself of a reputation that has been acquired over years.*

divest sb **of** sth *formal*

to officially take away someone's power or rights ● *There's a growing movement to divest the monarchy of its remaining privileges.*

divide by divides, dividing, divided

divide sth **by** sth

if you divide a larger number by a smaller number, you calculate the number of times that the smaller number fits into the larger one ● *21 divided by 3 is 7.*

divide into divides, dividing, divided

divide sth **into** sth

if you divide a smaller number into a larger number, you calculate the number of times that the smaller number fits into the larger one ● *What do you get if you divide 6 into 18?*

divide off divides, dividing, divided

divide off sth or **divide** sth **off**

to separate an area with a wall or other vertical structure ● *The end of the room was divided off by a tall screen.*

divide up divides, dividing, divided

divide up (sth) or **divide** (sth) **up**

to separate something into smaller parts or groups, or to form smaller parts or groups ● *She divided up the class into four groups.* ● *The world divides up into those who like cats and those who don't.*

divide up sth or **divide** sth **up**

to share something between a number of people or groups ● (often + **among**) *I think we should divide up the costs equally*

among us. ● (often + **between**) *They're proposing that the country be divided up between them.*

divvy up divvies, divvying, divvied

divvy up (sth) or **divvy** (sth) **up** *informal*

to share something between a number of people ● *They haven't yet decided how to divvy up the proceeds from the sale.*

do away with does, doing, did, done

do away with sth

to get rid of something, or to stop using something ● *These ridiculous rules and regulations should have been done away with years ago.*

do away with sb *informal*

to kill someone ● (often reflexive) *I tried to do away with myself but I couldn't.*

do down does, doing, did, done

do down sb or **do** sb **down** *British informal*

to criticize someone in order to make them feel ashamed or to make other people lose respect for them ● *It seemed that everyone at the meeting was trying to do her down.* ● (often reflexive) *Stop doing yourself down.*

do for does, doing, did, done

do for sb/sth *mainly British old-fashioned, informal*

to damage something so badly that it cannot be used any more, or to seriously hurt or kill someone ● *Driving on rough roads has really done for my car.*

done for *adj* (always after verb) *informal* ● *Driving conditions were so awful – I was convinced I was done for.* ● *We're done for if she ever finds out what really happened.*

do in does, doing, did, done

do in sb or **do** sb **in**

1 *informal* to make someone extremely tired ● *That walk's completely done me in.*
done in *adj* (always after verb) *informal* ● *When we got back home we were completely done in.*

2 *informal* to attack or kill someone ● *Phil had heard that his enemies were threatening to do him in.*

do out   does, doing, did, done

do out sth or **do** sth **out** *British & Australian*

to decorate or clean a room • *I'm off work next week so I'm going to do out the kids' rooms.*

do out of   does, doing, did, done

do sb **out of** sth *informal*

to stop someone from getting or keeping something, in a dishonest or unfair way • *Roz was convinced he was trying to do her out of her inheritance.*

do over   does, doing, did, done

do over sth or **do** sth **over**

1 *British informal* to go into a house and steal things from it • (usually passive) *In this area some of the houses have been done over many times.*

2 *mainly American* to decorate a room or a house in order to make it look more attractive • *They're getting some new appliances and want to do over their kitchen at the same time.*

3 *American & Australian* to do something again because you did not do it well the first time • *This is full of errors – I'm sorry but you'll have to do it over.*

do over sb or **do** sb **over** *British & Australian slang*

to attack someone • *Rumours were going about that they were going to do him over.*

do up   does, doing, did, done

do up sth or **do** sth **up**

1 to fasten something • *Can you help me do up my dress? • Do your laces up or you'll trip over.*

2 to repair something, or to improve the appearance of something, especially a building • *She and her husband were planning to buy an old country house and do it up.*

3 to wrap something [esp. present] in paper • (often + **in**) *She always does her presents up beautifully in gold paper.*

do up *British*

to become fastened • *Why won't this zip do up?*

do yourself up (always reflexive) *slightly informal*

to make yourself look more attractive • *Don't bother doing yourself up, we're only going for a pizza.*

do with   does, doing, did, done

do with sth

to put something somewhere • (usually in questions) *What have you done with my car keys? • I had his letter yesterday but I just can't remember what I did with it.*

do sth **with** yourself (always reflexive) *informal*

to spend your time in a particular way • *What are you going to do with yourself today? • I'm sure she won't know what to do with herself when the kids leave home.*

could do with sth/sb *informal*

to need or want something or someone • *Do you have time to talk? I could really do with some advice. • I could have done with a couple of people to help me out.*

I can't do with/I can't be doing with sth/sb (always negative) *British informal*

something that you say to tell someone that you are very annoyed by something or someone • *I really can't be doing with his constant complaining. • He's one person on telly I just can't be doing with.*

do without   does, doing, did, done

do without (sth/sb)

to manage without something or someone • *There's no milk left, so I'm afraid you'll just have to do without.*

I can/could do without sth *informal*

something that you say when something is annoying you or causing problems for you, because your situation at that time makes it difficult for you to deal with it • *I could really do without all that screaming and shouting from the kids while I'm trying to work.*

dob in   dobs, dobbing, dobbed

dob in sb or **dob** sb **in** *British & Australian informal*

to cause trouble for someone by telling someone in authority that they have done something wrong • *At school she was the sort of girl who was always dobbing people in.*

dole out   doles, doling, doled

dole out sth or **dole** sth **out** *informal*

to give something [esp. money] to several people or in large amounts • (often + **to**) *I can't keep doling out money to you kids.*

• *Beryl was in the kitchen doling out soup to hungry children.*

doll up   dolls, dolling, dolled

doll yourself up (always reflexive) *informal*
if a woman dolls herself up, she tries to make herself more attractive than usual by putting on special clothes and make-up • *She dolled herself up for the occasion in a little red dress.*
dolled up *adj informal* • *Sandra was there – all dolled up in a strappy black dress and heels.*

doom to   dooms, dooming, doomed

doom sb/sth **to** sth
to make someone or something sure to fail or suffer in a particular way • (usually passive) *The plan was doomed to failure from the start.* • *Does this mean that the present leadership is doomed to eventual defeat?*

dope up   dopes, doping, doped

dope up sb or **dope** sb **up**
to give someone so many drugs that they cannot think or speak in the usual way • (usually passive) *We visited her in hospital but she was so doped up she didn't even recognize us.*

dose up   doses, dosing, dosed

dose sb **up with** sth
to give someone a lot of medicine • *She dosed him up with a cold cure and put him to bed.*

doss about/around   dosses, dossing, dossed

doss about/around *British informal*
to spend your time doing very little • *I spent the whole afternoon just dossing around.*

doss down   dosses, dossing, dossed

doss down (always + *adv/prep*) *mainly British & Australian informal*
to sleep on the floor or somewhere you do not usually sleep because you have no home or because there is no bed available • *She dossed down in stations and doorways, anywhere that would shelter her from the cold.* • *You can doss down on our sofa for tonight if you like.*

dot about/around

be dotted about/around (swh) (always passive)
if things are dotted about an area or a place, they can be found in many different parts of that area or place • *We have offices dotted about all over the region.* • *I noticed a few photographs dotted around the room.*

dot with   dots, dotting, dotted

dot sth **with** sth
to put small amounts of something, especially food, on a surface in several places • *Dot the crust with butter and place in the oven.*

be dotted with sth (always passive)
if an area is dotted with things, it has many of them in different places • *We looked at the fields below dotted with tents.*

dote on/upon   dotes, doting, doted

dote on/upon sb
to love someone completely and believe that they are perfect • *She has a three-year old son who she just dotes on.*

double as   doubles, doubling, doubled

double as sth
if something doubles as something else, it also has the purpose of that thing • *The school's gymnasium doubles as a dining room.* • *A hard-wearing shirt for the daytime, it doubles as a light jacket for the evening.*

double back doubles, doubling, doubled
double back
to turn and go back in the direction that you have come from • *If we don't find it by the end of this road, we'll just double back.* • *It's a strange route because you effectively **double back** on yourself.*

double for doubles, doubled
double for sb (never in continuous tenses)
to look very similar to someone else, especially someone famous • *There was a guy in the gym last night who could have doubled for Arnold Schwarzenegger.*

double over/up doubles, doubling, doubled
double (sb) **over/up**
to suddenly bend your body forwards because you are laughing a lot or in a lot of pain, or to make someone do this • (often passive + **with**) *He has his audiences doubled up with laughter.* • *She doubled over, clutching her side.*

double up doubles, doubling, doubled
double up
to share something [esp. bedroom] with another person because there are not enough for everyone • *There are only three bedrooms so some of us will have to double up.* • (often + **with**) *Jane, would you mind doubling up with Anna when the others arrive?*

double up as doubles, doubling, doubled
double up as sth
if something doubles up as something else, it also has the purpose of that thing • *Our spare bedroom doubles up as a study.*

doze off dozes, dozing, dozed
doze off *informal*
to gradually start to sleep, especially during the day • *He dozed off in front of the TV.*

draft in drafts, drafting, drafted
draft sb **in** or **draft in** sb
to bring people, often extra people, somewhere to do a particular job • (often passive) *Every Christmas, thousands of people are drafted in to help with the post.*

drag away drags, dragging, dragged
drag sb **away** *informal*
to make someone stop doing something so that they can do something else • (usually + **from**) *I'll bring Melissa with me tonight – if I can drag her away from the TV.* • (often reflexive) *I'll perhaps meet you for a drink – if I can drag myself away from my studies.*

drag down drags, dragging, dragged
drag sb **down**
if an unpleasant or difficult situation drags someone down, it makes them feel unhappy or ill • *He's been unwell for a number of months now and it's starting to drag him down.* • *All that stress and conflict at work has really dragged him down.*

drag down sth or **drag** sth **down**
to make the level of something go down • *The earthquake will drag down the prices of property built on less stable ground.* • *One or two bad exam results may drag down the overall results.*

drag in/into drags, dragging, dragged
drag in sb/sth or **drag** sb/sth **in**
drag sb/sth **into** sth
1 to force someone or something to become involved in an unpleasant or difficult situation • *Think very carefully before you go dragging the police in.* • *It seems likely now that the whole region will be dragged into the war.*
2 to talk about someone or something when you are having an argument, especially when that person or thing is not connected with what you are arguing about • *Every time we discuss this you drag your mother in.* • *There's no point dragging all that into the argument – it's just not relevant.*

drag on drags, dragging, dragged
drag on
if an unpleasant or difficult situation or process drags on, it continues for too long • (often + **for**) *The war has already dragged on for six years and could drag on for a further six.* • *The talks might drag on for weeks before any concrete result is announced.*

drag out   drags, dragging, dragged

drag out (sth) or **drag** (sth) **out**
 to continue for longer than is necessary, or to make something do this ● (often + **for**) *It's looking as if the talks might drag out for several more days.* ● *She intended to drag out her thesis project for as long as she could.*

drag out of   drags, dragging, dragged

drag sth **out of** sb
 to make someone tell you something that they do not want to tell you ● *You never tell me how you feel – I always have to drag it out of you.*

drag up   drags, dragging, dragged

drag up sth or **drag** sth **up**
 to talk about something unpleasant that happened in the past in order to annoy or embarrass someone ● *All that stuff with Dave happened years ago. Why do you have to keep dragging it up?* ● *The press have dragged up some story about a woman that he was supposed to have hit.*

drag up sb or **drag** sb **up** *British humorous*
 if parents drag a child up, they are not very careful about teaching the child to behave correctly ● *Wine in cups? Who dragged you up?!*

dragoon into   dragoons, dragooning, dragooned

dragoon sb **into** doing sth *humorous*
 to make someone do something that they do not want to do ● *I've been dragooned into giving the after-dinner speech.*

draw back   draws, drawing, drew, drawn

draw back
1 to move away from someone or something, usually because you are surprised or afraid ● *Connie drew back, startled and frightened.* ● (often + **from**) *He drew back from the window when he saw the car arriving.*
2 to decide not to do something, especially because you think it would be bad for you ● (often + **from**) *He was a man who always drew back from conversation.* ● *They had intended to take him to court but had drawn back because of the costs involved.*

draw in   draws, drawing, drew, drawn

draw in *mainly British & Australian*
 if days, evenings, or nights draw in, it becomes darker earlier because autumn or winter is coming ● *The nights are really drawing in now.*

draw in/into   draws, drawing, drew, drawn

draw in sb/sth or **draw** sb/sth **in**
draw sb/sth **into** sth
 to make someone or something become involved in a difficult or unpleasant situation ● (usually passive) *If the conflict spreads and other countries are drawn in it could be very bad news.* ● *I'm not going to be drawn into that kind of argument.*

draw in

draw into swh
 if a train draws in, it arrives and stops at a station ● *She looked eagerly along the platform as the train slowly drew in.* ● *People gathered on the platform as the train drew into the station.*

draw off   draws, drawing, drew, drawn

draw off sth or **draw** sth **off**
 to remove a quantity of liquid from a larger amount ● *The next step is to draw the wine off into a clean barrel.*

draw on   draws, drawing, drew, drawn

draw on sth
 to breathe in smoke from a cigarette ● *He drew deeply on his cigar and then began to speak.*

draw on *slightly formal*
 if time or a period of time [e.g. time, day, year] draws on, it slowly passes or gets nearer to its end ● *As the evening drew on, she became more anxious.*

draw on/upon   draws, drawing, drew, drawn

draw on/upon sth
1 to use information or your knowledge or experience of something to help you do something ● *His early poetry **draws heavily on** his experience and memories of childhood.*
2 to use part of a supply of something ● *I have some money saved which I can draw on in an emergency.*

draw out   draws, drawing, drew, drawn

draw out sb or **draw** sb **out**
   to help someone who is shy to feel more
   confident ● *I tried to draw him out with
   some conversation.*

draw out sth or **draw** sth **out**
   to make something continue for longer
   than is usual or necessary ● *The director
   drew the meeting out for another hour
   with a series of tedious questions.*
   drawn-out *adj* ● *The signs indicate that
   it isn't going to be a long, drawn-out affair.*

draw out
1 *mainly British & Australian* if days, evenings, or nights draw out, it stays light
   until later because spring or summer is
   coming ● *I much prefer it when the evenings start to draw out again.*
2 if a train draws out, it gradually moves
   out of a station ● *I ran onto the platform
   just as the train began to draw out.*

draw up   draws, drawing, drew, drawn

draw up sth or **draw** sth **up**
1 to prepare something [e.g. list, plan, con-
   tract] by writing it ● *The new agreement
   was drawn up in secret by the Health Minister.* ● *I've drawn up a list of candidates
   I'd like to interview.*
2 to move a piece of furniture [esp. chair]
   near to something or someone ● *Their
   card game looked interesting so I drew up
   a chair to watch.*
3 to move your knees or legs closer to your
   body ● *Cold and miserable, he drew up his
   knees and held them tightly to his chest.*

draw up
   if a vehicle, or someone in a vehicle,
   draws up, they arrive somewhere and
   stop ● (usually + *adv/prep*) *With a screech
   of the brakes he drew up outside her house
   in a red sports car.*

draw yourself **up** (always reflexive)
   to stand up very straight, usually in
   order to make yourself seem bigger and
   more important ● *Miss Wilson drew herself up, stared at him in disgust and
   walked angrily out of the room.*

draw upon
   see **draw on/upon**

dream of

wouldn't dream of doing sth
   something that you say in order to tell
   someone that you would never do something because you think it is wrong or
   silly ● *I wouldn't dream of asking your
   mother to help us – she's much too busy.* ● *I
   wouldn't dream of leaving my car un-
   locked round here.*

dream on

dream on! *informal*
   something that you say in order to tell
   someone that what they are hoping for is
   not possible and will not happen ● *'When
   I win the lottery, I'm going to give up work
   and live in the south of France.' 'Dream
   on, Jenny!'*

dream up   dreams, dreaming, dreamt or dreamed

dream up sth or **dream** sth **up**
   to think of an idea or plan, especially one
   that is very imaginative or not really possible ● *They've asked a marketing company to dream up a name for their latest
   product.* ● *She's always dreaming up
   crazy schemes to get rich quick.*

dredge up   dredges, dredging, dredged

dredge up sth or **dredge** sth **up**
   to talk about something unpleasant that
   happened in the past in order to annoy or
   embarrass someone ● *He accused the
   press of dredging up lies about his past.*

dredge up sth/sb or **dredge** sth/sb **up**
   to search and find something or someone
   ● *We finally managed to dredge up some
   old family photos.* ● *Let's see if we can
   dredge up an eligible man for Helen.*

dress down   dresses, dressing, dressed

dress down
   to put on clothes that are not formal or
   special and that will not attract attention
   ● *This time he dressed down, having realised that the smart suit would be out of
   place.*

dress down sb or **dress** sb **down**
   to speak very angrily to someone because
   they have done something wrong ● (often
   + **for**) *He dressed them down for challen-
   ging his authority.*
   dressing-down *n* [C] ● *She gave me a
   dressing-down for being late.*

dress up   dresses, dressing, dressed

dress up (sb) or **dress** (sb) **up**

1 to put on formal or special clothes for a special occasion, or to put them on someone else • *Weddings are a great opportunity to dress up.* • *She was **dressed up to the nines** (= extremely dressed up) in a pink Chanel suit and high heels.* • (sometimes + **in**) *I used to hate it when my Mum would dress me up in pretty dresses.*

2 to put on someone else's clothes to make yourself look like someone else, or to make someone do this, usually as a game • (often + **in**) *When she was young, she loved to dress up in her mother's clothes.* • (often + **as**) *Matthew was dressed up as a cowboy for Luke's party.*
dressing-up n [U] *British* the game or activity of wearing old or special clothes • *Dressing-up is one of Robbie's favourite games at the moment.* • (used as *adj*) *Provide dressing-up clothes and ask the children to pretend to be a member of their family.*

dress up sth or **dress** sth **up**
to make something seem more interesting, acceptable, or attractive than it really is • (often + **as**) *They attempted to dress it up as a book with international relevance.* • (often + **in**) *A lot of so-called new products are simply the old products dressed up in new packages.*

drift apart   drifts, drifting, drifted

drift apart
if two friends drift apart, they gradually become less friendly and their relationship ends • *Jane used to be one of my best friends at school but we've drifted apart over the past few years.*

drift off   drifts, drifting, drifted

drift off
to gradually start to sleep • *As Tim started telling her about his holiday for the third time, she closed her eyes and drifted off.* • *I was just **drifting off to sleep** when there was a crash in the kitchen.*

drill into   drills, drilling, drilled

drill sth **into** sb
to tell someone something again and again so that they learn it • *It was drilled into us at an early age that we should*

never cross the road without looking.

drink in   drinks, drinking, drank, drunk

drink in sth or **drink** sth **in**
to look at, listen to, or experience something with all your attention and to enjoy it very much • *He gazed up at her adoringly, drinking in her every word.* • *We sat in a small café watching people pass by and drinking in the atmosphere.*

drink to   drinks, drinking, drank, drunk

drink to sb/sth
to hold up your glass before drinking from it in order to celebrate something or to wish someone success or happiness • *Let's drink to John and Annmarie and wish them every happiness in the future!* • *They raised their glasses and drank to the success of the project.*

drink up   drinks, drinking, drank, drunk

drink up (sth) or **drink** (sth) **up**
to completely finish your drink • *We'd better drink up – it looks like the pub's about to close.* • *Drink your coffee up, Paul, before it goes cold.*

drive at

be driving at sth (always in continuous tenses; always used in questions) *informal*
if you ask someone what they are driving at, you are asking them what they really mean • *What on earth is he driving at?* • *I just don't understand what you're driving at.*

drive away   drives, driving, drove, driven

drive away sb/sth or **drive** sb/sth **away**
to force a person or animal to leave or move away from somewhere • *The sheep were annoying her, so she clapped her hands to drive them away.*

drive away sb or **drive** sb **away**
to make people [e.g. tourists, customers] not want to go to a place • (sometimes + **from**) *Tourists have been driven away from our beaches by the threat of oil pollution.*

drive away sth or **drive** sth **away**
if something drives away a feeling or thought [e.g. sadness, worry, care], it stops you feeling or thinking it • *A trip to the seaside will drive your cares away.*

drive off drives, driving, drove, driven

drive off sb/sth or **drive** sb/sth **off**
to force someone or something that is coming towards you, or attacking or threatening you to stop and leave ● *The enemy attack was driven off by their army.*

drive off sb or **drive** sb **off** (sth)
to force a person or animal to leave or move away from somewhere ● *The farmer called in the police to drive the gypsies off his land.*

drive off
if someone playing golf drives off, they make the first hit at the start of a game or hole ● *Hogan drove off at the seventeenth.*

drive out drives, driving, drove, driven

drive out sb/sth or **drive** sb/sth **out**
to force someone or something to leave ● (often + **of**) *They were driven out of their homes and villages by the invading army.*

drone on drones, droning, droned

drone on
to talk for a long time in a very boring way ● (often + **about**) *She droned on for hours about her family history.*

drool over drools, drooling, drooled

drool over sth/sb
to look at something or someone in a way that shows you find them very attractive ● *We sat by the swimming pool, drooling over all the gorgeous young men.* ● *I left Sarah in the shop, drooling over a green silk dress.*

drop around/round drops, dropping, dropped

drop around/round mainly British & Australian informal
to make a short visit to someone in their home, usually without arranging it before ● *Is it OK if I drop round to pick up those photos?* ● *You should drop around sometime – it's ages since we've got together.*

drop around/round sth or **drop** sth **around/round** informal
to deliver something, usually something small ● *If you drop those papers around tomorrow, I'll have a look at them.*

drop away drops, dropping, dropped

drop away
1 *mainly British & Australian* if the amount of something [e.g. value, support, interest] drops away, it gradually becomes less ● *Contributions from the public have dropped away rapidly and now form only 20% of our income.*
2 *mainly British & Australian* if land drops away, it slopes down steeply ● (sometimes + **to**) *Behind the house the garden drops away to a small stream.*

drop back drops, dropping, dropped

drop back
if you are moving forward in a group of people and you drop back, you move to a position nearer the back ● *I dropped back to help my sister who was having trouble with her horse.* ● (sometimes + **to**) *She was in the lead at the end of the first lap but has now dropped back to fourth place.*

drop behind drops, dropping, dropped

drop behind (sb/sth)
1 to move forwards more slowly than the rest of a group of people, animals, or moving objects so that they get ahead of you ● *I couldn't run as fast as the others and soon dropped behind.* ● *He dropped behind the other cars when he had to stop to change a wheel.*
2 *British & Australian* to make less progress than someone or something else ● *Repeated illness caused him to drop behind at school.* ● (sometimes + **in**) *We've dropped behind our competitors in productivity and output.*

drop by drops, dropping, dropped

drop by British & Australian informal
to make a short visit to someone in their home, usually without arranging it before ● *He said he might drop by later this evening.*

drop in drops, dropping, dropped

drop in informal
to make a short visit to someone in their home, usually without arranging it before ● *Just drop in whenever you're in the area.* ● (often + **on**) *I dropped in on George* (= I went to George's house) *on my way home.* ● (often + **at**) *Could you drop in at Sarah's and pick up my books for me?*

drop sb **in it** *British & Australian informal*

to cause trouble for someone by doing something that makes someone else angry with them ● *Why did you have to tell her about my date with Sally? You've dropped me right in it.*

drop in/into   drops, dropping, dropped

drop in sth or **drop** sth **in** *British & Australian informal*

drop sth **into** swh *British & Australian informal*

to deliver something to a place or to someone ● *Jim can drop your books in at the library if you like.* ● *She dropped her skirt into the cleaner's this morning.*

drop in

drop into swh

to go into a place [e.g. shop, library, pub] for a short time ● *I need to drop in at the bank on my way home.* ● *I dropped into the book store to see if they had that book you wanted.*

drop off   drops, dropping, dropped

drop off sb/sth or **drop** sb/sth **off**

to take someone to a place that they want to go to, or to deliver something to a place, usually in a car, often when you are going somewhere else ● *I'm driving into town so I can drop you off on the way.* ● *If you're going past the library would you mind dropping off these books?*

drop off

1 *informal* to fall asleep ● *She dropped off in the armchair.* ● *I lay in bed hoping I'd **drop off to sleep** but I couldn't.*

2 if the amount, number, or quality of something drops off, it decreases ● *Orders have dropped off since Christmas.*

drop-off *n* [C] ● (often + **in**) *a drop-off in the number and quality of applicants*

drop out   drops, dropping, dropped

drop out

1 to not do something that you were going to do, or to stop doing something ● *Peter was coming with us to the theatre, but had to drop out at the last minute.* ● (often + **of**) *He dropped out of the race after two laps.*

2 if a student drops out, they stop going to classes before they have finished their course ● (often + **of**) *She dropped out of college and took a job in a riding stables.*

dropout *n* [C] ● *She runs informal classes for high school dropouts.*

3 to choose not to be involved in the usual activities of the society that you live in, especially by not having a job ● *He dropped out in the sixties and spent several years in India.*

dropout *n* [C] ● *The protesters are mainly hippies and dropouts.*

drop over   drops, dropping, dropped

drop over *informal*

to make a short visit to someone in their home, usually without arranging it before ● *I might drop over after work. Will you be in?*

drop round

see **drop around/round**

drown in/with   drowns, drowning, drowned

drown sth **in/with** sth

to cover something with a lot of liquid ● *As usual, Ben drowned his food in tomato sauce.*

drown out   drowns, drowning, drowned

drown out sth or **drown** sth **out**

if a loud noise drowns out another noise, it prevents it from being heard ● *I had to turn the music up to drown out the shouting.*

drown with

see **drown in/with**

drum into   drums, drumming, drummed

drum sth **into** sb

to force someone to believe in a particular idea, or to remember a particular fact by repeating it to them again and again ● (usually passive) *As a soldier, discipline and respect for rank is drummed into you from day one.* ● *They've had it drummed into them not to complain.*

drum out   drums, drumming, drummed

drum out sb or **drum** sb **out**

to force someone to leave an organization because they have done something wrong ● (usually passive + **of**) *She'd been drummed out of her job after having an affair with one of her students.*

drum up   drums, drumming, drummed

drum up sth

to increase interest in something or support for something • *He's just launched a campaign to drum up support for the cause.* • *Both companies are desperately trying to find new ways to drum up business.* (= get more customers)

dry off   dries, drying, dried

dry off (sb/sth) or **dry** (sb/sth) **off**

to make someone or something dry, or to become dry, especially on the surface • (sometimes reflexive) *Here, dry yourself off with this towel.* • *I like to dry off in the sun.*

dry out   dries, drying, dried

dry out (sth) or **dry** (sth) **out**

to make something dry, or to become dry • *Central heating dries out your skin.* • *If you don't keep food covered, it dries out.*

dry out *informal*

to stop being an alcoholic (= someone who cannot stop drinking alcohol) or drug addict (= someone who cannot stop taking drugs) • *She was in her late thirties when she finally dried out.*

dry up   dries, drying, dried

dry up (sth) or **dry** (sth) **up** *British & Australian*

to dry dishes, plates, etc. after they have been washed, using a cloth • *I was just drying up a few dishes.* • *Give me a teatowel and I'll dry up for you.*

drying up *n* [U] *British & Australian* • *I'll wash up if you'll* **do the drying up**.

dry up

1 if an area of water [esp. river, lake] dries up, the water in it disappears • *The pond had dried up over the long hot summer.* • *The wells have all dried up and people walk miles for water.*

2 if a supply of something dries up, it ends • *The flow of foreign money into the country has almost dried up.*

3 to stop speaking when you are acting or making a speech, especially because you suddenly forget what to say next • *My biggest fear is that halfway through my presentation I'll just dry up.*

dry up! (always an order) *informal*
something that you say to tell someone to be quiet when they are talking or complaining too much • *Oh dry up, for God's sake, you've done nothing but moan all morning!*

duck out   ducks, ducking, ducked

duck out

to leave somewhere quickly and quietly, often to avoid being seen • *At the sound of her mother's voice, Sane ducked out by the back door.*

duck out of   ducks, ducking, ducked

duck out of sth/doing sth *informal*

to avoid doing something that other people are expecting you to do • *I'm supposed to be going to a meeting but I might duck out of it.*

duff up   duffs, duffing, duffed

duff up sb or **duff** sb **up** *British informal*

to hurt someone by hitting or kicking them again and again • *They followed him out of a nightclub and duffed him up.*

duke out   dukes, duking, duked

duke it out *American slang*

if two people duke it out, they have a fight • *The two men were duking it out in the bar.*

dumb down   dumbs, dumbing, dumbed

dumb down sth or **dumb** sth **down** *informal*

to make something [e.g. textbook, curriculum] simpler and easier to understand • *They did not approve of dumbing down books as a way of encouraging children to read.*

dump on   dumps, dumping, dumped

dump on sb

1 *informal* to treat someone badly, especially by giving them too much to do ● *I really don't want to dump on you, but on the other hand the work has to be done.*

2 *American informal* to criticize someone severely and often unfairly ● *It's okay for me to dump on my family but I don't like anyone else doing it.*

dump (sth) **on** sb *mainly American informal*

to tell someone everything about your problems ● *I wish he wouldn't come and dump on me every time he's feeling depressed.* ● *Sam's in need of a good listener to dump his troubles on.*

dust down/off   dusts, dusting, dusted

dust down sth/sb or **dust** sth/sb **down** *British & Australian*

dust off sth/sb or **dust** sth/sb **off** *British, American & Australian*

to remove dust or dirt from something ● *He stood up, dusted his trousers off and shook his jacket.* ● (sometimes reflexive) *She dusted herself down and went on with her work.*

dust down sth or **dust** sth **down** *British & Australian*

dust off sth or **dust** sth **off** *British, American & Australian*

1 to use something from the past [e.g. idea, law, phrase], especially something that has already been used too much ● *Every time a great actor dies, critics dust off the same tired old clichés.*

2 to prepare something in order to be able to use it again after not using it for a long time ● *They brought out the old ambulances, dusted them down and put them back into service.*

dust yourself **down/off** (always reflexive)

to recover from a serious problem or a bad experience ● *You always have setbacks in life but you've just got to* **pick** *yourself up and dust yourself down.*

dwell on/upon   dwells, dwelling, dwelled

dwell on/upon sth

to think or talk about a particular subject for too long, especially one that is unpleasant or not important any more ● *I try not to dwell on the past.* ● *He was an alcoholic for five years but it's a subject that he'd rather not dwell on.*

94

E

ease off/up   eases, easing, eased

ease off/up

1 to gradually stop or become less ● *I'm
leaving soon but I'm just waiting for the
traffic to ease off a bit.* ● *At last the rain
began to ease up.*

2 to start to work less or do things with less
energy ● *John's been working really long
hours over the past month so the boss has
told him to ease off a little.* ● (often + **on**)
*The police are under political pressure to
ease up on their investigation.*

3 to start to treat someone less severely
than before ● *At first they were pretty hos-
tile towards me but when they found out
I'd helped the authorities they eased up a
bit.* ● (often + **on**) *Ease off on him will you,
he's not all that bad.*

ease out   eases, easing, eased

ease out sb or **ease** sb **out**

to make someone leave their job or position but in a way that makes it seem as if
they have chosen to leave ● (usually passive + **of**) *Mr Millard was eased out of his
job after a long campaign by parents and
teachers.*

ease up

see **ease off/up**

eat away   eats, eating, ate, eaten

eat away sth or **eat** sth **away**

to gradually destroy something by continuously damaging it or taking little
parts of it ● *The house was built on land
which the sea is slowly eating away.*

eat away at   eats, eating, ate, eaten

eat away at sb

if a memory or bad emotion [e.g. bitterness, shame] eats away at someone, they
think about it a lot and it makes them
very unhappy ● *The knowledge that I
killed him eats away at me inside.*

eat away at sth

to gradually destroy something by continuously damaging it or taking little
parts of it away ● *There is a belief that
routine eats away at love.*

eat in   eats, eating, ate, eaten

eat in

to have a meal at home, not in a restaurant ● *We're eating in tonight as we want to
go to bed early.*

eat into   eats, eating, ate, eaten

eat into sth

to use or take away a large part of something valuable [e.g. savings, profits, leisure time, business] ● *The high cost of living in London is eating into my savings.*
● *Increased administrative work can eat
into employees' free time.*

eat out   eats, eating, ate, eaten

eat out

to eat a meal in a restaurant, not at home
● *The cost of eating out is quite high here.*

eat out sb or **eat** sb **out** *American slang*
to tell someone angrily that they have
done something wrong ● *He eats out all
his students, so don't worry about it.*

eat up   eats, eating, ate, eaten

eat up sth or **eat** sth **up**

1 to eat all the food you have been given
● *Within two minutes she had eaten up all
the bread and cheese.*

2 to use all of something that is valuable
and that you are trying to keep ● *The increased cost of books eats up the school's*

budget. • *Any software that stores images will eat up a lot of disk space.*

3 *slightly informal* to use large amounts of fuel • *A big car like this eats up petrol.*

4 *American informal* to enjoy something [e.g. film, show] very much • *I didn't like the show but the kids really ate it up.*

eat up sb or **eat** sb **up**

if a memory or bad emotion [e.g. guilt, bitterness] eats someone up, they experience it so strongly that they are very badly affected by it • *He was so eaten up by guilt he became ill.* • *If you're not careful, bitterness can eat you up.*

Eat up! (always an order)

something that you say to someone, especially a child, in order to tell them to eat their food • *Come on, eat up! We haven't got all day.*

ebb away   ebbs, ebbing, ebbed

ebb away

to gradually disappear • *Our strength ebbed away under the hot sun.* • *His life was ebbing quickly away.*

edge out   edges, edging, edged

edge out sb/sth or **edge** sb/sth **out**

to cause someone or something to gradually lose their position and to replace them with someone or something else • *Mr James who was hired by the previous management was soon edged out by the new boss.* • (often + **of**) *Foreign car manufacturers are edging domestic companies out of the markets.*

edit out   edits, editing, edited

edit out sth or **edit** sth **out**

to remove part of a piece of writing or recorded material before it is printed or broadcast • *The new television channel adopted the policy of editing out sex, nudity and street language from the films it broadcasts.* • *Two paragraphs had been edited out of the article.*

eff off

Eff off! (always an order) *British & Australian taboo*

something that you say in order to tell someone very rudely to go away • *Just tell him to eff off!*

egg on   eggs, egging, egged

egg on sb or **egg** sb **on**

to encourage someone to do something, often something that is wrong, stupid, or dangerous • *A crowd of youths egged him on as he climbed the wall.* • *Egged on by his friends, Joe drank five pints of strong lager.*

eke out   ekes, eking, eked

eke out sth or **eke** sth **out** (never passive)

1 to use something slowly or carefully because you only have a small supply of it • *I added some tomato to eke out the meat sauce.*

2 to manage to get enough of what you need even though this is very difficult • *He ekes out a living* (= gets enough money to live) *by trading paintings for food.*

elbow out   elbows, elbowing, elbowed

elbow out sb/sth or **elbow** sb/sth **out**

to force someone or something out of a position or job • *The smaller countries of the region were elbowed out by their larger neighbours.*

emanate from/to   emanates, emanating, emanated

emanate from/to sb/sth *formal*

to come from or be produced by someone or something • *Angry voices emanated from a room upstairs.* • *Complaints about working conditions were emanating from factory staff.*

embark on/upon   embarks, embarking, embarked

embark on/upon sth *slightly formal*

to start something, especially something large, important, or new • *So does he have any advice for those about to embark on an acting career?* • *We are now embarked on the third and most important of the projects.*

embroider on   embroiders, embroidering, embroidered

embroider on sth

to add details which are not true to a description of events in order to make the description more interesting • *Admittedly I had embroidered on the truth a little but that's what story-telling is all about.*

empty out empties, emptying, emptied

empty out sth or **empty** sth **out**

1 if you empty out a container, you remove all the things that are inside it • *I've emptied out my pockets but it's not there.*

2 if you empty out things that are in a container, you remove them from it • *He tried to make the bottle lighter by emptying out half the water.*

empty out

if a place empties out, all the people in it leave • *Most of the offices in the city empty out at 5.30 on weekdays.*

encroach on/upon encroaches, encroaching, encroached

encroach on/upon sth

1 *formal* to gradually take away someone else's rights, or to take control of someone's time, work etc. • *What the government proposed encroaches on the rights of individuals.*

2 to gradually cover more and more of an area of land • *The new plans involve private land and do not encroach on country park territory.*

end in ends, ending, ended

end in sth

to finish in a particular way • *Her first, childless marriage ended in divorce.* • *(British) As for Sophie and Mark getting together, it'll end in tears.* (= the situation will end badly)

end up ends, ending, ended

end up (always + *adv/prep/adj*) *slightly informal*

to finally be in a particular place, state, or situation, especially without having planned it • *We ended up in Blackpool of all places.* • (often + **as**) *Illegally imported reptiles such as snakes and crocodiles often end up as shoes, belts and handbags.* • (often + **with**) *He ended up with an alcohol problem.* • *She'll end up pregnant at this rate.*

end up doing sth *slightly informal*

to finally do something, especially without having planned to • *I ended up paying for everyone on the table.*

endear to endears, endearing, endeared

endear sb **to** sb

if a quality in someone's character or

their behaviour endears them to you, it makes you like them • (often negative) *He has a sexist streak in him which is unlikely to endear him to his new colleagues.* • *It's the way that she laughs at herself that endears her to me.*

endow with endows, endowing, endowed

be endowed with sth (always passive)

to have a particular quality or feature • *Some lucky people are endowed with both brains and beauty.*

endow sb/sth **with** sth *formal*

to give a particular quality or feature to someone or something, or to make them seem to have it • *The author endowed his hero with extraordinary vigour and charm.*

engage in engages, engaging, engaged

engage in sth *formal*

to take part in something • *They've been engaged in a legal battle with the council for months.*

engage sb **in** sth

if you engage someone in conversation, you try to start a conversation with them • *He made no attempt whatsoever to engage either of us in conversation.*

engage on/upon engages, engaging, engaged

engage on/upon sth *formal*

if you engage on a particular activity, you do it • (usually passive) *So what projects are you engaged on at present?*

engage with engages, engaging, engaged

engage with sb/sth

to show interest in, and a wish to understand and give attention to, someone or something • *I want us to plan this trip together, but Charles just won't engage with it.*

enlarge on/upon enlarges, enlarging, enlarged

enlarge on/upon sth *formal*

to give more details about something that you have said or written • *The idea is to introduce the main points of your talk before you enlarge upon them.* • *Would you care to enlarge on what you've just said?*

enquire after   enquires, enquiring, enquired

enquire after sb/sth *formal*

to ask for information about someone or something, especially about someone's health ● *He always enquires after my father.*

enquire into   enquires, enquiring, enquired

enquire into sth *formal*

to try to discover the facts about something, or to try to discover if something you want to do is possible ● *I decided to enquire into the possibility of part-time work.*

enter into   enters, entering, entered

enter into sth

1 to start to become involved in something, especially a discussion ● *They refuse to enter into any discussion on the matter.* ● *The company had been invited to enter into settlement negotiations.* ● *We are sorry we cannot enter into personal correspondence.* ● *You've got to dance if you're going to **enter into the spirit of things**.* (= show your enthusiasm for a special occasion)

2 if you enter into an agreement, you officially agree to something ● *They have made it clear that they do not wish to enter into the agreement.* ● *That explains his reluctance to enter into such a contract.*

3 to affect a situation and be something that is important to consider ● (often negative) *The issue of money doesn't enter into it – it's whether you want to go that's important.*

enter on/upon   enters, entering, entered

enter on/upon sth *formal*

to start to do something, or to become involved in something ● *She never entered upon any action of importance without*

first consulting her husband.

even out   evens, evening, evened

even out (sth) or **even** (sth) **out**

to become equal, or to make something equal ● *He pays for some things and I pay for others and in the end it all evens out.* ● *The new system is aimed at evening out the differences between rich and poor colleges.*

even up   evens, evening, evened

even up sth or **even** sth **up**

to make a situation more equal or fair ● *Gavin's been on three trips this year so if you go on this one that evens things up a bit.*

expand on/upon   expands, expanding, expanded

expand on/upon sth

to give more details about something that you have said or written ● *He mentioned one or two ideas that he'd had but he didn't expand on them.*

explain away   explains, explaining, explained

explain away sth or **explain** sth **away**

to give a reason for something bad happening which makes other people think that it is not so bad or that it is not your fault ● *Six hundred pounds is missing – try explaining that away.*

eye up   eyes, eyeing, eyed

eye up sb or **eye** sb **up** *mainly British & Australian informal*

to look at someone in a way which shows that you are sexually interested in them ● *That guy in the green jacket's been eyeing you up all evening.*

eye up sth or **eye** sth **up** *mainly British & Australian informal*

to look closely at something, especially because you want it or are very interested in it ● *I saw you eyeing up that chocolate cake!*

98

face down   faces, facing, faced

face down sb/sth or **face** sb/sth
down
to deal with a powerful or threatening
person or thing strongly and confidently
• *She faced down her opponents with a
powerful speech explaining her ideas.*

face off   faced, facing, faces

face off *American*
if two people or two groups face off, they
disagree about something and start to
fight or oppose each other • (often +
over) *Increasingly, doctors and insurance
companies are facing off over health care.*
• *Amy and Mary Jo faced off in the street
ready to fight.*
face-off   *n*   [C]   *mainly   American*
• (usually singular) *an angry face-off between the neighbors*

face up to   faces, facing, faced

face up to sth
to accept that a difficult or unpleasant
situation exists • *She refuses to face up to
reality and still believes the project will be
a success.* • *You're going to have to face up
to the fact that you're not going to get that
job.*

factor in/into   factors, factoring,
factored

factor in sth or **factor** sth **in**
factor sth **into** sth
to include something when you are making a calculation or when you are trying
to understand something • *People are
earning more, but when inflation is factored in, they are no better off.* • *The age of
the subjects will not be factored into the
research results.*

factor out   factors, factoring, factored

factor out sth or **factor** sth **out** *American*
to not include something when you are

doing a calculation • *When you factor out
delays for rain, the game took four hours.*

fade away   fades, fading, faded

fade away
1 to gradually become less strong or clear
and then disappear • *As the years passed,
the memories of her grandfather slowly
faded away.* • *The voices became louder
and closer and then faded away again.*
2 if someone fades away, they become gradually weaker and then die • *He was taken
to hospital and faded away a few days
later.*

fade in   fades, fading, faded

fade in (sth) or **fade** (sth) **in**
if the sound or picture of a film or recording fades in, or if you fade it in, it becomes gradually louder or brighter so
that you can hear it or see it clearly • *As
the music faded in, the camera focussed on
the face of a young boy.*

fade out   fades, fading, faded

fade out
to gradually disappear or become less
common • *Interest in the product has now
almost completely faded out.* • *The fashion
for wearing old, ripped jeans faded out
very quickly.*

fade out (sth) or **fade** (sth) **out**
if the sound or picture of a film or recording fades out, or if you fade it out, it gradually becomes quieter or less clear until
you cannot hear or see it any more • *At
the end of the film the image of the city at
night faded out and the lights came on in
the cinema* • *The sound engineers were
told to fade the music out when the chairman stood up to speak.*

faff about/around   faffs, faffing,
faffed

faff about/around *British informal*
to spend time doing unimportant things
instead of doing what you should be
doing • *I wish you'd stop faffing about and
do something useful!*

fake out   fakes, faking, faked

fake out sb or **fake** sb **out** *American informal*
to trick someone, or to make someone believe something that is not true • *It*

looked like he was passing the ball to Jim,
but he faked us out and handed it to Tom.

fall about   falls, falling, fell, fallen

fall about *British & Australian informal*
to laugh a lot about something ● *She fell
about laughing when she saw his new
haircut.* ● (sometimes + **at**) *I told Mike
about Sue's car breaking down again and
he fell about at the news.*

fall apart   falls, falling, fell, fallen

fall apart
1 if something falls apart, it breaks or
breaks into pieces because it is old or
weak ● *I've only had these shoes three
months and they are already falling apart.*
● *She didn't realize the vase was cracked
and when she picked it up it fell apart in
her hands.*
2 if an organization, system, or agreement
falls apart, it fails or stops working effectively ● *His company fell apart in the market collapse of 1987.* ● *With the high rate of
unemployment and a failing economy, the
country seems to be **falling apart at the
seams.*** (= not working effectively any
more) ● *Their marriage was already falling apart even before his wife had an affair.* ● *After Julie's husband died, her
whole world fell apart.* (= she was so unhappy that she could not continue her life
in the normal way)
3 if someone falls apart, they experience extreme emotional problems and cannot
think or behave in the normal way ● *She
began to fall apart after the death of her
son.*

fall away   falls, falling, fell, fallen

fall away
1 if something [e.g. plaster] falls away, it
separates from the surface it is attached
to ● *Although the building was fairly new,
the plaster was already falling away in
places.* ● (often + **from**) *The house was
very damp and much of the plaster had
fallen away from the walls.*
2 mainly *British & Australian* if the
amount or rate of something falls away, it
becomes smaller or lower ● *Support for
the Prime Minister has fallen away over
the past few years.* ● (sometimes + **to**)
*Profits rose to £30 million in 1990, but fell
away to £20 million as the company was*

hit by recession.
falling-away *n* [C] *British & Australian* ● *There has been a noticeable falling-
away of audiences at the theatre.*
3 if an emotion or something which
controls your behaviour falls away, it
disappears ● *After a few minutes all her
inhibitions fell away and she joined in the
singing.*
4 if land falls away, it slopes down steeply
● *From the top of the hill, the road fell
away and the views of the surrounding
countryside were superb.*

fall back   falls, falling, fell, fallen

fall back
1 to move backwards away from someone
or something, often because you are
afraid ● *Anna saw the look of anger in his
eyes and fell back a step or two.* ● (often +
in) *The police fired tear gas into the crowd
and they fell back in confusion.*
2 if an army falls back, it moves away from
an enemy army in order to avoid fighting
them ● *The British troops suffered heavy
losses in the fighting and fell back.*
3 to fail to remain level with a group of
people that is moving forwards ● *They
were walking so fast that she could not
keep up with them and she soon fell back.*
● *Richards was in the lead for the first 200
metres of the race, but fell back to third
place just before the finishing line.*
4 *British & Australian* if the amount or
rate of something falls back, it becomes
smaller or lower ● *Production has fallen
back over the past six months.*

fall back on/upon   falls, falling, fell, fallen

fall back on/upon sth
to use something when other things have
failed, or when there are no other choices
● *Many families had lost their savings
during the war and had nothing to fall
back on.* ● *We'll have to fall back on our
original plan if this one doesn't work out.*
fallback *adj* (always before noun) ● *She
aims to be elected onto the committee, but
her fallback position is to influence the debate at the committee meeting.*
fallback *n* [C] ● *Their first choice for the
job is Amanda Martin, with Paul Davies
as the fallback.*

fall behind   falls, falling, fell, fallen

fall behind (sb)

1 to fail to remain level with a group of people that is moving forwards ● *She managed to keep up with them for the first few minutes but fell behind shortly afterwards.*

2 to fail to score as many points as another team or player in a competition ● *In the first half of the game, Middlesbrough had fallen behind Liverpool by two goals to one.* ● (often + **in**) *She finally managed to beat her opponent after falling behind in both sets.*

fall behind (sth/sb)

to fail to develop at the same rate as something else, or to fail to achieve a standard reached by other people ● *In the early 1990's, the company was falling dangerously behind its rivals.* ● *My parents told me I couldn't have a part-time job because I would fall behind at school.* ● (often + **in**) *The report claims that we have fallen behind the rest of the world in information technology.*

fall behind (sth)

to fail to do something fast enough or by a particular time ● *The project has fallen hopelessly behind schedule.* ● (often + **with**) *He was ill for six weeks and fell behind with his schoolwork.* ● (sometimes + **in**) *High interest rates have caused many people to fall behind in their mortgage payments.*

fall down   falls, falling, fell, fallen

fall down

1 to fall to the ground ● *In the strong winds they were worried that the tree in the garden would fall down.* ● *He stumbled a few metres and then fell down.*

2 to fail because of not being satisfactory for a particular purpose ● *The book falls down by failing to bring out the hero's true character sufficiently.* ● (often + **in**) *The government has been accused of falling down in its duty to prevent materials being sold abroad for the manufacture of weapons.*

downfall *n* [C] the sudden failure of a person or organization, or something that causes this ● (usually singular) *This series of military defeats brought about the downfall of the government.* ● *In the end, it was the continual drinking that was his downfall.*

be falling down (always in continuous tenses)

if a building is falling down, it is in extremely bad condition ● *Much of the city's housing that was built in the 60's is now falling down.*

fall for   falls, falling, fell, fallen

fall for sb/sth *informal*

to be attracted to someone or something ● *She fell for a tall, handsome Frenchman when she was on holiday in Paris.* ● *He fell for the romance of travelling by train while he was a student.*

fall for sth

to be tricked into believing something that is not true ● *She often falls for the extravagant claims of slimming products.* ● *He told me he had property worth £2 million, and I fell for it **hook, line and sinker**.* (= I believed what he said completely)

fall in   falls, falling, fell, fallen

fall in

1 if a structure [e.g. roof, ceiling] falls in, it drops to the ground because it is weak or damaged ● *Ten miners were trapped underground when the roof of the tunnel fell in.*

2 if soldiers fall in, they move into a line ● (often an order) *'Company fall in!'* shouted the sergeant-major.* ● (often + **behind**) *As Marco began marching off,*

the others fell in behind him.

fall in alongside/beside   falls, falling, fell, fallen

fall in alongside/beside sb
to start walking next to a person or group of people • *The girl fell in alongside Alice, and for a while they both remained silent.*

fall into   falls, falling, fell, fallen

fall into sth
1 to start doing something, often without intending to • *I fell into my job purely by chance.* • *While living in Spain, he had fallen into the habit of having a short sleep after lunch.* • *She fell into conversation with the man working behind the bar.*
2 to begin to be in a particular state • *He died in March, three months after falling into a coma.* • *Many of the houses along the seafront have fallen into disrepair.* (= are in a bad condition)
3 to belong to a particular group of things that have similar qualities • *The problems we face fall into two categories.* • *His work as a novelist falls into three distinct periods.*

fall in with   falls, falling, fell, fallen

fall in with sb *informal*
to become friends with someone after meeting them by chance • *Carol's parents didn't approve of the group of people she had fallen in with at school.*

fall in with sth
if you fall in with an idea or plan, you agree with it or accept it • *She claimed she only fell in with his plan because she was frightened of him.* • *I don't mind what we do – I'll just fall in with whatever you decide.*

fall off   falls, falling, fell, fallen

fall off
if the amount, rate, or quality of something falls off, it becomes smaller or lower • *The demand for new cars fell off in the first half of the year.* • *We used to enjoy going to our local French restaurant but the standard has really fallen off recently.*
fall-off *n* [C] • *Travel agents have reported a fall-off in business to the Caribbean.*

fall on   falls, falling, fell, fallen

fall on sth
to happen on a particular day or date • *My birthday falls on a Monday this year.*

fall on/upon   falls, falling, fell, fallen

fall on/upon sb
1 if a job or duty falls on someone, it becomes their responsibility • *The job of collecting the new tax will fall on local councils.* • (sometimes + to do sth) *It fell on Jane to make all the arrangements for their trip.*
2 to attack someone suddenly • *The gang of youths fell on him, kicking and punching him in the stomach.*

fall on/upon sth
to start eating food very eagerly • *They fell upon the bread and cheese as if they had not eaten for days.*

fall out   falls, falling, fell, fallen

fall out
1 to argue with someone and stop being friendly with them • *I haven't seen Karen since we fell out last month.* • (often + with) *He left home after falling out with his parents.* • (sometimes + over) *It's stupid to fall out over* (= because of) *such a small thing.*
falling-out *n* [C] *informal* • (usually singular) *Clare and Richard had a falling-out last week and they're still not speaking to one another.*
2 if your hair or a tooth falls out, it becomes loose and falls out of your head or mouth • *His hair began to fall out when he was only 25.* • *Most of Sophie's baby teeth have fallen out.*
3 if soldiers fall out, they move out of a line • (often an order) *'Fall out, men!' shouted the major.*

fall over   falls, falling, fell, fallen

fall over
1 if someone falls over, they fall to the ground • *He was walking along quite normally and then suddenly fell over.*
2 if something falls over, it falls onto its side • *If you make the cake too high it'll just fall over.*

fall over sth
if someone falls over something, they

knock their foot against it and this makes them fall to the ground ● *Be careful not to fall over the step on your way in.*

fall over yourself to do sth (always reflexive)

to be very eager to do something ● *He was falling over himself to make her feel welcome.*

fall through   falls, falling, fell, fallen

fall through

if a plan or agreement falls through, it fails to happen ● *The company had agreed to finance the project, but the deal is now in danger of falling through.* ● *Our plans to go on holiday together fell through when John became ill.*

fall to   falls, falling, fell, fallen

fall to sb

if a duty or job falls to someone, it is their responsibility to do it ● *The job of arranging the new schedule fell to Steven.* ● (often + to do sth) *It falls to me to thank the committee for their continued support of the group.*

fall to (sth/doing sth) *literary*

to start doing something ● *There was a lot of work to be done and they fell to it immediately.* ● *As we sat together, he fell to talking about the past.*

fall under   falls, falling, fell, fallen

fall under sth (never passive)

1 to be included in a particular group of things ● *This article falls under the general heading of media studies.*

2 to begin to be controlled by or feel the effects of something [e.g. influence, spell] ● *While he was at university he fell under the influence of one of the English professors.* ● *At the end of the war, the land fell under government control.* ● *I had only known her a week but I had already fallen under her spell.* (= I was already attracted by her charm and beauty)

fall upon

see **fall on/upon**

fan out   fans, fanning, fanned

fan out

if a group of people fans out, the people in the group walk forwards and move away from each other ● *The group of police of-*

ficers and volunteers fanned out so that they could search the area more effectively.

fan out (sth) or **fan** (sth) **out**

to move into the shape of a half circle, or to make something do this ● *He fanned the cards out on the table so that everyone could see them.*

farm out   farms, farming, farmed

farm out sth or **farm** sth **out**

to give work to other people instead of doing it yourself ● *He has decided to farm out most of the work to freelance designers.*

fart about/around   farts, farting, farted

fart about/around *informal*

to spend time doing silly or unimportant things ● *Tina spent the whole day farting around at home.*

fasten on to/onto   fastens, fastening, fastened

fasten on to/onto sb

to follow someone and stay with them, especially when they do not want you to be with them ● *She had fastened onto one of the actors at the party and kept asking him questions about famous film stars.*

fasten on/upon   fastens, fastening, fastened

fasten on/upon sth

to give attention to something, and usually decide that it is the cause of a problem ● *He fastened on the words 'group leader' in the document and wondered whether this referred to him.* ● *Looking for an explanation for the fighting, journalists fastened on extreme nationalism.*

fasten up   fastens, fastening, fastened

fasten up sth or **fasten** sth **up** *mainly British & Australian*

to join together the two sides of something [e.g. coat, bag] ● *You should fasten your coat up – it's freezing outside.*

fasten upon

see **fasten on/upon**

fathom out   fathoms, fathoming, fathomed

fathom out sth or **fathom** sth **out**
British & Australian
to understand something by thinking about it very carefully • *I spent hours trying to understand what he had meant but I just couldn't fathom it out.* • (often + question word) *Have you fathomed out how to make it work yet?*

fatten up   fattens, fattening, fattened

fatten up sth or **fatten** sth **up**
to give a lot of food to an animal so that it becomes fatter • *The cattle are fed a diet which is designed to fatten them up as cheaply as possible.*

fawn on/over   fawns, fawning, fawned

fawn on/over sb
to praise someone in a way that is false in order to get something from them or to make them like you • *The photographers were fawning over Princess Diana, trying to get her to pose for the cameras.*

fear for   fears, fearing, feared

fear for sth/sb *slightly formal*
to be worried about something, or to be worried that someone is in danger • *After 50 workers were laid off many people feared for their jobs.* • *John had not been seen for over 24 hours, and she feared for his safety.* (= she was afraid that he might not be safe) • *When their daughter was taken into hospital with an unknown disease, they feared for her.*

feast on/upon   feasts, feasting, feasted

feast on/upon sth
to enjoy something very much • *His fans will be able to feast on his biography which has just been published.*

feed off   feeds, feeding, fed

feed off sth
1 if an animal feeds off something, it uses it for food • *Hyenas feed off rotting flesh.*
2 to use something for your own advantage, often unfairly • *The popular press feeds off gossip about famous people.* • *Each project team feeds off the work that other teams have already completed.*

feed on/upon   feeds, feeding, fed

feed on/upon sth
1 if an animal feeds on a particular type of food, it usually eats that food • *Most beetles feed on live plants or plant material.*
2 if an idea, feeling, or process feeds on something, it grows stronger and larger because of it • *Extreme nationalism feeds on hatred of other ways of life.*

feed sb/sth **on/upon** sth *British & Australian*
to give a particular type of food to a person or animal • *The athletes were fed on a diet which was high in protein and carbohydrates.* • *You shouldn't feed your dog just on tinned food.*

feed up   feeds, feeding, fed

feed up sb/sth or **feed** sb/sth **up**
British & Australian
to give a lot of food to a person or animal, especially when they are ill, in order to make them strong and healthy • *Kate's very thin at the moment-we'll have to feed her up a bit.*

feed upon
see **feed on/upon**

feel for   feels, feeling, felt

feel for sb *slightly informal*
to feel sorry for someone because they are very unhappy or in a difficult situation • *I really feel for him having to take the exam all over again.* • *We felt for Jane, she seemed so miserable when Thierry left.*

feel out   feels, feeling, felt

feel out sb or **feel** sb **out** *informal*
to try to find out what someone thinks or feels about something, especially without asking them directly • *She wanted to feel out her manager about taking some time off.*

feel out sth or **feel** sth **out** *informal*
to try to decide what you think or feel about something • *They were feeling out the possibility of starting their own business.*

feel up   feels, feeling, felt

feel up sb or **feel** sb **up** *informal*
to touch someone in a sexual way without their permission • *It was the second time she had been felt up on the Metro.*

feel up to   feels, feeling, felt

feel up to sth/doing sth
to feel physically and mentally strong enough to do something ● *Jane wanted to do the tour but Andy didn't feel up to it.* ● *Do you feel up to coming to the party then?*

fence in   fences, fencing, fenced

fence in sth or **fence** sth **in**
1 to build a fence around an area ● *She decided to fence in her yard to make it more private.* ● (used as *adj*) *a small fenced-in garden*
2 to put an animal in an area which is surrounded by a fence ● (usually passive) *The sheep are always fenced in at night.*

fence off   fences, fencing, fenced

fence off sth or **fence** sth **off**
to build a fence around an area, especially in order to stop people or animals entering it ● (often passive + **from**) *A small area was fenced off from the rest of the beach.* ● (used as *adj*) *A fenced-off area in the garden contained a variety of rare plants.*

fend for   fends, fending, fended

fend for yourself (always reflexive)
to take care of yourself without needing help from other people ● *She's 83 years old and still fends for herself.* ● *A million commuters were left to fend for themselves yesterday when bus drivers went on strike all over the city.*

fend off

fend off   fends, fending, fended

fend off sth/sb or **fend** sth/sb **off**
1 to defend yourself from an attack or from harm by pushing something or someone away ● *Police used their riot shields to fend off bricks thrown by the crowd.* ● *She managed to fend off her attacker.*
2 to avoid dealing with someone or something that is unpleasant or difficult to deal with so that they cannot harm you ● *She only tells you what she wants you to know and fends off any difficult questions anyone tries to ask.* ● *Sophie spent the whole evening fending off all the young men at the party.*

ferret out   ferrets, ferreting, ferreted

ferret out sth or **ferret** sth **out**
to find something after searching for it ● *For the fancy-dress party, he ferreted out an old suit his father had worn in the 60s.*

fess up   fesses, fessing, fessed

fess up *American informal*
to admit that you have done something that someone else will not like ● *Fess up – you ate the last piece of cake, didn't you?*

fetch up   fetches, fetching, fetched

fetch up *old-fashioned, informal* (always + *adv/prep*)
to arrive somewhere, especially when you had not planned to go there ● (often + **in**) *After a whole hour driving around, we fetched up in the middle of nowhere.*

fetch up sth or **fetch** sth **up** (never passive) *British informal*
to vomit something ● *The dog fetched up its dinner all over the kitchen floor.*

fiddle about/around   fiddles, fiddling, fiddled

fiddle about/around
1 *informal* to use your hands in a series of small movements in order to try to do something ● *She was fiddling around in her bag looking for a comb.* ● *I fiddled about on my short wave radio to find the World Service.*
2 *informal* to spend time doing silly or unimportant things ● *They can no longer afford to fiddle around – it's time they acted.*

fiddle about/around with fiddles, fiddling, fiddled

fiddle about/around with sth *informal*
to try different ways of arranging or doing something until you find the right or best way • *Naomi, stop fiddling about with your hair. It looks just fine.* • *A good team captain will fiddle around with different combinations of players to find a winning side.*

fight back fights, fighting, fought

fight back
to defend yourself when someone or something attacks you or causes problems for you • *He might be 70 years old, but don't underestimate his ability to fight back.* • (often + **with**) *The company fought back with the argument that customers are capable of judging a product before they buy it.*

fight back sth or **fight** sth **back**
to try hard not to show an emotion, or to try hard not to let your emotions control what you do • *Somehow he fought back his anger and remained calm.* • *'I owe them over $3,000', he confessed, fighting back the tears.*

fight down fights, fighting, fought

fight down sth or **fight** sth **down**
to try hard not to do something that you want to do • *He had to fight down the desire to laugh.*

fight off fights, fighting, fought

fight off sb/sth or **fight** sb/sth **off**
to use violence so that someone or something goes away • *Officials say that villagers have had to fight off several attacks in the past year.*

fight off sth or **fight** sth **off**
to try hard to get rid of something unpleasant or unwanted, especially an illness or bad emotions • *People vary in their ability to fight off infections.* • *He spent many years fighting off painful memories from his childhood.* • *The company managed to fight off competition for the contract.*

fight out fights, fighting, fought

fight out sth or **fight** sth **out**
to come to an agreement about something, especially by arguing or by using

violence • *There's only one free ticket so you'll have to fight it out between you.* (= have a discussion to decide who will get the ticket) • *The salary issue is still being fought out.*

figure on figures, figuring, figured

figure on sth/doing sth *mainly American & Australian*
to expect that something will happen and to include it in your plans • *They figured on about 20 people coming to the party.* • *Nobody figured on the drought and its devastating effect on the corn crop.* • *We hadn't figured on staying up so late.*

figure out figures, figuring, figured

figure out sth/sb or **figure** sth/sb **out**
to understand something or someone, or to find the answer to something by thinking carefully • (often + question word) *I can't figure out why he did it.* • *I've never been able to figure Sue out.*

file away files, filing, filed

file away sth or **file** sth **away**
to put something that is written [e.g. document, letter] in a particular place so that you can find it easily • *He always files everything away very carefully, so the report shouldn't be hard to find.*

file for files, filing, filed

file for sth
to make an official request for a legal state, such as divorce or bankruptcy (= officially having no money) • *He was separated from his wife for six months before she filed for divorce.*

fill in fills, filling, filled

fill in sth or **fill** sth **in**

1 to write the necessary information on an official document [e.g. form, questionnaire] • *Please fill in the application form and send it back by November 2nd.*
2 to cover a hole in the surface of something and make it smooth by putting a substance in it • *Before painting, fill in all the cracks in the plaster.*

fill in sb or **fill** sb **in** *slightly informal*
to tell someone about the things that have happened while they have not been there, or to give someone the information they need in order to do something • (often +

on) *Let's go for a coffee and you can fill me in on what happened at the meeting.*

fill in

to do someone else's work for them because they cannot or will not do it themselves ● (usually + **for**) *Can you fill in for me for a couple of hours while I'm at the dentist's?* ● *Janet filled in while her boss was away on holiday.*

fill out   fills, filling, filled

fill out sth or **fill** sth **out**

to write the necessary information on an official document [e.g. form, questionnaire] ● *We were all asked to fill out a form.*

fill out

if someone fills out, their body becomes fatter or bigger and stronger ● *When John's a little older and fills out more, he'll be an outstanding athlete.*

fill up   fills, filling, filled

fill up (sth) or **fill** (sth) **up**

to become full, or to make something become full ● *Fill that bucket up with water and bring it over here.* ● *We'd better get to the restaurant early because it usually fills up around 8 o'clock.* ● *We need to fill up* (= put petrol in the car) *at the next gas station.*

fill-up *n* [C] *American* the action of filling something, for example filling a car with petrol ● *We need to stop at a gas station for a fill-up.*

fill up sb or **fill** sb **up**

if food fills someone up, it makes them feel as if they have eaten enough ● *Those potatoes have really filled me up. I couldn't eat another thing!*

film over   films, filming, filmed

film over

if a surface that you can normally see through films over, it becomes covered with a thin layer of something and becomes difficult to see through ● (often + **with**) *His eyes filmed over with tears when he heard the news.*

filter in   filters, filtering, filtered

filter in *British*

to join a line of moving traffic, driving carefully so that the other cars do not

have to stop to let you in ● *There's a lane closed ahead and we'll have to filter in to the middle lane.*

filter out   filters, filtering, filtered

filter out sth or **filter** sth **out**

to remove an unwanted substance from a liquid or gas by passing it through a piece of equipment or a special substance ● *Devices in the two chimneys are used to filter out poisonous gases from the smoke released into the air.*

filter out sth/sb or **filter** sth/sb **out**

to separate or remove something or someone that is not wanted from a group of things or people ● *The company claims that the device can filter out unwanted phone calls before the phone rings.* ● *These tests are designed to filter out unsuitable applicants.*

find against   finds, finding, found

find against sb/sth

if a judge finds against a person or organization that is involved in a court case, they decide that that person or organization is wrong and will lose the case ● *The jury found against the tobacco company and awarded £400,000 to the woman smoker's family.*

find for   finds, finding, found

find for sb/sth

if a judge finds for a person or organization that is involved in a court case, they decide that that person or organization is right and will win the case ● *Yesterday the judge found for two men on the assault charges they had made against the police.*

find out   finds, finding, found

find out (sth) or **find** (sth) **out**

to get information about something because you want to know more about it, or to learn a fact or piece of information for the first time ● (often + question word) *I need to find out exactly what went wrong.* ● *Ring the restaurant to find out if they still have a table free.* ● (often + **about**) *He knew that if his parents found out about the party he would never be allowed to stay in the house on his own again.* ● (often + **that**) *We found out that it was his birthday and so decided to buy him a small present.* ● *Learning to drive isn't* *easy, as you'll soon find out.* ● *He's often thought about having an affair, but is worried that his wife would find out.*

find out sb or **find** sb **out**
to discover that someone has done something wrong ● (usually passive) *He lived in dread of being found out.*

---

finish off   finishes, finishing, finished

finish off sth or **finish** sth **off**
1 to complete the last part of something that you are doing ● *I'll just finish this letter off before I go.* ● *We need some more tiles to finish off the bathroom wall.*
2 to eat or drink the last part of what you have been eating or drinking ● *Let's finish this one off before we open another bottle.*

finish off
to do or have as the last part of something ● (often + **with**) *We ate a huge meal, finishing off with banana cream pie.* ● *The bride's father spoke for half an hour and finished off by reading out the telegrams.*

finish off sb/sth or **finish** sb/sth **off**
slightly informal
1 to kill a person or animal, especially one that has already been injured ● *He lay on the ground waiting for the bullet that would finish him off.*
2 to defeat a person or team that you are competing against in a sporting event ● *A goal from Clough finished off the opposition in the last minutes of the game.*

finish off sb or **finish** sb **off**
to make someone so tired, weak, or unhappy that they are unable to continue what they were doing ● *The last game of tennis has really finished me off.* ● *It was the fact that his wife left him for another man that finished him off.* (= made him so unhappy that he could not continue his life in the normal way)

---

finish up   finishes, finishing, finished

finish up (always + *adv/prep/adj*) *mainly British & Australian slightly informal*
to finally be in a particular place, state or situation, especially without having planned it ● *She drank so much that she finished up in hospital.* ● *We did a ten-mile walk and finished up in a village on the other side of the river.* ● (often + **with**) *Amazingly she finished up with a seat in the Italian parliament.* ● (often + **as**) *He*

finished up as a gardener in a park.

finish up doing sth *British & Australian slightly informal*
to finally do something, especially without having planned to ● *We finished up paying twice as much for the trip as Nicki and Steve!*

finish up (sth) or **finish** (sth) **up**
1 to eat or drink all of what you are eating or drinking ● *Finish up your dinner and then you can watch television.*
2 *mainly American* to do the last part of something ● *He's currently finishing up his latest album which will be released next July.*

---

finish up with   finishes, finishing, finished

finish up with sth
to do or have as the last part of something ● *The President's week begins with a visit to Camp David and finishes up with an address to Congress.* ● *I ate three courses and finished up with a chocolate dessert.*

---

finish with   finishes, finishing, finished

finish with sb
1 *British & Australian informal* to end a romantic relationship with someone ● *Paula's just finished with her boyfriend after three years.*
2 to stop dealing with someone ● *One moment – I haven't finished with you yet.* ● *He'll wish he'd never come to see me by the time I've finished with him.* (= when I have finished punishing him)

finish with sth
to stop using or needing something ● *Have you finished with this magazine?* ● *I'll have the scissors when you've finished with them.*

---

fink on   finks, finking, finked

fink on sb *American old-fashioned*
to give someone secret information about someone else ● *How did the police know? Someone must have finked on him.*

---

fire away

Fire away! (always an order) *slightly informal*
something that you say in order to tell someone that you are ready for them to start asking you questions, or to start speaking ● *'I'd like to ask you some ques-*

tions about your childhood, if I may.' 'Fire away!'

fire off   fires, firing, fired

fire off sth or **fire** sth **off**

1 to fire a shot from a gun • *The rebels ran through the streets firing off shots into the air.*

2 to write and send an angry letter to someone • *After reading the newspaper article she fired off an angry letter to the editor.*

fire up   fires, firing, fired

fire up sb or **fire** sb **up**

to make someone become excited or angry • *The issue has fired up civil rights activists.* • *We had an argument about it and she got all fired up.*

fire up sth or **fire** sth **up**

1 *American* to make something start to burn [e.g. cigarette, barbecue] • *He paused and fired up another cigarette.* • *If we fire up the barbecue now dinner will be ready in an hour.*

2 *American* to start an engine • *She fired up the car engine, slipped it into gear, and went speeding off.*

firm up   firms, firming, firmed

firm up sth or **firm** sth **up**

1 to make something [e.g. agreement, details, prices] more definite or less likely to change • *Could we have a meeting so that we can firm up the details of our agreement?*

2 to make part of your body [thighs, buttocks] have less fat and become harder by doing exercise • *Swimming is one of the best ways to firm up your thighs.*

fish for   fishes, fishing, fished

fish for sth (never passive)

if you fish for something [e.g. compliments, information, invitation], you try to make someone tell you it or say it to you by asking them a question • (usually in continuous tenses) *Anne's brother was fishing for information about David, her new boyfriend.* • *He's always fishing for compliments.* • *It was embarrassing listening to them fishing for an invitation to her party.*

fish out   fishes, fishing, fished

fish out sth/sb or **fish** sth/sb **out** *informal*

to pull or take something or someone out of water • (often + **of**) *The police fished a body out of the river this morning.* • *The ball's fallen into the pond, can you fish it out?*

fish out sth or **fish** sth **out** *informal*

to pull or take something out of a bag or pocket, especially after searching • *He put his hand in his pocket and fished out a sweet.*

fit in   fits, fitting, fitted   (*American pt* also **fit**)

fit in

1 to feel happy in a group of people because you are similar to them • (often + **with**) *She seems to fit in well with everyone in the department.* • *I never felt that I fitted in at school.*

2 if one thing fits in with another thing, they look pleasant together or are suitable for each other • (often + **with**) *These colours don't fit in with the design of the room.*

3 to be part of a situation, system, or plan • *We need someone to drive the van. That's where Susan fits in.*

4 to be able to be done between other activities • (often + **around**) *Tennis has to fit in around her busy schedule of meetings.*

fit in sb/sth or **fit** sb/sth **in**

to find time to do something or see someone • *He'll fit in a TV interview before travelling to Paris.* • *The doctor's very busy, but she could fit you in tomorrow morning.*

fit into   fits, fitting, fitted   (*American pt* also **fit**)

fit into sth

1 to be part of a situation, system, or plan • *The new college courses fit into a national education plan.* • *Road development did not fit into his vision of the future.*

2 to be part of a group of people or things • *As a writer, she does not fit into any of the traditional categories.*

fit in with   fits, fitting, fitted   (American pt also **fit**)

fit in with sth

1 if one activity or event fits in with another, they exist or happen together in a way which is convenient ● *The chance to move to a bigger building fits in well with our plans to expand the business.* ● *Why should I change my habits to fit in with their way of life?*

2 if one activity or event fits in with another, it exists or happens in a way which shows that someone's plans and opinions have not changed ● *The latest bombings fit in with previous threats to increase terrorist activity.*

fit out   fits, fitting, fitted   (American pt also **fit**)

fit out sb/sth or **fit** sb/sth **out**

to provide someone [esp. soldier] or something [esp. ship] with all the equipment and other things they need ● *The ship is being fitted out for the voyage.* ● *We fitted him out with a smart new suit for the occasion.*

fit up   fits, fitting, fitted   (American pt also **fit**)

fit up sb/sth or **fit** sb/sth **up** *mainly British & Australian*

to provide a person or place [e.g. room, house] with equipment for a particular purpose ● *He fitted up a special pine-panelled bar in the room.* ● (often + **with**) *The new director asked to be fitted up with his own private plane.* ● *We fitted the children up with three speed bikes for the trip.*

fit up sb or **fit** sb **up** *British informal*

to make someone seem to be guilty of a crime when you know that they are not ● *The policemen were accused of fitting up a businessman on a false murder charge.*

fix on   fixes, fixing, fixed

fix on sth/sb

to decide to choose something or someone ● *We haven't fixed on a hotel yet for our wedding reception.*

fix up   fixes, fixing, fixed

fix up sth or **fix** sth **up**

1 to repair or arrange something [e.g. room, house] in order to improve it or to make it suitable for a particular purpose ● *Ella had fixed up one of the bedrooms for me to use as an office.* ● *They spent thousands of dollars fixing up an old house in the countryside.*

2 to arrange something [esp. meeting] ● *I'd like to fix up a meeting with you for some time next week if that's possible.*

3 *American & Australian informal* to solve a problem, or to end an argument or disagreement ● *Did you manage to fix up the problem with your lease?* ● *They fixed up their dispute with the builder and work on the house is underway again.*

fix up sb/sth or **fix** sb/sth **up**

to provide or arrange something for someone ● (often + **with**) *Could you fix us up with a place to stay for a few nights?* ● *If I still haven't found anyone to take to the dance, Paul said he'd be able to fix me up.* (= find a suitable partner for me)

fix yourself **up** (always reflexive) *American informal*

to make yourself look tidy and more attractive ● *She changed her clothes and brushed her hair, fixing herself up to go out.*

fix sb **up** *Australian informal*

to pay back money which you owe to someone ● *I haven't forgotten the $20 I owe you, can I fix you up tomorrow?*

fizzle out   fizzles, fizzling, fizzled

fizzle out *slightly informal*

to gradually end or disappear, especially in a disappointing way ● *When she went away to college, she stopped writing to her boyfriend and eventually their relationship just fizzled out.* ● *All the newspapers wrote about the scandal but public interest soon fizzled out.*

flag down   flags, flagging, flagged

flag down sth or **flag** sth **down**

to make a vehicle stop by waving at the driver ● *A police officer flagged the car down.* ● *We tried to flag down a taxi but they were all full.*

flake out   flakes, flaking, flaked

flake out *informal*

to suddenly fall asleep or feel very weak because you are extremely tired ● *The children had had an exhausting day, and flaked out on their beds.*

flare out   flares, flaring, flared

flare out *American informal*

to suddenly express strong emotion ● (usually + **at**) *He flared out at her, slamming his fist on the table.*

flare up   flares, flaring, flared

flare up

1 if something [e.g. violence, argument, anger] flares up, it suddenly happens and becomes very serious ● *Violence flared up again last night in many parts of the city.* ● *As soon as he saw Nina he could feel the anger flaring up in his heart.*

2 if someone flares up, they suddenly become very angry ● *'You can't stop me from saying what I think' she said, flaring up.*
flare-up *n* [C] ● *The possibility of a flare-up between the two governments remains very strong.*

3 if a disease that you had before flares up, you suddenly get it again ● *If it flares up again, you should go to see a doctor.*
flare-up *n* [C] ● *She experienced a flare-*

up of her arthritis problems.

flash around   flashes, flashing, flashed

flash around sth or **flash** sth **around**

to show something valuable [e.g. money, ring] to people because you want them to know about it or be jealous of you, especially in a way which makes you seem too proud ● *Did you see Judy flashing her diamond ring around?*

flash back   flashes, flashing, flashed

flash back

if your mind or thoughts flash back to something that happened to you in the past, you suddenly remember that thing ● (usually + **to**) *Her mind flashed back to the day of their wedding.*

flashback *n* [C] an occasion when you suddenly remember something that happened to you in the past ● *A year after the accident he was still having flashbacks.*

flashback *n* [C] a scene in a film which shows something that happened in the past ● *The film begins with a flashback to the hero's childhood.*

flash on   flashes, flashing, flashed

flash on sth *American informal*

to suddenly have a thought or an idea ● *Wait, I just flashed on a possible solution to our scheduling problem.*

flash out   flashes, flashing, flashed

flash out sth or **flash** sth **out**

to suddenly express a strong emotion [esp. anger] ● *Tom's eyes flashed out a look of hatred.*

flatten out   flattens, flattening, flattened

flatten out (sth) or **flatten** (sth) **out**

1 to become flat, or to make something become flat ● *Matthew flattened out his newspaper and began to read.* ● *The path is steep here but flattens out at the top of the hill.*

2 if the rate of something flattens out, or if something flattens it out, it stops increasing and decreasing and begins to stay at the same level ● *Interest rates have begun to flatten out.*

flesh out   fleshes, fleshing, fleshed

flesh out sth or **flesh** sth **out**

to add more details or more information

to a piece of writing, especially in order to make it more interesting • (often + **with**) *Can you flesh out your report with some figures?*

flick over   flicks, flicking, flicked

flick over *British informal*
to quickly change from one television or radio channel to another • *She flicked over to see if the film had begun.*

flick through   flicks, flicking, flicked

flick through sth
1 to look briefly at the pages of something [esp. book, magazine] • *I passed the time flicking through glossy magazines.* • *He picked up my photo album and started flicking through it.*
2 to change quickly and repeatedly from one television or radio channel to another • *I've just been flicking through the channels but there's nothing I want to watch.*

fling into   flings, flinging, flung

fling yourself **into** sth (always reflexive)
to start to spend a lot of your time and energy doing something • *He's really flung himself into his work since his relationship with Isobel ended.*

fling off/on   flings, flinging, flung

fling off/on sth or **fling** sth **off/on**
to take off or put on something, e.g. clothes or a cover, quickly and without being careful • *She just had time to fling her clothes off and dive into the shower.* • *I flung on my shirt and ran out of the door.*

flip off   flips, flipping, flipped

flip off sb or **flip** sb **off** *American slang*
to make an extremely rude sign by holding your hand out towards someone and raising your middle finger, in order to show that you do not care what they are doing or saying • *He laughed sarcastically and flipped them off.*

flip out   flips, flipping, flipped

flip out *mainly American informal*
to suddenly start to behave in a very excited or strange way • *The kids really flipped out the first time they saw the new computer games.* • *He flipped out in court, yelling and screaming about his rights.*

flip through   flips, flipping, flipped

flip through sth
to look briefly at the pages of something [esp. book, magazine] • *I was just flipping through my new cookbook while the kettle boiled.*

flirt with   flirts, flirting, flirted

flirt with sb
to talk and behave towards someone in a way that is sexually attractive and which shows that person that you are sexually attracted to them • *He likes to flirt with the young women in the office.*

flirt with sth
to consider doing something, or to be interested in something for a short period of time • *He's flirted with the idea of going back to college but whether he'll actually do it I don't know.* • *As a young man he flirted briefly with communism.*

float about/around   floats, floating, floated

float about/around
if an idea or story floats about, it is discussed or repeated by a lot of people • *Rumours about his condition had been floating about for a long time.*

be floating about/around (always in continuous tenses)
if you say something is floating around, you mean that you have seen it somewhere, but you do not know exactly where it is • *I'm sure I saw your list floating around somewhere.*

flood back   floods, flooding, flooded

flood back
if memories flood back, you suddenly remember very clearly a lot of things about an experience or period in the past • *Seeing where I used to live brought so many memories flooding back.* • *I only have to smell the polish they used at my school and it all comes flooding back.*

flood in/into   floods, flooding, flooded

flood in

flood into sth
to arrive or enter somewhere in very large numbers or amounts • *More and more hotels are being built as tourists from Germany and Japan flood in.*

• *Letters of complaint have been flooding into the office.*

flood out floods, flooding, flooded

flood out sb or **flood** sb **out**

to force someone to leave their home because of floods • *Several families living on the seafront were flooded out during the storm.*

flood with floods, flooding, flooded

flood sth **with** sth

to provide or send something in large numbers or amounts, often more than is necessary • *Thousands of the paper's loyal readers flooded its offices yesterday with faxes of support.* • *The international market is flooded with tea and coffee.*

flounder about/around flounders, floundering, floundered

flounder about/around

to have a lot of difficulty trying to move in water or mud • (often + **in**) *He floundered around in the deep water, desperate to reach the shore.*

flow from flows, flowing, flowed

flow from sth

to be the result of a particular situation or event • *Problems flowing from his recent illness have made the family's life very difficult.*

fluff out/up fluffs, fluffing, fluffed

fluff out/up sth or **fluff** sth **out/up**

to make something [e.g. cushion, feathers] bigger by hitting or shaking it so that it fills with air • *The parakeets looked bigger than ever having fluffed out their feathers.* • *Fluff the pillows up when you make the bed.*

flunk out flunks, flunking, flunked

flunk out *American & Australian informal*

to have to leave school or college because your work is not good enough • *Dan won't be going back to college next year – he flunked out.*

flush out flushes, flushing, flushed

flush out sb/sth or **flush** sb/sth **out**

to force a person or animal to come out of the place they are hiding in • (often + **from**) *Their dog flushed the rabbits out from their holes* • *Troops launched a*

dawn raid to flush out resistance fighters.

flush out sth or **flush** sth **out**

to clean something by putting a large amount of liquid through it • *Heavy rain had flushed out the drains, taking sewage and other pollutants out to sea.*

flutter about/around flutters, fluttering, fluttered

flutter about/around

if a bird or insect flutters about, it moves its wings up and down very quickly and lightly • *Butterflies fluttered about in the sunlight.*

fly about/around flies, flying, flew, flown

fly about/around (swh)

if statements [esp. rumours, accusations] fly about, they are made a lot in a way which makes people excited • (usually in continuous tenses) *Nobody knew where George had gone, but there were all sorts of rumours flying around.* • *There's a ridiculous story about Jane having a drinking problem flying about the office.*

fly at flies, flying, flew, flown

fly at sb

1 to attack someone suddenly and violently • *When she saw her daughter's killer, she flew at him screaming and scratching.*

2 to suddenly speak to someone very angrily • *He will fly at anyone who dares to disagree with him.*

fly into flies, flying, flew, flown

fly into sth

if someone flies into a particular state [e.g. rage, temper, panic], they are suddenly in that state • *When I refused to move my car he flew into a rage and threatened to call the police.*

fob off fobs, fobbing, fobbed

fob off sb or **fob** sb **off** *informal*

1 to persuade someone to accept something that is of lower quality or that is different from what they really want • (usually + **with**) *She really knows about jewellery. You won't be able to fob her off with false diamonds.*

2 to persuade someone to go away or to stop causing you difficulties, especially by making an excuse or telling a lie • *The*

manager of the shop tried to fob us off by telling us to complain directly to the manufacturer. ● *The children refused to be fobbed off with promises of chocolate.*

fob off sth or **fob** sth **off** *informal*
to persuade someone to accept something you do not want yourself ● (usually + **on/onto**) *Who can I fob off all these old books onto?*

focus on/upon   focuses, focussing, focussed

focus (sth) **on/upon** sth

1 to give a lot of attention to one particular activity, situation, or idea ● *He has given up running in order to focus on the long jump.* ● *Scientists are focussing their research upon areas with high levels of cancer patients.*

2 to make your eyes or a piece of equipment [esp. camera, microscope] give a clear picture of something ● *I focussed the telescope on the moon.* ● *All eyes were focussed upon him.*

fog up   fogs, fogging, fogged

fog up (sth) or **fog** (sth) **up**
if something made of glass [e.g. windscreen, glasses] fogs up, or if something fogs it up, it becomes covered with small drops of water and you cannot see through it any more ● *The steam from all this cooking has fogged up the windows.* ● *My glasses fogged up when I came into the warm room.*

foist on   foists, foisting, foisted

foist sth **on** sb
to force someone to accept something that they do not want ● *Parents should not try to foist their values on their children.* ● *His friends tried to foist a goodbye party on him, but he preferred to leave quietly.*

fold away   folds, folding, folded

fold away (sth) or **fold** (sth) **away**
to fold the parts of a piece of furniture [e.g. chair, table] so that it is smaller and can be stored somewhere, or to be able to be folded in this way ● *The van's seats can be folded away to make more room.* ● *He bought a bicycle which folds away and fits in the back of his car.*
    fold-away *adj* (always before noun) ● *a fold-away bed*

fold in   folds, folding, folded

fold in sth or **fold** sth **in**
to mix food [esp. flour, egg whites] into another food mixture by turning it carefully with a spoon so that there is air in the mixture ● *Beat the eggs and butter, then fold in the flour.*

fold into   folds, folding, folded

fold sth **into** sth
to mix food [esp. flour, egg whites] into another food mixture by turning it carefully with a spoon so that air is held in the mixture ● *Fold the egg whites into the chocolate mixture.*

fold up   folds, folding, folded

fold up (sth) or **fold** (sth) **up**
to make something [e.g. cloth, paper, chair] into a smaller, neater and usually flatter shape by folding it, or to be able to be folded in this way ● *Can you help me fold up these sheets?* ● *The road map folds up and fits in my bag.* ● *Fold that chair up and put it in here.*
    fold-up *adj* (always before noun) ● *a fold-up*

follow on   follows, following, followed

follow on

1 *mainly British & Australian* to happen or exist as the next part of something ● (usually + **from**) *This document follows on from the discussions we had last month.*
    follow-on *n* [singular] *mainly British & Australian* ● (often + **from**) *My research project is a follow-on from earlier work.*

2 to leave later than someone else in order to go somewhere, with the intention of meeting them there ● *David has already left and we'll be following on later.*

follow through   follows, following, followed

follow through (sth) or **follow** (sth) **through**

1 to do something as the next part of an activity or period of development ● *The group had one successful song but failed to follow through with another hit record.*

2 to make certain that something [e.g. plan, promise] is completed, or that it really happens ● (usually + **on**) *We hope that they will follow through on their commitment to better working conditions.*

• *Scientists plan to follow through on their investigations into the cause of the disease.*

3 to complete the movement of hitting, kicking, or throwing a ball by continuing to move your arm or leg in the same direction • *She needs to follow through more on her backhand if she is going to improve it.*

follow up   follows, following, followed

follow up sth or **follow** sth **up**

1 to do something in order to make the effect of an earlier action or thing stronger or more certain • (often + **with**) *If you make a hotel booking by phone, follow it up with written confirmation.* • *We are worried that terrorists will follow up their threats with bomb attacks.*

follow-up *n* [singular] • (usually + **to**) *The meeting was a follow-up to the West Africa summit talks.*

2 to find out more about something and take action connected with it • *The police were quick to follow up allegations of fraud.*

fool about/around   fools, fooling, fooled

fool about/around

1 to spend time having fun or behaving in a silly way • *We spent the afternoon fooling around on the beach.* • (often + **with**) *You should never fool about with matches.*

2 to have a sexual relationship with someone who is not your usual sexual partner • (usually + **with**) *She's fooling around with someone at work.*

fool with   fools, fooling, fooled

fool with sth *American & Australian informal*

to touch or play with something dangerous • *Don't fool with that gun – it's loaded!*

footle about/around   footles, footling, footled

footle about/around *British*

to spend time doing unimportant things • *She spent the whole morning footling around in the kitchen.*

force back   forces, forcing, forced

force back sth or **force** sth **back** (never passive) *mainly British & Australian*

to try not to show your emotions • *When she saw her sister again she had to force back the tears.*

force on/upon   forces, forcing, forced

force sth **on/upon** sb

to make someone accept something that they do not want • *I wasn't going to eat a dessert but Julia forced it on me.* • *When she accepted the promotion she had many new responsibilities forced upon her.*

force yourself **on/upon** sb (always reflexive)

to make someone allow you to stay with them or do something with them • *I couldn't stay at their house – I'd feel as if I was forcing myself on them.*

forge ahead   forges, forging, forged

forge ahead

1 to move forwards suddenly • *Just 100 metres from the finishing line Jackson forged ahead.*

2 to suddenly make a lot of progress with something • *They are forging ahead, building a mile a day of the railway line.* • (often + **of**) *The company has forged ahead of its rivals with record profits.* • (sometimes + **with**) *The department has promised to forge ahead with its plan to build a new airport.*

fork out   forks, forking, forked

fork out sth or **fork** sth **out** *informal*

to pay or give money for something, especially when you do not want to • *She couldn't persuade her father to fork out for a plane ticket home.*

fork over/up   forks, forking, forked

fork over/up sth or **fork** sth **over/up** *American & Australian informal*

to give something [esp. money] to someone, especially when you do not want to • *Guests had forked over $2000 for the privilege of eating with the presidential candidate.* • *I know you have my book, now fork it over.*

foul up   fouls, fouling, fouled

foul up sth or **foul** sth **up** *informal*

to cause something to stop working properly • *The new program fouled up our computer system.*

foul-up *n* [C] *informal* • *There was a foul-up which meant that she never* *received the message.*

foul up (sth) or **foul** (sth) **up** *informal*
to do something badly, or to fail at something ● *Too often management fouls up and then blames others.* ● *He fouled up his resignation speech.*

found on/upon

be founded on/upon sth (always passive)
to be based on a particular idea or belief ● *He claims that a society founded on socialist principles could never work.* ● *Her ideas are all founded upon a belief in the supreme importance of the family.*

freak out   freaks, freaking, freaked

freak out (sb) or **freak** (sb) **out** *informal*
to suddenly feel extremely surprised or afraid, or to make someone suddenly feel this way ● *She just assumed from his appearance that he was a girl and it freaked her out to hear him speak.* ● *She saw all those faces looking up at her and just freaked out.*

freak out *informal*
to suddenly start behaving in a very strange or violent way ● *He freaked out totally and attacked Peter.*

free up   frees, freeing, freed

free up sth or **free** sth **up**
to make time or money available for a particular use by not using it in another way ● *I cancelled my meeting to free up the afternoon to write my report.* ● *If the developed nations cut their military spending it would free up huge resources.*

free up sb or **free** sb **up**
to do something for someone so that they are available to do something else ● *If I can get Dan to do my filing, that'll free me up to get on with writing those letters.*

freeze off

be frozen off (always passive) *British*
if a sporting event is frozen off, it cannot start because the ground is frozen ● *Racing at Taunton was frozen off again today.*

freeze out   freezes, freezing, froze, frozen

freeze out sb or **freeze** sb **out**
1 to make someone feel that they are not part of a group by being unfriendly towards them, or to stop someone from being included in an arrangement or activity ● *She wanted to be a member of the group but the others were freezing her out.* ● *He believed that organizations such as theirs were being frozen out.*

2 *mainly American* to stop someone from being included in an arrangement or activity, especially in business ● *The government wants to help home buyers who are frozen out of high-priced markets.*

freeze over   freezes, freezing, froze, frozen

freeze over
if water freezes over, it becomes covered with ice ● *The lake would freeze over in the winter and we would go skating.*

freeze up   freezes, freezing, froze, frozen

freeze up
1 if something [e.g. pipe, lock] freezes up, it becomes blocked with ice and stops working ● *It was so cold that the pipes froze up and I thought they were going to burst.* ● *When I tried to get into my car I found that the locks had frozen up.*

2 *American & Australian* if a piece of machinery or a lock freezes up, it stops working properly because its parts are stuck and cannot move ● *The lock had frozen up and wouldn't open until I put some oil on it.*

3 to suddenly become so afraid that you cannot do anything ● *In front of the man she had admired for so long she froze up completely and was unable even to speak.*

freshen up   freshens, freshening, freshened

freshen up sth or **freshen** sth **up**
to make something look cleaner and more attractive ● *I've painted the bedroom to freshen it up a little.*

freshen up
to quickly wash yourself so that you feel clean ● *Would you like to use the bathroom to freshen up a little?* ● (sometimes reflexive) *Just let me freshen myself up and then we can go.*

frig about/around   friggs, frigging, frigged

frig about/around British & Australian slang

to behave stupidly, or to waste time doing unimportant things • *Stop frigging about, you idiot!*

frig around with   friggs, frigging, frigged

frig around with sth Australian slang

to touch or change something in a careless way or without any particular purpose • *He's been frigging around with the lawnmower all morning!*

frig around with sb Australian slang

to have a sexual relationship with someone who is not your usual sexual partner • *Tom's been frigging around with his best friend's wife.*

frig up   friggs, frigging, frigged

frig up sth or **frig** sth **up** Australian slang

to damage or break something • *You were supposed to fix it, not frig it up.*

frig-up n [singular] Australian slang a mess or confusion • *What a frig-up!*

frighten away/off   frightens, frightening, frightened

frighten away/off sb/sth or **frighten** sb/sth **away/off**

1 to make a person or animal so afraid that they go away • *Be quiet or you'll frighten the deer away.*

2 to make a person or organization so worried that they decide not to do what they were going to do • *Tourists were frightened off by reports of street crime.*

fritter away   fritters, frittering, frittered

fritter away sth or **fritter** sth **away**

to waste something [esp. money, time] by using it in a careless way for unimportant things • (often + **on**) *She fritters so much money away on expensive make-up.* • (sometimes + doing sth) *Jane and Len frittered their time away arguing about who should go.*

frizzle up   frizzles, frizzling, frizzled

frizzle up (sth) or **frizzle** (sth) **up** British & Australian informal

to become dry or burnt, or to make something become dry or burnt • *I can't eat this bacon – it's all frizzled up!*

frolic about/around   frolics, frolicking, frolicked

frolic about/around

to behave in a happy and playful way • *The children spent all day frolicking around in the sea.*

front for   fronts, fronting, fronted

front for sb/sth

to be the person or organization that represents someone or something to the public, especially in order to hide an illegal activity • *There were rumours that she was fronting for international gangsters.*

front on/onto   fronts, fronting, fronted

front on/onto sth

if a building fronts on something [e.g. sea, lake] it faces in that direction • *Their house fronts onto the lake.*

front up   fronts, fronting, fronted

front up Australian informal

to go or be somewhere for a short time, even though you may not really want to • *I'm dreading the party, but I'll still front up.*

frost over/up   frosts, frosting, frosted

frost over/up

to become covered with frost (= the thin white layer of ice which forms when the temperature is below freezing) • *The car windows were frosted up.*

frown on/upon   frowns, frowning, frowned

frown on/upon sth

to believe that something is wrong and that you should not do it • *Many people tend to frown on smoking nowadays.* • (usually passive) *Divorce is still frowned upon in many countries.*

fry up   fries, frying, fried

fry up sth or **fry** sth **up**

to fry food in order to make a quick meal • *Shall we just fry up last night's meat and potatoes?*

fry-up n [C] British informal a quick meal made of fried food • *We had a big fry-up for breakfast.*

fuck about/around   fucks, fucking, fucked

fuck about/around *taboo*
  to behave stupidly, or to waste time doing unimportant things • *Just stop fucking around and listen to me, will you!*

fuck sb **about/around** *taboo*
  to treat someone badly by wasting their time or causing them problems • *You shouldn't fuck him about like that.*

fuck off   fucks, fucking, fucked

Fuck off! (always an order) *taboo*
  something that you say when you are very angry in order to tell someone to go away • *Just fuck off and leave me alone!*

fuck sb **off** *taboo*
  to annoy or upset someone very much • *It really fucks me off the way he thinks he can talk to people like that!*

fuck over   fucks, fucking, fucked

fuck over sb or **fuck** sb **over** *American taboo*
  to treat someone very badly or unfairly • *Mitchell fucked us all over when he ran off with the money.*

fuck up   fucks, fucking, fucked

fuck up (sth) or **fuck** (sth) **up** *taboo*
  to spoil or damage something, or to do something very badly • *He's worried he fucked up the job interview.* • *That was a disaster – I really fucked up!*

  fuck-up *n* [C] *taboo* • *It's been one fuck-up after another since she became manager!*

fuck up sb or **fuck** sb **up** *taboo*

  to make someone experience extreme emotional problems • *Maria's been really fucked up by her parents' divorce.*

fuel up   fuels, fuelling, fuelled   (*American* also **fuels, fueling, fueled**)

fuel up
  to put fuel into a vehicle • *We can drive for another 20 miles and then we'll need to fuel up.*

fumble about/around   fumbles, fumbling, fumbled

fumble about/around
  to move awkwardly, especially using your hands, usually because you are trying to find something • *She fumbled around in the dark until she found the light switch.* • *The woman fumbled around in her handbag looking for the keys.*

fur up   furs, furring, furred

fur up *British*
  if something [e.g. kettle, water pipe] furs up, the inside of it becomes covered with a hard, light grey substance formed from chemicals in water • *The water is so hard around here, our kettle is always furring up.*

fuss at   fusses, fussing, fussed

fuss at sb *American*
  to complain about someone or something again and again in an annoying way • *Those two are continually fussing at each other over nothing.* • *Don't fuss at me, I'm working as fast as I can.*

fuss over   fusses, fussing, fussed

fuss over sb/sth

  to pay too much attention to someone or something, especially because you want to show that you like them • *Tim watched, embarrassed at the way she fussed over him.*

gad about/around gads, gadding, gadded

gad about/around (swh) *informal, old-fashioned*

to visit a lot of different places, enjoying yourself and having few worries ● (usually in continuous tenses) *Most of our weekends were spent gadding about London.* ● *While you were gadding around with your friends I was at home cooking for ten people!*

gadabout *n* [C] *humorous, old-fashioned* ● *Where have you been, you young gadabout!*

gain on/upon gains, gaining, gained

gain on/upon sb/sth

to get nearer to someone or something that you are chasing ● *You'll have to speed up – they're gaining on us!* ● *I was now gaining rapidly on the yacht in front of me.*

gang up gangs, ganging, ganged

gang up *informal*

to form a group in order to attack or oppose someone, often unfairly ● (often + **on**) *She says the other kids in her class have been ganging up on her.* ● (often + **against**) *I think I felt sorry for him because the rest of the family were ganging up against him.*

gas up gases, gassing, gassed

gas up (sth) or **gas** (sth) **up** *American informal*

to put fuel in a car or other vehicle ● *We'll need to gas up before we get on the thruway.* ● *You go gas up the van and then we can leave.*

gather around/round gathers, gathering, gathered

gather around/round (sb/sth)

to form a group surrounding someone or something ● *A crowd gathered around*

her. ● *In the evenings we would gather round the campfire and sing songs.* ● (sometimes + to do sth) *Hundreds of office workers gathered around to watch the firemen control the blaze.*

gather in gathers, gathering, gathered

gather in sth or **gather** sth **in**

to collect a group of things [esp. crops, harvest] and put them together in a safe place ● *We watched them gathering in the harvest.*

gather round

see **gather around/round**

gather up gathers, gathering, gathered

gather up sth or **gather** sth **up**

to collect several things, especially from different places, and put them together ● *She gathered up the newspapers that were scattered around the floor.* ● *I'll just gather my things up and then we can go.*

gather sb **up** *literary*

to put your arms around someone and hold them to you in order to show you love them ● *He gathered her up in a warm embrace.*

gather yourself **up** (always reflexive) *literary*

to stand up ● *He gathered himself up and left the room.*

gear to/towards gears, gearing, geared

gear sth **to/towards** sth/sb

to design or organize something so that it is suitable for a particular purpose, situation, or group of people ● (usually passive) *Most public places are simply not geared to people with disabilities.* ● *The old education system was geared towards exams.*

gear up gears, gearing, geared

gear up (sth/sb) or **gear** (sth/sb) **up**

to prepare for something that you have to do or want to do ● (often + to do sth) *Employees are already gearing up to cope with an increased workload.* ● (sometimes reflexive) *I'm gearing myself up to ask him to give me my money back.* ● (often + **for**) *The singer and his group are gearing themselves up for a world tour.*

gee up   gees, geeing, geed

gee up sb or **gee** sb **up** *British informal*
to encourage someone to feel more enthusiasm for what they are doing and to try
harder to succeed ● *We hadn't been playing well and our captain was trying to gee
us up.*

Gee up! (always an order) *British*
something that you say to a horse when
you want it to move more quickly ● *Gee
up, Neddy!*

gen up   gens, genning, genned

gen up *British*
to find out as much information as possible about something ● (usually + **on**) *I
thought I'd better gen up on the company
before my interview.*

get about   gets, getting, got   (*American* *pp* also **gotten**)

get about
1 *mainly British & Australian informal* to
travel to a lot of different places ● *So
you've just come back from Japan and
now you're off to Canada? You get about a
bit, don't you?*
2 to be able to go to different places without
difficulty, especially if you are old or
have been ill ● *Annie's finding it much
more difficult to get about these days.*
3 *mainly British* if news or information
gets about, a lot of people hear about it
● *News certainly gets about quickly in
these parts!*
4 *informal* to have sexual relationships
with a lot of different people ● *He gets
about a bit, does Alex. I never seem to see
him with the same woman twice.*

get above   gets, getting, got   (*American* *pp* also **gotten**)

get above yourself (always reflexive)
mainly British
to behave as if you are better than other
people ● (usually in continuous tenses)
*She's really getting above herself since she
got that promotion.*

get across   gets, getting, got   (*American* *pp* also **gotten**)

get across sth or **get** sth **across**
to successfully communicate an idea to
other people ● *There's only so much you
can get across in a short advertisement.*

● (often + **to**) *This is the message that we
want to get across to the public.*

get after   gets, getting, got   (*American* *pp* also **gotten**)

get after sb/sth *American*
to chase a person or animal ● (often an
order) *Get after Shirley and tell her not to
wait for us.*

get after sb (never passive) *American*
to keep asking someone to do something,
or keep telling them how to do something
● *I'll have to get after that plumber.*
● (often + **about**) *You should get after the
kids about the mess in their rooms.*

get ahead   gets, getting, got   *American* *pp* also **gotten**

get ahead
to be successful in the work that you do
● (often + **in**) *It's tough for any woman
who wants to get ahead in politics.*

get along   gets, getting, got   (*American* *pp* also **gotten**)

get along
1 if two or more people get along, they like
each other and are friendly to each other
● *Vicky and Ellen seem to be getting along
much better these days.* ● (often + **with**) *I
really don't get along with my sister's husband.* ● *We've been **getting along like a
house on fire**.* (= very well)
2 to deal with a situation, especially successfully ● *I wonder how Julie got along
in her interview.* ● (sometimes + **with**)
*How are you getting along with your
Spanish?* ● (sometimes + **without**) *It's not
going to be easy but I reckon we can get
along without him.*

be getting along (always in continuous
tenses) *old-fashioned*
if you say that you must be getting along,
you mean that you need to leave somewhere, usually because you have a lot of
things to do ● *Anyway, I must be getting
along, I've got so much to do at home.*

get around   gets, getting, got   (*American pp* also **gotten**)

get around
1 to travel to a lot of different places
● *Spain, Germany and Italy in one month?
You certainly get around!*
2 if news or information gets around, a lot

of people hear about it ● *I don't want it to get around that I'm leaving.* ● *Word* (= the news) *got around that Jeanette and Dave were having an affair.*

3 *informal* to have sexual relationships with a lot of different people ● *So he gets around quite a bit, does he? Lucky sod.*

get around sth

to find a way of dealing with or avoiding a problem ● *Don't worry about the problem with the catering, we'll get around it somehow.* ● *Our lawyer found a way of getting around the adoption laws.*

get around sb

to persuade someone to do what you want by being kind to them ● *And don't think you can get around me by buying me flowers!*

get around (swh)

to be able to go to different places without difficulty ● *We managed to get around and see quite a bit of the island.* ● *It's difficult to get around the city if you don't have a car.*

get around/round to   gets, getting, got   (*American pp* also **gotten**)

get around/round to sth/doing sth

to do something that you have intended to do for a long time ● *I finally got round to sorting out that cupboard yesterday.* ● *I'll mention your name when I write to him – if I ever get around to it.*

get at   gets, getting, got   (*American pp* also **gotten**)

get at sb

1 *British informal* to criticize someone in an unkind way ● *He keeps getting at me and I really don't know what I've done wrong.* ● (used as *adj*) *I think she felt a bit got at during the meeting.*

2 to use threats or payments in order to persuade someone to make the decision you want them to make, especially in a court of law ● (usually passive) *The accused claimed that the witness had been got at.*

be getting at sth (always in continuous tenses; always used in questions) *informal*

if you ask someone what they are getting

at, you are asking them what they mean, usually because they have expressed something indirectly ● *What are you getting at, Andy? Do you think I was wrong to tell her?*

get at sth

1 to be able to reach or get something ● *I've put that cake on a high shelf so Tom can't get at it.* ● *She's inherited a lot of money but she's not allowed to get at it till she's 21.*

2 to discover information about something, especially the truth about a situation ● *I just don't believe the explanation I've been given – I'm determined to get at the truth.*

get away   gets, getting, got   (*American pp* also **gotten**)

get away

1 to leave a place or person, often when the situation makes it difficult for you to do this ● *What time did you finally get away last night?* ● (often + **from**) *We walked to the next beach to get away from the crowds.*

2 to escape ● *We ran after them but they got away.* ● *They got away in a stolen car.* ● (sometimes + **with**) *Everyone's saying they got away with $500,000.*

getaway *n* [C] *informal* ● *The thieves made a getaway through a back exit.* ● (used as *adj*) *The three men jumped into a getaway van and drove off.*

3 *informal* to go somewhere to have a holiday, especially because you need to rest ● (usually + *adv/prep*) *I just need to get away for a few days and think things over.* ● *We decided to go up to Scotland to get away from it all.* (= have a relaxing holiday)

Get away! *British informal, old-fashioned* something that you say when you do not believe what someone has just said ● *'Nicky, doing a parachute jump?' 'Get away!'*

get away from   gets, getting, got   (*American pp* also **gotten**)

get away from sth

1 to do something in a different way from what is usual or expected ● *The problem with being a fast-food outlet is that it's difficult to get away from the greasy burger image.*

2 to begin to talk about something different from what you should be talking about • *I think we're getting away from the main issue here.*

get away with · gets, getting, got
*(American pp also **gotten**)*

get away with sth/doing sth

1 to succeed in not being criticized or punished for something wrong that you have done • *If I thought I could get away with it, I wouldn't pay tax at all.* • *He shouldn't treat you like that – don't let him get away with it.* • *He **gets away with murder** (=* he does a lot of bad things and is never punished) *just because he's cute.*

2 to do something successfully even though it is not the best way of doing it • *Do you think we could get away with only one coat of paint on that wall?*

get back · gets, getting, got · *(American pp also **gotten**)*

get back

to return to a place after you have been somewhere else • *What time did you get back last night?* • (often + **to**) *By the time we got back to the hotel, Lydia had already left.* • (sometimes + **from**) *The letter was at home waiting for me when I got back from work.*

get back sth *or* get sth back

if you get something back, something that you had before is given to you again • *I wouldn't lend him anything, you'll never get it back.*

Get back! (always an order)

something that you say in order to tell someone to move away from something or someone, usually because there is a danger • *Get back, Josh, or you'll get hurt!*

get sb back *informal*

to do something unpleasant to someone because they have done something unpleasant to you • *I want to get him back for embarrassing me yesterday in front of Robert.*

get back at · gets, getting, got
*(American pp also **gotten**)*

get back at sb

to do something unpleasant to someone because they have done something unpleasant to you • (often + **for**) *I think he's*

trying to get back at her for those remarks she made in the meeting.*

get back into · gets, getting, got
*(American pp also **gotten**)*

get back into sth

to begin doing something again after not doing it for a period of time • *She worked as a doctor for a few years but eventually decided to get back into research.*

get back to · gets, getting, got
*(American pp also **gotten**)*

get back to sb

if you get back to someone, you talk to them, usually on the telephone, in order to give them some information that they have asked you for, or because you were not able to speak to them before • *I'll get back to you later this afternoon with more details.* • *He said he'd get back to me in a couple of days.*

get back to sth

to start talking about something again, or to start doing something again • *To get back to the question of funding, there are one or two matters that concern me.* • *Anyway, I'd better get back to work.* • *It was ages before I got back to sleep.*

get behind · gets, getting, got
*(American pp also **gotten**)*

get behind

if you get behind with work or with payments, you have not done as much work or paid as much money as you should by a particular time • *I don't want her to have too much time off school or she'll get behind.* • (often + **with**) *They got behind with the house payments when the interest rates went up.*

get behind sb/sth *mainly American*

to support someone or something in order to help them succeed • *The whole neighborhood got behind the proposal to install traffic lights at the school.*

get by · gets, getting, got · *(American pp also **gotten**)*

get by

1 to have just enough money to pay for the things that you need, but nothing more • (often + **on**) *I don't know how he gets by on so little money.*

2 to have or know just enough of something

to be able to deal with a particular situation but not have or know as much as you would like ● (often + **with**) *We can just about get by with four computers but ideally we'd have another.* ● *I can get by in Italian but I'm by no means fluent.*

get down gets, getting, got (American *pp* also **gotten**)

get sb **down** (never passive)
to make someone feel unhappy ● *All this uncertainty is really getting me down.* ● *The house is always untidy and it's starting to get me down.*

get down sth or **get** sth **down** (never passive)
1 to write something, especially something that someone has said ● *I didn't manage to get down every word she said.* ● *Did you get that telephone number down?*

2 to manage to swallow something, especially when this is difficult ● *Her throat was so swollen she couldn't get anything down.*

get down
1 to move your body so that you are sitting, kneeling, or lying on the ground ● *'Get down! He's got a gun.'* ● *I'm not going to get down on my knees and beg him to come.*

2 *mainly British informal* if children ask to get down after they have finished eating, they are asking permission to leave the table ● *Can I get down now please Mummy?*

get down to gets, getting, got (American *pp* also **gotten**)

get down to sth/doing sth
to start doing something seriously and with a lot of your attention and effort ● *I've got loads of work to do but I can't seem to get down to it.* ● *It's time you got down to looking for a job.*

get in gets, getting, got (American *pp* also **gotten**)

get in
1 to succeed in entering a place, especially a building ● *I used Bob's keys to get in.* ● *We wanted to see the new Spielberg film but we couldn't get in.* (= we were not allowed in because all the seats were full)

2 to arrive at your home or at the place

where you work ● *What time did Chuck get in last night?* ● *Just give me five minutes to organize myself – I've only just got in.*

3 if a train, plane, or other vehicle gets in at a particular time, that is when it arrives ● *What time does your train get in?* ● *His plane doesn't get in till ten o'clock.*

4 if a political party or a politician gets in, they are elected ● *Do you think the Conservatives will get in again?* ● *Bush got in with a small majority.*

5 to succeed in getting a place at a school, college, or organization ● *He wanted to go to Oxford but he didn't get in.*

6 *British* to succeed in becoming a member of a team ● *You have to be pretty good for the first team. Not many people get in.*

get in sb or **get** sb **in**
to ask someone to come to your home or the place where you work in order to do something for you, especially to repair something ● *There's obviously a problem with the wiring – we'll have to get an electrician in.*

get in sth or **get** sth **in**
1 to buy food or other supplies so that you have what you will need ● *I must get some extra milk in at the weekend.*

2 to manage to say something even though it is difficult to do this because other people are talking ● *I finally managed to get a word in.* ● *She was chattering away and I **couldn't get a word in edgeways**.* (= I couldn't say anything because she was talking all the time) ● *I'll try to get my suggestion in at the start of the meeting.*

3 *informal* to manage to do something even though you do not have much time because you are busy doing other things ● *Do you think we could get a game of tennis in before lunch?* ● *I managed to get in a couple of hours work before the meeting.*

get in on gets, getting, got (American *pp* also **gotten**)

get in on sth *informal*
to start to become involved in an activity that other people are already doing, often without being invited to ● *A Japanese company tried to get in on the deal.* ● *They've seen the advantages and now they're trying to **get in on the act**.* (= become involved)

get into   gets, getting, got   (*American pp* also **gotten**)

get into sth

1 to become interested in an activity or subject, or to start being involved in an activity ● *She's been getting into yoga recently.* ● *How did you get into journalism?*

2 to succeed in getting a place at a school, college, or organization ● *Did she get into university?*

3 *British* to succeed in becoming a member of a team ● *He's hoping to get into the school team.*

4 to start to have a particular habit or way of behaving ● *I got into the habit of having a snack at about 11 each morning.* ● *We had to get into a completely different routine once the baby arrived.*

5 *informal* to be thin enough to be able to put your clothes on ● (usually negative) *I've put on so much weight that I can't get into any of my clothes any more.*

6 to start discussing something, especially something complicated or different ● *We will also need to plan the student party, but there's no time to get into that now.*

get (sb) into sth (never passive)

to become involved in a difficult situation, often without intending to, or to make someone do this ● *He'd drunk too much and got into a fight outside the restaurant.* ● *Can't you do something, Rob? You got us into this mess!* ● *Business was bad during the recession and we got into debt.* ● (sometimes reflexive) *She got herself into trouble with the police.*

get into sb *Australian informal*

to criticize someone ● *That's right Jo, you get into him!*

get in with   gets, getting, got (*American pp* also **gotten**)

get in with sb *informal*

to become friendly with someone, especially because you think that they can help you ● *I think she's trying to get in with Sue because she thinks it will be good for her career.* ● *He was always very keen to get in with the right people.*

get off   gets, getting, got   (*American pp* also **gotten**)

get off (sth)

1 to leave a bus, train, aircraft, or boat ● *She got off the bus and ran towards him.* ● *The plane was still on the runway but people were already beginning to get off.* ● *You need to get off* (= leave the train/bus) *at Camden Town.*

2 to leave the place where you work, usually at the end of the day ● *I'll see if I can get off early this afternoon.* ● *What time do you get off work?*

get (sb) off (sth)

to avoid being punished for something that you have done wrong, or to help someone avoid being punished for something that they have done wrong ● *She was charged with fraud, but her lawyer managed to get her off.* ● (sometimes + **with**) *He got off with a $20 fine.* ● *Considering that it was his second offence I think he got off lightly* . (= he was not punished severely)

Get off (sb/sth)! (always an order)

mainly British informal something that you say in order to tell someone to stop touching someone or something ● *If he tries putting his arm round you again, just tell him to get off.*

get off

1 to leave a place in order to start a journey or go somewhere ● *If we can get off by seven the roads will be clearer.* ● *Anyway, I must get off to the shops.*

2 *American slang* to become extremely

happy and relaxed because you have taken a drug • (usually + **on**) *He likes to get off on cocaine.* • *How can we get off if we don't have any gear?*

get (sb) off

1 *informal* to start sleeping, or to help a baby to start sleeping • *I've been trying to get Sam off for an hour now.* • *What time did you finally get off to sleep?*
2 *American slang* to have an orgasm (= the moment of greatest pleasure in sexual activity), or to make someone do this • *Last night we got off at the same time.*

get off sth

1 if someone gets off the phone, they stop using it • *I'm waiting for Adrian to get off the phone so that I can call Dom.*
2 *American* to say or write something funny [e.g. joke] • *Joan got off two quick jokes about the manager before he arrived.*

get sth off *informal*

to send a letter or parcel to someone • *I got that letter off this morning.*

Get off it! *American informal*

something that you say in order to tell someone that you do not believe them or that you disagree with them • *Get off it! I don't believe a word you've said.*

get it off *American slang*

to have sex or to have an orgasm (= the moment of greatest pleasure in sexual activity) • (often + **with**) *So did he get it off with anyone?*

---

get off on   gets, getting, got   (*American pp* also **gotten**)

get off on sth *informal*

to become very excited by something • *Dave likes power – he gets off on it.*

---

get off with   gets, getting, got
(*American pp* also **gotten**)

get off with sb *British & Australian slang*

to begin a sexual relationship with someone • *She'd got off with some bloke at the party.*

---

get on   gets, getting, got   (*American pp* also **gotten**)

get on (sth)

to go onto a bus, train, aircraft, or boat • *I got on the wrong bus and ended up horribly lost.* • *I got on* (= I went onto the train) *at Clapham Junction.* • *The plane was almost full by the time I got on.*

get on

1 *mainly British & Australian* if two or more people get on, they like each other and are friendly to each other • *Sue and I have always got on well.* • (often + **with**) *It's a shame she doesn't get on better with her colleagues.* • (sometimes + **together**) *Do James and your father get on together?*
2 to deal with a situation, or to deal with a situation successfully • (often in continuous tenses) *She seems to be getting on fine at school.* • (often + **with**) *How are you getting on with the painting?*
3 to continue doing something, especially work • (usually + **with**) *I think I'll get on with some work while the kids are out.* • *I've told you what to do – now just get on with it!* • *I'll leave you to get on then, shall I?*
4 *mainly British & Australian* to be successful in your work • *He came to this company with the attitude that he wanted to get on.* • (sometimes + **in**) *You have to make some sacrifices if you're going to get on in the business world.*

be getting on (always in continuous tenses)

1 *informal* if someone is getting on, they

are old ● *How old's George, then? He must be getting on.*

2 *mainly British & Australian informal* if you say that time is getting on, you mean that it is getting late ● *Time's getting on and he's still not here.* ● *Anyway, it's getting on – I'd better go.*

get it on *mainly American slang*
to have sex ● (often + **with**) *Did you get it on with her?*

get on at gets, getting, got (*American pp* also **gotten**)

get on at sb (never passive)
to criticize someone in an unkind way ● *You're always getting on at me!*

get on for

be getting on for sth (always in continuous tenses) *British & Australian*
to be almost a particular number, amount, or time, especially a large number or amount, or a time that is late ● *He must be getting on for 90 now.* ● *There must have been getting on for 200 people at the wedding.* ● *It's getting on for nine now and it takes half an hour to get there.*

get on to/onto gets, getting, got (*American pp* also **gotten**)

get on to/onto sth
1 to start talking about a subject after discussing something else ● *It didn't take long before we got onto the subject of babies.* ● *How did we get onto that subject?*

2 to be elected as a member of an organization ● *Taylor has threatened to resign if she gets on to the committee.*

3 if someone gets on to the television or radio, they are invited to appear or speak on the television or radio ● *He got on to local radio with the story.*

get on to/onto sb (never passive)
1 to speak or write to a person or organization, especially because you want them to help you in some way ● *We'd better get on to a plumber about that leak in the bathroom.* ● *Did you get onto the passport office?*

2 if someone in authority gets on to you, they find out about something that you have done that you were trying to keep secret ● *It only took a couple of months before the Immigration Office got on to her.*

get on toward gets, getting, got (*American pp* also **gotten**)

be getting on toward sth (always in continuous tenses) *American*
to be almost a particular time, especially a time that is late ● *It must be getting on toward closing time.* ● *It's getting on toward seven.*

get out gets, getting, got (*American pp* also **gotten**)

get out
1 to move out of a vehicle ● *I'll stop at the lights and you can get out.* ● *As he got out of the car his wallet fell out of his pocket.*

2 to go out to different places and meet people in order to enjoy yourself ● *She doesn't get out so much now that she's got the baby.*

3 if news or information gets out, people hear about it even though someone is trying to keep it secret ● *There'll be trouble with the unions if news of the redundancies gets out.* ● *Word* (= the news) *got out that Matthew was intending to resign.*

get (sb) **out**
to escape from or leave a place, or to help someone do this ● *I left the door open and the cat got out.* ● (often + **of**) *They're trying to get the hostages out of the country.* ● (often an order) *Just get out* (= leave this place)*, will you!* ● *A lot of people who've been in prison find it difficult to get a job when they get out.* (= are allowed to leave prison).

get out sth or **get** sth **out**
1 to remove dirt or an unwanted substance from a piece of material ● (often + **of**) *I*

can't get those coffee stains out of the table-cloth.

2 to succeed in making a product so that it is available for people to buy, especially a book or record • *We've really got to get this book out by the end of the year.*

3 to succeed in saying something, especially when this is difficult • *He was so overcome with shock he could hardly get the words out.*

get out of   gets, getting, got   (*American pp* also **gotten**)

get out of sth/doing sth

to avoid doing something that you should do, often by giving an excuse • *I've got a meeting this morning but I'll see if I can get out of it.* • *You're just trying to get out of doing the housework!*

get out of sth

to stop a habit or regular activity • *I used to do a lot of swimming but I've got out of the habit these past few months.* • *If you get out of a routine it's very hard to get back into it.*

get sth **out of** sb

to persuade or force someone to give or tell you something • *He was determined to get the truth out of her.* • *Daniel must know what happened – I'll try to get it out of him.* • *Did you get a refund out of the travel agent for that trip you had to cancel?*

get sth **out of** sth/doing sth

to enjoy something or to think that something is useful • *She gets a lot of pleasure out of her garden.* • *It was an interesting course but I'm not sure I got much out of it.*

get over   gets, getting, got   (*American pp* also **gotten**)

get over sth

1 to begin to feel better after an experience that has made you unhappy • *I don't suppose you ever really get over the death of a child.* • *It took her months to get over the shock of Richard leaving.*

2 (never passive) to feel better after having an illness • *She was only just getting over the flu when she caught chickenpox.*

3 to find a solution to a problem • *They had to get over one or two technical problems before filming could start.*

get over sth or **get** sth **over**

to successfully communicate ideas or in-

formation to other people • *He frequently uses humour to get over serious messages.* • *Did you manage to get your points over?*

can't/couldn't get over sth (always negative) *informal*

if someone can't get over something, they are very surprised or shocked that something has happened or that something is true • *I couldn't get over how much weight Dave had lost.* • *He was so incredibly rude to her – I couldn't get over it.*

get over with   gets, getting, got   (*American pp* also **gotten**)

get sth **over with**

to do and complete something difficult or unpleasant that must be done • *I'll be glad to get these exams over with.* • *I wanted to give my paper at the start of the week so that I could get it over with.* • *I'd rather do it now and **get it over and done with**.* (= complete it)

get round   gets, getting, got   (*American pp* also **gotten**)

get round *mainly British & Australian*

if news or information gets round, a lot of people hear about it • *Word* (= the news) *had got round that Helena was leaving the company.* • *For obvious reasons I don't want it to get round that I've applied for the post.*

get round sth *mainly British & Australian*

to find a way of dealing with or avoiding a problem • *We're making progress but there are still one or two obstacles to get round.* • (sometimes + **by**) *They got round the problem of overcrowding by opening up an alternative location.*

get round sb *mainly British & Australian*

to persuade someone to do what you want by being kind to them • *I don't think Liz is too keen on the idea at the moment but don't worry, I'll get round her.*

get round to

see **get around/round to**

get through   gets, getting, got   (*American pp* also **gotten**)

get through

to manage to talk to someone on the telephone • *I tried phoning her earlier, but I couldn't get through.* • (often + **to**) *He got* *through to the wrong department.*

get through sth *mainly British & Australian*

1 to use a lot or all of something, especially food, drink, or money ● *We nearly got through a whole jar of coffee last week.* ● *Have you got through that box of cornflakes already?* ● *He gets through over £50 every time he goes out.*

2 to finish something that you are doing ● *I get through a lot more work when I'm on my own.* ● *It took me ages to get through that book she lent me.*

get (sb/sth) **through** sth (never passive) to succeed in an examination or competition, or to help someone or something do this ● *She didn't get through her first year exams.* ● *You'll never get that car through the road test unless you fix the exhaust.*

get (sb) **through** sth (never passive) to deal with a difficult or unpleasant experience, or to help someone do this ● *I don't know how I got through the first couple of months after Andy's death.* ● *We need to conserve our supplies so that we can get through the winter.* ● *We'll get you through this, Karen.*

get (sth) **through** (sth) .if a law or proposal gets through, or if someone gets a law or proposal through, it is officially accepted by a government or organization ● *It took several months to get the bill through Parliament.* ● *If these proposals get through, we'll have to rethink our strategies.*

get through to gets, getting, got
(American pp also **gotten)**

get through to sb to succeed in making someone understand or believe something ● (often negative) *I just don't seem to be able to get through to him these days.*

get through to sth to succeed in reaching the next stage in a competition ● *If they win this they'll get through to the final.* ● *I didn't even get through to the second interview stage.*

get to gets, getting, got   *(American pp* also **gotten)**

get to sb *informal* to make someone feel upset or angry ● *I know he's annoying, but you shouldn't let*

him get to you. ● *This heating is starting to get to me – I don't know how much more I can bear.*

get to (always used in questions) *informal* if you ask where someone or something has got to, you are asking where they are because they have not arrived or they are not where you expected them to be ● *I wonder where my glasses have got to.* ● *So where's Annabel got to? She should have been here an hour ago.*

get to doing sth to start to do something ● *I got to thinking about his childhood and how different it must have been to mine.*

get together   gets, getting, got
(American pp also **gotten)**

get together (sb) or **get** (sb) **together** if two or more people get together, or if someone gets two or more people together, they meet in order to do something or spend time together ● *We should get together and go for a drink some time.* ● *I'm planning to get a few friends together for a dinner party.* ● (often + to do sth) *The whole team got together to discuss the matter.* ● (sometimes + **with**) *We got together with our solicitor to look at the contract.*

get-together n [C] *informal* an informal meeting or party ● *I suppose you'll be having the usual family get-together over Christmas.*

get together if two people get together, they begin a romantic relationship ● *I always thought that Shirley and Alan would get together.* ● (often + **with**) *Eight years ago I got together with a girl who worked at the hospital.*

get yourself **together** (always reflexive) to begin to control your emotions so that you behave more calmly ● *I just need a few minutes to get myself together.*

get it together

1 *informal* to succeed in controlling what happens to you in life so that you do all the things that you have planned ● *I thought he'd really got it together last time I saw him – he'd got a job, found somewhere to live and seemed pretty happy.* ● *She had a lot of plans for her career but*

she never really got it together.

2 *informal* if two people get it together, they begin a sexual or romantic relationship with each other • *They finally get it together about two minutes before the end of the film.*

get together sth or get sth together

1 to collect several things and put them together in one place • *Can you just give me a couple of hours so that I can get my things together?*

2 to prepare or arrange something • *Can you get together a quick report and bring it to the meeting? • I'd really like to do the course but I'm not sure I can get the fees together.* (= arrange to get the amount of money needed)

get up   gets, getting, got   (American pp also gotten)

get (sb) up

to wake up and get out of bed, or to make someone do this • *I had to get up at five o'clock this morning. • Can you get the kids up?*

get up

1 to stand up • *The whole audience got up and started clapping. • I keep having to get up to answer the phone.*

2 *British & Australian* if the wind gets up, it starts to become much stronger • *The wind's getting up – do you think there's going to be a storm?*

get up sth or get sth up

1 to organize something • *They're getting up a petition against the new motorway.*

2 *American* to learn something or develop your knowledge of something • *She's getting up her French before she leaves for a job in Montreal.*

get sb up *informal*

1 (always + *adv/prep*) to dress someone in a particular type of clothing, especially unusual clothing • (often reflexive) *He'd got himself up as a Roman emperor for a fancy dress party. • All the kids had been got up in teddy-bear suits.*

getup *n* [C] *informal* • *He was in a sort of Santa Claus getup with a red suit and white beard.*

2 *American informal* to prepare someone for a sporting activity or event by training them or by increasing their confi-

dence • (often + **for**) *Her trainer was determined to get her up for the marathon.* • *The coach gets the players up before the game.*

get it up *informal*

if a man gets it up when he is sexually excited, his penis is harder and bigger than usual and points up • (usually negative) *He was so drunk he couldn't even get it up!*

Get up! (always an order) *American*

something that you say to a horse in order to tell it to start to move or to go faster • *Get up, Nelly.*

get up to   gets, getting, got   (American pp also gotten)

get up to sth

1 *mainly British & Australian* to do something, especially something that other people think is wrong • *Did you find out what the kids had been getting up to? • She's been getting up to all sorts of mischief lately.*

2 to reach a particular place in something that you are doing and to stop there • *I got up to chapter 4. • Which question did you get up to in the test?*

get with   gets, getting, got   (American pp also gotten)

Get with it! (always an order)

humorous something that you say in order to tell someone that they should be more modern • *Get with it, dad, they're the biggest band since the Beatles. You must have heard of them!*

giddy up

Giddy up! (always an order)

something that you say to a horse when you want it to move more quickly • *Giddy up, horsey!*

ginger up   gingers, gingering, gingered

ginger up sth or ginger sth up

to make something more exciting or more interesting • *The problem is that it makes dull reading – I think we ought to ginger it up somehow.*

give away   gives, giving, gave, given

give away sth or give sth away

1 to give something to someone without asking for payment • (often + **to**) *I gave away my old pans to a friend who's just*

set up home. • *We're giving away free shampoo samples as a promotion.*

give-away n [C] something given free to a customer • *I was amazed by the number of give-aways you get when you fly first-class.* • (used as *adj*) *He'd seen adverts for leather jackets at give-away prices.* (= very low prices)

2 to let someone know something that should be kept secret, often by mistake • *If you tell her any more you'll give the end of the film away.* • *It was meant to be a surprise until Caroline gave it away.* • *You don't want to give too much away about a product before it's on the market.* • *Don't tell him too much or you'll **give the game away**.* (= tell someone something that should be secret)

give-away n [singular] something that makes you aware of a fact that someone else was trying to keep secret • *'So how do you know she's smoking again?' 'Well, the cigarette packets lying around are a give-away!'* • *informalIt's the unnatural orange colour of fake-tan – it's a **dead give-away**.* (= it is very obvious that it is false)

3 to give your opponent in sport an advantage [e.g. goal, penalty] by playing badly • *Luton's poor defense gave away three goals to Coventry.*

give sb **away**

to do something by accident that lets someone know something about yourself that you were trying to keep secret • *His voice seems quite calm but his trembling hands give him away.* • (often reflexive) *You give yourself away by trying too hard to seem cheerful.*

give away sb or **give** sb **away**

1 to formally bring a bride (= a woman who is getting married) to her husband at the front of the church and give permission for her to marry • *The bride's father usually gives her away.*

2 *British & Australian* to give a baby to someone else so that they can look after that child as their own until he or she is an adult • *Her first child, born when she was 17, was given away at birth.*

---

give back   gives, giving, gave, given

give back sth or **give** sth **back**

to return something to the person who

---

gave it to you • *I must give you back that book you lent me.*

give sb sth **back**

to make someone have a quality or ability again after they had lost it or after it was taken away from them • *She will undergo an operation which will give her her sight back.* • *Nothing could give him his dignity back.*

---

give in   gives, giving, gave, given

give in

1 to finally agree to what someone wants after a period when you refuse to agree • *He nagged me so much to buy him a new bike that eventually I just gave in.* • (often + **to**) *The government cannot be seen to give in to terrorists' demands.*

2 to accept that you have been defeated and agree to stop competing or fighting • *She knew she'd lost the argument but she wouldn't give in.* • *You'll never guess the answer. Do you give in?*

give in sth or **give** sth **in**

to give a piece of written work or a document to someone for them to read, judge, or deal with • *Have you given in your essay yet?* • *We want to get 5000 signatures before we give the petition in.*

---

give in to   gives, giving, gave, given

give in to sth

if you give in to an emotion or desire, you stop trying not to feel it and you allow your actions to be controlled by that emotion or desire • *Certainly he felt the pull of*

self-pity, but he never once gave in to it.
• *I've been craving chocolate all morning but I refuse to give in to it.*

give of   gives, giving, gave, given

give of yourself/sth *formal*

if you give of yourself, or if you give of your time or money, you do things for other people without expecting them to do anything for you • *He was remembered as a kind, generous man who would always give of himself.* • *The club is run entirely by volunteers who give of their free time during the summer holidays.*

give off   gives, giving, gave, given

give off sth

1 to produce heat, light, a smell, or a gas • *I've only got a small radiator in my room and it doesn't give off much heat.* • *The petrol tank was on fire and it was giving off clouds of thick black smoke.*

2 if someone gives off a particular quality, their behaviour or appearance makes you believe that they have that quality • *Although he came from a working-class family, he gave off a certain air of nobility.*

give onto   gives, giving, gave, given

give onto sth *mainly British & Australian*
if a window, door, room etc. gives onto a place, it opens in the direction of that place or has a view of it • *The patio doors give onto a small courtyard.*

give out   gives, giving, gave, given

give out sth or **give** sth **out**

1 to give something to a large number of people • *I've said I'll give out leaflets for them in town.* • *One of the government's proposals is to give out condoms in high schools.*

2 to tell people information • (usually passive) *The winners' names were given out on the radio last night.*

give out

1 if a supply of something gives out, it finishes and there is none left • *The food supplies will give out by the end of the week.* • *Eventually my patience gave out and I shouted at her.*

2 if something gives out, it stops working because it is old, damaged, or has been used too much • *It was on the twenty-first mile that my legs gave out.* • *I'll stop*

speaking now because I think my voice is about to give out. • *The car's at the garage – the clutch has finally given out.*

3 if a road or path gives out, it ends at a particular place • *The trail gave out half way around the lake.*

give out sth

1 *literary* to make a sound • *He gave out a low moan.* • *Suddenly she gave out a loud scream and clutched at me.*

2 to produce light, heat, or a gas • *Is that radiator giving out any heat?* • *Fluorescent lamps give out a brighter light for the same amount of electricity.*

give over

Give over! (always an order) *British informal*
something that you say in order to tell someone to be quiet, or to stop doing something that is annoying you • *'Can I have 50p to buy some sweets, Mum?' 'Oh, give over! I've given you £2 already today.'*

give over to

be given over to sth (always passive)
to be used only for a particular purpose or activity • *A whole wing of the museum has been given over to the Matisse exhibition.* • *The whole evening was given over to eating and drinking.*

give yourself **over to** sth (always reflexive)
to spend all your time or energy doing an activity • *When she started her career, she gave herself over to her job.*

give over sb/sth **to** sb or **give** sb/sth **over to** sb
to give the responsibility for something or someone to someone else • *The keys to the property were given over to us at the solicitors'.* • *On her mother's death, Kay was given over to her aunt to be looked after.*

give up   gives, giving, gave, given

give up (sth) or **give** (sth) **up**

if you give up a habit [e.g. smoking, drinking] or give up something unhealthy [e.g. cigarettes, alcohol], you stop doing it or having it • *I gave up smoking six months ago.* • *Don't offer him a cigarette – he's given up.* • *I gave up alcohol while I was pregnant.*

give up sth or **give** sth **up**

1 to stop doing a regular activity or a job
• *Are you going to give up work when you have your baby?* • *I had to give up French classes because I just didn't have time.*

2 to stop owning and using something • *They were forced to give up their home because they couldn't pay the mortgage.* • *He gave up his seat on the bus so that a woman with a baby could sit down.*

3 to use time that you would usually spend enjoying yourself to do something that helps other people • (often + to do sth) *She gave up every Saturday afternoon to work in a charity shop.*

give up (sth/doing sth) or **give** (sth) **up**

to stop doing an activity or piece of work before you have completed it, usually because it is too difficult • *I had to give up halfway through the race because I was so tired.* • *I've given up trying to persuade Sara to come – she's just not interested.*

give up

to stop trying to think of the answer to a joke or question • *I give up – what's the capital of Sudan? • Do you give up?*

give yourself **up** (always reflexive)
to allow the police to catch you, or to allow enemy soldiers to take you as a prisoner • (sometimes + **to**) *The gunman finally gave himself up to the police.* • *The rebels had to give themselves up because they'd run out of supplies.*

give up sb or **give** sb **up**

1 to give a baby to someone else so that they can look after it until it is an adult • *She was very young when she gave birth to a son and her parents made her give him up.*

2 to stop being friendly with someone, or to stop having a relationship with someone • *He wanted me to give up all my male acquaintances and I just wouldn't do it.*

give up on   gives, giving, gave, given

give up on sb

to stop hoping that someone will do what you want them to do • *You're here at last. We'd almost given up on you!* (= we had started to think that you were not coming) • *He'd been unconscious for so long that the doctors had given up on him.*

give up on sth

to stop hoping that something will achieve what you want it to achieve • *I've given up on aerobics. It just wasn't making any difference to my body.*

give up to   gives, giving, gave, given

give yourself **up to** sth (always reflexive)

1 *literary* to spend all your time and energy doing something • *After 1851 he gave himself up entirely to his historical publications.*

2 *literary* to let yourself be controlled completely, especially by an emotion • *After his death she gave herself up to grief.*

glance off   glances, glancing, glanced

glance off (sth)

if something [e.g. ball, bullet, light] glances off an object, it touches the object quickly and lightly at an angle and bounces away in another direction • *The ball grazed his left wrist and glanced off his jaw.*

glance over   glances, glancing, glanced

glance over sth

to look at something, especially something written, very quickly • *Could you just glance over this letter and tell me if you think it's all right?*

glaze over   glazes, glazing, glazed

glaze over

if someone or someone's eyes glaze over, they stop showing emotion because they are bored or tired and have stopped listening to what someone is saying • *He started telling her about the different rates of interest on savings accounts and her eyes glazed over.* • *I'm sure I just glaze over every time he starts talking about his job.*

glom onto   gloms, glomming, glommed

glom onto sth *American informal*

1 to get or take something that you want • *She glommed onto some of my tapes after the party and hasn't given them back yet.*

2 to become very interested in something, for example a new idea or fashion • *Young people are quick to glom onto any new fashion in clothes.*

glory in   glories, glorying, gloried

glory in sth

to enjoy something and be very proud of it ● *Other people might not want such a fearsome reputation but Davies seems to glory in it.*

gloss over   glosses, glossing, glossed

gloss over sth

to avoid discussing something, or to discuss something without talking about the details in order to make it seem unimportant ● *The company's profits dropped dramatically last year, a fact which the director was keen to gloss over.*

glue to

be glued to sth (always passive)

to be watching something [esp. television] with all your attention ● *Everyone was glued to the TV set as the election results came in.*

gnaw at   gnaws, gnawing, gnawed

gnaw at sb

to make someone feel more and more anxious or annoyed ● *I thought I trusted him, but a growing doubt kept gnawing at me.*

gnaw at sth

to gradually have a harmful effect on something ● *Violent crime and drug culture continue to gnaw at the fabric of society.*

go about   goes, going, went, gone

go about sth/doing sth

to start to do something or deal with something ● (often used in questions) *How can we go about solving this problem?* ● *I'd like to help, but what's the best way to go about it?*

go about sth

to continue with an activity ● *In spite of last night's bomb attack most people seem to be going about their business as usual.* ● *She tends to whistle as she goes about her household chores.*

go about doing sth

if someone goes about doing something, they spend their time behaving badly or doing something that is unpleasant for other people ● *I wish she wouldn't go about telling people that I'm depressed.*

● *You can't go about treating people like that!*

go about

1 *mainly British* if an illness goes about, a lot of people get it ● (usually in continuous tenses) *There seems to be a lot of flu going about at the moment.*

2 *mainly British* if a story or piece of news goes about, a lot of people are talking about it ● (usually in continuous tenses) *Don't believe anything you hear, there're all kinds of rumours going about.*

3 (always + *adv/prep*) *mainly British* to dress or behave in a particular way ● *Everyone went about in fur coats and thermal boots.*

4 *mainly British* if a boat or ship goes about, it turns around ● *The boat went about as it came close to the shore.*

go about together/with   goes, going, went, gone

go about together *mainly British*

go about with sb *mainly British*

to spend a lot of time with someone because they are your friend ● *We used to go about together when we were at school.*

go after   goes, going, went, gone

go after sb

to follow or chase someone in order to try to catch them ● *I got on my bike and went after him.* ● *She looks upset, do you think we should go after her?*

go after sth

to try to get something that you want [e.g. job] ● *Are you planning to go after Simon's job when he leaves?*

go against   goes, going, went, gone

go against sth

if something goes against a rule or something you believe in, it does not obey it or agree with it ● *It goes against my principles to respect someone just because they're in a position of authority.* ● *The EU says the decision goes against European trade rules.* ● *It **goes against the grain** (=* it is not usual) *for Sarah to admit that she's wrong.*

go against sth/sb

to do the opposite of what someone has asked or advised you to do ● *I went against my father's advice and bought the house.* • *I really don't want to go against my boss.*

go against sb

if a decision or vote goes against someone, they do not get the result that they needed • *If the vote goes against him, it could be the end of his political career.* • *If the verdict goes against him he could face up to five years in prison.*

go ahead   goes, going, went, gone

go ahead

1 to start to do something • *The preparations are complete but we can't go ahead without government money.* • (often + **with**) *We're going ahead with the offer unless we're told we can't proceed.*

go-ahead *n* [U] permission for something to start • *The government has **given the go-ahead** for a multi-billion pound road-building project.* • *We've got to **get the go-ahead** from our director before we take on more people.*

go-ahead *adj* (always before noun) using new methods and ideas to succeed • *Some of the more go-ahead companies even allow job-share.*

2 *slightly informal* something that you say to someone to give them permission to start to do something • *'Do you mind if I take some of this paper?' 'Sure, go ahead.'* • *'May I use your computer for a moment?' 'Go right ahead.'*

3 if an event goes ahead, it happens • *The majority of French people want the trial to go ahead.* • *The president's visit will go ahead* (= will happen) *despite the political situation.*

go along   goes, going, went, gone

go along

1 to go to a place or to an event, usually informally and without careful planning • *'Do you use the bar much?' 'I sometimes go along after work.'* • (often + **to**) *I thought I might go along to the party for an hour or so.*

2 (always + *adv/prep*) *slightly informal* to happen or develop in a particular way • *She was happy at work and happy in her relationship. In fact everything was going along quite nicely.*

go along with   goes, going, went, gone

go along with sth/sb

to support an idea, or to agree with someone's opinion • *She'll go along with anything he says just for a quiet life.* • *I go along with Martin on this one – I think the scheme's a disaster.*

go around   goes, going, went, gone

go around doing sth

if someone goes around doing something, they spend their time behaving badly or doing something that is unpleasant for other people • (usually in continuous tenses) *Someone's been going around spraying graffiti on the walls.* • *Please don't go around telling everyone what I said.*

go around (swh)

1 if an illness goes around, a lot of people get it • *There's a nasty flu virus going around at the moment.* • *I think I've caught that cold that's been going around the office.*

2 if a story or piece of news goes around, a lot of people are talking about it • *What's this story going around about Matthew leaving home?* • *There's a rumour around these parts that he's been having an affair.*

go around

1 (always + *adv/prep*) *mainly American* to visit someone at the place where they are living, staying, or working • *'Have you seen Amanda recently?' 'Yes, we went around to her place for dinner last week.'*

2 to be enough for everyone in a group of people • *Will there be enough cake to go around or should I get some more?*

3 (always + *adv/prep*) to dress or behave in a particular way • *He usually goes around in shorts and a T-shirt.* • *Ever since she got that job she's been going around with a big smile on her face.*

go around together/with   goes, going, went, gone

go around together

go around with sb

to spend a lot of time with someone because they are your friend • *Do they still go around together?* • *They don't approve of the people she goes around with.*

go at   goes, going, went, gone

go at sth (never passive) *informal*

to start doing something with a lot of energy and enthusiasm • *I had a good session in the gym today – I really went at it.* • *(British) I've never heard them argue like that before – they really **went at it hammer and tongs**.*

go at sb (never passive) *informal*

to attack someone physically • *She really went at him with her fists!*

go away   goes, going, went, gone

go away

1 to leave a place • (often an order) *Look, just go away and leave me alone, will you?*
2 to leave your home in order to spend time in a different place, usually for a holiday • (usually + *adv/prep*) *She usually looks after the house when we go away in the summer.* • *He goes away on business a lot.*
3 if something unpleasant goes away, it disappears • *Sometimes the symptoms go away on their own without treatment.* • *I've got this bad feeling about the relationship and it won't go away.*

go back   goes, going, went, gone

go back

1 to return to a place where you were or where you have been before • *I'd been away from Canada for three years and thought it was time I went back.* • (often + **to**) *When are you going back to Paris?* • *'So you didn't enjoy your meal?' 'No, we won't be going back there again!'*
2 if schools or students go back, the schools are open and the students start going to lessons again after the holidays • (usually + *adv/prep*) *The schools all go back in the second week of April.* • *When do you go back to university?*
3 *informal* if something that you have bought or borrowed goes back, you return it to the place from which you got it • *That shirt's going back – I found a hole in it.* • *When do these books have to go back?*

go back sth

1 *informal* if people go back a number of years, they have been friends for that many years or since that time • *Stef and Delia go back almost twenty years.* • *Trevor and me – we **go back a long**

way. (= have known each other for a long time)
2 if something goes back a number of years, it was started or made at that time • *Britain's links with this country go back centuries.*
3 if you go back a number of years, you think about how something was at that time • *Going back a couple of hundred years, this place would not have been inhabited.*

go back on   goes, going, went, gone

go back on sth

to not do something that you promised or said you would do • *I promised him I'd be there and I don't like to go back on my promises.* • *He said he'd pay you the money and I don't think he'll **go back on his word**.* (= break his promise)

go back over   goes, going, went, gone

go back over sth

to examine or think about something again or after it has happened • *I went back over the figures just to check that they were correct.* • *As she lay in her bed she went back over the events of the day.*

go back to   goes, going, went, gone

go back to sth

1 to start doing something again that you were doing before • *She went back to work when her daughter was two.*
2 to start talking or thinking about a particular subject again • *Going back to the first point that I made, we're all going to have to speed up.* • *To go back to what Sue said earlier...*
3 if a situation goes back to a particular state, it returns to that state • *If things go back to the way they were last year we'll have to make some changes.*
4 if you go back to a time in the past, you think about how something was at that time • *If you go back to the turn of the century, ten to fifteen people would have lived in a house this size.*
5 if something goes back to a time in the past, it started or was made at that time • *Parts of the church go back to the eleventh century.*

go back to sb

to start a relationship again with a person who you had a romantic relationship with in the past • *'Would you ever go back to Darren?' 'He wouldn't have me back.'*

go before   goes, going, went, gone

go before (always in past tenses; never in continuous tenses)

to have happened before • *This performance was a marked improvement on what had gone before.* • *Whatever has gone before is irrelevant.*

go before sb

if someone or something goes before a judge or other person in authority, the facts about that person or thing are considered by the judge so that a decision or judgement can be made about them • *This was the first case of its kind to go before an English jury.* • *He's due to go before the judge next week.*

go beyond   goes, going, went, gone

go beyond sth

to be much better, more detailed, more serious etc. than something else • *He has ambitions which go beyond the mere production of catchy pop records.*

go by   goes, going, went, gone

go by

1 if time goes by, it passes • *As each month goes by, the economic situation just gets worse.* • *Time went by and hopes for the hostages' safety began to fade.*

bygone adj (always before noun) *formal* from the past • *I don't have much patience with the romanticizing of bygone days.* • *The monarchy are just a relic of a bygone era.*

2 to walk past • *I'm just sitting here **watching the world go by**.* (= watching a lot of people walk past)

go by sth (never passive)

1 to use information or experience that you have of someone or something in order to help you decide what to do or what to think about that person or thing • *'How much pasta do you cook for 6 people?' 'I tend to go by what it says on the packet.'* • *If last year's was anything to go by it should be a great party.*

2 to obey the rules of something • *We'd better go by the rules – I don't want any trouble.* • *Mike's like that – he always **goes by the book**.*(= he obeys every rule)

go by swh *American & Australian*

to stop somewhere while you are going somewhere else, in order to do or get something • *I thought I'd go by the store on my way home and get some food.*

go down   goes, going, went, gone

go down

1 to become lower in level • *House prices went down in July following an increase in the previous two months.*

2 to become worse in quality • *It used to be a really good restaurant but it's really gone down recently.*

3 if something that is filled with air [e.g. tyre] goes down, some of the air comes out and it becomes smaller and softer • *That back tyre's gone down again – it must have a puncture.*

4 if part of your body that is bigger than usual because of an illness or injury goes down, it starts to return to its usual size • *My throat's still very sore although my glands have gone down now.*

5 if lights go down, they become less bright • *The audience grew quiet as the lights went down.*

6 when the sun goes down, it moves down in the sky until it cannot be seen any more • *We sat on the balcony sipping drinks and watching the sun go down.*

7 if a ship goes down, it sinks • *1513 people drowned when the Titanic went down in 1912.*

8 if an aircraft goes down, it falls out of the sky • *The plane went down just three miles from the airport.*

9 to travel south to a place • (often + **to**) *We might go down to Brighton at the weekend and see Johnny.*

10 (always + adv/prep) to be considered or remembered in a particular way • *I think my speech went down rather well, don't you?* • *(British) My joke about the fat couple **went down like a lead balloon**.* (= no one liked it) • (sometimes + **as**) *This will go down as one of the most important soccer matches ever played.* • *His contribution to world peace will **go down in history**.* (= will be remembered in the future)

11 (always + adv/prep) if food or drink goes down, it is enjoyable or easy to eat • *I'm so hot. A glass of cold beer would go down*

really well right now.

12 *mainly British* to lose in a sports competition ● *They're playing so badly, it's obvious they're going to go down.* ● (often + **to**) *England went down 4-2 to France in last night's match.*

13 if a computer goes down, it stops working ● *The computers went down and we lost a whole day's work.*

14 *British & Australian informal* to be sent to prison ● *You could go down for five years if they catch you.*

15 *American informal* to happen ● *I tried to warn him about what was going down, but he wouldn't listen.*

16 *British formal* to leave university, especially Oxford or Cambridge University ● *He went down in 1954 and joined the army.*

17 to touch someone's sexual organs with the mouth and tongue in order to give them sexual pleasure ● (often + **on**) *Quietly, he went down on her.*

go down on   goes, going, went, gone

go down on sth (always + *adv/prep*)
  to move into a position in which you are near to the ground and supported by your knees or by your knees and hands ● *She likes me to **go down on all fours** (= on hands and knees) and give her horse-rides.* ● *Please come tonight – I'll **go down on my knees** and beg you.* ● *So how did he propose, then? Did he **go down on one knee?***

go down with   goes, going, went, gone

go down with sth *British informal*
  to become ill, usually with a disease that is not very serious ● *James had gone down with the flu just before they went away.*

go for   goes, going, went, gone

go for sth
1 to choose something ● *When you're buying a computer, go for one with a lot of memory.*
2 if something goes for a particular amount of money, it is sold for that amount ● *One-bedroom apartments go for about $80,000 in this part of town.* ● *I found this silver tray in a local junk shop where it was **going for a song**. (= being sold very cheaply)*

3 to try to get or achieve something ● *As he was going for the ball, he tripped and fell.* ● *I've decided to go for that job in the sales department.* ● (informal) 'Do you think I should apply for that job?' 'Yeah, **go for it!'***

go for sb/sth
1 (never in continuous tenses) to like a particular type of thing or person ● *Chris tends to go for older women.* ● *I go for plain-coloured clothes rather than patterned ones.*
2 (never passive) if a statement about someone or something goes for someone or something else, it is also true about that other person or thing ● *Oh, do be quiet Sam! And that goes for you too, Emma!*

go for sb
1 *informal* to attack someone ● *As he opened the door one of the dogs went for him.*
2 to criticize someone strongly ● *I don't know what I've done to offend Pam but she really went for me in the meeting today.*

go forth   goes, going, went, gone

go forth *literary*
  to leave the place where you are in order to do something ● *The time had come to go forth to battle.*

go forward   goes, going, went, gone

go forward
1 if a planned activity goes forward, it begins to happen ● *Their marriage can now go forward.*
2 to win one stage of a competition and to compete in another stage ● (often + **to**) *The three regional winners will go forward to the semi-finals next week.*
3 *mainly British* when the clocks go forward, the time shown on clocks is changed to an hour later in the spring ● *Is this the weekend when the clocks go forward?*
4 if someone's name goes forward, it is suggested that that person should compete for an elected position or a job ● *The local party is selecting a candidate for the election and Daryl's name has gone forward.*

go forward with　goes, going, went, gone

go forward with sth (never passive)

to start to do something that you have planned to do ● *The publishing company is going forward with its plans to take over the magazine.*

go in　goes, going, went, gone

go in

1　to enter a place ● *I had a look in the window but I didn't go in.*

2　to enter a dangerous place in order to try to help ● *Fighting broke out in the region yesterday and troops have gone in to restore order.*

3　to go to the place where you work, or to go to hospital for treatment ● *If you don't feel well, don't go in.* ● *When does she go in for her eye operation?*

4　to go to the centre of the town or city that you live in ● *I usually go in on the bus, rather than have the car to worry about.*

5　if the sun or moon goes in, it becomes hidden behind a cloud ● *The sun went in just as I sat down on the terrace.*

6　*informal* if a fact or piece of information goes in, you understand it and remember it ● *You can tell her something ten times, but it still doesn't go in.*

7　if a ball goes in during a ball game [e.g. football, hockey, golf], a player kicks, throws, or hits the ball into the right area or hole and they score a point ● *His first shot narrowly missed the goal but his second shot went in.*

go in (sth)

to fit inside a container, an object, or a hole ● *Is this too big to go in the suitcase?* ● *I tried all the keys in the lock, but none of them would go in.*

go in for　goes, going, went, gone

go in for sth

1　to like a particular thing, or to do a particular activity because you enjoy it ● (often negative) *I don't really go in for party games.* ● *They go in for chess a lot in Russia.*

2　to choose a particular type of work as your job ● *Have you ever thought of going in for teaching?*

3　to compete in a competition, or to do an exam ● *Are you going in for the First Certificate this month?*

go into　goes, going, went, gone

go into swh

1　to enter a place ● *Mike went into the kitchen to start cooking the dinner.*

2　to go to the place where you work, or to go to hospital for treatment ● *I'm not going into the office today.* ● *He's going into hospital next week to have his tonsils out.*

3　to go to the centre of the town or city that you live in ● *I'm going into town this afternoon. Do you need anything?*

go into sth

1　(never passive) to start an activity, or start to be in a particular state or condition ● *He was in first place as he went into the final.* ● *A new model of the car has just gone into production.*

2　(never passive) to join a particular company, or to start to do a particular type of work ● *She's going into the family business when she graduates.* ● *You're not thinking of going into politics, are you?*

3　(never passive) to suddenly start to show a strong emotion ● *He went into a mad rage at the news.* ● *Kathy went into peals of laughter when I told her.*

4　(never passive) if an aircraft or a vehicle goes into a sudden uncontrolled movement [e.g. spin, nosedive], it starts to do that movement ● *The pilot suddenly lost control of the plane and it went into a nosedive.*

5　to describe, discuss, or examine something in a detailed way ● *She mentioned that she'd had an accident but she didn't go into it in any detail.* ● *The issues involved are highly complex and I don't want to go into them right now.*

6　(never passive) if a vehicle goes into something [e.g. tree, lamppost], it hits it ● *The truck swerved off the road and went into a lamppost.*

7　(never passive) if a number goes into a larger number, the second number can be divided by the first ● *Five goes into thirty six times.*

8　if an amount of time, money, or effort goes into a product or an activity, it is used or spent creating that product or doing that activity ● *Over $50 million has gone into designing the new aircraft.*

• *Clearly, a lot of effort has gone into pro-ducing this book.*

go in with   goes, going, went, gone

go in with sb

to become someone's business partner • *I've decided to go in with a friend of mine who's just started a software company.*

go off   goes, going, went, gone

go off

1 if a bomb or gun goes off, it explodes or fires • *Two people were seriously injured when a bomb went off in the main station.*

2 if a light or machine goes off, it stops working • *All the lights suddenly went off and the house was plunged into darkness.* • *I've set the heating to go off at 11 p.m.*

3 to leave a place and go somewhere else • (sometimes + **to**) *I'm going off to Vancouver next week to see my sister.* • (sometimes + to do sth) *Tim went off to make us both a cup of coffee.*

4 *British & Australian* if food or drink goes off, it is not good to eat or drink any more because it is too old • *These sausages smell rather strange – I think they've gone off.*

5 if a warning device [e.g. alarm] goes off, it suddenly makes a loud noise • *The alarm went off in the middle of the night.* • *My alarm clock didn't go off this morning.*

6 (always + *adv/prep*) *informal* to happen in a particular way • *I thought the per-formance went off rather well.* • *The dem-onstration went off peacefully with no ar-rests.*

7 *British & Australian* to become worse in quality • *I enjoyed the first hour or so of the film but I thought it went off a little towards the end.*

go off sb/sth *British & Australian*

to stop liking someone or something • *I used to eat a lot of fish but I've gone off it a bit recently.* • *I'm not going to go off you after one argument!*

go off with   goes, going, went, gone

go off with sth

informal to steal something, or to take something without asking • *Someone's gone off with my pen.*

go off with sb

to leave your husband, wife, or the per-son you are having a romantic relation-ship with in order to have a relationship with someone else • *Apparently, he's left his wife and gone off with his next-door neighbour.*

go on   goes, going, went, gone

go on

1 to continue to exist or happen • *The music festival goes on until August 31.* • (often + **for**) *The war had been going on for three years and there was still no sign of peace.* • (sometimes + doing sth) *Let's hope the situation will go on improving.* • *The path just seemed to **go on and on**.* (= it was very long) • *I know she's upset about losing her job, but, you know, **life must go on**.* (= she must try to continue her life in the usual way)

ongoing *adj* • *The study is part of an on-going research project about women and employment.* • *Smoking is an ongoing problem in the school.*

2 to continue doing something • (often + doing sth) *We can't go on living here for much longer.* • (sometimes + **with**) *He looked up at me as I came into the room and then went on with what he was doing.* • *Clive and I haven't spoken to each other for weeks – we can't go on like this.* (= we can't continue to behave in this way)

3 to happen • (often in continuous tenses) *Why isn't Mel here? What's going on?* • *I don't know what went on last night but they're not speaking to each other this morning.*

goings-on *n* (plural) *informal* strange or amusing events or activities • *There've been some strange goings-on in the house next door.*

4 to talk in an annoying way about some-thing for a long time • (often + **about**) *I've just spent an hour listening to Anne going on about all her problems.* • *Anita does go on, doesn't she!*

5 to continue moving or travelling in a par-ticular direction • *We must go on if we want to reach home before it gets dark.* • *Helen had a short rest while the rest of the group went on ahead of her.*

6 if a light or other electrical device goes on, it begins to work • *The heating goes on at about 7 o'clock.*

Go on!

1 *informal* something that you say to encourage someone to do something ● *'I don't really feel like going to this party.' 'Oh, go on, it'll be great fun!'*

2 *informal* something that you say in order to agree to do or allow someone something that you did not want to do or allow before ● *'Are you sure you wouldn't like another drink?' 'Oh, go on then, but just a small one.'* ● *'Can I go out to the cinema, Dad?' 'Oh, go on, but don't be late back.'*

3 *informal* something that you say to tell someone that you do not believe what they have just told you ● *'Apparently, she got so drunk that she sat on Colin's knee.' 'Go on, she didn't!'*

go on sth

to use a piece of information in order to help you discover or understand something ● *I'm not certain if Jack still lives at that address – I'm just going on what a friend told me.* ● *We don't have much to go on at the moment, but we are continuing our research.*

go on sth/doing sth (never passive) *British*

if an amount of money goes on something, it is spent on that thing or doing that thing ● *I should imagine most of his money goes on beer and cigarettes.*

be going on sth (always in continuous tenses) *informal*

to be almost a particular age ● *She's probably sixteen going on seventeen.*

go on to do sth

to achieve something important after having been successful in the past ● *After his surprise win in the first round he then amazed everyone by going on to win the championship.*

go on (sth)

to start talking again after stopping for a short time, or to continue what you are saying ● *I'm sorry, I interrupted you. Please go on.* ● (often + **with**) *He paused to light a cigarette and then went on with his story.* ● *'We used to be good friends,' Val went on, 'but we've completely lost touch now.'* ● (sometimes + to do sth) *He explained that there had been a gas leak but went on to reassure us that we would not be affected.*

---

go on at goes, going, went, gone

go on at sb

to criticize someone continuously ● (often + to do sth) *She'd been going on at him for ages to have his hair cut.* ● (often + **about**) *I wish you wouldn't go on at me about my clothes.*

go on to goes, going, went, gone

go on to swh

to go to a particular place after going somewhere else ● *We plan to spend a week in Sydney before going on to Melbourne.*

go on to sth

to start to do something after you have finished something else ● *Are you planning to go on to university after you finish school?* ● *Let's go on to the second point on today's agenda.*

go out goes, going, went, gone

go out

1 to leave a place in order to go somewhere else ● *You've got to go out on a Saturday night.* ● (often + **for**) *Do you fancy going out for a beer some time?* ● (often + to do sth) *He's just gone out to collect his mother from the station.*

2 to become old-fashioned, or to stop existing or being used ● *Baggy jeans went out years ago.* ● (often + **of**) *You spend all this money on a piece of clothing and then it goes out of fashion.*

3 if news or a message goes out, it is officially announced or sent to someone ● *A flood alert went out last night.* ● (often + **to**) *Dismissal notices have gone out to one in five of the company's employees.*

4 if a light goes out, it stops giving light ● *In the middle of dinner the lights suddenly went out.*

5 if something which is burning [e.g. fire] goes out, it stops burning ● *Have you got a light? My cigarette's gone out.* ● *Shall I put some more wood on the fire or let it go out?*

6 if a radio or television programme goes out, it is broadcast (= sent out) ● *The new series is scheduled to go out on Saturday evenings at 9 o'clock.*

7 if the sea or the tide (= movement of the sea in and out) goes out, it moves away from the beach ● *A few small boats were left stranded on the beach as the tide went out.*

8 *British* to lose when you are playing in a sports competition, so that you must stop playing in the competition ● (often + **to**) *Connors went out to Bjorg in the semi-finals.*

9 to refuse to work because you disagree with your boss about your pay or working conditions ● *It was rumoured that the miners were about to go out on strike.*

go out for　goes, going, went, gone

go out for sth *American*

to try to be chosen for a place on a sports team, or to take part in some other activity ● *He went out for football in his freshman year and made the team.* ● *Are you going out for chorus this year?*

go out of　goes, going, went, gone

go out of sb/sth

if a quality, especially a good quality, goes out of someone or something, they do not have it any more ● *All the life and energy has gone out of her since she lost her job.* ● *After 25 years together all the excitement had gone out of our marriage.*

go out to　goes, going, went, gone

go out to swh

to travel to another country, often to stay there for a long time ● *He's going out to Japan to start a teaching job.*

go out to sb

if your thoughts or sympathies go out to someone, you feel very sorry for them when they are in a difficult situation ● *Louisa's death was a tragedy, our deepest sympathies go out to her husband and three children.* ● *Our thoughts go out to all the people who cannot be with their families at this special time of year.* ● ***My heart goes out to*** (= I feel very sorry for) *anyone in that position.*

go out together/with　goes, going, went, gone

go out together

go out with sb

to have a romatic relationship with someone ● *They'd been going out together for years before they got married.* ● *How long have you been going out with him now?*

go over　goes, going, went, gone

go over sth

1 to talk or think about something in order to explain it or make sure that it is correct ● *We don't have much time so I'll quickly go over the main points of the document.* ● *I'd like to go over your essay with you when you've half an hour to spare.*

2 to think about something that has happened or something that was said ● *You can go over the same old things again and again in your head.* ● *In bed last night I kept going over what you'd said to me at lunch.*

3 to examine a building ● *The police had been over his apartment looking for drugs.* **going-over** n [singular] ● *He's going to give the car a good going-over.*

4 to clean something, especially a surface ● *I usually just go over the floor with a damp cloth.* **going-over** n [C] ● (usually singular) *The bedrooms shouldn't be too bad because I gave them a good going-over* (= cleaned them carefully) *last week.*

go over

1 (always + *adv/prep*) to visit someone who lives near you ● *I haven't seen Patrick for a while – I thought I might go over for an hour or so later on.*

2 to visit a different country, especially one that is across an area of sea ● *So when are you going over to Paris?*

3 (always + *adv/prep*) to be thought of in a particular way ● *I wonder how a play like this would go over in Britain?* ● *(American) Our new design is expected to go over big with our customers.*

go over to　goes, going, went, gone

go over to sth

1 to change to a new system or new way of doing things ● *The company that I work for has recently gone over to flexi-time.* ● *We used to have electric heating but we've recently gone over to gas.*

2 to leave one group or organization and join a group or organization that is competing against them ● *Some key party members have already gone over to the opposition.* ● *She has a few enemies ever since she went over to the other side.* (= joined an opposing group)

go round goes, going, went, gone

go round doing sth *mainly British*

if someone goes round doing something, they spend their time behaving badly or doing something that is unpleasant for other people • *You can't go round telling everyone he's a liar.* • *Someone's been going round writing on the walls.*

go round (swh)

1 *mainly British* if an illness goes round, a lot of people get it • *There's a nasty flu virus going round the office at the moment.* • *Have you had the throat infection that's been going round?*

2 *mainly British* if a story or piece of news goes round, a lot of people are talking about it • *The news went round the school that two pupils had been expelled.*

go round

1 (always + *adv/prep*) *mainly British* to visit someone at the place where they are living, staying or working • *I might go round after work and see how he's doing.*

2 *mainly British* to be enough for everyone in a group of people • *Do you think there'll be enough wine to go round?*

3 (always + *adv/prep*) to dress or behave in a particular way • *He usually goes round in jeans and a T-shirt.* • *She's been going round with a big smile on her face.*

go round together/with goes, going, went, gone

go round together *mainly British*

go round with sb *mainly British*

to spend a lot of time with someone • *As kids, they always went round together.* • *He's been going round with some really weird types recently.*

go through goes, going, went, gone

go through sth

1 to experience an unpleasant or difficult situation or event • *She went through absolute hell during her divorce.* • *My younger son is going through rather a difficult phase.*

2 to experience or complete each part of a process until the whole process is finished • *All new patients are required to go through a medical examination.*

3 to carefully examine the contents of something or a collection of things in order to find something • *Customs officers*

went through her suitcase looking for drugs. • *Someone's been going through my papers because they're all over my desk.*

4 to perform a particular series of movements • *Do you want me to go through those dance steps with you?*

5 to carefully read or discuss every part of something in order to make sure that it is correct or acceptable • *When I went through my bank statement, I found I'd been charged too much interest.* • *Why don't we go through it together and see if you've missed anything?*

6 to quickly use a lot of something, or to use something so much that it cannot be used any more • *New York's an expensive city and we went through over $400 while we were there.* • *I used to go through 40 cigarettes a day.* • *He's gone through three pairs of shoes this year already.*

go through sb/sth

to ask a person or organization to deal with something for you, or to give you permission to do something • *You have to go through the switchboard if you want to phone Mike at work.* • *All changes in the practices of the Church of England have to go through Parliament.* • *If you want to make a complaint, you'll have to go through the proper channels.* (= you must follow the official way of making a complaint)

go through

1 if a law, plan, or deal goes through, it is officially accepted or approved • *All handguns will be banned if this bill goes through.* • *The deal will only go through if 51% of shareholders agree to it.*

2 *mainly British* to win one part of a competition and to be allowed to compete in the next part • (often + **to**) *Wigan won their game and went through to the final.* • *If she plays like this tomorrow she should go through without any difficulty.*

go through with goes, going, went, gone

go through with sth

to do something unpleasant or difficult which you have planned or promised to do • *The union is determined to go through with the strike, despite the threat of job losses if it does.* • *She realized she couldn't go through with the abortion and so she decided to keep her baby.*

go to   goes, going, went, gone

go to sth

1 to start to do something, or to start to be in a particular state ● *The United Nations has intervened to try to stop the two countries from going to war.* ● *Does anyone want to finish the potatoes? I don't want them going to waste.*

2 to make a lot of effort to do something for someone ● *Please don't go to a lot of trouble to cook for us.* ● (often + to do sth) *He went to great pains to check every fact in the book.* ● *Her parents went to great expense* (= spent a lot of money) *to send her to boarding school.*

go to sb

if money or a prize goes to a person or an organization, it is given to them ● *All of the money raised will go to a local charity.* ● *The award for Best Actor went to Tom Hanks.*

go to it *American informal*

to start to do something in a very active way ● (often an order) *Go on, there's cleaning to be done. Go to it!* ● *I'd better go to it and make up for time lost.*

go together   goes, going, went, gone

go together

1 (never in continuous tenses) if two types of thing or people go together, they are usually found with each other ● *People tend to think that politics and corruption go together.* ● *Hollywood and glamour went together during the 1940s.*

2 (never in continuous tenses) if two pieces of clothing or two types of food go together, they look or taste good when you wear or eat them at the same time ● *Do you think that this blue shirt and these green trousers go together?* ● *Tomatoes and basil go together wonderfully.*

3 *informal* if two people go together, they are having a romantic relationship ● (usually in continuous tenses) *They had been going together since they were 17.*

go towards   goes, going, went, gone

go towards sth/doing sth (never passive)

if an amount of money goes towards something, it is used to pay part of the cost of that thing or activity ● *My parents gave me $1000 to go towards my college tuition.* ● *£3 billion of this year's budget will go towards cleaning up the environment.*

go under   goes, going, went, gone

go under

1 to sink below the surface of the water ● *The ship went under just minutes after the last passenger had been rescued.*

2 if a company or business goes under, it fails financially ● *The government has refused any financial assistance to stop the company from going under.* ● *Thousands of small businesses went under during the recession.*

go up   goes, going, went, gone

go up

1 if an amount, rate, or standard goes up, it rises ● *The government is trying to prevent interest rates from going up.* ● (often + by) *The price of fuel has gone up by five cents a gallon.* ● (sometimes + to) *The jobless total went up to two million this year.*

2 if a building or sign goes up, it is built or it is fixed into position ● *New hotels and apartments are going up all along the coast.* ● *Posters have gone up all over the city advertising the free concert.*

3 to suddenly explode ● *There's a gas leak and the whole building could go up at any moment.* ● *There was a loud explosion and the car went up in flames.* (= suddenly began to burn)

4 if a shout [e.g. cheer, cry, groan] goes up, a lot of people make that noise at the same time ● *Huge cheers went up when the result was announced.*

5 to move towards someone or something in order to speak to them or do something ● (often + to do sth) *Afterwards, several members of the audience went up to congratulate her.* ● (often + to) *He went up to the microphone and announced the winners of the competition.*

6 to travel north to a place, or to travel to the city near to where you live ● (usually + to) *I'm thinking of going up to Scotland for my holidays this year.* ● *'When are you going to London next?' 'I'm going up next Saturday to do some shopping.'*

7 *British formal* to begin studying at a university, especially Oxford or Cambridge

University • (often + **to**) *He spent a year travelling in India before going up to Cambridge.*

go up to   goes, going, went, gone

go up to sth

to reach as far as a particular place • *During the flood, the water went up to the top of the bridge.*

go with   goes, going, went, gone

go with sth

1 if one thing goes with another, they suit each other or they look or taste good together • *That red tie doesn't go with your suit – why don't you wear the green one?* • *The company needs a new logo to go with its updated image.* • *What sort of wine do you think goes best with Chinese food?*

2 if one problem, activity, or quality goes with another one, they often happen or exist together and the first thing is often caused by the second • *Petty crime often goes with drug addiction.* • *Are you aware of all the health problems that go with smoking?*

3 if food or drink goes with another type of food or drink, it is provided with it so that you can eat or drink them together • *Would you like a drink to go with your meal?*

go with sth/sb (never passive) *slightly informal*

to accept a plan or an idea, or to support the person whose ideas you agree with • *I think we should go with Sue's proposal.* • (sometimes + **on**) *I go with Amanda on this one – it would be much cheaper to update our existing system than buy a new one.*

go with sb (never passive) *informal*

to have a romantic relationship with someone, or to have sex with someone • *Pete was the first man I ever went with.* • *Did Tessa go with anyone else while you were married?*

go without   goes, going, went, gone

go without (sth)

to not have something which you usually have • *I don't like to go without sleep.* • *I can't afford to buy her a new coat this year, so she'll have to go without.*

goad on   goads, goading, goaded

goad on sb or **goad** sb **on**

to make someone do something, often something bad, by encouraging or annoying them until they do it • *He was goaded on by the taunts and jeers from the crowd.*

gobble down/up   gobbles, gobbling, gobbled

gobble down/up sth or **gobble** sth **down/up** *informal*

to eat food very quickly • *We've got half an hour for lunch so you don't need to gobble it down.* • *He was so hungry that he'd gobbled up his food before she'd even started hers.*

gobble up   gobbles, gobbling, gobbled

gobble up sth or **gobble** sth **up**

1 *informal* to use a lot of something, especially money • *My rent gobbles up two thirds of my monthly salary.*

2 *informal* if a large organization gobbles up a smaller organization, it takes control of the smaller organization • *Independent magazines are increasingly being gobbled up by large publishing groups.*

goof around   goofs, goofing, goofed

goof around *mainly American & Australian informal*

to spend your time doing unimportant or silly things • *We spent the afternoon goofing around by the pool.*

goof off   goofs, goofing, goofed

goof off *American informal*

to avoid work, or to spend time in a lazy, pleasant way • *They've goofed off and gone to a ballgame.*

goof-off n [C] *American informal* • *That guy is the biggest goof-off – he'll be lucky if he keeps his job.*

goof up   goofs, goofing, goofed

goof up (sth) or **goof** (sth) **up** *American & Australian informal*

to make a mistake, or to spoil something by making a mistake or doing it badly • *He goofed up the deal by insisting on too high a price.* • (often + **on**) *Sally always goofs up on school tests.*

gouge out   gouges, gouging, gouged

gouge out sth or **gouge** sth **out**

to remove something by digging or cutting it from the surrounding surface, often violently • *Several of the victims had had their eyes gouged out.* • *I spent the morning gouging the flesh out of pumpkins.*

grab at   grabs, grabbing, grabbed

grab at sb/sth

to quickly try to get hold of someone or something • *She grabbed at the balloon as the wind blew it away.* • *A hand grabbed at me from behind as I ran forward.*

grab at sth

to quickly use or accept an opportunity to do or have something • *If I were you I'd grab at the chance to work in the U.S.*

grapple with   grapples, grappling, grappled

grapple with sth

to try to deal with or understand a difficult problem or subject • *I've been grappling with the finer points of Spanish all morning.* • *This is one of many problems that the committee is having to grapple with.*

grasp at   grasps, grasping, grasped

grasp at sth

1 to try to quickly get hold of something • *I grasped at the pole to try and steady myself.*

2 to quickly use or accept an opportunity to do or have something, especially because you are unhappy with the present situation • *They grasp at every new idea put for-*

ward. • *When the doctor has told you you've a year to live, you **grasp at straws**.* (= you try anything even though you are not likely to succeed)

grass on/up   grasses, grassing, grassed

grass on sb *British & Australian*

grass up sb or **grass** sb **up** *British & Australian*

if someone grasses on someone else, they tell the police or someone in authority about something bad that that person has done • *He'd grassed on other members of the band.* • *You wouldn't grass him up, would you?*

grass over   grasses, grassing, grassed

grass over sth or **grass** sth **over**
mainly British & Australian

to plant grass over an area of land • *We could grass over the whole area and make it into a lawn.*

grass up

see **grass on/up**

grate on   grates, grating, grated

grate on sb/sth

if something, especially someone's voice or way of behaving, grates on you, it annoys you • *She has one of those nasal voices that really grates on me.* • *After a while the baby's crying began to **grate on his nerves**.*

gravitate to/towards   gravitates, gravitating, gravitated

gravitate to/towards sth/sb

to be attracted to something or someone, or to move in the direction of something or someone • *She does tend to gravitate towards older men.*

grind away   grinds, grinding, ground

grind away *slightly informal*

to work hard for long periods, especially doing things that are boring • *Many authors grind away for years to produce books that scarcely sell a copy.*

grind down   grinds, grinding, ground

grind down sb or **grind** sb **down**

to gradually cause someone to have no confidence or hope any more • *Ground down by years of abuse, she no longer had the will to leave him.* • *They had been ground down by years of harsh dictatorship.*

grind out   grinds, grinding, ground

grind out sth or **grind** sth **out**
to produce the same thing, especially a boring thing, again and again ● *The orchestra ground out the same tunes that they've been playing for twenty years.*

gronk out   gronks, gronking, gronked

gronk out *informal*
1 if someone gronks out, they become very tired or ill or they fall asleep ● *We watched a movie, then gronked out for the night.*
   gronked-out *adj* ● *I was totally gronked-out with the flu.*
2 if a machine or piece of equipment gronks out, it stops working ● *My washing machine just gronked out.*
   gronked-out *adj* ● *He makes a living repairing gronked-out televisions.*

grope for   gropes, groping, groped

grope for sth *informal*
to try hard to think of something [e.g. words, solution], often without success ● *I found myself groping for words to try to express how I felt.* ● *The government is still groping for a solution to the problem.*

gross out   grosses, grossing, grossed

gross out sb or **gross** sb **out** *American informal*
if something grosses you out, you think it is very unpleasant or disgusting ● *Your room really grosses me out – at least pick up the dirty clothes!*

ground in/on

be grounded in/on (always passive)
to be based on something ● *What I don't like about his films is that they're not grounded in reality.*

grow apart   grows, growing, grew, grown

grow apart
if people who are good friends grow apart, they gradually become less friendly, often because they do not have the same interests and opinions any more ● *We were good friends at school but we've grown apart over the years.* ● *The fact is that people change and sometimes this*

causes them to grow apart.

grow away from   grows, growing, grew, grown

grow away from sb
if you grow away from a good friend, you become less friendly with that person, often because you do not have the same interests and opinions any more ● *A lot of them are people I knew at school and I've just grown away from them.*

grow into   grows, growing, grew, grown

grow into sth
1 if children grow into clothes, they become big enough for the clothes to fit them ● *The trousers are a bit big now but he'll soon grow into them.*
2 if you grow into a new activity or situation, you gradually become more confident and better at dealing with it ● *It takes a while but you gradually grow into the job.* ● *At first motherhood felt a little odd but I've sort of grown into the role.*

grow on   grows, growing, grew, grown

grow on sb *informal*
if something or someone grows on you, you like them more and more, although you did not like them at first ● *I wasn't sure about that painting when you bought it, but it's growing on me.* ● *He didn't seem all that attractive at first but he's starting to grow on me.*

grow out of

grow out of   grows, growing, grew, grown

grow out of sth

1 if children grow out of clothes, they become too big to fit into the clothes • *If you buy something that only just fits her now she'll have grown out of it in a couple of months.*

2 to develop from something or because of something • *The idea for the film grew out of a dream that I'd had as a child.* • *The book grew out of lectures he first gave in Cambridge in 1943.*

3 if a child grows out of an interest, way of behaving, or illness, they stop having or doing it because they have become older • *She went through a phase of speaking in silly voices but thankfully grew out of it.* • *Hay fever is one of those illnesses you often grow out of as you get older.*

grow up   grows, growing, grew, grown

grow up

1 to gradually change from being a child to being an adult • *She grew up in New Zealand.* • *What do you want to be when you grow up?* • *Learning to take disappointments is all part of growing up.*

   grown-up n [C] a child's word for an adult • *Daddy, why are all the grown-ups laughing?*

   grown-up adj fully developed as an adult, or behaving or appearing like an adult • *The couple, married for 32 years, had four grown-up children.* • *I hadn't seen her for three years and she suddenly looked so grown-up.*

2 to begin to exist and then become bigger and more important • (usually + adv/prep) *The city grew up originally as a crossing point on the river.* • *A tremendous closeness had grown up between all those involved in the crisis.*

Grow up! informal

something that you say to an adult in order to tell them to stop behaving stupidly • *Oh grow up, for God's sake, it's really not that funny!*

grow up on   grows, growing, grew, grown

grow up on sth

if you grow up on a particular type of thing, it is that type of thing that you do or have when you are a child • *These comedy shows from the 70's are funny to us because that's what we grew up on.*

grub about/around   grubs, grubbing, grubbed

grub about/around informal

to search for something by digging or by looking under things • *She watched the dog grubbing around for something in the mud.* • *Grubbing about in my bag for the ticket, I found a half-eaten chocolate bar.*

grub out/up   grubs, grubbing, grubbed

grub out/up sth or grub sth out/up

to dig something out of the ground, often in order to eat it or to get rid of it • *She spent the morning in the garden grubbing up weeds.*

guard against   guards, guarding, guarded

guard against sth

to try to prevent something from happening, or to try to prevent something from harming you • *Emotional dependency is something you have to guard against in a relationship.* • *I have to guard against the temptation to socialize when I should be studying.*

guess at   guesses, guessing, guessed

guess at sth

to try to imagine something when you have little knowledge or little experience of it • (often + question word) *There are no photographs of him so we can only guess at what he looked like.* • *You can only guess at the difficulties a blind person might encounter.*

gum up   gums, gumming, gummed

gum up sth or gum sth up informal

1 to prevent something from working or opening in the usual way by covering it with a sticky substance • (usually passive) *When I woke up this morning my eyes were all gummed up.*

2 to prevent a system or process from working properly • *A few strikers have managed to gum up production at the factory.*

gun down   guns, gunning, gunned

gun down sb or gun sb down

to shoot someone and kill or seriously injure them, often when they cannot defend themselves ● *He was gunned down in front of his wife and child by two masked assassins.*

gun for

be gunning for sb (always in continuous tenses) *informal*

to try to harm someone or cause trouble for someone ● *He's been gunning for me ever since I got the promotion he wanted.*

gussy up   gussies, gussying, gussied

gussy up sb/sth or **gussy** sb/sth **up**
American informal

to put special clothes on someone, or to improve the appearance of something ● *He was gussied up in a bright, new shirt for the party.* ● *They bought a cheap house and gussied it up with all sorts of appliances.*

gutter out   gutters, guttering, guttered

gutter out

1 if a candle gutters out, the flame becomes weaker and it goes out ● *The candles were burnt down and guttering out.*

2 *American* to gradually become less active and then stop ● *His career as a writer guttered out.*

hack into hacks, hacking, hacked

hack into sth

to get into someone else's computer system without permission in order to look at information or do something illegal • *A student had managed to hack into some top-secret government data.*

hack off hacks, hacking, hacked

hack off sb or **hack** sb **off** *British informal*

to annoy someone • *It really hacks me off, the way he just expects me to do everything for him.*

hacked-off *adj British informal* • *What are you looking so hacked-off* (= annoyed) *about?*

hail from hails, hailed

hail from swh (never in continuous tenses) *formal*

to have been born in or to come from a particular place • *Where do you hail from with an accent like that?*

ham up hams, hamming, hammed

ham it up *informal*

to perform or behave in a false way, especially in a way that makes people laugh • *Lawrence plays the part of a film star, hamming it up hilariously in every scene.* • *They hammed it up for the TV cameras, gazing lovingly at each other throughout the interview.*

hammer away at hammers, hammering, hammered

hammer away at sth

to work very hard at something for a long period of time • *Poor Mark's been hammering away at his report all weekend.*

hammer away at sth/sb

to repeat something again and again • *She hammers away at the same point for three whole pages.* • *He kept hammering away at the witness.*

hammer in/into hammers, hammering, hammered

hammer in sth or **hammer** sth **in**

hammer sth **into** sb

to repeat something again and again in order to make someone understand it • *It's an important principle and it has to be hammered in.*

hammer out hammers, hammering, hammered

hammer out sth or **hammer** sth **out**

if two people hammer out something [e.g. agreement, deal], they talk or argue a lot about it until they agree with each other • *Our lawyers expect to hammer out an agreement with the industry within a few months.*

hand around/round hands, handing, handed

hand around/round sth or **hand** sth **around/round**

to offer something, especially food or drink, to each person in a group of people • *Could you hand these mints round with the coffee?*

hand back hands, handing, handed

hand back sth or **hand** sth **back**

1 to give something that you are holding back to the person who gave it to you • *'No, I've never seen him before', I said, handing the photograph back.*

2 to give something back to the person it first belonged to • *She had broken the rules of the contest and had to hand back the prize.*

hand (sb) **back**

if someone who is talking on the radio or television hands back, they stop talking so that the programme can go back to the person or place where it started • *'No more news at the scene of the accident, so I'll hand you back to the London studio.'*

hand down hands, handing, handed

hand down sth or **hand** sth **down**

1 to give or teach something to someone who will be alive after you have died • *These traditions have been handed down from generation to generation.* • *She had some jewellery which had been handed down from her grandmother.*

2 to announce an official decision, often a

decision about how someone should be punished [e.g. verdict, sentence] ● *The judge is expected to hand down a life sentence this week.*

3 to give something to someone who is below you ● *You stand there and I'll hand them down to you.*

hand in   hands, handing, handed

hand in sth or **hand** sth **in**

1 to give a piece of written work [e.g. essay] to a teacher ● *All essays must be handed in on time.*

2 to give something to someone in authority ● *Please hand your passport in at the office, they will be returned to you later.* ● *The terrorists must hand in their weapons if the peace process is to succeed.*

3 to tell your boss officially that you do not want to do your job any more ● *As soon as this project is over, I'll be **handing in my notice**.* ● *I feel like **handing in my resignation.***

hand on   hands, handing, handed

hand on sth or **hand** sth **on**

1 to give something that you do not want or have finished dealing with to someone else so that they can deal with it ● *The papers are signed by an official before being handed on to the next department.*

2 to give or teach something to someone who will be alive after you have died ● *These are dances which have been handed on from one generation to the next.*

hand out   hands, handing, handed

hand out sth or **hand** sth **out**

1 to give something to each person in a group of people ● *They stood on the street corner handing out leaflets.* ● *Some hospitals hand out free samples of baby milk.*

handout *n* [C] something, especially money, clothing, or food, that is given to poor people in order to help them ● *We don't expect handouts, only what is rightfully ours.*

handout *n* [C] a piece of paper that is given to people who go to a talk or class and which has information on it about the subject dealt with in the talk or class ● *If you can't attend the lecture, make sure someone gives you a copy of the handout.*

2 if you hand out something [e.g. advice, criticism, punishment], you give it to

someone, usually when they do not want it ● *Prisoners complained about the harsh treatment handed out to them.* ● *She's good at handing out criticism but she can't take it.*

hand over   hands, handing, handed

hand over sth or **hand** sth **over**

to give something to someone else ● *The driver was forced to hand over the car keys and was left standing on the roadside.*

hand over (sth/sb) or **hand** (sth/sb) **over**

to give someone else responsibility for or control of something or someone ● (often + **to**) *He announced his decision to resign and hand over to his junior.* ● *Dr Clarke will be handing over responsibility for her patients from next month.* ● *All prisoners of war will be handed over after the ceasefire.*

handover *n* [C] ● (usually singular) *I think we're all hoping for a peaceful handover.*

hand round

see **hand around/round**

hang about

Hang about! (always an order) *British & Australian informal*

something that you say to tell someone to stop doing or saying something ● *Hang about! You can't just take it without asking her.*

hang about/around/round   hangs, hanging, hung

hang about/around/round (swh) *informal*

to spend time somewhere, usually without doing very much ● *I spent quite a bit of my youth just hanging about on street corners.* ● *I had to hang around the station waiting for his train to arrive.*

hang about/around/round *British & Australian informal*

to be slow to do something ● *If you hang about any more, you'll miss your train.* ● *Once he's decided to do something, he doesn't hang around.*

hang about/around/round together hangs, hanging, hung

hang about/around/round together *informal*

if people hang around together, they spend time together • *There were ten of us who used to hang around together.*

hang about/around/round with hangs, hanging, hung

hang about/around/round with sb *informal*

to spend time with someone • *I've got no idea who she hangs around with these days.*

hang back hangs, hanging, hung

hang back

1 to be unwilling to do something • (often + **from**) *Hadley was hanging back from signing the agreement.*

2 to not move forwards, usually because you are shy or afraid • *The others rushed over but I hung back and watched to see what would happen.*

hang in hangs, hanging, hung

hang in there *British, American & Australian*

hang in *American*

informal to continue to try to do something even though it is very difficult • (usually an order) *Hang in there – things will get better.* • *Try to hang in a little longer.*

hang on hangs, hanging, hung

hang on

1 *informal* to wait, especially for a short time • *We're a bit busy at the moment – can you hang on a minute?* • *We asked for a quick decision but they've kept us hanging on for weeks.*

2 to hold something or someone tightly, usually in order to stop yourself from falling • *Hang on tight, it's going to be a bumpy ride!* • (often + **to**) *Hang on to the rail as you go down the ramp.*

3 to continue doing something even when it is difficult • *It's all about hanging on and trying not to let the situation get to you.* • (*informal*) *If you just **hang on in there** things will get better.*

Hang on! (always an order) *informal*

something that you say when you are

confused or surprised by something and you need to think • *Hang on, I thought Pete was in Paris at the moment.* • *Hang on a minute, who's Matt Collins and what's his connection with the company?*

hang sth **on** sb *American old-fashioned*

to blame someone for doing something, often unfairly • *He was afraid the police would hang the break-in on him.*

hang on to/onto hangs, hanging, hung

hang on to/onto sth/sb

1 to hold something or someone tightly, often in order to stop yourself from falling • *We hung onto the side of the boat while John swam to the bank.*

2 to keep something • *You should hang on to that painting, it might be worth a lot of money one day.* • *At least she's managed to hang onto her job.*

hang on/upon hangs, hanging, hung

hang on/upon sth

to depend on something • *The project's future hangs mainly on the outcome of a recent grant application.*

hang out hangs, hanging, hung

hang out (always + *adv/prep*) *informal*

to spend a lot of time in a particular place, or to spend a lot of time with someone • *It's where all the students hang out.* • (often + **with**) *Mainly he hangs out with kids his own age.*

hang-out n [C] *informal* • *The café was a favourite hang-out for artists.*

hang out sth or **hang** sth **out**

to hang things that you have washed on a piece of string outside so that they become dry • *What a pain! – It's raining and I've just hung the washing out.*

hang out for hangs, hanging, hung

hang out for sth *Australian informal*

to wait until you get what you are asking for and not accept anything less • *He's hanging out for his asking price of $250,000.* • *If I were you I'd hang out for a better deal.*

hang over hangs, hanging, hung

hang over sb/sth

if a problem or threat hangs over a person or situation, it exists and makes people worry about what is going to happen • *The prospect of famine hangs over many areas of the world.* • *I've got this job interview **hanging over my head***. (= making me feel worried)

hang round
see **hang about/around/round**

hang round together
see **hang about/around/round together**

hang round with
see **hang about/around/round with**

hang together   hangs, hanging, hung
hang together
1 if people hang together, they help each other and work together to achieve something • *We've all got to hang together if we're going to win this one.*
2 if the parts of something hang together, they are well organized or they seem to be true or correct • (often negative) *Somehow her story just doesn't quite hang together.* • *It was an interesting film but, for me, it didn't quite hang together as a whole.*

hang up   hangs, hanging, hung
hang up
to end a telephone conversation, often suddenly, by putting the part of the telephone that you speak into back into its usual position • *Can I talk to Joanne again before you hang up?* • (sometimes + **on**) *Why did you hang up on me?* (= end the conversation suddenly)

hang up sth or **hang** sth **up**
to hang something, especially clothes, on a hook • *She hung up her coat on a hook by the door.* • *Let me hang those things up for you.*

be hung up (always passive) *informal*
to be very worried about something and spend a lot of time thinking about it • (often + **about**) *Why are so many women so hung up about food?*
hang-up n [C] *informal* a feeling of embarrassment or fear about something, often when it is not necessary to feel that way • (often + **about**) *He's got a hang-up about his lack of education.*

hang up sb/sth or **hang** sb/sth **up** *American*
to delay someone or something

• *Computer problems have been hanging us up all week.* • *We were hung up in traffic for over an hour.*

hang it up *American informal*
to stop doing something • *If the job doesn't get better I'm going to hang it up.*

hang upon
see **hang on/upon**

hang with   hangs, hanging, hung
hang with sb *American slang*
to spend time with someone • *Who's that guy I saw you hanging with?*

hanker after/for   hankers, hankering, hankered
hanker after/for sth
to want something very much, especially something that you know you should not want • *Even after all these years I still hanker after a motorbike.*

happen along/by/past   happens, happening, happened
happen along/by/past (swh) *mainly American*
to go to a place without planning to go there • *I'd have drowned if he hadn't happened along and pulled me out of the river.* • *We happened by your house last night but you were out.*

happen on/upon   happens, happening, happened
happen on/upon sb/sth
to find something or meet someone without planning to • *I just happened on it in a second-hand bookshop and I had to have it.*

harden to
be hardened to sth (always passive)
to gradually become less upset by something unpleasant because it happens a lot • *After two years of war, these people have become hardened to the horrors of bombing.*

hare off   hares, haring, hared
hare off *British & Australian informal*
to run or leave a place very quickly • *He hared off down the road.*

hark at

Hark at you! *British humorous*
something that you say to someone who has criticized a person for something that they are guilty of themselves • *Hark at him, calling me lazy when he never even walks anywhere if he can drive!*

hark back to   harks, harking, harked

hark back to sth
1 if someone harks back to something in the past, they talk about it again and again, often in a way which annoys other people • (often in continuous tenses) *She's always harking back to when she was young and saying how much better it was then.*
2 (never in continuous tenses) if something harks back to something in the past, it is similar to it • *And yet his latest offering harks back to his earlier films.*

harp on   harps, harping, harped

harp on *informal*
to talk continually about something in a way that other people find boring or annoying • (usually + **about**) *He keeps harping on about declining standards in education.*

hash out   hashes, hashing, hashed

hash out sth or **hash** sth **out** *American informal*
to discuss something in order to make a decision or solve a problem • *Important management issues are hashed out in monthly meetings.*

hash over   hashes, hashing, hashed

hash over sth or **hash** sth **over** *mainly American informal*
to discuss something for a long time or many times • *This issue has been hashed over again and again, and we still have no solution.*

hash up   hashes, hashing, hashed

hash up sth or **hash** sth **up** *American & Australian informal*
to spoil something by doing it badly • *She hashed up her next shot and lost the game.*

haul before   hauls, hauling, hauled

haul sb **before** sb/sth *informal*
to force someone to go somewhere or see someone in order to be punished or to answer questions about their behaviour • (usually passive) *She was hauled before the courts and ordered to pay a fine.*

haul in   hauls, hauling, hauled

haul in sth or **haul** sth **in**
to pull something heavy towards you through water • *When the fishermen hauled in their nets they found them empty.*

haul in/into   hauls, hauling, hauled

haul in sb or **haul** sb **in**
haul sb **into** swh
if someone, especially the police, hauls someone in, they force that person to go somewhere to answer questions about their behaviour • (often + **for**) *The police hauled him in for questioning.*

haul off   hauls, hauling, hauled

haul off sb or **haul** sb **off**
to take someone somewhere by force • *The traders were investigated, found guilty, and hauled off to jail.*

haul up   hauls, hauling, hauled

haul up sb or **haul** sb **up** (always + *adv/prep*) *informal*
to force someone to go somewhere or see someone in order to be punished or to answer questions about their behaviour • (usually passive) *Ministers were hauled up in front of a special committee, in an attempt to discover what had gone wrong.* • (often + **before**) *His son was hauled up before the courts and given a three year sentence.*

have against   has, had

have sth **against** sb/sth (never in continuous tenses)
to dislike or disagree with someone or something for a particular reason • (usually negative) *I have nothing against her – I just don't find her very easy to talk to.*

have around/round   has, having, had

have sb **around/round** *mainly British & Australian*
if you have someone around, they come to your house for a social visit • *We're having some friends around on Friday night.* • *Shall we have your parents round for dinner next weekend?*

have away has, having, had

have it away *British slang*
    to have sex with someone • *She's been having it away with some bloke at work.*

have down as has, having, had

have sb **down as** sth (never in continuous tenses)
    to think that someone is a particular type of person, especially when they are not in fact like that • *For some reason I didn't have him down as the partying type.* • *I had you down as a sporty sort of person.*

have in has, having, had

have in sth or **have** sth **in** (never in continuous tenses)
    to keep a supply of something [e.g. food, drink] in your house • *We must make sure we have enough food in for the holiday weekend.* • *Do we have any wine in?*

have in sb or **have** sb **in**
1 to ask someone [e.g. builder, electrician, auditor] to come to your house or business to do some work • *We had the builders in last month to do the kitchen extension.*
2 *American & Australian* if you have someone in, they come to your house to visit you • *We had Anna and David in for a drink last night.*

have off has, having, had

have off sth or **have** sth **off**
    to spend time away from work • *I'm having a couple of weeks off in September.* • *Could I have Friday afternoon off?*

have it off *British & Australian slang*
    to have sex with someone • *They had it off in the back seat of his car.*

have on has, having, had

have on sth or **have** sth **on**
1 (never in continuous tenses; never passive) if you have clothes or shoes on, you are wearing them • *I was okay because I had my winter coat on.* • *I didn't have any clothes on at the time.*
2 (never in continuous tenses; never passive) if you have an electrical device [e.g. television, radio, iron] on, it is operating so that you can use it • *He has the TV on the whole time.*

have sth **on** (never in continuous tenses)
    to have an arrangement to do something • *Do we have anything on this Thursday night?* • *I've got a lot on* (= I am very busy) *at work this month.*

have sb **on** *British & Australian informal*
    to persuade someone that something is true when it is not, usually as a joke • (usually in continuous tenses) *That's not really his wife – you're having me on!*

have sth **on** you (never in continuous tenses)
    to be carrying something with you, usually in your pockets or in a bag • *Do you have any money on you?* • *Luckily, Alan had his keys on him, so we were able to get into the flat.*

have sth **on** sth/sb (never in continuous tenses; never passive) *informal*
    to have information about something or someone, usually connected with something bad or illegal that they have done • *Do you have anything on this organization?*

have out with has, having, had

have it out with sb *informal*
    to talk to someone about something that they have said or done that has made you angry in order to improve the situation • *Wouldn't it be better to have it out with him, rather than build up all this resentment?*

have over has, having, had

have sb **over**
    if you have someone over, they come to your house to visit you • *We had some friends over last night.*

have round

see **have around/round**

have up has, having, had

have sb **up** *British & Australian informal*
    to take someone to court for a trial • (usually passive) *He was had up for armed robbery.*

hawk about/around/round hawks, hawking, hawked

hawk about/around/round sth or **hawk** sth **about/around/round** (swh)
    to take things to several places in order to

try to sell them • *They hawked the paintings around the local shops and split the money they made between them.*

haze over   hazes, hazing, hazed

haze over

to become covered with a thin layer of water, smoke, or dust • *It was a beautiful clear morning but it's beginning to haze over now.*

head off   heads, heading, headed

head off sb/sth or **head** sb/sth **off**

to force someone or something to change the direction in which they are moving • *They had failed in their attempt to head off the incoming missiles.*

head off sth or **head** sth **off**

to prevent a difficult or unpleasant situation [e.g. strike, conflict] from happening • *The company is increasing wages in an attempt to head off a strike.*

head off/out   heads, heading, headed

head off *British, American & Australian*

head out *American*

to start a journey or leave a place • *As soon as the school year ended, the whole family headed off to the mountains.* • *We're heading out early – make sure you're here on time.*

head up   heads, heading, headed

head up sth or **head** sth **up**

to be in charge of an organization • *He heads up a multi-national corporation.*

heal over   heals, healing, healed

heal over

if a wound heals over, new skin grows over it • *Try to protect that cut until it heals over completely.*

heal up   heals, healing, healed

heal up

if a wound or injury heals up, the injured part repairs itself and it becomes healthy again • *I'm not supposed to use my arm till the bone has healed up completely.*

heap on/upon   heaps, heaping, heaped

heap sth **on/upon** sb/sth

to praise or criticize someone or something a lot • (usually passive) *Much praise has been heaped on this talented young musician.* • *He deals well with all the criticism heaped on him.*

heap up   heaps, heaping, heaped

heap up sth or **heap** sth **up**

to put a large amount of something in a pile • *Our coats and scarves were all heaped up in the corner.*

hear from   hears, hearing, heard

hear (sth) **from** sb

1 to receive news or information from someone, usually by letter or telephone • *Have you heard from Peter recently?* • *Please write soon. I look forward to hearing from you.* • *You'll be hearing from my lawyers.*

2 to be given someone's description of an event or their opinion about something, often officially • *The police would like to hear from anyone who might have witnessed the crime.* • *The enquiry heard from several former employees.*

hear of   hears, hearing, heard

have/had heard of sb/sth (always in perfect tenses)

to know a little about someone or something because you have read, seen, or been told something about them before • (often negative) *I'd never even heard of him.* • *It's a tiny country that most people have never heard of.* • *We'd heard of one another but had never met.*

not hear of sth or **not hear of** sb doing sth (always negative; never in continuous tenses)

not to allow something, or not to allow someone to do something • *She'd wanted to go to a late-night concert but her mother wouldn't hear of it.*

hear out   hears, hearing, heard

hear sb **out**

to listen to someone until they have said everything they want to say • *At least hear me out before making up your mind.*

heat up   heats, heated, heating

heat up sth or **heat** sth **up**

to make food hot so that it can be eaten • *I was just heating up some soup for lunch.*

heat up (sth) or **heat** (sth) **up**

to become warm or hot, or to make something warmer or hotter • *Electricity heats up the cables as it passes through them.*

heat up

if a situation in which people are arguing or competing with each other heats up, it becomes more serious or more violent • *United Nations forces were called in as the conflict heated up.* • *As growth in the business slows, competition is heating up.*

heave up   heaves, heaving, heaved

heave up (sth) or **heave** (sth) **up**
(never passive) *informal*
to vomit • *I found her heaving up in the toilets five minutes before the performance.*

hedge about/around/round with   hedges, hedging, hedged

hedge about/around/round sth **with** sth or **hedge** sth **about/around/round with** sth
if an agreement, statement, or situation is hedged about with things that control or limit it [e.g. conditions, restrictions], they make it more complicated or difficult • (usually passive) *The committee's conclusions were uncertain and hedged about with reservations.*

hedge against   hedges, hedging, hedged

hedge against sth
to do things which will prevent financial problems or changes from having a bad effect on you • *Investors are hedging against a possible stockmarket crash.* • *Raising taxes might be one way to hedge against economic recession.*

hedge in   hedges, hedging, hedged

hedge in sth/sb or **hedge** sth/sb **in**
to prevent someone from moving or acting freely, or to limit something, such as an agreement • (usually passive) *We have permission to sell, but it is hedged in with strict conditions.* • *I feel a bit hedged in at work.*

hedge round with
see **hedge about/around/round with**

heel over   heels, heeling, heeled

heel over
if a boat heels over, it leans very far to one side • *The ship heeled over in the strong winds.*

hell around   hells, helling, helled

hell around (swh) *American slang*
to behave in a noisy, wild way without considering the people around you • *It isn't much fun walking back home with young kids helling around the streets.*

help along   helps, helping, helped

help sth **along**
to encourage something to happen more quickly or easily • *Ice-cream sales are up 50 percent, helped along by the hot weather.*

help off with   helps, helping, helped

help sb **off with** sth
to help someone remove a piece of outer clothing [e.g. coat] • *Let me help you off with your coat.*

help on with   helps, helping, helped

help sb **on with** sth
to help someone to put on a piece of clothing • *Could you help the kids on with their coats?*

help out   helps, helping, helped

help out (sb) or **help** (sb) **out**
to help someone, especially by giving them money or by doing work for them • (often + **with**) *I thought I could help out with the childcare one or two afternoons a week.* • *If we were really short of money I'm sure my parents would help us out.*

help to   helps, helping, helped

help sb **to** sth
to put food on a plate or drink in a glass

and give it to someone • *Can I help you to some more dessert?*

hem in   hems, hemming, hemmed

hem in sb or **hem** sb **in**

to prevent someone from moving, or from doing what they want to do • (usually passive) *The crowd was hemmed in on all sides by the police.* • *We're hemmed in by so many regulations at work.*

hem in sth or **hem** sth **in**

to surround a place • (usually passive) *The city is hemmed in by mountains and the Adriatic Sea.*

hew to   hews, hewing, hewed

hew to sth *American*

to follow or be guided by particular rules, beliefs, or principles • *Our local newspaper has always hewed to the government line.* • *The present administration hews to an old, narrow view of business and competition.*

hide away   hides, hiding, hid, hidden

hide away sth or **hide** sth **away**

to put something in a secret place so that other people cannot find it • *I've got my own store of paper hidden away in a drawer.*

hide away

to go to a place where other people will not find you • *I thought I'd rent a cottage in the country and hide away for a while.*

hideaway *n* [C] a place where someone goes to be alone • *By the time the press arrived he'd already retreated to his country hideaway in Yorkshire.*

hide out   hides, hiding, hid, hidden

hide out

to go to a secret place in order to escape from someone who is looking for you • (usually + *adv/prep*) *The killer hid out in the mountains as the police launched a nationwide search.*

hideout *n* [C] a place where someone goes when they do not want to be found • *The guerillas operated from a secret hideout in the hills.*

hike up   hikes, hiking, hiked

hike up sth or **hike** sth **up**

1 *informal* to increase a price or rate suddenly and by a large amount • *The new* electricity company immediately hiked up their prices by 30%. • *The Chancellor hiked up interest rates from 7.5% to 11% in less than a year.*

2 *American* to lift something heavy with a strong, quick pull • *If we can hike the piano up over the step, we can get it into the house.*

3 *mainly American* to quickly lift up a piece of clothing you are wearing • *She hiked up her skirt and showed me the bruise.*

hinge on/upon   hinges, hingeing, hinged

hinge on/upon sth (never in continuous tenses)

1 if one thing hinges on another, the first thing depends on the second thing or is very influenced by it • *The prosecution's case hinged upon the evidence of a boy who had witnessed the murder.* • (sometimes + question word) *The future of the company hinges on whether sufficient sponsorship can be found.*

2 if a story or situation hinges on an idea or subject, it develops from that idea, or that is the most important subject in it • *The plot of the film hinges on a case of mistaken identity.* • *The whole election campaign hinged on the single issue of taxes.*

hint at   hints, hinting, hinted

hint at sth

to suggest something in an indirect way • *She hinted at the possibility that they might be taking on more staff in the near future.* • *What are you hinting at, Mark? Do you think I should lose weight?*

hire out   hires, hiring, hired

hire out sth or **hire** sth **out** *British & Australian*

to allow someone to use something for a short period of time after they have paid you money • *Several places now hire out bikes to tourists during the summer season.*

hire out sb or **hire** sb **out**

to arrange for someone to work for someone else • *She knew of a detective agency that also hired out security guards.* • (sometimes reflexive) *He's decided to go freelance and hire himself out as a computer programmer.*

hit back   hits, hitting, hit

hit back
to criticize or attack someone who has criticized or attacked you ● (often + **at**) *In tonight's speech, he is expected to hit back at critics who have attacked his handling of the crisis.*

hit for   hits, hitting, hit

hit sb **for** sth *American informal*
to ask someone for something, especially money ● *They're hitting all the parents for a contribution to the school appeal.*

hit off   hits, hitting, hit

hit it off *informal*
if two or more people hit it off, they like each other and become friendly immediately ● *Lynn and Elaine hit it off at once.* ● (sometimes + **with**) *I didn't really hit it off with his friends.*

hit on   hits, hitting, hit

hit on sb
1 *American slang* to talk to someone in a way that shows that you are sexually attracted to them ● *Some guy hit on me while I was standing at the bar.*
2 *American slang* to ask someone for something, especially money ● (often + **for**) *There were a couple of tramps outside the building hitting on people for money.*

hit on/upon   hits, hitting, hit

hit on/upon sth (never in continuous tenses)
to have a good idea, especially one that solves a problem ● *That's when I hit on the idea of giving the work to Caroline.*

hit out   hits, hitting, hit

hit out
1 to hit or try to hit someone suddenly with your hands in an uncontrolled way ● (often + **at**) *When she gets into a rage, she hits out at me and I can't control her.*
2 to criticize something or someone strongly, or to speak or behave in a way that hurts someone emotionally ● (usually + **at**) *The Medical Association yesterday hit out at government cuts in healthcare services.*

hit up   hits, hitting, hit

hit up *American & Australian informal*
to put illegal drugs [e.g. heroin] into your blood using a needle ● (often + **on**) *His parents are worried that he's been hitting up on heroin.* ● *They hang around the derelict buildings, hitting up.*

hit up sb or **hit** sb **up** *American slang*
to ask someone for something, especially money ● (often + **for**) *He hit me up for $20 but I didn't have it.* ● *Every time I see her she tries to hit me up.*

hit upon
see **hit on/upon**

hit with   hits, hitting, hit

hit sb **with** sth *informal*
to shock someone by telling them something which they did not expect, or by demanding a lot of money from them ● *That's when she hit us with the news that she was leaving.* ● *He spent twenty minutes checking over the car and then he hit me with a bill for £120!*

hive off   hives, hiving, hived

hive off sth or **hive** sth **off**
to separate one part of a company from the rest of the company, usually by selling it ● *The plan is to hive off individual companies once they are profitable.* ● *It is not known what will happen to the rest of the company once the shipyard has been hived off.*

hoard away   hoards, hoarding, hoarded

hoard away sth or **hoard** sth **away**
to put a supply of something in a safe place so that you can use it in the future ● *She had carefully hoarded away her wages each week.*

hoard up   hoards, hoarding, hoarded

hoard up sth or **hoard** sth **up**
to collect a large amount of something so that you can use it in the future ● *Many families are hoarding up tinned goods after warnings of possible food shortages.*

hoe in/into   hoes, hoeing, hoed

hoe in

hoe into sth
1 *Australian informal* to begin to do something in a determined way ● *She didn't want to waste any time so she hoed straight in.* ● *Jo loves school – you should see the way he hoes into his homework.*
2 *Australian informal* to start eating food,

especially in a hungry way • *The food's on the table, so hoe in everyone!* • *You should have seen the way those kids hoed into the cake.*

hoe into   hoes, hoeing, hoed

hoe into sb *Australian informal*

to criticize someone strongly • *Disappointed shareholders hoed into the management at the general meeting.*

hold against   holds, holding, held

hold sth **against** sb

to like or respect someone less because they have done something wrong or behaved badly • (often negative) *He certainly made a mistake, but I don't hold it against him.*

hold back   holds, holding, held

hold back sb/sth or **hold** sb/sth **back**

1 to prevent someone or something from moving forwards, or to force someone or something to remain in a place • *The police held back the crowds as the procession went past.* • *At the mouth of the reservoir, water is held back by a concrete dam.*

2 to prevent something from working effectively, or to prevent someone or something from making progress • *There are fears that higher interest rates in Europe could hold back the world economy.* • *I was reluctant to get a full-time job when I had young children, but nothing's holding me back now.*

hold back sth or **hold** sth **back**

1 to not give information to someone on purpose • (often + **from**) *Information is sometimes held back from patients when it is thought it might upset them.* • *The army are still holding back details of their casualties.*

2 to stop yourself from showing a feeling or emotion [e.g. tears] • *He cried bitterly, not even attempting to hold back the tears.* • *I held back my irritation and tried to speak slowly and calmly.*

3 to not give part of an amount of money to someone until an agreed time • *30% of the payment will be held back until completion of the work.*

hold (sb) **back**

if you hold back, or if something holds you back, you do not do or say something that you wanted to do or say because you

do not want to make a situation worse or because you are nervous • (often + **from** + doing sth) *I've always held back from interfering in their arguments.* • *She wanted to disagree with what they were saying but something held her back.*

hold down   holds, holding, held

hold down sb/sth or **hold** sb/sth **down**

to keep someone or something in a particular place or position and to stop them from moving • *He was struggling so much that it took four police officers to hold him down.* • *The roof consists of three layers of plastic sheeting, held down by bricks.*

hold down sth or **hold** sth **down**

1 to control the level of something [e.g. prices, costs, inflation] and to prevent it from increasing • *Car manufacturers are holding down their prices in an attempt to boost sales.* • *The government is trying to hold down public spending.*

2 *American informal* if you tell someone to hold down the noise, you want them to stop talking or to make less noise • (often an order) *Hold down the noise in there, I'm trying to get to sleep!* • *Can you hold it down a bit, kids.*

3 if you hold down a job, you keep it for a period of time • *Although he was an alcoholic, he managed to hold down a job for many years.*

4 to keep food in your stomach without vomiting, usually when you are ill • (usually negative) *She can't hold anything down at the moment.*

hold down sb or **hold** sb **down**

to limit the freedom of a group of people • *The satellite states were previously held down by a strong central government.*

hold forth   holds, holding, held

hold forth

to talk about a particular subject for a long time, often in a way that other people find boring • (often + **on**) *She held forth on a variety of subjects all through lunch.* • *I sat quietly in a corner while Greg held forth.*

hold off   holds, holding, held

hold off sb or **hold** sb **off**

to prevent someone from attacking you, or to prevent someone from defeating you in a competition • *A small group of guerrilla forces managed to hold off the government army.* • *The 100 metres champion successfully held off the other runners and finished in record time.*

hold off (sth/doing sth) (never passive)
to delay something or doing something • *Small investors would be wise to hold off and wait for the economy to improve.* • *You should probably hold off buying until house prices come down.* • *The board has decided to hold off its decision until next week.*

hold off
if bad weather [e.g. rain, snow] holds off, it does not start although it looks as if it might • *Luckily, the rain held off and we had the party outside as planned.*

hold on   holds, holding, held
hold on
1 to wait for a short time • (often an order) *Hold on – I'll be ready in a minute!* • *We held on another five minutes but in the end we had to leave without her.*
2 to hold something or someone firmly using your hands or arms • *I held on tight as the bike went over a bumpy bit of ground.* • (often + **to**) *Hold on to that rail, Polly.*
3 to continue doing something even though it is difficult • *The two teams were evenly matched, but Leeds held on and won the match 2-1.*

Hold on! (always an order)
something you say to show that you are surprised or confused about something and that you need to think about it for a short time • *Hold on, how much did you say you would pay him?* • *Hold on a minute – if Sarah's not coming, why are we booking a table for six?*

hold on to/onto   holds, holding, held
hold on to/onto sth/sb (never passive)
to hold something or someone firmly using your hands or arms • *The path's rather steep here so you'll need to hold on to the rail.* • *They held onto each other and kissed passionately.*

hold on to/onto sth (never passive)
1 to keep something that you have • *We sold most of the furniture but we held on to the kitchen table and chairs.* • *It was a*

tough fight but he managed to hold onto his title.
2 to continue to have a belief or principle • *Even the older members of the party have held onto their youthful idealism.*

hold out   holds, holding, held
hold out sth or **hold** sth **out**
to hold something in front of you • *She held out her glass for a refill.* • *He held out his hand for me to shake.*

hold out sth
if you hold out hope of something, you believe that it could happen • (often negative) *I don't hold out much hope that the situation will improve.*

hold out
1 if a supply of something [esp. food, money] holds out, you have enough for a particular period of time • *We're hoping that our money will hold out until the end of the month.* • *Our food supplies will only hold out for another two weeks.*
2 to continue to defend yourself against an enemy or attack • (often + **against**) *The city held out against the bombing for several months.* • *The longer the rebels hold out, the more publicity they'll receive for their cause.*

hold out against   holds, holding, held
hold out against sth
to refuse to accept something that you do not want • *Some teachers are still holding out against the recent changes in the education system.*

holdout n [C] *American* a person who refuses to accept an agreement • *The Senator was the only holdout against the new fuel tax.*

hold out for   holds, holding, held
hold out for sth
to wait until you get what you want and to refuse to accept anything less • *We could sell now or we could hold out for a better offer.* • *The strike continues as post office workers continue to hold out for better conditions.*

hold out on   holds, holding, held
hold out on sb
1 *informal* to not give information to someone when they have asked for it • *I'll be*

really angry if I find out you've been holding out on me.

2 *American informal* to not give someone the money you owe them ● *Liam was holding out on us when he could have paid.*

hold over holds, holding, held

hold over sth or **hold** sth **over**

1 to delay something and to arrange to do it at a later time ● (often passive) *The match had to be held over because of heavy rain.* ● (sometimes + **for**) *We held the meeting over for a week so that more people could attend.*

2 *American* to have more performances of a film or play than were originally planned because it is so successful ● (often passive) *The movie is so popular that it's being held over.* ● (sometimes + **for**) *They will hold the show over for another week.*

hold sth **over** sb

to use secret information which you have about someone in order to threaten them ● *His employers know that he is an illegal immigrant and they hold it over him.*

hold to holds, holding, held

hold sb **to** sth

1 to make someone do what they have agreed to do ● *They held me to the exact terms of the contract.* ● *'I'll give you that money next week.' 'I'll hold you to that.'*

2 to prevent your opponent in a sports competition from winning more points than you ● (usually passive) *In the second round, Davis was held to 2-2 by John Reeves.*

hold together holds, holding, held

hold (sth) **together**

if a country, organization, or group of people hold together, or if they are held together, they continue to exist as a group even though it is difficult ● *Successive rulers held the country together by force.* ● *The new coalition appears to be holding together.*

hold up holds, holding, held

hold up sth or **hold** sth **up**

to support something and to prevent it from falling down ● *The roof was held up by two steel posts.*

hold up sth/sb or **hold** sth/sb **up**

1 to delay something or someone ● *Lack of funding could hold up the building of the tunnel.* ● *The match was held up for ten minutes as police cleared fans off the pitch.* ● (used as *adj*) *I was late for the meeting because I got held up in the traffic.*
  hold-up n [C] ● *The new bypass is designed to reduce traffic hold-ups.*

2 to steal money from a building [esp. bank], a person, or a vehicle, by using violence or by threatening to use violence ● *Four armed men held up the bank and escaped with $4 million.* ● *He was held up at gunpoint by a gang of youths.*
  hold-up n [C] ● *There was a hold-up at our local post office last week.*

hold up

to remain in a healthy or successful state ● *If my knee holds up, I'll join you on that walk tomorrow.* ● *The leisure industry hasn't held up too well in the recent recession.*

hold up as holds, holding, held

hold sb/sth **up as** sth

to use someone or something as an example of something, especially something very good ● (usually passive) *Sweden is often held up as an example of a country with a high standard of living.* ● *The black community held him up as a role model for younger generations.*

hold with holds, held

not hold with sth (always negative, never in continuous tenses)

to approve of an idea or activity ● *She doesn't hold with people living together before they're married.*

hole up holes, holing, holes

hole up (always + *adv/prep*) *informal*

to hide in a place in order to escape from someone who is looking for you or in order to avoid an unpleasant situation ● *She holed up at a small hotel near the beach to avoid journalists.*

hollow out hollows, hollowing, hollowed

hollow out sth or **hollow** sth **out**

to make a space in something solid by removing the inside part of it ● *Hollow out the tomatoes and stuff them with the rice mixture.*

home in on   homes, homing, homed

home in on sth

1 to give a lot of attention to something and to examine or discuss it in detail • *The camera homes in on the woman's face and you can see that she's crying.* • *The new administration has already homed in on some issues badly in need of attention.*

2 if a weapon homes in on an object or place, it moves directly towards it • *Soldiers on the ground watched the missile home in on its target.*

honk up   honks, honking, honked

honk up (sth) or **honk** (sth) **up** (never passive) *British slang*
to vomit • *He came home drunk and honked up all over the floor.* • *She spent the night honking her guts up.* (= vomiting)

hook into   hooks, hooking, hooked

hook sb **into** sth/doing sth *American informal*
to persuade someone to do something that they do not want to do • *He's been hooked into working at the school fair.*

hook up   hooks, hooking, hooked

hook up sth/sb or **hook** sth/sb **up**
to connect a machine to a power supply or to another machine, or to connect a person to a piece of medical equipment • (often passive) *Is your computer hooked up yet?* • (often + **to**) *His wife lay on the couch, hooked up to a dialysis machine.*

hook-up n [C] a connection between two or more machines, places, or people using electronic equipment • *We hope to bring you a live report via our satellite hook-up.*

hook up

1 *American informal* to become friendly with someone and to spend time with them, or to meet someone for a particular purpose • *When did Laura and Bob hook up?* • (often + **with**) *Do you want to hook up with us when you come to Seattle?*

2 *informal* to agree to work with an organization or person • (often + **with**) *Many large British companies are hooking up with American partners.*

horn in   horns, horning, horned

horn in *American & Australian informal*
to try to become involved in a discussion or activity when you are not wanted • (often + **on**) *Anna's always horning in on our conversations!*

horse about/around   horses, horsing, horsed

horse about/around *informal*
to behave in a stupid or careless way • *He was horsing around in the kitchen and broke one of my favourite mugs.*

hose down   hoses, hosing, hosed

hose down sth or **hose** sth **down**
to clean something with water from a hose (= a long plastic pipe) • *Could you hose the car down?*

hot up   hots, hotting, hotted

hot up *mainly British & Australian informal*
if an event or situation hots up, it becomes more exciting and there is a lot more activity • *A few days before the election, the pace began to hot up.* • *Competition from European markets is just starting to hot up.*

hound out   hounds, hounding, hounded

hound out sb or **hound** sb **out**
to force someone to leave a job or place • (usually + **of**) *He claims he was hounded out of his job by a group of students who disapproved of his views.*

huddle up   huddles, huddling, huddled
huddle up

to move closer to other people, or to hold your arms and legs close to your body, usually because you are cold or frightened • *We huddled up together for warmth.* • *Terrified by the noise, she huddled up in a corner of the room.*

hunger after/for   hungers, hungering, hungered
hunger after/for sth *literary*

to want something very much • *I've never hungered after power.* • *She hungered for his touch.*

hunker down   hunkers, hunkering, hunkered
hunker down

1 *American* to sit close to the ground with your knees bent • *We hunkered down around the campfire toasting marshmallows.*

2 *American* to make yourself comfortable or to get ready so that you can stay in a place for a long time • *The audience hunkered down with their popcorn waiting for the movie to start.*

hunt down   hunts, hunting, hunted
hunt down sb or **hunt** sb **down**

to search for someone until you find them, usually in order to kill or punish them • *Chandler's mission was to hunt down and kill a German agent in Switzerland.*

hunt out   hunts, hunting, hunted
hunt out sth or **hunt** sth **out**

to find something after you have searched for it for a long time • *I'll try to hunt out those old photos for you.* • *We managed to hunt out the only Indian restaurant in Boston.*

hunt up   hunts, hunting, hunted
hunt up sth or **hunt** sth **up** (never passive)

to manage to find something that is difficult to find • *She tried to help him with his research by hunting up his references.*

hurry along   hurries, hurrying, hurried
hurry sb/sth **along**

to make someone do something more quickly, or to make something happen more quickly • *Can you hurry Fiona along a bit? She's spent over an hour in the bathroom.* • *We want to move into the house next month so John's trying to hurry the work along.*

Hurry along! (always an order) *old-fashioned*

something you say to tell someone, especially a child, to go somewhere quickly • *Hurry along now, Helen, or you'll be late for school!*

hurry on   hurries, hurrying, hurried
hurry on (sth)

to continue speaking quickly so that someone else cannot interrupt you • *He saw the shock on her face and hurried on.* • *'But that's all in the past now,' she hurried on.*

hurry up   hurries, hurrying, hurried
hurry up

to do something more quickly • (often an order) *Hurry up, Martin – we're already late!* • (sometimes + **with**) *Can you hurry up with that report? I need it by lunchtime.*

hurry-up *adj* (always before noun) *American informal* • *You'd better send him a hurry-up message – it's time he was here!*

hurry up sb/sth or **hurry** sb/sth **up**

to make someone do something more quickly, or to make something happen sooner • *Can you hurry the kids up because their dinner's getting cold.* • *I'd like to get this contract signed. Can't you hurry things up a bit?*

hush up   hushes, hushing, hushed
hush up sth or **hush** sth **up**

to stop the public from finding out about something bad that has happened • (usually passive) *There was some financial scandal involving one of the ministers but it was all hushed up.*

hush up *informal*

to stop talking and be quiet • *'Right, hush up and listen now, everybody,' said the teacher.*

hype up   hypes, hyping, hyped
hype up sth or **hype** sth **up**

informal to make something seem more

important than it really is • *The England match has been hyped up out of all proportion.*

hyped-up *adj informal* • *It's just one of those hyped-up action movies with a lot of special effects.*

ice down   ices, icing, iced

ice down sth or **ice** sth **down** *American informal*

to put ice on an injured part of the body ● *You'll need to ice your ankle down to reduce the swelling.*

ice over/up   ices, icing, iced

ice over/up

if something [e.g. lake, road, window] ices over, it becomes covered with a layer of ice ● *Winter is coming and the lakes will soon start icing over.* ● *The car's windows had iced up in the freezing cold.*

ice up   ices, icing, iced

ice up

if a machine or device [e.g. engine, lock] ices up, ice covers it and prevents it from moving or working properly ● *Our flight was delayed because the plane's engine had iced up.*

identify with   identifies, identifying, identified

identify with sb/sth

to feel that you are similar to someone, or to feel that you have similar feelings to someone and that you can understand them because of this ● *Many women feel unable to identify with the super-thin models in glossy magazines.* ● *Readers can easily identify with the hero's sense of frustration at the beginning of the novel.*

identify sb/sth **with** sth

to believe that someone or something is closely connected or involved with something ● (usually passive) *Saul Bellow and his novels are usually identified with Chicago.* ● *Many football fans are unfairly identified with violence.*

idle away   idles, idling, idled

idle away sth or **idle** sth **away**

to spend a period of time relaxing and doing very little ● (often + doing sth) *He was idling away the afternoon sitting on the grass and reading.*

imbue with   imbues, imbuing, imbued

imbue sb/sth **with** sth *formal*

to fill someone or something with a particular feeling, quality, or idea ● (usually passive) *Everyone in the department is imbued with a sense of pride in their work.* ● *His poetry is imbued with deep religious feeling.*

immerse in   immerses, immersing, immersed

immerse sb **in** sth

to involve someone completely in an activity or subject ● (usually passive) *He is totally immersed in family life and has no wish to work.* ● (sometimes reflexive) *At college, she immersed herself in the ideas of Mill, Locke and Voltaire.*

impact on/upon   impacts, impacting, impacted

impact on/upon sth/sb *slightly formal*

to have a noticeable effect on something or someone ● *Any problems with the computers will impact on our schedules.* ● *Falling export rates have impacted on the economy.*

impinge on/upon   impinges, impinging, impinged

impinge on/upon sth/sb *formal*

to have an effect on something or someone, usually in a way that limits it or that limits that person's freedom ● *The new regulations impinge upon our right to free* speech. • *The riots in the city impinged on the daily lives of ordinary people.*

impose on/upon   imposes, imposing, imposed

impose sth **on/upon** sb *formal*

to force a group of people to accept something, or to give someone a punishment [e.g. fine, ban] • *Strict financial controls were imposed on the BBC.* • *The settlers imposed their own culture and religion on the native people.* • *The court imposed a £10,000 fine on the newspaper for printing the story.*

impose on/upon sb

to expect someone to do something for you or to spend time with you when they do not want to or when it causes them problems • *I think Alex imposes on you too much – he's perfectly capable of doing his own cooking and washing.* • *Are you sure it's alright if I come and stay? I don't want to impose on you.*

impress on/upon   impresses, impressing, impressed

impress sth **on/upon** sb

to make someone understand the importance of something • *One of the things my father impressed on me was to stand up for myself.* • *The importance of patients' rights should be impressed upon all medical staff.*

improve on/upon   improves, improving, improved

improve on/upon sth

to do something in a better way or with better results than when it was done before • *He hopes to improve on his bronze medal and win the gold in the next Olympics.* • *I don't think the design of this bike can be improved upon.*

impute to   imputes, imputing, imputed

impute sth **to** sb/sth

1 *formal* to believe that someone or something has a particular characteristic, quality, or meaning • *She made the mistake of imputing stupidity to her critics.*

2 *formal* to say that someone is responsible for something that has happened, or to say that something is the cause of something else • *They imputed the error to the*

lawyer who was handling the case. • *Doctors have imputed people's breathing problems to high levels of pollution in the area.*

indulge in   indulges, indulging, indulged

indulge in sth

to allow yourself to do or have something that you enjoy • *I indulged in some duty-free shopping at the airport.* • *She was furious with her boss and indulged in fantasies of revenge.*

inform on   informs, informing, informed

inform on sb

to give information about someone who has done something wrong to a person in authority, especially the police • *The terrorist group warned that anyone who informed on them would be killed.*

infringe on/upon   infringes, infringing, infringed

infringe on/upon sth *formal*

if something infringes on someone's rights or freedom, it takes away some of their rights or it limits their freedom • *He warns that the new law will infringe upon the rights of minority groups.* • *They claim that censorship has infringed on freedom of expression.*

ink in   inks, inking, inked

ink in sth or **ink** sth **in**

to write or draw something in ink • *I inked in the date of their wedding in my diary.* • *She was busily inking in her pencil drawings of the house.*

ink in sth/sb or **ink** sth/sb **in** *informal*

to decide to do or have something, or to decide to use someone or something for a particular purpose • *I've inked in the party for June 23rd.* • *The team captain has inked in most of the players for Saturday's game.*

ink out   inks, inking, inked

ink out sth or **ink** sth **out**

to cover words with ink so they cannot be read • *Several lines of the document were inked out.*

inquire after   inquires, inquiring, inquired

inquire after sb/sth *formal*

to ask for information about someone or

something, especially about someone's health ● *He politely inquired after all her family.* ● *She phoned her sister to inquire after their mother's health.*

inquire into   inquires, inquiring, inquired

inquire into sth *formal*
to try to discover the facts about something, or to try to discover if something you want to do is possible ● *When the authorities inquired into his background, they found he had a criminal record.* ● *We're inquiring into the possibility of buying the apartment we're renting.*

insist on/upon   insists, insisting, insisted

insist on/upon sth/doing sth
to demand something and to make it clear that you will not accept anything else ● *She insisted on seeing her lawyer.* ● *He insists on the freshest produce for his restaurant.*

insure against   insures, insuring, insured

insure against sth
to do something in order to prevent something unpleasant from happening or from affecting you ● *You need to take precautions to insure against possible failure.* ● *They'd insured against rain by putting up a tent where their guests could shelter.*

interest in   interests, interested

interest sb **in** sth (never in continuous tenses)
to try to persuade someone that they want something ● *Can I interest you in a quick drink before lunch?* ● *The salesman tried to interest me in a new car.*

interfere with   interferes, interfering, interfered

interfere with sth
1 to prevent something from working effectively or from developing successfully ● *He tried not to let his personal worries interfere with his work.* ● *She decided not to have children because they would have interfered with her dancing career.*
2 if something interferes with radio messages or signals, it stops them from being heard or received clearly ● *His mobile phone produced radio emissions that interfered with other phones.*

interfere with sb *British & Australian*
to touch a child sexually, or to try to have sex with a child ● *He was sent to prison for interfering with young boys.*

invalid out   invalids, invaliding, invalided

invalid out sb or **invalid** sb **out** *mainly British & Australian*
to make someone leave a job, especially a military job, because they are ill or injured ● (usually passive) *He joined the army in 1994 and was invalided out the following year.* ● (often + **of**) *She was invalided out of the fire service because of injuries she'd received in a fire.*

inveigh against   inveighs, inveighing, inveighed

inveigh against sth/sb *formal*
to criticize something or someone strongly ● *He inveighed against the injustice of the legal system.*

invest in   invests, investing, invested

invest sth **in** sth
to use a lot of time or effort trying to achieve something or trying to make something successful ● *We've all invested a lot of time in this project.*

invest in sth *informal*
to buy something that you think is expensive and that you will use for a long time ● *I think it's time we invested in a new washing machine.* ● *Most schools in the region have now invested in computers with CD-ROMs.*

invest sth **in** sb *formal*
to officially give power or authority to someone ● (usually passive) *I am using the power invested in me to call an inquiry.*

invest with   invests, investing, invested

invest sb **with** sth *formal*
to officially give authority or power to someone ● (usually passive) *On 23rd April 1957 he was invested with a royal title.* ● *She has demanded that her commission be invested with the power of arrest.*

invest sth/sb **with** sth *formal*
to make something or someone seem to have a particular characteristic ● (usually

passive) *In his poems, everyday reality is invested with wonder and delight.*

invite along   invites, inviting, invited

invite along sb or **invite** sb **along**

to ask someone if they would like to go with you to an event or activity ● *We were all going out to the cinema so I invited Adrian along.* ● (often + **to**) *I usually get invited along to a few parties at the golf club.*

invite around/round   invites, inviting, invited

invite around/round sb or **invite** sb **around/round**

to ask someone to come to your home ● (often + **for**) *I've invited Clea and Alan round for dinner on Saturday.* ● (often + **to**) *We've been invited around to David's house tomorrow night.* ● (often + to do sth) *They invited us round to watch their wedding video.*

invite back   invites, inviting, invited

invite back sb or **invite** sb **back**

to ask someone to come to your home after you have been out somewhere together ● (often + **for**) *Jane invited us back for coffee after the show.* ● (often + **to**) *I was hoping to be invited back to Ian's place.*

invite out   invites, inviting, invited

invite out sb or **invite** sb **out**

to ask someone to go with you to a place, for example a restaurant or the cinema ● (often + **for**) *I've been invited out for dinner by an old friend of mine.* ● (often + **to**)

Harry invited her out to a club.

invite over   invites, inviting, invited

invite over sb or **invite** sb **over**

to ask someone to come to your home ● *We haven't invited John's parents over yet.* ● (often + **for**) *They invited us over for Christmas dinner.*

invite round

see **invite around/round**

iron out   irons, ironing, ironed

iron out sth or **iron** sth **out**

to find a way of solving small difficulties or problems, or to find a way of ending a disagreement ● *We're still trying to iron out some problems with our computer system.* ● *The committee's aim is to iron out the differences between the rival factions.*

issue forth   issues, issuing, issued

issue forth *literary*

to come out of a place ● *As she opened the lid of the desk, a great flood of papers issued forth.*

issue from   issues, issuing, issued

issue from swh *formal*

if something issues from a place, it comes out of that place ● *I noticed a cloud of smoke issuing from the chimney.* ● *A terrible scream issued from the room.*

itch for   itches, itching, itched

itch for sth *informal*

to want something very much ● *By four o'clock I was itching for the meeting to end.* ● *I could tell he was itching for a fight.*

jabber away   jabbers, jabbering, jabbered

jabber away *informal*
  to speak quickly in a way that is difficult to understand ● *They were all jabbering away in Italian and I couldn't understand a word.*

jack in   jacks, jacking, jacked

jack in sth or **jack** sth **in** *British informal*
  to stop doing something, especially a job ● *I've decided to jack in my job and go travelling.*

jack off   jacks, jacking, jacked

jack off *American taboo*
  if a man jacks off, he gives himself sexual pleasure by rubbing his penis ● *She found him jacking off over some porn magazines.*

jack up   jacks, jacking, jacked

jack up sth or **jack** sth **up**
1 to lift a heavy object [esp. car] off the ground by using a jack (= a piece of equipment for lifting) ● *We had to jack up the car to change the tyre.*
2 *informal* to increase a price or rate suddenly and by a large amount ● *Once tourists start visiting a place, the restaurant*

owners jack up their prices. ● *The Chancellor jacked up interest rates by 4.5%.*

jack up *Australian informal*
  to refuse to do something or go somewhere ● (often + **on**) *I asked Mary to clean my car but she jacked up on me and told me to do it myself.* ● *My aunt's invited us for dinner – I only hope the kids don't jack up.*

jam up

be jammed up (always passive)
1 if a place is jammed up, it is blocked because it is so full of people or vehicles ● *The entrance to the street was all jammed up with police cars.*
2 if part of a machine is jammed up, it does not move properly and it prevents the machine from working ● *The paper feeder in the printer is jammed up again.*

jar on   jars, jarring, jarred

jar on sb
  if something, especially a noise, jars on you, it annoys you ● *That squeaky voice of hers really jars on me.* ● *Their whispering and giggling had started to **jar on her nerves.***

jazz up   jazzes, jazzing, jazzed

jazz up sth or **jazz** sth **up** *informal*
  to make something more attractive or interesting ● *A nice colourful scarf will jazz that jacket up a bit.* ● (sometimes + **with**) *I bought a plain pizza and jazzed it up with a few olives and anchovies.*

jerk around   jerks, jerking, jerked

jerk around sb or **jerk** sb **around** *American slang*
  to treat someone badly, especially by causing them problems or by deceiving them ● *The public are tired of being jerked around by this government.*

jerk around *American slang*
  to behave in a stupid way ● *He used to jerk around a lot in class.*

jerk off   jerks, jerking, jerked

jerk off
1 *taboo* if a man jerks off, he gives himself sexual pleasure by rubbing his penis ● *He often jerks off in the bath.*
2 *American slang* to spend time doing stupid or unimportant things instead of

working • *They're always jerking off and they never get much done.*

jib at   jibs, jibbing, jibbed

jib at sth/doing sth *mainly British old-fashioned*

to be unwilling to do something or to continue with something • *She jibbed at the prospect of working extra hours.* • *Although the new tax is unpopular, the government has jibbed at abolishing it completely.*

jibe with   jibes, jibing, jibed

jibe with sth *American & Australian informal*

if one statement or opinion jibes with another, it is similar to it • *Her description of the man didn't jibe with what she told the police earlier.*

jockey into   jockeys, jockeying, jockeyed

jockey sth **into** sth *American*

to move a vehicle or large object until it is in the position where you want it • *They jockeyed the truck into a space in front of the store.*

jog along   jogs, jogging, jogged

jog along *British & Australian informal*

if something jogs along, it develops at a slow but regular speed • *My research is jogging along quite nicely.*

join in   joins, joining, joined

join in (sth)

to become involved in an activity with other people • *She watches the other kids playing but she never joins in.* • *You all seemed to be having such a good time that I thought I'd join in the fun.*

join up   joins, joining, joined

join up

1 to join the army, navy, or airforce • *He joined up as soon as he'd left school.*

2 if two organizations or groups of people join up, they start working together, or they meet in order to go somewhere or do something together • *The two design companies are planning to join up and create a new range of footwear.* • (often + **with**) *We joined up with another couple from the hotel and hired a boat for the day.*

join up (sth) or **join** (sth) **up**

if you join up two or more things, or if they join up, they become connected • *By 1980 the two motorways had been joined up.* • (often + **with**) *Ozone is formed when single oxygen atoms join up with two-atom oxygen molecules.*

join with   joins, joining, joined

join with sb *formal*

to say or do something with other people • (usually + **in** + doing sth) *I'm sure everyone will join with me in wishing Chris and Dawn a happy future together.* • *The police have joined with the drugs squad in trying to catch major drug traffickers.*

jolly along   jollies, jollying, jollied

jolly along sb or **jolly** sb **along** *informal*

to keep someone in a good mood so that they continue to work well or so that they will do something • *I think it's one of my jobs as a manager to jolly the staff along.* • *She didn't really want to go to the party so we jollied her along a bit.*

jot down   jots, jotting, jotted

jot down sth or **jot** sth **down**

to write something quickly on a piece of paper so that you remember it • *I always carry a notebook with me so that I can jot down any ideas.*

juice up   juices, juicing, juiced

juice up sth or **juice** sth **up**

1 *American informal* to make something more exciting or interesting, or to make the engine of a vehicle more powerful • *You can always juice up a story by adding some sexy dialogue.* • *He's going to juice up the car's engine and go racing in it.*

2 *American slang* to put petrol in a car • *I've gotta juice up the car for the trip.*

jumble up   jumbles, jumbling, jumbled

jumble up sth or **jumble** sth **up**

to mix things together in an untidy way • (usually passive) *His clothes were all jumbled up in the suitcase.*

jump at   jumps, jumping, jumped

jump at sth

to eagerly accept a chance to do or have something • *I jumped at the chance of a free trip to Paris.* • *I thought he'd jump at the offer, but he wasn't interested.*

jump in jumps, jumping, jumped

jump in
1 to interrupt someone when they are speaking • *I wish you'd stop jumping in and finishing my sentences all the time.*
2 to become involved in a situation very quickly • *The record company jumped in with a multi-million dollar deal.* • *It's just like me, isn't it, to **jump in with both feet!*** (= become involved in the situation without thinking about it)

jump on jumps, jumping, jumped

jump on sb *informal*
to criticize someone as soon as they have done something wrong or said something which you disagree with • *She jumps on*

me for the smallest mistake.

jump out at jumps, jumping, jumped

jump out at sb
if something jumps out at you, you notice it immediately • *As I scanned the books on the shelf, one of the titles jumped out at me.*

jump up jumps, jumping, jumped

jump up
to suddenly stand up from a sitting position • *She jumped up and ran to the door.*

jut out juts, jutting, jutted

jut out
to stick out from a surface or beyond the edge of something • (often + **from**) *Gibraltar juts out from the southern coast of Spain.* • (sometimes + **of**) *We could see the tips of icebergs jutting out of the water.*

keel over keels, keeling, keeled

keel over

1 if a boat keels over, it turns upside down in the water ● *Their boat keeled over in a storm.*

2 to fall over ● *He finished the bottle of whiskey, got up to leave and keeled over.*

keep after/at keeps, keeping, kept

keep after/at sb *American*

to try to make sure that someone does something by asking or telling them again and again to do it ● *She keeps after me to buy her a television for her bedroom but so far I've resisted.*

keep ahead keeps, keeping, kept

keep (sb) **ahead**

to continue to be more advanced and successful than other people, or to make sure that someone is more advanced or successful than other people ● (usually + **of**) *The selling power of the name alone will keep them ahead of their rivals.* ● *They'll have to work hard to keep ahead in the opinion polls.*

keep at keeps, keeping, kept

keep (sb) **at** sth

to continue working hard at something difficult or something which takes a long time, or to make someone continue to work hard ● *Learning a language is hard work – you have to keep at it.* ● *It was work that required intense concentration and he kept us at it all afternoon.*

keep away keeps, keeping, kept

keep away (sb/sth) or **keep** (sb/sth) **away**

to not go somewhere or near something, or to prevent someone or something from going somewhere or near something ● (usually + **from**) *There was a notice warning people to keep away from the edge of the cliff.* ● *The new campaign is aimed at keeping young people away from drugs.*

keep away sth or **keep** sth **away**

to prevent an illness from infecting you ● *He takes garlic tablets every morning to keep colds away.*

keep back keeps, keeping, kept

keep back (sb/sth) or **keep** (sb/sth) **back**

to not go near something, or to prevent someone or something from going past a particular place ● *Barriers were built to keep back the flood water.* ● *Once a firework is lit, you should keep well back.*

keep back sth or **keep** sth **back**

1 to not tell someone everything you know about a situation or an event that has happened ● *I suspected she was keeping something back.*

2 to not use the whole amount of something so that there is a small amount to use later ● *Fry the onions in two-thirds of the butter, keeping back a third for the sauce.*

3 *mainly British & Australian* to not pay someone all the money you owe them so that you can use part of the money for another purpose ● *Your employers will keep back 7% of your salary to pay into your pension.*

keep down keeps, keeping, kept

keep down sth or **keep** sth **down**

1 to stop the number, level, or size of something from increasing ● *The government are desperate to keep inflation down.* ● *I have to exercise to keep my weight down.* ● *I'm trying to keep numbers down* (= not invite many people) *as the room is quite small.*

2 if you keep the noise of something [e.g. music, voice] down, you stop it from becoming too loud ● (often an order) *Keep your voice down, would you?* ● *Could you keep the noise down? I'm trying to sleep.*

3 (never passive) to be able to eat or drink something without vomiting ● (usually negative) *For three days after the operation, she couldn't keep anything down.*

keep down sb or **keep** sb **down**

to prevent a person or group of people from having any power or freedom ● *It's all part of a conspiracy to keep women down.*

keep from   172

keep from   keeps, keeping, kept

keep sth **from** sb

to not tell someone about something • *Is there something you're keeping from me?* • *I tend to keep things like that from Trish because it just upsets her.*

keep sb **from** sth

to prevent someone from doing something, especially work, by spending time with them • *Well, I'd better go – I don't want to keep you from your studies.*

keep sb/sth **from** doing sth

to prevent someone from doing something, or to prevent something from happening • *I had to put my hand across her mouth to keep her from shouting.* • *A drop of oil in the pan will keep the spaghetti from sticking together.*

keep in   keeps, keeping, kept

keep sb **in**

1 to make a child stay at school or at home, especially as a punishment • *He was often kept in after school for bad behaviour.* • *The doctor told me to keep her in for a day or so until her temperature comes down.*

2 to make someone stay in hospital because they are not well enough to leave • *The doctors thought she was all right but they kept her in overnight for observation.*

keep in sth or **keep** sth **in**

to prevent yourself from showing your feelings or expressing your opinions • *I'd been feeling such intense frustration for so long and I just couldn't keep it in any more.*

keep in *British & Australian*

to stay near the side of a road • (usually an order) *Keep in! There's a car coming.*

keep in with   keeps, keeping, kept

keep in with sb *British & Australian*

to continue to be friendly with someone, especially because they can help you • *It's always good to keep in with ex-employers – you never know when you're going to need them.*

keep off   keeps, keeping, kept

keep (sb/sth) **off** sth

to not go onto an area, or to stop someone or something going onto an area • *Motorists have been advised to keep off*

the busy main roads. • *I wish she'd keep her dog off my lawn.*

keep off sth or **keep** sth **off** (sth/sb)

to stop something from touching or harming something or someone • *She wore a hat to keep the sun off.* • *He'd put a cloth over the plates to keep flies off the food.*

keep (sb) **off** sth

1 to not eat, drink or use something that can harm you, or to stop someone from eating etc. things that can harm them • *I'm keeping off cheese and fatty food generally.*

2 *mainly British & Australian* to not talk about a particular subject, or to stop someone from talking about a particular subject • *I tried to keep him off politics because once he starts, there's no stopping him.*

keep off *British*

if bad weather [e.g. rain, snow] keeps off, it does not start although it looks as if it might • *We're playing tennis this afternoon, if the rain keeps off.*

keep on   keeps, keeping, kept

keep on doing sth

to continue to do something, or to do something again and again • *She kept on asking me questions the whole time.* • *I keep on thinking I've seen him before somewhere.*

keep on sb or **keep** sb **on**

to continue to employ someone • *They got rid of most of the staff but kept one or two people on.*

keep on

1 *slightly informal* to talk in an annoying way about something for a long time • (usually + **about**) *He kept on about how much he was earning till we were all sick of hearing about it.*

2 to continue to go somewhere, usually going in the same direction • *We'll just keep on and hope that we see a signpost.*

keep on at   keeps, keeping, kept

keep on at sb (never in continuous tenses)

to talk to someone about something many times, usually because you want to complain about something they have done or not done • *I wish she wouldn't keep on at me, it's not my fault.* • (often + **about**) *He keeps on at me about the kind of clothes I wear.* • (sometimes + to do sth) *The boss keeps on at me to sort out the filing system.*

keep out   keeps, keeping, kept

keep out (sb/sth) or **keep** (sb/sth) **out**
to not go into a place, or to stop something from going into a place • *We hung up a thick curtain to keep out the draught.* • (often an order) *Unsafe building. Keep out.*

keep out of   keeps, keeping, kept

keep (sb/sth) **out of** sth
to not become involved in something, or to stop someone or something from becoming involved • *When they start arguing I just keep out of it.* • *That should keep you out of trouble for a while.* • *I tend to think that we should keep politics out of sport.*

keep to   keeps, keeping, kept

keep to sth
1 to stay in one particular area • *I was in a hurry so I thought I'd better keep to the main roads.*
2 if you keep to a particular subject, you only talk about that subject • *I was trying to keep to safe subjects, like the weather and the family.* • *I wish she'd keep to the point when she's telling you something.*
3 to do what you have promised or planned to do • *Once we've signed the contract, we have to keep to the terms of the agreement.* • *I'm finding it rather difficult keeping to my diet.* • *If we'd kept to our original plan we wouldn't be in this mess.*

keep sth **to** sth
if you keep something to a particular number or amount, you make sure that it does not become larger than that • *I'm trying to keep costs to a minimum.* • *If we keep the dinner party to six it'll be easier to cook for.*

keep sth **to** yourself (always reflexive)
to keep something secret and not tell anyone else about it • *She tends to keep her opinions to herself.* • *I told him I was leaving but asked him to keep it to himself.*

keep up   keeps, keeping, kept

keep up
1 to go at the same speed as someone or

something that is moving forward, so that you stay level with them • (often + **with**) *She was walking so fast that I couldn't keep up with her.*

2 to increase or to make progress at the same speed as something or someone else so that you stay at the same level as them • *Prices have been rising very fast and wages haven't kept up.* • *Because I'm new to the job, I have to work twice as hard as everyone else just to keep up.* • (often + **with**) *He finds it difficult to keep up with the rest of the class.*

3 to be able to understand or deal with something that is happening or changing very fast • *We've received so many orders for our products that our staff can't keep up.* (= can't deal with the orders fast enough) • (often + **with**) *My Italian friends talk so fast, I simply can't keep up with what they're saying.*

keep up (sth) or **keep** (sth) **up**
to continue without stopping or changing, or to continue something without allowing it to stop or change • *It's been wonderful weather this spring – let's hope it keeps up.* • *People are having difficulties keeping up the repayments on their loan.* • *We must keep up the pressure on the government to change this law.* • **Keep up the good work!** (= continue working hard and well)

keep up sth or **keep** sth **up**
1 to not allow something that is at a high level to fall to a lower level • *Make sure you eat properly – you've got to keep your strength up.* • *Demand for property in this area keeps the prices up.* • *Keep your spirits up.*
2 to practise a skill that you learned in the past so that you continue to be good at it • *I've tried to keep up my Spanish by going to evening classes.*
3 to keep a building in good condition, usually by providing money to repair it • *It takes a lot of money to keep up an old house.*

upkeep n [U] • *The tenant is responsible for the upkeep of the farm buildings.*

keep sb **up**
to make someone go to bed later than they usually do • *Anyway, I don't want to keep you up – you look tired.*

keep it up

to continue to do something, especially to work hard or to do good work • *I've been working flat out this morning and I can't keep it up much longer.* • (often an order) *You're doing very well, everybody, keep it up.*

key in/into   keys, keying, keyed

key in sth *or* **key** sth **in**

key sth **into** sth

to put information into a computer using a keyboard • *I've got all the data now but it still needs to be keyed in.* • *The forms are all filled in and the information is then keyed into the system.*

key to   keys, keying, keyed

key sth **to** sth *mainly American*

to arrange or plan something so that it is suitable for a particular person or situation • (usually passive) *Each player is paid a salary keyed to his position and ability.*

kick about/around   kicks, kicking, kicked

kick sb **about/around**

to treat someone badly, especially someone who is in a less powerful position than you • *I'm just sick of being kicked around by employers.*

kick about/around sth *or* **kick** sth **about/around** *informal*

to discuss one of several ideas with a group of people, informally • *Once a week the whole team gets together to kick around a few ideas.*

kick about/around (swh)

to spend time in a place, or travel around a place, without doing anything very important • *She kicked around the States for a year or so, then came home.*

be kicking about/around (swh) (always in continuous tenses) *informal*

if something is kicking around somewhere, it is in a particular place but nobody is using it or paying any attention to it • *I think there's an old lawnmower kicking about in the back of the shed somewhere.* • *We've probably got a copy of it kicking around the office somewhere.*

kick against

see **kick (out) against**

kick around with   kicks, kicking, kicked

kick around with sb *mainly Australian informal*

to spend a lot of time with someone • *They were just a couple of guys I used to kick around with.*

kick back   kicks, kicking, kicked

kick back *American informal*

to relax • *Tonight I just want to kick back and watch some baseball on TV.*

kick back sth *or* **kick** sth **back** *American*

to illegally pay part of an amount of money that you have obtained to the person who helped you to obtain it • (often + **to**) *She kicked back part of her fee to the agent who introduced the client to her.*

kickback n [C] *American* • *The customs officer was accused of receiving bribes and kickbacks.*

kick down   kicks, kicking, kicked

kick down sth *or* **kick** sth **down**

to kick a door or wall hard until it falls down • *He threatened to kick the door down if I didn't open it.*

kick down (sth) *or* **kick** (sth) **down** *American informal*

to make a vehicle go slower by changing the engine to a slower speed • *You'll have to kick down to a lower gear on the hill.*

kick in   kicks, kicking, kicked

kick in sth *or* **kick** sth **in**

to kick something vertical [esp. door, window] until it breaks into pieces • *They'd kicked the door in and got in that way.*

kick in (sth) *or* **kick** (sth) **in** *American & Australian informal*

to share the payment or work that is needed to buy or to do something between a group of people • *If everyone kicks in $15, we can rent the boat for a whole day.*

kick in *slightly informal*

to start to have an effect, or to start to happen • *We're still waiting for the air conditioning to kick in.* • *It takes about half an hour for the tablets to kick in.*

kick off   kicks, kicking, kicked

kick off

1 if a game of football or American football kicks off, it starts • *What time do they kick off?*

kickoff *n* [C] • (usually singular) *We got to the ground about five minutes before kickoff.* • *The kickoff's at 2.00.*

2 *American & Australian slang* to die • *He was in his 90's when he kicked off.*

3 *British informal* to start making trouble, usually shouting • *If you suggest increasing the workload, Steve is bound to kick off.*

kick off (sth) *informal*

to start • *The jazz festival kicks off next week.* • (often + **with**) *I'd like to kick off the discussion with a few statistics.*

kick off sth or **kick** sth **off**

to remove your shoes by shaking your feet • *She kicked off her shoes and danced barefoot.*

kick on   kicks, kicking, kicked

kick on *Australian informal*

to continue an activity • (usually + *adv/prep*) *The party was great – we kicked on until the early hours of Sunday morning.*

kick out   kicks, kicking, kicked

kick out sb or **kick** sb **out**

to force someone to leave a place or an organization • *If he's not paying his rent why don't you just kick him out?* • (often + **of**) *He was kicked out of college in the second year.*

kick out against   kicks, kicking, kicked

kick (out) against sth

to show that you are angry about something or opposed to something, especially something that you cannot control • *You've got to kick against the system – it's part of being a student.*

kick over   kicks, kicking, kicked

kick over sth or **kick** sth **over**

to make something fall on its side by kicking it • *He stood up and in his rage kicked the chair over.*

kick over *American informal*

if a vehicle's engine kicks over, it begins to work • *The engine isn't kicking over.*

kick sth **over** *Australian informal*

to complete a job or piece of work • *Don't worry about the washing-up, we'll kick that over in no time.*

kick up   kicks, kicking, kicked

kick up sth or **or kick** sth **up**

1 to cause dust or sand to rise into the air, often by walking or running • *The horses had kicked up a cloud of dust.*

2 *American informal* to increase prices, costs, or profits • *We're afraid the delays for building approval will kick our costs up.* • *The landlord has kicked up the rent.*

kick up *American informal*

if a part of your body or a machine kicks up, it causes you pain or trouble because it is not working as it should • *My knee is starting to kick up again after yesterday's run.*

kick up sth

to complain and show that you are angry about something • *She **kicked up a fuss** about the poor service in the hotel.* • *Some journalist had **kicked up a stink** about the police's treatment of them.*

kid around   kids, kidding, kidded

kid around *American informal*

to behave in a silly way • *Stop kidding around and listen to me!*

kill off   kills, killing, killed

kill off sth/sb or **kill** sth/sb **off**

to cause the death of a lot of living things, often so that there are none left alive • *She showed how the use of pesticides is killing off birds, fish and other wildlife.*

• *The bacteria in raw meat is killed off during cooking.*

kill off sth or **kill** sth **off**

1 to make it impossible for something to continue to exist • *The government had effectively killed off the local coal industry by allowing cheap imports.*

2 *mainly American & Australian informal* to finish an amount of food or drink • *There's hardly any wine left – let's kill off the bottle.*

kill off sb or **kill** sb **off**

if a writer kills off a character during a story, film etc., he or she makes that character die in the story • *Conan Doyle got bored with Sherlock Holmes and decided to kill him off.*

kip down   kips, kipping, kipped

kip down (always + *adv/prep*) *British & Australian informal*

to sleep in a place that is not your home or on something that is not a bed • (often + **on**) *Is it all right if we kip down on your floor tonight?*

kiss off   kisses, kissing, kissed

Kiss off! (always an order) *American slang* something you say to tell someone to go away • *Why don't you tell him to kiss off?*

kiss-off *n* [singular] *American slang* • *He's the latest of her admirers to get the kiss-off.* (= to be got rid of)

kiss off sb/sth or **kiss** sb/sth **off** *American informal*

to consider someone or something to be unimportant or not as good as other similar people or things • *A lot of doctors don't give alternative therapies a chance – they just kiss them off.* • (often + **as**) *In her report she kissed the researchers off as careless and inexperienced.*

kiss up to   kisses, kissing, kissed

kiss up to sb *American informal*

to try to make a person in a position of authority like you by saying and doing things that will please them • *I want the promotion but I'm not prepared to kiss up to Mike in order to get it.*

kit out   kits, kitting, kitted

kit out sb/sth or **kit** sb/sth **out**

to supply someone or something with the clothes or equipment that are needed for a particular purpose • (usually passive) *They were all kitted out in waterproof jackets and hiking boots.*

kneel down   kneels, kneeling, knelt or kneeled

kneel down

to lower your body by bending your knees until one or both of your knees are resting on the ground • *We knelt down to pray.*

be kneeling down (always in continuous tenses)

to be in a position in which one or both of your knees are resting on the ground • *She was kneeling down beside the bed.*

knit together   knits, knitting, knitted or knit

knit together (sth) or **knit** (sth) **together**

to join together firmly so that the things that are joined form a whole • *Broken bones take time to knit together.*

knock about/around   knocks, knocking, knocked

knock sb **about/around**

1 *informal* to hit or kick someone several times • *Her husband used to knock her about.*

2 *Australian informal* to make someone feel very tired • *A long-haul flight like that can really knock you around.*

knock about/around (swh) *informal*

to spend time relaxing and doing very little • *I spent most of my time knocking about the house.* • *So what have you been doing today – just knocking around?*

knock about/around sth or **knock** sth **about/around**

1 *British* if two or more people knock a ball about, they hit or kick it to each other for pleasure but not in a serious way • *We knocked a ball about on the beach for half an hour.*

knock-about *n* [C] *British informal* • *We usually have a knock-about before the match to warm up.*

2 *slightly informal* to discuss one of several ideas with a group of people, informally • *We knocked around a few ideas but we didn't make any firm decisions.*

knock about/around swh *informal*
to travel to different places ● *We spent the summer knocking about Europe.*

be knocking about/around (swh) (always in continuous tenses) *informal*
if something is knocking around somewhere, it is in a particular place but nobody is using it or paying any attention to it ● *Isn't there a spanner knocking about here somewhere?*

**knock about/around together/
   with** knocks, knocking, knocked

knock about/around together

knock about/around with sb
informal to spend a lot of time with someone, either because they are your friend or because you are having a romantic relationship with them ● *Dan's never really knocked around with girls his own age.* ● *We used to knock around together at college.*

knock back knocks, knocking, knocked

knock sb **back** (sth) *British & Australian informal*
to cost someone a large amount of money ● *Nice watch you've got there – I bet that knocked you back a bit!* ● *A car like that would knock you back a few thousand.*

knock sb **back** *British & Australian*
to shock or surprise someone ● *Jack's death really knocked her back.*

knock back sth or **knock** sth **back** *informal*
to quickly drink a lot of alcohol ● *She was knocking back the champagne at Marty's last night.* ● *I didn't realise how much Ted drinks – he can really knock it back.* (= he drinks a lot of alcohol)

knock back sb/sth or **knock** sb/sth **back** *Australian informal*
to refuse an offer that someone has made ● *He knocked back my offer of $2,000 for his car.* ● *I offered him $10,000 for it but he knocked me back.*

knock down knocks, knocking, knocked

knock down sb or **knock** sb **down**
to hit someone with a vehicle and injure or kill them ● (usually passive) *A nine-year-old boy was knocked down while crossing the road in Holbeach.* ● *She got knocked down by a motorbike.*

2 *mainly American & Australian* to cause someone to fall to the ground by pushing or hitting them ● *He punched his attacker in the face and knocked him down.*

knock down sth or **knock** sth **down**
to destroy and remove a building or part of a building [esp. wall] ● *They've knocked down the old cinema and built a supermarket in its place.* ● *We're going to knock down that old wall and build a new one.*

knock down sb/sth or **knock** sth/sb **down** (sth)
to reduce a price, or to persuade someone to reduce the price of something that they are selling ● *We got them to knock the price down because of the damage.* ● *Can't you manage to knock him down a few pounds?* ● (often + **to**) *She wanted £200 but I knocked her down to £175.*

knockdown *adj* (always before noun) *British & Australian* ● *It said in the window 'cookers and microwaves at knockdown prices'.*(= very cheap)

knock off knocks, knocking, knocked

knock off (sth) *informal*
to stop working, usually at the end of a day ● *I don't knock off until six.* ● *What time do you knock off work?* ● *It was getting late so I thought I might knock off for the day.*

Knock it off! (always an order) *informal*
something you say to tell someone to stop doing something which is annoying you ● *Oh knock it off Alex, I'm really not in the mood for your jokes.*

knock off sth or **knock** sth **off** (sth)
to take a particular amount away from something, especially a price ● *The manager knocked five pounds off because it was damaged.* ● *If you go on the motorway it knocks an hour off your journey.*

knock off sth or **knock** sth **off**
1 to produce something, especially a piece of work, quickly and easily ● *He could knock off a drawing in about five minutes.* ● *She can knock off* (= write) *a novel in a couple of weeks.*

2 *slang* if someone knocks something off, they steal it, or if someone knocks off a place, they steal something from that place ● (sometimes + **from**) *He's got a stack of computer equipment which he's*

knocked off from various shops. ● *The local supermarket was knocked off by a gang of youths.*

knock-off *adj British slang* ● *Are you sure you're not receiving knock-off* (= stolen) *goods?*

3 *American informal* to make a copy of a popular product, to sell at a cheaper price than the original one ● *They knock off any brand name clothing and sell it at a third of the price.*

knockoff *n* [C] *American informal* ● *Is that Armani you're wearing or is it a knockoff?* (= a cheap copy)

4 *Australian informal* to eat or drink something, often very quickly ● *I've seen Jim knock off a bottle of whisky in one night.*

knock off sb or **knock sb off**

1 *slang* to murder someone ● *She was causing too much trouble so he hired a hit man to knock her off.*

2 *American informal* to defeat someone in a competition ● *Albany knocked off Syracuse 14-7.*

3 *British & Australian slang* to have sex with someone ● *There wasn't much else to do besides drinking and knocking off each others wives.*

---

knock out knocks, knocking, knocked

knock out sb or **knock sb out**

1 to make someone become unconscious or to make someone fall asleep ● *Those sleeping tablets knocked me out for 15 hours.* ● *He was knocked out by a punch in the first round.*

knockout *adj* (always before noun) ● *The doctor gave me some knockout pills.* (= pills to make me sleep)

knockout *n* [C] in a boxing match, the act of hitting the other fighter so that they fall to the ground and are unable to get up again within ten seconds ● *He won the fight by a knockout in the tenth round.* ● (used as *adj*) *He finally delivered the knockout punch after one and a half rounds.*

2 to defeat a person or team in a competition so that they have to stop taking part in it ● *The former champions were knocked out during the third round.* ● (often + of) *Leeds United caused an upset by knocking Aston Villa out of the competition.*

knockout *n* [C] *British & Australian* a competition in which only the winners of each stage play in the next stage, until one person or team is the final winner ● *The tournament was a straight knockout.* ● (used as *adj*) *It's a knockout competition.*

knock sb out

1 *informal* to make someone feel a lot of admiration ● *I've never been so impressed by a performance – it really knocked me out.*

knockout *n* [C] *mainly American informal* someone who is extremely attractive ● *Your sister's a real knockout!*

2 *informal* to shock someone so much that they cannot think clearly and do not know what to say or do ● *I had some news today that really knocked me out.*

3 *American & Australian informal* to make someone very tired ● *All this walking has really knocked me out.* ● (often reflexive) *worked in the garden all day and really knocked myself out.*

knock out sth or **knock sth out**

1 to damage or destroy equipment so that it cannot be used any more, especially equipment used in wars ● *Enemy aircraft have knocked out 25 tanks.*

2 *informal* to produce something, especially a piece of work, quickly and without paying too much attention to details ● *I've knocked out a first draft of the report which we can amend at a later date.*

---

knock out of knocks, knocking, knocked

knock sth out of sb

if a quality is knocked out of someone they lose that quality because the situation they are in does not allow it to exist ● (usually passive) *Any creativity I had was soon knocked out of me at school.*

---

knock over knocks, knocking, knocked

knock over sb or **knock sb over**

to hit someone with a vehicle and injure or kill them ● (usually passive) *She was knocked over and killed on her way to school.* ● *He got knocked over by a taxi when he was running for the bus.*

knock over sth/sb or **knock sth/sb over**

to hit or push something or someone, especially accidentally, so that they fall to the ground or onto their side • *I knocked a bottle of wine over while I was reaching for a dish.* • *He banged into me so hard, he nearly knocked me over.*

knock over sth or knock sth over *American & Australian slang*

to steal from a place, attacking or threatening the people who work there • *The bank was knocked over by a gang armed with sawn-off shotguns.*

knock together   knocks, knocking, knocked

knock together sth or **knock** sth **together** *British & Australian*

if you knock two houses together, you remove the wall that joins them so that they become one building • *The two cottages had been knocked together and an extension added at the side.*

knock together/up   knocks, knocking, knocked

knock together/up sth or **knock** sth **together/up**

to make something, especially food, quickly and without much effort, using things that can easily be found • *I could knock up a quick snack if you wanted.*

knock up   knocks, knocking, knocked

knock sth **up** or **knock up** sth *British informal*

to make something quickly • *I'll just knock up a salad for our lunch.*

knock up sb or **knock** sb **up** *British informal*

to wake someone up by knocking on the door of their house or bedroom • *What time do you want me to knock you up?* • *The police came and knocked him up at three o'clock in the morning.*

knock up *British*

to practise before beginning a game of tennis, squash or badminton by hitting the ball etc. to each other • *The players have a couple of minutes to knock up before the match starts.*

knock-up *n* [C] *British* • *Shall we have a quick knock-up before the game?*

knock sb **up** *mainly American slang*

to make a woman pregnant • *So who knocked her up?* • *You don't want to get*

knocked up by some guy you don't even know.

know from   knows, knowing, knew, known

know sth **from** sth

to know the difference between something and something else, so that you can recognize either of them • (usually negative) *Call yourself a computer expert? You don't know a mouse from a modem!*

know of   knows, knowing, knew, known

know of sb/sth

to have heard of someone or something and to be able to give some information about them, but not very much • *I know of her but I've never actually met her.* • *The thing about this café is that it's hidden away in a back street so most people don't even know of its existence.* • *'Is anybody else going to the concert?' 'Not that I know of.'* (= I don't think so)

knuckle down   knuckles, knuckling, knuckled

knuckle down

to start to work or study hard, especially if you have not been working very hard before • *If we're going to meet this deadline, we're really going to have to knuckle down.* • (often + **to**) *I thought it was time to knuckle down to some serious studying.*

knuckle in on   knuckles, knuckling, knuckled

knuckle in on sth *Australian informal*

to force your way into a situation or activity even though your involvement is not wanted • *Don't tell Doug what's going on or he'll try to knuckle in on the deal.*

knuckle under   knuckles, knuckling, knuckled

knuckle under

to accept that someone has power over you and do what they tell you to do • *Did you really expect him to knuckle under and accept your terms without a fight?* • (often + **to**) *This government will not knuckle under to pressure from international organizations.*

kowtow to   kowtows, kowtowing,
  kowtowed

kowtow to sb
  to be too eager to please or obey someone
  in authority ● *He wants promotion but
  he's not prepared to kowtow to people
  higher up in the company to get it.*

labour/labor under labours, labouring, laboured/labors, laboring, labored

labour under sth *British & Australian*
labor under sth *American & Australian*

1 if you labour under something [e.g. delusion, illusion, misapprehension], you believe it even though it is not true • *He was labouring under the misapprehension that progress was being made.*
2 if you labour under something that is a problem for you, you try to continue with what you are doing even though the situation is very difficult • *The company is labouring under a debt of more than $4 million.*

lace up laces, lacing, laced

lace up sth *or* **lace** sth **up**

to fasten shoes, boots, or a piece of clothing by tying the laces (= long thin cords) • *She laced her boots up tightly.*
lace-up *adj* (always before noun) • *lace-up shoes*
lace-ups *n* (plural) *mainly British & Australian* shoes or boots which are fastened with laces • *I prefer lace-ups to slip-ons.*

lace with laces, lacing, laced

lace sth **with** sth

1 to secretly put alcohol or a drug into food or drink • (usually passive) *They gave him a glass of orange juice laced with vodka.*
2 to give a speech or piece of writing a particular quality • (usually passive) *His speech was laced with irony.* • *Her writing is laced with the melancholy that comes from an unhappy childhood.*

ladle out ladles, ladling, ladled

ladle out sth *or* **ladle** sth **out**

1 to serve food [e.g. soup, stew] with a very large spoon • *She was busy ladling out the soup into bowls.*

2 to give a large amount of something [esp. money] to someone, or to give advice to someone when it is not wanted • *The company has been ladling out cash to arts organizations.* • *I wish Gary would stop ladling out advice when he doesn't understand the situation.*

lag behind lags, lagging, lagged

lag behind (sb)

to move so slowly when you are with a group of people that you are behind them • *Louis was so exhausted that he soon began to lag behind.* • *She's now **lagging way behind** and has no hope of winning the race.*

lag behind (sb/sth)

to fail to achieve as much as someone or something else • *Sales figures confirmed that they still lagged behind their competitors.*

lam into lams, lamming, lammed

lam into sb/sth *informal*

to hit someone or something hard • *She swerved to avoid the bike and lammed into a lamppost.*

lam into sb *informal*

to criticize someone strongly or to shout at someone angrily • *The other driver started lamming into me for braking suddenly.*

land in lands, landing, landed

land (sb) **in** sth

to be in a difficult situation, or to cause someone to be in a difficult situation or an unpleasant place [e.g. prison] • (often + **with**) *Sam has landed in trouble with her teacher again.* • *His work for the group landed him in prison for six months.*

land sb **in it** *informal*

to cause trouble for someone by telling someone else that they have done something wrong • (often + **with**) *His letter of complaint really landed me in it with my boss.*

land up lands, landing, landed

land up (always + *adv/prep/adj*) *informal*

to finally be in a particular place, state, or situation, especially without having planned it • *Who knows where they may land up in the future.* • *If he carries on drinking like that, he'll land up penniless.*

land up doing sth *informal*
to finally do something, especially without having planned to • *I always land up talking to really boring people at Teri's parties.*

land with   lands, landing, landed

land sb **with** sth/sb *mainly British & Australian informal*
to make someone have to deal with something or someone that causes them problems • *Be careful that you don't get landed with a stolen car.* • *He invited his sister to stay and then landed me with her for a whole week.*

lap up   laps, lapping, lapped

lap up sth or **lap** sth **up**
1 to enjoy something [e.g. atmosphere, praise] very much • *We walked around the city and lapped up the atmosphere.* • *Everyone clapped and cheered and you could see that he was lapping it up.*
2 if an animal laps up a liquid, it drinks it by using a lot of quick movements of its tongue • *The cat was lapping up the last drops of milk from its bowl.*

lapse into   lapses, lapsing, lapsed

lapse into sth
1 to start speaking or behaving in a less active or less acceptable way • *Herbert lapsed into silence for a while.* • *When she's tired, she lapses into her regional dialect.*
2 to gradually get into a worse state or condition • *The country has lapsed into economic crisis.*

lard with

be larded with sth (always passive) *formal*
if speech or a piece of writing is larded with a particular type of language, it has too much of that type of language in it • *Her speech was larded with controversial statements.*

lark about/around   larks, larking, larked

lark about/around *informal*
to behave in a stupid or playful way • *We were all larking around, laughing and giggling.*

lash down   lashes, lashing, lashed

lash down
if rain lashes down, it falls very heavily • *For hours and hours the rain lashed down outside.*

lash down sth or **lash** sth **down**
to tie something firmly in a particular position, especially by using ropes • *She securely lashed down the sheet of plastic that was covering the wood.*

lash into   lashes, lashing, lashed

lash into sb/sth
to criticize someone or something very strongly • *Jennie lashed into him for arriving over an hour late.*

lash out   lashes, lashing, lashed

lash out
1 to criticize someone or something in an angry way • (often + **at**) *She lashed out at Pedro for wasting so much of their money.* • (sometimes + **against**) *In the article, Wilson lashed out against privatization.*
2 to suddenly try to hit someone • (often + **with**) *The horse lashed out with its hind leg.*

lash out (sth) *Australian informal*
to spend a lot of money on something which is very pleasant but which you do not need • (often + **on**) *I lashed out $100 on a new dress.* • *We usually live quite cheaply, but we do lash out occasionally.*

last out   lasts, lasting, lasting

last out (sth)
1 to manage to stay alive, or to manage to deal with a difficult situation for a particular period of time • *He was so ill that no one expected him to last out the night.* • *We can't last out much longer without fresh supplies.*
2 *British & Australian* if a supply of something lasts out, there is enough of it for a particular period of time • *If everyone continues to drink at this rate, the beer isn't going to last out the evening.*

latch on   latches, latching, latching

latch on *British & Australian informal*
to understand something • (often + **to**) *It took her a long time to latch on to the fact that they were teasing her.* • *Explain slowly and clearly or they'll never latch on.*

latch on to/onto   latches, latching, latched

latch on to/onto sb
to spend time with someone, especially when they do not want you with them ● *She had latched onto a group of Toby's friends at the party.*

latch on to/onto sth
1 to decide that something is so good or interesting that you start using it ● *They have latched on to tourism as a way of boosting the local economy.* ● *Fashion designers have latched onto the idea that women want to feel more feminine and so are now using light, pretty fabrics.*
2 to become connected to something ● *The bacterium latches onto the stomach wall.*

laugh off   laughs, laughing, laughed

laugh off sth or laugh sth off
to laugh about something unpleasant in order to make it seem less important or serious ● *Eleanor tried to laugh off their remarks but the sadness showed in her eyes.*

launch into   launches, launching, launched

launch into sth
to start doing or saying something [e.g. speech, story] in a very enthusiastic way ● *He launched into his usual long speech about industry and the environment.*

lavish on/upon   lavishes, lavishing, lavished

lavish sth on/upon sth/sb *slightly formal*
to give a large amount of something [e.g. money, attention] to something or someone ● *Huge sums of money were lavished on ambitious housing projects.* ● *She lavishes a lot of attention on her pet dog.*

lay about   lays, laying, laid

lay about sb *old-fashioned*
to attack someone ● (often + **with**) *She laid about him with her stick after she saw him breaking a window.*

lay aside   lays, laying, laid

lay aside sth or lay sth aside
1 to keep something [esp. money] so that you can use it in the future ● *She was try-ing to lay aside money to start her own business.*
2 to stop doing or thinking about something, especially for a short period of time ● *Ellen was so opposed to the plan that we decided to lay it aside for a while.* ● *He had laid aside all hopes of ever seeing them again.*

lay by   lays, laying, laid

lay by sth or lay sth by
to keep something [esp. money] so that you can use it in the future ● *I'm trying to lay by some money for my trip to the States.*

lay down   lays, laying, laid

lay down sth or lay sth down
1 to officially establish a rule, or to officially state the way in which something must be done ● *The military authorities have laid down strict rules which must be followed.* ● *New guidelines about dealing with patients have been laid down for doctors and nurses.* ● *She's always laying down the law about keeping the house tidy.* (= forcefully stating that she thinks it should be done)
2 if someone lays down their weapons, they stop fighting ● *The mediators have persuaded both sides to lay down their arms.*
3 to store wine for drinking in the future ● *Should I lay this claret down, or can I drink it now?*

lay in   lays, laying, laid

lay in sth or lay sth in
to store a supply of something because you will need it in the future ● *They were starting to lay in food for the winter.*

lay into   lays, laying, laid

lay into sb
to attack or criticize someone in an angry way ● *She laid into anyone who tried to oppose her ideas.* ● *He knocked me to the ground and began laying into me with his feet.*

lay off   lays, laying, laid

lay off sb or lay sb off
to stop employing someone because there is no work for them to do ● *Many factories have been forced to lay off workers over the summer period.* ● *Jo was laid off seven*

*weeks ago and she hasn't had any work
since then.*
lay-off *n* [C] • *The recession has led to a
large number of lay-offs in the building industry.*

lay off (sb) *informal*
to stop annoying, upsetting, or hurting
someone • (often an order) *Look, just lay
off will you! Can't you see how upset he is?*
• *I told them to lay off her but they just
wouldn't listen.*

lay off sth/doing sth
informal to stop using or doing something • *You'd better lay off alcohol while
you're pregnant.* • *The doctor advised him
to lay off eating and drinking excessively.*
lay-off *n* [C] *informal* a period of time in
which you stop doing something • *The
band has had a three-year lay-off between
albums.*

lay on   lays, laying, laid

lay on sth or **lay** sth **on**
to provide or supply something for a
group of people • (often + **for**) *On Sunday
lunchtimes he lays on sandwiches for all
the club members.* • *We'll be laying on a
coach from the airport to the hotel for all
the guests.*

lay it on *informal*
to describe something or complain about
something in a way that makes it seem
much more important or serious than it
really is • *Did you hear him telling Kim
all his problems? Apparently he really laid
it on.* • *She **laid it on a bit thick** when
she was telling Richard about her accident.*

lay sth **on** sb
1 *American & Australian slang* to tell someone something surprising that they did
not know before • *I hate to be the one to
lay this on you, but your girlfriend has
just left with another guy.*
2 to ask someone to do something that is
difficult or that they are unlikely to want
to do • *Sorry to lay this on you Kate, but
we need someone to work in Edinburgh
next week.*

lay out   lays, laying, laid

lay out sth or **lay** sth **out**
1 to put or arrange something on a flat surface • *He laid the map out on the floor.*

• *She was busy laying the food out on the
table.*
2 to design the way in which a house, city,
or garden is built or created • (usually
passive) *Most of Manhattan is laid out in
a grid pattern.* • *The gardens were laid
out in the early 19th century by Capability
Brown.*
layout *n* [C] the way in which the parts
of something are arranged • *The thieves
must have known the layout of the building.* • *Can you improve the layout of the
document?*
3 to describe or explain something very
clearly, especially in writing • *He wrote a
letter in which he laid out his financial
proposal.*
4 *informal* to spend money, especially a
large amount of money • (often + **on**)
*What's the point of laying out so much
money on a dress that you'll only wear
once?* • *He was not prepared to lay out a
penny unless she agreed to sign the contract.*

lay out sb or **lay** sb **out**
1 to prepare a dead person's body before it
is buried • *When she had been laid out in
her coffin, she looked no bigger than a
child.*
2 *informal* to hit someone so hard that they
fall down and become unconscious
• *Tyson was laid out for several minutes
by a blow to the head.*

lay over   lays, laying, laid

lay over
American to stay somewhere for a short
time before continuing a long journey,
especially a plane journey • (often + **in**)
*We have to lay over in Los Angeles on our
way to New Zealand.*
layover *n* [C] *American* • (often + **in**) *We
had layovers in New York and Rome.*

lay up   lays, laying, laid

be laid up (always passive) *informal*
to be so ill that you have to stay in bed
• (often + **with**) *She's been laid up with
flu for a week.*

lay up sth or **lay** sth **up**
if you lay up trouble or problems, you do
something that will cause you problems
in the future • *She's laying up trouble for
herself by ignoring her health problems.*

be laid up

lay up (sth) or **lay** (sth) **up**
to stop using a boat for a period of time
● *We had to lay up in Portsmouth for repairs.* ● *Fishermen are demanding compensation to lay up their boats.*

laze about/around   lazes, lazing, lazed

laze about/around
to relax and enjoy yourself by doing very little ● *They took a picnic and lazed around on the grass.* ● *You can't laze about for the rest of your life – you'll have to get a job some time!*

lead into   leads, leading, led

lead into sth
if a subject you are talking about or a discussion leads into another subject or discussion, it is the reason why you start talking about the second subject or start the second discussion ● *Tony's comment about air pollution led into a general discussion about the environment.*

lead off   leads, leading, led

lead off (sth) or **lead** (sth) **off**
to begin a discussion or meeting ● (often + **with**) *She led off the discussion with a progress report.* ● (sometimes + **by** + doing sth) *I'd like to lead off by thanking Ted Williams for all his support.*

   lead-off   *adj* (always before noun) *American* ● *The fire-department expert was the lead-off* (= first) *witness for the defence.*

lead off sth
if a room leads off another room, you enter it from the other room ● *The apart-*

ment consists of a living room, a kitchen, and a bedroom with a bathroom leading off it.

lead on   leads, leading, led

lead on sb or **lead** sb **on**
1 to make someone do something bad by encouraging them or annoying them until they do it ● *She didn't want to go through with it but the other girls led her on.*
2 to make someone believe something that is not true ● *She led him on and made him believe she loved him when she was only interested in his money.*

lead on to/onto   leads, leading, led

lead (sb) **on to/onto** sth (never passive)
mainly British & Australian
if one action or event leads on to something, it causes that thing to happen or exist, or it causes or encourages someone to do that thing ● *It is hoped that these discussions will lead on to an agreement between the two countries.* ● *The success of the charity dinner led him onto further fund-raising activities.*

lead to   leads, leading, led

lead to sth (never passive)
if an action or event leads to something, it causes that thing to happen or exist ● *The disagreement between the union and management could lead to a strike.* ● *Reducing speed limits should lead to fewer road deaths.*

lead up to   leads, leading, led

lead up to sth
1 if a period of time or a series of events leads up to an event or activity, it happens until that event or activity begins ● *Police are trying to discover where the boy had been in the hours which led up to his disappearance.* ● *The pilot had no recollection of the events leading up to the crash.*

   lead-up   *n* [C] *British & Australian* the period of time before an event or activity ● (usually + **to**) *Both parties are campaigning hard in the lead-up to the election.*

2 to prepare to talk about something or ask a question about something by mentioning the subject you want to talk about ● *I*

could tell he was leading up to a question about Marie by his constant references to divorce.

leaf through   leafs, leafing, leafed

leaf through sth

to turn the pages of a book or magazine and look at them quickly, without reading them in detail • *The waiting room was full of people leafing through magazines.*

leak out   leaks, leaking, leaked

leak out

if secret information leaks out, people who should not know this information find out about it • *Details of the controversial report had leaked out.*

lean on   leans, leaning, leant or leaned

lean on sb *informal*

to try to make someone do what you want by threatening or persuading them • *He leant on me so hard that I agreed to do it.* • (often + to do sth) *The US government was leaning on them to release their prisoners.*

lean on/upon   leans, leaning, leant or leaned

lean on/upon sb/sth

to use someone or something to help you, especially in a difficult situation • *It's good to have people you can lean on in a crisis.* • *You'll have to lean on your previous teaching experience to do this job.*

lean towards/toward   leans, leaning, leant or leaned

lean towards sth/doing sth *British, American & Australian*

lean toward sth/doing sth *American*

to support or begin to support a particular set of ideas or a particular political party • *The country was leaning increasingly towards Communism.* • *I'm leaning towards supporting the Democrats this time.*

lean upon

see **lean on/upon**

leap at   leaps, leaping, leapt or leaped

leap at sth

to eagerly accept the chance to do or have something • *She leapt at the opportunity*

to live in Japan.

leap on/upon   leaps, leaping, leapt or leaped

leap on/upon sth

to immediately show a lot of interest in something, especially because you think it will give you an advantage • *The clothes manufacturers who leapt on this trend made a lot of money.* • *Landlords have leapt on the clause in the contract which prevents them from having to pay.*

leap out at   leaps, leaping, leapt or leaped

leap out at sb

if something leaps out at you, you notice it immediately • *As I turned the page, his photo leapt out at me.*

leap upon

see **leap on/upon**

leave aside   leaves, leaving, left

leave aside sth or **leave** sth **aside**

to not discuss or consider a particular subject so that you can discuss a different subject • *Let's leave aside the matter of who's to blame for the moment.* • *Leaving aside the question of cost, how many people do we need on the job?*

leave behind   leaves, leaving, left

leave behind sth/sb or **leave** sth/sb **behind**

to leave a place without taking something or someone with you, either because you have forgotten them or because you cannot take them with you • *We left in a hurry and I must have left my keys behind.* • *He was forced to flee the country, leaving behind his wife and son.*

leave behind sth or **leave** sth **behind** (sb)

1 if you leave behind an activity or situation, you do not do it or experience it any more • *He used to drink heavily but he's left that behind him now.* • *She had built up quite a large social circle and was sorry to be leaving it all behind.*

2 to cause a situation to exist after you have left a place • *The army left, leaving a trail of destruction behind them.*

leave behind sb or **leave** sb **behind**

to make progress much faster than someone else • *Japan is leaving the rest of the world behind in technological developments.*

leave off   leaves, leaving, left

leave off (sth/doing sth)

to stop, or to stop doing something • *This film begins where the first one leaves off.* • *I've decided to leave off eating meat for a while.*

Leave off! (always an order) *British & Australian informal*

something you say to tell someone to stop doing something which is annoying you • *Leave off, would you! You've been nagging at me all day.*

leave out   leaves, leaving, left

leave out sb/sth *or* **leave** sb/sth **out**

to not include someone or something • *I'd rather invite everyone in the office than leave someone out.* • *I've left out the nuts in this recipe because Delia's allergic to them.*

left out *adj* (always after verb) if someone feels left out, they are unhappy because they have not been included in an activity or conversation • *The older children went off to play upstairs and she felt left out.*

Leave it out! (always an order)

1 *British slang* something you say to tell someone to stop doing something • *Leave it out, you two, somebody's going to get hurt!*

2 *British slang* something you say to someone when you do not believe what they have just said • *Leave it out – she's not fifty-two!*

leave over

be left over (always passive)

1 if an amount of money or food is left over, it remains when the rest has been used or eaten • *There was £10 left over after we'd bought the present so we bought some flowers as well.* • *We had loads of food left over from the party.*

leftovers *n* (plural) food that was prepared for a meal but not eaten • *I was eating leftovers from the party for days afterwards.*

leftover *adj* (always before noun) • *I made myself a sandwich with some of last*

night's leftover chicken. • *If you have any leftover foreign currency* (= money that you have not spent), *you can exchange it when you get back home.*

2 to exist from an earlier time • *Sometimes there are snowbanks along the side of the roads, left over from winter.*

leftover *n* [C] • (usually + **from**) *The powers of the monarchy are a leftover from a bygone age.* • *He looks like a leftover from the 1960's with his long hair and open sandals.*

leave to   leaves, leaving, left

leave sb **to** sth *informal*

to go away from someone so that they do something by themselves or so they can continue what they are doing • *She told me what I had to do and then left me to it.* • *I just want to tell you some news and then I'll leave you to your meal.*

lend out   lends, lending, lent

lend out sth *or* **lend** sth **out**

if an organization lends out something, it allows people to borrow that thing • *The bank lent out over $700 million last year.* • *The library has a very rare collection of books which can't be lent out.*

lend to   lends, lending, lent

lend itself **to** sth (always reflexive) *formal*

to be suitable for a particular purpose, or to be likely to be used in a particular way • *The novel's complex, imaginative style does not lend itself to translation.* • *The current regulations are not strict enough and therefore lend themselves to abuse.*

let down   lets, letting, let

let down sb *or* **let** sb **down**

1 to disappoint someone by failing to do what you agreed to do or what you were expected to do • *I promised to go to the party with Jane, and I can't let her down.* • *Many farmers feel the government has let them down badly in the negotiations.* • *(British & Australian) All her family had gone to university and she felt she would **let the side down** (= disappoint her family) if she didn't go too.*

letdown *n* [C] something which is not as good as you thought it would be • (usually singular) *The holiday was a real letdown – the hotel was dirty and it* *rained all week.*

2 (always + *adv/prep*) to give someone bad news in a kind way so that you do not upset them ● *He let her down gently, saying that she hadn't got the job but that he had been very impressed by her application.* ● *Robert had really been looking forward to this trip, so I tried to let him down as lightly as I could.*

let down sb/sth or **let** sb/sth **down**
to make someone or something unsuccessful by failing to achieve a good enough standard ● *The film has a good script but is let down by poor acting.* ● *Becker said that he had lost the match because his forehand had let him down.*

let down sth or **let** sth **down**
1 *mainly British & Australian* to allow the air to escape from an object that is filled with air [e.g. tyre, ball] ● *When he went back to his car, he found that someone had let his tyres down.*

2 to make a piece of clothing longer by removing the sewing from the bottom folded edge and then sewing closer to the edge of the material ● *That skirt is much too short for you. Why don't I let it down a bit?*

let in   lets, letting, let

let in sb/sth or **let** sb/sth **in**
to allow a person or animal to enter a room or building, usually by opening the door for them ● *I knocked on the door and Michelle let me in.*

let in sth or **let** sth **in** (never passive)
if something lets in water, air, or light, it allows water, air, or light to enter it through a hole or opening ● *I need a new pair of shoes because these ones are letting in water.* ● *He opened the window to let in some fresh air.*

inlet *n* [C] the part of a machine which water enters through ● *Remove the inlet from the washing machine and check that there are no obstructions.*

let in for   lets, letting, let

let sb **in for** sth *slightly informal*
to cause someone to do or become involved in a difficult or unpleasant activity ● (often reflexive) *Do you know how much work you're letting yourself in for by doing this exam?* ● *A lot of people agreed to*

take part in the project without knowing exactly what they had let themselves in for.

let in on   lets, letting, let

let sb **in on** sth *informal*
to tell someone about something that is secret, or to allow someone to become involved in something which only very few people are involved in ● *Debbie agreed to let me in on her plans.* ● *Why don't we let Mick in on the act?* (= allow him to become involved in what we are doing)

let into   lets, letting, let

let sb/sth **into** sth
to allow a person or animal to enter a room or building, usually by opening the door for them ● *We were asked to show some identification before they would let us into the building.*

let sth **into** sth *British*
to put something into a flat surface [e.g. wall] so that it does not stick out from the surface ● (usually passive) *A large safe had been let into the wall between the bookshelves.*

let sb **into** sth *British & Australian*
if you let someone into a secret, you tell them something other people do not know ● *Shall I let you into a secret? I've decided to give up work at the end of the year.*

let off   lets, letting, let

let off sb or **let** sb **off**
to not punish someone who has committed a crime or done something wrong, or to not punish someone severely ● *I'll let you off this time, but I don't ever want to catch you stealing again.* ● (often + **with**) *She thought she would be sent to prison, but the judge let her off with* (= gave her) *a £1000 fine.* ● *The police only gave him a warning – he was let off lightly.* (= he was given a less serious punishment than he deserved)

let off sb or **let** sb **off** (sth)
to allow someone not to do an unpleasant job or duty, or to allow someone not to pay you money that they owe you ● *I'm letting you off your homework today because it's almost the end of term.* ● *I've found someone else to work on Christmas Eve, so you've been let off the hook.*

(= you do not have to work)

let off sth or **let** sth **off**

to make an exploding device [e.g. bomb, firework] explode, or to fire a gun • *A group of kids were letting off crackers in the street.* • *As the protestors came closer, the soldiers let off a round of machine-gun fire into the air.*

let off (sth) or **let** (sth) **off** British & Australian slang

to allow gas to escape from your bottom • *There's an awful smell in here. Who's let off?*

---

let on   lets, letting, let

let on *slightly informal*

to tell someone about something which was supposed to be a secret • *I think Dave knows more about this than he's letting on.* • (sometimes + **to**) *She let on to a friend that she'd lied in court.*

---

let out   lets, letting, let

let out sb/sth or **let** sb/sth **out**

to allow a person or animal to leave somewhere, especially by opening a locked or closed door • *I stopped the car to let Susie out.* • (often + **of**) *Rosie lets her hamster out of its cage every night.* • *He was let out after serving just two years of his four-year prison sentence.*

let out sth or **let** sth **out**

1 to allow air or water to come out of something • (often + **of**) *You need to let some air out of those tyres.*
  outlet *n* [C] • *a waste water outlet*

2 to make a particular sound • *She let out a cry of delight when she opened the present.* • *Gary let out a groan when I told him what he had to do.*

3 to express or get rid of an angry emotion by doing a particular activity • *Sports such as football and rugby provide a good opportunity for people to let out their aggression.*
  outlet *n* [C] • (usually singular) *Writing provided him with an outlet for the frustration he was feeling.*

4 to tell someone about something which was supposed to be a secret • *Wouldn't you know that Mary would let the secret out!*

5 British & Australian if you let out a building or part of a building that you own,

you allow someone to pay you money so that they can live in it or use it • *Kate decided to let out her London flat while she was working in Boston.* • (often + **to**) *You could make some money by letting out your spare room to students.*

6 to make a piece of clothing wider by removing the sewing from the side edges and then sewing closer to the edge of the material • *I'm going to have to let this skirt out – I've put on so much weight recently.*

---

let out sb or **let** sb **out**

to allow someone not to get involved in a difficult or unpleasant situation, or to allow someone not to do something which they have agreed to do • *Jan's got to look after the kids on Saturday evening, so that lets her out.* • (often + **of**) *They refused to let him out of his written contract.*

let-out *n* [C] • *I didn't want to go on the trip and John being ill was the perfect let-out.*

let-out *adj* (always before noun) British & Australian • *The contract has a let-out clause in case you change your mind.*

---

let out American

if something that people go to [e.g. school, movie] lets out, it ends and everyone leaves • *The movie let out at 9.00 and we all went for a pizza.* • *When does school let out for Christmas?*

---

let up   lets, letting, let

let up

1 *informal* if bad weather or an unpleasant situation lets up, it stops or improves • *Let's go for a walk once the rain lets up.* • *This current fall in sales shows no sign of letting up.*
  let-up *n* [C] *informal* • (usually singular) *The cold, windy weather will continue this week with no let-up in sight.* • (often + **in**) *There has been no let-up in the recent wave of demonstrations and strikes.*

2 *informal* to stop doing something which you have been doing continuously or in a determined way • (usually negative) *Neil's been complaining about his job all evening – he just won't let up!* • (often + **on**) *Film companies are not letting up on their campaign against people who sell pirate videos.*

level against
levels, levelling, levelled
(*American & Australian* also **levels, leveling, leveled**)

level sth **against** sb
if you level something [e.g. charge, criticism] against someone, you publicly criticize them or state that they have done something bad ● (usually passive) *Charges of corruption have been levelled against him.*

level at
levels, levelling, levelled
(*American & Australian* also **levels, leveling, leveled**)

level sth **at** sb/sth
to aim a gun at someone or at part of someone's body ● *She was grabbed from behind and a pistol was levelled at her head.*

level sth **at** sb
if you level something [e.g. charge, criticism] at someone, you publicly criticize them or state that they have done something bad ● (usually passive) *She decided to resign after a wave of criticism had been levelled at her.*

level off/out
levels, levelling, levelled
(*American & Australian* also **levels, leveling, leveled**)

level off/out
1 if a rate or amount levels off, it stops rising or falling and it stays at the same level ● *European exports have now levelled off after soaring during the 1980's.* ● *House prices are finally levelling out after the steep falls of the past two years.*
2 if an aircraft levels off, it begins to travel at a fixed height after having moved up or down ● *The plane rose sharply before levelling off as it left the coast.*

level off/out (sth) or **level** (sth) **off/out**
to become flat, or to make the surface of something smooth and flat ● *They've put a wooden seat where the ground levels off, halfway up the hill.* ● *Add six spoonfuls of sugar, levelling off each spoonful with a knife to ensure the precise amount.*

level with
levels, levelling, levelled
(*American & Australian* also **levels, leveling, leveled**)

level with sb *informal*
to tell someone the truth about something ● *I asked Carol to level with me and tell me exactly what was going on.*

lie about/around
lies, lying, lay, lain

lie about/around *informal*
to spend time lying down and doing very little ● *I spent a week in Spain lying around on the beach.* ● *They lay about drinking wine and smoking cigarettes all day.*

lie about/around (swh)
if things are lying around, they are untidily left in places where they should not be ● (usually in continuous tenses) *I wouldn't leave money lying around the house if I were you.* ● *Has anyone seen my keys lying about?* (= does anyone know where my keys are)

lie ahead
lies, lying, lay, lain

lie ahead
if an event or situation that will cause problems lies ahead, it will happen in the future ● *He's under no illusions about the difficulties that lie ahead for the industry.*

lie around
see **lie about/around**

lie back
lies, lying, lay, lain

lie back
to move from a sitting position to a lying position by lowering the top half of your body ● *She lay back in the dentist's chair and tried to relax.*

lie before
lies, lying, lay, lain

lie before sb *literary*
if something lies before you, it will happen to you in the future ● *Had I known the troubles that lay before me, I would not have been so cheerful.*

lie behind
lies, lying, lay, lain

lie behind sth
to be the real reason for something ● *I wonder what lay behind her sudden decision not to go.*

lie down   lies, lying, lay, lain

lie down

to move into a position in which your body is flat, usually in order to sleep or rest ● *She lay down on her bed and cried.* ● *I thought I might go upstairs and lie down for a while.*

lie-down *n* [singular] *informal* ● *Why don't you go upstairs and have a lie-down?* (= rest on a bed)

be lying down (always in continuous tenses)

to be in a position in which your body is flat on the ground or on a surface ● *You can do these exercises lying down.* ● *The dog was lying down in its basket, chewing a bone.*

lie in   lies, lying, lay, lain

lie in sth *British & Australian*

to exist or be found in something ● *His skill lies in his ability to communicate quite complex ideas.* ● *The play's interest lies in the questions it raises about sexuality.*

lie in

to stay in bed in the morning later than you usually do ● *I like to lie in on the weekend.* ● *I lay in till eleven o'clock this morning.*

lie-in *n* [singular] *British & Australian informal* ● *I'm not working tomorrow so I can have a lie-in.*

lie up   lies, lying, lay, lain

lie up *British*

to hide from people who are looking for you [e.g. police, soldiers] ● *The escaped prisoners lay up in a barn for a few weeks until the search had been called off.*

lie with   lies, lying, lay, lain

lie with sb

1 if something [e.g. responsibility, blame, decision] lies with someone, it is their responsibility or decision ● *Responsibility for the whole disaster lies with the government.* ● *In cases like this, the fault lies with the parents.*

2 *old use* to have sex with someone ● *Jacob lay with Rachel.*

lie with sb/sth

if a problem lies with someone or something, they cause it ● *The problem lies*

with the gun laws that allow such people to own firearms.

lift off   lifts, lifting, lifted

lift off

if a spacecraft or aircraft lifts off, it leaves the ground ● *The space shuttle Atlantis is scheduled to lift off next Thursday.*

lift-off *n* [singular] the moment when a spacecraft leaves the ground ● *Twenty seconds to lift-off.*

light on/upon   lights, lighting, lighted or **lit**

light on/upon sth *formal*

to suddenly find something or think of something ● *She lit upon a small wooden box hidden under the leaves.* ● *I lit upon the right solution entirely by accident.*

light out   lights, lighting, lighted or **lit**

light out *American informal*

to leave a place quickly ● (often + **of**) *When he saw the police arriving, he lit out of there as fast as he could.* ● (often + **for**) *When she was sixteen she left home and lit out for California.*

light up   lights, lighting, lighted or **lit**

light up sth or **light** sth **up**

1 to shine light on something ● *We stood by the river and watched the fireworks light up the night sky.* ● *The church looks beautiful at night when it is lit up.*

2 to make a place seem more attractive or interesting ● *A series of brightly coloured paintings lit up the dark corridor.*

light up (sth) or **light** (sth) **up**

1 if your face or eyes light up, or if something [e.g. smile] lights them up, you suddenly look very happy or excited ● (often + **with**) *His face lit up with pleasure as Helen walked into the room.* ● *A radiant smile lit up her face.*

2 to make a cigarette start burning and to begin smoking it ● *The airport is a no-smoking area, and you can be fined $200 for lighting up.* ● *He made himself a coffee, lit up a cigarette, and settled down to watch TV.*

light up

if part of a machine lights up, it begins to shine brightly ● *When you turn on the computer, the screen lights up and it's ready to use.* ● *An arrow lit up on the car dashboard showing that the oil was low.*

light upon
see **light on/upon**

lighten up   lightens, lightening, lightened

lighten up sth or **lighten** sth **up**

to make a speech or piece of writing less serious • *He needs a few jokes to lighten up his talk.*

Lighten up! (always an order) *informal*
something you say to tell someone to stop being so serious or annoyed • *Lighten up, would you! She didn't mean to break the vase.*

liken to   likens, likening, likened

liken sb/sth **to** sb/sth

to compare a person or thing to someone or something that you believe has similar qualities or characteristics • *The 18-year-old has been likened to a young Keanu Reeves.* • *Critics have likened her narrative style to that of Virginia Woolf.*

limber up   limbers, limbering, limbered

limber up

1 to do simple exercises in order to stretch your muscles and prepare your body for doing a physical activity • *You should limber up for at least ten minutes before the race.*

2 to prepare yourself for a job or competition which will be difficult to do or win • (often + **for**) *Around the country, politicians are limbering up for the election.*

line up   lines, lining, lined

line up (sb/sth) or **line** (sb/sth) **up**

to arrange people or things in a row, or to stand in a row • *The soldiers lined their prisoners up against the wall.* • *The books were lined up neatly on the shelves.* • *A fight broke out behind me as we lined up to receive our food rations.*
line-up *n* [C] *mainly American & Australian* a row of people that includes someone who is believed to have committed a crime and whom a person who saw the crime tries to recognize • *She spotted the man who had mugged her in the line-up.*

line up sb/sth or **line** sb/sth **up**

to arrange for someone to perform at an event or to compete in a sports competi-
tion, or to organize an event or activity • *We've lined up a jazz band to play at the party.* • *Sampras is lined up against Becker in the next round.* • *Have you got anything lined up for the weekend?*
line-up *n* [C] a group of people who are chosen to perform at an event or play for a sports team, or a set of events or programmes • (usually singular) *Italy has selected a multi-national line-up for their team.* • *The BBC has an impressive line-up of comedy and drama this autumn.*

line up sth or **line** sth **up**

to move something in order to make it straight or level with something else • *The two parts won't fit together if they're not lined up properly.*

line up (always + *adv/prep*)

to be ready to support or oppose someone or something • *Unions lined up with* (= supported) *management in the fight to keep the factory open.* • *Some of the president's advisers were lining up against* (= opposing) *him.*

link up   links, linking, linked

link up (sth/sb) or **link** (sth/sb) **up**

if two or more things or people link up, or if you link them up, they form a connection so that they can operate or work together • *A network of ski lifts links up the three resorts.* • (often + **with**) *The government has encouraged British firms to link up with foreign partners.* • (sometimes + to) *You can use your phone line to link up to the office computer.*
link-up *n* [C] • *The nine-year-old gave evidence to the court by a video link-up.*

link up

to meet someone in a particular place so that you can travel somewhere together • (usually + **with**) *I travelled to Paris on my own and linked up with the rest of the group a week later.*

liquor up   liquors, liquoring, liquored

liquor up (sb) or **liquor** (sb) **up** *American informal*

to drink too much and become drunk, or to make someone do this • *You'll find him in the bar, liquoring up.* • *She was sure he'd try to liquor her up.*

listen in   listens, listening, listened

listen in
1   to secretly listen to a conversation, especially a telephone conversation ● *Jo had picked up the extension phone and was listening in.* ● (often + **on**) *I was sure that someone was listening in on our conversation.* ● (often + **to**) *The Secret Services are able to listen in to conversations on mobile phones by using a special device.*
2   to listen to a radio programme ● *The programme is very popular and thousands of people listen in every week.* ● (often + **to**) *I usually listen in to the 9 o'clock news as I'm driving to work.*

listen out for   listens, listening, listened

listen out for sth
to make an effort to hear a noise which you are expecting ● *Would you listen out for the phone while I'm in the bath?*

listen up

Listen up! (always an order) *mainly American informal*
something you say to tell people to listen to what you are going to say ● *Okay, everyone, listen up! This is your assignment for the weekend.*

litter with

be littered with sth (always passive)
if something is littered with a particular type of thing, it has or contains a lot of that thing ● *The book is littered with printing errors.* ● *Legal history is littered with cases of innocent people being found guilty.*

live by   lives, living, lived

live by sth
if you live by particular rules or beliefs, these rules or beliefs influence your behaviour ● *These people have decided not to live by society's rules.* ● *I always try to live by what I believe in.*

live down   lives, living, lived

live down sth or **live** sth **down**
to stop feeling embarrassed about something you have done by waiting until people forget about it ● *Such a bad reputation is hard to live down.* ● (often negative) *I'll never live it down if Richard refuses to go out with me.*

live for   lives, living, lived

live for sth/sb
to believe that something or someone is the most important thing or person in your life ● *Andrea just lives for parties.* ● *The couple live for each other.*

live in   lives, living, lived

live in
if a student or employee lives in, they live at the place where they study or work ● *The college is building a new accommodation block so that more students can live in.*

live-in *adj* (always before noun) ● *We have a live-in nanny who looks after the children.*

live off   lives, living, lived

live off sth/sb
to have enough money for the things you need by taking it from a supply of money or from another person ● *I had to live off my savings while I was looking for a job.* ● *She lives off her rich grandfather.*

live off sth
to only eat a particular type of food ● *I lived off curries and pizzas when I was a student.*

live on   lives, living, lived

live on sth
1   to have a particular amount of money in order to buy the things you need ● *He and his family live on £70 a week.* ● *I had to take an evening job because we didn't have enough money to live on.*
2   to only eat a particular type of food ● *Martin lived on peanut butter sandwiches while we were staying in New York.*

live on
to continue to exist ● *The memory of Pete will live on.* ● *That is one of the only traditions that still lives on.*

live out   lives, living, lived

live out sth
1   to remain in a particular place or in a particular condition until the end of your life ● (usually + *adv/prep*) *It was sad that she had to live out her last years in a nursing home.* ● *He lived out the final months of his life as a recluse.*
2   if you live out something that you want to do [e.g. fantasy, ambition], you do it or

live through

194

experience it ● *We dressed up in glamorous costumes and lived out our fantasies for one night.* ● *He was trying to live out his own ambitions through his son.*

live out *British & Australian*
if a student or employee lives out, they do not live at the place where they study or work ● *Most second-year students choose to live out.*

live through · lives, living, lived

live through sth
to experience a difficult situation or event ● *My grandparents lived through two world wars.* ● *He had lived through a horrible ordeal with great courage.*

live together · lives, living, lived

live together
if two people live together, they live in the same house and have a sexual relationship with each other, but are not married ● *They lived together for two years before they got married.*

live up · lives, living, lived

live it up *informal*
to spend time doing exciting and enjoyable things ● *He's living it up in the Bahamas for the next two weeks.*

live up to · lives, living, lived

live up to sth
if someone or something lives up to people's expectations or a particular standard, they are as good as they were expected to be ● *Did the trip live up to your expectations?* ● *He's striving to live up to his reputation as a world-class athlete.*

live with · lives, living, lived

live with sb
if one person lives with another, they live in the same house and have a sexual relationship with each other, but are not married ● *How long did you live with Will for?*

live with sth
to accept a difficult or unpleasant situation and continue with your life while it exists ● *For many years the population had lived with the threat of war.* ● *The doctor said he couldn't give me anything for the pain – I've just got to live with it.*

liven up · livens, livening, livened

liven up (sth) or **liven** (sth) **up**
to become more interesting and exciting, or to make something become like this ● *The party livened up as soon as Bob arrived.* ● *We're trying to think of ways in which we can liven up this book cover.*

liven up (sb) or **liven** (sb) **up**
to become more energetic or cheerful, or to make someone feel this way ● *Take that gloomy look off your face and liven up!* ● *Ted's jokes soon livened the kids up.*

load down · loads, loading, loaded

load down sb or **load** sb **down**
1 to give someone too many things to carry ● (usually passive + **with**) *I was loaded down with shopping so I thought I'd take a taxi home.*
2 to give someone too much work or too many responsibilities ● (usually passive + **with**) *It seemed to me that the staff were loaded down with work.*

load up · loads, loading, loaded

load up (sth) or **load** (sth) **up**
to put a lot of things into a vehicle or machine ● *If you bring the car up to the door, we'll start loading up.* ● *Could you load up the dishwasher for me?*

loaf about/around · loafs, loafing, loafed

loaf about/around *informal*
to spend your time doing very little ● *He just loafs around all day, watching TV and reading comics.*

loan out · loans, loaning, loaned

loan out sth or **loan** sth **out**
to lend something to someone ● *The library loans out books, CDs, and videotapes.*

lock away · locks, locking, locked

lock away sth or **lock** sth **away**
to put something in a safe place and lock the door so that no one else can get it ● *He locks his gun away at night.* ● *Her jewellery was locked away in a safe.*

lock away sb or lock sb away

to put someone in prison or in a hospital for people who are mentally ill • *Dangerous criminals need to be locked away from society.*

lock yourself **away** (always reflexive)

to go to a room or building where you can be alone, usually so that you can work • *I'm going to have to lock myself away in the library to get this essay written.*

lock in   locks, locking, locked

lock in sb or lock sb in

to prevent someone from leaving or entering a room or building by locking the door • *As a punishment she would take him up to his bedroom and lock him in.* • (sometimes reflexive) *He ran up to the bathroom and locked himself in.*

lock-in *n* [C] *British informal* a lock-in is when a pub locks its doors and allows people to continue drinking after the time when it should have closed • *Our local pub had a lock-in last Friday night.*

lock onto   locks, locking, locked

lock onto sth

if a missile (= flying weapon) locks onto the object it is aimed at, it finds the exact position of the object and then follows it closely • *The missile locked onto the hot exhaust outlet from the aircraft.*

lock out   locks, locking, locked

lock out sb or lock sb out

1 to prevent someone from entering a building by locking the door • *He broke into the house because his girlfriend had*

locked him out.

2 to prevent workers from entering their place of work until they agree to particular conditions given by the employer • *Management has threatened to lock out the workforce if they do not accept the proposed changes.*

lockout *n* (C/U) • *A series of lockouts ended with the workers' acceptance of the new terms.* • *The General Strike in Britain in 1926 was caused by the lockout of coalminers.*

lock yourself **out** (always reflexive)

to accidentally prevent yourself from getting into a building or vehicle by leaving the keys inside when you shut the door • *I can't believe I've locked myself out again.*

lock up   locks, locking, locked

lock up (sth) or lock (sth) up

to lock all the doors and windows of a building when you leave it • *Don't forget to lock up when you leave.* • *It's my responsibility to lock up the shop at night.*

lock-up *adj* (always before noun) *British & Australian* a lock-up garage or shop is one that you can rent • *The drugs were found in a lock-up garage in East London.*

lock up sth or lock sth up

to put something in a safe place and lock the door so that no one else can get it • *It makes sense to lock up any valuables before you go away.*

lock up sb or lock sb up

to put someone in prison or in a hospital for people who are mentally ill • *At present youths can only be locked up for crimes such as murder and rape.* • *The man's mad – he should be locked up!* • *After what she did to those children, they should* **lock her up and throw away the key.** (= keep her in prison for the rest of her life)

lockup *n* [C] *American informal* a prison or a room in a prison • *A couple of drunks were brought in and thrown in the lockup.*

be locked up (always passive)

if your money is locked up, it is not available for spending because it has been invested • (often + **in**) *He's a wealthy man but most of his money is locked up in shares.*

log in/into   <small>logs, logging, logged</small>
log in

log into sth

 to connect a computer to a system of computers by typing your name, usually so that you can start working • *Log in using your own name and password.*

log off   <small>logs, logging, logged</small>
log off (sth)

 to stop a computer being connected to a computer system, usually when you want to stop working • *Could you all log off for five minutes, please?* • *Log off the system and then shut down.*

log on/onto   <small>logs, logging, logged</small>
log on

log onto sth

 to connect a computer to a system of computers by typing your name, usually so that you can start working • *Anyone can log onto this computer.*

log out   <small>logs, logging, logged</small>
log out

 to stop a computer being connected to a computer system, usually when you want to stop working • (often + **of**) *There was a problem and everyone had to log out of the system.*

loll about/around   <small>lolls, lolling, lolled</small>
loll about/around

 to sit or lie somewhere in a relaxed way, doing very little • (usually + *adv/prep*) *I spent most of the weekend lolling about on the beach.* • *Neil went out jogging while I lolled around at home.*

look after   <small>looks, looking, looked</small>
look after sb/sth

 to take care of someone or something by doing what is needed to keep them well or in good condition • *Do you think you could look after the cat while we're away?* • *If you look after your clothes, they last a lot longer.* • (sometimes reflexive) *Don't worry about Jenny, she can look after herself.* • (used as *adj*) *I made sure that the animals were well looked after.*

look after sth

1 to be responsible for dealing with something • *The transport department looks after roads and railways.*

2 if you look after something that belongs to someone else, you make sure that it is not lost, stolen, or damaged • *Could you look after my things while I go for a quick swim?*

look ahead   <small>looks, looking, looked</small>
look ahead

 to think about what will happen in the future and plan for these events • *Like any company, we've got to look ahead and plan for the future.* • *We're trying to look ahead and see what our options are.*

look around/round   <small>looks, looking, looked</small>
look around/round (swh)

 to walk through a building or around a place and look at the things in it • *I didn't have time to look round the shops.* • *It's such a beautiful city, it's a shame we didn't have more time to look around.*

look around/round

 to try to find something you want [e.g. job] by asking different people or by looking in different places • (usually + **for**) *I've been looking around for a new job.* • *Have you started looking round for a new apartment yet?*

look at   <small>looks, looking, looked</small>
look at sth

1 to read something quickly and not very carefully • *Would you mind looking at my report before I submit it?*

2 to consider a subject carefully in order to make a decision about it • *We need to look carefully at the advantages and disadvantages of the new system.* • *We are looking at all the options.*

3 if an expert [e.g. doctor] looks at something, they examine it and decide how to deal with it • *Did you ask the doctor to look at your knee?* • *We'll have to get a plumber to look at the central heating.*

4 to consider something in a particular way • *I suppose if I'd been a mother, I might have looked at things differently.* • *He's either being very foolish or very brave, depending on the way you look at it.*

not look at sth/sb (always negative)

 to not be prepared to accept an offer, or to not be interested in someone or something • *The people selling the house won't look at anything less than their asking price.* ● *She only likes men with blonde hair – she **wouldn't look twice at** (= would not be interested in) you.*

Look at sb/sth**!** (always an order) *informal* something you say when you give an example of someone or something in order to prove that what you have just said is true ● *Your life doesn't come to an end just because you've got a baby. Look at Catrin and Simon!*

look back   looks, looking, looked

look back
to think about or remember something that happened in the past ● *When I look back, I'm amazed that I coped so well after his death.* ● (often + **on**) *It wasn't such a bad experience when I look back on it.*

look down on   looks, looking, looked

look down on sb/sth
to think that someone is less important than you, or to think that something is not good enough quality for you to use ● *You shouldn't look down on him just because he left school at 16.* ● *She tends to look down on anything that is mass-produced.*

look for   looks, looking, looked

look for sth/sb

to try to find something or someone, either because you have lost them or because you need them ● *Have you seen my gloves? I've been looking for them all week.* ● *I was looking for Andy. Do you know where he is?* ● *How long have you been looking for a job?*

look for sth
if you are looking for a solution to a problem, you are trying to decide what that solution is ● *Both governments are looking for a peaceful solution to the crisis.*

look forward to   looks, looking, looked

look forward to sth/doing sth

to feel pleased and excited about something that is going to happen ● *We're really looking forward to seeing Andy again.* ● *I'm not looking forward to Christmas this year.*

look in   looks, looking, looked

look in
to visit a person for a short time, usually when you are on your way somewhere else ● (often + **on**) *I thought I might look in on Sally when I'm in York.* ● *Can you look in on the kids before you go to bed and make sure they're alright?*

look into   looks, looking, looked

look into sth
to discover and examine the facts about a problem or situation ● *Police are reported to be looking into the case.* ● *We're looking into the possibility of merging the two departments.*

look on   looks, looking, looked

look on
1 to watch an activity or event without becoming involved in it ● *Demonstrators tore down the statue as police calmly looked on.* ● (often + **in**) *The crowd looked on in disbelief as the player walked off the pitch.*

onlooker *n* [C] a person who watches an activity or event without becoming involved in it ● *A crowd of curious onlookers gathered round to see what was happening.*

2 *American* to share a book or document with another person in a group ● (usually + **with**) *Can you look on with Sam because we don't have enough books for everyone?* ● *I don't have a copy of the music. Can I look on?*

look on/upon

look on/upon sth/sb
to consider something or someone in a particular way ● (usually + **as**) *You shouldn't look upon this as a failure.* ● *We look on her as a daughter.* ● *He wouldn't **look kindly on** (= he would be angry with) anyone who attempted to interfere in the matter.*

look out   looks, looking, looked

look out sth or **look** sth **out** (never passive) *British & Australian*
to search for and find something ● *I'll look out the recipe and send it to you.*

Look out! (always an order)
something you say or shout in order to tell someone that they are in danger

• *Look out, Russ, there's a car coming!*
lookout *n* [C] a person who is watching for danger • *The lookout was standing on the corner while the two men broke into the store.*

lookout *n* [C] a high place where a person can look at what is happening in the area around them, especially in order to watch for any danger • *There's a lookout at the top of the cliff.*

look out for   looks, looking, looked

look out for sb/sth
 to carefully watch the people or things around you so that you will notice a particular person or thing • *Remember to look out for Anna – she said she'd be there.* • *Can you look out for a present for Ed while you're out shopping?*

look out for sb
 to take care of someone and do what will be best for them • *I come from a large family and we all look out for each other.* • (often reflexive) *Tom just looks out for himself.* (= he only does what will be good for himself) • *She certainly knows how to **look out for number one**.* (= she only does what will be good for herself)

look over   looks, looking, looked

look over sth/sb or **look** sth/sb **over**
 to quickly examine something or someone • *I had a few minutes before the meeting to look over what he'd written.* • *She looked the boy over and sent him to join the other children.*

look round

 see **look around/round**

look through   looks, looking, looked

look through sth
1 to carefully examine the contents of something or a collection of things in order to find something • *I've looked through her drawers but I can't find the letter.* • *Why don't you look through these files and see if the document's there?*
2 to read something quickly and not very carefully • *Could you look through these figures and see if I've made any obvious errors?*

look through sb
 to not notice someone that you know, or to pretend that you have not noticed

someone, even though you are looking directly at them • *I said hello but she looked straight through me.*

look to   looks, looking, looked

look to sb to do sth
 to hope that someone will do something for you • *We're looking to you to advise us on how to proceed.*

look to for   looks, looking, looked

look to sb **for** sth
 to hope that someone will provide something for you • *They looked to the government for additional support.*

look up   looks, looking, looked

look up sth or **look** sth **up**
 to look at a book or computer in order to find a piece of information • *Can you look up the French word for 'marrow'?* • *I'm not sure what his number is. You'll have to look it up in the telephone directory.*

look up
 if a situation is looking up, it is improving • (usually in continuous tenses) *Things are looking up now you've got your promotion.* • *The housing market seems to be looking up at last.*

look up sb or **look** sb **up**
 to visit someone who you have not seen for a long time when you are visiting the place where they live • *You'll have to look me up the next time you're in Los Angeles.*

look up to   looks, looking, looked

look up to sb
 to respect and admire someone • *Kate has always looked up to her father.*

look upon

 see **look on/upon**

loom ahead   looms, looming, loomed

loom ahead
 if something unpleasant looms ahead, it will happen soon and it makes you feel worried or frightened • *I've got my exams in June looming ahead.*

loom up   looms, looming, loomed

loom up
 to appear as a large but not clear shape, often in a way that seems frightening • (usually + *adv/prep*) *A figure suddenly*

loomed up out of the darkness. • *The mountains loom up against the skyline.*

lose out to (= are less successful than) *those who can.*

loose on/upon

be loosed on/upon sb/sth (always passive) *literary*
if a destructive force is loosed on people or a place, it is suddenly allowed to have its full effect on them • *Anarchy would be loosed on our roads if we didn't have police to enforce the rules.*

lounge about/around   lounges, lounging, lounged

lounge about/around (swh)
to spend your time in a relaxed way, doing very little • *Most days were spent lounging around the pool.* • *I've just been lounging around in front of the television.*

loosen up   loosens, loosening, loosened

loosen up (sth) or **loosen** (sth) **up**
to prepare your body muscles for a physical activity by stretching and doing simple exercises • *I like to do a few exercises to loosen up before I run.* • *We're just going to do a few stretches to loosen up those muscles.*

loosen up *slightly informal*
to start to feel less embarrassed and to become more relaxed when you are with other people • *She loosened up after a couple of glasses of wine.* • *We get the students to loosen up at the start of the course by making them talk about their families.*

louse up   louses, lousing, loused

louse up (sth) or **louse** (sth) **up** *mainly American & Australian informal*
to do something very badly • *She's taking her driving-test this afternoon, so let's hope she doesn't louse it up again.*

luck into   lucks, lucking, lucked

luck into sth *American informal*
to get something that you want by chance • *We lucked into two tickets for the World Series.*

luck out   lucks, lucking, lucked

luck out *American informal*
to be very lucky • *We got the last two tickets – we really lucked out there.*

lop off   lops, lopping, lopped

lop off sth or **lop** sth **off**
1 to cut off a part of something with a quick movement • *We lopped off the biggest of the branches.*
2 *informal* to reduce a price or the amount of time taken to do something by a particular amount • *A fall in demand has lopped 12 cents off a barrel of oil.* • *She lopped three seconds off the world record for the 400 metres.*

lull into   lulls, lulling, lulled

lull sb **into** sth/doing sth
to gradually give someone confidence or make them feel safe, usually by deceiving them • *Most exercise classes start gently, lulling you into thinking that you're fit.* • *The economic success of the last few years has **lulled** the government **into a false sense of security**.* (= made it feel confident when it has no reason to be)

lord over   lords, lording, lorded

lord it over sb *slightly informal*
to behave as if you are better than someone else and have the right to tell them what to do • *He likes to lord it over the more junior people in the office.*

lumber with   lumbers, lumbering, lumbered

lumber sb **with** sth *British & Australian slightly informal*
to give someone a problem or difficulty which they must deal with • (usually passive + **with**) *You don't want to get lumbered with the job of clearing up after the party.* • (sometimes reflexive) *She's lumbered herself with too many responsibilities.*

lose out   loses, losing, lost

lose out
to not have an advantage that other people have • *The new tax means that married women will lose out.* • (often + **on**) *If you leave now, you'll lose out on the company pension scheme.* • (often + **to**) *Children who cannot write correct English*

lump together   lumps, lumping, lumped

lump together sth/sb or **lump** sth/sb **together**

to consider that two or more different things or people belong to the same group, or to combine different things or people to make one group ● (usually passive) *American and Canadian authors tend to be lumped together in the same category.* ● *Children of varying abilities are lumped together in one class.*

lust after   lusts, lusting, lusted

lust after sb

to feel sexual desire for someone that you are not having a sexual relationship with

● *She's been lusting after Adam for months.*

lust after sth *slightly informal*

to want something very much, especially something expensive ● *I'd been lusting after one of their silk shirts for ages and I finally bought one.*

luxuriate in   luxuriates, luxuriating, luxuriated

luxuriate in sth *formal*

to spend time getting as much pleasure as you can from an enjoyable experience ● *I buried my head in the sheets, luxuriating in their warmth and softness.* ● *For a moment she said nothing, but luxuriated in their praise.*

magic away magics, magicking, magicked

magic away sth or **magic** sth **away**
   to make something disappear so quickly that it seems as if you have used magic • *A spot of make-up will magic away any shadows and imperfections.*

major in majors, majoring, majored

major in sth *American & Australian*
   to study something as your main subject at university • *She majored in French at Middlebury.*

make after makes, making, made

make after sb/sth (never passive)
   to chase someone or something • *We made after him in a van.*

make away with makes, making, made

make away with sth (never passive)
   to steal something • *Thieves raided the premises and made away with $10,000 in cash.*

make for makes, making, made

make for swh (never passive)
   to go in the direction of a place • *He got up and made for the exit, looking fairly ill.*

make for sth (never passive; never in continuous tenses)
   to cause a particular result or situation • *Poor service does not make for satisfied customers.* • *Ironically, food rationing made for a healthier population.* • *Reports of the trial make for gruesome reading.* (= they are very unpleasant to read)

make of makes, made

make of sth/sb (always used in questions; never in continuous tenses)
   if you ask someone what they make of someone or something, you want to know their opinion about that person or thing, usually because there is something strange about them • *What do you make of this letter?* • *There seems to be a lot of conflict in their household. I'm not sure what to make of it all.* • *She's a bit of a mystery – I've never known what to make of her.*

make off makes, making, made

make off
   to leave somewhere quickly, especially in order to escape • *The burglars made off as soon as the police arrived.*

make off with makes, making, made

make off with sth (never passive) *slightly informal*
   to steal something and take it away • *Somebody broke into the shop and made off with several TVs and videos.*

make out makes, making, made

make out sth/sb or **make** sth/sb **out**
   to be able to see or hear something or someone, usually with difficulty • *We could just make out a building through the trees.* • *I listened but couldn't make out what they were saying.*

make out sth or **make** sth **out**
1 (never passive) to understand something, especially the reason why something has happened • (often + question word) *Nobody can make out what their motives were.* • *Can you make out how they did it?*
2 to write all the necessary information on an official document [e.g. cheque, application, ticket] • *The applications for shares were made out in different names.* • *I made out a cheque for £50.*

make out sth
   to claim falsely that something is true • (often + **that**) *He made out that he'd been living in Paris all year.* • *She made out as if they were really good friends when I happen to know she's only met him twice.*

make sb/sth **out to be** sth
   to describe someone or something in a false way • *British food isn't as bad as it's made out to be.* • *The book makes him out to be a complete crook.*

make out sb or **make** sb **out** (never passive)
   to understand why someone behaves in the way that they do • *I thought James*

would be pleased to see us. I can't make him out at all.

make out

1 *American informal* to deal with a situation, especially in a successful way ● (often used in questions + **with**) *How is Don making out with his new school?* ● *She'll make out all right – don't worry about her.*

2 *American informal* to kiss, touch and hold someone in a sexual way ● *Those two were too busy making out to notice anyone else.* ● (often + **with**) *Sam was making out with Cindy in the back of the car.*

3 *American & Australian informal* to succeed in having sex with someone ● (often + **with**) *He's only interested in making out with her.*

make over   makes, making, made

make over sth or **make** sth **over**
to give money or possessions to someone in an official way, so that they own them legally ● (usually + **to**) *He made over his fortune to his wife.* ● *Her family tried to stop her making her estate over to a conservation charity.* ● *Make the cheque over to D. Glennon.*

make over sb/sth or **make** sb/sth **over** *American informal*
to change someone or something [e.g. house, apartment] to give them a different appearance or a new use ● *Once they've bought the apartment they can make it over to suit themselves.* ● *The hair stylist wants to make Carla over.*

make-over n [C] if someone has a make-over, they have their appearance changed by a specially trained person ● *She was furious – he suggested she get a haircut and a make-over.*

make towards   makes, making, made

make towards sth *mainly British & Australian slightly formal*
to go in the direction of something ● *He made towards the door but then stopped and turned to face me.*

make up   makes, making, made

make up sth or **make** sth **up**

1 to say or write something that is not true [e.g. excuse, report, story] in order to deceive someone ● *I'd made up some story*

about having to go home to see my sick mother.* ● *Can't you make up an excuse?*

2 to invent something [e.g. story, game] ● *Sometimes I'll read her a story from a book and sometimes I'll make one up.* ● *We haven't fixed a programme for the concert. We'll just make it up as we go along.* (= as each part is finished we'll decide what to do next)

made-up *adj* ● *We gave ourselves made-up names.*

3 to make an amount of something complete or as big as it should be ● *If I'm late for work I'll just make up the time tomorrow.* ● *We are hoping to make up time* (= become less late) *on the return journey.* ● *I had £20 but needed £25, so my parents said they'd make up the difference.*

make-up n [C] *American* a school test that you were not present for and that you take later ● *She was sick when we had the French test but she can take a make-up.* ● (used as *adj*) *When's the make-up test?*

4 to prepare something so that it is ready to be used ● *We made up twenty packets of sandwiches for the walkers.* ● *We made up a bed for her on the sofa.*

make up sth

to form the whole of something ● *Women make up nearly 50% of medical school entrants.* ● *Muscle fibres are made up of* (= contain) *two proteins.*

make-up n [U] the combination of things which form something ● *Membership of the committee does not reflect the racial make-up of the city.*

make up

to forgive someone who you have argued with and to become friendly with them again ● *We argue a lot, but we always have fun making up!* ● (often + **with**) *Have you made up with Daryl yet?*

make up sb or **make** sb **up**

to put make-up (= a substance that you use on your face to improve or change your appearance) on someone ● (usually passive) *We are inviting three lucky winners to be made up by a leading make-up artist.* ● *He was made up as an old man, with heavy lines on his face and a grey wig.*

make-up n [U] ● *It takes her ages to put on her make-up in the morning.* ● *I forgot* *to take my make-up off before I went to bed.*

make up for   makes, making, made

make up for sth

1 to replace something that has been lost, or to provide something good in order to make a bad situation better • *This year's good harvest will make up for last year's bad one.* • *He seems to be making up for an empty childhood by surrounding himself with expensive possessions.* • *I didn't travel much when I was younger, but I'm certainly **making up for lost time** now.* (= doing all the travelling I didn't do before)

2 if someone makes up for something bad that they have done, they do something good so that the bad thing does not cause a problem any more • *He bought me dinner to make up for being late the day before.*

make up to   makes, making, made

make it up to sb

to do something good for someone who you have done something bad to in the past, or to someone who has done something good for you • *I'm really sorry about the way I behaved last night – I'll make it up to you, I promise!* • *She's given me so much. I don't know how I'm ever going to make it up to her.*

make up to sb (never passive)

to try to make a person in authority like you and approve of you by doing and saying things which will please them • *Have you seen the disgusting way she makes up to the boss?*

map out   maps, mapping, mapped

map out sth or **map** sth **out**

to plan something in detail • *By the age of fourteen he had his future mapped out before him.*

march on   marches, marching, marched

march on swh

to walk to a particular place in a large group in order to attack it or to express your opposition to something • *Thousands of antiwar demonstrators have marched on the Pentagon.* • *Armed rebels marched on the capital to seize power.*

mark down   marks, marking, marked

mark down sth or **mark** sth **down**

1 to write something on a piece of paper in order to make a record of it • *He was marking down my responses to certain questions.*

2 to reduce the price of something in order to encourage people to buy it • *Women's shoes have all been marked down by 25% this week.* • (used as adj) *He runs a shop that sells marked-down designer clothes.*
   markdown n [C] • *We're offering a 10% markdown on selected items.*

mark sb **down as** sth

to consider someone as a particular type of person • *I'd marked her down as a Labour Party supporter, but I was completely wrong.* • *I must say I didn't have him marked down as a feminist.*

mark down sb or **mark** sb **down**

to give someone a lower result in an exam or competition because they have made a mistake or done something wrong • (often + for) *Do they mark you down for spelling errors?* • *Our team was marked down for* (= because of) *going over the time limit.*

mark off   marks, marking, marked

mark off sth or **mark** sth **off**

1 to separate an area by putting something around it • *The police had marked off the area where the body was found with white tape.*

2 to put a symbol next to something on a list, or to draw a line through something to show that it has been dealt with • *I like to make a list of all the jobs I've got to do and then mark them off as I do them.* • *When I was a child, I used to mark off the days to my birthday on the calendar.*

mark off sb/sth or **mark** sb/sth **off**

if a particular quality marks off someone or something, it makes that person or thing different from other people or things of a similar type • (usually + from) *It's the intelligence of her insight that marks her off from other writers of this genre.*

mark out   marks, marking, marked

mark out sth or **mark** sth **out**

to show the shape or position of something by drawing a line around it • *He'd marked out a volleyball court on the beach with a stick.*

mark out sb/sth or **mark** sb/sth **out**
(always + *adv/prep*) *mainly British*
if a particular quality marks out someone or something, it makes that person or thing different from or better than other people or things • (sometimes + **as**) *His ability to change his views according to the situation marked him out as a survivor in the world of politics.* • (sometimes + **from**) *It's her enthusiasm that marks her out from her colleagues.*

mark out for   marks, marking, marked

mark sb **out for** sth
to believe that someone is likely to achieve something in the future • (usually passive) *He was marked out for success at an early age.*

mark up   marks, marking, marked

mark up sth or **mark** sth **up**
1 to increase the price of something • *They buy these goods cheaply overseas and then mark them up to resell at home.*
mark-up *n* [C] • *The mark-up on wine in restaurants is often as high as 70%.*
2 to write instructions on or make changes to a piece of writing or music • *As director, I usually spend the first couple of rehearsals marking up my copy of the play.*

marry above   marries, marrying, married

marry above yourself (always reflexive)
old-fashioned
to marry someone of a higher social class than your own • *She'd married above herself and we knew it would end badly.*

marry beneath   marries, marrying, married

marry beneath yourself (always reflexive) *old-fashioned*
to marry someone of a lower social class than your own • *Her uncle was afraid that by marrying Mr Watts she would be marrying beneath herself.*

marry into   marries, marrying, married

marry into sth
if you marry into a family, especially a rich family, you marry a member of that

family • *She married into a wealthy farming family.*

marry off   marries, marrying, married

marry off sb or **marry** sb **off**
to make sure that someone, especially a female member of your family, gets married or that they marry the person you have chosen • (often + **to**) *She was married off to the local doctor by the age of 16.*

marry out   marries, marrying, married

marry out *British old-fashioned*
to marry someone whose religion is different to yours • *There's a lot of disgrace attached to marrying out.*

marry up   marries, marrying, married

marry up (sth) or **marry** (sth) **up**
if two things marry up, or if you marry them up, they match or join together • *I listened to the film in German whilst reading the English subtitles, but the two versions didn't seem to marry up.*

mash up   mashes, mashing, mashed

mash up sth or **mash** sth **up**
to crush food until it is soft and smooth • *For his lunch, just mash up a banana with a fork and give him that.*

match against   matches, matching, matched

match sb/sth **against** sb/sth
to make two people, teams, or things compete with each other • (usually passive) *France is matched against Ireland in next week's semi-final.*

match up   matches, matching, matched

match up
1 if two pieces of information match up, they are the same and this shows that the information is likely to be correct • *They both described what had happened that night but their stories didn't quite match up.*
2 to be as good as something or someone else • (usually + **to**) *Nothing that he wrote after this point ever quite matched up to his early work.*

match up sb/sth or **match** sb/sth **up**
to find someone or something that will be suitable for a particular person, activity, or purpose • (usually + **with**) *They look*

at your interests and they try to match you up with someone suitable.

max out   maxes, maxing, maxed

max out (sth) or **max** (sth) **out** *mainly American informal*
to use almost all that is available of something, especially money ● *We've maxed out all our credit cards.*

measure against   measures, measuring, measured

measure sb/sth **against** sb/sth
to judge someone or something by comparing them with someone or something else ● *Our city's transport problems are minor when measured against capitals like London and New York.* ● (sometimes reflexive) *Women have always been encouraged to measure themselves against other women physically.*

measure out   measures, measuring, measured

measure out sth or **measure** sth **out**
to take a small amount of something from a larger amount, first weighing or measuring it in order to make sure that it is the right amount ● *Measure out 300 grams of flour and place in a bowl with the egg yolks.*

measure off   measures, measuring, measured

measure off sth or **measure** sth **off**
to mark the length of something, especially cloth, from a larger piece and to cut it ● *The assistant measured off a length of cloth that would be enough for both curtains.*

measure up   measures, measuring, measured

measure up (sth) or **measure** (sth) **up**
to find the exact size of something, for example a window or a room ● *They're measuring up for new carpets.* ● *We need new curtains for that window if you could measure it up some time.*

measure up
to be good enough ● (often negative) *Production targets are high and managers*

who don't measure up, don't last. • (often
+ **to**) *People started to realize how poorly
their country measured up to the standards of the outside world.*

meet up   meets, meeting, met

meet up
1 to meet another person in order to do
something together • *We quite often meet
up after work and go for a drink.* • (often
+ **with**) *I met up with a few friends and
went for a meal.*
2 if roads or paths meet up, they join at a
particular place • (often + **with**) *This
path meets up with the main road at the
bridge.*

meet with   meets, meeting, met

meet with sb *mainly American*
to have a meeting with someone in order
to discuss or arrange something • *Brown
has met with the senator several times in
recent weeks to discuss the proposals.*
• *Each student meets with an advisor at
the beginning of the school year.*

meet with sth
1 *slightly formal* to cause a particular reaction or result • *Both proposals have met
with fierce opposition.* • *Sadly, the campaign met with little success.* • *I trust the
arrangements* **meet with your approval.**
(= I hope that you like them)
2 *slightly formal* to experience something,
especially something unpleasant • *If you
meet with any difficulties, just let the manager know.* • *It was on this day that he met
with an accident that was to shape the rest
of his life.*

mellow out   mellows, mellowing, mellowed

mellow out (sb) or **mellow** (sb) **out**
American informal
to relax and stop worrying about things,
or to make someone do this • *I'm gonna
go home, pour myself a martini, put on
some music and mellow out.* • *Marriage
seems to have mellowed him out.*

melt down   melts, melting, melted

melt down sth or **melt** sth **down**
if you melt something down, especially a
metal object, you heat it until it changes
to liquid • *Stolen gold rings are often melt-
ed down to make new ones.*

meltdown *n* (C/U) a dangerous situation in a nuclear power station when the
material becomes so hot that it melts,
burns through its container, and radi-
ation (= energy very harmful to living
things) escapes • *The inspectors feared a
meltdown of Chernobyl proportions.*

merge in   merges, merging, merged

merge in
if something merges in, it looks similar to
its surroundings so that you do not notice
it • (often + **with**) *The museum was
designed to merge in with the architecture
around it.*

merge into   merges, merging, merged

merge into sth
if something merges into its surroundings, it looks similar to them so that you
do not notice it • *Her dark form merged
into the night.*

mess about/around   messes, messing, messed

mess about/around
1 *informal* to spend time playing or doing
things with no particular purpose • *He
spends his weekends messing about in his
boat on the Thames.*
2 *informal* to behave stupidly or to waste
time doing unimportant things • *Daniel,
will you stop messing around and tidy
your room!*

mess sb **about/around** *informal*
to treat someone badly, especially by
changing your mind a lot or not doing
what you have promised • *I'm just tired of
being messed around by men who don't
know what they want.* • *She's fed up with
the guy she works for – he's messed her
about so much.*

mess about/around with   messes, messing, messed

mess about/around with sb *informal*
to have a sexual relationship with someone who is not your usual partner
• *That's what happens when you mess
about with married men.*

mess about/around with sth *informal*
to try to change or improve something,
usually with bad results • *I don't want
him coming in here and messing around
with our computers.* • *Why would you*

want to mess around with hair as beautiful as yours?

mess up   messes, messing, messed

mess up (sth) or **mess** (sth) **up**
to spoil or damage something, or to do something badly ● *You don't want to mess up your career.* ● *It's the politicians who always mess things up for ordinary people.* ● *He's really messed up this time, I don't know how we're going to sort this one out.*

mess up sth or **mess** sth **up**
to make something untidy or dirty ● *I've got the kitchen looking perfect so don't go messing it up again.* ● *The problem with wearing a hat is that it messes up your hair.*

mess up sb or **mess** sb **up**
informal to cause someone to suffer from emotional and mental problems ● *Drugs can really mess you up.*
    messed-up adj informal ● *The newspapers portrayed him as a messed-up junkie.*

mess with   messes, messing, messed

mess with sb/sth *informal*
to become involved with someone or something that is dangerous ● *If you mess with drugs you're asking for trouble.*

mess with sth
to try to change or repair something, usually without success ● *Phil's been messing with the TV and it's not working.*

mess with sb *informal*
to annoy someone, treat them badly, or start an argument with them ● *I've warned you already – don't mess with me!*

mete out   metes, meting, meted

mete out sth or **mete** sth **out** *formal*
to give someone a punishment, or to make someone receive unfair treatment ● (usually passive) *Women's groups were outraged at the 5-year jail sentence meted out to the man who had killed his wife.*

militate against   militates, militating, militated

militate against sth *formal*
to make something less likely to happen ● *The fall in consumer spending this month militates against economic recovery.*

mill about/around   mills, milling, milled

mill about/around (swh)
to walk around a particular place or area, usually while waiting for something ● *A crowd of reporters were milling about the gates of the actor's Hollywood mansion.* ● *There was the usual group of fans milling around outside the theatre.*

mind out

Mind out! (always an order) *British & Australian*
something that you say in order to tell someone to be careful or to warn someone of a danger ● *Mind out, this plate's very hot!*

minister to   ministers, ministering, ministered

minister to sb/sth *formal*
to care for someone who is ill or who needs help ● *The church has always played a major role in ministering to the poor and sick.* ● *I spent the weekend in a five-star hotel and a crowd of hotel staff ministered to my every need.*

minor in   minors, minoring, minored

minor in sth *American*
to study another subject as well as your main subject at university ● *She majored in French and minored in history in college.*

miss out   misses, missing, missed

miss out
to not do or get something that you would enjoy or that would be good for you, or to not have something that other people have ● (often + **on**) *If you leave early for Christmas you'll miss out on all the partying.* ● *There are some real bargains to be had in the sale, so don't miss out.* ● *We didn't have a TV at home when I was young, and I felt as though I missed out.*

miss out sb/sth or **miss** sb/sth **out**
British & Australian
to fail to include someone or something ● *Could you look at this list of names and check that I haven't missed anyone out?* ● *You've missed out an 'n' in 'Susannah'.*

mist over   mists, misting, misted

mist over
if your eyes mist over, they become filled with tears which stop you from seeing clearly ● *Her eyes mist over as she starts to talk about her son.*

mist over/up   mists, misting, misted

mist over/up
if something made of glass [e.g. windscreen, window, glasses] mists over, it becomes covered with very small drops of water so that you cannot see through it easily ● *You'll need to turn the car fan on to stop the windscreen misting over.*

mix in   mixes, mixing, mixed

mix in *American informal*
to meet and talk with other people, especially people you do not know well ● *It's very hard to make friends if you're not willing to mix in.*

mix up   mixes, mixing, mixed

mix up sth/sb or **mix** sth/sb **up**
to confuse two people or things by thinking that one person or thing is the other person or thing ● *Kim and Wendy were almost identical as children and I often used to mix them up.* ● *We both wear black wool coats and it's very easy to get them mixed up.* ● (often + **with**) *I was often mixed up with Tom at school because we had the same surname.*

mix-up *n* [C] a mistake caused by confusion which prevents something from being done or causes something to be done incorrectly ● (often + **over**) *There's been a bit of a mix-up over the arrangements for the trip.*

mix up sth or **mix** sth **up**
1 to cause a group of things to be untidily arranged ● *I've just spent two hours sorting those papers so please don't mix them up.* ● *We've got loads of photos but they're all mixed up together in a huge cardboard box.*
2 to combine different substances together, especially food, so that they become one substance ● *And the next thing you do is you put the chocolate, butter and egg in a bowl and mix them all up.*

mix up sb or **mix** sb **up** *American & Australian informal*
to make someone feel confused ● *It doesn't take much to mix her up!* ● *He had so much conflicting advice he was really mixed up by it all.*

mix up in

be mixed up in sth (always passive) *informal*
to be involved in an illegal or unpleasant activity ● *The film's main character is a writer who gets mixed up in the violent world of drug-dealing.* ● *You don't want to be mixed up in his dodgy business affairs.*

mix up with

be mixed up with sb (always passive)
to be involved with someone who has a bad influence on you ● *How did she get mixed up with such unpleasant people?*

mix with   mixes, mixing, mixed

mix it with sb *mainly British informal*
to compete against someone, or to argue with them about something serious ● *Despite his age, he still has the ability to mix it with the younger tennis players.*

mock up   mocks, mocking, mocked

mock up sth or **mock** sth **up**
to make a model of something in order to show people what it will look like or how it will work ● *They mocked up the newly designed car so that its shape could be studied in more detail.*

mock-up *n* [C] ● *New pilots are often trained in a mock-up of an aircraft.* ● (used as *adj*) *A mock-up control room was created in order to test the effects of light on workers.*

model on/upon   models, modelling, modelled   (*American* also **models, modeling, modeled**)

model sth **on/upon** sth
to design or develop something by basing it on another thing or system ● (usually passive) *The Sheldonian Theatre in Oxford is modelled on an idea of the classical theatre.* ● *She has proposed the introduction of a new education system modelled on the German system.*

model yourself **on/upon** sb (always reflexive)

to copy the behaviour or characteristics of another person who you admire ● *As a young actor, he modelled himself on Jack Nicholson.*

monkey about/around   monkeys, monkeying, monkeyed

monkey about/around *informal*

to behave in a silly way ● *They were monkeying around in the kitchen and the younger boy banged his head against the cupboard.*

mooch about/around   mooches, mooching, mooched

mooch about/around (swh) *mainly British & Australian informal*

to spend your time doing very little or doing nothing important ● *I spent my holidays reading and mooching about.* ● *I mooched around second-hand bookshops.*

moon about/around   moons, mooning, mooned

moon about/around (swh) *informal*

to spend your time in a lazy way doing very little, often because you are unhappy ● *He spent the whole weekend just mooning about at home.*

moon over   moons, mooning, mooned

moon over sb

to spend all your time thinking about someone that you love ● *He spent most of the summer mooning over some girl he'd met on the beach.*

mop up   mops, mopping, mopped

mop up (sth) or **mop** (sth) **up**

to use a cloth to remove a liquid that has been dropped or that has spread ● *I was just mopping up the milk that you spilt in the kitchen.* ● *Hundreds of villagers have been mopping up after last weekend's flood.*

mop up sth or **mop** sth **up**

1 to eat the small amount of soup or sauce which remains on a plate or in a dish by using a piece of bread to lift up the liquid ● *Leave the fish to cool and serve with French bread to mop up the juices.*

2 to use what remains of an amount of something ● *Buying clothes for the kids*

usually mops up any spare money I have at the end of the month.

3 *informal* to deal with something ● *I've just got a few things to mop up before I leave the office tonight.* ● *It was left to him to mop up the mess caused by the scandal.*

mop up sb or **mop** sb **up**

to kill the remaining soldiers from an enemy army, or to take them as prisoners ● *Government soldiers are now mopping up rebel forces in the rural north.* ● (used as *adj*) *21 rebels fighters were killed in a mopping-up operation.*

mouth off   mouths, mouthing, mouthed

mouth off *informal*

to talk about a subject as if you know more than everyone else, or to complain a lot about something ● (often + **about**) *Tim was his usual tedious self, mouthing off about the middle-classes and how much he hates them.* ● *I had to sit there and listen to Michael mouthing off over lunch.*

move ahead   moves, moving, moved

move ahead

1 if a process or plan moves ahead, it advances or develops, often after a pause or delay ● *The judge's decision will allow the case to move ahead after two years of delays.* ● *Reform should move ahead more quickly after the election.*

2 to start or continue to do something that you have planned to do ● *The change in law means that cable TV companies can move ahead and offer phone services.* ● (often + **with**) *We need his permission before we can move ahead with the project.* ● (sometimes + **on**) *Despite safety concerns over the building, the company has decided to move ahead on construction.*

move along   moves, moving, moved

move sb **along**

if someone in authority [e.g. police officer, guard] moves you along, they ask you to leave a place ● *Police officers at the scene of the accident were asking passers-by to move along.*

move (sth) **along**

if a process moves along, or if you move a process along, it develops in a satisfactory way ● *It took a long time for the project to get going but things are really moving along now.* ● *We're trying to move the case along as quickly as possible.*

move away   moves, moving, moved

move away
to leave the place or area where you live and go and live in another place • *The village's population has fallen sharply in the past ten years as young people have moved away.*

move away from   moves, moving, moved

move away from sth/doing sth
to stop using or doing something and to begin to use or do something else instead • *Campaigners are encouraging the government to move away from nuclear power and use alternative sources.* • *A lot of young people in Britain are moving away from eating meat.*

move down   moves, moving, moved

move down (sb) or **move** (sb) **down**
British & Australian
if a student moves down, or if a teacher moves them down, they are put into a lower level or class • *If you failed your end-of-term exams you were moved down.* • *If he finds the work too difficult he can always move down to a lower class.*

move in/into   moves, moving, moved

move in

move into sth
1 to begin living in a new house or area • *They've made a lot of alterations to the house since they moved in.* • *Some friends of mine have just moved into our street.*
2 to become involved in a particular business for the first time • *In 1984, Renault moved into the executive car market.* • *The drugs trade increased rapidly during the 1960s and London gangsters soon moved in.*

move in (sb) or **move** (sb) **in**

move (sb) **into** swh
if a group of people in authority [e.g. police, troops] move in, or if someone moves them in, they go to a place in order to deal with a difficult or dangerous situation • *The area is under rebel control and government troops are about to move in.* • *Preparations are being made to move the army into the region.*

move in on   moves, moving, moved

move in on sb/sth
to approach a group of people or a place where people are staying in order to attack them • *There are reports that the police are moving in on the terrorists.* • *Government troops have moved in on the rebel stronghold.*

move in on sth
if a large company moves in on a particular business, they become involved in it for the first time, taking business away from smaller companies • *A large American corporation is planning to move in on the newly privatised British electricity industry.*

move in together/with   moves, moving, moved

move in together

move in with sb
to start living in the same house as someone you are having a romantic relationship with • *She's just moved in with her boyfriend.* • *Moving in together is a big step in a relationship.*

move on   moves, moving, moved

move on
1 to leave the place where you have been staying and go somewhere else • *I'd been in Paris long enough and thought it was time to move on.*
2 to start doing a new activity • *After three years working as a junior reporter, she was ready to move on.* • (often + **to**) *We're about to move on to the second stage of the project.*
3 to become better or more advanced • *Fashion photography hasn't really moved on since the 1950s.* • (often + **from**) *You can now phone abroad in seconds – things have really moved on from the days when you had to wait hours to be connected.*

move on sb or **move** sb **on**
if someone in authority [e.g. police officer, guard] moves you on, they ask you to leave a place • *You can't spend the night in the station because the police will move you on.*

move out   moves, moving, moved

move out
1 to stop living in a particular house • *She*

wants to move out and find a place on her own.

2 to stop being involved in a particular business ● (often + **of**) *The company has decided to move out of the electronics business due to increased competition.*

3 if a vehicle moves out, it moves to the right or left side of the road, usually in order to go past another vehicle ● *As I moved out to overtake the truck, I suddenly saw a car coming towards me at high speed.*

4 *American informal* to leave a place ● *Let's move out guys – they're closing the bar.*

move out sb or **move** sb **out**

if someone in authority [e.g. police, government] moves people out of a place, they arrange for them to leave that place ● *The American government finally decided to move its troops out.*

move over   moves, moving, moved

move over

1 to change the place where you are sitting or standing so that there is space for someone else to sit or stand ● *If you move over a bit, Tess can sit next to me.* ● *Tim moved over so that I could sit down.*

2 to leave your job so that someone who is younger or who has new ideas can do it instead ● *It's time she moved over and let someone else chair the committee.* ● *Our next guest is a 19-year-old with a wonderful voice and a great new record so move over, Madonna!* (= this person is younger and better than you)

3 (always + *adv/prep*) to start a new job which involves similar work to the work you did before ● (often + **to**) *She began work as a radio journalist and then moved over to television.*

4 (always + *adv/prep*) *mainly British & Australian* to start using a different system ● (often + **from**) *We've recently moved over from oil to gas heating.*

move towards   moves, moving, moved

move towards sth/doing sth

if you move towards something, the preparations for achieving it have begun and it is likely to happen soon ● *The government is moving further towards democracy.* ● *The board of directors has moved towards accepting the demands of the union.*

move up   moves, moving, moved

move up

British & Australian to move slightly so that there is enough space for someone else ● *Could you move up, Joe, so that Emily can sit down?*

move up (sb) or **move** (sb) **up**

1 to get a more important job, or to give someone a more important job ● (often + **to**) *James Webb has been moved up to senior editor.* ● *She moved up last month to become deputy manager.*

2 if a student moves up, or if a teacher moves them up, they are put in a higher level or class ● (often + **to**) *She was doing so well in class that she was moved up to the next grade.*

mow down   mows, mowing, mowed
pp also **mown**

mow down sb or **mow** sb **down**

to kill people, usually in large numbers, by shooting them or driving into them in a vehicle ● (usually passive) *Forty people were mowed down when gunmen opened fire at the funeral.* ● *Hundreds of cyclists each year are mown down by careless drivers.*

muck about/around   mucks, mucking, mucked

muck about/around *mainly British & Australian informal*

to waste time doing silly things ● *He was always in trouble for mucking about in class.* ● *I wasn't really working – I was just mucking around on the computer.*

muck sb **about/around** *British & Australian informal*

to treat someone badly, especially by changing your mind a lot or not doing what you have promised ● *I'm fed up with them mucking us around and cancelling our arrangements.* ● *That boyfriend of hers really mucks her around.*

muck about/around with   mucks, mucking, mucked

muck about/around with sth *British & Australian informal*

to try to change or improve something, usually with bad results ● *I wouldn't muck about with the engine if I were you – I'd take it to the garage.* ● *Tom's been mucking about with the video and I can't get it to work.*

muck in   mucks, mucking, mucked

muck in

British & Australian informal to share the work that needs to be done • *If we all muck in we can probably get the place cleaned up in a couple of hours.* • *And although he's the boss, he's not afraid to muck in with the rest of us.* (= he does not consider himself too important to work with everyone else)

muck out   mucks, mucking, mucked

muck out (sth) or **muck** (sth) **out**

to clean the place where a large animal lives [e.g. stables] • *For a bit of extra money she helps muck out a friend's racing stables.*

muck up   mucks, mucking, mucked

muck up sth or **muck** sth **up**

1 mainly British & Australian informal to do something very badly • *I'm going to prepare for this interview because I really don't want to muck it up like the last one.* • *I mucked up the whole exam.*
   muck-up n [C] British & Australian informal (usually singular) *I made a real muck-up of my first driving test.*
2 mainly British & Australian informal to spoil something, for example a plan or a system • *The car's broken down so that's mucked up our plans for the weekend.* • *If I had a baby now it would muck up my career.*
3 informal to make something dirty • *I was going to wear my new beige jacket but I've gone and mucked it up.*

muck up Australian informal

if someone, especially a child, mucks up, they behave badly • *Pete was always mucking up at school and getting in trouble.*

muck up sb or **muck** sb **up** Australian informal

to treat someone badly, especially by changing your mind a lot or not doing what you have promised • *Jan's late again. She's always mucking me up.*

muddle along/on   muddles, muddling, muddled

muddle along/on

to continue doing something with no clear purpose or plan • *I don't think he knows where his career is going – he just muddles along from day to day.*

muddle through   muddles, muddling, muddled

muddle through

to succeed in doing something even though you have difficulties because you do not really know how to do it • *Nothing really prepares you for looking after a small baby but somehow you muddle through.* • *None of us has had any formal training but we've managed to muddle through.*

muddle up   muddles, muddling, muddled

muddle up sth or **muddle** sth **up**

to spoil the order or arrangement of a group of things • *I arranged these cards alphabetically and she's gone and muddled them up.* • *If you don't put pairs of socks together they all get muddled up in the drawer.*

muddle up sb/sth or **muddle** sb/sth **up**

to confuse two people or things in your mind • (usually passive) *The two older brothers look very similar and I get them muddled up.* • *You've muddled up the Italian word with the Spanish one.*

mug up   mugs, mugging, mugged

mug up (sth) or **mug** (sth) **up** British informal

to quickly try to learn the main facts about a subject, especially before an exam • *He has to mug up his history for an exam tomorrow.* • (often + **on**) *I'd better mug up on my French before the interview.*

mull over   mulls, mulling, mulled

mull over sth or **mull** sth **over**

to think carefully about something for a long time, often before making a decision • *I need time to mull things over before I decide what to do.* • *I left Johnny mulling over the menu and went to look for Cleve.*

muscle in   muscles, muscling, muscled

muscle in
to force your way into a situation or activity in order to get an advantage, even though your involvement is not wanted ● (often + **on**) *When other companies saw how well she was doing they muscled in on the act.*

muscle into   muscles, muscling, muscled

muscle into sth
to force your way into a situation in order to get an advantage, even though your involvement is not wanted ● *Criminal gangs are muscling into the lucrative world of the car boot sale.*

muscle out   muscles, muscling, muscled

muscle out sb or **muscle** sb **out** *American informal*
to use power and influence to force someone out of a larger group ● *The electronics firm managed to muscle out several competitors to win the contract.* ● *He was muscled out of the planning committee by local businessmen.*

muster in/into   musters, mustering, mustered

muster in sb or **muster** sb **in** *American formal*

muster sb **into** sth *American formal*
to formally join the army or navy ● (usually passive) *He was mustered into the army last fall.*

muster out   musters, mustering, mustered

muster out sb or **muster** sb **out** *American formal*
to officially arrange for someone to leave their work, especially in the army or navy ● (usually passive) *Now that the war is over troops are being mustered out and sent home.*

muster up   musters, mustering, mustered

muster up sth or **muster** sth **up**
if you muster up braveness or energy, you try hard to find that quality in yourself because you need it in order to do something ● (often + to do sth) *She finally mustered up the courage to ask him for more money.* ● *I'm trying to muster up the energy to go for a walk.*

muss up   musses, mussing, mussed

muss up sth or **muss** sth **up** *mainly American informal*
to make something untidy or spoil its appearance ● *She's worried the wind will muss up her hair.*

N

naff off

Naff off! (always an order) *British slang*
something that you say in order to tell
someone to go away because they are annoying you • *Just tell those reporters to
naff off!*

nail down   nails, nailing, nailed

nail down sb or **nail** sb **down**
to make someone give you exact details
or a decision about something • (often +
to) *They've agreed to do it but we haven't
managed to nail them down to a date yet.*
• *I don't know what his position is on this
– I'm going to have to nail him down.*

nail down sth or **nail** sth **down**
1 *American* to succeed in getting or achieving something • *There is some doubt as to
whether they will be able to nail down the
financing for the project.*
2 *American* to understand something completely, or to describe something accurately • *It's difficult to nail down exactly
what are the weaknesses of the system.*

name after/for   names, naming, named

name sb/sth **after** sb/sth *British,
American & Australian*

name sb/sth **for** sb/sth *American*
to give someone or something the same
name as someone or something else
• (usually passive) *Thomas was named
after his grandfather.* • *The Brendan
Byrne Arena was named for the former
Governor of New Jersey.*

narrow down   narrows, narrowing, narrowed

narrow down sth or **narrow** sth
down
to make something [e.g. list, choice, op-
tion] smaller and clearer by removing the
things that are less important • *The police department attempted to narrow down
the list of suspects.* • (often + **to**) *The*
*committee had narrowed the choices down
to two.*

nibble away at   nibbles, nibbling, nibbled

nibble away at sth
to slowly reduce something • *Even when
inflation is low, it nibbles away at people's
savings.*

nick off   nicks, nicking, nicked

nick off *Australian informal*
to leave • *See you later, we're nicking off
to the pub.*

Nick off! (always an order) *Australian informal*
something you say to tell someone that
you want them to leave • *Just nick off and
leave us in peace!*

nick out   nicks, nicking, nicked

nick out *Australian informal*
to leave somewhere for a short time • *Bill
just nicked out for a second. He'll be back
soon.*

nod off   nods, nodding, nodded

nod off *informal*
to fall asleep when you do not intend to
go to sleep • *I nodded off just before the
end of the film.*

nose about/around   noses, nosing, nosed

nose about/around (swh) *informal*
to look around a place, often in order to
find something • *I don't like the idea of
someone nosing around in my bedroom.* • *I*

was just nosing around his office.

nose out   noses, nosing, nosed

nose out sth or **nose** sth **out** *mainly British & Australian*

to discover information by searching carefully • *She seems to have a gift for nosing out people's secrets.*

nose out sb or **nose** sb **out** *informal*

to defeat someone by a small amount, especially in an election or a sport • *He was nosed out of second place by a former colleague.*

notch up   notches, notching, notched

notch up sth or **notch** sth **up**

to achieve something [e.g. victory, points] • *She has recently notched up her third win at a major tennis tournament.*

note down   notes, noting, noted

note down sth or **note** sth **down**

to write words or numbers, often so that you do not forget them • *I noted down the telephone number of the agency.* • *Did you note down the address?*

number among   numbers, numbering, numbered

number (sb/sth) **among** sth *formal*

to include someone or something in a particular group, or to be included in a particular group • *Reeves numbered among the intellectuals who were members of the group.* • *The city numbers among the most active trading centres in the country.*

nut out   nuts, nutting, nutted

nut out sth or **nut** sth **out** *Australian informal*

to understand something, or to find the answer to something by thinking about it • *It took all morning but I finally managed to nut it out.*

nuzzle up   nuzzles, nuzzling, nuzzled

nuzzle up

to rub your head or nose against someone, especially to show that you like them • (often + **against**) *He got into bed and nuzzled up against her.*

room, area, or road, you can enter one from the other directly ● *The square opens off the main street of the town.*

open onto   opens, opening, opened

open onto sth

if a room, window, or door opens onto a place, it opens in the direction of that place or has a view of it ● *The kitchen opens onto a large breakfast room.* ● *The windows at the back open onto fields.*

open out   opens, opening, opened

open out (sth) or **open** (sth) **out**

1 to unfold, or to unfold something ● *We need one of those sofas that opens out into a bed.* ● *He opened the map out and studied it carefully.*

2 to begin to involve more people or things than before, or to make something do this ● *In the last three chapters of the book, the argument opens out to encompass the whole of Western literature.* ● *The debate should be opened out into a general discussion on environmental policy.*

open out

if a road or path opens out, it becomes wider ● (often + **into**) *As you emerge from the wood, the path opens out into a wide track.* ● *The long tunnel of overhanging branches opens out into a clearing.*

open up   opens, opening, opened

open up (sth) or **open** (sth) **up**

1 to open the door of a building, often by unlocking it ● *We've arranged for the caretaker to open up the building.* ● *Open up – we know you're in there!*

2 if a country or area opens up, or is opened up, it becomes easier to travel around it or sell things to it ● *Cheaper air travel has opened up all kinds of new holiday destinations.* ● (often + **to**) *Eastern European markets are opening up to Western investment.*

3 to create a new opportunity or possibility ● *This latest discovery opens up almost unlimited possibilities for research.* ● *When you've got a qualification like that, so many career opportunities open up.*

4 to start a new shop or business ● *Several banks have recently opened up new branches in the city centre.* ● *Fast food restaurants are opening up everywhere you look.*

object to   objects, objecting, objected

object to sth/sb/doing sth

to feel or say that you oppose or dislike something or someone ● *What I object to is being spoken to as if I'm a complete idiot.* ● *Someone in the meeting objected to his use of the word 'girl' instead of 'woman'.*

occur to   occurs, occurring, occurred

occur to sb

if a thought or idea occurs to you, it comes into your mind ● (often + **that**) *It didn't occur to me that he might be offended.* ● (often + to do sth) *Did it ever occur to you to ask where she'd been?* ● *The thought did occur to me.*

offend against   offends, offending, offended

offend against sth *formal*

to go against a principle, or to go against what people consider to be morally right ● *The channel was banned on the grounds that it 'offended against good taste and decency'.*

offer up   offers, offering, offered

offer up sth or **offer** sth **up**

if you offer up a prayer or a sacrifice (= something offered to God in a ceremony), you pray to God or you sacrifice something ● *Prayers of thanksgiving were offered up each morning.*

open into   opens, opening, opened

open into sth

if a room or door opens into a room or other space, it opens in the direction of that place ● *The door opened into a tiny hallway.* ● *Their bedroom opens into the bathroom.*

open off   opens, opening, opened

open off sth

if a room, area, or road opens off another

open up sth or open sth up

1 to show something that was hidden or not previously known • *The security council debate could open up sharp differences between the countries.* • *Getting to know Patrick opened up a whole new world for me.*

2 to increase the number of points by which one competitor is winning • *Davis opened up a gap of ten points over the defending champion.* • *Latest surveys show the Labour party opening up a clear lead in the opinion polls.*

open up

1 to start to talk more about yourself and your feelings • (often + **to**) *I've never opened up to anyone like I do to you.* • *He's quite a private person – it took quite a while for him to open up.*

2 to start firing a weapon • *Enemy guns opened up as the planes flew in.* • (sometimes + **on**) *A lone gunman opened up on the crowd.*

open up sb/sth or open sb/sth up

to cut open the body of a person or animal in order to do a medical operation • *When the doctors opened her up they couldn't find anything wrong with her.*

opt in/into   opts, opting, opted

opt in *British & Australian*

opt into sth *British & Australian*

to choose to become involved in an arrangement or activity [esp. plan, scheme] • *I've decided to opt into the company's pension scheme.* • *People were told about the research project and asked whether they wanted to opt in.*

opt out   opts, opting, opted

opt out

to choose not to be part of an activity or arrangement [esp. plan, scheme], or to stop being involved in it • (often + **of**) *He's decided to opt out of the company's pension scheme.* • *Given the option of leaving government control, many schools have decided to opt out and become independent.*

order about/around   orders, ordering, ordered

order sb **about/around**

to tell someone what they should do all the time • *You can't just come in here and start ordering people around.*

order in   orders, ordering, ordered

order in sth or **order** sth **in** *American*

to order food that is ready to eat to be brought to your house or the place where you work • *We stayed in last night, watched a video and ordered in a pizza.*

order out   orders, ordering, ordered

order out *American*

to order food that is ready to eat to be brought to your house or the place where you work • (usually + **for**) *We ordered out for sandwiches and worked through lunch.*

own up   owns, owning, owned

own up

to admit that you have done something wrong, especially something that is not important • (often + **to**) *Someone obviously broke the machine but no-one will own up to it. Come on, own up! Who's been using my mug?*

pace off/out   paces, pacing, paced

pace off/out sth or **pace** sth **off/out**
(never passive)
to measure a distance by taking steps of equal size across it and counting them ● *I was just pacing out the room to see where the bed would fit.*

pack away   packs, packing, packed

pack away sth or **pack** sth **away**
1 to put something into a bag or container, or to put something in the place where it is usually kept ● *Come on, James, pack away your toys now, please.* ● *All her clothes and belongings had been packed away in trunks and boxes.*
2 *informal* to eat a lot of food ● *For a small person she can pack away an impressive amount of food.*

pack in   packs, packing, packed

pack in sth or **pack** sth **in** *informal*
1 to stop doing something, especially a job ● *My job was really boring so I decided to pack it in.*
2 to manage to do a lot of activities in a period of time ● *We were only there four days but we packed so much in.*

Pack it in! (always an order) *British & Australian informal*
something that you say in order to tell someone to stop doing something that is annoying you ● *Pack it in, you two! You've been arguing all morning.*

pack in sb or **pack** sb **in**
1 if a film, play, or performance packs people in, a lot of people come to see it ● (sometimes + **at**) *The rock show 'Hot Stuff' is already packing them in at a London theatre.*
2 *British informal* to end a romantic relationship with someone ● *They're not seeing each other any more – she's packed him in.*

pack into   packs, packing, packed

pack sth **into** sth
to manage to do a lot of activities in a period of time ● *We packed a lot of sight-seeing into our weekend in New York.*

pack off   packs, packing, packed

pack off sb or **pack** sb **off** *informal*
to send someone away, usually because you do not want them to be with you ● (usually + **to**) *When they were eleven, the twins were packed off to boarding school.* ● *I packed him off to the doctor's.*

pack out   packs, packing, packed

pack out sth or **pack** sth **out** *British*
to make a place very full ● *100,000 football supporters packed out Wembley Stadium to see the game.*

packed out *adj* (always after verb)
● *The cinema was absolutely packed out.*

pack up   packs, packing, packed

pack up (sth) or **pack** (sth) **up**
to collect your things together and put them into bags or boxes, especially when you have finished doing something ● *I just need a few minutes to pack up my equipment, and then we can leave.* ● *I got to the market just as it was closing and everyone was packing up.*

pack up
1 *British informal* if a machine packs up, it stops working ● *Our car's packed up again.*
2 *informal* to finish work ● *I usually pack up early on Friday afternoons.*

pad out   pads, padding, padded

pad out sth or **pad** sth **out**
to make a piece of writing or a speech longer by adding more information or words, usually in a way that does not improve it ● (often + **with**) *If your essay is on the short side, you can always pad it out with a few quotations.*

page through   pages, paging, paged

page through sth *American*
to turn the pages of a book or magazine and look at them quickly, usually without reading them ● *She watched the official page through her passport.*

pair off   pairs, pairing, paired

pair off

if two people pair off, they start a romantic relationship ● *Two months into the course, everyone started pairing off.*

pair off with   pairs, pairing, paired

pair sb **off with** sb

to introduce two people to each other, hoping that they will start a romantic relationship ● *I think she was trying to pair me off with her brother.*

pair up   pairs, pairing, paired

pair up

to join another person for a short time in order to do something ● (often + **with**) *We had to pair up with another person for a couple of the activities.*

pal around   pals, palling, palled

pal around *American informal*

to spend time with someone that you are very friendly with ● (often + **with**) *He had a glamorous life palling around with famous people.*

pal up   pals, palling, palled

pal up *British & Australian informal*

to become friends with someone ● (usually + **with**) *She's palled up with some people from work and they're going on holiday together.*

palm off   palms, palming, palmed

palm off sb or **palm** sb **off**

to give someone an explanation for something that is not true but which you hope will satisfy them ● (usually + **with**) *I feel I've just been palmed off with a series of excuses.*

palm off as   palms, palming, palmed

palm sth **off as** sth

to try to persuade someone that something has a particular quality or value that it does not have ● *He was trying to palm it off as an original when it clearly wasn't.*

palm off on/onto   palms, palming, palmed

palm off sth/sb **on/onto** sb or **palm** sth/sb **off on/onto** sb

to give or sell something to someone because you want to get rid of it ● *So you've got a newer, better computer and you're trying to palm the old one off on me!* ● *They're always palming their kids off onto other people.*

pan out   pans, panning, panned

pan out (always + *adv/prep*)

to develop or happen in a particular way ● *We'll have to see how things pan out.*

pander to   panders, pandering, pandered

pander to sb/sth

to do or provide what someone wants, although you know that it is wrong ● *I'm not really interested in pandering to male fantasies.*

paper over   papers, papering, papered

paper over sth

to hide a disagreement or difficulty and try to make people believe that there is no problem ● *Respective governments have papered over many of the disagreements between the two countries.* ● *He accused Walker of 'trying to **paper over the cracks** in (= hide the difficulties with) his party's policy'.*

parcel out   parcels, parcelling, parcelled (*American* parceling, parceled)

parcel out sth or **parcel** sth **out**

to divide something into several parts and give them to different people ● *The remaining profits were parcelled out to six outside companies.*

parcel up   parcels, parcelling, parcelled

parcel up sth or **parcel** sth **up** *British*

to wrap something and make it into a parcel ● *Parcel up those tins and we'll send them off tomorrow.*

pare down   pares, paring, pared

pare down sth or **pare** sth **down**

to reduce the size or amount of something ● *A lot of companies have pared their staff down to a minimum.*

pared-down *adj* (always before noun) ● *It was a pared-down version of the play, lasting an hour and a half.*

parlay into   parlays, parlaying, parlayed

parlay sth **into** sth *American*

to use an advantage that you have, for example money or skills, to make a lot of money • *He bought a hamburger stand which he later parlayed into the third largest food service business in the country.*

part with parts, parting, parted
part with sth

to give something away, usually when you do not want to • *I was going to give away her old baby clothes but I couldn't bring myself to part with them.* • *You know how difficult it is getting Simon to part with his hard-earned cash.* (= to spend money)

partake of partakes, partaking, partook, partaken
partake of sth

1 *formal* to have similar qualities to something else • *Her fiction partakes of the vivid emotional world of a child.*
2 *formal* to eat or drink something • *Would you care to partake of a little refreshment?*

partition off partitions, partitioning, partitioned
partition off sth or **partition** sth **off**

to separate one part of a room from another using a thin wall or a piece of glass • (usually passive) *One part of the bedroom was partitioned off to form a study.*

partner off/up partners, partnering, partnered
partner off/up (sb) or **partner** (sb) **off/up** *mainly British & Australian*

to become someone's partner in a game, sport, or dance, or to make someone do this • (sometimes + **with**) *For most of the dances you had to partner off with someone.*

pass around/round passes, passing, passed
pass around/round sth or **pass** sth **around/round**

to offer something to each person in a group of people • *Take a copy for yourself and pass the rest around.* • *I thought it would be nice to have some chocolates to pass round.*

pass as/for passes, passing, passed
pass as/for sb/sth (never passive)

if someone or something passes as someone or something else, they appear like that person or thing • *She's fifteen but she could easily pass for eighteen.* • *Their food is really good, especially if you think about **what passes for** (= what is considered) food in most pubs.*

pass away passes, passing, passed
pass away

1 to die • *She passed away peacefully in her sleep.* • *I've lived on my own since my husband passed away five years ago.*
2 *slightly formal* if a period of time passes away, it stops existing • *The great age of coal mining in the region has long since passed away.*

pass by passes, passing, passed
pass by (sb/swh)

to go past a person or place without stopping • *He passes by our house on his way to work.* • *I just happened to be passing by when it happened.*

pass by (swh) (never passive) *British*

to visit somewhere for a short time, usually while you are going somewhere else • *I'll pass by the shop on my way home and buy a paper.* • *I told Helen that you'd pass by to collect the books.*

pass by

if time or a period of time passes by, it goes past • *Time seems to pass by so slowly when you're at school.* • *As the weeks passed by, I began to give up hope of ever seeing him again.*

pass sb **by**

if an event or opportunity passes you by, you do not notice it or you do not get any advantage from it • *I was so busy studying for my exams that the election passed me by completely.* • *You mustn't let an opportunity like that pass you by.* • *I sometimes get the feeling that **life is passing me by**.* (= that I am not doing the same interesting or enjoyable things as other people)

pass down passes, passing, passed
pass down sth or **pass** sth **down**

to teach or give something to someone who will be alive after you have died • (usually passive; often + **from**) *Tales such as these were passed down from generation to generation.* • *In the past, buttons were often kept and passed down from* *mother to daughter.*

pass for

see **pass as/for**

pass off   passes, passing, passed

pass off (always + *adv/prep*) *British & Australian*

if an event passes off in a good way, it happens in that way ● *The demonstration passed off peacefully, although there were over 200,000 people present.*

pass off as   passes, passing, passed

pass off sth/sb **as** sth/sb or **pass** sth/sb **off as** sth/sb

to pretend that something or someone is a better type of thing or person than they really are, especially in order to deceive someone ● *She'd tried to pass the painting off as a Picasso.* ● (often reflexive) *He then went to the States where he tried to pass himself off as an aristocrat.*

pass on   passes, passing, passed

pass on sth or **pass** sth **on**

1 to tell someone something that someone else has told you ● (often + **to**) *Did you pass on my message to Jeremy?* ● *They were in possession of vital information which they failed to pass on to the police.*

2 to give something to someone else ● (often + **to**) *Could you pass it on to Laura when you've finished reading it?*

3 to teach your skills or knowledge to younger people ● (often + **to**) *One of the pleasures of being a teacher is being able to pass on your knowledge of a subject.*

4 if someone passes on a disease or physical quality to their child, their child also has it ● (often + **to**) *It is thought that these cancer-causing genes can be passed on to the next generation.* ● *In the past, people with diseases that could be passed on were often advised not to have children.*

5 to give a disease to another person or animal ● (often + **to**) *Scientists are worried that BSE can be passed on to humans.* ● *The virus can be passed on through physical contact.*

6 if a company passes on savings or increased costs to its customers, it makes the prices it charges for goods lower or higher because the cost of producing the goods has become lower or higher ● (often + **to**) *The rise in the price of*

computer chips means that computer manufacturers will be passing on this increase to consumers.*

pass on

to die ● *Did you hear that Mrs Thomas had passed on?*

pass on to   passes, passing, passed

pass on to sth (never passive) *British & Australian*

to begin to talk about a new subject during a discussion ● *Let's pass on to the next item on the agenda.*

pass out   passes, passing, passed

pass out

1 to become unconscious ● *It was so hot in the stadium that I thought I was going to pass out.* ● *He came back drunk from Gav's party and passed out on the sofa.*

2 *British & Australian* to successfully finish a training course at a police or military college ● *He was posted to Northern Ireland a month after he passed out.*

passing-out *adj* (always before noun) *British & Australian* ● *The end of their six-month training course was marked by a passing-out parade.*

pass out sth or **pass** sth **out**

to give something to each person in a group of people ● *Could you pass those books out?*

pass over   passes, passing, passed

pass over sb or **pass** sb **over**

to not give someone a job or a higher position and give it to someone else who is younger or less experienced ● (usually passive) *Ms Williams claims that she was passed over because she was pregnant.* ● (often + **for**) *He decided to retire at the age of 55 after being passed over for promotion.*

pass over sth or **pass** sth **over**

to avoid discussing a particular subject, or to ignore something that someone has said ● *The media has been accused of passing over some of the most disturbing details of the case.* ● *Yes, well, we'll pass over that last comment.*

pass round

see **pass around/round**

pass to   passes, passing, passed

pass to sb *slightly formal*

if something passes to someone, they begin to own or be responsible for it • *On his aunt's death, all her property will pass to him.* • *The presidency of the EU will pass to the Netherlands next year.*

pass up   passes, passing, passed

pass up sth or **pass** sth **up**

to decide not to use an opportunity or a chance • (often + to do sth) *I can't believe she passed up the chance to go to Australia.* • *It's a great opportunity – you'd be a fool to pass it up.*

patch together   patches, patching, patched

patch together sth or **patch** sth **together**

1 to arrange something very quickly and not very carefully • *We managed to patch together a last-minute deal after the original deal collapsed.*

2 to create something quickly by joining several different things together • *After the civil war ended, a national army was patched together from three resistance groups.*

patch up   patches, patching, patched

patch up sth or **patch** sth **up**

1 to try to improve your relationship with someone after an argument • *Apparently, they're trying to patch up their marriage.* • *Has he managed to patch things up with Emma after their little fall-out?*

2 to quickly repair something • *I've patched up the hole in the shed roof with a piece of plastic.*

patch up sb or **patch** sb **up** *slightly informal*

to give basic medical treatment to someone who is injured • *The hospital had no drugs or equipment, but the doctors did their best to patch up the injured.*

paw at   paws, pawing, pawed

paw at sth

if an animal paws at something, it touches that thing again and again because it wants something • *The dog was pawing at the door, trying to get back in.*

paw at sb *informal*

to touch someone roughly in a sexual way, when they do not want you to do this • *The last thing you want is a group of drunken football-fans pawing at you.*

pay back   pays, paying, paid

pay back sb/sth or **pay** sb/sth **back**

to pay someone the money that you owe them • *Pay me back another time. I don't need the money just now.* • *Only borrow the money if you're sure you'll be able to pay it back.*

pay back sb or **pay** sb **back**

to do something unpleasant to someone because they have done something unpleasant to you • (usually + **for**) *I'm going to pay him back for all those things he said about me.*

pay for   pays, paying, paid

pay for sth

to be punished for doing something bad to someone else, or to suffer because of a mistake you have made • *He stopped me from getting that job and I'm going to make him pay for it.* • *I didn't bother having the car checked, a mistake **for** which I **paid dearly**.* (= a mistake which caused me a lot of problems)

pay in/into   pays, paying, paid

pay in sth or **pay** sth **in**

pay sth **into** sth

to put money into a bank account • *I still haven't paid that cheque in.* • *I've just got to pay some money into my account.*

pay off   pays, paying, paid

pay off sth or **pay** sth **off**

if you pay off a debt [e.g. loan, mortgage, overdraft], you pay back all the money you owe • *I'm planning to pay off my bank loan within five years.* • *It makes sense to pay off your credit card balance every month.*

pay off

if something that you have done to try to achieve something pays off, it is successful • *I was pleased to hear about your job offer – all that hard work has obviously paid off.*

pay-off n [C] • *The pay-off, as far as I'm concerned, is the freedom to use my time as I wish.*

pay off sb or **pay** sb **off**

1 to give someone money so that they will not do something • *The gang threatened to attack his business premises unless he paid them off.* • (sometimes + to do sth) *There were rumours that key witnesses had been paid off to keep quiet.*

pay-off n [C] • *He has been accused of making an illegal pay-off to the police to avoid prosecution.*

2 to tell a worker that there is no more work for them after paying them the money that you owe them for work already done • *The city council has decided to pay off 50 of its employees and take on temporary staff instead.*

pay-off n [C] • *She left her job as chief executive of the company with a £50,000 pay-off.*

pay out   pays, paying, paid

pay out (sth) or **pay** (sth) **out**

to spend a lot of money on something, or to pay a lot of money to someone • *I had to pay out £300 to get my car fixed.* • *If the insurers pay out, we should get about £600 for it.* • (sometimes + **in**) *An additional £265 million has been paid out in unemployment benefits this year.*

payout n [C] a payment made to someone who has won a competition or made a claim to an insurance company • *The winner of the lottery will receive a payout of £3 million.* • *The earthquake cost insurers millions of dollars in payouts.*

pay out sth or **pay** sth **out**

to release a piece of rope slowly and carefully • *I started the boat's engine while Alex paid out the rope.*

pay up   pays, paying, paid

pay up *informal*

to give someone the money that you owe them, especially when you do not want to • *If he doesn't pay up, I'll throw him out. It's as simple as that.* • (often an order) *That's fifty bucks you owe me. Come on, pay up!*

pay up sth or **pay** sth **up** *American*

to pay all the money that you owe for something • *We finally paid up the mortgage.*

peal out   peals, pealing, pealed

peal out

if bells peal out, they ring loudly • *It was 10 o'clock on a Sunday morning and the church bells were pealing out.*

peck at   pecks, pecking, pecked

peck at sth

to eat small quantities of food without any enthusiasm • *She only pecked at her food – I think she's upset about something.*

peel off   peels, peeling, peeled

peel off sth or **peel** sth **off**

1 to take off a wet or tight piece of clothing • *She peeled off her swimsuit and started drying herself with a towel.* • *He took off his thick coat and peeled off his gloves.*

2 to take some money from a large pile of bank notes that you are holding in your hand • *He peeled off five £10 notes and handed them to me.*

peel off

to move away from the group that you are travelling with and start travelling in another direction • *One of the planes peeled off and circled around to the left.*

peg away   pegs, pegging, pegged

peg away *old-fashioned*

to continue doing something that is difficult in order to achieve the result you want • (often + **at**) *Louise had been pegging away at her books* (= studying for a long time) *and was looking very tired.*

peg down   pegs, pegging, pegged

peg down sth or **peg** sth **down**

to fasten something [e.g. tent, net] to the

ground by using small metal or wooden sticks ● *Remember to peg your tent down well so the rain doesn't get in.*

peg out   pegs, pegging, pegged

peg out sth or **peg** sth **out**
British & Australian to fasten wet clothes or sheets to a washing line so that they become dry ● *Have you pegged out the washing yet?*

peg out
1 *British & Australian old-fashioned, informal* if a person pegs out, they die ● *My uncle Jack, now he pegged out at the age of 95.*
2 *British & Australian old-fashioned, informal* if a machine pegs out, it stops working ● *My car finally pegged out five miles from home.*

pelt down   pelts, pelting, pelted

pelt down *informal*
to rain very heavily ● *Take an umbrella with you – it's pelting down outside.* ● (sometimes + **with**) *It's been pelting down with rain all day.*

pen in

be penned in (always passive)
if someone is penned in, they feel that the situation they are in does not allow them to do what they want ● *I can't imagine myself penned in at home with small children.*

pen in/up   pens, penning, penned

pen in/up sth/sb or **pen** sth/sb **in/up**
to shut animals or people in a small, enclosed area ● (usually passive) *The rebel army was penned in on all sides by government troops.*

pencil in   pencils, pencilling, pencilled
(*American & Australian* also **penciling, penciled**)

pencil in sth/sb or **pencil** sth/sb **in**
to arrange for something to happen or for someone to do something on a particular date, knowing that the arrangement might be changed later ● (often + **for**) *I'll pencil in the meeting for next Friday and confirm it later.* ● *'Can you suggest someone who would speak at the conference?' 'Pencil in Barbara Glennon and I'll phone her to check.'*

pension off   pensions, pensioning, pensioned

pension off sb or **pension** sb **off**
if an organization pensions off someone who has worked for a long time, it makes them leave their job and it gives them their pension (= money paid to someone who is too old to work) ● *The company has decided to pension off all members of staff over the age of 55.*

pep up   peps, pepping, pepped

pep up sth/sb or **pep** sth/sb **up** *slightly informal*
to make something more interesting or attractive, or to make someone feel more active or energetic ● *You can pep up a plain outfit with a bright scarf.* ● *A good night's sleep will soon pep you up.*

pepper with   peppers, peppering, peppered

pepper sth **with** sth
1 if you pepper a speech or piece of writing with a particular style of language, you include a lot of that type of language ● (usually passive) *Her speeches are peppered with literary references.*
2 to fill an area with a lot of a particular type of thing ● (usually passive) *The southern coast is peppered with pretty villages and ports.*

pepper sb/sth **with** sth
to hit someone or something again and again with bullets ● *They peppered him with gunshot before leaving him to die.*

pepper sb **with** sth *American*
to annoy someone by asking them a lot of questions or by making a lot of requests or complaints ● *A crowd of reporters peppered the senator with questions as he left the building.*

perk up   perks, perking, perked

perk up (sb) or **perk** (sb) **up**
to suddenly become happier or more energetic, or to make someone feel this way ● *I felt really tired when I woke up, but I'd perked up a bit by lunchtime.* ● *A strong cup of coffee might perk you up.* ● (sometimes + **at**) *She perked up at* (= when she thought about) *the prospect of lunch.*

perk up

if something perks up, it improves or becomes more exciting • *Share prices on the stock exchange have perked up after last week's fall.* • *I thought the first hour of the film was a bit dull but it perked up in the second half.*

permit of permits, permitting, permitted

permit of sth (never passive) *formal*

to allow something to be possible • (usually negative) *This rule permits of no exceptions.* • *He must have taken the money; the facts permit of no other interpretation.*

pertain to pertains, pertaining, pertained

pertain to sth *formal*

to be connected with a particular subject, event, or situation • *The charges against him pertain to a series of illegal deals he made in 1992.* • *A reward has been offered for information pertaining to the incident.*

peter out peters, petering, petered

peter out

1 if an energetic activity or a strong emotion peters out, it gradually becomes less energetic or strong until it stops completely • *The fierce fighting in the capital has finally petered out.* • *Early enthusiasm for the project is now petering out as people realize how much work is involved.*

2 if a path peters out, it gradually becomes narrower until it ends completely • *The track petered out after three miles and we had to find our own way through the forest.*

phase in phases, phasing, phased

phase in sth or **phase** sth **in**

to make a new system, process, or law gradually begin to happen or exist • *The new tax will be phased in over five years.* • *The government is phasing in tougher safety standards for cars.*

phase out phases, phasing, phased

phase out sth or **phase** sth **out**

to gradually stop using or supplying something • *Sweden is planning to phase out its nuclear reactors by the year 2010.* • *Farm subsidies will be phased out over the next few years.*

phone around/round phones, phoning, phoned

phone around/round (sb) (never passive) *mainly British*

to telephone several people, often in order to find out information • *Why don't you phone around and see if any of your friends want to come?* • *I'll phone around a few travel agents and see if I can get a cheaper ticket.*

phone in phones, phoning, phoned

phone in

1 *mainly British* to telephone a radio or television station in order to express your opinion or ask a question during a programme that is being broadcast • *Listeners who want to speak to the Health Minister should phone in with their questions.* • *Over three hundred people phoned in to complain about the programme.*
phone-in n [C] *mainly British* • *I always listen to the late-night phone-in on Radio 1.* • (used as *adj*) *It's a radio phone-in show.*

2 *mainly British* to telephone the place where you work in order to tell your employer something • *You should phone in and tell Steve you're going to be late.* • *Anna's just **phoned in sick**.* (= telephoned to say she is ill and cannot come to work)

phone round

see **phone around/round**

phone up phones, phoning, phoned

phone up (sb) or **phone** (sb) **up** *mainly British*

to telephone someone • *I hadn't spoken to you for ages so I thought I'd phone you up.* • *Why don't you phone up and see if there are any tickets left for tonight?*

pick at picks, picking, picked

pick at sth

1 to eat only a small amount of a meal because you are not hungry or because you are feeling ill • *Bec was picking at her food in a dejected way.*

2 to pull something using your fingernails again and again • *If you pick at that scab on your knee it will never heal.* • *She sat nervously in the dentist's waiting-room, picking at the sleeve of her jumper.*

pick off   picks, picking, picked

pick off sb/sth or **pick** sb/sth **off**

1 to shoot and kill a person or animal that is in a group, or to shoot at and destroy a ship or aircraft that is travelling in a group • *A gunman picked off the soldiers one by one as they ran for cover.* • *Five ships were picked off by torpedo boats during the attack.*

2 to take the best person or thing from a group • *Several leading British scientists have been picked off by American universities.* • *The Japanese-owned bank has the resources to be able to pick off foreign banks when they become available.*

pick on   picks, picking, picked

pick on sb

to choose one person from a group of people to criticize or treat unfairly, especially when they are smaller or weaker than you • *He was picked on at school because he was much smaller than the other kids.* • *I felt I was being picked on.* • *(informal) Why don't you **pick on someone your own size**?* (= threaten someone who is as big or powerful as you)

pick out   picks, picking, picked

pick out sth/sb or **pick** sth/sb **out**

1 to choose one thing or person or several things or people from a large group • *She picked out a pink shirt for me to try on.* • *Over 200 people applied for the job and we had to pick out eight to interview.*

2 to recognize a person or thing from a group of people or things • *A witness picked out the attacker from police photos.* • *See if you can pick out the drawing that Joe did.*

3 to manage to see something or someone, but not clearly • *It was dark outside but I could just pick out the outline of the mountains.*

4 if a light picks out someone or something, it shines only on them so that they can be seen clearly • *She walked onto the stage, picked out by a spotlight.*

pick out sth or **pick** sth **out**

to manage to play a tune on a musical instrument slowly or with difficulty • *(often + on) Sing the tune and Steve will pick it out on the guitar.* • *I can't play the piano like Kath, but I can just about pick out a tune.*

be picked out (always passive) *mainly British & Australian*

if something [e.g. name, letter] is picked out in a particular colour, it can be seen clearly because it is brighter than what is around it, or it is a different colour • *(usually + in) The boat's name was picked out in bright gold letters.*

pick over   picks, picking, picked

pick over sth or **pick** sth **over**

1 to look carefully at a group of things, choosing what you want or getting rid of what you do not want • *By the time I got to the sales, most of the clothes had already been picked over.* • *Pick over the strawberries and throw out any mouldy ones.*

2 to examine or discuss something that has happened, showing a lot of interest in any unpleasant or embarrassing details • *For the past week, the press has been picking over the details of the murder.* • *No one likes having their past picked over in public.*

pick through   picks, picking, picked

pick through sth

to search through a pile of untidy things in order to find something you want • *He manages to survive by picking through other people's rubbish.* • *A team of investigators picked through the wreckage of the plane, trying to discover the cause of the crash.*

pick up   picks, picking, picked

pick up sth/sb or **pick** sth/sb **up**

1 to lift something or someone by using your hands • *I bent over to pick up my pen which had fallen on the floor.* • *If she starts to cry, pick her up and give her a cuddle.* • *She picked up the phone* (= the part of the telephone that you hold to your ear and mouth) *and dialled David's number.*

2 to collect someone who is waiting for you, or to collect something that you have left somewhere or that you have bought • *I'm just off to pick Stella up from the station.* • *Could you pick up my dry cleaning while you're in town?* • *Would you prefer to pick the tickets up*

or have them sent to you?

pick-up *n* [C] • *We arranged the pick-up for ten o'clock.* • (used as *adj*) *You can pay for your goods now and collect them later at the pick-up area.*

pickup *n* [C] *mainly American* a small vehicle with an open part at the back in which goods can be carried • *Jack's out in the pickup delivering potatoes to customers.* • (used as *adj*) *a pickup truck*

pick up sth or **pick** sth **up**

1 to get or buy something when you have gone to a place to do something else • *I picked up a leaflet on vitamin supplements while I was at the doctor's.* • *Should I pick up something for dinner while I'm in town?*

2 to buy something cheaply • *I picked up a half-price skirt in the sales.* • *You can pick up a decent camera for as little as $40.*

3 to learn a new skill or language by practising it rather than being taught it • *I picked up quite a lot of Spanish during my six-month stay in Madrid.* • *There's no formal training for a job like this – you just **pick it up as you go along.** (= you learn how to do the job as you work)*

4 if you pick up a way of speaking or behaving [e.g. accent, habit], you start to speak or behave in that way, usually because you have spent time in a particular place or with particular people • *Parents who smoke should discourage their children from picking up the habit.* • *I picked up a Canadian accent while I was living in Toronto.*

5 to learn interesting or useful information [e.g. idea, tip, gossip] from someone or something • *Did you pick up any interesting gossip from Emilio?* • *You can pick up some really useful tips from cookery programmes.*

6 to win a prize, or to get something that gives you an advantage [e.g. votes, support] • *Anthony Hopkins picked up the award for best actor.* • *The ruling party has picked up 70% of the vote in the elections.*

7 if someone picks up the total amount of money owed for something [e.g. bill, tab, cheque], they pay for it • (often + **for**) *If she loses the case, she'll have to pick up the bill for legal costs.* • *Taxpayers will be picking up the tab for an improved public*

transport network.

8 to get an infectious illness from someone or something • *Children pick up infections easily.* • *I picked up a bug while I was travelling in north Africa.*

9 if a device picks up a signal or programmes broadcast by a radio station, it receives them • *Antennas around the top of the ship picked up the radar signals.* • *You can pick up BBC Radio 4 in most of northern France.*

10 to become aware of a smell, or to notice something that someone has left which can help you to find them • *Police dogs picked up the scent of the two men from clothes they had left behind.* • *I lost their trail by the stream but picked it up again shortly afterwards.*

11 to notice a mistake in a piece of writing • *If there are any errors, the copy editor should pick them up.*

12 *informal* to earn a particular amount of money • *Top football players can expect to pick up around £200,000 a year.*

13 *American informal* to make a place tidy by putting things in the place where they are kept • *I've told the kids to pick up their rooms.*

pick up (sth) or **pick** (sth) **up**

to start something again [e.g. story, relationship] from the point where you had stopped • *He picked up the story at the point where Jill had been rushed to hospital.* • *I hoped that when Peter came back from the States, we'd just **pick up where we left off.** (= start our relationship again)*

pick up sb or **pick** sb **up**

1 *informal* to start talking to someone you do not know because you want to have a sexual relationship with them • *Do you often pick women up in bars?*

pick-up *n* [C] *informal* • *I just thought he was being friendly – it never occurred to me that it was a pick-up.* • (used as *adj*) *This bar has the reputation of being a pick-up joint. (= a place where people go to meet possible sexual partners)*

2 if you pick someone up while you are travelling in a vehicle or boat, you allow them to get in your vehicle or boat so that you can take them somewhere • *We picked up a hitchhiker on our way to Manchester.* • *A passing ship heard the*

distress call and picked up the crew.

3 if the police pick someone up, they arrest them or they take them somewhere in order to ask them questions • *The security police picked him up for questioning.* • *She was picked up by the police on suspicion of drug-dealing.*

pick yourself **up** (always reflexive)
to stand up again after you have fallen • *She picked herself up and carried on walking.*

pick up

1 if something [e.g. business, economy, trade] picks up, it improves or increases after a bad period • *Business is finally picking up after the recession.* • *In the past few months, house sales have started to pick up again.*

pick-up *n* [singular] an increase or improvement • *There has been no sign of a pick-up in sales.* • *This year has seen a dramatic pick-up in the housing market.*

2 if the wind picks up, it becomes stronger • *The wind had picked up and it was looking rather stormy.*

3 *informal* if you pick up, you answer the telephone • *I sat there for ages, hoping someone would pick up.*

pick up sth
if a vehicle or ship picks up speed or steam, it starts to go faster • *The train picked up speed as it came out of the tunnel.*

pickup *n* [U] *American & Australian* the amount of power that a car engine has for increasing speed • *He always complains when he drives my car that it doesn't have enough pickup.*

---

pick up after   picks, picking, picked

pick up after sb *informal*
to put things back in the place they are kept after someone has untidily left them in the wrong place • *Don't expect me to always pick up after you!*

---

pick up on   picks, picking, picked

pick up on sth

1 to notice something that a lot of other people have not noticed • *Chris had picked up on the tension between Wendy and me.* • *The research group has picked up on the trend of women having children at an older age.*

2 to react to something that you have noticed or something that has happened • *She was surprised that the press hadn't picked up on the story.*

3 to discuss something in detail that someone has talked about before • *I'd just like to pick up on a point that Sally made at the start of this meeting.*

pick sb **up on** sth *British & Australian*
to correct someone for having said or done something wrong or something that you disapprove of • *My Spanish teacher always picks me up on my pronunciation.* • *She picked him up on his sexist use of the word 'girl' instead of woman.*

---

piece together   pieces, piecing, pieced

piece together sth or **piece** sth **together**

1 to try to understand a situation or to try to discover the truth about something by collecting different pieces of information and considering them at the same time • *Police are now trying to piece together a profile of the murderer.* • *Clues from genes have helped us piece together the history of living things.*

2 to create something by joining different things together or by joining the separate parts of something together • (often + **from**) *The book has been pieced together from a number of interviews with Richards.* • *He pieced together the document from fragments found in the wastepaper bin.*

pig out

pig out pigs, pigging, pigged

pig out *informal*
to eat a lot of food ● *Every once in a while I go to a restaurant and really pig out.* ● (often + **on**) *I pigged out on pizza and chocolate last night.*

pig-out *n* [C] *informal* ● *I'm still full after that pig-out at lunch.*

pike out pikes, piking, piked

pike out *Australian informal*
to fail to do something, especially something you have agreed to do ● (often + **on**) *Carl piked out on the deal at the last minute.*

pile in/into piles, piling, piled

pile in

pile into swh
if a group of people pile in, they enter a place or vehicle quickly and not in an organized way ● *She opened the car door and four of us piled in.* ● *It started to rain so we all piled into a nearby cafe.*

pile on piles, piling, piled

pile on sth or **pile** sth **on**
1 *informal* if someone piles on something, especially something spoken, they give you more and more of it ● (usually + **the**) *You've really been piling on the praise tonight, Roger!* ● *We're approaching the deadline so our manager has been piling on the pressure.* ● (British) *He was **piling on the agony** about his childhood.* (= making it seem worse than it really was)
2 *mainly British & Australian informal* if you pile on weight, you become fatter and heavier ● *I piled on ten pounds over Christmas.* ● *She's really **piled on the pounds** (= become fatter) since I last saw her.*

pile out piles, piling, piled

pile out
if a group of people pile out, they leave a place or vehicle quickly and not in an organized way ● *The train doors opened and a crowd of people piled out onto the platform.* ● (often + **of**) *They were all piling out of a pub.*

pile up piles, piling, piled

pile up (sth) or **pile** (sth) **up**
1 to become a pile, or to make a lot of things into a pile by putting them on top of each other ● *I hadn't done the dishes for a while and plates were starting to pile up in the sink.* ● *Just pile the books up and leave them on the table.*
2 if something unpleasant [e.g. work, bills, losses] piles up, or if you pile it up, you get more and more of it ● *The bills are starting to pile up and I just can't pay them.* ● *Both companies have piled up huge losses this year.*

pile up *mainly American informal*
if vehicles travelling on a road pile up, they crash into each other ● *Two cars and seven trucks piled up in fog on the interstate.*

pile-up *n* [C] *slightly informal* ● *Fifteen people were injured in a massive pile-up on the A1.*

pin down pins, pinning, pinned

pin down sb or **pin** sb **down**
1 to make someone give you exact details or a decision about something ● (often + **to**) *Paul says he'll come and visit in the spring but I haven't managed to pin him down to a date yet.* ● (sometimes + **on**) *She refuses to be pinned down on how much her business lost in 1995.* ● *I've been trying to get a decision from Stephanie but she's proving difficult to pin down.*
2 to force someone to stay in a horizontal position by holding them ● *He pinned her down on the floor with her hands above her head.*
3 if soldiers are pinned down, they cannot escape from a place because they are surrounded by enemy soldiers and will be killed if they move from it ● (usually passive) *Government forces were pinned down by resistance fighters 30 miles north of the capital.*

pin down sth or **pin** sth **down**
1 to understand something completely, or to describe something accurately ● (often + question word) *Without proper research, it's hard to pin down what the long-term effects of this drug are.* ● (often negative) *David's certainly very charming, but I can't pin down the exact nature of his charm.*
2 to discover exact details about something ● *Investigators are trying to pin down the cause of yesterday's fire.* ● (sometimes +

question word) *There's obviously a gas leak but we can't pin down exactly where it's coming from.*

pin on   pins, pinning, pinned

pin sth **on** sb

if you pin a crime or the blame for something on someone, you accuse them of having done it, often when this is not true • *When the theft was discovered, he tried to pin the blame on one of his colleagues.* • *I wasn't even in the office when the incident happened so she can't pin it on me.*

pin up   pins, pinning, pinned

pin up sth or **pin** sth **up**

to fasten something [e.g. picture, photo, notice] to a wall using a pin • *She'd pinned up a photo of her boyfriend next to her bed.*

pin-up *n* [C] a photograph of an attractive person that appears in a magazine or newspaper and that people often stick on a wall, or a person who appears in these photographs • *The magazine contains a lot of pin-ups of semi-naked men.* • *He's become the latest teenage pin-up.* • (used as *adj*) *His last three girlfriends have all been pin-up girls.*

pipe down   pipes, piping, piped

pipe down *informal*

to talk more quietly, or to stop complaining • (often an order) *Will you two pipe down, I'm trying to read!*

pipe up   pipes, piping, piped

pipe up (sth)

if someone who is in a group of people pipes up, they suddenly say something when you are not expecting it • *Suddenly a voice from the back of the room piped up: 'Can I ask a question?'* • (sometimes + with) *I was amazed when Andrew piped up with the answer.*

piss about/around   pisses, pissing, pissed

piss about/around *British & Australian slang*

to spend time doing unimportant things, or to behave in a stupid way • *He's not working – he's just pissing about on his computer.* • (sometimes + with) *I wish he'd stop pissing around with my camera.*

piss sb **about/around** *British & Australian slang*

to treat someone badly, especially by changing your mind a lot or by not doing what you have promised • *He's really been pissing me about – this is the third time he hasn't turned up.*

piss away   pisses, pissing, pissed

piss away sth or **piss** sth **away** *slang*

to waste a large amount of money, or not to use an opportunity • *He was given a lot of money by his uncle but he pissed it all away.* • *You've been given a chance to start again, so don't piss it away!*

piss down   pisses, pissing, pissed

piss (it) down *British & Australian slang*

to rain very heavily • *We're going to get soaked – it's pissing down outside.* • *It's pissing it down out there.*

piss off   pisses, pissing, pissed

Piss off! (always an order) *slang*

something you say to tell someone that you are annoyed with them or that you want them to go away • *'Make us a cup of tea.' 'Piss off and make it yourself!'* • *I feel like telling him to piss off.*

piss off *British & Australian slang*

to leave somewhere • *Paul pissed off hours before the rest of us.*

piss off sb or **piss** sb **off** *slang*

to annoy someone • *He never does any work around the house and it's starting to piss me off.*

pissed off *adj slang* • *She looked a bit pissed off when I told her I was going away for a few days.* • (sometimes + with) *I'm really pissed off with work at the moment.*

pit against   pits, pitting, pitted

pit sb/sth **against** sb/sth

to make someone or something fight or compete against someone or something else • *It was a bitter civil war that pitted neighbour against neighbour.* • *She watched as the men pitted their strength against each other.*

pitch for   pitches, pitching, pitched

pitch for sth

to try to persuade someone to give you something [e.g. business, job] • *Firms are having to pitch for business in an international market.*

pitch in   pitches, pitching, pitched

pitch in

1 *informal* to help with work that needs to be done • *If we all pitch in, we can get the kitchen cleared up in half an hour.*

2 *informal* to give your opinion during a discussion • *Meetings work best when everyone pitches in rather than one person talking all the time.* • (sometimes + **with**) *The newspapers have all pitched in with advice about what the government should do.*

pitch into   pitches, pitching, pitched

pitch into sb *mainly British & Australian* to criticize someone strongly • *Halfway through the meeting he suddenly pitched into her and accused her of mismanagement.*

pitch up   pitches, pitching, pitched

pitch up *informal* to arrive in a place, usually late or in an unsuitable state • *Gerald finally pitched up two hours late, still wearing his work clothes.*

plague with   plagues, plaguing, plagued

plague sb **with** sth to annoy someone by asking them a lot of questions or by making a lot of requests or complaints • *Every time I meet her, she plagues me with questions about our family history.*

plan ahead   plans, planning, planned

plan ahead to make decisions or plans about something you will do or something that might happen in the future • *The new system allows schools to plan ahead.* • *I'm not very good at planning ahead.*

plan on   plans, planning, planned

plan on doing sth to intend to do something • *Are you planning on staying long in Berlin?* • *We'd planned on catching the early train.*

plan on sb/sth doing sth to realize that someone might do something or that something might happen and to make arrangements to deal with the situation • (usually negative) *I hadn't*

planned on the whole family coming to visit.

plan out   plans, planning, planned

plan out sth or **plan** sth **out** to decide in detail how you will do something or how you will spend a period of time • *It's a good idea to plan out your essay before you start writing.* • *I'm just planning out my day.*

plant out   plants, planting, planted

plant out sth or **plant** sth **out** to put a young plant that has been grown in a container into the ground • *Plant out the geraniums in early June.*

play about/around   plays, playing, played

play about/around

1 *informal* to behave in a stupid way • *Come on, stop playing about and get on with your homework.* • (sometimes + **with**) *You shouldn't play around with matches – didn't your mother ever tell you that?*

2 *informal* if someone who is married or who has a serious relationship plays around, they have sex with another person or with several other people • (usually + **with**) *Do you think he plays about with other women?* • *If I ever caught him playing around I'd divorce him.*

play about/around with   plays, playing, played

play about/around with sth *informal* to consider various ways of doing something or to try various types of thing before deciding which one to choose • *We've been playing around with ideas for a new TV show.* • *Why don't you play about with the different fonts on the computer and see which one you want to use.*

play along   plays, playing, played

play along to pretend to agree with someone, or to do what someone wants for a short time, in order to get something from them or to avoid making them angry • (often + **with**) *I wanted to find out more about their plans, so I played along with them for a while.* • *She knew that if she played along and cooperated, she wouldn't be harmed.*

play around
see **play about/around**

play around with
see **play about/around with**

play at   plays, playing, played

play at sth
1 to pretend to be a particular person or to do a particular thing, usually as a game • *As kids we used to play at being doctors and nurses.*
2 to do a job in a way which makes people think that you are not very serious about it • *He just plays at being a writer.*

be playing at sth (always in continuous tenses; always used in questions)
if you ask what someone is playing at, you ask what they are doing, in a way which shows that you are surprised and angry • *What do you think you're playing at?* • *I don't know what she was playing at, running off like that.*

play back   plays, playing, played

play back sth or **play** sth **back**
to listen to sounds or watch pictures that you have just recorded • *When I played back our conversation I realised I hadn't made myself clear.*
playback n [U] • *New techniques give smooth playback of audio and video.* • (used as *adj*) *Press the playback button.*

play down   plays, playing, played

play down sth or **play** sth **down**
to try to make people believe that something is not very important, or that it is not likely to happen • *Ministers played down the prospect of a spring election.* • *Military spokesmen tried to play down the seriousness of the incident.*

play off   plays, playing, played

play off
to play the last game in a sports competition in order to decide the winner, especially when the teams or competitors have the same number of points • *The final 16 teams will play off on Sunday.*
play-off n [C] • *Chelsea will meet Middlesbrough in a play-off at Stamford Bridge.* • (used as *adj*) *This Saturday sees a play-off match against Coventry.*

play off against   plays, playing, played

play sb **off against** sb
to encourage one person or group to compete against or argue with another, hoping that you can get some advantage from this situation • *If you get quotes from two different companies you can sometimes play them off against each other.*

play on   plays, playing, played

play on
1 *British & Australian* if someone who is in charge of a sports game instructs the players to play on, they order them to continue playing although someone seems injured or seems to have broken the rules • (often an order) *Play on!* • *The Italian rolled over in the penalty area but the referee waved play on.*
2 to continue to play a musical instrument • *The band played on even as the boat was sinking, or so the story goes.*

play on/upon   plays, playing, played

play on/upon sth
to use someone's fears or weaknesses in order to make that person do what you want, often in a way that is unfair • *She knows that men find her attractive and she plays on it shamelessly to get what she wants.* • *I hate marketing strategies that play on people's fears and prejudices.*

play out   plays, playing, played

be played out (always passive)
if an event, especially an exciting one, is played out, it takes place • (usually + adv/prep) *In fact the whole crisis has been played out under the glare of international television cameras.*

play out or **play itself out** *mainly American*
if an event plays out or plays itself out, it develops and then comes to an end • *The best thing to do is stand back and let the crisis play itself out.* • *The impact of the new trade agreement will take time to play out.*

play out sth or **play** sth **out**
1 if you play out a situation [e.g. scene, fantasy], you pretend that it is really happening • *This therapy enables people to play out violent fantasies in a safe environment.*
2 to play a sports match to the end • *They*

refused to play out the last three minutes after the floodlights failed.

play up   plays, playing, played

play (sb) **up** *British & Australian slightly informal*
if a part of your body plays up or plays you up, it causes you pain ● (usually in continuous tenses) *My stomach was playing up after all that fatty food.* ● *His knee's been playing him up again.*

play up
1 *British & Australian slightly informal* if someone, especially a child, plays up, they behave badly ● *If the children start playing up, just send them out to the park.*
2 *British & Australian slightly informal* if a machine or part of a machine plays up, it does not work as it should ● (usually in continuous tenses) *My car's been playing up again.*

play up sth
to emphasize something, especially a quality, and make it seem more important than it really is ● *It's said that he plays up his working-class background in order to broaden his appeal.*

play up to   plays, playing, played

play up to sb
to try to make someone like you by behaving in a way you think will please them ● *She played up to her admirers with a mixture of charm and wit.*

play up to sth
to try to make people think you are a particular sort of person by behaving in the way that such a person would behave ● *She looks like the typical dumb blonde and it's an image that she plays up to.*

play upon
see **play on/upon**

play with   plays, playing, played

play with sth
1 to keep touching something or moving it from one position to another, often when you are bored ● *Stop playing with your hair!* ● *She was just playing with her meal – she didn't eat a mouthful.*
2 if you play with the idea of doing something, you consider it, but usually do not do it ● (usually in continuous tenses) *We*

were playing with the idea of moving to Glasgow.
3 if you play with words or ideas, you use them and change them in a clever way, often in order to be humorous ● *The advert plays with the company's name very cleverly.*

play with sb/sth
to treat a person or their feelings in a way that is not serious, for example by pretending to love them ● *He's not serious about her at all – he's just playing with her.*

play with yourself (always reflexive) *informal*
to give yourself sexual pleasure by touching your sexual organs ● *He spent hours playing with himself under the bedclothes.*

plod along/on   plods, plodding, plodded

plod along/on *slightly informal*
to continue walking or working at the same, slow rate ● *I keep plodding on and one day the job will be finished.* ● *Small children plodding along under the weight of bulging schoolbags are a familiar sight.*

plod away   plods, plodding, plodded

plod away *slightly informal*
to continue working at the same, slow rate ● *I guess we'll just keep plodding away and see if it leads to anything.*

plod on
see **plod along/on**

plonk down   plonks, plonking, plonked

plonk down sth/sb or **plonk** sth/sb **down** *mainly British & Australian informal*
to quickly put something or someone down without taking great care ● *Just plonk your bags down for the moment and we'll unpack later.* ● *She plonked an enormous bowl of pasta down in front of me.*

plonk yourself **down** (always reflexive) *mainly British & Australian informal*
to sit down quickly and heavily, in order to relax ● *He just plonked himself down next to me on the sofa and started talking.* ● *Plonk yourself down wherever you can find a space.*

plot out   plots, plotting, plotted

plot out sth or **plot** sth **out**
to plan something in detail • *I remember him plotting out his career at the age of fourteen.*

plough/plow back   ploughs, ploughing, ploughed/plows, plowing, plowed

plough back sth or **plough** sth **back** *British, American & Australian*

plow back sth or **plow** sth **back** *American*
to put money that you have earned into a business in order to make the business bigger or better • (usually + **into**) *All the company's profits are ploughed back into it.*

plough/plow into   ploughs, ploughing, ploughed/plows, plowing, plowed

plough into sth/sb *British, American & Australian*

plow into sth/sb *American*
if a vehicle ploughs into something or someone, it hits them with a lot of force • *I couldn't stop in time and I ploughed straight into the car in front.* • *The train came off the rails and plowed into a nearby bank, killing 23 passengers.*

plough/plow on   ploughs, ploughing, ploughed/plows, plowing, plowed

plough on *British, American & Australian slightly informal*

plow on *American slightly informal*
to continue doing something even though it is difficult or boring • *We could stop somewhere for a snack or we could just plough on till we reach Bruges.* • (often + **with**) *I'd better plough on with the cooking or this meal will never get done.*

plough/plow through   ploughs, ploughing, ploughed/plows, plowing, plowed

plough through sth *British, American & Australian*

plow through sth *American*
1 to read or eat all of something, even though there is a lot of it • *It took me weeks to plough through the first 500 pages.* • *Once I've ploughed through two* whole courses I'm usually too full for a dessert.
2 to move through an area, using a lot of force • *The ship ploughed through the icy Arctic waters.* • *Somehow the ambulances managed to plow through the chaos.*
3 if a vehicle ploughs through something, it goes through it, damaging or destroying it • *In another Navy aircraft crash, a jet ploughed through an aircraft hangar.*

plough/plow up   ploughs, ploughing, ploughed/plows, plowing, plowed

plough up sth or **plough** sth **up** *British, American & Australian*

plow up sth or **plow** sth **up** *American*
to break the surface of the earth using a plough (= a large piece of farming equipment), usually to prepare the land for growing crops • *Large areas of grazing land have been ploughed up for growing wheat.*

pluck at   plucks, plucking, plucked

pluck at sth
to pull something with your fingers again and again, using quick, small movements • *She sat there in the meeting plucking nervously at her collar.*

plug away   plugs, plugging, plugged

plug away *informal*
to work hard at something for a long time • (often + **at**) *I seem to have been plugging away at this article for ages.*

plug in/into   plugs, plugging, plugged

plug in sth or **plug** sth **in**

plug sth **into** sth
to connect a piece of electrical equipment to a supply of electricity or to another piece of electrical equipment • *Could you plug the iron in for me?* • *You could plug the TV into the socket behind the radiator.* • *I've wired up the stereo system but I haven't plugged the speakers in yet.*

plug into   plugs, plugging, plugged

plug into sth
1 if a piece of electrical equipment plugs into a supply of electricity or another piece of electrical equipment, it works by being connected to that supply of electricity or that piece of equipment • *So where does the microphone plug into the tape*

recorder? • *Does it need batteries or does it plug into the wall socket?*

2 *American informal* to be or feel connected with something • *With virtual reality, you can plug into any world that you want to.*

plug on   plugs, plugging, plugged

plug on *Australian informal*
to continue doing something or working hard, often when it is difficult or unpleasant • *I'm going to have to plug on with this essay – it's due in tomorrow.*

plug up   plugs, plugging, plugged

plug up sth or **plug** sth **up**
to put something into a hole in order to fill it • *You can always plug up the holes with cement.*

plumb in   plumbs, plumbing, plumbed

plumb in sth or **plumb** sth **in**
to connect something [e.g. toilet, bath, washing machine] to a water supply • *We've had the dishwasher delivered but we're waiting to have it plumbed in.*

plump down   plumps, plumping, plumped

plump down or **plump** yourself **down** *informal*
to sit down quickly and heavily • *She plumped herself down next to me on the sofa.*

plump sth **down**
to quickly put something down, without taking great care • *She plumped her bags down next to her.*

plump for   plumps, plumping, plumped

plump for sth *informal*
to choose something, especially after thinking about it for a while • *Which film did you plump for in the end?* • *I'm going to plump for the salmon in white wine sauce.*

plump up   plumps, plumping, plumped

plump up sth or **plump** sth **up**
to make something [e.g. cushion, pillow] rounder and softer, especially by shaking it • *She sat up while the nurse plumped up the pillows behind her.* • *The treatment claims to plump up* (= make smooth) *fine lines and give the skin a fresh, youthful look.*

plunge in   plunges, plunging, plunged

plunge in
to suddenly start talking or doing something without preparing for it or worrying about it • *My approach in these situations is to plunge in and start talking.* • *He'd had no experience of teaching but he plunged in nonetheless.*

plunge into   plunges, plunging, plunged

plunged sth **into** sth
to quickly put something, especially your hand, deep into something else • *I plunged my hand into cold water to stop the burning.* • *He plunged his hands into his pockets.* • *If the peas are frozen, plunge them into boiling water for three minutes.*

plunge into sth
to suddenly become very involved in an activity • *Two months before his exams he suddenly plunged into his studies.*

plunge (sb/sth) **into** sth
to suddenly be in a bad situation or state, or to cause someone or something to suddenly be in a bad situation or state • *Overnight the country seemed to plunge into recession.* • *He was plunged into depression again when his lover of five years left him.*

plunk down   plunks, plunking, plunked

plunk down sth or **plunk** sth **down** *American informal*
to pay money to buy something • (often + **for**) *He plunked down $225 for used tools and then opened his own business.* • (often + **on**) *I'd just plunked $200 down on a new tape player.*

plunk down sth/sb or **plunk** sth/sb **down** *American informal*
to quickly put something or someone down without taking great care • *She plunked the kid down in the seat, and told her to stay there.* • *He plunked his books down and left the room.*

plunk down or **plunk** yourself **down** *American informal*
to sit down quickly and heavily • *Flo plunked down, out of breath from all the dancing.*

ply with   plies, plying, plied

ply sb **with** sth
1 to keep giving someone something, espe-

cially food or drink ● *I'm going to ply him with drink and then ask him what's going on.*

2 if you ply someone with questions, you keep asking them questions ● *She plied him with questions about his forthcoming film.*

point out   points, pointing, pointed

point out sb/sth or point sb/sth out

to make a person notice someone or something, usually by telling them where they are or by holding up one of your fingers towards them ● (often + **to**) *If you see her you must point her out to me.* ● *I'd made one or two mistakes that she pointed out to me.*

point out sth or point sth out

to tell someone a fact that they did not already know, especially one that is important in the present discussion or situation ● (often + **that**) *I pointed out that long term this would undoubtedly cost us more.* ● *He was careful to point out the possible disadvantages of the new system.* ● (sometimes + **to**) *I'd never noticed that about her till you pointed it out to me.*

point to   points, pointing, pointed

point to sth

to say something because you think it is important in a discussion ● *She also pointed to the need for better training.*

point to/towards   points, pointing, pointed

point to/towards sth

if something points to or towards a fact or event, it makes it seem likely that the fact is true or that the event will happen ● *They don't know for certain but the evidence points to suicide.* ● *All the indicators are pointing towards a June election.*

point up   points, pointing, pointed

point up sth or point sth up *formal*

to make a problem or a fact easy to notice so that people are aware of it ● *Both studies point up the disadvantages of the present system.*

poke about/around   pokes, poking, poked

poke about/around

1 *informal* to search for something by moving things and looking behind things ● *I was poking around in the cupboard, seeing what I could find.*

2 (always + *adv/prep*) *informal* to try to get information about other people in a way that annoys them ● (often + **in**) *It serves him right for poking around in other people's affairs.*

poke around   pokes, poking, poked

poke around (swh) *American*

to move or do things slowly and without much interest ● *I left her poking around some old book store.*

poke at   pokes, poking, poked

poke at sth

to push your finger or a pointed object into something, usually several times ● *I drank some more wine and poked at my salmon.*

polish off   polishes, polishing, polished

polish off sth or polish sth off *informal*

to finish something quickly and easily, especially a large amount of food or a piece of work ● *He's just polished off a pizza and half a loaf of bread.* ● *I polished off no fewer than three essays last week.*

polish off sb or polish sb off *mainly American & Australian informal*

to kill someone ● *He was accused of polishing off his former partner.*

polish up   polishes, polishing, polished

polish up sth or polish sth up

1 to practise and improve your skills or your knowledge of something that you learned in the past but have partly forgotten ● *I really must polish up my Italian before we go to Rome.*

2 to rub something with a piece of cloth in order to make it shine ● *Those old silver candlesticks would be lovely if you polished them up.* ● *The celebration is seen as an opportunity to polish up* (= improve) *the city's image.*

ponce about/around ponces, poncing, ponced

ponce about/around

1 *British & Australian informal* if a man ponces about or around, he behaves or dresses like a woman • *He spent the seventies poncing about in skin-tight pink lycra.*

2 *British & Australian informal* to waste time doing silly, unimportant things • *Stop poncing around and help me sort this mess out, would you!*

ponce off ponces, poncing, ponced

ponce sth off sb *British slang*

to get something by asking someone else for it instead of buying or getting it yourself • *He never buys his own cigarettes – he just ponces them off other people.*

pony up ponies, ponying, ponied

pony up sth or pony sth up *American informal, old-fashioned*

to pay an amount of money for something • *It's about time the US ponied up its share of the UN's operating budget.*

poop out poops, pooping, pooped

poop out

1 *American slang* to become so tired that you have to stop what you are doing • *After thirty miles of cycling, I pooped out and needed a ride home.*

2 *American slang* to fail to do something that you arranged to do with other people • (often + on) *She said she was coming. I hope she's not going to poop out on me at the last minute.*

pop in pops, popping, popped

pop in *informal*

to go into a place, especially a friend's house, just for a short time • (usually + adv/prep) *If you're passing by you should pop in for a chat some time.*

pop off pops, popping, popped

pop off

1 *informal, old-fashioned* to die • *You're all just waiting till I pop off so you can get your hands on my money.*

2 (always + adv/prep) *informal* to leave the place where you are and go somewhere, usually for a short time • *She's just popped off to get a sandwich if you want to wait for her.*

3 *American informal* to talk a lot in a loud way about something that makes you angry or upsets you • (often + about) *She's always popping off about her husband's relatives.* • (sometimes + at) *Don't keep popping off at me. It's not my fault that he's not here!*

pop out pops, popping, popped

pop out *informal*

to leave the place where you are and go somewhere for a short time • (usually + adv/prep) *I'm just popping out to get some milk.*

pop up pops, popping, popped

pop up *slightly informal*

if something pops up, it suddenly appears, often when you are not expecting it • *He's one of those actors who pops up time and again on the television.* • *A message just popped up on my screen saying 'fatal error'.*

pop-up *adj* (always before noun) a pop-up book is a book which has pictures that stand up from the pages when the book is opened • *Alice was given a Winnie-the-Pooh pop-up book for her birthday.*

pop-up *adj* (always before noun) a pop-up menu is a list of choices which appears on a computer screen when the user requests it • *Select the option you want from the pop-up menu.*

pore over pores, poring, pored

pore over sth

to study or look carefully at something, especially a book or a document • *I left Jeremy poring over his notes for his first accountancy exam tomorrow.*

pork out porks, porking, porked

pork out *American informal*

to eat a lot of food • *We went home and porked out on pizza.*

portion out portions, portioning, portioned

portion out sth or portion sth out

to share something between a group of people • *They were all watching me to see that I portioned the cake out fairly.*

pose as poses, posing, posed

pose as sb/sth

to pretend to be a particular person, type

of person, or thing, in order to deceive people • *Apparently there's a man who is going round the hospital posing as a doctor.*

post off   posts, posting, posted

post off sth or **post** sth **off** *British & Australian*
to send a letter or parcel by post • *If I post it off now it should reach you tomorrow.*

post up   posts, posting, posted

post up sth or **post** sth **up**
to put a notice on a wall so that it can be seen by a lot of people • *Company announcements are usually posted up on the notice-board.*

pot up   pots, potting, potted

pot up sth or **pot** sth **up**
to put a small growing plant or a piece cut from a plant into a pot (= container for plants) • *Take the geranium cuttings and pot them up in a mixture of peat and sand.*

potter about/around   potters, pottering, pottered

potter about/around (swh) *British & Australian*
to spend time in a pleasant, relaxed way, often doing small jobs in or around the house • *She spent the afternoon pottering about in the garden.* • *Sunday is usually spent pottering around the house.*

pounce on/upon   pounces, pouncing, pounced

pounce on/upon sth
1 to immediately criticize a mistake • *He knows that his critics are waiting to pounce on any slip that he makes.*
2 to accept something quickly and with enthusiasm • *I think if she were given the opportunity to work here she'd pounce on it.*

pour down   pours, pouring, poured

pour down
to rain heavily • *Take an umbrella – it's pouring down.* • *The rain's pouring down.*
downpour *n* [C] a sudden, heavy fall of rain • (usually singular) *The streets were flooded after the downpour.*

pour forth   pours, pouring, poured

pour forth *formal*
to appear from somewhere in large numbers or amounts • *Statistics poured forth from every specialist in the land.*

pour in/into   pours, pouring, poured

pour in

pour into swh
to arrive or enter somewhere in very large numbers • *As soon as the gates opened, visitors started pouring in.* • *Letters have poured in congratulating us on our success.* • *Over 20,000 refugees have poured into the region.*

pour into   pours, pouring, poured

pour sth **into** sth
to provide a lot of money for something over a long period • *He's poured so much money into the company.*

pour out   pours, pouring, poured

pour out sth or **pour** sth **out**
to fill a glass, cup etc. with a drink • *I'll wait till the tea's a little stronger before I pour it out.*

pour out
to leave a place in large numbers • (usually + *adv/prep*) *The game had just finished and people were pouring out of the stadium.* • *The crowd poured out into the street.*

pour out sth or **pour** sth **out**
if you pour out your feelings or thoughts, you talk very honestly about what is making you sad • *She listened quietly while he poured out his troubles.* • *She really **poured her heart out**.* (= talked very honestly about what was making her sad)
outpouring *n* [C] a strong expression of emotion • (usually singular) *an outpouring of emotion* • *She was taken aback by his sudden outpouring of grief.*

outpouring *n* [C] a long and emotional expression of what someone feels or thinks about something • *It wasn't a speech so much as an outpouring.* • *These writings are clearly the outpourings of a deeply troubled man.*

power up   powers, powering, powered

power up (sth) or **power** (sth) **up**
American
if something [e.g. computer] powers up,
or if someone powers it up, it is turned on
so that it is ready to use ● *Computers take
a few seconds to power up, after they've
been switched on.* ● *He powered the boat
up and headed for the open sea.*

predispose to/towards   predisposes, predisposing, predisposed

predispose sb **to/towards** sth *formal*
to make someone likely to behave or think
in a particular way or to suffer from a particular illness ● *They've now discovered a
gene that seems to predispose people to colon
cancer.*

predisposed to/towards *adj formal*
● *He's predisposed towards negotiation and
favours a peaceful resolution to the problem.*

preside over   presides, presiding, presided

preside over sth
1 *formal* to be in charge of an event or
situation and have official responsibility
for it ● *He presided over some of the most
far-reaching reforms his country has ever
seen.* ● *Judge Langdale is to preside over
the official enquiry into the case.*
2 *formal* to be in charge of a company or
other organization ● *She presides over a
business which has thrived even in the
recession.*

press ahead   presses, pressing, pressed

press ahead
to start or continue doing something in a
determined way, often despite problems
● (usually + **with**) *They're determined to
press ahead with the new road despite
opposition from environmental groups.*

press for   presses, pressing, pressed

press (sb) **for** sth
to try to persuade someone, usually someone in authority, to give you something
or to allow something to happen
● *Workers continue to press for better
working conditions.* ● *I'm being pressed
for a decision on the matter.*

be pressed for sth (always passive)
to have very little or not enough of some-

thing, especially time or money ● *I'd like
to talk, but I'm a bit pressed for time right
now.* ● *Ask me another time when I'm not
so pressed for cash.*

press forward   presses, pressing, pressed

press forward
to continue doing something in a determined way, usually in order to bring it to
a more advanced stage ● (often + **with**)
*They seem determined to press forward
with their programme of reform.*

press into   presses, pressing, pressed

press sb **into** sth/doing sth
to force someone to do something ● *She
was pressed into marriage by her parents.*
● *Don't be pressed into making a quick
decision by the salesman.*

press on   presses, pressing, pressed

press on
to continue doing something in a determined way ● (often + **with**) *They were
determined to press on with the campaign
despite the committee's objections.* ● *It was
pouring with rain but we pressed on
(= continued our journey) towards the
village.*

press on/upon   presses, pressing, pressed

press sth **on/upon** sb
to offer something to someone in a forceful way so that it is difficult for them to
refuse to accept it ● *All the children had
sweets and presents pressed on them by the
visitors.*

presume on/upon   presumes, presuming, presumed

presume on/upon sth *formal*
if you presume on a quality that someone
has, you use it in order to get an advantage ● *I shouldn't like to presume on your
generosity.*

pretend to   pretends, pretending, pretended

pretend to sth *formal*
to say that you have a particular quality
even though this may not be true
● (usually negative) *I don't pretend to any
great skill as an orator.*

prevail on/upon   prevails, prevailing, prevailed

prevail on/upon sb to do sth *formal*
to persuade someone to do something that they did not want to do ● *He was eventually prevailed upon to accept the appointment.*

prey on/upon   preys, preying, preyed

prey on/upon sth
if an animal preys on another animal, it catches it and uses it as its food ● *Spiders prey on flies and other small insects.*

prey on/upon sb
to hurt or deceive a particular group of people, especially people who are weak and can easily be hurt or deceived ● *He would attack at night, preying on lone women in their twenties and thirties.* ● *It's particularly contemptible that these sort of people prey on the elderly.*

prick out   pricks, pricking, pricked

prick out sth or **prick** sth **out**
to take young plants that have been grown together and put them in separate holes in the ground ● *In April, prick out the seedlings and pot them individually.*

pride on/upon   prides, priding, prided

pride yourself **on/upon** sth/doing sth
(always reflexive)
to be proud of a quality that you have or something that you do ● *I've always prided myself on being reasonably self-sufficient.* ● *They pride themselves on the speed and reliability of their delivery service.*

print off   prints, printing, printed

print off sth or **print** sth **off**
to print a particular number of copies of something ● *We printed off two hundred copies of the letter.*

print out   prints, printing, printed

print out (sth) or **print** (sth) **out**
to produce a printed copy of a document that has been written on a computer ● *I've just printed out the first draft of my essay.* ● (sometimes + **in**) *The captions should have printed out in italics.*
printout n [C] ● *Can you get me a printout of the latest sales figures?*

prise/prize out   prises, prising, prised/prizes, prizing, prized

prise sth **out** *British & Australian*
prize sth **out** *American, British & Australian*
to get something from someone with difficulty, especially information or money ● (usually + **of**) *She wasn't going to tell me – I really had to prize it out of her.*

proceed against   proceeds, proceeding, proceeded

proceed against sb *formal*
to start to take legal action against someone ● (sometimes + **on**) *The Crown decided not to proceed against him on three charges of indecent assault.*

proceed from   proceeds, proceeding, proceeded

proceed from sth *formal*
to exist as a result of something ● *These beliefs proceed from the conviction that all human life is sacred.*

proceed with   proceeds, proceeding, proceeded

proceed with sth *formal*
to start something that you have planned to do, or to continue doing something that you have already started ● *Shall we proceed with the plan as agreed?* ● *You may proceed with your cross-examination now, Mr Brinkworth.*

prod at   prods, prodding, prodded

prod at sth
to push your finger or a pointed object into something, usually several times ● *She prodded at the fish with her fork a few times but didn't eat a mouthful.*

profit by/from   profits, profiting, profited

profit by/from sth/doing sth
to get an advantage from something ● *I'm quite sure we could profit from her advice.* ● *I profited enormously by working with her.*

pronounce on/upon   pronounces, pronouncing, pronounced

pronounce on/upon sth *formal*
to give a judgement or opinion about something ● *I'd rather not pronounce on a*

subject that I know so little about.

prop up   props, propping, propped

prop up sth or **prop** sth **up**

1 to make something stay in a particular position by putting something underneath or against it • *He fetched a few cushions to prop up her head.* • (often + **with**) *We had to prop the bed up with some old books.*

2 to give support to something, especially a country or organization, so that it can continue to exist in a difficult situation • *For years the whole industry was propped up by the government.*

prop yourself **up** (always reflexive)
to support yourself by leaning on or against something • *He groaned and propped himself up on his elbows.*

proportion to   proportions, proportioning, proportioned

proportion sth **to** sth *formal*
to make something be the correct size, amount, or value in relation to something else • (usually passive) *Your new salary has been proportioned to the cost of living.*

provide against   provides, providing, provided

provide against sth *formal*
to make plans in order to prevent or deal with a bad situation • *Banks are being encouraged to provide against third world debt.* • *Beach owners do not have a legal obligation to provide against injury or drowning.*

provide for   provides, providing, provided

provide for sb
to give someone the things they need, such as money, food, or clothes • *He has a wife and two young children to provide for.*

provide for sth

1 *formal* to make plans in order to deal with a possible event in the future • *We must provide for depreciation when calculating the costs.*

2 *formal* if a law or agreement provides for something, it allows it to happen or exist • *Current legislation provides for the detention of those suspected of terrorism.*

prowl about/around/round   prowls, prowling, prowled

prowl about/around/round (swh)
to move around a place quietly, trying not to be seen or heard and often looking for something or someone • *At night in bed I would imagine him prowling around outside my house.*

psych out   psychs, psyching, psyched

psych out sb or **psych** sb **out** *informal*
to talk or behave in a very confident way in order to make someone you are competing against less confident and less likely to succeed • *Both athletes were trying to psych each other out before the race.*

psych up   psychs, psyching, psyched

psych yourself **up** (always reflexive) *informal*
to try to make yourself feel confident and ready to do something well • *I have a couple of minutes on my own before I go on stage to psych myself up.*

psyched up adj mainly American informal • *Davis was psyched up* (= mentally prepared) *to go in and win the game.*

puff away   puffs, puffing, puffed

puff away *informal*
to smoke a cigarette or a pipe • (usually in continuous tenses) *She sat there, puffing away at her cigarette.*

puff out   puffs, puffing, puffed

puff out sth or **puff** sth **out**
to make your chest or your cheeks become rounder by filling them with air • *He puffed out his cheeks and sat back in his chair.*

puff up   puffs, puffing, puffed

puff up (sth) or **puff** (sth) **up**
to become larger and full of air, or to make something become larger in this way • *The soufflé should puff up and bake to a golden brown colour.*

puff up
if a part of your body puffs up, it becomes larger because it is infected or injured • *The medication had made her face puff up.*

puke up   pukes, puking, puked

puke up (sth) or **puke** (sth) **up** (never passive) *informal*
  to vomit or to vomit something • *He staggered into the kichen and puked up all over the floor.*

pull ahead   pulls, pulling, pulled

pull ahead
  to suddenly get in front of another car or person that was previously driving or running at the same speed as you • *It was on the final lap that Marsh pulled ahead.*

pull apart   pulls, pulling, pulled

pull apart sb/sth or **pull** sb/sth **apart**
  to separate people or animals that are fighting • *They went for each other with their fists and had to be pulled apart.*

pull apart sth or **pull** sth **apart**
  to say that something, especially a piece of written work, is very bad • *The last essay I gave him he completely pulled apart.*

pull sb **apart**
  to make someone feel very upset • *It just pulls me apart to see him treat her like this.*

pull at   pulls, pulling, pulled

pull at sth
  to pull something several times, usually with quick, light movements • *My four-year-old son was pulling at my sleeve, wanting us to leave.*

pull away   pulls, pulling, pulled

pull away
1 if a vehicle pulls away, it starts moving • *I just had time to leap on the bus before it pulled away.*
2 to suddenly get in front of another car or person that was previously driving or running at the same speed as you • (often + **from**) *With just a hundred meters to go, Black pulls away from the Italian and takes the lead.*
3 if you pull away from someone who is holding you, you suddenly move your body backwards, away from them • *As he went to kiss her she pulled away.*
4 if something pulls away from something else, it becomes separated from it • (often + **from**) *The radiator has started to pull away from the wall.*

pull back   pulls, pulling, pulled

pull back sth or **pull** sth **back** *British*
  if a team that is losing pulls a goal back or pulls points back, it scores a goal or wins some points • *Two minutes after half-time, Paul Brinkworth pulled a goal back.*

pull back (sth) or **pull** (sth) **back**
  if an army pulls back or is pulled back, it moves away from the enemy • *Its troops have pulled back from the border.*
  pullback n [singular] *American* • *The talks produced an immediate pullback of troops from both sides.*

pull back
1 if you pull back from someone who is holding you, you suddenly move your body backwards, away from them • *At the mention of Melissa she suddenly pulled back.*
2 *mainly American* if a company pulls back from something, it decides not to do something that it was previously going to do, usually because it will be bad for the company • (often + **from**) *It is rumoured that the company intends to pull back from petrochemicals.*

pull down   pulls, pulling, pulled

pull down sth or **pull** sth **down**
  to destroy a building or other structure because it is not being used or it is not wanted any more • *Most of the old buildings were pulled down to make room for the new shopping centre.* • *Protesters took to the streets and pulled down a statue of the country's former leader.*

pull down sb or **pull** sb **down** *American*
  if an unpleasant or difficult situation pulls someone down, it makes them feel unhappy or physically weak • *Her divorce really pulled her down.*

pull down sth *American informal*
  to earn an amount of money • *Between them they must be pulling down about $100,000 a year.*

pull for   pulls, pulling, pulled

pull for sb *American informal*
  to support someone and encourage them to be successful when they are doing something, especially when they are playing a sport • (often + **to do** sth) *The fans*

were all there, pulling for their team to win.

pull in   pulls, pulling, pulled

pull in sb or **pull** sb **in**

1 *informal* if the police pull someone in, they take that person to a police station because they think they have done something wrong ● *The police pulled in dozens of protestors during the demonstration.*

2 if an event, especially a show, pulls people in, a lot of people go to see it ● *It's the longest-running show in the West End and it's still pulling in the crowds.*

pull in sth or **pull** sth **in**

to earn a large amount of money ● *The bank pulls in over £390 million in a year.*

pull in/into   pulls, pulling, pulled

pull in

pull into swh

1 if a train pulls in or pulls into a station, it arrives there ● *The train pulling in on platform 6 – that should be hers.*

2 if a car pulls in or pulls into a place, it moves to the side of the road or to another place where it can stop ● *Pull in behind this truck and I'll get out and walk the rest of the way.* ● *We pulled into the first garage that we came to.*

pull-in *n* [C] *British informal* a place at the side of a main road where you can stop your car and buy food and drink ● *We stopped at a pull-in on the way here and had a bite to eat.*

pull off   pulls, pulling, pulled

pull off sth or **pull** sth **off**

to succeed in doing or achieving something difficult ● *It's a clever plan and if he pulls it off he'll earn a lot of money.* ● *So you're going to Madrid all expenses paid. How did you pull that off?*

pull off (sth)

if a car pulls off or it pulls off a main road, it leaves that main road, often in order to turn into a smaller road ● *We pulled off the motorway at Reigate.*

pull off

if a vehicle pulls off, it starts moving ● *I watched as the car pulled off and sped up the road.*

pull on   pulls, pulling, pulled

pull on sth

to put on clothes quickly ● *I pulled on some jeans and ran downstairs to answer the door.*

pull out   pulls, pulling, pulled

pull out

1 if a train pulls out, it starts to leave a station ● *I got to the platform just as the train was pulling out.*

2 to drive onto a road, either from another road or from the side of the road where you have stopped ● *I was just waiting for a gap in the traffic so that I could pull out.*

3 to drive to a different part of the road, usually a part where the vehicles are travelling faster ● *He pulled out in front of me without even looking.*

pull out (sth/sb) or **pull** (sb/sth) **out**

1 to stop being involved in an activity or
agreement • (often + **of**) *After lengthy
negotiations the company pulled out of the
deal.* • *They've pulled all their athletes out
of the competition.*

2 if soldiers or an army pull out of an area,
or if someone pulls them out, they move
out or are ordered to move out of that
area • (often + **of**) *There was a rumour
that they were about to pull out of the
region.* • *If we pull our troops out now, we
are admitting defeat.*

pull-out n [C] • *The government has ordered an immediate pull-out of troops from
the area.*

pull over   pulls, pulling, pulled

pull over

to drive a car to the side of the road in
order to stop • *I was looking for somewhere to pull over so I could have a look at
the map.*

pull over sb/sth or **pull** sb/sth **over**

if the police pull someone who is driving
a car over, they order them to drive the
car to the side of the road and stop • *I was
pulled over by the police and asked to show
my driving licence.*

pull through   pulls, pulling, pulled

pull (sb) **through** (sth)

to succeed in dealing with a difficult
period of your life, or to help someone
else to do this • *It was Glyn who pulled me
through the bad times.* • *They weren't the
happiest days of our lives but somehow we
pulled through.*

pull (sb) **through**

to recover from a serious illness, or to
help someone to do this • *I was so ill, they
didn't even know if I was going to pull
through.* • *I felt confident that the doctors
would pull him through.*

pull to   pulls, pulling, pulled

pull sth **to**

to close a door or window by pulling it towards you • *Pull the door to, would you, it
keeps banging.*

pull together   pulls, pulling, pulled

pull yourself **together** (always reflexive)
to become calm after being so angry or
upset that you were unable to behave in a
sensible way • (often an order) *Pull
yourself together, now. There's no point in
crying.*

pull together

to work as a group in order to achieve
something • *It's going to be a rush but if
we all pull together I'm sure we can get the
job finished on time.*

pull together sth or **pull** sth **together**

1 to improve something by making all the
different parts operate together • *A
strong government would pull the country
together.*

2 if you pull together a lot of facts or ideas,
you consider all of them when you are
writing about or discussing an idea
• *Really the book was an attempt to pull
together a lot of data that I'd collected over
the years.*

pull up

pull up   pulls, pulling, pulled

pull up

if a car pulls up, it stops, often for a short time ● *A car pulled up next to the church and two men got out.*

pull up sth or **pull** sth **up**

to move a piece of furniture [esp. chair] near to something or someone ● *Why don't you pull up a chair and join us.*

pull sb **up**

to tell someone that they have done something wrong ● (often + **on**) *She pulled me up on my use of the term 'mankind' instead of 'humankind'.*

pump in/into   pumps, pumping, pumped

pump in sth or **pump** sth **in**

pump sth **into** sth

to give a lot of money to a plan or organization ● *The government has pumped in billions of dollars over the last three years.* ● *New investors were being encouraged to pump capital into the company.*

pump out   pumps, pumping, pumped

pump out (sth) or **pump** (sth) **out** *informal*

to continuously produce a lot of something, especially music ● *Then there are the radio stations, pumping out nationalist songs and government propaganda.* ● *Dance music was pumping out from two loudspeakers.*

pump up   pumps, pumping, pumped

pump up sth or **pump** sth **up**

1 to fill something with air by using a pump ● *I must remember to pump up the tyres on my bike.*

2 *informal* to increase something ● *They slashed their prices in a desperate attempt to pump up sales.*

pump up sb or **pump** sb **up** *American informal*

to make someone excited and ready to do something ● *The auctioneer worked hard at pumping up the crowd.*

punch in   punches, punching, punched

punch in sth or **punch** sth **in**

to put information into a computer or telephone by quickly pressing its buttons ● *As soon as the alarm sounded I rushed downstairs and punched in the code.*

punch in *American*

to put a card into a special machine that records the time you arrive at work ● *What time did you punch in this morning?*

punch out   punches, punching, punched

punch out sth or **punch** sth **out** *mainly American*

to put information into a computer or telephone by quickly pressing its buttons ● *She picked up the telephone and punched out the number for the taxi.*

punch out sb or **punch** sb **out** *American informal*

to hit someone hard and make them fall to the ground ● *He got into a fight and punched the guy out.*

punch-out *n* [C] *American informal* ● *The two boys had a real punch-out.*

punch out *American*

to put a card into a special machine in order to record the time you leave work ● *I usually punch out around five o'clock.*

punch up   punches, punching, punched

punch up sth or **punch** sth **up** *American informal*

to make something more interesting ● *It's the same song but punched up with a new arrangement.*

push about/around/round   pushes, pushing, pushed

push sb **about/around/round**

to tell someone what to do in a rude or threatening way ● *She wasn't going to let them push her about any more.* ● *I'm fed up of being pushed around.*

push ahead   pushes, pushing, pushed

push ahead

to continue doing something with a lot of effort and enthusiasm, especially when this is difficult ● *We hit one or two problems but still decided to push ahead.* ● (often + **with**) *The government intends to push ahead with plans to give more power to local government.*

push around

see **push about/around/round**

push aside pushes, pushing, pushed
push aside sth/sb or **push** sth/sb **aside**

to decide to forget about or ignore something or someone • *We can't just push these problems aside – we have to deal with them.* • *Annie felt that she was being pushed aside in favour of a younger member of staff.*

push for pushes, pushing, pushed
push (sb) **for** sth

to try to persuade someone, usually someone in authority, to give you something or allow something to happen • *Local residents are pushing for the road to be made safer.* • *The unions have been pushing management for wage increases.*

push forward pushes, pushing, pushed
push forward

to continue doing something with a lot of effort and enthusiasm • (often + **with**) *An additional grant enabled the team to push forward with research plans.*

push yourself **forward** (always reflexive)

to try to make other people notice you and pay attention to you • *She always seemed to be pushing herself forward and not giving anyone else a chance.*

push in pushes, pushing, pushed
push in

1 *British & Australian informal* to rudely join a line of people who are waiting for something by moving in front of some of the people who are already there • *I think he thought I was trying to push in.* • *Stop pushing in!*
2 to become involved in a group or activity where you are not wanted • *I hoped she didn't think I was pushing in – I genuinely thought I might be able to help out.*

push off pushes, pushing, pushed
Push off! (always an order) *British & Australian informal*

something that you say when you are angry to tell someone to go away • *I was in such a bad mood, I just told him to push off.*

push off *informal*

1 to leave a place • *I'll push off now and collect the kids.*

2 if a boat pushes off, or if someone in a boat pushes off, the boat moves away from the edge of an area of water • *We pushed off and drifted along the canal.*

push on pushes, pushing, pushed
push on

1 to continue travelling somewhere • *We'll have to push on if we're going to get there before it gets dark.*
2 to continue doing something with a lot of effort • *Come on, let's push on. We still have a lot of this to get through.* • (often + **with**) *They are pushing on with their campaign for improved childcare facilities.*

push out pushes, pushing, pushed
push out sb or **push** sb **out**

to make someone leave a job or stop being involved in an activity by being unpleasant to them • (often + **of**) *She felt she'd been pushed out of the job.*

push over pushes, pushing, pushed
push over sb/sth or **push** sb/sth **over**

to push someone or something so that they fall to the ground • *One of the big kids pushed him over.*

push round
see **push about/around/round**

push through pushes, pushing, pushed
push through sth or **push** sth **through** (sth)

to make a plan or suggestion be officially accepted • *The president is trying to push through various tax reforms.* • *We're trying to push this deal through as quickly as possible.*

push to pushes, pushing, pushed
push sth **to**

to close a door or window by pushing it • *Can you push the door to? – I can feel a draft.*

push towards pushes, pushing, pushed
push (sb) **towards** sth/doing sth

to try to do or achieve something, or to try to make someone do or achieve something • *New employment laws are expected to push more women towards voting Labour.* • *Three of the countries in the European Union are pushing towards a single currency.*

push up   pushes, pushing, pushed

push up sth or **push** sth **up**
to increase the amount, number, or value of something ● *Increases in indirect taxes will push inflation up.*

put about   puts, putting, put

put about sth or **put** sth **about** *British & Australian*
to tell a lot of people news or information that might not be true ● *Rumours have been put about that the princess is thinking of getting remarried.* ● *Government sources have put it about that the opposition is planning to raise taxes if they win the election.*

put about
if a ship or boat puts about, it turns around ● *The wind was getting much stronger so we decided to put about and return to port.*

put it about *British slang*
to have sexual relationships with a lot of different people ● (usually in continuous tenses) *She's been putting it about a bit recently, hasn't she?*

put across   puts, putting, put

put across sth or **put** sth **across**
to explain or express something clearly so that people understand it easily ● *The government needs to put across the message that the economy is starting to recover.* ● *Good teachers are the ones who are able to put things across well.*

put yourself **across** (always reflexive)
to express your ideas and opinions clearly so that people understand them easily and realize what sort of person you are ● *I don't think I managed to put myself across very well in that interview.*

put around/round   puts, putting, put

put around/round sth or **put** sth **around/round**
to tell a lot of people news or information that might not be true ● *Rumours have been put around that the company is going to be bought by an American firm.* ● *Who's been putting it around that I'm going out with Chris?*

put aside   puts, putting, put

put aside sth or **put** sth **aside**
1 to save money for a particular purpose ● *She puts aside £100 a month for clothes.*
2 to ignore a problem or a disagreement so that you can achieve something ● *The opposition parties have finally put aside their differences and formed an alliance.* ● *Putting aside practical difficulties, I think the proposal sounds really promising.*
3 to keep something so that you can use it later ● *Pour half of the milk into the mixture and put the rest aside for the sauce.*

put at   puts, putting, put

put sth **at** sth
to roughly calculate that something will cost a particular amount or that something is a particular size or amount ● *Initial estimates put the cost of the earthquake damage at $17 million.* ● *The death toll was unofficially put at 2,200.*

put away   puts, putting, put

put away sth or **put** sth **away**
1 to put something in the place where it is usually kept ● *I'll wash and dry the dishes, if you put them away.* ● *She folded up the towels and put them away in the cupboard.*
2 to save an amount of money ● *I try to put a little away every month.*
3 *informal* if you put away a lot of food or drink, you eat or drink it ● *I can't believe how much Alex put away at lunch!* ● *Sam and I put away a whole bottle of whisky last night.*
4 *informal* to score a goal in a sport by kicking or hitting the ball into the net ● *The third goal was put away by Williams.*
5 *American informal* to kill an animal because it is old or ill ● *The dog's injuries were so terrible it had to be put away.*

put away sb or **put** sb **away**
1 *informal* to send someone to prison, or to a hospital for people who are mentally ill ● (usually passive) *He was put away for five years for armed robbery.* ● *They were charged with murder but there wasn't enough evidence to put them away.* ● *In the past, people who suffered from schizophrenia were often put away.*

2 *American slang* to kill someone • *The robber who put away the bank manager has been caught.*

put back   puts, putting, put

put back sth or **put** sth **back**

1 to put something where it was before it was moved • *You will put the books back when you've finished with them, won't you?* • *Joey, put that back, there's a good boy.*

2 to change the date or time of an event so that it happens later than planned • *That meeting has had to be put back till December 8th.*

3 to cause something to happen later than it should happen • *This latest problem might put back our finishing date by a whole month.*

4 if you put a watch or clock back, you make it show an earlier time • *We'll be landing in about five minutes – I'd better put my watch back.*

5 *informal* to quickly drink a lot of alcohol • *He can put back nine or ten beers on a good night.*

put before   puts, putting, put

put sth **before** sb

1 to give more attention to one thing than another because you think it is more important • *I'd never put my work before my family.*

2 if you put facts or ideas before people in authority, you formally tell or explain them to them • *We've got to put our proposal before the committee.*

put behind   puts, putting, put

put sth **behind** sb

if you put an unpleasant experience behind you, you forget it so that it does not affect your life • *Like any divorce, it was a painful business, but I've put all that behind me now.*

put by   puts, putting, put

put by sth or **put** sth **by**

to save an amount of money in order to use it later • *If you put a little by every week, it soon adds up.*

put down   puts, putting, put

put down sb/sth or **put** sb/sth **down**

to put something or someone that you

are holding onto the floor or onto another surface • *I'll just put my bag down – it's rather heavy.* • *'Put me down, daddy!'* • *Put that knife down – you're making me nervous.*

put down sb or **put** sb **down**

1 to make someone feel stupid or unimportant by criticizing them • *Why do you have to put me down in front of everyone like that?* • (sometimes reflexive) *You put yourself down too much.*

put-down *n* [C] • (usually singular) *That was a bit of a put-down, wasn't it, referring to Julia as 'that girl who types Derek's letters'?*

2 to put someone's name on a list or document, usually in order to arrange for them to do something • (often + **for**) *You have to put a child down for nursery almost as soon as they're born.* • (sometimes + to do sth) *I've put myself down to do French classes next term.* • (sometimes + **as**) *He'd put me down as next of kin so I was the first to be informed of his death.*

3 *British & Australian old-fashioned* to stop a vehicle and let someone get out of it or off it • *Ask the driver to put you down outside the church.*

put down sth or **put** sth **down**

1 if you put the phone down, you put the part of the telephone that you speak into back into its usual position after your conversation has ended • *It was only after I'd put the phone down that I realised what I'd said.* • (sometimes + **on**) *He put the phone down on me* (= suddenly ended the telephone conversation) *in the middle of what I was saying.*

2 to pay part of the total cost of something • *Have you got enough money to put a deposit down on a house?*

3 to kill an animal because it is very old or very ill • *Eventually the poor cat was in such pain that we had to have her put down.*

4 to write something • *If anyone wants to go to the seminar on Friday afternoon, could they put their name down on this list, please?* • *There are feelings you can't talk about and sometimes it helps to put it all down on paper.*

5 to use force to stop people opposing the government • *Tanks had been brought in to put down the last popular uprising.*

put sb **down**
  to put a baby in its bed so that it can sleep
  ● *I usually put Harry down for a nap in the afternoon.*

put down (sth) or **put** (sth) **down**
  to land in an aircraft, or to make an aircraft land ● *I ran out of fuel and had to put down in the middle of a field.*

put down as   puts, putting, put

put sb **down as** sth
  to think that someone is a particular type of person, especially someone that you do not know very well ● *I suppose I'd taken one look at his appearance and put him down as the artistic type.*

put down to   puts, putting, put

put sth **down to** sth
  to think that a problem or bad experience is caused by something else ● *She did seem quiet at the time but I put it down to the problems she was having at work.* ● *And that lack of confidence I'd always put down to his strange upbringing.*

put forth   puts, putting, put

put forth sth or **put** sth **forth**
1 *formal* to state an idea or opinion, or to suggest a plan, so that it can be considered or discussed ● *In her thesis, she completely rejects the ideas put forth by Chomsky.* ● *They have put forth a plan for improving public services.*
2 *formal* if a plant or tree puts forth new leaves etc, they begin to appear on the plant or tree ● *The plant resembles a small log which puts forth leaves when watered.*
3 *mainly American* to make a strong physical or mental effort to do something ● *The team put forth an inspired effort to win the championship.*

put forward   puts, putting, put

put forward sth or **put** sth **forward**
1 to state an idea or opinion, or to suggest a plan, so that it can be considered or discussed ● *A number of theories have been put forward about the possible causes of cancer.* ● (sometimes + **for**) *The US has put forward a five-point plan for peace in the Middle East.*
2 to change the date or time of an event so that it happens earlier than planned

● *They decided that they would have to put forward some of the events.*
3 if you put forward a clock or watch, you make it show a later time ● *London is five hours ahead of New York, so you'll need to put your watch forward.*

put forward sb/sth or **put** sb/sth **forward**
  if you put forward someone or someone's name, you officially suggest that they should be considered for a particular position or job ● (sometimes + **for**) *Barry Taylor's name has been put forward for the post of chairman.* ● (sometimes + **as**) *Helen Wilson has been put forward as a possible candidate for the position.*

put in   puts, putting, put

put in sth or **put** sth **in**
1 to make an official request or offer to have or do something ● *David's put in a request to be transferred to the Boston office.* ● *A French firm has put in a bid of $4 million.*
2 to fix new equipment or a new system in the correct place in a room or building ● *I've just had a new kitchen put in.* ● *We're having some problems with the wiring system that was put in last week.*

put in sth
  to say something while someone else is speaking ● *'But I don't think she's the right person for the job', she put in.*

put in for   puts, putting, put

put in for sth
  to make an official request to have or do something ● *Richard's finally put in for his driving test.*

put in/into   puts, putting, put

put in sth or **put** sth **in**
put sth **into** sth/doing sth
  if you put time, work, or effort into something, you spend a lot of time or effort doing it ● *We've all put a lot of effort into this project and we want it to succeed.* ● *Jean put a lot of work into finishing her book.* ● *Many charities rely on volunteers who put in hours of unpaid work.*

put in sth or **put** sth **in**
put sth **into** sth
  to provide money for an organization or activity ● *Investors need to put in a min-*

imum of $2,000. • Additional resources must be put into the health service.

put in sb or put sb in

put sb into sth

to elect a political party, or to officially choose someone to do a particular job • (usually passive) The Republicans were put in again, but with a smaller majority. • Within a year of being put into office, he was charged with corruption.

put sb in/into sth

to make someone go to prison, a particular type of school, or a place where they can be cared for • She was charged with driving while drunk and put in prison for 18 months. • They put both their children into boarding school from the age of eleven. • My mother can't cope on her own any more, and so I've decided to put her in a nursing home.

put in

put into sth

if a ship puts in, it stops in a port for a short time • If the wind gets any stronger, we should put in.

put off   puts, putting, put

put off sth/doing sth or put sth off

to decide or arrange to do something at a later time • (often + until) They had decided to put the wedding off until her brother came home from abroad. • I've put off talking to him about this for far too long.

put off sb or put sb off

1 to tell someone that you cannot see them or do something for them until a later time • We can't keep putting them off, they'll think we don't like them.
2 British & Australian if a vehicle [e.g. bus] puts someone off, it stops to let them get off • There's a bus which'll put you off at the end of our street.

put off sb or put sb off (sb/sth/doing sth)

to make someone not like someone or something, or not want to do something • A lot of young people are put off joining because the members all seem so old. • What put me off him was the way he only talked about himself. • I can't watch this any more, it's putting me off my food.

off-putting adj • Even those who agree with most of what he says may find his style a little off-putting.

put-off n [C] • The beach was beautiful but the polluted sea was a real put-off.

put off sb or put sb off (sth)

to cause someone to be unable to continue what they are doing by stopping them from giving all their attention to it • Please just be quiet, you're putting me off. • The thought that she would be arriving later that day had put him off his work.

off-putting adj • It's very off-putting having someone looking over your shoulder while you're writing.

put on   puts, putting, put

put on sth or put sth on

1 to put a piece of clothing onto your body • Put your coat on if you're going outside, it's cold. • She put on her glasses and stared intently at the photograph.
2 to put make-up or cream onto your skin • Is there a mirror somewhere? I need to put my make-up on.
3 to make a device [e.g. light, fire] work by pressing a switch • Put the light on, would you? • What time do you want me to put the oven on?
4 to pretend to have a particular feeling, or to behave in a way which is not real or natural for you • I don't think he's really upset – he's just putting it on. • Anthea often puts on a funny voice when she answers the phone.

put-on n [C] American informal • She's

not really angry – it's just a put-on.

5 to organize a play, show, or competition
• *They were putting on a concert to raise money for the new church roof.*

6 to begin to cook food • *Can you put the potatoes on while I make a salad?*

7 to put something that sounds or pictures are recorded onto [e.g. CD, video] into a machine which makes you able to hear or see the recording • *Why don't you put your new CD on?* • *I'll put on a video for the kids to watch.*

8 (never passive) if a person or animal puts on weight, they become heavier • *Have you seen Trevor recently, I think he's really putting weight on.* • *She put on over ten pounds in just 2 months.*

9 to provide something for people to use • *They've put on a late-night bus service for students.* • *They're putting on a new computing course at the regional college.*

put on sb or **put** sb **on** (sth)
to give someone the telephone so that they can speak to the person who is on it
• *Can you put Wendy on?* • *When she felt herself beginning to cry, she put Laurie on the phone.*

put sb **on** sth
1 to take someone to a train, bus etc. and to make sure that they get on it • *I put her on the 9:30 train so she should have arrived by now.*

2 to decide that someone should do a particular job • *Tracey's really exhausted since they put her on the night shift.* • *Alex and I have been put on the planning committee.*

3 to give someone a particular type of medical treatment or food • *They've put me on a low-fat diet.*

put sth **on** sth
1 to risk an amount of money by saying who you think will win a race or competition or what you think will happen in the future • *Can you put £5 on Mr. Bigwig in the last race for me?*

2 to add an amount to the cost or value of something • *They're putting another ten pence on cigarettes.*

put sb **on** (never passive) *American informal*
to persuade someone that something is true when it is not, usually as a joke

• *You didn't believe him did you? He was just putting you on.*

put-on *n* [C] *American informal* • *Is this one of your put-ons, Matt, or has she really been fired?*

put sb **on to/onto** sth
to tell someone about something or someone that could help them, often something or someone they did not know about before • *Andy and Fiona put us onto a really good garage in Hammersmith.*

put out sth or **put** sth **out**
1 to make a light stop shining by pressing a switch • *I'm rather tired – shall we put the light out?* • *Could you put that torch out?*

2 to make something that is burning [e.g. fire, cigarette] stop burning • *You'd better put your cigarette out before Terry sees it.* • *Ben grabbed the fire extinguisher and put the fire out.*

3 to put something in a place where people will notice it so that they can use it if they want to • *Did you put clean towels out for the guests?* • *I thought I'd put out some food for people to have with their drinks.*

4 to produce information [e.g. statement, warning, press release] and make it available for everyone to read or hear • *Earlier in the day the palace had put out a statement denying the rumour.* • *Police have put out a warning to people living in the area.*

5 to put something outside the house, especially so that it can be collected • *I must remember to put the rubbish out on Wednesday night in time for the collection.* • *Did you put the cat out last night?*

6 to produce or publish something for the public to buy or use • *The sort of books that they put out are never likely to be best-sellers.*

7 to broadcast a programme or film on television or radio • *Most of the films that they put out on the movie channel you wouldn't even want to watch.*

8 to injure a part of your body [e.g. back, shoulder] by making a bone move from its usual place • *Careful how you lift those boxes or you'll put your back out.*

put out sb or **put** sb **out**

1 to cause trouble or extra work for someone ● (usually negative) *If we could bring Sam that would be great but I don't want to put you out at all.* ● (sometimes reflexive) *It has to be said of Matthew that he doesn't put himself out for anyone.* (= he will not help someone else if it causes him trouble)

2 to make someone unconscious before a medical operation ● *I think I'd rather they put me out for the whole procedure.*

be put out (always passive)
to be annoyed, often because of something that someone has done or said to you ● *He seemed a bit put out at not having been included in the plans.*

put out

1 if a boat or ship puts out, it starts to sail ● *We waited for the storm to die down and then put out to sea.*

2 American slang if a woman puts out, she is willing to have sex with a man ● *He expects a woman to put out if he so much as buys her a drink.*

put over   puts, putting, put

put over sth or **put** sth **over**
to express an idea clearly so that people understand it ● *Did you feel that you managed to put over your point of view?*

put round

see **put around/round**

put through   puts, putting, put

put sth/sb **through** sth
to test something or someone in order to see if they can do what they should be able to do ● *We put all new models of car through a rigorous series of tests.*

put sb **through** sth

1 to make someone experience or do something unpleasant or difficult ● *Doctors are reluctant to put her through the ordeal of another operation.* ● *New recruits are put through a gruelling six-month training programme.*

2 to pay for someone to study at college or university ● *You'll need to save a lot of money if you want to put both your daughters through college.* ● (sometimes reflexive) *He worked in a bank four days a week to put himself through law school.*

put through sb or **put** sb **through**
to connect a telephone caller to the person they want to speak to ● *Hold the line, I'm just putting you through.* ● (often + **to**) *Can you put me through to customer services, please?*

put through sth or **put** sth **through**
if someone puts through a planned new law, it is formally accepted by an elected group of politicians ● *In March, the government put through a law to make strikes illegal.*

put to   puts, putting, put

put sth **to** sb

1 to suggest an idea or plan to someone so that they can consider it or discuss it ● *The peace plan was first put to the Prime Minister last week.* ● *We will be putting the latest offer to the negotiating committee.*

2 to ask someone a question, or to state an opinion to someone which they are likely to disagree with ● *Do you have any questions that you would like to put to the senator?* ● *She put it to the defendant that he was not telling the truth.*

put sb **to** sth
to make someone have to spend a lot of time or money doing something that they do not want to do ● *Are you sure you can pick me up from the party? I don't want to put you to any trouble.* ● *Losing your passport on holiday can put you to a good deal of inconvenience.*

put together   puts, putting, put

put together sth or **put** sth **together**

1 to put the parts of something in the correct place and join them to each other ● *Sally helped me put my futon together.* ● *I've knitted the entire sweater – I've just got to put the thing together now.*

2 to prepare a piece of work by collecting several ideas and suggestions and organizing them ● *We've put together a proposal which we want to put before the committee.*

3 to make a group or team by choosing several people ● *A team is being put together to carry out investigatory work.*

put towards   puts, putting, put

put sth **towards** sth

to use an amount of money to pay part of the cost of something • *My mother gave me some money which I'm going to put towards a new coat.*

put under   puts, putting, put

put sb **under** *American*

to make someone unconscious before a medical operation • *You won't be put under until the operation is about to start.*

put up   puts, putting, put

put up sth or **put** sth **up**

1 to build a structure [e.g. wall, building, statue] • *Most of the old buildings were pulled down so that blocks of apartments could be put up.* • *They're putting up a statue in town in his honour.*

2 to stick or fasten a piece of paper [e.g. notice, poster] to a wall so that it can be seen • *They put staff notices up on the board near reception.* • *This room looks very bare – I might put up one or two posters.*

3 to fasten a piece of furniture [e.g. shelves, cupboard] to a wall • *I might ask Guy to put some shelves up in the lounge.*

4 to spread something that is folded or rolled up [e.g. tent, umbrella] so that it is ready to be used • *Are you any good at putting tents up?* • *I'll just put my umbrella up.*

5 *British & Australian* to increase the price or value of something • *They're going to put up the price of petrol.* • *Our landlord has just put our rent up.*

6 to explain a suggestion or argument to people so that they can decide whether they like it or agree with it • *It was Bob Taylor who originally put up the idea of the exhibition.*

put up sth

1 to oppose something, or to fight against something that is happening • *We'd heard that they were against the plan but in fact they put up very little resistance.* • *I'm not going to make it easy for them – I intend to put up a fight.*

2 to provide a large amount of money for a particular purpose • *The money for the hospital was put up by an anonymous donor.*

put up sb or **put** sb **up**

1 to let someone stay in your home for a short period • (often + **for**) *If you need somewhere to stay, we can certainly put you up for the night.* • *She asked if we knew anyone who could put her up over the summer.*

2 to officially offer someone as one of the people to be elected to a position • *They've put up a new candidate – Bill Cronshaw, I think his name is.*

put up (always + *adv/prep*) *mainly British old-fashioned*

to stay somewhere for a short time • *We could always put up at a cheap hotel for the night.*

put upon   puts, putting, put

put upon sb *British & Australian*

to treat someone unfairly, usually by making extra work for them to do • *I know you've got a lot of work to do – I really don't want to put upon you.*

put-upon *adj* • *Really she's doing two people's work at once and I think she's beginning to feel put-upon.* • *Stewarts plays the part of the put-upon wife.*

put up to   puts, putting, put

put sb **up to** sth

to encourage someone to do something stupid or wrong • *I'm sure Ben wouldn't have thought of this on his own – someone must have put him up to it.*

put up with   puts, putting, put

put up with sb/sth

to accept unpleasant behaviour or an unpleasant situation, even though you do not like it • *He's not easy to live with – I think Jo puts up with a lot.* • *I can put up with a house being untidy but I don't like it to be dirty.* • *He's impossible! How do you put up with him?*

putt along   putts, putting, putted

putt along *American old-fashioned*

if a vehicle with a small engine [e.g. motorcycle, motor boat] putts along, it moves slowly forwards • *They were putting along through the streets looking for a restaurant.*

putter about/around   putters, puttering, puttered

putter about/around (swh) *American*

to spend time in a pleasant, relaxed way, often doing small jobs in the house • *We didn't go anywhere – we just puttered around the boat all day.*

puzzle out   puzzles, puzzling, puzzled

puzzle out sth or **puzzle** sth **out**

to find the solution to a problem by thinking carefully about it • *The whole thing is a mystery to me, I'll leave you to puzzle out an explanation.* • *I've thought long and hard about this problem, but I really can't*

quarrel with
quarrels, quarrelling, quarrelled (*American & Australian* also **quarrels, quarreling, quarreled**)

quarrel with sth

to disagree with an idea, statement, or decision ● *I'm not quarrelling with the idea that good childcare should be available to all who need it.*

queue up
queues, queueing, queued

queue up *British & Australian*

to stand in a line in order to wait for something ● (often + to do sth) *We queued up to get tickets for the concert.*

queue up to do sth *British & Australian slightly informal*

to want to do something very much ● *Some of the world's most respected musicians were queueing up to play with him.*

quiet/quieten down
quiets, quieting, quieted/quietens, quietening, quietened

quiet down (sb/sth) or **quiet** (sb/sth) *American*

quieten down (sb/sth) or **quieten** (sb/sth) **down** *British*

to become quieter or calmer, or to make a person or animal become quieter or calmer ● *Come on, quieten down now please everyone.* ● *The speaker attempted to quiet down the audience.*

quit on
quits, quitting, quit/quitted

quit on sb

1 *American & Australian informal* to stop working for someone or being friends with them, often at a time when they need your support ● *One of my staff has quit on me without any warning.* ● *He's the sort of guy who will quit on you just when you need him most.*

2 *American informal* if a machine quits on someone, it stops working ● *If the motorcycle quits on him in Montana, he's in real trouble.*

rabbit on   rabbits, rabbiting, rabbited

rabbit on *British informal*
to talk for a long time about things that are not interesting to other people ● (usually + **about**) *He's always rabbiting on about his stamp collection.*

rack off

Rack off! (always an order) *Australian slang*
something that you say in order to tell someone to go away because they are annoying you ● *Rack off you idiot!*

rack up   racks, racking, racked

rack up sth or **rack** sth **up**
1 *informal* to get a large amount or large number of something ● *They had racked up losses of about one million dollars.*
2 *American informal* to damage something ● *He swerved off the road and racked up the car.*

raffle off   raffles, raffling, raffled

raffle off sth or **raffle** sth **off**
to offer something as a prize in a raffle (= a competition in which prizes are won with numbered tickets) ● *They were raffling off some theatre tickets to raise money for the local hospice.*

rail against/at   rails, railing, railed

rail against/at sb/sth *formal*
to complain angrily about someone or something ● *The hero of the book rails at the injustices of the world but does nothing about them.*

rain down   rains, raining, rained

rain down (sth) or **rain** (sth) **down** *literary*
to fall suddenly in large amounts ● (often + **on**) *Bombs rained down on the besieged city.* ● *Her attacker rained down blows on her.* (= hit her again and again)

rain off/out

be rained off (always passive) *British & Australian*

be rained out (always passive) *American*
if a sport or other outside activity is rained off, it cannot start or continue because it is raining ● *Most of the day's matches at Wimbledon were rained off.* ● *Last night's baseball game was rained out.*

rake in   rakes, raking, raked

rake in sth or **rake** sth **in** *informal*
to earn large amounts of money, especially without doing much work ● *Tanya will rake in around $21,000 for three TV appearances.* ● *He's really **raking it in**.* (= earning a lot of money)

rake off   rakes, raking, raked

rake off sb or **rake** sb **off**
Australian informal to cheat someone by making them pay too much money for something ● *It's difficult in a tourist area like this to find a restaurant where they won't try to rake you off.*
rake-off n [C] *Australian informal* ● *Did you really pay $120 for that shirt? What a rake-off!*

rake over   rakes, raking, raked

rake over sth or **rake** sth **over** *informal*
to talk or think about something unpleasant again and again ● *I don't want to rake over all the old arguments with you.* ● *If she keeps raking over the past she'll remain very bitter.*

rake up   rakes, raking, raked

rake up sth or **rake** sth **up**
1 *informal* to think and talk about things that happened in the past, especially things that embarrass or upset someone ● *Newspapers are always raking up old scandals which are better forgotten.*
2 *informal* to get something although this is difficult to do ● *How much money did you manage to rake up?*

rally around/round   rallies, rallying, rallied

rally around/round (sb)
if a group of people rally around someone who has problems, they all try to help that person ● *His friends all rallied round*

when his wife died. • *If one of the family has a crisis we all rally around them.*

rally around/round sth/sb

if a group of people rally around a particular aim or someone who has a particular aim, they all give their support to that aim or to that person • *During the crisis they rallied around their leader.*

ramble on   rambles, rambling, rambled

ramble on

to talk or write for a long time about things that are not interesting to other people • (often + **about**) *Sarah gets very bored listening to her grandparents rambling on about old times.*

ramp up   ramps, ramping, ramped

ramp sth **up** or **ramp up** sth

to increase the speed, power, cost or amount of something • *The company has ramped up production of its new sports car.* • *He's started to ramp up the number of miles he is running each day.*

range against   ranges, ranging, ranged

range against sb/sth

if a group of people range against a particular person or idea, they all say publicly that they are against that person or idea • (usually passive) *Most of the state Democratic party were ranged against the President.* • *Ranged against the new law are politicians from all the different parties.*

rank among   ranks, ranked

rank (sth) **among** sth (never in continuous tenses)

to have a particular position in a list that has been arranged in order of quality • *California's universities rank among the best in the country.* • *Where fitness is concerned, the British are ranked among the worst in Europe.*

rap out   raps, rapping, rapped

rap out sth or **rap** sth **out**

to say something [e.g. order, question] suddenly and loudly and often in an angry way • *The sergeant rapped out an order to the waiting soldiers.*

rat on   rats, ratting, ratted

rat on sb *informal*

if you rat on someone who has done something wrong, you cause trouble for that person by telling someone in authority what they have done • *Prisoners are encouraged to rat on each other.*

rat on sth *British informal*

to fail to do something that you promised to do • *The government have ratted on their promises to the poor.*

rat through   rats, ratting, ratted

rat through sth *Australian informal*

to search for something in a careless way, usually because you do not have much time • *I came into the office to find him ratting through my papers.*

ration out   rations, rationing, rationed

ration out sth or **ration** sth **out**

to divide something between a group of people so that each person gets a small amount • *Supplies of food were low and we had to ration out the little that was left.*

rattle around   rattles, rattling, rattled

rattle around (swh) *slightly informal*

to be in a building or room that is much too big for you • (often + **in**) *There are just the two of them now rattling around in this enormous house.*

rattle off   rattles, rattling, rattled

rattle off sth or **rattle** sth **off**

to say a list or something that you have learned [e.g. speech, poem] quickly and without stopping • *She can rattle off the names of all the team's players.*

rattle on   rattles, rattling, rattled

rattle on *informal*

to talk for a long time about things that are not interesting to other people • (often + **about**) *I had to listen to Ian's mother rattling on about the neighbours for half the evening.*

rattle through   rattles, rattling, rattled

rattle through sth *informal*

to speak or do something very quickly in order to finish as soon as possible • *She rattled through her speech as if she were in a hurry to leave.*

rave up   raves, raving, raved

rave it up

British old-fashioned to celebrate by drinking, dancing and making a lot of noise • *They were raving it up at the office party last night.*

rave-up n [C] *British* • *Judging by the noise, they're having another one of their rave-ups next door.*

reach down   reaches, reaching, reached

reach down sth or **reach** sth **down**
mainly British
to get something that is above your head by reaching with your hand • *Could you reach those books down for me, Mike?*

reach out   reaches, reaching, reached

reach out (sth) or **reach** (sth) **out**
to stretch your arm in front of your body, usually in order to get or touch something • (often + to do sth) *She reached out to grab him but it was too late.* • *He reached out a hand to stroke the cat.*

reach out for   reaches, reaching, reached

reach out for sth
to try extremely hard to achieve a new or better situation • *The whole nation is reaching out for change.*

reach out to   reaches, reaching, reached

reach out to sb
1 to offer help and support to someone • *The rich have to reach out to the poor.*
2 to ask someone for help or support • *But I reached out to you and you just weren't there.*

read back   reads, reading, read

read back sth or **read** sth **back**
to read a short piece of writing for the second time, usually to make sure that you have understood it • *When I read back what I'd written, I understood why he'd been offended.*

read into   reads, reading, read

read sth **into** sth
to believe that an action, remark, or situation has a particular importance or meaning, often when this is not true • *It would be stupid to read too much into anything she says.* • *It's a very ambiguous statement – you can read what you want into it.*

read off   reads, reading, read

read off sth or **read** sth **off**
to look at the number that is being shown on a measuring device • *The pressure is then read off electronically.*

read out   reads, reading, read

read out sth or **read** sth **out**
1 to read something and say the words aloud so that other people can hear • *He read out the names of the winners.* • *Read out the numbers and I'll key them in.*
2 *mainly American* if a device reads out information, it shows that information to the person who is using the device • *The data collected by the vehicle movement detectors are being read out now.*

read-out n [C] • *The plane's computer read-out was inaccurate.*

read over/through   reads, reading, read

read over/through sth or **read** sth **over/through**
to read something from the beginning to the end in order to find any mistakes or to understand it better • *I read over my essay to check for errors.* • *She hadn't even made the effort to read my report through before the meeting.*

read up on   reads, reading, read

read up on sth
to read a lot about a particular subject in order to learn about it • *He was told to read up on world affairs before the interview.*

rear up   rears, rearing, reared

rear up
if a large animal [esp. horse] rears up, it suddenly lifts the front of its body by standing on its back legs • *There was a gunshot and the horse reared up.*

reason out   reasons, reasoning, reasoned

reason out sth or **reason** sth **out**
to think carefully about something in order to decide what to do, or in order to understand it • *She had reasoned out that doing this work would provide good training for the future.* • *At first I didn't understand her motivation and it took me a while to reason it out.*

reason with   reasons, reasoning, reasoned

reason with sb

to try to persuade someone not to do something stupid by giving them good reasons not to • *I've tried reasoning with him but he just won't listen.* • *The police pleaded and reasoned with the man to come down from the roof top.*

rebound on/upon   rebounds, rebounding, rebounded

rebound on/upon sb

if a negative action rebounds on someone, it has a bad effect on the person who did it and they do not achieve what they were trying to achieve • *Her jealous behaviour can only rebound on her in the future.*

reckon in   reckons, reckoning, reckoned

reckon in sth or **reckon** sth **in** *mainly British*

to include something in your calculations • *When you reckon in all your overtime, then your total pay is very good.*

reckon on   reckons, reckoning, reckoned

reckon on sth/doing sth

to think that something is going to happen and make it part of your plans • *We're reckoning on about two hundred people for dinner.* • *He is reckoning on your continued support.* • *They reckoned on beating their enemy.*

reckon up   reckons, reckoning, reckoned

reckon up sth or **reckon** sth **up** *mainly British old-fashioned*

to calculate the total amount of something • *I'll just reckon up how much you owe me.*

reckon with   reckons, reckoning, reckoned

reckon with sb/sth

to have to deal with someone or something that is difficult to deal with • *The rescue flight had to reckon with strong winds and freezing temperatures.* • *If he harms her in any way, he'll have me to reckon with.* • *When they realised she was **a force to be reckoned with** (= a serious threat they must deal with) they threw her off the land.*

not reckon with sb/sth *(always negative)*

to fail to realize that you are going to have to deal with someone or something • *We had not reckoned with an enemy as formidable as Zeldon.*

reckon without   reckons, reckoning, reckoned

reckon without sth

to fail to think about something when you are making plans and therefore not be prepared to deal with it • *We had expected an easy two-hour drive but had reckoned without the rain.*

reduce to   reduces, reducing, reduced

reduce sb **to** sth

1 to upset or surprise someone so much that they cry or are silent • *His classmates' jeers reduced him to tears.* • *The shock had reduced us all to silence.*

2 to force someone into a lower state or condition than they were in before • *(usually passive) The whole family were reduced to poverty by their father's gambling.*

reduce sb **to** doing sth

if someone is reduced to doing something that they think is bad, they do it even though it makes them feel ashamed, because nothing else is possible • *(usually passive) We've had to sell the car so I'm now reduced to travelling on buses.* • *I'd run out of cigarettes and was reduced to smoking the butts left in the ashtrays.*

reduce sth **to** sth

1 to destroy something that has been built [e.g. building, city] • *Constant bombing has reduced the city to ruins.* • *The inside of the building was reduced to ashes by the heat of the fire.*

2 to put something into a form that is shorter and easier to understand • *He was able to reduce the problem to three simple questions.*

3 to make something change to a weaker state or condition • *Clouds of burning oil reduced the sun to a feeble orange circle.*

reek of   reeks, reeked

reek of sth *(never in continuous tenses)*

if something reeks of an unpleasant quality, it seems to have that quality • *The whole affair reeks of hypocrisy.*

reel in   reels, reeling, reeled

reel in sth or **reel** sth **in**

if a person who is fishing reels in a fish or a fishing line (= a long thin piece of nylon used to catch fish), they pull it towards them by turning a handle on a wheel-shaped object that has the fishing line around it • *The boy slowly reeled in the fish.* • *Reel in the line when the fish bites.*

reel in sb or **reel** sb **in** *informal*

to offer someone something that is very attractive to them, in order to persuade them to do what you want them to do • *She's a high achiever and has reeled in some very big clients.* • *Channel 4 are hoping the film will reel the viewers in.*

reel off   reels, reeling, reeled

reel off sth or **reel** sth **off**

1 *informal* to say a long list of things quickly and without stopping • *She amazed everyone by reeling off the names of all the American Presidents.* • *They reeled off a list of all the places they hoped to visit.*

2 *American informal* to win several games or points one after the other in a sports competition • *The Wildcats reeled off 14 consecutive points and won.*

reel out   reels, reeling, reeled

reel out sth or **reel** sth **out**

to make something which is long, for example a rope or wire, come off a wheel-shaped object which it is rolled on • *The fireman reeled out the hoses to put out the fire.*

refer to   refers, referring, referred

refer to sb/sth

1 to talk about or mention someone or something • *In his autobiography he repeatedly refers to his unhappy school days.* • (often + **as**) *He always referred to his father as 'the old man'.*

2 if writing or information refers to someone or something, it describes or is about that person or thing • *The figures below refer to UK sales alone.*

refer to sth

to read something in order to get information • *Refer to the users' guide if you have any problems.* • *She spoke for an hour without once referring to her notes.*

refer sb/sth **to** sb/sth

to send someone or something to a different place or person in order to get information or help or in order to be dealt with • *Her doctor wants to refer her to a specialist.* • *They are hoping their case will be referred to the European Court.*

reflect on/upon   reflects, reflecting, reflected

reflect on/upon sth *slightly formal*

to think very hard about something, or to express your thoughts about something in what you say or write • *Anyone who reflects upon the nature of human existence may come to the same conclusion.* • *Reflecting on the sales department's performance this year, he singled out Andrew West for special praise.*

reflect on/upon sb/sth

if something reflects on someone or something, it affects other people's opinion of that person or thing • *The whole affair reflects badly on the government.*

regale with   regales, regaling, regaled

regale sb **with** sth *formal*

to entertain a person or group of people by telling them things [e.g. stories, tales] • *Adrian regaled us all with stories about his trip to Amsterdam.*

rein in   reins, reining, reined

rein in sb/sth or **rein** sb/sth **in**

to control someone or something more strictly in order to stop them from causing trouble • *Consumers have reacted to the slow growth in income by reining in their spending.*

rein in sth or **rein** sth **in**

if you rein in a horse, you make it go more slowly, or you stop it by pulling the reins (= long thin pieces of leather fastened around the horse's head) • *She reined in her pony and dismounted to open the gate.*

rejoice in   rejoices, rejoicing, rejoiced

rejoice in sth *formal*

to be very happy about something • *We all rejoice in your success and wish you every happiness in the future.*

relate to   relates, relating, related

relate to sb

1 to understand someone and be able to have a friendly relationship with them • *Many parents find it hard to relate to their teenage children.*
2 to affect someone • *What I'm interested in is how these proposals relate to me personally.*

relate to sth

1 to be connected to a particular subject, or to be about a particular subject • *Documents relating to the case were stolen from the defence lawyer's car.* • *Chapter nine relates to the effects of inflation on consumers.*
2 to understand a situation or someone's feelings because you have experienced a similar situation or similar feelings • *The culture that he describes is so different from mine that I sometimes find it difficult to relate to.*

relieve of   relieves, relieving, relieved

relieve sb of sth

1 *formal* to take a problem away from someone • *I was glad to be relieved of the responsibility for making that decision.*
2 *formal* to dismiss someone from a position or job because they have done something wrong • *The general was relieved of his command and sent home in disgrace.*
3 *humorous* to help someone by taking something heavy [e.g. bag] from them • *Let me relieve you of your bag.*

rely on/upon   relies, relying, relied

rely on/upon sth/sb

1 to need something or someone in order to survive, be successful, or work correctly • *This organization relies entirely on voluntary donations.* • (often + to do sth) *We'll rely on you to keep the conversation going.* • (often + for) *They rely on Mick's income for basics like food.*
2 to trust someone or something to do what you need them to do • *I need someone I can rely on.* • *You can't rely on the weather at this time of year.* • (often + to do sth) *Can I rely on you to get here on time?*

remember to   remembers, remembered

remember sb to sb (never in continuous tenses)

if someone asks you to remember them to someone else, they are asking you to give a greeting from them to that person • *Remember me to your parents when you see them next.*

remind of   reminds, reminded

remind sb of sb/sth (never in continuous tenses)

to cause someone to think of someone or something • *Something in his face really reminded me of an old boyfriend of mine.* • *Doesn't the countryside round here remind you of Holland?* • *She reminds me of a teacher I used to have.*

render down   renders, rendering, rendered

render down sth or render sth down *British*

to melt fat until it is liquid • (usually passive) *The fat is rendered down and then used as a base for cosmetics.*

render into   renders, rendering, rendered

render sth into sth *formal*

to change a piece of writing into another language • *The letter had been rendered into French by an inexpert translator.*

renege on   reneges, reneging, reneged

renege on sth *formal*

if you renege on something that you have agreed to do [e.g. promise, contract], you do not do it • *By increasing taxes, the government has reneged on the promises it made during the election campaign.*

rent out   rents, renting, rented

rent out sth or rent sth out

if you rent out something that you own [e.g. house], you allow someone to pay you money so that they can use it • *They rent out one floor of their apartment.* • (often + to) *She rents out boats to tourists during the summer season.*

repair to   repairs, repairing, repaired

repair to swh *old-fashioned*

to go to a place, often a different room • *Shall we repair to the drawing room for coffee?*

report back   reports, reporting, reported

report back

to give someone information about something that they asked you to find out about ● (often + **on**) *I've been asked to report back on what goes on at the meeting.*

report to   reports, reporting, reported

report to sb

if you report to someone at work, that person is your boss ● *As head of the sales team she reports only to the managing director.*

reside in   resides, resided

reside in sb/sth (never in continuous tenses) *formal*

if a quality or power resides in someone or something, they have that quality or power ● *The power ultimately resides in the army that put this government into office.*

resign to   resigns, resigning, resigned

resign yourself **to** sth (always reflexive)

to accept that something you do not want to happen will happen ● *Eventually you just resign yourself to being single.* ● *He's definitely coming over to stay so I'll just have to resign myself to it.*

resolve into   resolves, resolving, resolved

resolve (sth) **into** sth

to separate a substance into parts ● *The mixture gradually resolves into two separate compounds.*

resolve itself **into** sth (always reflexive)

to gradually change to become something different ● *As you watch it, this mass of coloured dots resolves itself into a definite shape.*

resonate with   resonates, resonating, resonated

resonate with sth *formal*

to have a lot of a particular quality or feeling ● *This building, standing in the oldest quarter of the town, resonates with historic significance.*

resort to   resorts, resorting, resorted

resort to sth/doing sth

to do something bad in order to achieve what you want, often because it is the only thing you can do to achieve it ● *I had to resort to threats to get my money back.* ● *I've got to find some way of raising money without resorting to selling the house.*

rest on/upon   rests, resting, rested

rest on/upon sth

to depend on something, or to be based on something ● *The prosecution's case rests almost entirely on the evidence of a convicted criminal.* ● *Christianity rests on the belief that Jesus was the son of God.*

rest on/upon sb/sth

if your eyes rest on someone or something, you look at that person or thing ● *His eyes rested on a short, slim, pretty woman.*

rest up   rests, resting, rested

rest up

1 *mainly British & Australian old-fashioned* to rest for a period of time, usually after you have been ill ● *The doctor had said she should rest up for a while.*

2 *mainly American & Australian* to rest and relax in order to have enough energy for a special event, especially a sport ● *You'd better go home and rest up before the game this afternoon.*

rest upon

see **rest on/upon**

rest with   rest, rested

rest with sb (never in continuous tenses)

if a responsibility [esp. decision] rests with a person, that person is responsible for it ● *The final decision rests with the patient.*

result in   results, resulting, resulted

result in sth

to cause something to happen, or to make a situation exist ● *Last year in the Philippines, earthquakes and tidal waves resulted in the deaths of more than 6000 people.*

rev up   revs, revving, revved

rev up sth or **rev** sth **up**

to make a vehicle's engine work faster while the vehicle is not moving ● *He revved up the engine and drove off.*

revved-up adj (always before noun) *mainly American* ● *He's put a new revved-up engine in the used car he bought.*

rev up (sb/sth)or **rev** (sb/sth) **up** *mainly American & Australian*
to become more active, or to make someone or something become more active ● *Both teams are revving up for the championships.* ● *They hope the new musical will rev up ticket sales for the summer season.*

revved-up adj (always before noun) *mainly American & Australian* ● *The Americans are facing competition from revved-up European airlines.*

revel in   revels, revelling, revelled
(American & Australian also **revels, reveling, reveled**)

revel in sth
to enjoy a situation or activity very much, especially one that people do not usually enjoy ● *He seems to revel in the attention of the mass media.* ● *She revelled in her new found freedom.*

revenge on   revenge, revenging, revenged

revenge yourself **on** sb *formal*

be revenged on sb *formal*
to punish someone because they have hurt you or been unkind to you ● *This only increased his desire to be revenged on the murderous duke.*

revert to   reverts, reverting, reverted

revert to sth/doing sth
1 to start talking about a subject that you were talking about before ● *Why does the conversation have to revert to money all the time?* ● *We reverted to talking about babies again.*
2 to go back to a previous condition or activity, especially a worse one ● *Only one of the former prisoners reverted to criminal behaviour.* ● *The last two summers have been very hot but this year the British weather has **reverted to type**.* (= is cooler, as it usually is)

revert to sb
if property reverts to someone, it legally belongs to the person who owned it be-

fore ● *When I die the house will revert to you.*

revolve around/round   revolves, revolving, revolved

revolve around/round sth/sb
if an activity or conversation revolves around something or someone, that thing or person is the main reason for the activity, or the main subject of the conversation ● *The conversation revolved mainly round the problems of childcare.* ● *Her life revolves around her husband and six children.* ● *The trouble with John is that **he thinks the world revolves around him**.* (= he thinks that he is more important than anyone else)

rid of   rids, ridding, rid or ridded, rid

rid sth/sb **of** sth
to remove something or someone unpleasant from a person, place, or organization ● *The new government promised to rid the country of corruption.* ● (often reflexive) *Recently he's been trying to rid himself of his playboy image.*

riddle with   riddles, riddling, riddled

riddle sb/sth **with** sth
to fill someone or something with holes or bullets, especially by shooting them ● (usually passive) *The car was damaged by fire and riddled with bullets.* ● *He wore an old jacket riddled with holes.*

be riddled with sth (always passive)
to be full of something, especially something unpleasant or bad ● *These poor animals are riddled with disease.* ● *The old regime was riddled with corruption.*

ride on   rides, riding, rode, ridden

ride on sth
if something important [e.g. reputation, money] rides on something else, it depends on it ● *There was $600,000 riding on the outcome of the deal.* ● *Thousands of jobs may ride on these seemingly unimportant decisions.*

ride out   rides, riding, rode, ridden

ride out sth or **ride** sth **out**
if someone rides out a difficult situation, they continue to survive during it, or are not badly affected by it ● *Many companies did not manage to ride out the recession.*

• *The government seem confident that they'll **ride out the storm**.* (= not be harmed by the difficult situation)

ride up   rides, riding, rode, ridden

ride up
if an piece of clothing rides up, it gradually moves up so that it is not covering as much of your body as it should • *That kind of dress always seems to ride up at the back.*

riffle through   riffles, riffling, riffled

riffle through sth *mainly American informal*
to search quickly through papers • *He riffled through his notes trying to find the information she wanted.*

rifle through   rifles, rifling, rifled

rifle through sth
to search quickly through something [e.g. papers, drawers], often in order to steal something • *Thieves had rifled through their luggage, but had taken nothing.*

rig out   rigs, rigging, rigged

rig out sb or **rig** sb **out** *old-fashioned, informal*
to dress someone in a particular type of clothes, especially clothes which are unusual or special • (usually passive) *I don't know where she was going but she was rigged out in the most amazing silver suit.*
rig-out n [C] *British old-fashioned, informal* • *Patrick himself was in the most extraordinary rig-out.*

rig up   rigs, rigging, rigged

rig up sth or **rig** sth **up** *informal*
to make a piece of equipment, or to fit a piece of equipment into a particular place, often for a short period of time and using whatever objects you can find • *Johnny had managed to rig up a cooker in the corner of the barn.*

ring back   rings, ringing, rang, rung

ring (sb) **back** (never passive) *mainly British & Australian*
to telephone someone for the second time, or to telephone someone who rang you earlier • *Brendan rang while you were out and asked if you'd ring him back.* • *I'm rather busy now, Alistair – could you ring back later?*

ring in   rings, ringing, rang, rung

ring in *British & Australian*
to telephone someone at your place of work, usually to explain why you are not there • *Linda rang in to say that she'd be late this morning.* • *Daniel just **rang in sick**.* (= rang to say that he was ill and could not come to work)

ring off   rings, ringing, rang, rung

ring off *British & Australian*
to end a telephone call by putting down the part of the telephone that you speak into • *I only thought to tell her about Stan after she'd rung off.*

ring out   rings, ringing, rang, rung

ring out
if a noise [e.g. gunshot, bells, voice] rings out, it can be heard loudly and clearly • *Three shots suddenly rang out.* • *The cathedral bells rang out across the square.*

ring round   rings, ringing, rang, rung

ring round (sb) (never passive) *British & Australian*
to telephone several people, often in order to find out information • *I thought I'd ring round a few airlines and get the cheapest flight.* • *I'll ring round and see if anyone can babysit on Saturday.*

ring up   rings, ringing, rang, rung

ring up (sb) or **ring** (sb) **up** *mainly British & Australian*
to telephone someone • *Ring him up and ask him what he's doing tonight.* • *Whenever I ring up it's always Bill who answers.*

ring up sth or **ring** sth **up**
to record the amount of money that is being put into a cash register (= machine used in shops for storing money) by pressing its buttons • *The sales assistant rang up $48 when the price tag said $38.*

ring up sth *American informal*
to achieve a particular amount of things • *The Yankees rang up five runs in the third inning.*

rinse out   rinses, rinsing, rinsed

rinse out sth or **rinse** sth **out**
1 to put something that you have washed in soapy water [e.g. cloth, sweater] into clean water in order to get rid of the soap

● *You haven't rinsed this sweater out properly.*

2 to quickly wash the inside of something [e.g. cup, glass] with clean water ● *I'll just rinse these glasses out and leave them to dry.*

rip into   rips, ripping, ripped

rip into sb/sth *informal*

to criticize someone or something in an unkind way, or to speak angrily to someone for doing something that you think is bad or wrong ● *His latest novel has really been ripped into by the critics.* ● (sometimes + **for**) *John's mother ripped into him for using her car without telling her.*

rip off   rips, ripping, ripped

rip off sb or **rip** sb **off**

informal to cheat someone by making them pay too much money for something ● *Taxi drivers love foreigners because they know they can rip them off.* ● *There's always that feeling when you're in an expensive restaurant that you're being ripped off.*

rip-off *n* [C] *informal* ● *Twenty dollars for a pizza is a rip-off whichever way you look at it.*

rip off sb/sth or **rip** sb/sth **off**

informal to copy someone or something by stealing their ideas or style, especially in order to make money ● *As a singer he has nothing at all he can call his own – he just rips off Michael Jackson.*

rip-off *n* [C] *informal* ● *Genuine Hard Rock T-shirts sell for about £25. The rip-off costs £6.*

rip off sth or **rip** sth **off**

1 to remove a piece of clothing very quickly and carelessly ● *He turns to face the camera and smiles that smile that makes you want to rip his shirt off.*

2 to steal something ● *He rips stuff off from supermarkets all the time.*

rip through   rips, ripping, ripped

rip through sth

if something harmful [e.g. bomb, bullet, hurricane] rips through a place, or building, it moves through it or destroys it quickly and violently ● *The bomb ripped through the building, leaving eleven people dead.* ● *This is nothing compared to* the hurricane which ripped through the Caribbean last month.

rip up   rips, ripping, ripped

rip up sth or **rip** sth **up**

1 to tear something [e.g. paper, cloth] into small pieces ● *He ripped up all her letters and photos.* ● *I'd better rip it up and start again.*

2 to remove something [e.g. carpet] from a floor ● *We ripped up the carpets and laid a new wooden floor.*

rise above   rises, rising, rose, risen

rise above sth

1 to not allow something bad that is happening or being done to you to upset you or to affect your behaviour ● *He has taken a lot of criticism in the press recently but miraculously has risen above it.* ● *As a politician you have to rise above personal considerations and think about what's best for people generally.*

2 to be much better or more successful than other people or other things of the same kind ● *The writing has an intelligence and humour which means that it rises above the level of most romantic fiction.*

rise up   rises, rising, rose, risen

rise up

1 if the people of a country rise up, they try to defeat their government or king ● (often + **against**) *He called on the people to rise up against their oppressors.*

2 *literary* to appear as a very tall shape ● *Snow-capped mountains rise up in the distance.*

rock up   rocks, rocking, rocked

rock up *informal*

to arrive somewhere doing something which makes other people notice you ● *Andy rocked up two hours late and extremely drunk.* ● (often + **to**) *She rocked up to the party dressed in tight leather trousers.*

roll about/around   rolls, rolling, rolled

roll about/around *informal*

to laugh a lot about something ● *Jim told us a funny story and he had us rolling about.* ● *We spent the whole journey **rolling around laughing**.*

roll around/round   rolls, rolling, rolled

roll around/round *informal*

if something that happens regularly rolls around, time passes and it happens again • *By the time the weekend rolls round I can't wait to get away from the office.* • *When the next election rolls around the Democrats will be in a stronger position.*

roll back   rolls, rolling, rolled

roll back sth or **roll** sth **back**

1 to decrease the amount of power or control that a particular system has • *A new economic policy which would roll back state ownership of resources.*
   roll-back n [singular] • *the roll-back of communism*

2 *American* to reduce the cost or price of something • *The steel industry rolled back prices last month.*

roll back

if an army rolls back, it moves back from its position • *The attacking troops rolled back.*

roll in   rolls, rolling, rolled

roll in

1 if money or requests for money [e.g. bills] roll in, they arrive in large numbers • (usually in continuous tenses) *He only set up the business last year and the money's already rolling in.* • *The bills were rolling in and we wondered how we could ever pay them.*

2 if bad weather [e.g. clouds, fog] rolls in, it appears in large amounts • *The sky darkened as the clouds rolled in.*

roll in/into   rolls, rolling, rolled

roll in

roll into swh

1 if heavy vehicles [esp. tanks] roll in, a lot of them arrive somewhere • *People fled the city as the enemy tanks rolled in.* • *Armoured vehicles rolled into the town square.*

2 *informal* if someone rolls in, they arrive somewhere in a relaxed way, usually later than they should • (usually + *adv/prep*) *Toby had been drinking and rolled in at three in the morning.* • *He rolled into work at 11.00 in the morning without a word of explanation.*

roll on   rolls, rolling, rolled

roll on

if time or an event rolls on, it continues to happen • *The years rolled on and the children grew up and left home.* • *The war rolls on with more and more casualties.*

Roll on sth! *British informal*

something that you say to show that you very much want a time or event to happen • *Roll on the weekend!*

roll out   rolls, rolling, rolled

roll out sth or **roll** sth **out**

1 to make an uncooked food mixture [e.g. pastry] flat and thin by rolling a tube-shaped object over it and pressing it down • *Roll out the pastry and place it in the bottom of a pie dish.*

2 to unfold something that is in a roll and put it flat on the ground • *The boys rolled out the ground sheet for the tent and laid it on the grass.*

3 *mainly American* to produce a new product or service, and get it ready for the public to buy • *Cosmetic companies roll out new make-up colors every few months.*
   roll-out n [singular] • *the official roll-out of their new computer software*

roll out sb or **roll** sb **out** *mainly American informal*

to arrange for someone important to speak or do something to help you • *They rolled out their best speakers for the fundraiser last night.*

roll over   rolls, rolling, rolled

roll (sb/sth) **over**

to turn from lying on one side of your body to the other side, or to make someone or something turn from one side to the other • *She yawned, rolled over and went back to sleep.* • *They rolled over the body to see who it was.*

roll over sth or **roll** sth **over**

1 if you roll over the money that you have invested with a bank for a particular period of time, you invest it again in the same way when this period of time ends, instead of taking the money back • *When their savings bond matures, they'll roll it over for a new one.*

2 *mainly American & Australian* to delay paying a debt until a later date • *The banks agreed that debts from my father's*

estate could be rolled over.

roll-over n [singular] *mainly American*
• *At issue is a roll-over of 15 million dollars of debt.*

3 *British* to add the prize money from one week to the next week's prize money in the national lottery (= competition in which people buy tickets to try to win money) • *If nobody wins they just roll over the prize money to the next week.*

roll-over n [C] *British* • *This week it's a roll-over – you can win £20 million.* • (used as *adj*) *It's a roll-over week.*

roll round

see **roll around/round**

roll up   rolls, rolling, rolled

roll up sth or **roll** sth **up**

1 to wrap something around itself to make the shape of a tube or ball • *Could you roll up that string for me?* • *She rolled up her sleeping bag as soon as she got up.*

roll-up n [C] a cigarette that you make by rolling a piece of paper around tobacco • *She's smoking roll-ups these days.*

2 to fold the edges of a piece of clothing that you are wearing [e.g. sleeves, trousers] in order to make them shorter • *He rolled up his trousers and waded into the water.*

roll up

to arrive somewhere, often in large numbers • *Crowds rolled up to see the stars arriving at the charity ball.* • *By the time you rolled up in your drunken state, the party was almost finished.*

Roll up! (always an order) *British* something that you shout to people in order to persuade them to come and pay to see a public event • *Roll up, roll up! See the famous headless chicken.*

romp through   romps, romping, romped

romp through sth *mainly British informal*

to do something quickly or easily • *Rory romped through his exams.* • *The researchers romped through all the data using the lab computer.*

root about/around   roots, rooting, rooted

root about/around (sth)

to search for something, especially by

looking among other things • *Bears often root around the garbage cans looking for food.* • *She was rooting around in her drawer for a red pencil.*

root for   roots, rooting, rooted

root for sb *informal*

to show support for someone in a competition, or to hope that someone will succeed in doing something difficult • *Good luck! We're all rooting for you.* • *The fans were out in large numbers to root for their team.*

root in

be rooted in sth (always passive)

to be based on something, or to be caused by something • *Children's education should be rooted in their own culture and heritage.* • *His prejudices are all rooted in ignorance.*

root out   roots, rooting, rooted

root out sth/sb or **root** sth/sb **out**

1 to find and get rid of the thing or person that is causing a problem • *It is our aim to root out corruption.*

2 *informal* to search and find something or someone that is difficult to find • *He rooted out an old pair of shorts to lend me.*

root up   roots, rooting, rooted

root up sth or **root** sth **up**

to take a whole plant out of the earth, including its roots • *He's spent all afternoon rooting up last year's spinach plants.*

rope in/into   ropes, roping, roped

rope in sb or **rope** sb **in**

rope sb **into** sth/doing sth

informal to persuade someone to help you with something, especially when they do not want to • *We needed a few people to help with the food, so we roped John's dad in.* • *She's been roped into giving a presentation at the conference.*

rope off   ropes, roping, roped

rope off sth or **rope** sth **off**

to put ropes around an area in order to stop people entering it • (usually passive) *Several parts of the museum had been roped off because of the fire damage.*

rough in · rough, roughing, roughed

rough in sth or **rough** sth **in**
to add something to a drawing without showing all the details ● *If you look closely you can see where she roughed in a few trees next to the lake.*

rough out · roughs, roughing, roughed

rough out sth or **rough** sth **out**
if you rough out a drawing or an idea, you draw or write the main parts of it without showing the details ● *I've roughed out a little play for the children to perform.* ● *She began her painting by roughing out the mountains in the background.*

rough up · roughs, roughing, roughed

rough up sb or **rough** sb **up** *informal*
to hurt someone by hitting them ● *They didn't kill him, they just roughed him up a bit as a warning.*

round down · rounds, rounding, rounded

round down sth or **round** sth **down**
to reduce a number to the nearest whole or simple number ● (often + **to**) *They rounded it down to 30,000.*

round off · rounds, rounding, rounded

round off sth or **round** sth **off**
1 to do something as a way of finishing an event or activity in a satisfactory way ● *To round off the lesson we had a quiz on the new words we'd learnt.* ● (often + **with**) *We rounded the meal off nicely with some coffee and mints.*
2 to make something that is pointed or sharp into a smooth, curved shape by rubbing it ● *He used a special machine to round off the corners of the old table.*
3 to reduce a number to the nearest whole or simple number ● *The total had been rounded off to make the calculations easier.*

round on/upon · rounds, rounding, rounded

round on/upon sb
to suddenly turn and attack someone or shout at someone angrily ● *Potter rounded upon the journalists with a stream of abusive comments.* ● *I saw her suddenly round on him, kicking and scratching furiously at him.*

round out · rounds, rounding, rounded

round out sth or **round** sth **out**
to make something more complete ● *He bought a pair of porcelain plates to round out the collection.*

round up · rounds, rounding, rounded

round up sb/sth or **round** sb/sth **up**
to find and gather together a group of people or animals ● *We watched as the dogs rounded up the sheep.* ● *I asked Mum to round up the kids while I got our things together.*

round-up *n* [C] ● (usually + **of**) *The president ordered the round-up and imprisonment of all opposition politicians.*

round up sth or **round** sth **up**
to increase a number to the nearest whole or simple number ● (often + **to**) *It's £19.50 but we'll round that up to £20.00*

round upon

see **round on/upon**

rout out · rout, routing, routed

rout out sb/sth or **rout** sb/sth **out**
to make someone come out of the place where they are ● (often + **of**) *His wife had to rout him out of bed.*

rub along · rubs, rubbing, rubbed

rub along *British old-fashioned, informal*
if people rub along, they live or work together without any problems ● (often + **together**) *They seem to rub along together okay even though the flat is very small.*

rub down · rubs, rubbing, rubbed

rub down sb/sth or **rub** sb/sth **down**
to make someone or something clean and dry by rubbing them with a cloth, or to make a surface smooth by rubbing it with sandpaper (= strong paper which is very rough on one side) ● *Rub down the window frames before you paint them.* ● *Is it okay if I use this towel to rub the dog down?*

rubdown *n* [C] *British* ● (usually singular) *Just let me give the table a quick rubdown.*

rub down sb or **rub** sb **down**
to rub someone's body, especially after they have been exercising, in order to make them relax ● *The coach rubbed him down after the long race.*

rubdown *n* [C] • (usually singular) *She went for a rubdown after the game.*

rub in   rubs, rubbing, rubbed

rub sth **in** *informal*

to talk to someone about something which you know they want to forget because they feel bad about it • *Look, I know it was stupid of me but there's no need to keep rubbing it in.*

rub in/into   rubs, rubbing, rubbed

rub in sth or **rub** sth **in**

rub sth **into** sth

1 to put a substance [e.g. ointment] onto the surface of something and to rub it so that it goes into the surface • *She gently rubbed the ointment in.*

2 to mix fat and flour together by rubbing them gently with your fingers • *Rub in the fat and then slowly start to add the water.*

rub off   rubs, rubbing, rubbed

rub off

if a quality or characteristic of a particular person rubs off, other people begin to have it because they have been with that person • (usually + **on**) *None of his parents' kindness and honesty seems to have rubbed off on him.*

rub out   rubs, rubbing, rubbed

rub out sth or **rub** sth **out**

to remove writing from something by rubbing it with a piece of rubber or with a cloth • *It's in pencil so you can rub it out if you need to.*

rub out sb or **rub** sb **out** *American & Australian slang*

to murder someone • *Her husband had been rubbed out by the Mafia.*

rub up against   rubs, rubbing, rubbed

rub up against sb

to touch someone with your body in a sexual way • *He remembered how she had rubbed up against him at the party.*

ruck up   rucks, rucking, rucked

ruck up (sth) or **ruck** (sth) **up** *British*

if cloth rucks up, or if you ruck it up, it pushes up into folds and moves out of its correct position • (usually passive) *Maria's dress was all rucked up at the back.*

ruffle up   ruffles, ruffling, ruffled

ruffle up sth or **ruffle** sth **up**

to make something that is smooth become uneven • *Sensing danger, the bird ruffles up its feathers.*

rule off   rules, ruling, ruled

rule off (sth) or **rule** (sth) **off** *British & Australian*

to draw a line underneath a piece of writing or a drawing in order to separate it from the next one • *She ruled off a space for the picture.* • *Rule off under the last piece of work.*

rule out   rules, ruling, ruled

rule out sb/sth or **rule** sb/sth **out**

to decide that something or someone is not suitable for a particular purpose, or to decide that something is impossible • *I'm afraid we can't rule out the possibility that she may have the disease.* • *The police had not ruled him out as a suspect.*

rule out sth or **rule** sth **out**

to make it impossible for something to happen • *The recent wave of terrorism has ruled out any chance of peace talks.* • *Dad's leg injury rules out a skiing holiday this year.*

rumble on   rumbles, rumbling, rumbled

rumble on

if a difficult situation or process rumbles on, it continues to exist for a long time • *The scandal over his will had been rumbling on for years.*

run across   runs, running, ran, run

run across sb

to meet someone you know when you are not expecting to meet them • *I ran across an ex-boyfriend of mine in town the other day.*

run after   runs, running, ran, run

run after sb/sth

to chase someone or something that is moving away from you • *I ran after him with a pile of papers that he'd left behind* • *Our dog's too lazy to run after cats.*

run after sth

to try very hard to get or achieve something ● *She'd spent her whole life running after fame and fortune.*

run after sb *informal*
to try to start a sexual relationship with someone ● *He's always running after unsuitable women.*

run along

Run along! (always an order) *old-fashioned*
something that you say to children to tell them to go away ● *Run along now children, I've got work to do.*

run around/round   runs, running, ran, run

run around/round *informal*
to be very busy doing a lot of different things ● (often + doing sth) *All week I've been running around getting things ready for this party we're having.*

run around/round after   runs, running, ran, run

run around/round after sb *informal*
to do a lot of things for someone else, especially when they should be able to do more for themselves ● *I seem to spend most of my time running around after the kids.*

run around with   runs, running, ran, run

run around with sb *old-fashioned, informal*
to spend a lot of time with someone, especially someone other people do not like ● *I'm not sure I like the gang he's running around with.*

run away   runs, running, ran, run

run away
1 to leave somewhere by running ● *He turned and ran away as fast as he could.*
2 to secretly leave a place because you are unhappy there ● *I was so unhappy at school, I even thought of running away.* ● (often + **from**) *When she was thirteen she ran away from home.*
   runaway *n* [C] someone who has run away or escaped from somewhere ● *Police recaptured the runaway.* ● *a hostel for runaways*
3 to avoid dealing with a problem or difficult situation ● (usually + **from**) *You're*

never going to solve problems by running away from them.
4 *informal* to leave somewhere in order to avoid having to do something ● *I might need you in a moment, David, so don't run away.*

run away with   runs, running, ran, run

run away with sb
1 to secretly leave a place with someone in order to live with them or marry them, especially when other people think this is wrong ● *She ran away with him when she was just seventeen.*
2 if something [e.g. emotions, imagination, enthusiasm] runs away with someone, it makes them do or think stupid things ● *It's important when you're making a speech not to let your emotions run away with you.* ● *Sometimes my imagination runs away with me and I convince myself they're having an affair.*

run away with sth
1 *mainly American* to steal something or to take something without asking ● *His partner ran away with all the money they had worked so hard to make.*
2 *informal* to win a competition or prize very easily ● *Once again Steve Joachim runs away with the title.*
3 *mainly American* to perform, for example in a play, in a way that makes you receive more praise and attention than anyone else ● *The audience loved them – their double act **ran away with the show!***

run by   runs, running, ran, run

run sth **by** sb *informal*
to repeat something, or to tell someone about something, so that they can give their opinion of it or hear it again ● *If you've got a moment I'd like to run a few ideas by you.* ● *Could you run those names by me again?*

run down   runs, running, ran, run

run down sb or **run** sb **down**
to hit someone with a vehicle and injure or kill them ● (usually passive) *He was run down as he was crossing the road.*

run down sb/sth or **run** sb/sth **down**
1 *informal* to criticize someone or something, often unfairly ● (often reflexive) *You shouldn't run yourself down like that!* ● *Whatever the government do, the press is*

going to run them down.

2 *informal* to find someone or something that you have been trying to find for a long time • *After five or six phone-calls I managed to run him down at an address in Rome.*

run down sth or **run** sth **down**

1 *British & Australian* to gradually reduce the size of an organization, especially in order to close it completely in the future • *He had decided to run the business down.*
rundown *n* [C] *British* • (usually singular) *They were protesting at the rundown of the Youth Training Scheme.*

2 *British & Australian* to reduce a supply of goods or money by using or selling it • *Shops are starting to run down their stocks.*

run down (sth) or **run** (sth) **down**

if a machine or device [e.g. clock, battery] runs down, or if something or someone makes a machine or device run down, it gradually loses power • *It doesn't work so well because the batteries are running down.* • *If you leave your car lights on you'll run the batteries down.*

run down sth

if you run down a list, you quickly look at it, or you quickly read and say all the things on it • *Just running down the list of candidates here, I can exclude four of them straight away.*

run for   runs, running, ran, run

run for sth *mainly American*

to try to get elected to a public position • *He ran for Governor of the state four years ago.*

run for it *informal*

to start running very quickly in order to escape from someone or something • (often an order) *There's someone coming. Run for it!*

run in   runs, running, ran, run

run in sb or **run** sb **in** *informal*

if the police run in someone who has done something illegal, they find them and take them to a police station • (usually passive) *The leader of the gang was run in last summer.*

run in sth or **run** sth **in** *British & Australian*

to drive a vehicle carefully and slowly for

a short time when it is new, so that you do not damage its engine • *I'm still running the car in so I tend to drive fairly slowly.*

run into   runs, running, ran, run

run into sb

to meet someone that you know when you did not expect to meet them • *I ran into an old neighbour of mine at the garage this afternoon.*

run into sth

1 to accidentally hit something while you are driving a vehicle • *I couldn't stop in time and ran into the car in front.*

2 if the amount or cost of something runs into thousands, millions etc., it reaches that level • *Production costs often run into hundreds of thousands of pounds.* • *Independent sources say the civilian death toll runs into hundreds.*

3 if you run into difficulties or problems, you begin to experience them • *Both companies have since run into financial difficulties.* • *We'd probably run into legal problems if we advertised for a woman.*

run off   runs, running, ran, run

run off

1 to leave somewhere by running • *We would throw stones at the window and then run off.*

2 *informal* to leave somewhere for ever, often secretly or suddenly • *Her husband ran off and left her with three small children to bring up.* • *She ran off to Canada and never came back again.*

3 *informal* to leave somewhere in order to avoid having to do something • *You're not going to run off and leave me to do this on my own are you?*

run sb/sth **off** (sth)

to force a person or animal to leave a place • *We had to run the cows off the field before we could play football.* • *If anyone comes sneaking around the buildings, they'll soon be run off.*

run (sth) **off** sth

if a machine runs off a supply of power, or if you run a machine off a supply of power, it uses that power in order to work • *It runs off batteries.*

run off sth or **run** sth **off**

1 to print several copies of something • *I'll run off a few copies of the article and circulate it.*

2 to quickly and easily write something that is usually difficult to write [e.g. poem, speech] • *She can run off a poem on any subject you like in a few minutes.*

run off with   runs, running, ran, run

run off with sb

to secretly leave a place with someone in order to live with them or marry them, especially when other people think this is wrong • *Her first husband ran off with his secretary.*

run off with sth

to steal something or to take something without asking • *He ran off with half the company's funds.* • *Someone's run off with my pen.*

run on   runs, running, ran, run

run on

1 to continue for longer than expected • (usually + *adv/prep*) *I don't want this meeting to run on too long.* • *The talk ran on till after 3 o'clock.*

2 *American* to talk for a long time about one subject, especially in a way that is boring for the people who are listening • (usually + **about**) *She ran on at great length about her operation.*

run (sth) **on** sth

if a machine runs on a supply of power, or if you run it on a supply of power, it uses that power to work • *The first car ran on alcohol.*

run out   runs, running, ran, run

run out

1 to use all of something so that there is none left • *Could you get some more milk? We're about to run out.* • (often + **of**) *We've run out of paper for the photocopier.* • *(British) I'm going to finish work in a moment as I'm rapidly **running out of steam**.* (= I have no more energy or enthusiasm left) • *(American) The team was **running out of gas**.* (= was losing its energy and enthusiasm)

2 if a supply of something runs out, there is none left because it has all been used • *We had to come home because our money ran out.* • *He'd better apply for the job soon – time's running out.* • *I'm afraid my patience with him is about to run out.*

3 if a document or official agreement runs out, the period of time it lasts for comes to an end • *My contract runs out in September and I don't know whether to renew it.* • *Did you know that your passport runs out next year?*

run out on   runs, running, ran, run

run out on sb

to suddenly leave someone who you are having a relationship with, usually causing problems for them • *Her husband ran out on her when the kids were very young.*

run over   runs, running, ran, run

run over sb/sth or **run** sb/sth **over**

to hit someone or something with a vehicle and drive over them, injuring or killing them • (usually passive) *He was run over and killed.*

run over sth

1 to quickly read something or repeat something in order to remember it or to make sure that it is correct • *We'd better run over what we're going to say as our introduction.*

2 to quickly explain something to someone • *I'll just run over the main points of the article.*

run over

1 if a container runs over, there is so much liquid in it that it flows over the edges • *I turned the taps off because the bath was almost running over.*

2 to continue past the expected finishing time • *I don't want this meeting to run* *over so I'll be brief.*

run round
see **run around/round**

run round after
see **run around/round after**

run through   runs, running, ran, run
run through sth

1 to repeat something in order to practise it or to make sure that it is correct • *We had to stay behind at the end of the rehearsal to run through a couple of scenes.*
run-through *n* [C] • *We'll certainly need time for a run-through before the concert.*

2 to explain or read something to someone quickly • *I'll just run through what I've written with you and see if you've anything to add.* • *He ran through a list of names but I didn't recognize any of them.*

3 if you run through money, you spend a lot of it very quickly • *In just under six months he'd run through all the money his father had left him.*

4 if a quality runs through something, it is in all of that thing • *The theme of the domineering mother-figure runs through all his work.* • *Sadly, racism runs right through society.*

run through sb
if a feeling of fear or excitement runs through a group of people, it is suddenly felt by them • *As the actor said the line, a shiver ran through the audience.*

run sb through *literary*
to push a sword (= long thin metal weapon) through someone's body • *He lunged forward and ran him through with his sword.*

run to   runs, running, ran, run
run to sb

to ask someone to help or protect you when you should be helping yourself • *I'm thirty-one – I can't keep running to my parents every time something goes wrong.*

run to sth (never in continuous tenses)

1 to reach a particular amount, usually a large amount • *A document like this can run to twenty or thirty pages.* • *A meal with wine might run to £60 a head.*

2 *British & Australian* if you or your money runs to a particular thing, you have enough money to buy that thing • (usually negative) *He earns a decent wage but it certainly doesn't run to two houses.* • *I bought a cooker but I couldn't run to new kitchen units too.*

3 if your taste runs to something, that is the type of thing that you enjoy • *I should imagine that your musical taste doesn't run to opera.*

run up   runs, running, ran, run
run up

to run to where a person is • *I ran up behind him and slapped him on the back.* • (often + **to**) *She ran up to me and put this package in my hands.*

run up sth or run sth up

1 if you run up a debt [e.g. bill, deficit], you do things which cause you to owe a large amount of money • *We ran up the most enormous bill in the first restaurant we went to.* • *He ran up a lot of debts while he was unemployed.*

2 to make something very quickly, especially a piece of clothing, by sewing • *She can run up a dress in a couple of hours on her sewing machine.*

3 to raise a flag to the top of its pole • (usually passive) *The British flag was run up on the roof.*

4 to make the price or value of something [e.g. stocks] increase • *Heavy buying ran the price of stocks up higher than expected.*

run up against   runs, running, ran, run
run up against sth

if you run up against problems or difficulties, you begin to experience them • *The community scheme has run up against local opposition.*

sack out   sacks, sacking, sacked

sack out *American informal*
to go to bed or to go to sleep • *It's late – I'm going to sack out.*

saddle up   saddles, saddling, saddled

saddle up (sth) or **saddle** (sth) **up**
to put a saddle (= a seat made of leather) on a horse so that you can ride it • *We saddled up and set off down the path.* • *I asked him to saddle up the pony.*

saddle with   saddles, saddling, saddled

saddle sb **with** sth
to give someone a job, problem, or responsibility which will cause them a lot of difficulty or work • *I've been saddled with the task of sorting out all the books in the library.* • (often reflexive) *The company has saddled itself with a lot of debt.*

safeguard against   safeguards, safeguarding, safeguarded

safeguard against sth
to do things that you hope will stop something unpleasant happening • *To safeguard against theft, please deposit your money and jewellery in the hotel safe.*

sail through   sails, sailing, sailed

sail through (sth)
to succeed very easily, especially in a test, examination etc. • *Rachel sailed through all her exams with top marks.*

sally forth/out   sallies, sallying, sallied

sally forth/out *literary*
to leave your house or a safe place in a brave or confident way in order to do something • *The villagers sallied forth, armed with knives and guns to defend their land.* • *Jemima sallied out in spite of the weather.*

salt away   salts, salting, salted

salt away sth or **salt** sth **away** *informal*
to put money into a safe place so that you can use it in the future • *People say that he's salted away millions of dollars in a Swiss bank account.*

sand down   sands, sanding, sanded

sand down sth or **sand** sth **down**
to rub a surface with sandpaper (= strong paper with a rough substance stuck to one side of it) in order to make it smooth • *I sanded down the door before repainting it.*

sandwich between

be sandwiched between sb/sth
(always passive) *informal*
to be in a small space in the middle of two people or things • *Kim was sandwiched between her brothers in the back of the car.* • *The small church was sandwiched between two tall buildings.*

save on   saves, saving, saved

save (sth) **on** sth
to avoid using something [e.g. electricity, food] so that you do not have to pay for it • *He used to go to bed very early to save on his electricity bills.* • *To save money on bus fares, she went everywhere by bike.*

save up   saves, saving, saved

save up (sth) or **save** (sth) **up**
to keep money so that you can buy something with it in the future • *If you want a new bike, you'd better start saving up.* • *It*

took me ages to save up enough money to buy a new car. • (often + **for**) *Daniel's saving up for a computer with a CD-ROM.*

save up sth or **save** sth **up**

to collect and keep similar things so that you can use them in the future • *Once you've saved up 50 tokens, the supermarket will give you £5 off your shopping.*

scale down/back   scales, scaling, scaled

scale down sth or **scale** sth **down**
British, American & Australian

scale back sth or **scale** sth **back**
American

to make something [e.g. project, production, budget] smaller than it was or than it was planned to be • *Since the end of the Cold War, most European countries have scaled down their armed forces.* • *The sports center is scaling back children's programs because it is short of money.*

scaled-down *adj* (always before noun)
• *a scaled-down model of the building*

scaling-down *n* [singular] • *There will be a scaling-down of production over the next 18 months.*

scare away/off   scares, scaring, scared

scare away/off sb/sth or **scare** sb/sth **away/off**

to make a person or animal so frightened that they go away • *She managed to scare off her attacker by screaming loudly.* • *He ran out into the garden clapping his hands to scare the birds away.*

scare away/off sb or **scare** sb **away/off**

to make someone worried about something so that they decide not to do what they had planned to do • *The firm's current problems have scared away potential investors.* • *Many travellers have been scared off by the airline's latest fare increases.*

scare up   scares, scaring, scared

scare up sb/sth or **scare** sb/sth **up**
American informal

to manage with a lot of difficulty to find someone or something that you need • *Can you scare up a few volunteers to sell tickets for the concert?* • *He's hoping to scare up some money and join us on our next trip.*

scarf down   scarfs, scarfing, scarfed

scarf down sth or **scarf** sth **down**
American slang

to eat or drink something very quickly • *We scarfed down a few beers and left.*

scarf up   scarfs, scarfing, scarfed

scarf up sth or **scarf** sth **up** *American slang*

1 to eat or drink something very quickly • *Who scarfed up all the sandwiches?*

2 to take all of something quickly and eagerly • *Eager fans scarfed up the concert tickets in just two hours.*

scoop out   scoops, scooping, scooped

scoop out sth or **scoop** sth **out**

to remove something that is inside something else by using a spoon or your curved hand • *Cut the tomato in half and scoop out the seeds with a spoon.*

scoop up   scoops, scooping, scooped

scoop up sth/sb or **scoop** sth/sb **up**

to lift something or someone by using your hands or arms, or to collect something by using a container • *I scooped up my belongings into my handbag.* • *She scooped up the children and ran back into the house.* • *He found a bucket and scooped up some water.*

scoop up sth or **scoop** sth **up** *informal*

to win or get a large number of something [e.g. prizes, votes] very easily • *The film scooped up three awards at the Cannes film festival.* • *The Republicans are expected to scoop up votes in the southern states.*

scoot over   scoots, scooting, scooted

scoot over *American informal*

to move along a seat in order to make a space for someone else • *If you scoot over, Jon can sit down too.*

scope out   scopes, scoping, scoped

scope out sb/sth or **scope** sb/sth **out**
American informal

to look carefully at someone to see if they are interesting or attractive, or to consider something carefully • *She scoped out the men standing near the bar.* • *I need to scope out all the possibilities before I make a decision.*

score off   scores, scoring, scored

score off sth or **score** sth **off** British &
Australian
to draw a line through something that is
written to show that it has been dealt
with ● *Score off the names on the list as I
read them out.*

score off sb British & Australian
to try to make someone seem stupid or
less intelligent than you by making a
clever or funny remark ● *She tried to
score off him by quoting from an American
journal which she knew he hadn't read.*

score out   scores, scoring, scored

score out sth or **score** sth **out** British &
Australian
to draw a line through something that is
written to show that it is not needed ● *He
scored out Michael Brown's name and
wrote in Ruth Hardy's instead.*

scout about/around/round   scouts, scouting, scouted

scout about/around/round (swh)
to look in different places in order to try
to find something ● *Go and scout around
and see if you can find some matches.*
● (often + **for**) *We scouted about Edinburgh for a suitable house to rent.*

scout out   scouts, scouting, scouted

scout out sth or **scout** sth **out**
to search for something that you need
● *She works for a rental agency, scouting
out new properties.*

scout round

see **scout about/around/round**

scout up   scouts, scouting, scouted

scout up sb/sth or **scout** sb/sth **up**
American
to try to find someone or something that
you need ● *You'd better scout up someone
to take Bob's place on the team.*

scrabble about/around/round   scrabbles, scrabbling, scrabbled

scrabble about/around/round
1 to make small quick movements with
your fingers in order to find something
that you cannot see ● (often + **in**) *She
scrabbled around in her bag, trying to find
her keys.* ● (often + **for**) *He was on the
floor scrabbling round for his glasses.*

2 to try to get something very quickly that
you need ● (often + **for**) *He scrabbled
around for a suitable excuse.*

scrape along   scrapes, scraping, scraped

scrape along
to manage to live when you do not have
much money ● (often + **on**) *After he lost
his job, his family had to scrape along on
£95 a week.*

scrape by   scrape, scraping, scraped

scrape by
1 to manage to live when you do not have
much money ● (often + **on**) *She has to
scrape by on what she earns as a cleaner.*
● *He earns just enough money as a writer
to scrape by.*
2 *mainly American* to manage with a lot of
difficulty to get a successful result in an
exam ● *He scraped by with a C.*

scrape in/into   scrapes, scraping, scraped

scrape in British & Australian

scrape into sth British & Australian
to manage with a lot of difficulty to be accepted as a student in a college or to get a
job ● *She scraped into college with very
poor grades.* ● *In the election, the Labour
candidate scraped in by only seven votes.*

scrape through   scrapes, scraping, scraped

scrape through (sth)
to manage with a lot of difficulty to succeed in something [e.g. exam] ● *I managed to scrape through my English exam
even though I hadn't done much work.* ● *It
looked as if Becker might lose the match
but he scraped through in the final set.*

scrape together   scrapes, scraping, scraped

scrape together sth/sb or **scrape**
sth/sb **together**
to manage with a lot of difficulty to collect an amount of money or to find someone or something that you need ● *I've
finally scraped together the $250 I need for
the trip.* ● *Do you think we can scrape
together a team for the game on Saturday?*

scream out screams, screaming, screamed

scream out sth or **scream** sth **out**
to shout something loudly because you are frightened, angry, or excited • *He screamed out 'Stop!' and ran into the street.*

screen off screens, screening, screened

screen off sth or **screen** sth **off**
to separate part of a room from the rest of the room by using a curtain or a wall that can be moved • *We can screen off part of the living room and use it as an office.* • (sometimes + **from**) *The sleeping area is screened off from the living area.*

screen out screens, screening, screened

screen out sb or **screen** sb **out**
if an organization screens someone out, it refuses to employ them or help them because it thinks they are not suitable • *Applicants over the age of 55 were screened out.*

screen out sth or **screen** sth **out**
to stop something [esp. light] from entering somewhere • *She drew the curtains to screen out the sunlight.* • *The ozone layer screens out the sun's ultraviolet rays.*

screw about/around screws, screwing, screwed

screw sb **about/around** *slang*
to treat someone badly, especially by changing your mind a lot or not doing what you have promised • *I wish Paul would stop screwing me around and decide what he wants!*

screw around screws, screwing, screwed

screw around *taboo*
to have sex with a lot of different people • *She threatened to divorce him when she found out he'd been screwing around.*

screw down screws, screwing, screwed

screw down sth or **screw** sth **down**
to fix something firmly to something else using screws, or to close a lid firmly by turning it until it is very tight • *You should screw down any loose floorboards.* • *Make sure the top is screwed down well before you put the bottle away.*

screw out of screws, screwing, screwed

screw sth **out of** sb *informal*
to persuade someone in a forceful way to give you money or information • *She managed to screw an extra £1,500 a year out of her company.* • *It took the police several hours to screw a confession out of him.*

screw sb **out of** sth *informal*
to trick someone in order to stop them from getting something that should be theirs • *He screwed me out of my share of the profits.*

screw over screws, screwing, screwed

screw over sb or **screw** sb **over** *American slang*
to deceive or trick someone, especially in order to get money from them dishonestly • *The company screwed him over by not paying him all the money they owed him.*

screw up screws, screwing, screwed

screw up sth or **screw** sth **up**
1 to twist and crush paper or material with your hands • *He screwed up the letter and threw it in the bin.*
2 to make your eyes narrower, or to twist your face into a different shape, often in order to show an emotion • *She screwed up her eyes because the light was so bright.* • *He screwed up his face in disgust at the terrible smell.*

screw up (sth) or **screw** (sth) **up** *informal*
to make a mistake, or to damage or spoil something • *If you screw up again, you'll be in trouble!* • *I really screwed up my exams last year.* • *Drugs like heroin and cocaine can really screw your body up.*
  screw-up *n* [C] *informal* • *There's been a real screw-up with our tickets.* • *Jim? No way! I'm not having that screw-up working on this project.*

screw up sb or **screw** sb **up** *informal*
to make someone feel confused or unhappy about themselves and their life • *Her parents have screwed her up emotionally.* • *It really screwed him up when his wife left him.*
  screwed-up *adj informal* • *She's a lonely, screwed-up woman.*

scribble down scribbles, scribbling, scribbled

scribble down sth or **scribble** sth **down**

to write something very quickly on a piece of paper • *I scribbled down his address in the back of my diary.*

scrounge around scrounges, scrounging, scrounged

scrounge around *American & Australian informal*

to look in different places for something that you need • (often + **for**) *They were scrounging around for wood to light a fire on the beach.* • (sometimes + **in**) *Look what I found while I was scrounging around in the attic.*

scrounge up scrounges, scrounging, scrounged

scrounge up sth/sb or **scrounge** sth/sb **up** *American & Australian informal*

to manage with a lot of difficulty to collect an amount of money or to find someone or something that you need • *They haven't scrounged up enough money for their vacation yet.*

scrub out scrubs, scrubbing, scrubbed

scrub out sth or **scrub** sth **out**

to clean the inside of something by using a brush, soap and water • *The bath is filthy – you'll have to scrub it out before you use it.*

scrub up scrubs, scrubbing, scrubbed

scrub up

if a doctor or nurse scrubs up, they wash their hands and arms very carefully before doing a medical operation • *The surgeon only had a few minutes to scrub up before his next operation.*

scrunch up scrunches, scrunching, scrunched

scrunch up sth or **scrunch** sth **up**

1 to crush a piece of paper or material into a small round shape • *He read the note quickly and then scrunched it up.*

2 *informal* to twist your face or part of your face into a different shape often in order to show an emotion • *She scrunched up her nose as the smell became stronger.*

scrunch up *American informal*

if people scrunch up, they move closer together • *Everyone scrunched up close to the stage to hear the band.*

seal off seals, sealing, sealed

seal off sth or **seal** sth **off**

to prevent people entering or leaving a place • *Police immediately sealed off the streets around the hotel as they searched for the bomb.*

seal up seals, sealing, sealed

seal up sth or **seal** sth **up**

to fasten something so that nothing can get in or out • *He sealed the parcel up with sticky tape.* • *The dirt and noise from the traffic was so bad that we had to seal up the windows.*

search out searches, searching, searched

search out sb/sth or **search** sb/sth **out**

to look for someone or something for a long time until you find them • *While I was in Australia, I searched out my cousin who I hadn't seen for 20 years.*

secure against secures, securing, secured

secure sth **against** sth/sb

1 to prevent a place from being attacked or from being entered illegally • *A wall was built around the village to secure it against attack.* • *We need to secure the building against intruders.*

2 if you secure a loan (= money that you borrow) against something that you own, you legally promise to give that thing to the organization that you borrowed the money from if you cannot pay back the money • (usually passive) *The house was worth £62,000 and a loan of £30,000 was secured against it.* • *The company has secured its bank loans against its hotel business.*

see about sees, seeing, saw, seen

see about sth

to deal with something, or to arrange for something to be done • *It's getting late – I'd better see about dinner.* • *You should see about getting your hair cut.*

see in   sees, seeing, saw, seen

see sth **in** sb/sth

to believe that someone or something has a particular quality ● *I can't understand what you see in Susan.* (= what qualities you like) ● *You can see a strong sense of morality in his writing.*

see in/into   sees, seeing, saw, seen

see in sb or **see** sb **in**

see sb **into** sth

to go with someone to a room or building in order to make sure that they arrive ● *Mr Wilson is expecting you in his office. I'll see you in.* ● *I saw Helen into her house and then I took the bus home.*

see off   sees, seeing, saw, seen

see off sb or **see** sb **off**

1 to go to the place that someone is leaving from in order to say goodbye ● *My parents came to the airport to see me off.*

2 to force someone to leave a place ● *If anyone tries to come in here, the dogs will soon see them off.*

see off sb/sth or **see** sb/sth **off** British & Australian informal

if you see off an opponent or an attempt by someone to compete against you [esp. challenge], you defeat them or stop them from competing against you ● *Germany saw off their opponents with a goal in the last minute.* ● *The president has seen off several challenges to his leadership this year.*

see out   sees, seeing, saw, seen

see out sb or **see** sb **out**

to go with someone to the door of a room or building when they are leaving ● *My secretary will see you out.* ● (often reflexive) *Don't worry. I can see myself out.* (= leave the building without anyone coming with me)

see out sth or **see** sth **out**

1 to continue doing something until a difficult period of time or an unpleasant event has finished ● *She's determined to see out her three-year contract even though she dislikes her work.* ● *The industry needs more investment if it's going to see out the recession.*

2 if a supply of something sees out a period of time, you have enough of it to use until the end of that period of time ● *We've got just enough food to see the week out.*

see over   sees, seeing, saw, seen

see over sth British & Australian

to examine a building in order to decide if you want to buy it ● *Some people are coming to see over our house tomorrow.*

see through   sees, seeing, saw, seen

see through sb/sth

if you see through someone who is trying to deceive you, or if you see through someone's behaviour, you realize what they are really like and what they are trying to do ● *He told me he was incredibly rich and owned a Ferrari, but I saw through him at once.* ● *She was so convincing that I didn't see through her lies until it was too late.*

see sb **through** (sth)

to help or support someone during a difficult period in their life ● *He was a prisoner of war for five years, but his courage saw him through.* ● *My brother's lent me £200 to see me through the next few weeks.*

see sth **through**

to continue doing a job or activity until it is finished, especially when it is difficult ● *The course would take me three years to complete, but I was determined to see it through.*

see to   sees, seeing, saw, seen

see to sth/sb

to deal with something that needs doing or to help someone who needs your help ● *The cats need feeding twice a day, but Paula's seeing to that.* ● *Would you like any help or are you being seen to?* ● *Please see to it that no one enters without identification.*

seek out   seeks, seeking, sought

seek out sb/sth or **seek** sb/sth **out**

to look for someone or something for a long time until you find them ● *She tried to seek out her real mother when she discovered she was adopted.* ● *Many shoppers are now seeking out environmentally-friendly products.*

seize on/upon   seizes, seizing, seized

seize on/upon sth

to use something in an enthusiastic way

because it will help you or give you an advantage • *Her story was seized upon by the press.* • *You should seize on every new opportunity to improve your qualifications.*

seize up   seizes, seizing, seized

seize up

if part of your body or a machine seizes up, it stops moving or working in the normal way • *His right leg suddenly seized up during the race.* • *I couldn't get my suitcase open because the lock had completely seized up.*

seize upon

see **seize on/upon**

sell off   sells, selling, sold

sell off sth or **sell** sth **off**

1 to sell all or part of a business • *The company announced that it would be selling off its hotel business.*
   sell-off n [C] • *The sell-off of the electricity industry has raised millions of pounds for the government.*

2 to sell something at a low price because you do not want it or because you need some money • *The shop is selling off damaged books at bargain prices.*

sell on   sells, selling, sold

sell sb **on** sth *informal*

to make someone like an idea or plan • (usually passive) *She's really sold on the idea of going abroad to study.*

sell on sth or **sell** sth **on** *mainly British*

to sell something soon after you have bought it • *Are you going to keep your shares or sell them on?* • (often + **to**) *The company buys electricity from the central generator and then sells it on to customers.*

sell out   sells, selling, sold

sell out

1 if a shop sells out, it has no more of a particular product available to buy • (often + **of**) *Book stores had sold out of the new edition within a few hours.* • *I went to the local shop to get some milk but they'd sold out.*

2 if a supply of something sells out, there is no more of that thing available to buy • *The first issue of the magazine sold out in two days.*

3 if a performance or popular event sells

out, all the tickets for it have been sold • *Her concerts always sell out months in advance.* • *The Cup Final was sold out weeks ago.*
sell-out n [C] • *Over 200,000 people watched the game which was a complete sell-out.* • (used as *adj*) *The group had a sell-out tour of the US.*

4 to sell your business or your part of a business • (often + **to**) *They decided to sell out to their competitors.*

5 *informal* to do something that you used to think was wrong in order to earn more money • *She thinks that actors who've gone to Hollywood to make films have sold out.*
sell-out n [C] *informal* • *Some writers turn to popular fiction to make money but he regards it as a sell-out.*

sell out sb or **sell** sb **out** *informal*

to disappoint someone by failing to do what you were expected to do, or by helping or supporting someone else instead • *French farmers feel they've been sold out by their government in the negotiations.*
sell-out n [C] *informal* • *Both sides see the peace agreement as a sell-out.*

sell up   sells, selling, sold

sell up (sth) or **sell** (sth) **up** *British & Australian*

to sell your house or business in order to go somewhere else or do something else • *He decided to sell up and retire to the south of France.* • *She left the country after selling up most of her assets.*

send away for   sends, sending, sent

send away for sth

to write to an organization to ask them to send you something • *If you collect three tokens, you can send away for a free watch.*

send back   sends, sending, sent

send back sth or **send** sth **back**

to return something to the company you bought it from because it is unsuitable or damaged • *The trousers were the wrong size, so I sent them straight back.*

send down   sends, sending, sent

send down sb or **send** sb **down**

1 *British informal* to send someone to prison

● (usually passive) *He was sent down for armed robbery.* ● (often + **for**) *She was sent down for three years.*

2 *British* to make a student leave a university because they have done something wrong ● (usually passive) *He was sent down after failing his second year exams.* ● (often + **from**) *She was sent down from Oxford for taking drugs.*

send for sends, sending, sent

send for sb
to send someone a message asking them to come to see you ● *Do you think we should send for the doctor?* ● *I was really worried when my boss sent for me.*

send in sends, sending, sent

send in sb or **send** sb **in**
to send a group of people with special skills [e.g. police, troops] to deal with a difficult situation ● *Peace-keeping troops were sent in as the situation got worse.* ● *We are sending in a medical team to deal with the latest epidemic.*

send in sth or **send** sth **in**
to send something to an organization ● *Viewers were asked to send in photographs of their pets.* ● *Please send in completed forms before January 31st.*

send in for sends, sending, sent

send in for sth
to write to an organization to ask them to send you something ● *I've sent in for a full illustrated brochure.*

send off sends, sending, sent

send off sth or **send** sth **off**
to send a letter, document, or parcel by post ● *Have you sent off your application form yet?*

send off sb or **send** sb **off** *British & Australian*
to order a sports player to leave the playing area during a game because they have done something wrong ● (often + **for**) *He was sent off for swearing at the referee.*

sending-off *n* [C] *British & Australian* ● *He has contacted the Football Association about his sending-off in last week's game.*

send off for sends, sending, sent

send off for sth
to write to an organization to ask them to send you something ● *I've sent off for lots of holiday brochures.*

send on sends, sending, sent

send on sth or **send** sth **on**
to send a document that you have received to another person, or to send someone's letters to their new address ● (often + **to**) *I thought Jill would be interested in the article and so I've sent it on to her.* ● *I've asked the new owners to send on my mail.*

send out sends, sending, sent

send out sth or **send** sth **out**
1 to send something to a lot of different people at the same time ● *How many invitations are you sending out?* ● *Electricity bills are sent out every three months.*
2 to produce light, a sound, or a signal ● *The torch sends out a powerful beam of light.* ● *The ship's crew sent out a distress call.*
3 if a plant sends out something [e.g. roots, shoots], it grows ● *This plant sends out long roots and so it needs to be planted in deep soil.*

send out for sends, sending, sent

send out for sth
to telephone a restaurant to ask for food to be delivered to you ● *Do you want to send out for a pizza?*

send up sends, sending, sent

send up sb/sth or **send** sb/sth **up** *informal*
to make someone or something seem stupid by copying them in a funny way ● *He loves sending up some of the more serious teachers.* ● *The book sends up the British obsession with class.*

send-up *n* [C] *informal* ● *The programme is a hilarious send-up of the James Bond films.*

send up sb or **send** sb **up** *American informal*
to put someone in prison ● (usually passive + **for**) *He was sent up for 3 years.*

separate off   separates, separating, separated

separate off sth or **separate** sth **off**
to remove something from a large group of things • *The infected cattle were separated off from the rest of the herd.*

separate out   separates, separating, separated

separate out sb/sth or **separate** sb/sth **out**
to divide a group of people or things into smaller groups • (often + **into**) *The children were separated out into three small groups.* • *A machine is used to separate the seeds out according to size and type.*

separate out sth or **separate** sth **out**
to remove something from other things • *A chemical process separates out and purifies the gold.*

serve as/for   serves, serving, served

serve as/for sth
to be used for a particular purpose, often because there is nothing else more suitable • *The hut had wooden benches along the walls which served as beds.* • *My umbrella will serve for a weapon, should the occasion arise.*

serve on   serves, serving, served

serve sth **on** sb
to send or give a legal document to a person or organization, demanding that they go to a court of law, or that they obey an order • *Finally he served a writ on Slater, claiming damages for alleged loss of royalties.*

serve out   serves, serving, served

serve out sth
to continue doing something until the end of a fixed period of time, especially spending time in prison • *She served out almost all of the 13-year sentence.* • *He served out his apprenticeship before moving to a different firm.*

serve out sth or **serve** sth **out** *British & Australian*
to put food on plates and in dishes for people to eat • *Can you carve the meat while I serve out the vegetables?*

serve up   serves, serving, served

serve up sth or **serve** sth **up**
1 to put food on plates and in dishes for people to eat • *I'm just about to serve up the food if anyone's interested.* • *It's no worse than the sort of food that's served up in any self-service canteen.*
2 to provide information or entertainment for people, especially television or radio programmes • *The new channel serves up a mixture of movies, pop music and chat shows.*

set about   sets, setting, set

set about sth/doing sth
to start doing something, especially something that uses a lot of time or energy • *I got home and immediately set about cleaning the house.*

set about sth
to start dealing with something in a particular way • *I think they're setting about the problem the wrong way.* • *I need to find a job but I don't know how to set about the task.*

set about sb *literary*
to attack someone physically • (often + **with**) *They dragged him into an alley and set about him with their fists.*

set against   sets, setting, set

be set against sth/doing sth (always passive)
to be opposed to doing or having something • *French public opinion is set against war.* • *Why is Martin so set against signing the contract?* • *She's **dead set against** (= is strongly opposed to) going to college.*

be set against sth (always passive)
if a story, film, or play is set against a particular event or period, the action takes place during that event or period • *It's the story of young love, set against the background of growing fascism.* • *The film is set against the backdrop of the American civil war.*

set sth **against** sth
1 to consider how one thing is affected by another thing • *The advantages of the scheme are few when set against the disadvantages.*
2 if you set something of one colour against something of another colour, you put it in

front of it so that the difference in colours is very noticeable • (usually passive) *There's a striking picture of her on the wall, her blond hair set against a plain black background.*

set sb **against** sb

to make one person or group of people start to fight or argue with another person or group • *This is a war that has set neighbour against neighbour.*

set ahead sets, setting, set

set sth **ahead** *American*

to change the time on clocks and watches in the spring so that it is an hour later • *When do we set the clocks ahead? Is it in March?* • *Did you remember to set your watch ahead this morning?*

set apart sets, setting, set

set apart sb/sth or **set** sb/sth **apart**

if a quality sets someone or something apart, it makes them different from and usually better than others of the same type • (usually + **from**) *It's their intelligence that sets them apart from other rock bands.*

set apart sth or **set** sth **apart**

to use something, especially time, for one purpose and no other purpose • *I like to set apart a couple of hours each week to write my journal.*

set aside sets, setting, set

set aside sth or **set** sth **aside**

1 to use something, especially time or money, for one purpose and no other purpose • (often + to do sth) *I set aside half an hour every evening to hear Erika read.* • (often + **for**) *He had some money in an account that he'd set aside for his kids.*

2 if you set aside your own feelings or opinions, you decide that you will not be influenced by them because they are not important at that time • *In times of war people tend to set aside political differences.*

3 if a judge or court sets aside a previous decision, they state that it does not now have any effect • *His conviction was set aside by the court of appeal.*

set back sets, setting, set

set back sb/sth or **set** sb/sth **back**

to make something happen more slowly,

or to make something happen later than it should happen • *A war would inevitably set back the process of reform.* • *We've had a couple of staff leave so that's set us back a few months.* • *The completion date for the project has been set back by a few weeks.*

setback n [C] • *We've suffered a number of setbacks since the start of the project.* • *The knee injury is the latest in a series of setbacks for the 23-year old player.*

set sb **back** (sth) *informal*

to cost someone a particular amount of money, usually a large amount of money • *One of these machines, new, would set you back a thousand pounds.* • *That car of yours looks as if it set you back, Ted.*

be set back (always passive)

if a building is set back, it is a long distance from the road • (often + **from**) *Emma's house is set back from the road so you can't see it as you approach.*

set back sth or **set** sth **back** *American & Australian*

to change the time on clocks or watches in the autumn so that it is an hour earlier • *You set the clocks back in the fall when the days get shorter.*

set down sets, setting, set

set down sth or **set** sth **down**

1 to make a record of something, especially your thoughts or feelings, by writing about them • *I've got various complaints so I thought I'd set them all down in a letter.* • *Sometimes it helps to set down your thoughts in writing.*

2 to state in an official document how something must be done • *It was proposed that passengers' rights be set down in a charter.* • *They have asked the board to reconsider the rules set down for the contest.*

set down sb or **set** sb **down** *British & Australian*

to stop a vehicle and let someone get out of it or off it • *Ask the taxi-driver to set you down on the corner of Mill Road and Stockwell Street.*

set down (sth) or **set** (sth) **down**

to land an aircraft, or to land in an aircraft • *We set down on a strip of land to the west of the city.* • *The pilot set the plane down at the edge of the airfield.*

set forth   sets, setting, set

set forth sth *formal*
to clearly state an opinion, idea, or set of facts ● *He set forth his views in various critical works.*

set forth *literary*
to start a journey ● *We set forth at daybreak, our packs strapped to our backs.*

set in   sets, setting, set

set in
if something unpleasant sets in, it begins and seems likely to continue ● *This rain looks as if it has set in for the rest of the day.* ● *It was when I realised how many people I was speaking to that the panic set in.*

set off   sets, setting, set

set off
to start a journey ● *What time are you setting off tomorrow morning?* ● (often + **for**) *I'm just about to set off for the station.*

set off sth or **set** sth **off**
1 to cause a loud noise or explosion [e.g. bomb, firework, alarm] to begin or happen ● *Terrorists set off a bomb in the city centre, killing two people.* ● *The smoke had set off the fire alarm.*
2 to cause a series of events or a lot of activity, often without intending to do this ● *The minister's comments have set off a flurry of debate.* ● *The shootings set off a wave of rioting in the inner cities.*
3 to make something look attractive, usually by providing a very different colour ● *I thought I'd wear the white dress to set off my suntan.* ● *That red scarf would set off your beige jacket beautifully.*

set sb **off** (doing sth) *slightly informal*
to make someone start to laugh, cry, or talk about something that they often talk about ● *Amanda started crying and of course that set me off.* (= I started crying too) ● *Every time I think about you on that bike it sets me off laughing.* ● *I didn't mention Darren – I thought it might set Julia off again.*

set off against   sets, setting, set

set sth **(off) against** sth
to make an official record of the money that you have spent in connection with

your job in order to reduce the amount of money that you have to pay ● *You can set your heating expenses off against tax.*

set on/upon   sets, setting, set

set (sth/sb) **on/upon** sb
to attack someone, or to make a person or animal attack someone ● *He was set upon by a mob as he left the club.* ● *She'd threatened to set the dog on him if he came any closer.*

set out   sets, setting, set

set out
1 to start a journey ● *It was quite sunny when we set out.* ● *They said they'd set out at about 7 o'clock, so they should be here soon.*
2 to start an activity, especially when you have already decided what you want to achieve ● (often + **with**) *She'd set out with the aim of becoming the youngest ever winner of the championship.* ● (often + to do sth) *Like so many young people before them, they set out to change the world.*
outset n [singular] ● *We knew from* **the outset** *that it wasn't going to be easy.*

set out sth or **set** sth **out**
to give all the details of something, or to explain something clearly, especially in writing ● *Your contract will set out the terms of your employment.* ● (often passive + **in**) *His plans for the coming year are set out in this document.*

set to   sets, setting, set

set to
1 *old-fashioned* to start working or dealing with something with a lot of energy and enthusiasm ● *If we all set to we should be able to finish the job this afternoon.*
2 *old-fashioned* if two people set to, they begin to fight ● *The boys suddenly set to with fists and feet.*
set-to n [C] *informal* ● (usually singular) *We had a bit of a set-to with the neighbours about their playing loud music at all hours.*

set up   sets, setting, set

set up sth or **set** sth **up**
1 to start a company or organization ● *At the age of 29 he set up a commercial property business.* ● *A committee has been set up to investigate the problem.*

set-up n [C] ● (usually singular) *It's important that clients see that you have a professional set-up.*

2 to make arrangements so that something can happen or exist ● *Could we set up a meeting for some time next week?* ● *A fund has been set up for the victims of the earthquake.*

set-up n [C] *slightly informal* the way that something is arranged ● (usually singular) *It took me a while to get used to the set-up in my new job.*

set up sb or **set** sb **up**

1 to trick someone in order to make them do something, or in order to make them seem guilty of something that they have not done ● *Jensen has always maintained that he was set up.* ● *I set him up – I got him to go to the party without telling him that Isobel would be there.*

set-up n [C] ● *Drugs were found in her luggage but she claimed that it was all a big set-up.*

2 to give someone the money that they need to start a business ● (often + **with**) *Her father set her up with a catering company when she left college.* ● *An inheritance like that should really **set you up for life**.* (= provide you with enough money for the rest of your life)

set up or **set** yourself **up**

to start working for yourself in your own company ● (usually + **as**) *I hear John's set up as a freelance journalist.* ● *I think you should set yourself up as an interior designer.* ● *He used to work for us but he's since set up on his own.*

set up (sth) or **set** (sth) **up**

to get all the necessary equipment ready for a particular activity ● *I need one or two people to help me set up the stand.* ● *We only had a couple of hours to set up before the exhibition opened up.*

set-up n [C] the way in which equipment for a particular activity is set up ● (usually singular) *In an efficient set-up, the same computer could perform all these different tasks.*

set sb **up**

if something [e.g. sleep, breakfast] sets you up, it prepares your body for the day by making you feel healthy and energetic ● *A good breakfast sets you up for the day.*

set upon

see **set on/upon**

settle down   settles, settling, settled

settle down

1 to start living in a place where you intend to stay for a long time, usually with the same partner, especially after a period in which you have travelled a lot or changed partners ● *Eventually I'd like to settle down and have a family, but not yet.* ● *When he meets the right person he'll settle down, you'll see.*

2 to start to feel happy and confident with a new situation ● *It took him a while to get used to his new school but I think he's settled down now.* ● *Has she settled down in her new job?*

settle (sb) **down**

to become quiet and calm or to make someone do this ● *The kids were so excited that it took me over an hour to settle them down again.* ● *Come on children, stop chatting and settle down, please!* ● *The office was pretty hectic before Christmas but things seem to have settled down now.*

settle for   settles, settling, settled

settle for sth

to accept something, often something that is not exactly what you want, or is not the best ● *It looks like she'll probably have to settle for second place.* ● *They've demanded a 10% pay rise and they're not going to settle for anything less.*

settle in/into   settles, settling, settled

settle in (sb) or **settle** (sb) **in**

settle (sb) **into** sth

to begin to feel relaxed and happy in a new home, job, or school ● *When we've settled in you'll have to come round for dinner.* ● *How's your new place? Are you settling in okay?* ● *It always takes a while to get settled into a new job.*

settle on   settles, settling, settled

settle sth **on** sb *formal*

to formally give money or property to someone ● *A small sum of money was settled on each grandchild when their grandmother died.*

settle on/upon   settles, settling, settled

settle on/upon sth

to agree on a decision • *Have they settled on a name for the baby yet?* • *We still haven't settled on a place to meet.*

settle up   settles, settling, settled

settle up

to pay someone the money that you owe them • (often + **with**) *I still haven't settled up with you for those tickets you bought.* • *You pay for this now and we'll settle up later.*

settle upon

see **settle on/upon**

sew up   sews, sewing, sewed, sewn or sewed

sew up sth or **sew** sth **up**

1 to close or repair something by sewing the edges together • *Ask her if she'll sew up the hole in your jeans.*
2 *slightly informal* to complete all the arrangements for a business agreement that you are sure will bring you success • (usually passive) *He was hoping to get the deal sewn up on Friday and fly back from Hong Kong on Saturday.*
3 to make sure that you win or get control of something • (usually passive) *The Democrats appear to have this election sewn up.* (= they are certain to win) • *Between them, the two companies would seem to have the market all sewn up.*

shack up   shacks, shacking, shacked

shack up (always + *adv/prep*) *mainly American informal*

to live in a place for a short time because you need somewhere to stay • *As itinerant workers, they shacked up in rented rooms and company dorms.* • *Western tourists in Tibet shack up at the Everest Hotel.*

shack up together/with   shacks, shacking, shacked

shack up together *informal*

shack up with sb *informal*

to start living in the same house as someone you are having a romantic relationship with • *I suppose we could always shack up together.* • *I heard he'd shacked up with some woman in the village.*

shade in   shades, shading, shaded

shade in sth or **shade** sth **in**

to make part of a picture darker • *She shaded in the background to make the figures stand out more.*

shake down   shakes, shaking, shook, shaken

shake down

1 to become organized as a group that works successfully together • *Give them a month or two to shake down and they'll be a pretty effective team.* • (often + **into**) *He reported that the unit had shaken down into an efficient, functioning organization.*
   shakedown *n* [C] • (usually singular) *After the shakedown of the new management team, the company took a lead in world markets.*
2 *British old-fashioned* to sleep on the floor or somewhere you do not usually sleep because you have no home or because there is no bed available • *In the summer he would shake down in a doorway or under the arch of a bridge.*

shake down sb or **shake** sb **down** *American informal*

if criminals shake someone down, they get money from them by using threats or tricks • *Together they would shake down neighborhood stores, demanding protection money.*
   shakedown *n* [C] *American informal* • *He'd been expecting some sort of shakedown from the mob.*

shake down sb/sth or **shake** sb/sth **down** *American & Australian informal*

if the police shake down someone or shake down a place, they search them in order to try to find things that are illegal or stolen • *Troops have been brought into the region to man checkpoints and shake down suspicious characters.* • *We can't shake down the whole building, only the suspect's apartment.*
   shakedown *n* [C] *American & Australian informal* • *Two policemen gave his place a real shakedown.*

shake off   shakes, shaking, shook, shaken

shake off sth or **shake** sth **off**

to get rid of an illness or something that is causing you problems • *I've had this cough for weeks and I just can't seem to shake it off.* ● *The actor was quoted as having said that he wanted to shake off his bad-guy image.*

shake off sb or **shake** sb **off**

to succeed in escaping from someone who is following you ● *I turned into a back street to try to shake him off.*

shake out   shakes, shaking, shook, shaken

shake out sth or **shake** sth **out**

to hold something made of cloth at one end and move it up and down in order to get rid of dust or dirt or to make it smooth ● *She took the dress out of the bag and shook it out.*

shake up   shakes, shaking, shook, shaken

shake up sth or **shake** sth **up**

1 to mix things inside a container by moving the container quickly up and down ● *You just put oil, vinegar and lemon juice in a jar, shake them up and you've got an instant salad-dressing.*

2 to make big changes to an organization in order to improve it ● *A Japanese-trained manager was brought in to shake up the organization.* ● *The government has shaken up the capital markets too.*
   shake-up n [C] ● *In the recent shake-up at Acme Communications, five senior managers lost their jobs.*

shake up sb or **shake** sb **up**

1 if an unpleasant experience shakes someone up, it makes them feel shocked and upset ● *She was quite shaken up by the accident.*

2 to shock someone in order to make them work harder or behave better ● *There are a lot of lazy, complacent people round here and they need shaking up.*

shape up   shapes, shaping, shaped

shape up

1 *slightly informal* to develop or improve, especially in the way that you want ● *I was watching Dom play squash at lunch – he's shaping up nicely.* ● *Overall, I think the project's shaping up quite well.*

2 *slightly informal* to improve your work or behaviour in order to reach an acceptable standard ● *If she doesn't shape up, she'll have to go.* ● *(American & Australian) It's a question of **shape up or ship out**.* (= improve or leave)

share out   shares, sharing, shared

share out sth or **share** sth **out**

to divide something into smaller amounts and give one amount to each person or thing in a group ● *We're trying to make sure that the work is shared out equally.* ● (often + **among**) *Profits are shared out among the members of the group.* ● (often + **between**) *The jobs were shared out between the two departments.*

sharpen up   sharpens, sharpening, sharpened

sharpen up (sb/sth) or **sharpen** (sb/sth) **up**

to improve something, especially by working hard or practising a lot ● *I need to sharpen up my game before I take Mark on at tennis.* ● *He's taking a course in public speaking so that should sharpen him up.* ● *We're not the leaders in the field but we're certainly sharpening up.*

shave off   shaves, shaving, shaved

shave sth **off** sth

to reduce something by a small amount ● *She managed to shave 0.29 seconds off the previous record.*

sheer off/away   sheers, sheering, sheered

sheer off/away

to move or break away suddenly and go in a different direction ● *A bolt sheered off the engine and became stuck in the blades.*

shell out   shells, shelling, shelled

shell out (sth) or **shell** (sth) **out**
informal

to pay or give money for something, especially when you do not want to ● (often + **for**) *Having shelled out fifty pounds for the tickets I wasn't going to miss it.*

shift for   shifts, shifting, shifted

shift for yourself (always reflexive) *old-fashioned, informal*

to look after yourself without help from anyone else ● *Well, if I'm away for a few days he'll just have to shift for himself.*

shin/shinny down   shins, shinning, shinned/shinnies, shinnying, shinnied

shin down sth *British, American & Australian*

shinny down sth *American*
    to quickly climb down something using your hands and legs • *I caught him shinning down a drainpipe at the back of the house.*

shin/shinny up   shins, shinning, shinned/shinnies, shinnying, shinnied

shin up sth *British, American & Australian*

shinny up sth *American*
    to quickly climb up something using your hands and legs • *He could shin up a tree faster than any kid I knew.*

shine out   shines, shining, shone

shine out
1 to shine brightly • *The lights of the chapel shone out through the misty gloom.*
2 if a person or a quality shines out, that person or quality is noticeable because they are very good • *It's a strong cast but one or two actors in particular shine out.*

shine through   shines, shining, shone

shine through (sth)
    if a quality that someone has shines through or shines through something, that quality is very easily noticed • *And it's this sense of humour that shines through everything he writes.* • *She has an intelligence that somehow shines through no matter what role she's playing.*

shinny up

    see **shin/shinny up**

ship off   ships, shipping, shipped

ship off sb/sth or **ship** sb/sth **off**
    to send someone or something to a place in a ship • (usually + **to**) *In those days British convicts were often shipped off to Australia.*

ship off sb or **ship** sb **off** *informal*
    to send or take someone somewhere • *When she told her parents she was pregnant, they shipped her off to live with her older brother.*

ship out   ships, shipping, shipped

ship out sth/sb or **ship** sth/sb **out**
    to send something or someone to a place in a ship • *We shipped the books out on Thursday.*

ship out
    to leave somewhere • *Ok, we're ready to ship out.*

shoot down   shoots, shooting, shot

shoot down sb/sth or **shoot** sb/sth **down**
1 to destroy an aircraft or make it fall to the ground by firing bullets or weapons at it • *They shot down two enemy planes during the raid.* • *He was shot down over enemy territory.*
2 *informal* to criticize someone's ideas or suggestions and refuse to consider them • *Any suggestions that I made in the meeting were shot down.*

shoot down sb or **shoot** sb **down**
    to kill or injure someone by firing a bullet at them, especially when they cannot defend themselves • *Five protesters were shot down by police during the anti-government demonstration.*

shoot for   shoots, shooting, shot

shoot for sth *mainly American informal*
    to try to achieve something • *He's shooting for a contract with a major record company.*

shoot off   shoots, shooting, shot

shoot off *British & Australian informal*
    to leave somewhere very quickly • *I'm going to have to shoot off – my train leaves in ten minutes.*

shoot through   shoots, shooting, shot

shoot through
    Australian informal to leave a place suddenly and often secretly, especially to avoid something • *He went to collect the money from them but they'd shot through.*

shoot through with

be shot through with sth (always passive)
    if a piece of writing is shot through with an emotion or a quality, that emotion or quality is in every part of it • *The lyrics of many of her songs are shot through with bitterness.*

shoot up   shoots, shooting, shot

shoot up

1 if the number, amount, or rate of something shoots up, it increases very quickly
• *The number of university students in Britain has shot up in the past few years.* • *House prices in the area have shot up recently.* • (sometimes + **to**) *In July the temperature shoots up to 35 degrees.*

2 if a child shoots up, he or she grows taller very quickly • *Karl has really shot up since I last saw him.*

3 *slang* to put illegal drugs [e.g. heroin] into your blood using a special needle • *I saw a guy shooting up in the square.*

shoot up sth or **shoot** sth **up**

to damage a building or to injure part of a person's body by firing bullets at it
• *Shells and machine-gun fire had shot up the city's schools and main hospital.* • *He came home from the war with both his legs badly shot up.*

shop around   shops, shopping, shopped

shop around

to compare the price and quality of the same item or service from different shops or companies before deciding which one to buy • (sometimes + **for**) *I shopped around for my computer and ended up paying $200 less than David.* • *Mortgage-hunters should shop around for the best deal on interest rates.*

shore up   shores, shoring, shored

shore up sth or **shore** sth **up**

1 to strengthen or improve an organization, agreement, or system that is not working effectively or that is likely to fail
• *Millions of dollars have been spent trying to shore up the company.* • *The government is relying on military power to shore up the fragile political system in the country.*

2 to stop a wall or a building from falling down by supporting it with building materials such as wood or metal • *A sagging wall was shored up with pieces of timber.*

shout down   shouts, shouting, shouted

shout down sb or **shout** sb **down**

to shout in order to prevent someone who is saying something that you disagree with from being heard • *One of the speakers was shouted down when she tried*

to discuss the issue of abortion.

shout out   shouts, shouting, shouted

shout out (sth) or **shout** (sth) **out**

to suddenly say something in a loud voice
• *I turned round in surprise as someone in the crowd shouted out my name.* • *She saw the police car approaching and shouted out to warn him.*

shove off

Shove off! (always an order) *informal*

something that you say when you are angry to tell someone to go away • *Just shove off, will you!*

shove off *informal*

to leave somewhere • *I have to shove off – I'll see you later.*

show around/round   shows, showing, showed, shown

show sb **around/round** (swh)

to go with someone to a place that they have not visited before and show them the interesting parts • *Let me know when you're coming to Boston and I'll show you around.* • *Ellie showed me around her new apartment with its beautiful roof terrace.*

show in/into   shows, showing, showed, shown

show in sb or **show** sb **in**

show sb **into** swh

to lead a visitor into a room where they have arranged to meet or wait for someone • *I was shown into a small dingy office.* • *Would you show the next candidate in, please?*

show off   shows, showing, showed, shown

show off

to try to make people admire your abilities or achievements in a way which other people find annoying • *He was the kind of kid who was always showing off to his classmates.* • *You're just showing off.*
  show-off n [C] *slightly informal* • *Peter ordered his dinner in Turkish, the show-off.* • *Nobody likes a show-off, Andrew.*

show off sb/sth or **show** sb/sth **off** (never passive)

to show someone or something that you are proud of to a group of people • *Chris was there, showing off his new sports car* to everyone. • *Sarah invited us round to dinner to show off her Italian boyfriend.*

show off sth or **show** sth **off** (never passive)

if one thing shows off another thing, it makes the attractive qualities of the other thing more noticeable • *The dark blue velvet of her dress showed off her blonde hair beautifully.* • *White shows off a tan.*

show out   shows, showing, showed, shown

show out sb or **show** sb **out**

to lead a visitor who is leaving to the door of a room or building • *My secretary will show you out.* • (often + *of*) *Could you show Mr Taylor out of the building?*

show over   shows, showing, showed, shown

show sb **over** swh *British & Australian*

to lead someone around a place which they are visiting officially or formally while telling them about it • *A police officer showed the detectives over the murder scene.*

show round

see **show around/round**

show through   shows, showing, showed, shown

show through

if a feeling shows through, it becomes obvious to other people, often when you are trying to hide it • *She smiles for the camera but somehow her sadness shows through.*

show up   shows, showing, showed, shown

show up

1 *informal* to arrive, especially at a place where people are expecting you • (usually + *adv/prep*) *He was supposed to be there at 8 o'clock and he didn't show up till ten.* • *She didn't show up for the meeting, I noticed.* • *Do I have to make an appointment to see the doctor or do I just show up at the surgery?*

2 if something shows up, it can be seen clearly or easily • *If there had been an abnormality, it would have shown up in the tests.*

show up sth or **show** sth **up**

to cause something to be seen or noticed • *A cream-coloured carpet would only show up the dirt.* • *What this case has shown up is the inadequacies of the legal system.*

show up sb or **show** sb **up** *slightly informal*

to make someone that you are with feel ashamed, often by doing or saying something stupid • *I didn't want my parents there, showing me up in front of all my friends.*

shrink from   shrinks, shrinking, shrank, shrunk   (*American & Australian pt* also **shrunk,** *American & Australian pp* also **shrunken**)

shrink from sth/doing sth

to avoid doing something that is difficult or unpleasant • (often negative) *He's no one to shrink from responsibilities.* • *She does not shrink from expressing controversial opinions.*

shrivel up   shrivels, shrivelling, shrivelled   (*American & Australian* also **shriveling, shriveled**)

shrivel up

if something shrivels up, it becomes smaller and its surface becomes covered with lines because it is dry or old • *Left too long in the sun, the leaves had all shrivelled up.*

shrug off   shrugs, shrugging, shrugged

shrug off sth or **shrug** sth **off**

to not worry about something and treat it as unimportant • *She has an amazing capacity to shrug off criticism.* • *Mr L shrugged off allegations that he had acted unfairly.*

shuck off   shucks, shucking, shucked

shuck off sth or **shuck** sth **off**

1 *American informal* to take off a piece of clothing • *She shucked off her clothes and dumped them on the floor.*

2 *American informal* to get rid of something, especially a belief or habit, and not let it influence you any more • *He shucked off his left-wing beliefs years ago.*

shut away   shuts, shutting, shut

shut away sb/sth or **shut** sb/sth **away**

to put someone or something in a special place from which they cannot leave or be taken away • *In the past, people with mental illnesses were often shut away.*

shut yourself **away** (always reflexive)

to go to a room where you can be alone for long periods • (often + **from**) *If I want to do any serious studying I have to shut myself away from the kids.*

shut down   shuts, shutting, shut

shut down (sth) or **shut** (sth) **down**

1 if a factory or business shuts down, or if someone shuts it down, it closes and stops working • *Both chemicals factories were shut down for safety reasons.* • *Three thousand people will lose their jobs if the car manufacturer shuts down.*

shutdown *n* [C] • *An electrical fire forced the shutdown of the company's nuclear power plant.*

2 if a machine shuts down or someone shuts it down, it stops operating • *The crew shut down the aircraft's right-hand engine when a fire broke out.* • *The computer system shuts down automatically at 8pm.*

shutdown *n* [C] • *The reasons for the engine shutdown have not yet become clear.*

shut in   shuts, shutting, shut

shut sb/sth **in** (sth)

to prevent someone or something from leaving a place by shutting the door or gate • *The cats had to be shut in the house all weekend while we were away.* • *The kids hate being shut in* (= having to stay inside the house) *all day.*

shut yourself **in** (sth) (always reflexive)

to go into a room and shut the door so that no one else can enter • *She shut herself in her bedroom and refused to talk to anyone.*

shut off   shuts, shutting, shut

shut off (sth) or **shut** (sth) **off**

if a machine shuts off, or if someone shuts it off, it stops operating • *The engine shuts off automatically when the desired speed is reached.* • *The test site was*

ordered to shut off its equipment for three days. • (used as *adj*) *The system has an automatic shut-off valve.*

shut off sth or **shut** sth **off**

1 to prevent supplies or goods from being available to the people that usually use them • *Gas supplies were shut off for four hours while the leak was repaired.*

2 to prevent a view from being seen by putting something in front of it • *A row of tall fir trees shut off the view of the street in front.*

shut yourself **off** (always reflexive)

to stop speaking to other people or becoming involved with them • (usually + **from**) *Since her row with her mother she's more or less shut herself off from the rest of the family.*

shut off from

be shut off from sth (always passive)

to be separated from other people or things so that you are not affected by them • *The town's wealthy people live in large houses, shut off from the outside world by high fences.*

shut out   shuts, shutting, shut

shut out sth or **shut** sth **out**

1 to prevent a sound or light from being heard or seen • *Could you close the curtains and shut out some light?* • *These windows shut out most of the traffic noise.*

2 to stop yourself from thinking about something or from feeling an emotion, usually because it causes you to suffer • *You've got to deal with these feelings – you can't just shut them out.* • *There are memories so painful that you have to shut them out.*

shut out sb or **shut** sb **out**

1 to not include someone in an activity, or to not tell someone about your thoughts and feelings • (often + **of**) *A lot of women feel that they have been shut out of higher-paid jobs.* • *I try to get him to tell me how he feels but he just shuts me out.*

2 *American* to prevent the person or team you are playing against in a sports competition from scoring any points • *The Orioles' pitcher shut the Red Sox out in a 7-0 victory.*

shutout *n* [C] *American* • *The game was a shutout, 3-0, to the Toronto Rangers.*

shut out sb/sth or **shut** sb/sth **out**

to prevent a person or animal from entering a place, usually by closing a door or gate • *I'd just shut the dog out because I was cleaning the kitchen floor.*

---

shut up   shuts, shutting, shut

shut (sb) **up**

to stop talking or making a noise, or to make someone do this • (often an order) *(informal) Just shut up and get on with your work!* • *Once he starts talking it's impossible to shut him up.* • *In the end I gave him some money just to shut him up.* (= stop him complaining)

shut up sb/sth or **shut** sb/sth **up**

to keep a person or animal somewhere and prevent them from leaving • (usually + **in**) *He was shut up in a lunatic asylum for the first twenty years of his life.* • *How would you like to be shut up in a tiny cage with no light and no room to move?*

shut up sth or **shut** sth **up** *British & Australian*

to close a shop or other business for a period of time when you are not using it • *Most of the shops were shut up for the winter.* • *Basically, the business wasn't making money any more and I thought it was time we **shut up shop**.* (= closed the business)

---

shy away from   shies, shying, shied

shy away from sth/doing sth

to avoid doing something, usually because you are afraid or you lack the confidence to do it • *He tends to shy away from anything that involves public speaking.*

---

sic on   sics, siccing, sicced

sic sb/sth **on** sb *American*

to tell a dog to attack someone, or to encourage someone to catch or attack another person • *They sic their dog on anyone who approaches the house.* • *He's going to sic the police on us if we don't move our operation on.*

---

sick up   sicks, sicking, sicked

sick up sth or **sick** sth **up** *British informal*

if someone, especially a baby, sicks up their food, they vomit • *Fifi had sicked up a load of milk all over my black silk shirt.*

---

side against   sides, siding, sided

side against sb

to oppose a person or group in an argument • *I felt that they were siding against me in the meeting this morning.*

---

side with   sides, siding, sided

side with sb

to support a person or group in an argument • *If ever there was any sort of argument, she'd always side with my father.*

---

sidle up   sidles, sidling, sidled

sidle up

to walk towards someone slowly and nervously as if you do not want anyone to notice • (usually + **to**) *I saw him sidle up to her and whisper something in her ear.*

---

sift out   sifts, sifting, sifted

sift out sth or **sift** sth **out**

to separate something from a group of other things • *We've looked through all the applications and sifted out the best.* • (often + **from**) *It's difficult to sift out the good stuff from the bad.*

---

sift through   sifts, sifting, sifted

sift through sth

to examine a large collection of something, especially papers, usually in order to discover something or to decide what is important • *We had to sift through hundreds of files before we found the relevant information.* • *I was sifting through a pile of photographs and I came across one of Dave.*

---

sign away   signs, signing, signed

sign away sth or **sign** sth **away**

to give someone else your property or legal rights to something by signing an official document • *He had signed away his rights to publish the research.*

---

sign for   signs, signing, signed

sign for sth

1 to sign a document to show that you have received something • *Could someone sign for this parcel?*

2 *British* if a footballer signs for a team, he signs a formal agreement saying that he will play for that football team • *The 21-year-old goalkeeper has signed for Chelsea on a month's trial.*

sign in   signs, signing, signed

sign in (sb) or **sign** (sb) **in**
to write your name or someone else's name in a book when you arrive in a building, especially a club, office, or hotel ● *Visitors please sign in at reception.* ● *I'd better sign you in since you're no longer a member.*

sign in
to type your name, and usually a secret word, onto a computer screen so that you can start using a computer system ● *Before you can look at your account details online, you must sign in.*

sign off   signs, signing, signed

sign off (sth)
1 to give a final message at the end of a letter or a television or radio programme ● *It's getting late so I'd better sign off now. Lots of love, Bec xxx* ● *She signed off her show by wishing all her listeners a happy new year.*
2 *British* to sign a form at a government office which states that you now have a job and do not need to receive unemployment benefit (= money paid by the government) ● *I signed off at the end of November when I got that building job.* ● *Investigations into fraudulent claims led to 65,000 people signing off the dole.*

sign off *American informal*
to stop doing something and leave ● (usually + *adv/prep*) *I'm signing off early today – I'll see you tomorrow.*

sign off sb or **sign** sb **off** *British*
if a doctor signs someone off, he sends a note to their employer saying that they are ill and that they are unable to go to work for a period of time ● *She was signed off by her doctor for a month.*

sign off on   signs, signing, signed

sign off on sth *American*
to agree to a plan, often by writing your name on a piece of paper ● *The director hasn't signed off on the budget proposal yet.*

sign on   signs, signing, signed

sign on
1 to sign a document saying that you will work for someone ● (often + **with**) *She's signed on with a temp agency.*
2 *British* to sign a form at a government office which states that you do not have a job and that you want to receive unemployment benefit (= money paid by the government) ● *You can sign on at your nearest Job Centre.*
3 *American* to arrange to take part in an activity ● *I've signed on to help at the school fair.*
4 to type your name, and usually a secret word, onto a computer screen so that you can start using a computer system ● *Once you sign on, you can see the whole list of available items.*
5 *American* to start to broadcast on television or radio at the beginning of the day. ● *He signs on each morning with exactly the same phrase.* ● *What time does the station sign on?*

sign on sb or **sign** sb **on** *American & Australian*
to arrange for someone to sign an agreement which states that they will work for you ● *We've signed on three new instructors.*

sign out   signs, signing, signed

sign out sth or **sign** sth **out**
to sign a form or a book in order to say that you have taken or borrowed something ● *You'll need to sign those books out.*

sign out (sb) or **sign** (sb) **out**
to write your name or someone else's name in a book when you leave a building, especially a club, office, or hotel ● *Don't forget to sign out before you leave.* ● *Could you sign our guests out?*

sign over   signs, signing, signed

sign over sth or **sign** sth **over**
to give someone else your property or legal rights to something by signing an official document ● (usually + **to**) *Two years before her death she signed her property over to her two children.*

sign up   signs, signing, signed

sign up
1 to arrange to take part in an activity ● (often + **to do sth**) *I've signed up to do scuba diving.* ● (often + **for**) *She's signed up for a couple of night classes at the local college.*
2 to sign a document stating that you will work for someone ● *He's signed up with*

an agency who are fairly confident that they'll find him some work.

sign up sb or sign sb up

to arrange for someone to sign a document stating that they will work for you ● (usually passive) *She's been signed up by a modelling agency.*

sign with   signs, signing, signed

sign with sth

1 if a musician signs with a company, he or she signs an official agreement which allows that company to record and sell his or her work ● *In this year he signed with Columbia Records and released his first recording.*
2 *mainly American* to officially agree to play or work for one particular team or person ● *Rogers signed with a Montreal team and left the US.*

silt up   silts, silting, silted

silt up (sth) or silt (sth) up

if an area of water [e.g. river, dam, harbour] silts up or something silts it up, it becomes blocked with sand or earth ● *A new port had to be built when the river silted up.*

simmer down   simmers, simmering, simmered

simmer down

to become less angry or excited about something ● (usually an order) *Simmer down, kids! Come on, now, get on with your work.*

sing along   sings, singing, sang, sung
(*American pt* also **sung**)

sing along

to sing a piece of music while someone else is singing it or while it is being broadcast or performed ● (often + **with**) *She was singing along with the car radio.*

singalong *n* [C] a singalong is when a group of people sing songs together for enjoyment ● *After dinner, we all had a good singalong around the piano.* ● (used as *adj*) *Abba had a talent for writing great singalong pop songs.* (= songs that people like singing)

sing out   sings, singing, sang, sung
(*American pt* also **sung**)

sing out (sth) or sing (sth) out

to say something loudly and clearly ● *'Is that you, Charles?' sang out a woman's voice from the garden.* ● *I'll be downstairs, so just sing out if you want anything.*

sing out

to sing loudly ● *The choir sang out across the courtyard.*

sing up   sings, singing, sang, sung
(*American pt* also **sung**)

sing up

to sing more loudly so that people can hear you ● *Sing up a bit Ashley, I can hardly hear you.*

single out   singles, singling, singled

single out sb/sth or single sb/sth out

to choose one person or thing from a large group in order to criticize or praise them ● (often + **for**) *The report singled out three government ministers for criticism.* ● (sometimes + **as**) *His company was singled out as the most successful small business in the region.*

sink in   sinks, sinking, sank, sunk

sink in

if a fact or idea, especially a surprising or unpleasant one, sinks in, you gradually start to believe it or realize what effect it will have on you ● *It was a few minutes before the news finally sank in.* ● (sometimes + **that**) *It still hasn't really sunk in that I'm never going to see her again.*

sink into   sinks, sinking, sank, sunk

sink into sth

to gradually get into a worse state ● *As the months went by, he sank into a deep depression.* ● *Over the past six months, the company has sunk deeper into debt.*

sink sth into sth

to spend a large amount of money on a business or other piece of work ● *When the firm went bankrupt, he lost all of the $200 000 he had sunk into it.* ● *The government has sunk millions of dollars into such schemes.*

siphon away

see **siphon/syphon away/off**

siphon/syphon away/off   siphons,
siphoning, siphoned/syphons, syphoning,
syphoned

siphon away/off sth or **siphon** sth
away/off *British, American & Australian*

syphon away/off sth or **syphon** sth
away/off *British & Australian*

to succeed in taking something [e.g. business, votes] from another organization or
person ● *The new out-of-town supermarket
has siphoned off business from the town
centre.* ● *If she stands for election, she
could siphon off votes that would otherwise
go to the Republican candidate.*

siphon/syphon off   siphons,
siphoning, siphoned/syphons, syphoning,
syphoned

siphon off sth or **siphon** sth **off** *British, American & Australian*

syphon off sth or **syphon** sb/sth **off**
British & Australian

to dishonestly take money from an organization or other supply and use it for a
purpose for which it was not intended ● *It
was later discovered that he had siphoned
off 400 million from the company pension
fund.*

sit about/around   sits, sitting, sat

sit about/around (swh)

to spend time sitting down and doing
very little ● (often + doing sth) *We sat
around most of the afternoon drinking coffee and chatting.* ● *It's no good sitting
around the house all day doing nothing.*

sit back   sits, sitting, sat

sit back

1 to relax in a chair so that your back is
against the back of the chair ● *You sit
back and relax – you've been working all
day.*

2 to wait for something to happen without
making any effort to do anything yourself
● *You can't just sit back and wait for job
offers to come to you.*

sit by   sits, sitting, sat

sit by

to fail to take action to stop something

wrong happening ● *We can't sit by and
watch the country slide further into civil
war.*

sit down   sits, sitting, sat

sit down

1 to move your body so that the lower part
of it is resting on a seat or on the ground
● *Would you like to sit down?* ● *I sat down
on the sofa next to Barbara.* ● *It was after
9 o'clock when we finally **sat down to
dinner**.* (= to eat dinner)

sit-down *n* [C] a short rest in which you
sit down ● *I'd like to go somewhere where I
can have a sit-down.*

sit-down *n* [C] a situation in which a
group of people refuse to leave a place
until someone agrees to give them what
they want ● *Over 100 students staged a sit-
down over a ban on smoking in the college.*
● (used as *adj*) *Workers are threatening to
hold a sit-down strike to protest about proposed job losses.*

sit-down *adj* (always before noun) a
sit-down meal is a formal meal served to
people who are sitting at a table ● *After
the wedding ceremony there was the usual
sit-down meal.*

2 to spend a lot of time discussing a subject
in order to solve a problem or make a
decision ● (often + **with**) *You've got to sit
down with your boyfriend and get to the
bottom of what it is that's upsetting you.*
● (sometimes + **together**) *Management
and staff have got to sit down together and
reach a compromise.*

be sitting down (always in continuous
tenses)

to be in a sitting position with the bottom
half of your body resting on a seat or on
the ground ● *And these exercises are perfect for the office or the car because you can
do them while you're sitting down.*

sit sb **down**

to help someone who has difficulty moving to sit down, or to make someone sit
down ● *I helped her onto the train and sat
her down on a seat by the window.* ● *I sat
him down to tell him the bad news.*

sit yourself **down** (always reflexive)
slightly informal

to move your body so that the lower part
of it is resting on a seat or on the ground
● (often an order) *Sit yourself down and*

I'll make a nice pot of tea. • *He sat himself down near the fire and warmed his hands.*

sit for   sits, sitting, sat

sit for sb/sth

to be a model for an artist or a photographer and stay in the same position while they paint you or take photographs of you • *Elizabeth Siddal sat for many of the Pre-Raphaelite painters.* • *In the past ten years he's sat for over 50 portraits.*

sit for sb *mainly American*

to look after young children, or to have an arrangement with their parents to do this, usually for a small payment • *The kids really love it when Terry sits for them.* • *She doesn't sit for the Walkers anymore – the children were too difficult.*

sit in   sits, sitting, sat

sit in

1 to be present in a meeting or class without taking part in it • (usually + **on**) *Two observers from the United Nations sat in on the meeting.* • *You could sit in on a class to see if it was the type of thing that would interest you.*

2 if a group of people sit in, they go to a public building and refuse to leave it in order to complain about something • *The factory was occupied by demonstrators sitting in as a protest against the arms trade.*
sit-in *n* [C] • *Campaigners staged a sit-in outside the British embassy.*

sit in for   sits, sitting, sat

sit in for sb

to do someone's job while they are absent • *The minister has attended all the talks except one when his deputy sat in for him.*

sit on   sits, sitting, sat

sit on sth

1 to be an official member of a group of people that represents or controls an organization [e.g. committee, board, panel] • *She sat on the company's board for five years.* • *He sits on a number of committees.*

2 *informal* to delay dealing with something • *I still haven't had a reply from the council – they've been sitting on my letter for weeks.*

3 to prevent people from knowing a piece of information • *The government will presumably sit on the report until the police*

finish their investigation.

be sitting on sth (always in continuous tenses)

to own something very valuable, often without knowing its full value • *The house alone is probably worth £500 000 – she must be sitting on a fortune.* • *When he finally took the paintings to be valued, he found that he'd been **sitting on a goldmine**.* (= that they were extremely valuable)

sit out   sits, sitting, sat

sit out sth or **sit** sth **out** (never passive)

1 to be unable to take part in a physical activity, especially a sport, usually because you are injured • *Monica Seles had to sit out the doubles competition because of a broken wrist.* • *I've been dancing for over an hour so I thought I might sit the next one out.*

2 to wait for something unpleasant to finish before taking any action • *The government is prepared to sit out the strike rather than agree to union demands.*

sit over   sits, sitting, sat

sit over sth

if you sit over a meal or a drink, you eat or drink it in a very slow and relaxed way • *We sat over dinner that night, talking for a long time.*

sit through   sits, sitting, sat

sit through sth

to listen to or watch a whole meeting, speech, or performance that is very long or boring • *We had to sit through two hours of speeches before dinner was finally served.*

sit up   sits, sitting, sat

sit up

1 to move into a sitting position after you have been lying down ● *He thought he heard a noise and sat up in alarm.* ● *She sat up and switched on the bedside light.*

sit-up *n* [C] an exercise in which you move from lying on the floor to a sitting position ● *I do 50 sit-ups every morning to keep my stomach trim.*

2 to straighten your back when you are in a sitting position ● *Stop slouching now – sit up straight.*

3 to stay awake and not go to bed even though it is late ● (often + doing sth) *We sat up half the night just talking.* ● *I won't be home till late so don't sit up for me.*

4 if something interesting or surprising makes someone sit up, it makes that person give their attention to it ● *His lectures really made people sit up and think.* ● *That was the record that made me **sit up and take notice** of Coldplay.*

be sitting up (always in continuous tenses)

to be in a sitting position ● *When we went to see her yesterday she was sitting up, reading a book.*

size up   sizes, sizing, sized

size up sb/sth or **size** sb/sth **up**

to carefully examine a situation or person in order to make a judgement ● *It's one of those stores where the sales assistants size you up as you walk through the door.* ● *I'm still trying to size up the situation.*

skate around/over/round   skates, skating, skated

skate around/over/round sth

to avoid discussing a subject or problem or not give it enough attention, usually because it is too difficult or embarrassing ● *I noticed that he skated round the issue of redundancies.*

sketch in   sketches, sketching, sketched

sketch in sth or **sketch** sth **in**

1 to give more information about something ● *I'll start by outlining the proposal and then sketch in a few more details later.*

2 if you sketch in a part of a picture, you draw it quickly and roughly ● *When you look closely at the painting you can just make out where he started to sketch in a few trees.*

sketch out   sketches, sketching, sketched

sketch out sth or **sketch** sth **out**

1 to give a short, general description of an idea or plan ● *He sketched out his ideas in an essay and sent it to various publishers.* ● *The guide sketched out a plan of the week's activities.*

2 to draw all the main features of something without showing the exact details ● *He sketched out a few designs for us to look at.*

skim off   skims, skimming, skimmed

skim off sth or **skim** sth **off**

to remove an amount of money from a larger amount of money, usually in order to keep it for yourself ● (sometimes + **from**) *Hains is accused of skimming off money from government grants.*

skim over/through   skims, skimming, skimmed

skim over/through sth

to read a piece of writing quickly in order to understand the main points, without studying the details ● *I didn't have much time so I just skimmed through the article.*

skimp on   skimps, skimping, skimped

skimp on sth

to not spend enough time or money on something, or not use enough of something ● *A lot of old people skimp on food and heating so that they can pay their bills.* ● *We've got plenty of cheese so don't skimp on it.*

skin up   skins, skinning, skinned

skin up *British slang*

to make a cigarette using marijuana (= a drug) and a thin piece of paper to wrap around it ● *You're not skinning up again, are you?*

skip off/out   skips, skipping, skipped

skip off/out *American & Australian informal*

to leave a place suddenly and often secretly, especially to avoid something ● *They skipped out after the meal without paying the bill.* • (sometimes + **with**) *Someone has skipped off with (= taken and kept) the book I left on the table.*

skip out on   skips, skipping, skipped

skip out on sb *American & Australian informal*

to suddenly leave your husband, wife, or your partner and end your relationship with them • *Her husband skipped out on her when the kids were small.*

skirt around/round   skirts, skirting, skirted

skirt around/round sth

1 to go around the edge or outside of something • *I skirted round the side of the building and got in via a back entrance.*

2 to avoid discussing a subject or problem, usually because it is too difficult • *I felt that he skirted around the most important issues.*

skive off   skives, skiving, skived

skive off (sth) *British informal*

to avoid doing your work by not going to the place where you should be working • *Where's Martin? Is he skiving off again?* • *Why does everyone just assume that I was skiving off work?*

slack off   slacks, slacking, slacked

slack off

to work less hard than usual • *I think we all slack off a bit towards the end of the week.*

slacken off   slackens, slackening, slackened

slacken off

to become slower or less active • *We expect demand to slacken off in the new year.* • *I'm waiting for the rain to slacken off before I venture outside.*

slag off   slags, slagging, slagged

slag off sb/sth or **slag** sb/sth **off** *British informal*

to criticize someone or something in an unpleasant way • *He's always slagging her off behind her back.* • *People seem all too eager to slag off British movies.*

slam down   slams, slamming, slammed

slam down sth or **slam** sth **down**

to put something down with a lot of force,

especially the part of the telephone that you talk into • *I guessed he was pretty angry because he slammed the phone down.*

slap around   slaps, slapping, slapped

slap sb **around** *informal*

to hit someone often • *Her first husband used to slap her around.*

slap down   slaps, slapping, slapped

slap down sb or **slap** sb **down**

to criticize someone unpleasantly, especially by telling them that their ideas or suggestions are not good • *I tried to give my opinion about the plans but was immediately slapped down.*

slap on   slaps, slapping, slapped

slap on sth or **slap** sth **on** *informal*

to quickly put or spread something on a surface • *It won't take five minutes to slap on a bit of make-up and brush my hair.* • *I just had time to slap a piece of cheese on some bread and eat it.*

slap sth **on** sth

to suddenly announce a new charge or law, especially one that is not fair • *A duty of 8.5 % has been slapped on wine imports.* • *They slapped an injunction on the press preventing publication of the report.*

slave away   slaves, slaving, slaved

slave away

to work very hard with little or no rest • (often + **at**) *I've been slaving away at the the housework all morning.* • *(humorous) I don't know, you two are off having fun and here's me, **slaving away over a hot stove!** (= doing a lot of cooking)*

slaver over   slavers, slavering, slavered

slaver over sb/sth *informal*

to look at someone or something with great excitement and interest, in a way that is unpleasant to other people • *Nigel, of course, was slavering over some blonde at the bar.*

sleep about/around   sleeps, sleeping, slept

sleep about/around *informal*

to have sex with a lot of different people without having a serious relationship with any of them • *He used to sleep around a lot at college.* • *I don't know if it's very wise to sleep around these days.*

sleep in   sleeps, sleeping, slept
sleep in

to sleep longer in the morning than you normally do • *I like to sleep in on Saturdays.*

sleep off   sleeps, sleeping, slept
sleep off sth or **sleep** sth **off**

to sleep until you feel better, especially after too much alcohol • *He's probably still in bed, sleeping off his hangover.*

sleep on   sleeps, sleeping, slept
sleep on sth

if someone sleeps on a decision or problem, they wait until the next day before they decide what to do about it • *Let's not make any hasty decisions, let's sleep on it.*

sleep out   sleeps, sleeping, slept
sleep out

to sleep outside • *I'd like to sleep out tonight, under the stars.*

sleep over   sleeps, sleeping, slept
sleep over *informal*

to sleep in someone else's home for a night • *If you don't want to drive home tonight, you're welcome to sleep over.*

sleep-over *n* [C] *mainly American* a party at which several young people sleep at a friend's house for a night • *Tyler was invited to a sleep-over at her friend's house.*

sleep through   sleeps, sleeping, slept
sleep through sth

if someone sleeps through a noise or an activity, the noise or activity does not wake them • *I didn't even hear the alarm go off – I just slept straight through it.* • *Don't worry about Jim – he can sleep through anything.*

sleep together   sleeps, sleeping, slept
sleep together *informal*

if two people sleep together, they have sex • *We started sleeping together a couple of weeks after we met.* • *Do you think they sleep together?*

sleep with   sleeps, sleeping, slept
sleep with sb *informal*

to have sex with someone, especially someone who is not your usual sexual partner • *He found out that she'd been sleeping with his best friend.*

slice off   slices, slicing, sliced
slice off sth or **slice** sth **off** (sth)

to remove something by cutting it • *She sliced off a piece of the sausage and handed it to me.*

slice up   slices, slicing, sliced
slice up sth or **slice** sth **up**

1 *British & Australian* to cut something into flat thin pieces • *Slice up the vegetables and fry them.*

2 to cut or divide something into parts • *The woods around the farm house had been sliced up into quarter acre plots of land.*

slick up   slicks, slicking, slicked
slick up sb/sth or **slick** sb/sth **up** *American*

to make someone or something look more attractive, especially by making them tidier • *What are you all slicked up for? Are you going out?* • *I need to slick up the apartment before having anyone over.*

slim down   slims, slimming, slimmed
slim down

to become thinner • *He's really slimmed down over the last few months.*

slim down (sth) or **slim** (sth) **down**

to become smaller in size, often by employing fewer people, or to make something smaller • *Obviously, one way to make a saving is to slim down the workforce.* • (used as *adj*) *The new slimmed-down organization is far more efficient.*

slip away   slips, slipping, slipped
slip away

1 if someone's power or the possibility of them winning or achieving something slips away, it disappears • *Just one goal ahead, they're determined not to let victory slip away.*

2 if a period of time slips away, it seems to pass quickly • *As the months slipped away I began to forget what he looked like.*

slip by   slips, slipping, slipped
slip by

1 if a period of time slips by, it seems to

pass quickly ● *The months slipped by and still there was no news of him.*

2 if a chance to do something slips by, you do not make use of it ● *You mustn't let an opportunity like that slip by.*

slip down   slips, slipping, slipped

slip down (sth) (always + *adv/prep*)
slightly informal
if an alcoholic drink or soft food slips down, you enjoy drinking or eating it ● *This Bordeaux is delicious – it slips down the throat very easily.*

slip in   slips, slipping, slipped

slip in sth or **slip** sth **in**
to add a remark to your conversation or speech in a quick, informal way that does not attract too much attention ● *Did you notice the way she managed to slip in a reference to her famous brother?* ● *I usually slip in one or two jokes during a talk just to liven things up a bit.*

slip into   slips, slipping, slipped

slip into sth
1 to quickly put on clothes or a piece of clothing, especially after removing a different set of clothes ● *Would you wait for me while I go and slip into something cooler?* ● *I'll just slip into something more comfortable.*
2 if you slip into a bad state or a bad way of behaving, you gradually start to be in that state or start to behave in that way ● *The figures suggest that the economy is in danger of slipping into recession.* ● *I was afraid that if he started drinking he might slip into his old habits.*

slip off   slips, slipping, slipped

slip off
to leave a place quietly so that other people do not notice you going ● *She just slipped off without telling us.* ● (sometimes + **to**) *I can't find Alan – do you think he's slipped off to the pub?*

slip off sth or **slip** sth **off**
to take off your shoes, clothes, or a piece of clothing ● *She slipped off her bathrobe and stepped into the shower.*

slip on   slips, slipping, slipped

slip on sth or **slip** sth **on**
to put on shoes, clothes, or a piece of

clothing quickly ● *She slipped on her shoes and ran out to meet him.*

slip-on *adj* (always before noun) ● *slip-on shoes*

slip-ons *n* (plural) shoes which do not have fasteners and which can be put on and taken off quickly ● *What sort of shoes are you looking for: slip-ons or lace-ups?*

slip out   slips, slipping, slipped

slip out
slightly informal if a piece of information slips out while you are talking to someone, you tell it to them without intending to ● *I really didn't mean to tell her that Ellen was pregnant – it just slipped out.*

slip up   slips, slipping, slipped

slip up *informal*
to make a mistake ● *These figures don't make sense – have we slipped up somewhere?*

slip-up *n* [C] *informal* ● *I want this job done properly. We can't afford any more slip-ups.*

slob about/around   slobs, slobbing, slobbed

slob about/around *British informal*
to behave in a lazy way, doing very little ● *We didn't do much really – we just slobbed around in front of the TV.*

slobber over   slobbers, slobbering, slobbered

slobber over sb *informal*
to show a lot of sexual interest in someone in a way that is embarrassing for other people ● *All the men were slobbering over Amanda's sister, who happens to be very blond and very pretty.*

slog away   slogs, slogging, slogged

slog away *informal*
to keep working very hard, usually for a long time ● (usually + **at**) *If she's got a job to do, she'll just slog away at it until it's finished.*

slop about/around   slops, slopping, slopped

slop about/around (swh) *British & Australian informal*
to behave in a lazy way, doing very little ● *Jeans are all right for slopping around*

the house but I wouldn't wear them for work.

slop out   slops, slopping, slopped

slop out (sth) *British*

if prisoners slop out, they empty the containers that they have used as toilets during the night • *Inmates of the prison still have to slop out their chamber-pots every morning.*

slopping-out *n* [U] *British* • *Slopping-out is the part of the prison routine that prisoners most object to.*

slope off   slopes, sloping, sloped

slope off *British & Australian*

to leave somewhere quietly so that you are not noticed, especially when you are avoiding work • (often + **to**) *They must have sloped off to the bar while we weren't looking.*

slot in/into   slots, slotting, slotted

slot in sb/sth or **slot** sb/sth **in**

slot sb/sth **into** sth

to find a time for someone or something in a period of time that has already been planned • *Doctor Sewards is busy this morning but she might be able to slot you in around one o'clock.*

slouch about/around   slouches, slouching, slouched

slouch about/around (swh)

to behave in a lazy way, doing very little • *There were the usual gang of youths slouching around the town square.*

slough off   sloughs, sloughing, sloughed

slough off sth or **slough** sth **off**

formal

1 to get rid of something that you do not want any more • *In recent years the magazine has been trying to slough off its old-fashioned image.*

2 if an animal [e.g. snake] sloughs off its outer skin, its outer skin comes off through a natural process • *The old skin is sloughed off as the new skin grows.*

slow down   slows, slowing, slowed

slow down

to become less physically active than you were before • *I think my body's telling me that I've got to slow down a little.*

slow down (sb/sth) or **slow** (sb/sth) **down**

to become slower, or to make something or someone slower • *Slow down, you two, I can't keep up with you.* • *I was carrying some heavy bags so that slowed me down.* • *It seems likely that the economy will slow down over the next twelve months.*

slowdown *n* [C] • (usually singular) *Even the prime minister acknowledged that the slowdown in the economy had been sharper than expected.*

slow up   slows, slowing, slowed

slow up (sth/sb) or **slow** (sth/sb) **up**

to become slower, or to make something or someone slower • *The car slowed up at the traffic lights.* • *If we have to get their approval every time we do something it slows things up.*

slug out   slugs, slugging, slugged

slug it out

1 *informal* if two people slug it out, they fight • *I can't understand why people pay to watch two sweaty men slugging it out in a ring.*

2 *informal* to argue with someone or compete against someone until you defeat them • *If a couple can't settle these matters between them, they'll slug it out in the courts.* • *Either the two companies merge now or they slug it out in the market and one goes bust later.*

sluice down/out   sluices, sluicing, sluiced

sluice down/out sth or **sluice** sth **down/out** *British & Australian*

to wash something with large amounts of water • *We had to sluice out the garage to get rid of the smell of petrol.*

smack of   smacks, smacking, smacked

smack of sth

if something smacks of an unpleasant quality [e.g. desperation, hypocrisy], it seems to have that quality • *The whole thing smacks of hypocrisy.* • *To me, the statement smacks of desperation.*

smarten up   smartens, smartening, smartened

smarten up (sb/sth) or **smarten** (sb/sth) **up**
to make a person or a place look tidier • *You'll have to smarten up a bit for your interview.* • (often reflexive) *I'll just have a wash and smarten myself up.* • *They've really smartened the town centre up since I was last there.*

smarten up *American & Australian*
to become more clever and more aware of things • *I know I'm going to have to smarten up to keep up with the class.*

smash down   smashes, smashing, smashed

smash down sth or **smash** sth **down**
to hit a door or wall hard until it falls down • *When I wouldn't let him in he threatened to smash the door down.*

smash in   smashes, smashing, smashed

smash in sth or **smash** sth **in**
to break or damage something by hitting it hard many times • *The windows of the car had been smashed in.* • *(informal) Right now I'd like to **smash his face/head in**.* (= hit his face/head very hard)

smash up   smashes, smashing, smashed

smash up sth or **smash** sth **up**
to badly damage or destroy something by hitting it many times • *A load of football fans had come in and smashed the place up.*
smash-up *n* [C] *slightly informal* a serious road or train accident • *There was a terrible smash-up on the motorway this morning.*

smell of   smells, smelling, smelled
(*British and Australian pt & pp* also **smelt**)

smell of sth
if something or someone smells of a particular thing, they have that smell • *You smell of garlic.* • *His breath smelled of alcohol.* • *When Graham's been to stay the whole house smells of cigarettes.*

smell out   smells, smelling, smelled
(*British and Australian pt & pp* also **smelt**)

smell out sth or **smell** sth **out**
if an animal smells something out, it finds that thing by smelling • *I bet your dog could smell those rabbits out.*

smell out/up   smells, smelling, smelled
(*British and Australian pt & pp* also **smelt**)

smell out sth or **smell** sth **out** *British & Australian informal*

smell up sth or **smell** sth **up** *American informal*
to fill a room with a smell, especially an unpleasant one • *That curry you had last night has smelt the whole place out.*

smile on   smiles, smiling, smiled

smile on sth
to accept behaviour that is slightly bad because you do not think it important and because you like the person who is responsible for it • *Americans had tended to smile on the misdemeanours of their presidents.*

smoke out   smokes, smoking, smoked

smoke out sb/sth or **smoke** sb/sth **out**
to force a person or animal to come out of a place by filling it with smoke • *If any are left in the forest, they're usually smoked out.*

smoke out sb or **smoke** sb **out**
to succeed in finding someone who is causing a problem • *The finance minister has announced a tougher approach to smoking out tax dodgers.*

smooth away   smooths, smoothing, smoothed

smooth away sth or **smooth** sth **away**
to remove the difficulties from something • *I always had my mother there to smooth away any little problems.*

smooth down   smooths, smoothing, smoothed

smooth down sth or **smooth** sth **down**
to press your hair or your clothes with your hands in order to make them flat • *He straightened his tie and smoothed down his hair.*

smooth out   smooths, smoothing, smoothed

smooth out sth or **smooth** sth **out**
1 to make a piece of cloth or paper flat by moving your hands across it and pressing it • *I was just trying to smooth out the creases in your shirt.*
2 to reduce the changes or difficulties in a process or situation • *We're looking for ways to smooth things out during this transition period.*

smooth over   smooths, smoothing, smoothed

smooth over sth or **smooth** sth **over**
to make a disagreement or problem seem less serious or more easy to deal with, especially by talking to the people involved in it • *Would you like me to smooth things over between you and Nick?* • *He was keen to smooth over the argument and continue with the negotiations.*

smother in/with   smothers, smothering, smothered

smother sth/sb **in/with** sth
to cover the whole surface of something with a large amount of something else • *Two of my aged aunts were there to greet me so I was smothered with kisses.* • *She'd helped herself to a huge slice of chocolate cake and smothered it in cream.*

snack on/off   snacks, snacking, snacked

snack on sth *British & Australian*

snack off sth *American*
to eat small amounts of a particular food • *If you eat three meals a day, you're less likely to snack on cakes and biscuits.* • *We snacked off milk and cookies when we got home.*

snap out of   snaps, snapping, snapped

snap out of sth *informal*
to force yourself to stop feeling sad and upset • *He's been suffering from depression since his wife died and he just can't snap out of it.*

snap to   snaps, snapping, snapped

Snap to it! (always an order) *informal*
something you say to tell someone to do something quickly • *I want this place cleaned up by this evening so snap to it!*

snap up   snaps, snapping, snapped

snap up sth or **snap** sth **up** *slightly informal*
to buy or get something quickly because it is very cheap or because it is exactly what you want • *It was half-price in the sales so I snapped it up.* • *The rights to the story have been snapped up by a Sunday newspaper.*

snap up sb or **snap** sb **up** *informal*
to successfully persuade someone to join your team or company before other people can do so • *The association is concerned that the richer football clubs will snap up all the best players.*

snarl up   snarls, snarling, snarled

snarl up
informal if traffic or a road snarls up, the traffic cannot move freely because the road is blocked or because there is so much traffic • *It only takes one accident for the whole road to snarl up.*
snarl-up n [C] *informal* • *There was a huge snarl-up on the road going into town.*
snarled up adj *informal* • *Traffic is snarled up in both directions.*

snatch at   snatches, snatching, snatched

snatch at sth *British & Australian*
to try to use an opportunity quickly before it disappears • *Naturally I snatched at the chance of a promotion.* • *You have to snatch at happiness when you can.*

sneak up

sneak up   sneaks, sneaking, sneaked
(*American and Australian pt* & *pp* also **snuck**)

sneak up
to move close to someone without them seeing or hearing you • *He sneaked up from behind and surprised her.* • (often + **on**) *Don't sneak up on me like that – you really scared me!*

sniff around/round   sniffs, sniffing, sniffed

sniff around/round swh
to look for information or for something you want in a particular place • *A couple of detectives were sniffing around the hotel, asking questions.*

sniff at   sniffs, sniffing, sniffed

sniff at sth
1 *informal* to disapprove of something • *A lot of people still sniff at comics and think them a juvenile habit.* • *Still, a free weekend in Amsterdam is an offer **not to be sniffed at**.* (= is worth having)
2 *informal* to show that you are interested in buying something • *A number of big computer firms are sniffing at our new software.*

sniff out   sniffs, sniffing, sniffed

sniff out sth or sniff sth out
if a dog used by the police or army sniffs out hidden drugs or explosives, it finds them by smelling them • *Customs officers used dogs to sniff out the drugs which were hidden in the truck.*

sniff out sth/sb or sniff sth/sb out
informal to discover information about something, or to find something or someone after searching for them • *He's been trying to sniff out what we've been doing.* • *She goes round the big fashion shows, sniffing out talent for a modelling agency.*

snow in/up

be snowed in/up (always passive)
if a person or place is snowed up, there is so much snow that it is impossible to travel anywhere or leave that place • *We were snowed in for five days in January.* • *The airport was snowed up and all flights had been diverted to Edinburgh.*

snow under

be snowed under (always passive)
informal
to have so much work that you have problems dealing with it • (often + **with**) *I couldn't finish the report on time because I was snowed under with work.* • *You look snowed under. Would you like some help?*

snow up
see **snow in/up**

snuff out   snuffs, snuffing, snuffed

snuff out sth or snuff sth out
1 to stop a candle or small flame from burning by covering it with something or by pressing it with your fingers • *One by one, she snuffed out the candles.*
2 *informal* to suddenly end something • *Italy's third goal snuffed out any hopes England had of winning the game.* • *Both rebellions were snuffed out as quickly as they started.*

snuff out sb or snuff sb out *American & Australian slang*
to kill someone • (usually passive) *He was snuffed out in the first five minutes of the movie.*

snuggle down   snuggles, snuggling, snuggled

snuggle down
to make yourself warm and comfortable in your bed • *I turned off the light and snuggled down under the covers.*

snuggle up   snuggles, snuggling, snuggled

snuggle up
to move into a warm and comfortable position • (usually + *adv/prep*) *She snuggled up on the sofa with a magazine and a cup of tea.* • (often + **to**) *He snuggled up to her during the film and put his arm round her.*

soak up   soaks, soaking, soaked

soak up sth or soak sth up
1 if a dry substance soaks up a liquid, it absorbs it • *Fry the aubergines until they soak up all the oil.* • *The dry ground quickly soaked up the rain.*
2 to enjoy the effects of an experience • *We arrived early at the pop festival to soak up the atmosphere.* • *I spent two weeks in*

*Greece **soaking up the sun**.* (= lying in the sun)

3 *informal* if something soaks up a supply of something [esp. money], it uses all or a lot of the supply ● *The repairs on our house soaked up all our savings.* ● *The festival has been criticized for soaking up too much public money.*

sober up   sobers, sobering, sobered

sober up (sb) or **sober** (sb) **up**
to become less drunk, or to make someone less drunk ● *I went for a walk to try to sober up.* ● *Here, have a black coffee – that should sober you up.*

sober up
to become calmer and more serious ● *He's sobered up a good deal since his wild teenage days.*

sock away   socks, socking, socked

sock away sth or **sock** sth **away**
American & Australian informal
to save money by putting it in a bank or by investing it ● *He's socked away hundreds of dollars in a savings account.*

sock in   socks, socking, socked

sock in sth/sb or **sock** sth/sb **in**
American
if bad weather socks in an airport or a person, the airport has to close or the person cannot travel because of the bad weather ● (usually passive) *Boston was socked in with fog and the plane had to land at Hartford.*

sock to   socks, socking, socked

sock it to sb
1 *informal* to hit someone hard ● *Go on, sock it to him!*
2 *informal* to do or say something in a way that has a strong effect ● *It's a powerful advertisement that really socks it to the public.*

sod off

Sod off! (always an order) *British & Australian slang*
something you say to tell someone that you are annoyed with them or that you want them to go away ● *"All right, gorgeous?" "Oh, sod off!"* ● *Next time he says something like that, tell him to sod off.*

soften up   softens, softening, softened

soften up sb or **soften** sb **up** *informal*
to do things that will please someone so that they will do what you want ● *She tried to soften him up with a nice meal before asking him for the job.*

soldier on   soldiers, soldiering, soldiered

soldier on
to continue doing something, although it is difficult or unpleasant ● *She had a cold and a high temperature but she knew she had to soldier on.* ● (sometimes + **with**) *He soldiered on with his job, long after he should have retired.*

sort out   sorts, sorting, sorted

sort out sth or **sort** sth **out**

1 to successfully deal with a problem or difficult situation ● *Initially we had some problems with our computer system but they've been sorted out now.* ● *She spent several days sorting out disagreements among the staff.*

2 to arrange or organize things which are untidy ● *My first task was to sort out a pile of papers.*
sort-out *n* [singular] *British informal* ● *This cupboard needs a really good sort-out.*

3 to separate one type of thing from a group of things ● *Sort out the books you want and put them on the table.* ● (sometimes + **from**) *You'll need to sort out the whites from the rest of the washing.*

4 to make a decision about something by discussing it with someone else or by considering it carefully ● (usually + question word) *We need to sort out what we're doing about accommodation.*

sort yourself **out** (always reflexive) *British & Australian informal*
to spend time dealing with your personal problems or organizing your things ● *He needs a bit of time to sort himself out before he even thinks about working.* ● *Just give me five minutes to sort myself out and I'll be with you.*

sort out sb or **sort** sb **out** *British slang*
to attack someone in order to punish them for behaving badly ● *Do that again, mate, and I'll sort you out!*

sound off   sounds, sounding, sounded

sound off informal
to express your opinions loudly, especially in order to complain about someone or something • (usually + **about**) *He's always sounding off about the way this place is run.*

sound out   sounds, sounding, sounded

sound out sb/sth or **sound** sb/sth **out**
to talk to someone in order to discover what they think about an idea or plan • (often + **about**) *I sounded her out about working for us but she wasn't interested.* • *We need to sound out his views on the project before we go ahead.*

soup up   soups, souping, souped

soup up sth or **soup** sth **up**
informal to improve something by making it more powerful or more interesting • *Circuit boards can be used to soup up existing machines.*
souped-up adj (always before noun) *informal* • *He patrols the nightclubs on a souped-up scooter.*

space out   spaces, spacing, spaced

space out sth or **space** sth **out**
to arrange things so that there is enough space or time between them • *The plants need to be spaced out evenly in the border.* • *The best way to take the tablets is to space them out throughout the day.*

space out American informal
to be unable to think clearly or be aware of what is happening around you • *The way he spaces out makes me think he's on drugs.*
spaced-out adj American informal • *I usually feel a bit spaced-out after a long flight.*

spark off   sparks, sparking, sparked

spark off sth or **spark** sth **off**
if something sparks off an activity [e.g. fighting, violence] or a state, it causes it to suddenly happen or exist • *The riot sparked off violence in the rest of the city.* • *A series of TV programmes sparked off a lot of interest in the subject.*

speak out   speaks, speaking, spoke, spoken

speak out
to publicly express your opinions, especially in order to criticize or oppose someone or something • (often + **against**) *He lost his job after he spoke out against his employers.* • *The Environment Secretary has spoken out in defence of the new policies.*
outspoken adj if someone is outspoken, they express their opinions even though other people might be offended by them • *She is an outspoken critic of the government.* • *He's quite outspoken in his views.*

speak up   speaks, speaking, spoke, spoken

speak up
1 to publicly express your opinions about something or someone, especially in order to support them • (usually + **for**) *She has often spoken up for the rights of working mothers.*
2 to begin to speak more loudly • (often + an order) *Speak up, Gemma, I can't hear what you're saying.*

speed up   speeds, speeding, speeded or sped

speed up (sth) or **speed** (sth) **up**
to happen or move more quickly, or to make something happen or move more quickly • *You can speed up the application process by faxing us your form.* • *One of the effects of the drug is to make your heart rate speed up.*

spell out   spells, spelling, spelled or spelt

spell out sth or **spell** sth **out**
1 to explain something in detail and in a clear way • *The document clearly spells out the correct procedure for dealing with complaints.* • (often + question word) *She never spelt out what the contract involved.*
2 to say or write the letters that form a particular word in their correct order • *We live on Lynton Road. Would you like me to spell that out for you?*

spew up   spews, spewing, spewed

spew up (sth) or **spew** (sth) **up** mainly British & Australian slang
to vomit • *I was spewing up all night after*

eating that curry.

spice up   spices, spicing, spiced

spice up sth or **spice** sth **up**

to make something more interesting or exciting ● (sometimes + **with**) *He'd spiced up his speech with a few rude jokes.* ● *There was an article in the paper about spicing up your sex life.*

spill out   spills, spilling, spilt or spilled

spill out

1 to flow or fall out of a container ● (often + **of**) *400,000 gallons of oil have spilled out of the pipeline.* ● *My suitcase had burst open while it was being unloaded and the contents spilt out.*

2 if people spill out of a place, large numbers of them come out of that place ● (often + **of**) *The wedding guests spilled out of the church onto the pavement.* ● (sometimes + **onto**) *He got to the pub just as everyone was spilling out onto the street.*

spill out (sth) or **spill** (sth) **out**

if you spill out an emotion or if emotion spills out, you express it, usually by talking in an uncontrolled way ● *He listened quietly as she spilled out all her anger and despair.*

spill over   spills, spilling, spilt or spilled

spill over (sth)

if the liquid in a container spills over, it flows over the edge of the container ● *That soup's going to spill over if you're not careful.*

spill over

if a bad situation or problem spills over, it begins to have an unpleasant effect on another situation or group of people ● (usually + **into**) *There was a growing concern that the war might spill over into the country's southern republic.* ● (sometimes + **to**) *The hostilities could spill over to minority groups in Britain.* **spillover** n [singular] ● *What we don't want to see is a spillover of the war.* ● (used as *adj*) *The bad weather in February and March could have a spillover effect on farmers in April.*

spin off   spins, spinning, spun

spin off sth or **spin** sth **off**

1 to produce a useful but unexpected result from an activity or piece of work in addition to the expected results ● *The American space program spun off a lot of new computer technology.*
spin-off n [C] ● *The development of the country's air transport system has had useful spin-offs for other service industries.* ● (used as *adj*) *One of the spin-off benefits from tourism in the region has been the creation of 200 jobs.*

2 to form a separate company from parts of an existing company ● *The company was spun off from the Asda superstore group last year.* ● *The bank is planning to spin off its investment-management division.*
spin-off n [C] ● *The research firm is a spin-off from a big drugs company.* ● (used as *adj*) *Two senior managers will run the new spin-off company.*

3 to create a new television show using characters from a successful show ● *The show attracts 15 million viewers a week and has spun off two other TV comedies.*
spin-off n [C] ● *He has been offered a part on the new 'Star Trek' spin-off.* ● (used as *adj*) *The show is so popular that a spin-off TV series has been planned.*

spin out   spins, spinning, spun

spin out sth or **spin** sth **out**

to make something continue for as long as possible ● *There's probably about three days work left so I'm trying to spin it out.*

spirit away   spirits, spiriting, spirited

spirit away sb/sth or **spirit** sb/sth **away**

to remove someone or something from a place quickly and secretly ● *He was spirited away by four police officers in the middle of the night.*

spit out   spits, spitting, spat   *(American pt & pp also* **spit***)*

spit out sth or **spit** sth **out**

1 to get rid of something in your mouth by blowing it out ● *I took a bite of the melon and then spat out the seeds.*

2 to say something in a very angry way ● *He spat the word out like a bullet.*

• *'Don't touch me!' she spat out, turning to face him.*

Spit it out! (always an order) *informal*
something you say to encourage someone to tell you something which they do not want to tell you • *Come on, spit it out! What are you trying to say?*

spit up   spits, spitting, spat or spit

spit up (sth) or **spit** (sth) **up** *American & Australian informal*
if someone, especially a baby, spits up, they vomit a small amount of a substance • *I was worried about the baby because she'd been spitting up her milk.*

splash down   splashes, splashing, splashed

splash down
if a space vehicle splashes down, it lands in the sea after a space flight • *They splashed down in the Pacific Ocean.*
splashdown *n* [C] • *The splashdown on July 19 marked the end of the series of Apollo flights.*

splash out   splashes, splashing, splashed

splash out *informal*
to spend a lot of money on something which is very pleasant but which you do not need • (often + **on**) *The wedding was cheaper than we expected so we splashed out on a honeymoon in the Caribbean.* • *I hadn't been to a restaurant for ages so I decided to splash out.*

split off   splits, splitting, split

split off (sth) or **split** (sth) **off**
if something splits off, or if someone splits something off, it becomes separated from something else • *Small pieces of rock split off as she touched the cave walls.* • *The company has announced plans to split off its chemicals division.*

split off
to stop belonging to a particular group or political party and form a separate one • (often + **from**) *The Renaissance Party is the latest group to split off from the ruling party.* • *Several disillusioned members split off to form a new party.*

split on   splits, splitting, split

split on sb *British & Australian informal*
to tell a person in authority about some-

one who has done something wrong • *Don't split on me, will you?*

split up   splits, splitting, split

split up (sth) or **split** (sth) **up**
to divide into smaller parts or groups, or to divide something into smaller parts or groups • (often + **into**) *The class was too big so we split up into two smaller groups.* • *The railway network was split up in preparation for privatization.*

split up
if two people who are married or who have a romantic relationship split up, they end their marriage or relationship • *My parents split up when I was seven.* • (sometimes + **with**) *She'd just split up with her boyfriend and was feeling a bit low.*

spoil for

be spoiling for sth (always in continuous tenses)
if someone is spoiling for trouble or a fight, they are very eager to have an argument or fight • *Coming home drunk like that was just spoiling for trouble, wasn't it?* • *You're spoiling for a fight, you are, speaking to me like that!*

sponge down   sponges, sponging, sponged

sponge down sth or **sponge** sth **down**
to clean something by rubbing it with a wet sponge (= soft substance full of holes) • *That stain should disappear if you sponge it down with a little detergent.*

sponge off/on   sponges, sponging, sponged

sponge off/on sb *informal*
to get money from someone without intending to pay it back or without doing anything for them • *He's always sponging off his mates.* • *She was going on about people sponging on the state.*

spoon out   spoons, spooning, spooned

spoon out sth or **spoon** sth **out**
to put an amount of food onto a plate or dish using a spoon • *Do you want to help yourselves to potato or shall I just spoon it out?*

spout off   spouts, spouting, spouted

spout off *informal*

to talk about something in a boring or annoying way without really thinking about what you are saying • *She doesn't know anything about football, so I don't know why she was spouting off like that.*

sprawl out   sprawls, sprawling, sprawled

sprawl out

to sit or lie with your arms and legs spread out in a relaxed way • *He sprawled out on the sofa next to me.*

spread out   spreads, spreading, spread

spread out

1 if a group of people spread out, they move away from each other so that there is a wide space between them • *We spread out and began to search through the woods.* • *If you spread out more, you won't get in each other's way.*

2 (never in continuous tenses) if a town or city spreads out, it covers a large area • *The city centre is quite small but the suburbs spread out for miles.*

be spread out (always passive)

1 if people or things are spread out, they are in different parts of a large area and are not close together • (usually + *adv/prep*) *Most of Canada's population is spread out along its border with the United States.* • *Our offices are spread out over a very wide area.*

2 (always + *adv/prep*) if a view of something is spread out below you or in front of you, you can see all of it clearly • *We stood at the top of the hill and gazed at the valley spread out below us.*

spread out (sth) or **spread** (sth) **out**

to gradually cover a large area, or to make something cover a large area • (often + **over**) *The oil spread out over the surface of the water.* • *He spread the straw out so that it covered the stable floor.*

spread out sth or **spread** sth **out**

1 to open something that is folded [e.g. map, towel] and put it down flat on a surface • *He spread the map out and showed me where the village was situated.* • (often + **on**) *She spread out her towel on the sand and lay down.*

2 to arrange a group of things on a surface so that each one can be seen clearly • *She*

spread out her photos on the table so that everyone could see them.

3 if you spread out your arms, legs, or fingers, you stretch them so that there are wide spaces between them • *He pushed back his chair and spread out his legs.*

4 to arrange for something to happen in stages during a period of time • (usually + **over**) *The job losses will be spread out over the next year.* • *You can spread the payments out over a period of time if you prefer.*

spread over   spreads, spreading, spread

spread sth **over** sth

to arrange for something to happen in stages during a period of time • *I've spread the loan repayments over two years.* • *The museum has been promised a £2 million grant which will be spread over ten years.*

spring back   springs, springing, sprang, sprung   (*American & Australian pt also* sprung)

spring back

if something that has been pressed down springs back, it quickly goes back to its original position, shape, or size • *As she brushed her hair, her curls sprang back into place.* • *If the cake is cooked properly, it will spring back when you press it with your finger.*

spring for   springs, springing, sprang, sprung   (*American & Australian pt also* sprung)

spring for sth *American informal*

to pay for food or drink for other people • *Let me spring for the drinks.*

spring from   springs, springing, sprang, sprung   (*American & Australian pt also* sprung)

spring from sth

to be caused by something • *His desperate need to be liked springs from a deep sense of insecurity.*

spring from swh (always used in questions) *informal*

if you ask where someone or something has sprung from, you mean you are surprised because they have appeared very suddenly • *Where did you spring from? I didn't hear anyone come in.* • *Where have all these posters sprung from?*

spring on   springs, springing, sprang, sprung   (*American & Australian pt* also sprung)

spring sth on sb
to tell someone some news that surprises them • *I hope he's not going to spring any unpleasant surprises on us in the meeting.*

spring up   springs, springing, sprang, sprung   (*American & Australian pt* also sprung)

spring up
if something springs up, it suddenly appears or begins to exist • *Thousands of new businesses have sprung up in the past few years.* • *New, open markets have sprung up on the outskirts of the city.*

sprout up   sprouts, sprouting, sprouted
sprout up
if a large number of things sprout up, they suddenly appear or begin to exist • *New office buildings seem to be sprouting up all over the city.*

spruce up   spruces, sprucing, spruced
spruce up sb/sth or spruce sb/sth up
to make someone or something look more attractive by cleaning and tidying them • (often reflexive) *I'd just like to spruce myself up a bit before we go out.* • *They've spent thousands of pounds sprucing up the town centre.*

spur on   spurs, spurring, spurred
spur on sb or spur sb on
to encourage someone to try harder in order to achieve something • *Spurred on by the crowd, Coventry scored two goals in the first 30 minutes.* • (sometimes + to) *One success should spur him on to even greater achievements.* • (sometimes + do sth) *You lose a bit of weight and it spurs you on to lose even more.*

spurt out   spurts, spurting, spurted
spurt out
if liquid spurts out, it flows suddenly in a fast stream • *The blood spurted out.*

• (often + of) *Water was spurting out of a pipe.*

spy on/upon   spies, spying, spied
spy on/upon sb/sth
to watch someone or something secretly in order to discover information about them • *I think my neighbours have been spying on me.* • *He was arrested for spying on American air bases.*

square away   squares, squaring, squared
square away (sth) or square (sth) away *American*
to finish dealing with something • *She'll join us after she's squared away the arrangements for tomorrow's meeting.*

square off   squares, squaring, squared
square off *American*
to prepare to fight, compete, or argue with someone • *Sampras and Becker will square off next Saturday in the final.* • (sometimes + against) *The police squared off against a crowd armed with bricks and bottles.*

square up   squares, squaring, squared
square up
1 *British & Australian* to prepare to fight, compete, or argue with someone • (often + to) *A group of police officers and a crowd of youths were squaring up to each other.* • (often + for) *Europe and the United States squared up for another dispute over trade restrictions.*
2 *informal* to pay someone the money you owe them • *Do you want to square up now?* • (often + with) *If you pay for the meal, I'll square up with you later.*

square up to   squares, squaring, squared
square up to sth *British & Australian informal*
to accept that you must deal with a problem or accept a responsibility • *He needs to square up to his responsibilities.* • *The first thing the new government must do is to square up to its economic problems.*

square with   squares, squaring, squared
square (sth) with sth
to match, or to accept as being able to exist together • (usually negative) *The problem is that her story doesn't square*

with the evidence. • These recent revelations don't quite square with the image of him that's promoted in the press. • I don't think I could spend that much money on a piece of clothing – I couldn't **square it with my conscience**.

square sth **with** sb *informal*
to get permission from someone to do something • *If I take a day off I'll usually square it with my boss first.*

squash in/into squashes, squashing, squashed

squash in (sb) or **squash** (sb) **in**

squash (sb) **into** sth
to manage to get yourself or someone else into a very small space or place that is full of people • *If we all move up a bit, Polly can squash in.* • *Four of us squashed into the back seat of the car.* • *We can probably squash you in at the back.*

squash up squashes, squashing, squashed

squash up
if people who are sitting or standing together squash up, they move closer together in order to make space for someone else • *If we all squash up, there'll be room for Christine.*

squeak by squeaks, squeaking, squeaked

squeak by *American informal*
to manage with a lot of difficulty to achieve something or get a successful result • (sometimes + **with**) *Canada barely squeaked by with a 4-3 victory over Sweden.*

squeal on squeals, squealing, squealed

squeal on sb *slang*
to tell someone in authority about someone who has done something wrong • *Someone must have squealed on McGraw because the police arrested him that morning.*

squeeze in/into squeezes, squeezing, squeezed

squeeze in sth/sb or **squeeze** sth/sb **in**

squeeze sth/sb **into** sth
to manage to do something or see someone when you are very busy and do not have much time available • *I think we can squeeze in a quick drink before we go.* • *I was hoping the doctor might be able to squeeze me in this morning.* • *You seemed to squeeze a lot of sightseeing into your trip.*

squeeze out squeezes, squeezing, squeezed

squeeze out sth/sb or **squeeze** sth/sb **out**
to prevent something from being part of a system or organization, or to prevent someone from continuing with an activity • *The new ten-subject curriculum in schools means that subjects like art and Latin will be squeezed out.* • (often + **of**) *By lowering its prices, the airline hopes to squeeze smaller firms out of the market.*

squeeze out of squeezes, squeezing, squeezed

squeeze sth **out of** sb
to persuade or force someone to give you money or information • *The museum directors have managed to squeeze an extra £200,000 a year out of the arts council.* • *After several hours of questioning, the police finally squeezed a confession out of him.*

squirrel away squirrels, squirrelling, squirrelled *(American & Australian also squirreling, squirreled)*

squirrel away sth or **squirrel** sth **away** *mainly American*
to put something [esp. money] in a secret place so that you can use it later • *He's busy squirreling money away for his retirement.* • *She'd squirreled away the chocolates to eat later.*

stack up stacks, stacking, stacked

stack up sth or **stack** sth **up**
to arrange things in a tall pile • *If you stack the dishes up by the sink, I'll do them later.* • *She stacked up a pile of logs by the garage wall.*

stack up (sth) or **stack** (sth) **up** *mainly American*
if something stacks up, or if you stack it up, you gradually get more of it • *Every time you fly, you stack up points for free flights.* • *More and more problems are stacking up for the event organizers.*

stack up

1 if aircraft stack up, they fly over an air-port at different heights waiting to be told they can land • *Storms were causing the planes to stack up over Kennedy airport.*

2 (always + *adv/prep*) *American & Australian informal* if you describe how someone or something stacks up, you say if they are better or worse than someone or something else • (usually + **against**) *Our new car doesn't stack up against* (= is not as good as) *our old one.*

stake on   stakes, staking, staked

stake sth **on** sth/doing sth

to risk losing money or harming something important [e.g. reputation] if a plan does not succeed • *The president has staked his reputation on persuading his party to support the bill.* • *They'll never agree to compromise over this issue. **I'd stake my life on it.*** (= I am certain that this is true)

stake out   stakes, staking, staked

stake out sth or **stake** sth **out**

1 to mark the position of a piece of land or an area in order to show that you own it or that you are going to use it • *Many of the early settlers were involved in disputes as they staked out their territory.* • *We arrived early at the concert and staked out a place at the front.*

2 to state your opinion clearly and publicly • *Both parties are currently staking out their positions on the issue.*

3 *mainly American & Australian* if the police or reporters stake out a building where someone is living or hiding, they watch the building continuously in order to see who is leaving or entering it • *The police have staked out the apartment where the two terrorists are hiding.*

stakeout *n* [C] *mainly American & Australian* • *The incident occurred while police were on a stakeout of the suspect's house.*

stake to   stakes, staking, staked

stake sb **to** sth *American*

to give someone something they need • *Her father staked her to a loan so she could buy the house.*

stall off   stalls, stalling, stalled

stall off sb or **stall** sb **off** *American & Australian*

to prevent someone from doing something or going somewhere for a short time so that you have enough time to do something • *The thief broke into the office while his accomplice stalled off the security guard.*

stamp on   stamps, stamping, stamped

stamp on sth

to use force to get rid of something that you disapprove of • *The ruling party has stamped on all attempts at opposition.*

stamp out   stamps, stamping, stamped

stamp out sth or **stamp** sth **out**

to get rid of something that is considered wrong or harmful • *The government has brought in new laws to stamp out child prostitution.* • *A new campaign has been launched to stamp out malaria in the region.*

stand about/around/round   stands, standing, stood

stand about/around/round

to spend time standing in a place waiting for someone or doing very little • *We stood about in the cold for half an hour before we were allowed in.* • (often + doing sth) *After the lecture, we stood around chatting and drinking coffee.*

stand aside   stands, standing, stood

stand aside

1 to leave a job or position so that someone else can do it instead • *It's time he stood aside and let his son take over the company.*

2 to decide not to become involved in a difficult or dangerous situation • *If there is a war in the region, the neighbouring countries cannot afford to stand aside.*

stand back   stands, standing, stood

stand back

1 to move a short distance away from something or someone • *Stand well back while we light the fire.* • (sometimes + **from**) *I stood back from the painting so I could see all the details.*

2 to try to understand a situation or solve a problem by considering it in a way in

which someone who is not involved in it would consider it ● *We need to stand back and analyse where our research is going wrong.* ● *Being unemployed gave me the chance to stand back and think about my life.*

stand by   stands, standing, stood

stand by

1 to wait and be ready to do something or to help ● *Police in riot gear were standing by in case the demonstration got out of control.* ● (sometimes + **for**) *The pilot told the cabin crew to stand by for takeoff.*

  standby *n* (C/U) a person or thing that can be used if someone or something else is not available or cannot be used ● *Board games are a good standby to keep the children amused if the weather is bad.* ● *It is not yet known if there are any casualties, but hospitals in the area are on standby.* (= they are ready to deal with any injured people) ● (used as *adj*) *We have two standby generators in case of a power cut.*

  standby *n* [C] a cheap ticket for a flight or performance which is sold just before the flight or performance if there are any seats available ● *I got a standby and flew to New York for only $80.* ● (used as *adj*) *Standby tickets are available on the day of the performance from 6 pm.*

2 to do nothing to prevent something unpleasant from happening ● *How long can the world stand by and watch these atrocities?* ● *We cannot stand idly by while the environment is being destroyed.*

  bystander *n* [C] a person who sees something happening but who is not involved in it ● *Many innocent bystanders were injured in the explosion.*

stand by sb

  to continue to support or help someone when they are in a difficult situation ● *She has vowed to stand by her husband who has just been jailed for assault.* ● *He promised to stand by her if she decided to have the baby.*

stand by sth

  if you stand by an agreement or decision, you do what you have agreed or decided to do, or if you stand by something you have said, you continue to believe it is true ● *They are standing by their agreement to lower prices.* ● *I stand by what I*

said earlier: *patients need to be told about the risks associated with the drug.*

stand down   stands, standing, stood

stand down

1 *British & Australian* to leave an important job or official position so that someone else can do it instead ● *The Conservative MP announced that he would be standing down at the next election.* ● (sometimes + **as**) *She has decided to stand down as festival director.*

2 if a person who has been asked questions during a trial stands down, they leave the special place in court where they have been standing ● *The judge told the witness to stand down after she had been cross-examined.*

stand for   stands, standing, stood

stand for sth

1 (never in continuous tenses) if a letter stands for a word or name, it is the first letter of that word or name and it is used to represent it ● *UFO stands for unidentified flying object.* ● *The initials TH stand for Trinity House.*

2 if a group of people stand for a set of ideas, they support those ideas, or if something stands for a particular idea, it represents that idea ● *The party stands for low taxes and the private ownership of industries.* ● *The United States is often thought to stand for freedom of speech.*

3 to accept a situation or someone's behaviour without complaining or without trying to change it ● (usually negative) *I won't stand for this kind of behaviour in my house!*

4 *British & Australian* to compete in an election for an official position, or to try to be elected as a member of an organization [e.g. parliament] ● *He stood for mayor in the 1995 local elections.* ● *She's decided to stand for Parliament in the next election.*

stand in   stands, standing, stood

stand in

  mainly British & Australian to do someone else's job for a short period of time, or to take someone else's place at an event, because that person cannot be there ● (often + **for**) *The Foreign Secretary will be standing in for the Prime Minister at* *the funeral.* • *I can't come to the meeting, but one of my colleagues will be able to stand in.*

stand-in n [C] • (sometimes + **for**) *He was a regular stand-in for Terry Wogan before he was given his own chat show.*

stand off   stands, standing, stood

stand off sb (never passive)
American to stop someone who might attack or harm you from coming near you • *They armed themselves with clubs and knives to stand off any intruders.*

standoff n [C] *mainly American & Australian* an argument or fight in which no agreement is reached or in which neither side can get an advantage • *Many people feared the standoff between demonstrators and the police could turn violent.* • *The two countries have been locked in a diplomatic standoff.*

stand out   stands, standing, stood

stand out
1 to be much better than other similar things or people • (sometimes + **among**) *Two books stand out among the dozens recently published on the Royal Family.* • (sometimes + **from**) *We had a lot of good applicants for the job, but one stood out from the rest.*

outstanding adj extremely good, or of a very high standard • *She is a truly outstanding athlete.* • *He won an Oscar for his outstanding performance as a man dying of AIDS.*

standout n [C] *American* a person or thing that is much better than similar people or things • *Ann Stamford, as the detective investigating the murder, is a standout in a fine cast.* • *While all the desserts are good, the apple pie is the clear standout.*

2 if someone or something stands out, they are very noticeable because they look different or behave differently from other people or things • *Children are often anxious not to stand out.* • (sometimes + **against**) *The gold lettering stands out against the black background.* • *He likes to stand out from the crowd.* (= look different to most people)

stand out against   stands, standing, stood

stand out against sth *mainly British & Australian*
to strongly oppose a plan or idea that a lot of other people support • *He was one of the few politicians who stood out against the war.*

stand over   stands, standing, stood

stand over sb
to stand close to someone in order to watch what they are doing • *His mother stood over him while he finished his homework.*

stand round
see **stand about/around/round**

stand up   stands, standing, stood

stand up
1 to rise from a sitting or lying position to a standing position • *I stood up to greet her.*

stand-up adj (always before noun) a stand-up comedian is a person who tells jokes as a performance • *The film stars Robin Williams, one of America's best stand-up comedians.* • *She won an award for stand-up comedy at the Edinburgh Festival.*

2 if an idea or claim stands up, it is proved to be correct when it is examined carefully • (often + **to**) *This theory may not stand up to close investigation.* • *Do you think the evidence against him will stand up in court?* (= be accepted as correct in a court of law)

stand up sb or **stand** sb **up** *informal*
to fail to meet someone on purpose, especially someone with whom you were starting to have a romantic relationship • *I waited for an hour outside the cinema before I realised I'd been stood up.* • *There's nothing worse than being stood up.*

stand up for   stands, standing, stood

stand up for sth/sb
to defend something that you believe is important [e.g. principle, right], or to defend a person who is being criticized • *She always stands up for what she believes in.* • *The Prime Minister has promised to stand up for British interests abroad.* • (often reflexive) *You've got to*

stand up for yourself if you want people to respect you.

stand up to   stands, standing, stood

stand up to sb

if you stand up to a powerful person or organization, you state your opinions forcefully and refuse to agree with them or do what they want • *He was not afraid to stand up to his superiors if they had a difference of opinion.* • *She has been criticized for failing to stand up to the powerful right-wing of the party.*

stand up to sth

to be strong enough not to be damaged by something • *We need a carpet that will stand up to everyday use.* • *This type of plant stands up to the most severe winter weather.*

stare down/out   stares, staring, stared

stare down sb or **stare** sb **down** American

stare out sb or **stare** sb **out** British & Australian

to look into someone's eyes for a long time until they look away in embarrassment • *Callahan stared him out and he lowered his head in embarrassment.*

start off   starts, starting, started

start off (sth) or **start** (sth) **off**

to start happening, or to make something start happening • (often + **with**) *She started off the meeting with a report on the sales conference.* • *I'm going to start off by saying thank you all for coming here this evening.*

start off (always + adv/prep)

1 to start a life, existence, or profession in a particular way • (often + **as**) *He started off as a door-to-door salesman and look where he is now.* • *It started off as a bit of joke but then people started taking it seriously.*

2 to start a journey • (usually + adv/prep) *We started off down the road and I suddenly remembered that we'd forgotten Michael's book.*

start sb **off**

1 to help someone to start an activity, especially a piece of work • (often + **on**) *I'll start her off on some fairly basic stuff and see how she gets on.*

2 to make someone start to laugh, cry, or talk about something that they often talk about • *I could see Paul trying not to laugh and of course that started me off.* • (often + doing sth) *I didn't want to start her off crying again.*

start on   starts, starting, started

start on sth

to start to deal with something, or to start to use something • *I'm just about to start on the cleaning.* • *Shall we start on the wine or wait till Colin gets here?*

start on sb

to start complaining angrily to someone about something that they have done • *She went on and on to Andrew about how badly he'd behaved and then she started on Stewart.*

start on at   starts, starting, started

start on at sb

to start complaining angrily to someone about something that they have done • *She started on at him about the way that he's always looking at other women.*

start out   starts, starting, started

start out

to start a life, existence, or profession in a particular way • (often + **as**) *He started out as a teacher and only began writing in his thirties.* • *What started out as a part-time job became a full-time occupation.*

start out to do sth

to intend to do something from the start • *We didn't start out to build our own house – it just happened that way.*

start over   starts, starting, started

start over American

to start doing something again from the beginning because you did not do it well the first time • *This is just full of errors – I'm going to have to start over.*

start up   starts, starting, started

start up (sth) or **start** (sth) **up**

1 if a business or other organization starts up, or if someone starts one up, it is created and starts to operate • *Many small businesses started up in the 1980's to cater to this growing market.* • *We ought to start up a drama group.* • *We're starting up a number of projects early next year.*

start-up *adj* (always before noun) • *He founded the company with a start-up loan of $20,000 from the bank.*

start-up *n* [C] • (usually singular) *After its successful start-up, the company immediately began looking for ways to expand.*

2 if a vehicle or engine starts up, or if someone starts it up, it starts to work • *The car wouldn't start up this morning.* • *He looked in his mirror and started up the engine.*

3 if a sound or activity starts up, or if someone starts it up, it starts to happen • *The music had started up again.*

start up

1 to sit up or stand up suddenly because you are surprised • *When he saw me, he started up and looked highly embarrassed.*

2 (always + *adv/prep*) to begin to work or to manage a business • (usually + **in**) *He started up in business at the age of twenty-five.*

starve for

be starving for sth (always in continuous tenses) *American*
if you are starving for something that you want or need, you have not had it for a long time • *I'd been on my own all week and was starving for conversation.*

be starved for sth (always passive) *American & Australian*
if you are starved for something that you want or need, you have not had it for a long time • *I feel I've been starved for affection all these years.*

starve into   starves, starving, starved

starve sb **into** sth
to force someone to do what you want by not giving them any food or money until they do it • *Basically, they were starved into submission by the government* (= forced to do what the government wanted because they were given no money)

starve of   starves, starving, starved

starve sb **of** sth *British & Australian*
to not let someone have something that they want or need for a long time • (usually passive) *I feel I've been starved of your company.*

starve out   starves, starving, starved

starve out sb or **starve** sb **out**
to force people to leave a place by not letting them have any food • *Crops have been burned to starve out the rebels.*

stash away   stashes, stashing, stashed

stash away sth or **stash** sth **away**
slightly informal
to store something, especially money, in a safe or secret place • *He's got plenty of money stashed away in foreign bank accounts.*

stave off   staves, staving, staved

stave off sth or **stave** sth **off**
to stop something bad from happening or to try to make something bad happen later • *Here, have a sandwich – that should stave off the hunger.* • *They tried desperately to raise cash to stave off bankruptcy.*

stay ahead   stays, staying, stayed

stay ahead
to continue to be more advanced and successful than other people • (often + **of**) *We are always looking for new ways to stay ahead of our competitors.*

stay away   stays, staying, stayed

stay away
to not go to a place • (often + **from**) *People are staying away from the beaches because of the oil pollution.* • *He had been warned to stay away.*

stay away from   stays, staying, stayed

stay away from sth
to avoid something that has a bad effect on you • *I think he should stay away from drugs of any sort.*

stay behind   stays, staying, stayed

stay behind
to not leave a place when other people leave it • *I stayed behind to ask the teacher a couple of questions.*

stay down   stays, staying, stayed

stay down
if something that you eat when you are ill stays down, you can eat it without vomiting • *I've been feeding him dry toast because it's the only thing that stays down.*

stay in   stays, staying, stayed

stay in

to remain at home, especially in the evening • *I think I'm going to stay in tonight and have a quiet one.*

stay off   stays, staying, stayed

stay off (sth) *British & Australian*

to not go to work or school, usually because you are ill • *If I feel like this tomorrow I'll stay off.*

stay off sth

to not eat, drink or use something that can harm you [e.g. cigarettes, alcohol] • *I think I'm going to stay off the drink for a couple of weeks.*

stay on   stays, staying, stayed

stay on

1 to stay in a place longer than you planned or after other people have left it • *Susie flew back on the Monday but I stayed on for a couple of days.* • *They stayed on after India became independent.*

2 *British & Australian* to continue to study at school or university in order to get a higher qualification • *You can leave school at sixteen or stay on and take the exams that are required for university.*

3 to continue working in your job • *She had intended to retire, but her boss persuaded her to stay on for another year.*

stay out   stays, staying, stayed

stay out

1 to not come home at night, or to come home late • *I've got to be up early in the morning so I don't want to stay out too late.*

2 if workers who are on strike (= not working because of an argument with their employer) stay out, they continue to refuse to work • *The miners are prepared to stay out until their demands are met.*

stay out of   stays, staying, stayed

stay out of sth

to not become involved in a discussion or an argument • *It's really for Julia and Mark to sort out – I'd stay out of it if I were you.*

stay over   stays, staying, stayed

stay over

to spend the night somewhere instead of returning to your home or continuing your journey • *We've got an extra room so you can stay over any time.*

stay up   stays, staying, stayed

stay up

to go to bed later than usual • *Rosie was allowed to stay up till eleven o'clock.* • (often + to do sth) *We stayed up late to watch the Olympics on television.*

steady on

Steady on! (always an order) *British & Australian*

something that you say in order to tell someone that you think what they are saying is too extreme • *Steady on, Mike! That's rather strong language to use in the presence of ladies!*

steal away   steals, stealing, stole, stolen

steal away

to leave a place quietly without anyone knowing • *I waited till nobody was looking and stole away.*

steal over   steals, stealing, stole, stolen

steal over sb *literary*

if a feeling or emotion steals over someone, they gradually feel it • *I was tired, but a dreamy contentment stole over me.*

steal up   steals, stealing, stole, stolen

steal up (always + *adv/prep*)

to move quietly and secretly towards someone or something • (often + **on**) *She stole up on him when he wasn't looking.*

steam up   steams, steaming, steamed

steam up (sth) or **steam** (sth) **up**
  if a glass surface steams up, or if something steams it up, it becomes covered with very small drops of water ● *The bathroom mirror steamed up when I ran the hot water.*

steep in

be steeped in sth (always passive)
  to have a lot of a particular quality [e.g. history, tradition] ● *The city of York is steeped in Roman history.* ● *Italian cuisine is steeped in tradition.*

stem from   stems, stemming, stemmed

stem from sth
  if a problem or difficult situation stems from something, it is caused by it ● *Most of her problems stem from the difficult childhood she had.*

step aside   steps, stepping, stepped

step aside
  to leave your job or position, especially so that someone else can do it ● *I think they're hoping that he'll step aside so that a younger man can take over.*

step back   steps, stepping, stepped

step back
  to try to think about a situation in a new way, often by not being involved in it for a short time ● (often + **from**) *I think he should just step back from the whole situation for a while and think things over.*

step down   steps, stepping, stepped

step down
  to leave your job, especially so that someone else can do it ● (often + **as**) *Richardson is to step down as chairman of the company.* ● (often + **from**) *He has agreed to step down from his post as club manager.*

step down sth or **step** sth **down**
  to reduce the amount or rate of something ● (usually passive) *Production of this model of car is being stepped down.*

step forward   steps, stepping, stepped

step forward
  to offer to help ● (often + to do sth) *One by one, survivors have been stepping forward to talk about the tragedy.*

step in   steps, stepping, stepped

step in
  to get involved in an argument or a difficult situation, in order to try to stop it or to deal with it ● *I try not to step in and sort out the kids' arguments but sometimes I just have to.* ● (often + to do sth) *A Japanese bank stepped in to provide financial support for the project.*

step on

step on it! (always an order) *informal*
  something that you say to someone, especially someone who is driving, when you want them to hurry ● *Step on it, would you Les, we're already late.*

step out   steps, stepping, stepped

step out
1 to leave a place for a short period of time ● *Beth just stepped out for a few minutes – I'll get her to call you back.*
2 *British & Australian old-fashioned* to walk very quickly in an energetic way ● *If we step out we'll be able to catch up with the others.*

step out on   steps, stepping, stepped

step out on sb *American informal*
  to behave in a dishonest way towards your husband, wife, or usual sexual partner by having a sexual relationship with someone else ● *I don't know why she puts up with him, he's always stepping out on her.*

step up   steps, stepping, stepped

step up sth or **step** sth **up**
  to do more of an activity or to increase the speed of a process, usually in order to improve a situation ● *Security at the airport has been stepped up since the bomb scare.* ● *The police have stepped up their efforts to try to recover the stolen items.*

stick around   sticks, sticking, stuck

stick around *informal*
  to stay somewhere for a period of time ● *I'll stick around here a bit longer and see if Simon turns up.* ● *I didn't know what he wanted but I wasn't going to stick around to find out.*

stick at   sticks, sticking, stuck

stick at sth
  to continue to work hard at something

even though it is difficult or tiring ● *If you're going to learn to play a musical instrument you really have to stick at it.* ● *She never stuck at one job for more than a couple of months.*

stick by   sticks, sticking, stuck

stick by sb
to continue to support someone when they are having problems ● *I'll stick by you whatever happens.* ● *He's my husband and I'll **stick by him through thick and thin**.* (= whatever the situation)

stick by sth
to continue to support or use a decision, opinion, or plan ● *The government intends to stick by its planned cuts, despite criticisms.* ● *I'll stick by what I said.*

stick down   sticks, sticking, stuck

stick down sth or **stick** sth **down**
1 to fix two flat surfaces together by using glue etc. ● *The cover on that book was coming off so I stuck it down.*
2 to quickly write or draw something on a piece of paper ● *Could you stick my name down on the list?* ● *I was bored of filling in forms so I just stuck anything down.*

stick on

be stuck on sth (always passive) *informal*
to like an idea so much that you do not want to change it ● *Tony didn't want a traditional wedding but Sharon was stuck on the idea.*

be stuck on sb (always passive) *American & Australian informal*
to be very attracted to someone ● *She's really stuck on some guy in the office.*

stick out   sticks, sticking, stuck

stick out
1 if part of something sticks out, it comes out beyond the edge or surface of something ● *She'd be so pretty if her teeth didn't stick out.* ● (often + **of**) *A bright, spotted handkerchief was sticking out of his jacket pocket* ● (often + **from**) *I could see Bill's legs sticking out from underneath the car.*
2 if a quality or characteristic of someone or something sticks out, it is very easy to notice ● *She's new to the job and it really sticks out.* ● *She really hates Will and it **sticks out a mile**.* (= it is very obvious) ● *Andy and I dressed up for the party but*

*we **stuck out like a sore thumb**.* (= we looked very different to everyone else)

stick out sth or **stick** sth **out**
1 to push part of your body forward or out from the rest of your body ● *She sticks her bottom out when she walks.* ● *This little kid stuck his tongue out at me.* (= he showed me his tongue in order to be rude)
2 to continue doing something until you have completed it, even though it is unpleasant ● *I'm not sure if I can stick this job out for much longer.* ● *It's a tough course but if you can stick it out, the qualification is well worth having*

stick out for   sticks, sticking, stuck

stick out for sth *British & Australian*
to continue to demand a particular amount of money and refuse to accept less ● *The unions have said that they are going to stick out for a 10% pay rise.*

stick to   sticks, sticking, stuck

stick to sth
to limit yourself to doing or using one particular thing and not change to anything else ● *I'm sticking to my original plan.* ● *The others were all drinking champagne but I stuck to orange juice.* ● *Could you stick to the point please?* (= only talk about what you are supposed to talk about)

stick it to sb *American informal*
to treat someone unfairly ● *They really stick it to you when they realise you're a foreigner.*

stick together   sticks, sticking, stuck

stick together *informal*
if two or more people stick together, they support each other, especially when they are in a difficult situation ● *No family can stick together under the strain of so many pressures.* ● *We women have to stick together.*

stick up   sticks, sticking, stuck

stick up
if part of something sticks up, it comes up above the surface of something, or it points upwards ● *I can't go out with my hair sticking up like this.* ● *You see that branch sticking up out of the water?*

stick up for

320

stick up sb/sth or **stick** sb/sth **up**
American & Australian informal
to steal from a place or person, using a gun as a threat • *Those guys who stuck up the drugstore were on the news last night.*
stick-up n [C] *American & Australian informal* • *There was a stick-up at the post office last week.*

stick up for   sticks, sticking, stuck

stick up for sb *informal*
to defend a person when they are being criticized • *Why do you always feel you have to stick up for him?* • (often reflexive) *She certainly knows how to stick up for herself.*

stick up for sth *informal*
to defend or fight for something important [e.g. rights] • *You've got to stick up for your rights.*

stick with   sticks, sticking, stuck

stick with sth *informal*
to do or use something as you had planned and not change to something else • *I think we'd better stick with our original plan.*

stick with sb *informal*
1 to stay close to someone • (usually an order) *Stick with me and you won't get lost.*
2 if something that someone says sticks with you, you remember it • *One piece of advice she gave me has stuck with me ever since.*

stick with it *informal*
to continue doing something even though it is difficult • *I know it's hard but stick with it and you'll get there in the end.*

sting for   stings, stinging, stung

sting sb **for** sth
1 *informal* to charge someone too much money for something • *I could go overdrawn but the bank would sting me for charges.*
2 *British & Australian informal* to borrow a small amount of money from someone • *I'm going to have to sting you for a couple of quid.*

stink out/up   stinks, stinking, stank, stunk

stink out sth or **stink** sth **out** *British & Australian informal*

stink up sth or **stink** sth **up** *American informal*
to fill a room with a very unpleasant smell • *I'd better get my running shoes out of here before they stink the place out.*

stir in/into   stirs, stirring, stirred

stir in sth or **stir** sth **in**

stir sth **into** sth
to mix one substance into another by moving the substance round, usually with a spoon • *Remove the sauce from the heat and stir in the cream.* • *Gently stir the egg yolks into the mixture and leave to cool.*

stir up   stirs, stirring, stirred

stir up sth or **stir** sth **up**
1 to cause arguments or bad feeling between people, usually on purpose • *I think she just likes stirring up trouble.* • *He was accused of stirring up racial tensions.* • *She's trying to stir things up between you because she's jealous of your relationship.*
2 if something stirs up memories, it makes you remember events in the past, usually ones that make you feel sad • *Going back to South Africa had stirred up some painful memories for him.*
3 to make something [e.g. dust, sand] rise and move around in the air or water • *Our feet had stirred up a cloud of dust.*

stir up sb or **stir** sb **up**
to try to make a group of people feel angry • *He was regarded by the government as someone who might stir up the underclass.*

stitch up   stitches, stitching, stitched

stitch up sth or **stitch** sth **up**
1 to stitch together the two parts of something that have come apart • *It took ten minutes for the nurse to stitch up my finger.*
2 to complete a business agreement • (usually passive) *I reckon we'll get the deal stitched up by lunch time.*

stitch up sb or **stitch** sb **up** *British informal*
1 to make someone seem guilty of a crime when they are not, usually by giving false information • *He claims he was stitched up by the police.*
stitch-up *n* [C] *British informal* • (usually singular) *He still maintains that he's innocent and that the whole affair was a stitch-up.*
2 to cheat someone, usually by taking money from them • (usually passive) *You shouldn't have paid fifty quid for that, mate – you've been stitched up.*

stock up stocks, stocking, stocked
stock up
to buy a lot of something, often food or drink • (often + **on**) *We'd better stock up on food for the holidays.* • (often + **with**) *I usually stock up with alcohol in the duty-free shop at the airport.*

stoke up stokes, stoking, stoked
stoke up sth or **stoke** sth **up**
1 to make a fire burn better by adding more fuel or by moving it around with a stick • *I'll just stoke up the fire and get this room a bit warmer.*
2 if someone stokes up bad feelings, they encourage a lot of people to feel them • *He's been accused of stoking up old hostilities between the nations.*

stoop to stoops, stooping, stooped
stoop to sth/doing sth
to do something even though you know it is wrong, because you think it will give you an advantage • (usually negative) *I'm a desperate woman but I wouldn't stoop to blackmail.* • *No reputable company would stoop to selling the names of their clients to other companies.*

stop around/round stops, stopping, stopped
stop around/round *American*
to visit someone for a short time, especially at their home • *Why don't you stop around sometime?*

stop back stops, stopping, stopped
stop back *American*
to return to a place that you have been to earlier • *I'll stop back later when you have a little more time.*

stop behind stops, stopping, stopped
stop behind
to stay in a place for a short time after other people have left • *I stopped behind after the class to ask the teacher one or two things.*

stop by stops, stopping, stopped
stop by (swh)
to visit a person or place for a short time, usually when you are going somewhere else • *I thought I might stop by on my way home as I haven't seen you for ages.* • *I've got to stop by the bank.*

stop in stops, stopping, stopped
stop in
1 *informal* to visit a person or place for a short time, usually when you are going somewhere else • (often + **at**) *I stopped in at Justin's on the way home and returned his video.* • *I thought I'd stop in and say hello as I was passing your house.*
2 *British informal* to stay at home, especially in the evening • *I'm going to stop in tonight and write a couple of letters.*

stop off stops, stopping, stopped
stop off
to visit a place for a short time when you are going somewhere else • (often + **in**) *We could stop off in Paris for a couple of days before heading south.* • (often + **at**) *I'll stop off at the supermarket on the way home and get some wine.*

stop out stops, stopping, stopped
stop out *British & Australian informal*
to stay out at night and not come home, especially when other people are expecting you to come home • *If you're going to stop out will you let me know?*

stop over stops, stopping, stopped
stop over
1 to stop somewhere for a period of time when you are on a long journey • *We stopped over in Los Angeles for two nights on the way to New Zealand.*
stopover *n* [C] • *Our tickets to Australia included a two-night stopover in Singapore.*
2 *British informal* to stay somewhere for the night • *Why don't you come round for dinner one night and you can stop over?*

stop over swh *American*

to visit a person or place for a short time
• *I stopped over Annie's house this afternoon.* • *Jen's stopping over later.*

stop round

see **stop around/round**

stop up stops, stopping, stopped

stop up *British informal*

to go to bed later than usual • (usually + to do sth) *I stopped up to watch the late film.*

stop up sth or **stop** sth **up**

to fill a hole so that nothing can pass through it • *We found a mouse hole and stopped it up with plaster.*

store away stores, storing, stored

store away sth or **store** sth **away**

to put something in a safe place so that it can be used in the future • *Because it's summer all my sweaters are stored away at the back of the wardrobe.*

store up stores, storing, stored

store up sth or **store** sth **up**

1 to keep a lot of something in one place so that it can be used in the future • *These small rodents store up nuts in the winter.*

2 to remember things, usually so that you can tell people about them later • *I listen in to their conversations and store it all up to tell you later.*

store up sth

if you store up trouble or problems, you behave in a way that will cause trouble in the future • (usually + **for**) *If you don't deal with the matter now, you're just storing up trouble for the future.*

stow away stows, stowing, stowed

stow away

to hide on a ship, aircraft, or other vehicle, in order to travel secretly or without paying • *She stowed away on a freighter bound for Hong Kong.*

stowaway *n* [C] a person who stows away • *Checks revealed a stowaway on board.*

stow away sth or **stow** sth **away**

to put something in a safe place so that it can be used in the future • (often + **in**) *The camping equipment had been stowed away in the loft.*

straighten out straightens, straightening, straightened

straighten out (sth) or **straighten** (sth) **out**

to become straight, or to make something straight • *The road straightens out after a mile or so.* • *I'm trying to straighten out some of these tent pegs.*

straighten out sth or **straighten** sth **out**

to successfully deal with a problem or confused situation • *There are a few matters I need to straighten out with you before we start.*

straighten out sb or **straighten** sb **out** *informal*

to improve someone's behaviour • *And you really think a year in the army's going to straighten him out?* • (often reflexive) *He'd better straighten himself out if he wants a job.*

straighten up straightens, straightening, straightened

straighten up

to stand straight • *Something went click in my back and when I tried to straighten up it was agony.*

straighten up sth or **straighten** sth **up**

to make a place tidy • *Could you just straighten up the lounge before people start arriving?*

strap into

strap in/into   straps, strapping, strapped

strap in sb or **strap** sb **in**

strap sb **into** sth

to fasten someone into a seat using a strap • *The kids need strapping into their seats in the back.* • (sometimes reflexive) *He lowered himself into the cockpit and strapped himself in.*

strap up   straps, strapping, strapped

strap up sth or **strap** sth **up** *British & Australian*

to put a bandage around an injured part of the body • *He played the second set with his ankle strapped up.*

stretch away   stretches, stretching, stretched

stretch away (always + *adv/prep*)

if an area of land stretches away, it continues over a long distance • *Fields of golden corn stretch away as far as the eye can see.*

stretch out   stretches, stretching, stretched

stretch out

to lie with your arms and legs spread out in a relaxed way • *He stretched out on the sofa in front of the TV.*

stretch out sth or **stretch** sth **out**

to hold a part of your body straight out in front of you • *She stretched out a hand and lifted the glass to her lips.*

stretch out

if an area of land stretches out, it continues over a long distance • *On either side of us fields stretch out for miles.*

strike back   strikes, striking, struck

strike back

to attack someone who has attacked you • (sometimes + **at**) *The courts are now more sympathetic to women who strike back at violent husbands.*

strike down   strikes, striking, struck

strike down sb or **strike** sb **down**

1 to make someone very ill • (usually passive) *My training was going really well till I was struck down with flu.*

2 to make someone die • (usually passive) *He died in '63, struck down by an assassin's bullet.*

strike down sth or **strike** sth **down** *American*

if a judge or a court strikes down something [e.g. law, statute, conviction], they decide that it is wrong and should not be used • *The law restricting abortion was struck down in the Supreme Court last month.*

strike off

be struck off (always passive) *British & Australian*

if a doctor or lawyer is struck off, they are not allowed to work as a doctor or lawyer any more because they have done something bad • (often + **for**) *In 1989 he was struck off for professional misconduct.*

strike on

be struck on sb/sth (always passive) *British informal*

to like someone or something very much • *She seems very struck on this new man.* • (often negative) *I'm not that struck on Indian food.*

strike on/upon   strikes, striking, struck

strike on/upon sth

to think of a good idea • *He struck on the idea while he was working as a researcher in the States.*

strike out   strikes, striking, struck

strike out

1 (always + *adv/prep*) to start doing something that you have not done before • *As a company they've never been afraid to strike out in new directions.* • *She'd worked for her father for over ten years and thought it was time to strike out on her own.*

2 to try to hit someone • *I lost control and struck out.*

3 *American informal* to fail • *I really struck out with her – I didn't even get to kiss her goodnight.*

4 (always + *adv/prep*) to start walking in a particular direction in a determined way • *We struck out across the fields towards the village.*

strike out sth or **strike** sth **out**

to draw a line through something that you have written, usually because it is wrong • *The word had been struck out and another word written over it.*

strike up strikes, striking, struck

strike up sth

to start a conversation or relationship with someone ● (often + **with**) *I struck up a conversation with the guy who works behind the bar.* ● *He met her in '65 and struck up a friendship that was to last many years.*

strike up (sth)

to start to play a piece of music ● *Then a regimental band with bagpipes struck up the national anthem.* ● *A jazz band struck up and people started to dance.*

strike upon

see **strike on/upon**

string along strings, stringing, strung

string along sb or **string** sb **along**
informal

to deceive someone for a long time by pretending that you love them or that you will do what they want you to do ● *He strung her along for years, saying he'd marry her when he'd divorced his wife.* ● *He's never going to give you that money he owes you – he's just stringing you along.*

string along *informal*

to go somewhere with someone, usually because you do not have anything else to do ● (often + **with**) *I didn't have any other plans so I thought I'd string along with them.* ● *If you're going into town later is it okay if I string along?*

string out string, stringing, strung

be strung out (always passive)

if a group of things or people are strung out, they are positioned in a long line with spaces between them ● (usually + **along**) *Armed guards were strung out along the five-mile border.*

string out sth or **string** sth **out**
informal

to make an activity last longer than necessary ● *It's in the lawyer's interest to string out the case because he'll earn more fees.*

string together strings, stringing, strung

string together sth or **string** sth **together**

if someone strings words or sentences together, they manage to say something that other people can understand ● *I managed to string a few words together in Greek.* ● *He'd drunk so much he could hardly string two sentences together.*

string up strings, stringing, strung

string up sth or **string** sth **up**

to fasten something, especially a decoration, to two points so that it hangs high in the air ● *We put tables and chairs in the garden and strung up coloured lights in the trees.*

string up sb or **string** sb **up** *informal*

to kill someone by hanging them by the neck from a rope ● *If you want my opinion, I think he should be strung up from the nearest lamp post.*

strip away strips, stripping, stripped

strip away sth or **strip** sth **away**

1 if you strip away something which hides the true character of someone or something, you ignore it so that you can discover what the person or thing is really like ● *Strip away the jargon and you'll see that the competition is just an attempt to sell you something.*

2 to gradually get rid of traditions or rights which have existed for a long time ● *Workers' rights have been systematically stripped away by the government.*

strip down strips, stripping, stripped

strip down sth or **strip** sth **down**

to separate a vehicle or an engine into its different parts in order to repair it or clean it ● *He specializes in stripping down motorbikes and rebuilding them.*

strip of strips, stripping, stripped

strip sb **of** sth

to take away a prize, right, or position of power from someone as a punishment ● (usually passive) *He was stripped of his gold medal after it was discovered he had taken drugs before the race.* ● *Her native country stripped her of her citizenship after she fled in 1975.*

strip off   strips, stripping, stripped

strip off (sth) or **strip** (sth) **off**

to remove a piece of clothing or all the clothes that you are wearing ● *She stripped off and stepped into the shower.* ● *It was so hot that he stripped off his shirt.*

struggle on   struggles, struggling, struggled

struggle on

to continue doing something which is difficult ● *It's hard bringing up kids on your own when you've very little money but she struggles on.*

stub out   stubs, stubbing, stubbed

stub out sth or **stub** sth **out**

to stop a cigarette from burning by pressing the burning end against a hard surface ● *He stubbed out his cigar in the ashtray and stood up to leave.*

stuff up   stuffs, stuffing, stuffed

stuff up (sth) or **stuff** (sth) **up** *Australian slang*

to do something badly, or to make a mistake ● *I really stuffed that exam up.* ● *We're giving you another chance so don't stuff up this time.*

stuff-up n [C] *Australian slang* ● *Oh no, what a stuff-up!*

stumble across/on/upon   stumbles, stumbling, stumbled

stumble across/on/upon sth/sb

to discover something by chance, or to meet someone by chance ● *Customs offiers stumbled across heroin worth £5 million while doing a routine check.* ● *Scientists believe they might have stumbled upon a cure for the disease.*

stump up   stumps, stumping, stumped

stump up (sth) or **stump** (sth) **up** *British informal*

to provide money for something, especially when you do not want to ● *Shareholders are being forced to stump up another £50 million in order to finish the project.* ● *Maggie didn't have the money for her ticket so I had to stump up again.*

subject to   subjects, subjecting, subjected

subject sb/sth **to** sth

to make someone experience something unpleasant, or to treat something in a very severe way ● (usually passive) *While he was in prison, he was subjected to frequent beatings.* ● *The report has been subjected to detailed analysis.*

subscribe to   subscribes, subscribing, subscribed

subscribe to sth *formal*

to have a particular belief or opinion ● *I certainly don't subscribe to the view that women are necessarily more moral than men.* ● *Like many right-wing politicians, he subscribes to the view that the welfare state should be abolished.*

succeed in   succeeds, succeeding, succeeded

succeed in sth/doing sth

to achieve something that you have been trying to get or do ● *She succeeded in getting herself elected as mayor.* ● *He's finally succeeded in his ambition to learn how to fly.*

suck in/into   sucks, sucking, sucked

suck in sb or **suck** sb **in**

suck sb **into** sth

to make someone gradually become involved in an unpleasant situation or harmful activity ● (usually passive) *The government does not want to be sucked into another messy and expensive war.* ● *A lot of teenagers don't want to get involved with gangs, but they find themselves getting sucked in.*

suck off   sucks, sucking, sucked

suck off sb or **suck** sb **off** *taboo*

to move the tongue and mouth around and across someone's sexual organs to give them pleasure ● *He was watching a video of some woman sucking a guy off.*

suck up to   sucks, sucking, sucked

suck up to sb *informal*

to try to make someone who is in a position of authority like you by doing and saying things that will please them ● *At school she was always sucking up to the teachers.*

sucker in/into   suckers, suckering, suckered

sucker sb **in** *American informal*

sucker sb **into** sth/doing sth *American informal*

to trick someone into doing or expecting something ● *We were suckered into doing the work for free.* ● *Don't get suckered in by the guy.*

suit up   suits, suiting, suited

suit up *American*

to put on special clothes or a uniform in order to take part in a particular activity ● *The virtual reality viewer has to suit up in a headset and electronic glove.*

sum up   sums, summing, summed

sum up (sth/sb) or **sum** (sth/sb) **up**

to describe briefly the most important facts or characteristics of something or someone ● *The purpose of a conclusion is to sum up the main points of the essay.* ● *To sum up, we need to increase sales by 12% next year if the company is to stay in profit.* ● *He's a small man with a big ego – that about sums him up, doesn't it?*

sum up sb/sth or **sum** sb/sth **up**

1 if something sums up someone or something, it represents the most typical qualities of that person or thing ● *For me, her paintings sum up the restless spirit of America.*

2 to quickly decide what you think about someone or something ● *He tends to sum people up according to what books they read.* ● *I think she summed up the situation pretty quickly.*

sum up

if a judge in a law court sums up, he or she repeats the main ideas that were expressed and the most important facts that were given during the trial ● *The jury returned a 'not guilty' verdict after the judge summed up in the defendant's favour.*

summing-up n [C] ● (usually singular) *In his summing-up, the judge described the defendant as arrogant.*

summon up   summons, summoning, summoned

summon up sth or **summon** sth **up**

1 to try hard to find a particular quality [e.g. courage, energy] in yourself because you need it in order to do something ● *It took her six weeks to summon up the courage to report the incident to the police.* ● *I was so tired I couldn't summon up the energy to get out of bed.*

2 if something summons up a memory or an image, it makes you remember something or think about something ● *The smell of cut grass summons up images of hot summer afternoons.*

surge up   surges, surging, surged

surge up *literary*

if an emotion surges up, you suddenly experience it very strongly ● *She smiled at him and an overwhelming feeling of love surged up within him.*

suss out   susses, sussing, sussed

suss out sb/sth or **suss** sb/sth **out** *mainly British & Australian informal*

to discover what someone or something is really like, or to find out how a machine or a piece of equipment works ● *She's quite strange. I haven't been able to suss her out at all.* ● *I couldn't work out how to programme my video recorder, but Kate soon sussed it out.* ● (sometimes + question word) *Have you sussed out if there are any good bars near here?*

swallow up   swallows, swallowing, swallowed

swallow up sth or **swallow** sth **up**

1 if an organization or activity swallows up a large amount of money, it uses the whole amount of money ● *Defence spending swallows up 30% of the country's wealth.* ● (often passive + **in**) *It's a very expensive project to run: £10 million is swallowed up in administration costs alone.*

2 if a large organization or country swallows up a smaller one, the smaller one is made part of the larger one ● *Specialist publishers are increasingly being swallowed up by large publishing groups.*

3 to make something disappear ● (usually passive + **in**) *Beyond the light of the fire, everything was swallowed up in the darkness.*

swarm with   swarms, swarming, swarmed

swarm with sb/sth
if a place swarms with people or insects, it is full of large numbers of people or insects which are all moving about ● (usually in continuous tenses) *St Mark's Square in Venice is always swarming with tourists in the summer.*

swear by   swears, swore, sworn

swear by sth (never in continuous tenses)
to believe that something is very effective and that it will always work well ● *Have you tried their new moisturizer? Polly swears by it.* ● (often + **for**) *My mother swears by garlic for keeping colds away.*

swear in   swears, swearing, swore, sworn

swear in sb or swear sb in
to make someone promise to be honest or loyal during a trial in court, or during an official ceremony before they begin a new job ● (often passive + **as**) *She was sworn in as a member of the jury.*
swearing-in n [singular] ● *The formal swearing-in of the new US Ambassador to Moscow will take place this afternoon.* ● (used as *adj*) *After the swearing-in ceremony, she made a speech outside the presidential palace.*

swear off   swears, swearing, swore, sworn

swear off sth
to decide to stop using harmful substances [e.g. drugs, alcohol], or to promise to stop doing something dangerous ● *She swore off alcohol and cigarettes after her heart attack last year.*

sweat out   sweats, sweating, sweated

sweat it out *informal*
1 to wait nervously for an unpleasant situation to end or improve ● *I don't get my exam results till the end of June, so I just have to sweat it out till then.*
2 to exercise hard ● *Pete sweats it out in the gym for an hour every day after work.*

sweat out sth or sweat sth out
1 to get rid of an illness [e.g. cold, flu] by keeping very warm ● *I was ill with flu last week, so I went to bed and just sweated it out.*
2 if you sweat out a substance that is in your body, that substance leaves your body through your skin ● *I eat a lot of garlic but I sweat it out when I go running.*

sweat out of   sweats, sweating, sweated

sweat sth out of sb
to make someone tell you something by threatening them ● *The police finally sweated a confession out of him.*

sweat over   sweats, sweating, sweated

sweat over sth *informal*
to work very hard at something and spend a lot of time on it ● *I really sweated over that essay.*

sweep along   sweeps, sweeping, swept

sweep along
if something sweeps you along, it makes you feel involved in an activity and it makes you feel very enthusiastic about it ● (usually passive) *I was swept along by David's enthusiasm for the project.* ● *Both parties have been swept along on the tide of political change in the country.*

sweep aside   sweeps, sweeping, swept

sweep aside sth or sweep sth aside
to refuse to think about something that someone says and to treat it as unimportant ● *I tried to argue that the scheme was expensive and badly planned but my objections were swept aside.*

sweep aside sb or sweep sb aside
to easily defeat someone ● *England swept aside Holland 4-1 in the European Championship.* ● *Government troops were swept aside by the advancing rebel forces.*

sweep away   sweeps, sweeping, swept

sweep away sth or sweep sth away
to get rid of a system, rule, or tradition which is old-fashioned or unfair ● *Trade restrictions will be swept away under the new law.*

sweep away sb or sweep sb away
if an emotion sweeps someone away, they experience it so strongly that they are unable to think clearly or behave calmly ● (usually passive) *He was swept away by an overwhelming feeling of optimism.* ● *It was the first time that she had been in love*

*and she was **swept away on a tide of** passion.*

sweep out   sweeps, sweeping, swept

sweep out sth or **sweep** sth **out**

to clean the floor of a room by using a brush to remove the dirt • *I've been sweeping out the attic – it was so dusty.*

sweep up   sweeps, sweeping, swept

sweep up (sth) or **sweep** (sth) **up**

to remove rubbish or dirt, usually from the floor, using a brush • *We spent an hour sweeping up after the party.* • *I'd better sweep that glass up before someone cuts themselves.*

sweep up sth or **sweep** sth **up**

1 *informal* to win a large amount of money or a large amount of something that you want [e.g. votes, awards] • *$5 billion is swept up each year by lucky lottery winners.* • *In last month's elections, the socialists swept up 60% of the vote.*

2 if an emotion or activity sweeps you up, you feel it very strongly or become involved in it • (usually passive) *He was swept up by the general enthusiasm for the war.*

sweeten up   sweetens, sweetening, sweetened

sweeten sb **up** or **sweeten up** sb

to make someone happier and friendlier towards you, so that they are more likely to give you something or do something you want • *I was trying to sweeten Dad up before I asked him for a loan.*

swell up

swell up   swells, swelling, swelled, swollen/swelled

swell up

1 if a part of your body swells up, it becomes larger or rounder than usual, often because of an illness or injury • *He had a really bad toothache and the left-hand side of his face had swollen up.* • *My feet always swell up when I'm on a plane.*

2 if a feeling swells up, it gradually becomes stronger • *She felt a sense of pride swell up inside her as Jonathan went up to accept the award.*

swerve from   swerves, swerving, swerved

swerve from sth *formal*

if someone swerves from an aim or a principle, they stop trying to achieve that aim, or they stop obeying that principle • (usually negative) *He had wanted to be a doctor from a very young age and nothing had made him swerve from that intention.*

swill down   swills, swilling, swilled

swill down sth or **swill** sth **down** *informal*

to drink a large amount of alcohol quickly • *He's probably in some bar with his mates swilling down beer.*

swing around/round   swings, swinging, swung

swing around/round

1 to suddenly turn around so that you can see someone or something behind you • *She heard a voice behind her and swung round in surprise.*

2 to change your opinion about something • (usually + **to**) *The government has swung around to the view that education needs more funding.*

swing at   swings, swinging, swung

swing at sb

to try to hit someone with your hand or with something that you are holding • (sometimes + **with**) *One of the gang swung at him with an iron bar and he felt a violent pain in his stomach.*

swing at sth

to try to hit the ball when it is thrown towards you in a game such as baseball • *I swung at the ball but missed it completely.*

swing by　swings, swinging, swung

swing by swh *American & Australian informal*
to visit a person or place for a short time while you are going somewhere else
● *She's asked me to swing by the grocery store for some milk.*

swing round

see **swing around/round**

switch around/round　switches, switching, switched

switch around/round sth or **switch sth around/round**
to move two or more things so that each of them is now in the place that one of the others was in before ● *You've switched the furniture around in here.*

switch off　switches, switching, switched

switch off (sth) or **switch** (sth) **off**
to turn off an electrical device [e.g. light, radio] or an engine by using a switch
● *Could you switch that light off?* ● *The heating switches off automatically at 9 pm.*
● *Don't forget to switch off before you leave.*

switch off
to stop giving your attention to something or someone ● *When he starts going on about his emotional problems I just switch off.* ● *Most people in stressful jobs find it difficult to switch off when they come home.*

switch on　switches, switching, switched

switch on (sth) or **switch** (sth) **on**
to turn on an electrical device [e.g. light, radio] or an engine by using a switch ● *He switched on the bedside lamp and sat up,*

● *The heating switches on automatically at 6 am.* ● *Could you switch the TV on?*

switch over　switches, switching, switched

switch over

1 to change from one method, product, or situation to another ● (usually + **to**) *We've switched over to low fat milk.* ● *They're switching over to a new computer system.*
switch-over *n* [singular] ● (often + **to**) *The switch-over to the new system is unlikely to start for three years.*

2 to change from one television or radio station to another ● (often + **to**) *I'll switch over to the news after this.*

switch round

see **switch around/round**

swivel around/round　swivels, swivelling, swivelled　(*American & Australian* also **swivels, swiveling, swiveled**)

swivel around/round
to turn around so that you can see someone or something behind you ● *She swivelled around to see who had walked into the office.*

swot up　swots, swotting, swotted

swot up (sth) or **swot** (sth) **up** *British & Australian informal*
to learn as much as you can about something, especially before an exam ● (often + **on**) *He'll need to swot up on his maths if he's going to pass.* ● *I'm swotting up my geometry theorems.*

syphon off

see **siphon/syphon away/off** or **siphon/syphon off**

tack on/onto   tacks, tacking, tacked
tack on sth or **tack** sth **on**
tack sth **onto** sth

to add something that you had not planned to add • *The film is basically the same as the book but with a happy ending tacked on.*

tag along   tags, tagging, tagged
tag along *slightly informal*

to go somewhere with a person, especially when they have not asked you to go with them • (often + **with**) *Every time we went out he'd tag along with us and it was starting to annoy me.* • *If you're going to town do you mind if I tag along?*

tag on/onto   tags, tagging, tagged
tag on sth or **tag** sth **on**
tag sth **onto** sth

to add something to what you have said or written • *He mentioned the change in some remarks tagged onto the main interview.*

tail away/off   tails, tailing, tailed
tail away/off

if someone's voice tails away or off, it becomes quieter and then stops • *'I couldn't imagine life without him and I just, er,' her voice tailed off.*

tail back   tails, tailing, tailed
tail back *British*

if traffic tails back, it forms a long line and moves very slowly or stops • *The traffic is tailing back as far as the motorway exit.*
tailback n [C] *British* a long line of traffic that is moving very slowly • *a two-mile tailback on the M25*

tail off   tails, tailing, tailed
tail off

to decrease in amount or level • *Profits tailed off towards the end of the year.*

• *Initially there was a lot of interest in the case but it's begun to tail off.*

take aback   takes, taking, took, taken
take sb **aback**

if something takes you aback, you are very surprised by it • (usually passive) *I was a little taken aback at the directness of the question.* • *I was taken aback to discover that the insurance company had rejected my claim.*

take after   takes, took, taken
take after sb (never in continuous tenses)

1 to have a similar appearance or character as an older member of your family • *Peter's very tall – he takes after his father.* • *Erika takes after her mother with her bad temper.*

2 *American informal* to quickly follow someone in order to catch them • *He took after me but I managed to escape.*

take against   takes, taking, took, taken
take against sb *British*

to begin to dislike someone • *I think she took against me because I got the promotion she wanted.*

take along   takes, taking, took, taken
take along sb/sth or **take** sb/sth **along**

to take someone or something with you when you go somewhere • *Are you taking anyone along to Gavin's party?* • *We'd better take along a couple of bottles of wine.*

take apart   takes, taking, took, taken
take apart sth or **take** sth **apart**

to separate something into its different parts • *He spent the afternoon taking his bike apart and cleaning each bit.*

take apart sb or **take** sb **apart** *slightly informal*

1 to defeat someone very easily in a sport • *He took the English defence apart, scoring three goals in the first half.*

2 *mainly American* to attack someone • *If I see you around here again, I'll take you apart.*

take apart sb/sth or **take** sb/sth **apart**

to strongly criticize someone or something that someone has written • *She was taken apart by the opposition for her part in the political scandal.*

take around/round takes, taking, took, taken

take around/round sb or **take** sb **around/round** (swh)

to walk through a building or to visit a place with someone, showing them the most interesting or important parts • *Haven't you ever been to my office before? Let me take you around.* • *She took us round the house, showing us the different rooms.*

take aside takes, taking, took, taken

take aside sb or **take** sb **aside**

to separate someone from a group of people so that you can speak to them privately • *She took him aside after the meeting and asked him why he'd been late.*

take away takes, taking, took, taken

take away sth or **take** sth **away**

1 to remove something from where it was and put it somewhere else • *A waiter came to take our plates away.*

2 to remove something from a person or organization so that they do not have it any more • *The new law will take away the right of workers to strike.* • (often + **from**) *The report claims that large supermarkets are taking business away from small shops.*

3 to make a particular quality or feeling disappear • *It really takes my appetite away if someone smokes during a meal.*

4 if you take one number away from another one, you subtract the first number from the second • (usually + **from**) *'What do you get if you take two away from four?'*

5 if you take away something [e.g. memory, impression, message] from an event or performance, you remember or think about that thing after the event or performance has finished • *The impression I took away from the conference was that it had been rather badly organized.* • *So what message are you supposed to take away at the end of the film?*

6 *British & Australian* to buy food in a shop or restaurant and eat it somewhere else • *I'd like a hamburger and chips to take away, please.*

takeaway *n* [C] *British & Australian* a meal that you can buy and take somewhere else to eat, or a shop where you can buy this food • *I thought we might call at the Chinese takeaway on the way back.* • *Do you fancy a takeaway?*

Take it away! (always an order) *informal* something that you say in order to tell someone who is going to play music or sing to start performing • *We've got a great jazz trio playing for you tonight. So take it away, Steve and the boys!*

take away sb or **take** sb **away**

1 to make someone leave a place and go somewhere with you • *Two men with guns came to her house and took her away.* • *He has been taken away by the police for questioning.*

2 to stop someone from being somewhere or from doing an activity • (usually + **from**) *Her job takes her away from home a lot.* • *The problem with hobbies is that they take you away from your studies.*

3 to take someone with you when you stay somewhere for a short time • *I'm taking Tina away for a weekend in the country.*

take away from takes, taking, took, taken

take away from sth

to make something seem less good or successful • *I don't tend to analyse films too deeply – it takes away from the enjoyment.*

take back takes, taking, took, taken

take back sth or **take** sth **back**

1 to return something to the person or organization that you borrowed or bought it from • *I've got to take my library books back before January 25th.* • *I might take this coat back and get a larger size.*

2 if a shop takes back goods that it has sold to you, it agrees to give you money or goods for them because they are damaged or unsuitable • *They won't take back anything that looks as if it's been worn.*

3 to get possession or control of something which you used to possess or control, often by using force • *The army's task is to take back the land that was lost in the war three years ago.*

4 to admit that something you said was wrong • *I take back everything I said about George – he's been really nice to me recently.* • *I know I said he was arrogant*

and unfriendly but I take it all back now.

take back sb or take sb back

1 if something takes you back, it makes you remember a period or an event in the past • (often + to) *That piece of music takes me back to my childhood.* • *Seeing those photos of my sister's wedding really took me back.*

2 to agree to start a relationship with someone again or to employ someone again after a disagreement • *She's asked her husband to take her back.* • *The strike ended once the company agreed to take back the 50 workers it had fired.*

take down   takes, taking, took, taken

take down sth or take sth down

1 to remove something that is fixed to a wall • *Her bedroom used to be full of Oasis posters but she's taken them all down now.* • *The living room curtains need to be taken down tomorrow for cleaning.*

2 to remove a large temporary structure from a place by separating it into pieces and taking the pieces away • *We'll take the tent down after we've had lunch.* • *When are the builders coming to take the scaffolding down?*

3 to write something, especially something that someone says • *The police officer took my name and address down and said that he would contact me shortly.* • *Did you take down that number?*

4 to unfasten and lower your trousers without removing them completely • *He took down his trousers and showed me his scars.*

take in   takes, taking, took, taken

take in sb or take sb in

1 to let someone stay in your house • *Several families in the village have taken in refugee children.* • *You could earn some extra money by taking in foreign students.*

2 if an organization [e.g. school, hospital] takes someone in, it allows that person to study there, be treated there etc. • *The university is planning to take in 15% more students next year.* • *We will be able to take in more patients once the new wing of the hospital is built.*

intake *n* [C] the number of people who begin to study at a school or who join an organization at a particular time • *The*

college *has an annual intake of about 6,000 students.*

3 if the police take someone in, they make that person go with them to the police station in order to ask them questions • *She's been taken in for questioning by the police.*

4 to deceive someone, or to make someone believe something that is not true • (usually passive) *I can't believe she was taken in by him.*

take in sth or take sth in

1 to look at something carefully, noticing all the details • *We took a cable car to the top of the mountain and took in the magnificent views.*

2 to understand the meaning or importance of news or information, or to understand and remember facts • *She had to read the letter twice before she could take the news in.* • *It was quite an interesting lecture but there was just too much to take in.*

3 *mainly American* to go to watch a film or performance, or to visit a place [e.g. museum, gallery] for enjoyment • *I thought we might get something to eat and then take in a movie.* • *We took in a couple of galleries while we were in New York.*

4 to include something • *The three-week cruise will take in the islands of Corfu and Crete.* • *Her work takes in a wide range of subjects from motherhood to madness.*

5 to take your car or a faulty piece of equipment to a place where it can be examined and repaired • *I took my car in to have the exhaust repaired.*

6 to earn money by doing jobs at home [e.g. washing, sewing] for other people • *After her husband died, she supported herself by taking in washing.*

7 if people, animals, or plants take in a substance that they need [e.g. air, water, food], they make that substance enter their body, for example by breathing or swallowing • *Plants take in water through their roots.* • *He sat down quickly and took in several large gulps of air.*

intake *n* [singular] • *Increasing your intake of vitamin C can help to prevent colds.*

8 if a boat takes in water, water enters the boat through a hole • *A rock tore a hole in the side of the boat and we began to take in water.*

9 *mainly American* to receive or collect an

amount of money, especially for things that are sold or work that is done • *The movie took in about $50 million in ticket sales.* • *How much did you take in at the school fair?*

10 to make a piece of clothing narrower by removing the sewing from the edges and sewing closer to the middle of the material • *Since she's lost weight she's had to take a lot of her clothes in.*

take off   takes, taking, took, taken

take off sth or **take** sth **off**

1 to remove something, especially something that you are wearing • *She took off her clothes and stepped into the shower.* • *Aren't you going to take your glasses off to go swimming?* • *I always take my make-up off before I go to bed.*

2 to spend time away from your work • *I'm taking Friday off to get one or two things done around the house.* • *He needs to take some time off and get some rest.*

take off

1 if an aircraft, bird, or insect takes off, it moves from the ground and begins to fly • *I like watching planes take off.* • *A puffin will take off and land many times during feeding.*
take-off n (C/U) • *The majority of crashes happen on take-off or landing.*

2 to suddenly become successful or popular • *Her career as a jazz singer had just begun to take off.* • *The market for home fax machines really seems to have taken off.*

3 *slightly informal* to suddenly leave somewhere, especially without telling anyone that you are going • *I can't just take off without saying goodbye.*

take off sth or **take** sth **off** (sth)

to subtract a particular amount from a total • *They took another £10 off the sale price because of the damage.* • *Take half a mark off for every spelling mistake.*

take off sb/sth or **take** sb/sth **off**

1 *slightly informal* to copy the way a person behaves, or to copy the way something is done, often in order to make people laugh • *She's really good at taking people off.*
take-off n [C] *slightly informal* • (usually + **of**) *He does a really good take-off of Paul.*

2 *American slang* to steal from a person or place, especially by using violence • *They were just young kids who took off the liquor store.*

take sb **off** sth

1 to stop someone from doing a particular type of work, especially because they are not doing it well • *Both police officers involved have been taken off the case.* • *I might have to take him off the editing if his work doesn't improve.*

2 to stop giving someone a particular type of medical treatment or food • *He's been taken off the medication.*

take off sb or **take** sb **off**

to make someone leave a place and go somewhere with you • (often + **to**) *He was taken off to prison.*

take yourself **off** *informal*

to go somewhere • (usually + **to**) *I think you should take yourself off to the doctor's.* • *She left her job and took herself off to Tunisia.*

take on   takes, taking, took, taken

take on sb or **take** sb **on**

1 to begin to employ someone • *We usually take on extra staff over Christmas.* • *They only took her on because she's the manager's niece.*

2 to compete against someone or fight someone • *I might take you on at tennis some time.* • *The government took on the unions and won.*

take on sth or **take** sth **on**

1 to accept a particular job or responsibility and begin to do what is needed • *She's just taken on too much work.* • *When I took this job on I didn't expect it to take all this time.* • *I can't take on* (= begin to help with) *his problems as well as my own.*

2 if a vehicle takes on passengers, fuel, or goods, it stops so that the passengers can get on, or so that the fuel or goods can be put onto it • *The plane has two scheduled stops to take on passengers and fuel.*

take on sth

to begin to have a particular quality • *Her voice took on a troubled tone.* • *Words take on new meanings all the time.*

take out   takes, taking, took, taken

take out sth or **take** sth **out**

1 to remove something from a particular place or container ● *I was having problems with my wisdom teeth so the dentist took them out.* ● (often + **of**) *She took a clean handkerchief out of her pocket.*

2 to borrow a book from a library ● *How many books did you take out last time you were here?*

3 to get money from a bank ● *I took £50 out to spend over the weekend.*

4 to arrange to get an official document [e.g. insurance policy] from an organization or court of law ● *Chris and I took out a life insurance policy when we got our mortgage.* ● *She decided to take out an injunction against him.*

take out sb or **take** sb **out**

to go somewhere and do something with someone, usually something that you have planned or paid for ● (often + **to**) *We took the kids out to the zoo on Saturday.* ● (often + **for**) *The boss usually takes us out for a meal at Christmas.*

take out sb/sth or **take** sb/sth **out** *informal*

to kill someone, or to destroy something ● *He had been ordered to take the sniper out.* ● *All large military targets must be taken out.*

take out of   takes, taking, took, taken

take sth **out of** sb *informal*

to make someone feel very tired ● *Driving those sort of distances really **takes it out of** you.* ● *Her job is very demanding and I think it takes a lot out of her.*

take sb **out of** themselves *British & Australian*

to stop someone from thinking about what was making them feel unhappy ● *The great thing about music is the way it takes you out of yourself.*

take out on   takes, taking, took, taken

take out sth **on** sb or **take** sth **out on** sb

to treat someone badly because you are upset or angry, even though they have done nothing wrong ● *I know you've had a bad day, but there's no need to take it out on me!* ● *He tends to take out his frustration on the kids and it's just not fair.*

take over   takes, taking, took, taken

take over (sth) or **take** (sth) **over**

to start doing a job or being responsible for something that someone else was doing or was responsible for before you ● (often + **from**) *Who'll be taking over from Cynthia when she retires?* ● (often + **as**) *He took over as manager two years ago.* ● *Colin Lamb has taken over responsibility for the new project.* ● *If I've looked after the kids all day Steve will take over when he gets home.*

take over sth or **take** sth **over**

1 to get control of a company by buying most of its shares (= the equal parts into which the ownership of the company is divided) ● *The company he works for was recently taken over.* ● *British Airways has taken over two subsidiary airlines.*

   takeover *n* [C] ● *They were involved in a takeover last year.*

2 to get control of an area of land or a political organization, usually by using force ● *In January 1986 the government was taken over by a guerrilla army.*

   takeover *n* [C] ● (often + **of**) *She went into exile after the communist takeover of Romania.*

3 to start to use or live in a house or other building ● *I took over Jenny's flat when she went to Sweden.* ● *The premises have been taken over by a specialist retailer.*

take over

to become more successful or powerful than something or someone else that is involved in the same type of activity ● (usually + **from**) *France has taken over from Spain as Europe's favourite holiday destination.* ● *A 21-year-old sprinter has taken over from Graf as Germany's top sportswoman.*

take round

see **take around/round**

take through   takes, taking, took, taken

take sb **through** sth

to explain something to someone, or to show someone how to do something ● *I'll just take you through a couple of routines and then you can try yourselves.*

take to   takes, taking, took, taken

take to sb/sth

to start to like someone or something ● *I really took to him – I thought he was lovely.* ● *I tried cycling to work for a while but I didn't take to it.*

take to sth/doing sth

to start to do something often ● *I've taken to wearing jeans for work.* ● *In his depressed state he took to drink.* (= he started drinking too much alcohol too often)

take to swh

to go somewhere, usually because you are in a difficult or dangerous situation ● *The refugees took to the hills for safety.* ● *Every time she has the slightest headache, she takes to her bed.*

take up   takes, taking, took, taken

take up sth or **take** sth **up**

1 to start doing a particular job or activity ● *He's taken up golf in his spare time.* ● *Have you ever thought of taking up acting?*

2 to use a particular amount of time, space or effort ● *This desk takes up too much room.* ● *I'll be quick, I don't want to take up too much of your time.* ● (often passive + **with**) *His day was completely taken up with meetings.*

3 to remove something that is fixed to a surface [e.g. carpet] ● *We're going to take up these carpets and lay some different ones.*

4 *literary* to lift something and hold or carry it ● *Charlotte took up her pen and began to write.*

5 to discuss something, or to deal with something ● *A leading law firm took up his case.* ● (often + **with**) *I can't give you an answer, you'll have to take the matter up with your supervisor.*

6 to accept an offer or opportunity to do something ● *I think I'll take up Ann's offer to babysit.* ● *I'm not sure I'm ready to take up the challenge of motherhood just yet.*

7 to move to a particular position so that you are ready to do something ● *As the crowd grew, riot police took up their positions.*

8 to continue with an activity that has been interrupted ● *Ian took up the story where Sue had left off.*

9 to shorten a piece of clothing [e.g. skirt,

trousers] ● *Her dress was too long for me so I had to take it up a couple of inches.*

take up on   takes, taking, took, taken

take sb **up on** sth

1 to accept an offer that someone has made ● *Could I take you up on that offer of a lift, Rob?* ● *He's offered me a free ticket, but I'm not sure whether to take him up on it.*

2 to ask someone to explain something that they have just said or done, often because you think they are wrong ● *I should have taken her up on her comment but it didn't seem worth the trouble.*

take up with   takes, taking, took, taken

take up with sb

to become friendly or start a relationship with someone, especially someone who might have a bad influence on you ● *She was worried because her son had taken up with some older boys from across the street.* ● *When Angela left he took up with a girl from the hospital.*

be taken up with sth (always passive)

to be very busy doing something ● *She's completely taken up with moving house at the moment.*

take upon   takes, taking, took, taken

take sth **upon** yourself

to decide to do something without asking anyone first ● (usually + to do sth) *Craig **took it upon himself** to cancel my appointment, which didn't exactly please me.*

talk around/round   talks, talking, talked

talk sb **around/round** *British & Australian*

to persuade someone to agree with you or to do what you want them to do ● *Annie's not convinced about the idea but I think I can talk her round.* ● (sometimes + **to** + doing sth) *Do you think you can talk them round to lending us some money?*

talk around/round sth

to talk about a problem or subject in a general way and avoid dealing with the important parts of it ● *I just felt that he'd talked round the subject and hadn't really said anything of importance.*

talk at   talks, talking, talked

talk at sb

to talk to someone without listening to them or allowing them to speak ● *Charles is someone who doesn't talk to you, he talks at you.*

talk back   talks, talking, talked

talk back

if someone, especially a child, talks back, they reply rudely to someone they should be polite to ● (usually + **to**) *He knew better than to talk back to his father.*

backtalk n [U] *American* ● *That's enough of your backtalk, Tommy!*

talk down   talks, talking, talked

talk down sth or **talk** sth **down**

to talk about something in a way that makes it seem less important or successful than it really is ● *He began his presentation by talking down the initiatives of a rival company.*

talk down sb or **talk** sb **down**

1 to give instructions to someone who is flying an aircraft to help them bring the aircraft to the ground ● *The weather conditions were so bad that he had to be talked down by someone on the ground.*

2 to persuade someone who is threatening to kill themselves not to jump from a high place ● *The policeman talked the girl down after she had been on the roof for two hours.*

3 to speak loudly or without stopping in order to prevent someone else from speaking ● *I tried to explain, but he just talked me down.*

talk down to   talks, talking, talked

talk down to sb

to talk to someone as if they were less clever than you ● *He was always talking down to us like we were idiots.*

talk into   talks, talking, talked

talk sb **into** sth/doing sth

to persuade someone to do something ● *I've managed to talk him into buying a new bed.* ● *I don't know if he's very keen on the idea but I think I can talk him into it.*

talk out   talks, talking, talked

talk out sth or **talk** sth **out**

to discuss a problem or plan in order to find a solution or an agreement ● *They'd set up a therapy group where people could talk out their problems.*

talk yourself **out** (always reflexive)

to talk so much that you have nothing else to say ● *My parents lectured me until they had talked themselves out.*

talk out of   talks, talking, talked

talk sb **out of** sth/doing sth

to persuade someone not to do something ● *It was a crazy idea and we both tried to talk him out of it.* ● *So, has Roger talked you out of buying a second-hand car?*

talk over   talks, talking, talked

talk over sth or **talk** sth **over**

to discuss a problem or situation, especially before making a decision about it ● (often + **with**) *I'd like to talk things over with my wife first.* ● *I'll talk it over with Marty and see what he thinks.*

talk round

see **talk around/round**

talk through   talks, talking, talked

talk through sth or **talk** sth **through**

to discuss all the details of something so that you can understand it or make a decision about it ● *Let's talk things through before we do anything.* ● (often + **with**) *I'll talk it through with him and let you know.*

talk sb **through** sth

to help someone to understand something or deal with something by talking to them ● *If you call this number someone will talk you through the procedure.* ● *Talk the students through the notes as you write them on the blackboard.*

talk up   talks, talking, talked

talk up sth/sb or **talk** sth/sb **up** *mainly American*

to talk about something or someone in an enthusiastic way in order to make other people interested in them • *Whatever the product you're presenting, you've got to talk it up a bit.*

tamp down   tamps, tamping, tamped

tamp down sth or **tamp** sth **down**

to press something [e.g. earth, soil] so that it becomes firm • *We filled in the hole and tamped down the earth around the base of the post.*

tamper with   tampers, tampering, tampered

tamper with sth

to touch or change something without permission • *The lock on my drawer had been tampered with and some of my papers were missing.*

tangle up in

be tangled up in sth (always passive)

to be trapped in something [e.g. ropes, branches] and unable to move • *The kite got tangled up in the branches of a tree.*

tangle with   tangles, tangling, tangled

tangle with sb *mainly American & Australian*

to fight or argue with someone • *I wouldn't tangle with him if I were you – he's a big guy.*

tank up   tanks, tanking, tanked

tank up

1 *American informal* to fill a car with fuel • *We'd better tank up before we get on the thruway.*

2 *American informal* to drink a lot of an alcoholic drink • (often + **on**) *We'd spent all evening tanking up on scotch.*

    tanked up *adj* (always after verb) *informal* • *He was already tanked up (= drunk) when he arrived at the party.*

tap for   taps, tapping, tapped

tap sb **for** sth

1 *informal* to get money from someone • *I might be able to tap my father for a loan.*

2 *American informal* to choose someone to

do an important job • (usually passive) *He's been tapped for a top management job by his company.*

tap into   taps, tapping, tapped

tap into sth

to use part of a large supply of something for your own advantage • *They're hoping to tap into the very rich market for books on CD-ROM.* • *There's a vast store of information on the database, just waiting to be tapped into.*

tap out   taps, tapping, tapped

tap out sth or **tap** sth **out**

to hit a surface lightly, making a repeated pattern of sound • *He tapped out the rhythm on the table.*

tape up   tapes, taping, taped

tape up sth or **tape** sth **up**

1 to fasten a box or parcel by putting tape (= a narrow length of sticky material) around it • *I've taped up the box so the lid won't come off.*

2 *American & Australian* to put a bandage around an injured part of the body • *He came back onto the field with his ankle taped up.*

taper off   tapers, tapering, tapered

taper off

to gradually become less • *By September the burst in spending seemed to be tapering off.*

tart up   tarts, tarting, tarted

tart up sth or **tart** sth **up** *British & Australian informal*

to try to make something look more attractive by decorating it, in a way that makes it look cheap to some people • *They've tarted up a lot of those old buildings down near the canal.* • *It's really just a potato salad tarted up.*

tart yourself up (always reflexive) *British & Australian informal*

to try to make yourself look more attractive by putting on make-up, jewellery etc. • *You don't need to tart yourself up for me, love.*

tax with   taxes, taxing, taxed

tax sb **with** sth *formal*

to accuse someone of doing something wrong • *I taxed him with this offence, hoping that he might express some regret for his misconduct.*

team up   teams, teaming, teamed

team up
if two or more people team up, they form a group in order to do something together ● (usually + **with**) *I teamed up with Brendan for the doubles tournament.*

tear apart   tears, tearing, tore, torn

tear apart sth or **tear** sth **apart**
1 to pull something violently so that it breaks into two or more pieces ● *A dog can tear a rabbit apart in seconds.*
2 to destroy a building or room ● *The blast had torn the building apart.*
3 to destroy something that was united [e.g. party, country, family] by dividing it into two or more parts that fight or argue with each other ● *Ethnic rivalries threaten to tear this country apart.* ● (often reflexive) *He left, depressed at the way that the party was tearing itself apart.*

tear sb **apart**
to make someone feel very unhappy ● *I know that I'll never live with my kids and it tears me apart.*

tear at   tears, tearing, tore, torn

tear at sth
to try to pull pieces off something in a violent way ● *They rolled on the floor, tearing at each other's hair and clothes.*

tear away   tears, tearing, tore, torn

tear sb **away**
to force someone to stop doing something that they enjoy in order to do something else ● (usually + **from**) *I'll bring Gene with me, if I can tear him away from the television.* ● (often reflexive) *If you could tear yourself away from your studies, it would be great to see you.*

tear away sth or **tear** sth **away**
if the surface of something is torn away, it is violently pulled away from the thing that it is attached to ● (usually passive) *The front of the building had been torn away in the blast.*

tear down   tears, tearing, tore, torn

tear down sth or **tear** sth **down**
to destroy a building or other structure because it is not being used or it is not

wanted any more ● *They're going to tear down the old hospital and build a block of offices.* ● *The statue had been torn down in the revolution.*

tear into   tears, tearing, tore, torn

tear into sb/sth *informal*
to criticize someone or something strongly ● *She tore into me, accusing me of trying to destroy her career.*

tear off   tears, tearing, tore, torn

tear off sth or **tear** sth **off**
to remove clothing quickly and carelessly ● *He tore off his clothes and jumped into the water.*

tear off *informal*
to leave very quickly ● (usually + *adv/ prep*) *He tore off down the road in his car.*

tear up   tears, tearing, tore, torn

tear up sth or **tear** sth **up**
1 to tear something, especially paper or cloth, into a lot of small pieces ● *If he sends me any letters I just tear them up and throw them away.* ● *We had to tear up a sheet to make bandages.*
2 to destroy or damage something, especially an area of land ● *Acres of parkland are being torn up to make way for new developments.*
3 if you tear up an agreement or contract, you refuse to accept it or be controlled by it any more ● *Talks are on the verge of collapse with the rebels threatening to tear up the only agreement reached so far.*

tease out   teases, teasing, teased

tease out sth or **tease** sth **out**
1 to try to understand something that is hidden or not clear ● *After the speech, reporters tried to tease out precisely what she meant.*
2 to use your fingers in order to pull apart or straighten hairs or threads that are stuck together ● *I teased out the tangled knots in Rosie's hair.*

tee off   tees, teeing, teed

tee off
1 to hit a golf ball off the tee (= a short stick on which a golf ball is put to be hit), or to begin a game of golf by doing this ● *Ballesteros admitted to feeling nervous before teeing off.*

2 *American informal* to begin an event or start an activity ● *The exhibition is all ready and due to tee off in September.* ● (sometimes + **with**) *The new edition of the paper teed off with an editorial on crime.*

tee off sb or **tee** sb **off** *American informal*

to annoy someone ● *It really tees me off when she doesn't listen to me.*

teed off *adj* (always after verb) ● *They were fairly teed off with all the delays at the airport.*

tee off on   tees, teeing, teed

tee off on sb/sth *American informal*

to criticize someone or something in an angry way ● *Their teacher teed off on the sloppy work they'd handed in.*

teem down   teems, teeming, teemed

teem down

to rain very heavily ● *It's been teeming down all day.*

teem with   teems, teeming, teemed

teem with sth/sb

to contain large numbers of animals or people ● (usually in continuous tenses) *The town centre is usually teeming with tourists on a Saturday.*

tell against   tells, telling, told

tell against sb/sth *British & Australian formal*

to make someone or something more likely to fail ● *It's a reputation that might tell against him if he ever decides to change jobs.*

tell apart   tells, telling, told

tell sb/sth **apart**

to be able to see the differences between two similar things or people and judge which is which ● *When they were small, the twins looked so alike that I just couldn't tell them apart.* ● (sometimes + **from**) *It's impossible to tell a forged £10 note apart from a real one.*

tell from   tells, telling, told

tell sth/sb **from** sth/sb

if you can tell one person or thing from a similar person or thing, you are able to say which of them is which because you can see the differences between them

● *The two brothers looked so similar, I couldn't tell one from the other.* ● *I've always had a problem with telling my left from my right.*

tell off   tells, telling, told

tell off sb or **tell** sb **off**

to speak angrily to someone because they have done something wrong ● *She told him off for not doing his homework.* ● *You always get told off in Mr Warren's lesson.*

telling-off *n* [C] *British & Australian* ● *The nurse gave me a good telling-off.* ● (often + **from**) *She got a telling-off from her teacher for forgetting her book.*

tell on   tells, telling, told

tell on sb

1 to have a bad effect on someone's health or behaviour ● *He'd been three months in the job and the strain was beginning to tell on him.*

2 *informal* if you tell on someone who has done something wrong, you tell someone in authority what that person has done ● *I'll tell on you if you copy my homework again.* ● *I'm telling on you!*

tend to   tends, tending, tended

tend to sb/sth

to deal with the problems or needs of a person or thing ● *Surgeons in six operating rooms tended to the injured.* ● *Would you mind waiting? I'm tending to another customer at the moment.*

tend towards   tends, tending, tended

tend towards sth

1 to show more of a particular quality than others ● *Her taste in clothes tends towards the theatrical.*

2 to be likely to choose a particular thing ● *I tend towards the first of those two options.*

tense up   tenses, tensing, tensed

tense up

if you tense up or your muscles tense up, your muscles stiffen because you are not relaxed ● *I could feel myself tense up as he touched my neck.*

tensed up *adj* (always after verb) ● *You're all tensed up – I can feel it in your shoulders.*

test out   tests, testing, tested

test out sth or **test** sth **out**

to test a theory or new idea by seeing how it works in a practical situation or by finding out what other people think of it ● *The new procedures are being tested out in three different hospitals.*

thaw out   thaws, thawing, thawed

thaw out (sth) or **thaw** (sth) **out**

if frozen food thaws out, or if you thaw it out, it is taken out of a freezer so that it gradually becomes warmer and is not frozen any more ● *I can't start cooking until the chicken has thawed out.* ● *You're supposed to thaw food out completely before you use it.*

thaw out *slightly informal*

if someone thaws out, they become warmer after they have been outside and have got very cold ● *Why don't you sit by the fire and thaw out a bit?*

thin down   thins, thinning, thinned

thin down sth or **thin** sth **down**

to add water or another liquid to something to make it less thick ● *If the soup is too thick, thin it down a bit with some water or vegetable stock.*

thin down *informal*

if a person thins down, they become less fat ● *He's thinned down a lot since I last saw him.*

thin out   thins, thinning, thinned

thin out

if a large number of people or things thin out, they become fewer in number ● *The crowds thin out as you travel further south.* ● *As the land sloped down to the river, the trees began to thin out.*

thin out sth or **thin** sth **out**

to remove some plants from an area to make more space for the other plants to grow, or to remove part of a plant so that it becomes stronger and grows more quickly ● *I thinned out the strawberry plants in early spring.* ● *Thin out some of the larger clusters of apples so there is less weight on the branches.*

think ahead   thinks, thinking, thought

think ahead

to think carefully about what might hap-pen in the future, or to make plans for things you want to do in the future ● *Just concentrate on what you're doing now and try not to think too far ahead.* ● (sometimes + **to**) *I'm already thinking ahead to what I'll do when my exams are over.*

think back   thinks, thinking, thought

think back (always + *adv/prep*)

to think about things that happened in the past ● (often + **to**) *I thought back to the time when I was living in Montpellier.* ● (sometimes + **on**) *When I think back on what I did, I feel pretty stupid.*

think out/through   thinks, thinking, thought

think out/through sth or **think** sth **out/through**

to think carefully about something you are planning to do and to consider the possible results of it ● *He obviously hadn't thought it out properly.* ● *It sounds like a good idea but we need to spend some time thinking it through.*

think over   thinks, thinking, thought

think over sth or **think** sth **over**

to think carefully about an idea or plan before making a decision ● *She said she'd think it over and give me an answer next week.* ● *I need to think the matter over carefully.*

think through

see **think out/through**

think up   thinks, thinking, thought

think up sth or **think** sth **up**

to create an idea or plan by using your imagination and intelligence ● *I really don't want to go tonight and I'm trying to think up an excuse.* ● *It's one of those competitions where you have to think up a slogan for a product.*

thirst for   thirsts, thirsting, thirsted

thirst for sth *literary*

to want something very much ● *She thirsted for adventure and excitement.*

thrash out   thrashes, thrashing, thrashed

thrash out sth or **thrash** sth **out**

to discuss a problem, idea, or plan in detail until you find a solution, reach an agreement, or make a decision • *Talks are continuing between the two sides to thrash out a final agreement.* • *Over the next few weeks, the president's advisers will be thrashing out some new policies.*

thrive on   thrives, thriving, thrived
(*American pt* also **throve,** *pp* also **thriven**)

thrive on sth
to enjoy a particular situation or condition that other people find difficult or unpleasant [e.g. stress, pressure] and to deal with it successfully • *He was an exceptional leader who thrived on pressure.* • *Don't worry about Kate – she thrives on hard work.*

throttle back/down   throttles, throttling, throttled

throttle back/down (sth) or **throttle** (sth) **back/down**
to make a vehicle, aircraft, or boat travel more slowly by reducing the amount of fuel that flows into the engine • *The pilot throttled back as he came in to land.*

throw at   throws, throwing, threw, thrown

throw yourself **at** sb (always reflexive) *informal*
to make it very obvious to someone that you want to have sex with them • *She basically threw herself at him – it was quite embarrassing to witness.* • *Women just seem to throw themselves at him.*

throw away   throws, throwing, threw, thrown

throw away sth or **throw** sth **away**
1 to get rid of something because you do not want or need it any more • *I'm going to throw away those magazines if you've finished reading them.* • *These potatoes are past their best – I'd better throw them away.*

   throwaway *adj* (always before noun) a throwaway product is a product which you use once or for a short time and then throw away • *We were given some wine in a throwaway plastic bottle.* • *We're living in a **throwaway society.*** (= a society in which products are not made to last a long time)

2 to waste a skill or an opportunity to do something good • *You've spent years*

doing that training, and now you're going to throw it all away.* • *England had a chance to take the lead in the second half and they just threw it away.*

throw back on

be thrown back on sth/sb (always passive) *formal*
if you are thrown back on something or someone, you are forced to depend on them • *He was thrown back on his family during his illness.*

throw down   throws, throwing, threw, thrown

throw down sth or **throw** sth **down**
if soldiers throw down their weapons, they stop fighting • *More than 100 soldiers threw down their guns and surrendered.*

throw in   throws, throwing, threw, thrown

throw in sth or **throw** sth **in**
1 to add something extra when you are selling something without charging the buyer for it • *We booked our trip 10 months in advance so they threw the insurance in for free.*

2 if you are having a conversation and you throw in a remark, you suddenly say it without thinking carefully • *He threw in some comment about women being awful drivers.*

throw in/into   throws, throwing, threw, thrown

throw sb **in/into** swh
to force someone to go to prison • *Some of the protestors were thrown in jail.* • *The authorities had threatened to throw him into prison if he didn't cancel the demonstration.*

throw into   throws, throwing, threw, thrown

throw sth/sb **into** sth
to cause something or someone to suddenly be in a bad and confused state • *Their lives had been thrown into turmoil by the war.*

throw yourself **into** sth (always reflexive)
to start doing something with a lot of enthusiasm and energy • *She's really thrown herself into this new job of hers.*

throw off   throws, throwing, threw, thrown

throw off sth or **throw** sth **off**

1 to remove a piece of clothing quickly and not very carefully ● *We threw off our clothes and ran into the sea.*

2 *informal* to succeed in getting rid of a slight illness ● *I just can't seem to throw off this cold.*

3 to produce large amounts of heat or light ● *The lamp throws off a certain amount of heat as well as light.*

4 to free yourself from something that is limiting you in some way ● *Finally they could throw off the yoke of communism and join the rest of Europe.* ● *It's an unfortunate image and one that he's never quite managed to throw off.*

throw on   throws, throwing, threw, thrown

throw on sth or **throw** sth **on**

to put on a piece of clothing quickly and not very carefully ● *I'll just throw on a jacket and then I'll be with you.*

throw out   throws, throwing, threw, thrown

throw out sth or **throw** sth **out**

1 to get rid of something because you do not want or need it any more ● *If you don't want these books any more I'll throw them out.* ● *I threw those trousers out years ago.*

2 if people in authority throw out a plan or idea [e.g. bill, proposal] they refuse to accept or use it ● *There was a storm of protest about the bill and Parliament threw it out.* ● *The case got thrown out by the courts on the grounds of lack of evidence.*

3 to produce smoke, light, or heat and fill the surrounding air with it ● *I hate it when you get behind some great lorry that's throwing out clouds of black smoke.*

throw out sb or **throw** sb **out**

to force someone to leave a college, school, house or organization ● (often + **of**) *She was thrown out of college in the second year for not attending lectures.* ● *His parents told him that if he started taking drugs again they'd throw him out.*

throw over   throws, throwing, threw, thrown

throw over sb or **throw** sb **over** *old-fashioned*

to end a sexual or romantic relationship with someone ● *I heard he'd been thrown over for a younger man.*

throw together   throws, throwing, threw, thrown

throw together sth or **throw** sth **together**

to make or arrange something quickly and without much effort, using things that can easily be found ● *I hope the food's all right – I just threw it together.*

be thrown together (always passive)

if people are thrown together in a situation, that situation causes them to meet each other and to get to know each other ● *We were thrown together by chance at a conference.*

throw up   throws, throwing, threw, thrown

throw up (sth) or **throw** (sth) **up** (never passive) *informal*

to vomit ● *She'd spent half the night with her head down the toilet throwing up.* ● *I managed a slice of toast but threw it up ten minutes later.*

throw up sth or **throw** sth **up**

1 to produce new problems or ideas ● *I thought it was a good meeting – it threw up a lot of interesting ideas.* ● *The report has thrown up some worrying questions about the safety of air travel.*

2 to suddenly lift your arms or hands upwards, usually when you are very surprised or upset ● (sometimes + **in**) *He threw up his hands in amazement.*

3 to suddenly leave a job or position ● *He's thrown up his job and gone off travelling.*

4 to cause dust or water to rise into the air by moving over it ● *Thick clouds of dust were being thrown up by passing vehicles.*

thrust on/upon   thrusts, thrusting, thrust

thrust sth **on/upon** sb

to force someone to accept or deal with something ● (usually passive) *He felt as if fatherhood had been thrust on him.*

thumb through   thumbs, thumbing, thumbed

thumb through sth

to turn the pages of a book or magazine, looking at them quickly or reading small parts of them ● *I thumbed through the report on my way in to work on the train.*

tick away   ticks, ticking, ticked

tick away (sth)

if a clock ticks away, it makes a short sound every second ● (usually in continuous tenses) *At night all I can hear is the sound of the clock ticking away above my bed.* ● *Can you hear the clock ticking away the minutes?*

tick away/by   ticks, ticking, ticked

tick away/by

if time ticks away, it passes ● *With the final seconds ticking away, Chelsea scored a goal.* ● *The seconds ticked by and still she said nothing.*

tick off   ticks, ticking, ticked

tick off sth or **tick** sth **off**

to put a small mark next to a word on a list to show that you have dealt with it ● *I tend to tick off each item on the list as I do it.* ● *And you've already paid me so I'll tick your name off.*

tick off sb or **tick** sb **off**

1 *British & Australian* to tell someone that they have done something wrong and that you are angry about it ● (often + **for** + doing sth) *I had to tick him off for being late again.* ● *I got ticked off for not going to the meeting.*

   ticking off n [C] *British & Australian* ● (often + **for**) *She gave me a ticking off for leaving dirty dishes in the sink.* ● *I got a real ticking off from Susan when I got in.*

2 *American informal* to annoy someone ● *It really ticks me off the way these guys keep breaking their promises.*

   ticked off adj (always after verb) *American informal* ● (often + **at**) *I guess she was ticked off at Pete because he was late.*

tick over   ticks, ticking, ticked

tick over

1 *British & Australian* if the engine of a vehicle is ticking over, the engine is operat-

ing slowly although the vehicle is not moving ● (usually in continuous tenses) *I left the car with the engine ticking over.*

2 *British & Australian* if a business or system is ticking over, it is working but it is not producing very much ● (usually in continuous tenses) *For some months the financial markets have been just ticking over.* ● *Isobel will keep things ticking over in the office till I get back.*

tide over   tides, tiding, tided

tide sb **over** (sth) (never passive)

to help someone, usually by giving them money for a period of time when they have no money ● *Could you lend me £20 to tide me over till the weekend?* ● *I got some money in January which should tide me over the next couple of months.*

tidy away   tidies, tidying, tidied

tidy away sth or **tidy** sth **away** *British & Australian*

to put things in cupboards and drawers etc. after you have been using them ● *I usually get the kids to tidy their toys away before they go to bed.* ● *I just need to tidy a few things away in the kitchen.*

tidy out   tidies, tidying, tidied

tidy out sth or **tidy** sth **out** *British & Australian*

to make a space such as a room or cupboard tidy, by arranging things correctly and getting rid of the things that you do not want ● *I think it's time I tidied out that cupboard.* ● *I was just tidying out the spare room.*

tidy up   tidies, tidying, tidied

tidy up (sth) or **tidy** (sth) **up** *mainly British & Australian*

to make a room or a group of things tidy by putting things in the correct place ● *I'd better tidy up before our guests come.* ● *You can watch television when you've tidied up your room.*

   tidy-up n [C] *British & Australian informal* ● (usually singular) *I'm just having a quick tidy-up in the lounge.*

tidy up sb or **tidy** sb **up** *British & Australian*

to make someone look neat and clean by washing their hands and face, brushing their hair etc. ● (often reflexive) *Give me five minutes to tidy myself up a bit and I'll join you in the bar.*

tidy up sth or **tidy** sth **up** *British & Australian*

to correct mistakes and make small improvements to a piece of written work • *The article is basically well written – it just needs tidying up a bit.*

tie back   ties, tying, tied

tie back sth or **tie** sth **back**

to fasten something that usually hangs down [esp. hair] so that it is fixed in position and not hanging down • *I usually tie my hair back for work.*

tie down   ties, tying, tied

tie down sth/sb or **tie** sth/sb **down**

to fasten something or someone in a particular position, especially by using ropes • (sometimes + **to**) *They tied him down to the bed so he couldn't escape.* • *We loaded a ladder onto the roof of the van and tied it down with a length of rope.*

tie sb **down**

to stop someone from being free to do what they want to do • *He doesn't want to be tied down by a relationship.*

tie down sb or **tie** sb **down**

to prevent soldiers or police officers from going to a place where they are needed • *Half the army was tied down defending the north of the country from invaders.*

tie in   ties, tying, tied

tie in

if an idea or a statement ties in with something else that is said or written, it agrees with it or it is closely connected to it • (usually + **with**) *I don't understand how that statement ties in with the rest of his argument.* • *Michael's point about staffing numbers ties in with what you were just saying.*

tie in with   ties, tying, tied

tie in with sth

if one event ties in with another, it is planned so that both events happen at the same time • *There are a series of interviews planned to tie in with the publication of his latest novel.*

tie up   ties, tying, tied

tie up sb/sth or **tie** sb/sth **up**

to tie a part of a person or animal's body with a rope so that they cannot move or escape • *The security guard was left tied up in a cupboard.* • *I tied the dog up while I went into the shop.*

be tied up (always passive) *informal*

1 to be busy so that you are unable to see or speak to anyone else or go anywhere • *I'm a bit tied up at the moment, could you call back tomorrow?* • *I'm afraid she's tied up in a meeting at the moment.*

2 if money is tied up, it is used for one purpose and cannot be used for anything else • (usually + **in**) *He has plenty of money but most of it is tied up in property.*

tie up sth or **tie** sth **up**

1 to put string or rope around something so that it is fastened together • *I found a bundle of letters tied up with red ribbon at the back of her drawer.*

2 if you tie up your shoelaces, you join them with a knot • *I bent over to tie up my shoelaces.*

3 to use something continuously, preventing other people from using it • *He's had the printer tied up for the last half hour, printing out his reports.*

4 *American & Australian* to block a road or other track so that vehicles cannot move in the usual way • *The airport was tied up for 45 minutes, waiting for the Presidential plane to take off.*

tie-up *n* [C] *American* • *She was stuck in a tie-up on the interstate on her way home.*

tie up

to tie a boat to something using a rope or chain • *We tied up alongside the harbour wall.*

tie up with

be tied up with sth (always passive)

to be connected with something • *I suspect that the physical symptoms are all tied up with her mental state.*

tighten up   tightens, tightening, tightened

tighten up sth or **tighten** sth **up**

to fasten something that holds one thing to another [e.g. screw, bolt, strap] more firmly • *The mechanic went around tightening up any screws which had worked loose.*

tighten up (sth) or **tighten** (sth) **up**

1 to make rules more limiting and more difficult to avoid ● *New UK legislation is planned to tighten up the rules on mail-shots.* ● (sometimes + **on**) *The government is tightening up on safety standards.*

2 if your muscles tighten up, or you tighten them up, they become stiff, either because you have exercised a lot or because you are not relaxed ● *And this next exercise will really tighten up those tummy muscles.* ● *My right calf tightened up during the last mile and was starting to get painful.*

tighten up

if an organization or a sports team tightens up, they become more efficient, more controlled and make fewer mistakes ● *Chelsea's defence have really tightened up under their new manager.*

---

tinker about/around   **tinkers, tinkering, tinkered**

tinker about/around

to spend time doing small jobs or making small changes to things, usually trying to improve or repair them ● (often + *adv/prep*) *I was just tinkering about in the garage.*

---

tinker with   **tinkers, tinkering, tinkered**

tinker with sth

to make small changes to something, usually trying to improve or repair it ● *Every time I see Chris, he's tinkering with his car.* ● *Yeats was constantly tinkering with his poems, especially his earlier ones.*

---

tip off   **tips, tipping, tipped**

tip off sb or **tip** sb **off**

to warn someone secretly about something that will happen so that they can take action or prevent it from happening ● (often + **about**) *The prison governor had been tipped off about a possible escape plan.* ● *Someone must have tipped off the burglars that the house would be empty.*

  tip-off n [C] ● *Acting on a tip-off, the police raided the house and found £500,000 worth of heroin.*

---

tip over   **tips, tipping, tipped**

tip over (sth) or **tip** (sth) **over**

if something tips over, or if you tip it over, it falls onto its side ● *As I stood up I tipped my cup of coffee over.*

---

tip up   **tips, tipping, tipped**

tip up

if something tips up, it falls forwards or backwards, usually because a heavy object is put on one end of it ● *We put three heavy suitcases on the trolley and it tipped up.*

tip up sth or **tip** sth **up**

to turn a container upside down so that its contents come out ● *He tipped up the wheelbarrow and the sand poured into a heap on the ground.*

---

tiptoe around/round   **tiptoes, tiptoeing, tiptoed**

tiptoe around/round sb/sth

to avoid dealing with or talking about a difficult subject, problem or person ● *Things are very difficult with everyone tiptoeing around the subject of her illness.*

---

tire of   **tires, tiring, tired**

tire of sth/doing sth

to become bored with something that you used to enjoy ● *I wouldn't worry about the video games – he'll soon tire of them.* ● *I love all of Cary Grant's films and I never tire of watching them.*

---

tire out   **tires, tiring, tired**

tire out sb or **tire** sb **out**

to make someone very tired ● *The twelve-*

hour journey had tired me out.
• (sometimes reflexive) *You'll tire your-self out working so hard.*
tired out *adj* • *I think I'm going to go to bed – I'm absolutely tired out.*

toddle off   toddles, toddling, toddled

toddle off *British & Australian informal*
to leave somewhere and walk to another place • *It's getting late so I'm going to toddle off now.*

tog out/up   togs, togging, togged

tog out/up sb or **tog** sb **out/up** *British & Australian informal*
to put on clothes for a particular occasion or activity, or to put on special or stylish clothes • (often reflexive) *It was snowing outside, so I togged myself out in a thick jacket and boots.* • *Tony was all togged up in his new linen suit.*

toil away   toils, toiling, toiled

toil away
to work very hard on something for a long period of time • (often in continuous tenses) *I've been toiling away in the kitchen all afternoon.* • (often + **at**) *He's been toiling away at the same paper for what seems like months.*

tone down   tones, toning, toned

tone down sth or **tone** sth **down**
1 to make a piece of writing, a speech, or a performance less offensive or less critical • *Certain parts of the show have been toned down to make it suitable for a family audience.*
toned-down *adj* • *The film is a toned-down version of the original play.*
2 to start behaving or dressing in a way that attracts less attention • *He's had to tone down his flamboyant image since becoming a politician.*
3 to make a colour less bright • *You can tone down bright lipstick with a touch of face powder.*

tone in   tones, toning, toned

tone in *British & Australian*
if one piece of clothing or material tones in with another one, they look good together because their colours are similar • (often + **with**) *I'm looking for some curtains which will tone in with my new carpet.*

tone up   tones, toning, toned

tone up (sth) or **tone** (sth) **up**
to make your body or your muscles firmer and stronger by doing physical exercise • *Now this is a really good exercise for toning up those stomach muscles.* • *I don't want to lose weight, I just want to tone up.*

tool up   tools, tooling, tooled

tool up (sth) or **tool** (sth) **up**
if a business or factory tools up, or if someone tools it up, it is provided with the equipment it needs in order to produce goods • *The company has spent over $1 billion tooling up its 15 factories.* • (often + **for**) *Even for a small company, the costs of tooling up for production can be huge.*

top off   tops, topping, topped

top off sth or **top** sth **off**
to complete something in an enjoyable or successful way • *It had been such a nice evening and I thought a walk down by the lake would top it off nicely.*

top out   tops, topping, topped

top out *American*
if an amount or a rate tops out, it stops increasing after reaching a high level • (usually + **at**) *The hot weather continued yesterday with the temperature in New York topping out at 37 degrees C.*

top up   tops, topping, topped

top up sth or **top** sth **up**
to add more liquid to a container that is partly empty in order to make it full • *You've almost finished your drink. Let me top up your glass.* • (sometimes + **with**) *To make lemonade, mix together some lemon juice and sugar, then top it up with water.*

top up sb or **top** sb **up**
to put more drink into someone's glass or cup • *Can I top you up while I've got the wine in my hand?*
top-up *n* [C] • *Can I give you a top-up?*

topple over   topples, toppling, toppled

topple over
to fall to the ground because of not being very well balanced or because of being pushed • *Those books look as if they're going to topple over any minute.*

toss about/around　tosses, tossing, tossed

toss about/around sth or **toss** sth **about/around**

to discuss an idea or suggestion, without considering it in a serious way • *We haven't decided on our next project yet – we're just tossing some ideas around.*

toss back/down　tosses, tossing, tossed

toss back/down sth or **toss** sth **back/down**

to drink something very quickly, especially an alcoholic drink • *He tossed back a couple of glasses of whisky and left.*

toss for　tosses, tossing, tossed

toss (sb) **for** sth

to decide which person or team can do something or have something by throwing a coin in the air and guessing which side of the coin will be on top when it lands • *Who's going to bat first? Let's toss for it.* • *We'll each have a T-shirt and I'll toss you for the hat.*

toss off　tosses, tossing, tossed

toss off sth or **toss** sth **off**

to write something [e.g. letter, essay, article] very quickly, without thinking about it carefully • *I don't suppose it's very well written because I tossed it off in half an hour.*

toss off *British & Australian taboo*

if a man tosses off, he gives himself sexual pleasure by rubbing his penis • *Is that your idea of a sex-life – you toss off over porn mags?*

toss up　tosses, tossing, tossed

toss up

to decide which person or team can do something or have something by throwing a coin into the air and guessing which side of the coin will be on top when it lands • (often + to do sth) *Let's toss up to see which team will go first.*

toss-up n [singular] a situation in which two people or things seem equally likely to be chosen or two possible results seem equally likely to happen • (often + between) *I wouldn't like to say who'll get the job. It's a toss-up between Simon and Harry.*

tot up　tots, totting, totted

tot up sth or **tot** sth **up** *mainly British & Australian informal*

to add numbers or amounts together in order to get a total • *Let's tot up our scores to find out who's won.* • *Could you tot up what I owe you and I'll write a cheque?*

total up　totals, totalling, totalled
(*American & Australian* also **totals, totaling, totaled**)

total up sth or **total** sth **up**

to add numbers or amounts together in order to get a total • *We totalled up the money we had each earned and then shared it among the three of us.*

total up to　totals, totalling, totalled
(*American & Australian* also **totals, totaling, totaled**)

total up to sth

to be a particular total when amounts or numbers are added together • *The charity is well-supported, with annual contributions totalling up to $100 million a year.*

tote up　totes, toting, toted

tote up sth or **tote** sth **up** *American*

to add numbers or amounts together in order to get a total • *The company has toted up over $40 million in contracts in the past year.*

touch down　touches, touching, touched

touch down

when an aircraft touches down, it lands on the ground • *We touched down in Shannon airport.* • *The plane finally touched down at Heathrow after a ten hour delay.*

touchdown n (C/U) • *One of the plane's tyres burst on touchdown.*

touch for　touches, touching, touched

touch sb **for** sth *informal*

to borrow or take money from someone • *He touched me for ten dollars yesterday.*

touch off　touches, touching, touched

touch off sth

to make something suddenly begin, often a difficult or violent situation • *Cancellation of the elections touched off a wave of bombings, shootings and riots.*

touch on/upon   touches, touching, touched

touch on/upon sth
   to mention a subject briefly when speaking or writing about something ● *I'm only going to touch on the topic at this point but I shall be talking about it in more detail later.*

touch up   touches, touching, touched

touch up sth or **touch** sth **up**
   to improve something by making small changes or additions ● *I'm just going to go and touch up my make-up.* ● *The paintwork needs touching up in places.*

touch up sb or **touch** sb **up** *British informal*
   to touch someone's body without their permission in order to get sexual excitement ● *She was touched up on the train by some revolting old man.*

touch upon
   see **touch on/upon**

toughen up   toughens, toughening, toughened

toughen up (sb) or **toughen** (sb) **up**
   to become stronger and more able to deal with problems, or to make someone become this way ● *His father thought that a spell in the army would toughen him up.* ● *He'll toughen up once he gets to school.*

toughen up sth or **toughen** sth **up**
   to make rules more limiting and more difficult to avoid ● *The government want to toughen up existing drug laws.*

tout around/round   touts, touting, touted

tout around/round sth or **tout** sth **around/round** (sth)
   to take or send something to many different companies, hoping that they will buy it from you ● *Leeming has recently completed a book which he is currently touting around American publishers.*

tout for   touts, touting, touted

tout for sth
   to try to persuade people to buy your goods or services ● *There were hundreds of taxis at the airport, all touting for business.*

tout round
   see **tout around/round**

tower above/over   towers, towering, towered

tower above/over sb/sth
1 to be much taller or higher than someone or something else and make them look small ● *He's only 12 but he towers over his older brother.* ● *Canary Wharf towers above the Dockland area of London.*
2 to be much more successful than another person or organization that is doing the same thing ● *One computer manufacturer towers above all the rest.*

toy with   toys, toying, toyed

toy with sth
1 to think about an idea in a way that is not very serious, often not making a decision about it ● (usually in continuous tenses) *Dom and I are toying with the idea of going to Mexico this year.*
2 to keep touching an object, moving it from one position to another, usually while you are thinking about something else ● *She sat quietly for a moment, toying with her glasses.*

trace out   traces, tracing, traced

trace out sth or **trace** sth **out**
   to carefully and clearly write or mark something ● *You can trace out shapes by steering the marker pen around the paper.*

track down   tracks, tracking, tracked

track down sb/sth or **track** sb/sth **down**
   to find someone or something after searching for them in many different places ● *I'm trying to track down one of my old school friends.* ● *They've finally managed to track down that book I wanted.*

trade down   trades, trading, traded

trade down
   to sell something, especially a car or a house, and buy one that is cheaper ● (sometimes + **to**) *They plan to trade down to a smaller house when they retire.*

trade in   trades, trading, traded

trade in sth or **trade** sth **in**
   to give something as part of the payment for something else ● (usually + **for**) *He*

recently traded in his jeep for a new Mercedes.

trade-in *n* [C] *American & Australian*
• *Will you use your old car as a trade-in?*
• (used as *adj*) *(American & Australian) We got a good trade-in price for our old television.*

trade off   trades, trading, traded

trade off sth or **trade** sth **off**

to accept something that you do not want in order to have something else that you want • (often + **against**) *Buying in the sales often means trading off lower prices against restricted choice.*

trade-off *n* [C] • (often + **for**) *For some car owners, lack of space is an acceptable trade-off for a sporty design.* (= they will accept the lack of space because they like the design)

trade on/upon   trades, trading, traded

trade on/upon sth

to use a situation or a personal quality for your own advantage, especially in an unfair way • *People are always trading on her generosity.* • *Most good-looking people trade on their attractiveness to some extent.*

trade up   trades, trading, traded

trade up

to sell something, especially a car or house, and buy one that is more expensive • (often + **to**) *House owners are rushing to trade up to larger homes before prices rise again.*

trade upon

see **trade on/upon**

traffic in   traffics, trafficking, trafficked

traffic in sth

to buy and sell illegal goods, especially drugs • *Both men were charged with trafficking in illegal drugs.*

trail away/off   trails, trailing, trailed

trail away/off

if someone's voice trails away or off, it gradually becomes quieter and then stops • *He could see she was upset and his voice trailed away uncertainly.* • *"Without you, I ..." she trailed off and wiped a tear from her eye.*

train on/upon   trains, training, trained

train sth **on/upon** sb/sth

to aim something, especially a gun, in the direction of someone or something • *Anti-aircraft guns were trained on the jets flying overhead.*

train up   trains, training, trained

train up sb or **train** sb **up**

to teach someone a particular skill or subject • *More doctors and nurses need to be trained up to meet the growing demand.* • *Volunteers are trained up to deal with all kinds of emergencies.*

train upon

see **train on/upon**

traipse around/round   traipses, traipsing, traipsed

traipse around/round (swh) *informal*

to walk to many places slowly and unwillingly, usually because you are tired • *I've been traipsing around town for hours looking for a present for her.*

treat to   treats, treating, treated

treat sb **to** sth

to buy or pay for something for someone else • *He's got so few clothes – I thought I'd treat him to a new sweater.* • (often reflexive) *I'm going to treat myself to* (= buy myself) *a new pair of sandals.*

trick out

be tricked out (always passive; always + *adv/prep*) *literary*

to be decorated or dressed in a special way • *The hall was tricked out with war memorabilia.*

trick out of   tricks, tricking, tricked

trick sb **out of** sth

to take something away from someone by deceiving them • *He was tricked out of his inheritance by his brother.*

trifle with   trifles, trifling, trifled

trifle with sb/sth

to treat someone or something as if they are not important, or to not give very much attention to someone or something • (often negative) *Sally Palmer is not a woman to be trifled with.*

trigger off   triggers, triggering, triggered

trigger off sth or **trigger** sth **off**
to make something suddenly begin, often a difficult or violent situation • *The latest bomb is likely to trigger off more violent demonstrations in the capital.*

trip over   trips, tripping, tripped

trip over (sth)
to fall or almost fall because you have accidentally hit your foot against something while walking or running • *I kept tripping over tree roots as we walked through the forest.* • *She tripped over and sprained her ankle.*

trip up   trips, tripping, tripped

trip up (sb) or **trip** (sb) **up**
1 to fall or almost fall because you have hit your foot against something while walking or running, or to make someone do this • *I stumbled out of bed and tripped up on the edge of the carpet.* • *She stuck her foot out and tripped him up as he was walking past.*
2 to make a mistake, or to cause someone to make a mistake, especially by making them say something wrong • *Questions like that seem designed to trip you up.* • (sometimes + **on**) *I tripped up on the last question.*

triumph over   triumphs, triumphing, triumphed

triumph over sth/sb
to defeat something or someone, especially when this is very difficult • *This is the story of a man who triumphs over a series of disasters.* • *I believe that ultimately, good will triumph over evil.*

trot off   trots, trotting, trotted

trot off *informal*
if someone trots off, they go somewhere • (often + **to**) *I'm just trotting off to the shops if you want anything.*

trot out   trots, trotting, trotted

trot out sth or **trot** sth **out** *informal*
to say something that is not new and that you have not really thought about but are simply repeating • *She always trots out the same old excuses.* • *You trot out that argument whenever I try to discuss this*
matter with you.

true up   trues, trueing or truing, trued

true up sth or **true** sth **up** *American*
to make something [e.g. board, wall] straight or flat • *True up the boards before you lay the new flooring.*

truss up   trusses, trussing, trussed

truss up sb/sth or **truss** sb/sth **up**
to tie a person or animal very tightly so that they cannot move or escape • *The girls were trussed up and left in a cellar.*

trust in   trusts, trusting, trusted

trust in sth/sb *formal*
to believe in something or someone completely • *Trust in God.*

trust to   trusts, trusting, trusted

trust to sth
to rely on a particular thing [esp. luck], usually because nothing else is available to help you • *There's no guarantee we'll win – we'll just have to trust to luck.*

try back   tries, trying, tried

try (sb) **back** (never passive) *American informal*
to telephone someone again when you have already telephoned them but have not managed to speak to them • *Your sister called when you were out – she says she'll try back later.*

try for   tries, trying, tried

try for sth
to try to get something that you really want • *Aren't you going to try for that job in the sales department?* • *Apparently they'd been trying for a baby for over two years.*

try on   tries, trying, tried

try on sth or **try** sth **on**
to put on a piece of clothing to find out whether it fits you or whether you like it, especially before buying it • *I must have tried on everything in the shop, but nothing looked right on me.* • *Why don't you try on those yellow trousers?*

try it on *British & Australian informal*
if someone tries it on, they behave badly, especially in order to find out how badly they can behave before other people become angry • *The kids often try it on with*

a new babysitter.

try out　　tries, trying, tried

try out sth or **try** sth **out**
to test something in order to find out if it works or to decide whether you like it ● *They're trying out a new security system at the bank.* ● *We're going to try out a new restaurant tonight.* ● (often + **on**) *I've got a new recipe that I'm going to try out on you.*

try out *American & Australian*
to compete for a position in a sports team or a part in a play by playing or performing in front of other people ● (usually + **for**) *Luke's trying out for the college football team.* ● *She once tried out for the lead role in a television series.*

tryout *n* [C] *American & Australian* ● *They're holding tryouts tonight for the school cheerleaders.*

tuck away　　tucks, tucking, tucked

tuck away sth or **tuck** sth **away**
1 to put something in a safe place, especially something valuable ● (usually + **in**) *She gave him a £10 note which he tucked away in his inside pocket.* ● *He kept her letter tucked away in a desk drawer.*
2 *informal* to quickly eat large amounts of food ● *He usually tucks away a large meal a few hours before starting a race.*

be tucked away (always passive; always + *adv/prep*)
to be in a quiet or hidden place which not many people see or go to ● *The tiny laboratory was tucked away in the Suffolk countryside.* ● *We had a small kitchenette which was tucked away behind a folding screen.*

tuck in　　tucks, tucking, tucked

tuck in sth or **tuck** sth **in**
to push the loose end of a piece of clothing or material in something, usually to make it tidy ● *The nice thing about this shirt is that you can tuck it in or wear it out.*

tuck in *informal*
to start eating food ● (usually an order) *The food's on the table so tuck in before it gets cold.*

tuck in/up　　tucks, tucking, tucked

tuck in/up sb or **tuck** sb **in/up**
to make a child comfortable in bed by straightening the sheets and blankets ● *Tom usually likes his Dad to tuck him in.*

tuck into　　tucks, tucking, tucked

tuck into sth *informal*
to start eating ● *I was just about to tuck into an enormous pizza when you rang.*

tuck up　　tucks, tucking, tucked

tuck up sth or **tuck** sth **up**
to move your legs or feet underneath your body so that you are sitting on them ● *She sat in an armchair by the window, her legs tucked up underneath her.*

tucker out　　tuckers, tuckering, tuckered

tucker out sb or **tucker** sb **out**
American old-fashioned informal
to make someone very tired ● *She was tuckered out by the time she got home from work.*

tug at　　tugs, tugging, tugged

tug at sth
to give something a quick, strong pull ● *Joe was tugging at my sleeve.*

tumble down　　tumbles, tumbling, tumbled

tumble down
if a building or wall tumbles down, it falls to the ground ● *It looks as if the whole building could come tumbling down at any moment.*

tumbledown *adj* (always before noun)
a tumbledown building is in very bad condition and parts of it are falling down ● *There was a tumbledown shed at the bottom of the garden.*

tumble over　　tumbles, tumbling, tumbled

tumble over
to fall to the ground ● *He lost his balance and tumbled over.*

tumble to　　tumbles, tumbling, tumbled

tumble to sth *British informal*
to understand or realize something suddenly ● *I think he's tumbled to our plan.*

tune in   tunes, tuning, tuned

tune in
to turn on the radio or television in order to listen to or watch a particular programme • *Don't forget to tune in next week for another exciting episode!* • (often + **to**) *67 million people tune in to late night television.*

tune in sth *American*
to turn on the radio or television in order to listen to or watch a particular programme • *Did you tune in the ballgame last night?*

be tuned in (always passive)
to have a good understanding of what is happening in a situation or what other people are thinking • (usually + **to**) *She just doesn't seem to be tuned in to her students' needs.*

tune into   tunes, tuning, tuned

tune into sth
to turn on the radio or television in order to listen to or watch a particular programme • *Younger Cubans tend to tune into the American television networks.*

tune out   tunes, tuning, tuned

tune out sb/sth or **tune** sb/sth **out** *American informal*
to ignore someone or not give your attention to something that is happening around you • *He could tune Karen out and still look like he was listening to her every word.* • *You want to relax and tune out distractions from the TV or telephone.*

tune up   tunes, tuning, tuned

tune up (sth) or **tune** (sth) **up**
if musicians who are preparing to play tune up or tune up their instruments, they make changes to their instruments so that they produce the correct sounds • *The orchestra were just tuning up as we arrived.*

tune up sth or **tune** sth **up**
to make changes to a car's engine so that it works as well as possible • *They charge up to £500 to tune up a Porsche.*
tune-up n [C] • *Your engine needs a tune-up.*

turf out   turfs, turfing, turfed

turf out sb or **turf** sb **out** *mainly British & Australian informal*
to force someone to leave a particular place or organization • (often + **of**) *He was turfed out of the club for fighting.*

turf out sth or **turf** sth **out** *British & Australian informal*
to get rid of things that you do not want • *I turfed out a load of old shoes last week.*

turn against   turns, turning, turned

turn (sb) **against** sth/sb
to decide not to like or agree with someone or something, or to make someone do this • *Public opinion has turned against the war after six years of fighting.* • *The girl's natural father claims that her stepfather is turning her against him.*

turn around/round   turns, turning, turned

turn around/round sth or **turn** sth **around/round**
1 to change an unsuccessful business, plan, or system so that it becomes successful • *A new director has been brought in to turn the company round.* • *The opposition party is promising to turn round the economy in six years if they are elected.*
   turnaround n [C] a sudden improvement, especially in a business or the economy of a country • *Forecasts of an economic turnaround were challenged yesterday.*
2 to change the words or meaning of something that someone has said or written • *Whenever I say something he always manages to turn it round and make it sound stupid.*

turn around/round (sb/sth) or **turn** (sb/sth) **around/round**
to turn so that you are facing the opposite direction, or to make someone or something do this • *Someone called her name and she turned around.* • *He'd turned all her photographs round to face the wall.*

turn away   turns, turning, turned

turn away sb or **turn** sb **away**
1 to refuse to allow someone to enter a place, usually because there is no more space • *The camp was already full and many of the refugees had been turned*

away. ● Well-qualified students are being turned away because there just aren't the places.

2 to refuse to help someone ● *He's my son after all, I can't just turn him away.*

turn away from   turns, turning, turned

turn (sb) **away from** sth

to stop supporting something or being interested in something, or to make someone do this ● *More and more young people are turning away from the church.* ● *The reforms have tended to turn voters away from communist control.*

turn back   turns, turning, turned

turn back sth or **turn** sth **back**

to fold a part of something which bends easily [esp. pages, sheets] so that it covers another part ● *She'd turned the sheet back neatly over the blanket, like they do in hotels.*

turn back (sb) or **turn** (sb) **back**

to return to the place that you came from, or to make someone do this ● *We ran out of money halfway across America and had to turn back.* ● *Boatloads of refugees are being turned back before they reach the port.*

turn back

to change your plans ● (usually negative) *Once we've committed ourselves to this, there's no turning back.*

turn down   turns, turning, turned

turn down sb/sth or **turn** sb/sth **down**

to refuse an offer or request ● *He was offered the job but he turned it down because it involved too much travelling.* ● *Look, I'm offering you a free meal – you're surely not going to turn me down?*

turn down sth or **turn** sth **down**

to reduce the amount of sound or heat that is produced by a device [e.g. television, radio, oven] ● *Could you turn the radio down a little?* ● *Bring to the boil, then turn down the heat and simmer for 20 minutes.*

turn in   turns, turning, turned

turn in sth or **turn** sth **in**

1 to give something back to an organization or person in authority ● (often + **to**)

Hundreds of guns were turned in to the police after a national gun amnesty was declared.

2 *mainly American* to give a piece of written work to a teacher or employer ● *She's worried she won't be able to turn in her project on time.*

turn in sb or **turn** sb **in**

to take a criminal to the police ● (often reflexive) *After six months on the run, he turned himself in.* ● (sometimes + **to**) *She turned her husband in to the police the day after the accident.*

turn in *informal*

to go to bed ● *I'm going to turn in now – goodnight everyone.*

turn in sth

to produce results, especially good results ● *Both companies turn in pre-tax profits of over 5.5 million annually.* ● *He turned in a stunning performance as Hamlet at the National last year.*

turn into   turns, turning, turned

turn (sth/sb) **into** sth/sb

to change and become something or someone different, or to make something or someone do this ● *There are fears that this minor conflict could turn into a full-scale war.* ● *They're going to turn the old warehouse into a nightclub.* ● *Did you think I'd turned into a raging feminist overnight?*

turn off   turns, turning, turned

turn off sth or **turn** sth **off**

to touch a switch so that a machine or a piece of electrical equipment stops working, or to stop the flow or supply of something [e.g. water, electricity] ● *Make sure you turn off all the lights before you leave.* ● *We turned the water off at the mains when the pipes burst.* ● *Can you turn the TV off before you go to bed?*

turn off (sth)

to leave the road you are travelling on and travel along another one ● *You need to turn off at the next exit.* ● *We turned off the motorway and drove to a nearby garage.*

turn-off *n* [C] ● *I think there's a turn-off about half a mile up this road.*

turn off sb or turn sb off

to make someone feel that they are not interested in sex • *A lot of women say that explicit pornography actually turns them off.*

turn-off *n* [C] *informal* • *Hairy backs really are the ultimate turn-off.*

turn off sb or turn sb off (sth)

to make someone decide that they are not interested in something • *Bad teaching can turn children off poetry for life.* • *The title of the lecture was enough to turn most people off.*

turn-off *n* [C] *informal* • *Just the appearance of the food is a turn-off for a lot of people.*

turn on   turns, turning, turned

turn on sth or turn sth on

1 to touch a switch so that a machine or a piece of electrical equipment starts to work, or to start a flow or supply of something [e.g. water, electricity] • *Could you turn on the radio so we can listen to the news?* • *She shut the curtains and turned the lights on.* • *The oven's not working – have you turned the gas on yet?*

2 to start to show a particular quality, especially a quality such as affection or charm • *You really upset me and now you want me to be nice to you – I can't just turn it on like that.* • *When he thought I might be interested he really started to turn on the charm.*

turn on sb or turn sb on

1 to make someone feel sexually excited • *Aftershave really turns me on.*

turn-on *n* [C] *informal* • *I find leather a real turn-on.*

2 to make someone interested in something • *So what is it about science fiction that turns you on?* • *You like doing crosswords? – oh, well, **whatever turns you on**.* (= you may like doing crosswords but it wouldn't interest me)

turn on to   turns, turning, turned

turn sb on to sth/sb

to make someone start to be interested in something or someone • *It was an ex-boyfriend of mine who turned me on to jazz.*

turn on/upon   turns, turning, turned

turn on/upon sth

if an event or situation turns on something, it depends on it in order to work successfully • (often + question word) *The next election will turn on how people feel about the present economic situation.*

turn on/upon sb

to attack someone or criticize someone very strongly • *I tried to help her stand up but she turned on me, shouting 'Get off you bitch!'.*

turn out   turns, turning, turned

turn out

1 to happen in a particular way or to have a particular result • (often + *adv/prep*) *That dress I made turned out really well.* • *My trip to London didn't turn out quite as planned.* • (sometimes + to be sth) *Her granddaughter has turned out to be very musical.* • (sometimes + that) *It turned out that they'd been having an affair the whole time.*

2 if people turn out for an event or activity they go to watch it or take part in it • (often + to do sth) *Thousands of people turned out to welcome the England team home.*

turn-out *n* [C] the number of people who come to watch or take part in an event or activity • (usually singular) *There was a good turn-out for the match last Saturday.*

turn out sth or turn sth out

1 if a company or business turns out something, they make or produce it • *American film studios turn out hundreds of films each year.*

2 if you turn out a light, you touch a switch so that it stops working • *He turned out the light and went to sleep.*

3 if you turn out a container or the things that are in it, you empty it completely • *He opened the bag and turned the contents out onto the kitchen table.* • *I've turned out all the cupboards and drawers but I just can't find those photos.*

turn out sb or turn sb out

to make someone leave a place • (usually + **of**) *He was turned out of his flat because he couldn't pay the rent.*

turn over *turns, turning, turned*

turn over (sb/sth) or **turn** (sb/sth) **over**

to move so that you are facing in a different direction, especially when you are lying down, or or to move someone or something in this way • *Surely you're not going to just turn over and go to sleep?* • *Turn the postcard over and read what it says on the back.*

turn over sb or **turn** sb **over**

to take a criminal to the police or other authority • (usually + **to**) *A convicted terrorist was eventually turned over to the police, twelve hours after he had taken refuge in the Swiss Embassy.*

turn over sth or **turn** sth **over**

1 to give something to someone, especially someone in authority, or to make someone responsible for something • (usually + **to**) *All documents are to be turned over to the court.* • *He had intended to turn the business over to his son when he retired.*

2 to use or allow something to be used for a different purpose • (usually + **to**) *Grants are being offered to farmers who agree to turn over their land to woodland and forests.*

3 if a business or a company turns over an amount of money, it makes that amount in a particular period of time • *The company expects to turn over £11 million this year.*

turnover *n* [singular] the total amount of money made by a company or business in a particular period of time • *Green & Butler have an annual turnover of about £80 million.*

4 *British & Australian informal* to search a place or steal something from a place, making it very untidy or causing damage • *Their flat was turned over while they were away.*

turn over (sth) or **turn** (sth) **over**

1 to turn a page in a book so that the side which was facing down is now facing up • *If you turn the page over you can see a diagram which explains this.* • *Have you finished reading this page? Can I turn over now?*

2 *British* to change to a different channel on a television • *Do you mind if I turn over – there's a travel programme I want*

to watch on the other side.

3 if a car engine turns over, or if someone turns it over, it starts • *She turned the engine over and let it run for a few seconds.* • *I've tried everything but I can't even get it to turn over.*

turn round
see **turn around/round**

turn to *turns, turning, turned*

turn to sb

to ask someone for help, sympathy or advice • *I didn't want to burden him with my problems, but I had no-one else to turn to.* • *During the oil crisis, poorer countries turned to the richer ones for economic aid.*

turn to sth

to start to do or take something bad [e.g. crime, drugs, drink], usually because you are unhappy • *She turned to drugs after the break-up of her fifteen-year marriage.* • *In desperation, some young people are turning to crime.*

turn (sth) **to** sth

if someone turns to a particular subject, or if they turn their thoughts or attention to it, they begin to think, speak or write about it • *I would now like to turn to an issue which concerns us all – racism.* • *In the mid-eighties she began to turn her attention to the visual arts.*

turn up *turns, turning, turned*

turn up sth or **turn** sth **up**

1 to increase the amount of something, especially sound or heat, that is produced by a machine [e.g. television, radio, oven] • *Can you turn up the television a little – I can hardly hear it.* • *Turn the oven up to 200 degrees.*

2 to discover something, especially information, after a lot of searching • *Police have failed to turn up any new evidence about the murder.*

3 to shorten a piece of clothing [esp. trousers], by folding back and sewing the bottom edge of the material • *My legs are so short I've had to turn up every pair of trousers I've ever bought.*

turn-up *n* [C] *British* the piece of material at the bottom of a trouser leg that is folded back • *He won't wear trousers with turn-ups.*

turn up

1 if someone turns up somewhere, they arrive at that place • *Alex turned up late, as usual.* • *You can just turn up and buy a ticket on the door.*

2 if someone or something turns up, they appear or are found, either after a long time or when you are not expecting them • *Did your glasses ever turn up?* • *The children eventually turned up safe and well.*

3 if an opportunity to do something turns up, it becomes available, usually when you are not expecting it • *This job turned up just when I needed it.* • *You won't be out of work long. Something will turn up, you'll see.*

turn upon

see **turn on/upon**

type in/into   types, typing, typed

type in sth or **type** sth **in**

type sth **into** sth

to put information into a computer using a keyboard • *He typed in the licence plate number and her personal details flashed on the screen.* • *Responses to the questionnaire are typed directly into a computer.*

type out/up   types, typing, typed

type out/up sth or **type** sth **out/up**

to produce a copy of something you have written by typing it into a computer or by using a typewriter • *I drafted a letter and Aileen typed it out for me.* • *She's typed up all her notes on the computer to make them easier to read.*

do something ● *Diplomats urged the peace treaty upon the two sides.*

use up   uses, using, used

use up sth or **use** sth **up**

to finish a supply of something ● *Don't use up all the milk – we need some for breakfast.* ● *The earth's resources are being used up at an alarming rate.*

usher in   ushers, ushering, ushered

usher in sth *formal*

if an event ushers in a period of time in which new things or changes happen, it is at the beginning of that period or it causes those things to happen ● *A charity match ushers in the start of the new football season.* ● *The war ushered in a period of shortages and deprivation.*

urge on   urges, urging, urged

urge on sb or **urge** sb **on**

to encourage someone to do or achieve something ● *The crowd was cheering and urging her on.* ● *Urged on by his coach, he finished the race in record time.*

urge on/upon   urges, urging, urged

urge sth **on/upon** sb

to persuade or force someone to accept or

vamp up   vamps, vamping, vamped

vamp up sth or **vamp** sth **up** *informal*
to make something seem newer and more exciting by adding something to it • *It's basically the same musical but they've vamped it up with some new songs.*

vamp it up *informal*
if a woman vamps it up, she wears clothes which make her more sexually attractive to men • *She decided to vamp it up in a tight black dress and high heels.*

veer off   veers, veering, veered

veer off
to suddenly change direction • *The track we had been following veered off into the forest.* • *His life has veered off in a new and entirely unexpected direction.*

veg out   vegges, vegging, vegged

veg out *informal*
to relax and spend time doing very little • *After work I just veg out in front of the television.*

venture forth   ventures, venturing, ventured

venture forth *formal*
to leave your house or a safe place and go somewhere else • *Once the rain stops, I thought we might venture forth.*

venture on/upon   ventures, venturing, ventured

venture on/upon sth *formal*
to try to do something difficult or dangerous • *The wind was so strong that when we did finally venture on a walk, we were nearly swept away.*

verge on/upon   verges, verging, verged

verge on/upon sth
if something, especially a quality or feeling, verges on another more extreme thing, it is almost that thing • *It was a performance which, for me at least, verged on brilliance.* • *His interest in comic art verges on the obsessional.*

vest in   vests, vesting, vested

vest sth **in** sb *formal*
to officially give power or authority to a person or organization • (usually passive) *Real political power is vested in the presidency, not in the cabinet, as claimed.*

vie for   vies, vying, vied

vie for sth
to compete for something • (often in continuous tenses) *It's difficult when all three kids are constantly vying for your attention.* • *More than 30 different military groups are vying for power and control of the region.*

vie with   vies, vying, vied

vie with sb/sth
to compete with someone or something • (often + **for**) *Sports activities vie with music for time in the school day.* • (often + to do sth) *City firms vied with each other to hire the brightest young staff.*

visit on/upon   visits, visiting, visited

visit sth **on/upon** sb/sth *formal*
to cause damage or something very harmful to a person or place • (usually passive) *Death and destruction are daily visited on civilians caught in the war.*

visit with   visits, visiting, visited

visit with sb
1 *American* to spend time talking with someone that you know • *I hope there'll be time to visit with you both if I stop by tomorrow.*
2 *American* to spend the night in someone else's house • *My parents are visiting with us this weekend.*

vote down   votes, voting, voted

vote down sth or **vote** sth **down** *mainly American*
to decide as a group not to accept something [e.g. proposal, motion] • *I wanted to introduce stricter membership rules, but my proposal was voted down.*

vote in   votes, voting, voted

vote in sb or **vote** sb **in**
to decide as a group to give a person or group of people a particular job or pos-

ition of power ● (often + **as**) *She was voted in as party leader.* ● *The electorate chose to vote in a radical government.*

vote on   votes, voting, voted

vote on sth

to make a decision about something [e.g. proposal, motion] by counting the number of people for and against it ● *Delegates will vote on strike action tomorrow.*

vote out   votes, voting, voted

vote out sb or **vote** sb **out**

to decide as a group to remove a person or group of people from a particular job or position of power ● *Most of the more radical representatives were voted out at the last election.*

vote through   votes, voting, voted

vote through sth or **vote** sth **through**

to decide as a group to accept something [e.g. law, plan] ● *The reforms were voted through with a narrow majority.*

vouch for   vouches, vouching, vouched

vouch for sb

to say that you know someone and that you can promise that they have a good character or good skills ● *I can vouch for Angela Black – I've worked with her in the past and she's good.*

vouch for sth

to say that you know from experience that something is true or of good quality ● *I can give you a copy of the report but I can't vouch for its accuracy.* ● *I don't know what the cheesecake is like but I can certainly vouch for the lemon tart.*

wade in   wades, wading, waded

wade in

to start to do or say something in a forceful way, often without thinking about it carefully • (often + **with**) *When the crowd started throwing stones, the police waded in with tear gas.* • (sometimes + to do sth) *The large banks waded in to avert an economic crisis.*

wade into   wades, wading, waded

wade into sth

to become involved in a difficult situation, often without thinking about it carefully • *She has waded into one controversy after another.*

wade through   wades, wading, waded

wade through sth

to spend a lot of time and effort doing something boring or difficult, especially reading a lot of information • *We had to wade through pages of legal language before we found what we wanted.*

waffle on   waffles, waffling, waffled

waffle on *mainly British & Australian informal*

to talk or write a lot without giving any useful information • (often + **about**) *She waffled on about the public's right to information.*

wait about/around   waits, waiting, waited

wait about/around

to stay in one place without doing anything while you are waiting for something to happen • *I had to wait around for ages till someone could see me.*

wait behind   waits, waiting, waited

wait behind

to stay in a place after all the other people have left • *The teacher made us wait behind after school.*

wait in   waits, waiting, waited

wait in *British & Australian*

to stay at home because you are expecting someone or something to arrive • (often + **for**) *I had to wait in all day for the plumber.*

wait on   waits, waiting, waited

wait on sb/sth

1 *mainly American* to serve food and drink to someone in a restaurant or at a party • *The guests were waited on by a highly trained team of young staff.* • *She **waited on tables** (= served meals as a job) to earn money while she was at college.*

2 *American* to wait until someone arrives or until something is available • *I'm not waiting on Rachel any longer – I'm going home.*

wait on sb *American*

to sell goods to someone in a shop • *He's got a job waiting on customers in a large department store.*

wait on/upon   waits, waiting, waited

wait on/upon sb

to bring someone everything they want or need • *I'd like a maid to wait on me.* • *Greg **waited on me hand and foot** (= brought me everything I wanted) while I was pregnant.*

wait on/upon sth

to wait until you know the result of an activity or event before doing or deciding something • *The England team must wait on the outcome of Saturday's match between Germany and Brazil.*

wait out   waits, waiting, waited

wait out sth or **wait** sth **out** (never passive)

to wait until something unpleasant has ended • *There will be a long period of negotiation, but we're willing to wait it out.*

wait up   waits, waiting, waited

wait up

to stay awake because you are expecting someone to arrive • (often + **for**) *I'll be home late, so don't wait up for me.*

Wait up! (always an order) *mainly American*

something you say to tell someone to stop so that you can talk to them or go somewhere with them ● *Hey, Lennie, wait up! I need to talk to you.*

wait upon
see **wait on/upon**

wake up　wakes, waking, woke, woken
(*American pt & pp* also **waked**)

wake up (sb) or **wake** (sb) **up**

1 to become conscious after sleeping, or to make someone do this ● *I woke up with a dreadful headache.* ● *Stewart woke me up with his coughing.*

2 to begin to react to something after a period in which you have done very little, or to make someone begin to react to something ● *Companies need to wake up and take notice of the public's increasing concern with the environment.*

Wake up! (always an order) *informal* something you say to tell someone to listen to what you are saying when they have not been listening ● *Wake up, Susan! I've already explained all that.*

wake up to　wakes, waking, woke, woken　(*American pt & pp* also **waked**)

wake up to sth
to become aware of a situation or problem ● *She's going to have to wake up to the fact that she needs to do some work if she wants to pass her exams.*

walk away　walks, walking, walked

walk away
to stop being involved in a situation that is difficult to deal with or that does not give you any advantages ● (usually + **from**) *You can't walk away from a five-year relationship just because you're having a few problems.*

walk away with　walks, walking, walked

walk away with sth *informal*
to win a prize or competition very easily ● *He walked away with all three gold medals.* ● *A strong New Zealand team walked away with the match.*

walk in on　walks, walking, walked

walk in on sb
to go into a room and see what someone is doing when they did not want anyone

to see them ● *She walked in on me as I was getting undressed.*

walk into　walks, walking, walked

walk into sth
to get a job very easily ● *She walked straight into a well-paid job after leaving university.*

walk off　walks, walking, walked

walk off (sth)
to leave a place because you are angry or not satisfied with something ● *She threatened to walk off the film set if she didn't get any more money.* ● *Some of the workers wanted to walk off in protest at factory conditions.*

walk off sth or **walk** sth **off** (never passive)
to go for a walk in order to get rid of an illness [esp. headache] or the feeling of having eaten too much ● *I went to the beach to walk off my headache.* ● *Let's go and walk off our lunch.*

walk off with　walks, walking, walked

walk off with sth
1 *informal* to win a prize or competition very easily ● *He walked off with the most sought-after title in tennis.*

2 *informal* to steal something, or to take something without the owner's permission ● *I left my purse on the table and someone must have walked off with it.* ● *Did you walk off with my pen?*

walk out　walks, walking, walked

walk out
1 to leave a performance or meeting before it has ended because you do not like it or because you are angry ● *She was so disgusted by some of the language in the film that she walked out.* ● (often + **of**) *Some of the delegates walked out of the hall during her speech.*

2 to stop working because of a disagreement with your employer ● *Staff walked out after further job losses were announced.*
　　walk-out *n* [C] ● *Factory workers staged a walk-out to protest about rates of pay.*

3 to suddenly leave your husband, wife, or partner and end your relationship with them ● (often + **on**) *She walked out on her boyfriend after three years of abuse.* ● *I*

brought up my children on my own after my husband walked out.

walk through   walks, walking, walked

walk sb **through** sth

to explain something to someone slowly and carefully, or to carefully show someone how to do something ● *She walked me through the six-page document.* ● *He'll walk you through the procedure.*

wall off   walls, walling, walled

wall off sth or **wall** sth **off**

to build a wall around an area to separate it from another area ● (usually passive) *The offices were walled off and patrolled by security guards.*

wall up   walls, walling, walled

wall up sth or **wall** sth **up**

to fill a space in a building [e.g. window, doorway] with bricks ● (usually passive) *Some of the windows in the front of the house had been walled up.*

wallow in   wallows, wallowing, wallowed

wallow in sth

to remain in an unhappy emotional state without trying to get out of it, as if you are enjoying it or trying to get sympathy from other people ● *After a few weeks of wallowing in misery, I decided to look for a job.* ● *It doesn't do you any good to wallow in self-pity.*

waltz off with   waltzes, waltzing, waltzed

waltz off with sth *informal*

to take something without the owner's permission ● *David's just waltzed off with the only copy of the report.*

wander off   wanders, wandering, wandered

wander off

to leave the person or group of people you are with, without telling them where you are going ● *Small children tend to wander off if you don't watch them all the time.*

want for   wants, wanting, wanted

want for (always negative) *formal*

if someone does not want for anything, they have everything they need in order to have a satisfactory life ● *As a child, I*

wanted for nothing. ● *I made sure that they should never want for anything.*

want in   wants, wanting, wanted

want in

1 *informal* to want to be involved in a plan or activity ● *We've started an athletics club and a lot of local schools want in.* ● (sometimes + **on**) *When his business became successful, a lot of his friends wanted in on it.*

2 *American informal* to want to come inside a place ● *The cat wants in. Can you open the door?*

want out   wants, wanting, wanted

want out

1 *informal* to want to stop being involved in a plan or activity ● (often + **of**) *I want out of this deal before I lose all my money.*

2 *American informal* to want to leave a place ● (often + **of**) *I want out of here – the noise and the smoke are really getting to me.*

ward off   wards, warding, warded

ward off sth or **ward** sth **off**

to stop yourself from getting an illness, or to prevent something unpleasant from harming you ● *I eat an orange every day to ward off colds.* ● *She was given a magic charm to ward off evil spirits.*

warm over   warms, warming, warmed

warm over sth or **warm** sth **over**

1 *American* to heat food that has already been cooked ● *There's some food left from last night which I can warm over for lunch.*

2 *American* to use an idea or to discuss a subject that has been used or discussed before ● *Voters are bored with politicians warming over old policies.*

warmed-over *adj* (always before noun) *American* ● *His dissertation doesn't contain anything original, just warmed-over theories.*

warm to   warms, warming, warmed

warm to sth

to become more enthusiastic about an idea ● *She didn't want to move at first but I think she's warming to the idea.*

warm to sb

to start to like someone ● *Tom's so friend-*

ly that you can't help warming to him.

warm up   warms, warming, warmed

warm up (sth/sb) or **warm** (sth/sb) **up**

to become warmer, or to make something or someone warmer • *The room warms up fairly quickly once the heating is turned on.* • *Increased emissions of carbon dioxide are causing the Earth to warm up.* • *A hot cup of tea will soon warm you up.*

warm up (sth) or **warm** (sth) **up**

1 to prepare yourself for a physical activity by doing some gentle exercises • *You're less likely to injure yourself if you warm up before playing a sport.* • *I usually jog around the room to warm my leg muscles up.*

warm-up *n* [C] • *Stretching exercises form part of the warm-up.* • (used as *adj*) *I like to do a few warm-up exercises before playing squash.*

2 if an engine or machine warms up, or if you warm it up, it starts working so that it becomes warm enough to work well • *In cold weather, I usually warm up the engine before I set off for work.* • *The computer takes a couple of seconds to warm up.*

warm up sth or **warm** sth **up**

to heat food that has already been cooked • *I'll warm up the rest of yesterday's soup for lunch.*

warm up sb or **warm** sb **up**

to make a group of people who are going to watch a performance start to enjoy themselves by entertaining them for a short time before the performance • *He warmed the audience up by telling a few jokes.*

warm-up *n* [C] • *They booked a comedian for the studio audience warm-up.* • (used as *adj*) *Who was the warm-up act?*

warm up

1 to practise an activity for a short time before a performance, or to compete in a sports competition as a way of practising before an important competition • *She usually warms up in her dressing room by singing a couple of Beatles' songs.* • (often + **for**) *He warmed up for the title fight by beating Alex Brodie in two rounds in Los Angeles.*

warm-up *n* [C] • (often + **for**) *They're*

treating today's game as a warm-up for the cup final. • (used as *adj*) *Seles has decided not to compete in a warm-up match in Washington before the US Open.*

2 if an event or situation warms up, it gets more interesting and exciting • *We got to the party just as things were warming up.*

warm up to   warms, warming, warmed

warm up to sb/sth *mainly American*

to start to like a person, or to start to feel enthusiastic about an idea or situation • *By the end of the trip, Joey and I had finally warmed up to each other.* • *I think she's warming up to the idea of moving in with us.*

warn away   warns, warning, warned

warn away sb/sth or **warn** sb/sth **away**

to warn a person, ship, or aircraft not to come near a place because it is dangerous • (often + **from**) *Flashing lights are used to warn ships away from the rocks.*

warn off   warns, warning, warned

warn off sb or **warn** sb **off** (sth)

to warn someone not to do something or not to become involved with something, or to warn someone not to come near a place • *If you don't like violence, the title of the film is probably enough to warn you off.* • *Signs have been put up around the conservation area to warn off tourists.*

wash away   washes, washing, washed

wash away sth or **wash** sth **away**

if water [e.g. rain, flood] washes something away, it carries it away • *Whole villages were washed away in the floods.* • *Heavy rain had washed away most of the soil.*

wash down   washes, washing, washed

wash down sth or **wash** sth **down**

1 to drink something while you are eating food or taking medicine in order to help you swallow it • *She took a gulp of milk to wash the pills down.* • (often + **with**) *I had a large plate of cheese sandwiches washed down with a glass of cold beer.*

2 to clean a large object or surface [e.g. floor, walls] with a liquid • *The hospital floors are washed down with antiseptic every morning.*

wash out   washes, washing, washed

wash out sth or **wash** sth **out**
1 to clean the inside of a container with a liquid ● *Wash the pan out with detergent.*
2 to wash a dirty piece of clothing or cloth ● *He washed his socks out in the hotel sink.*
3 if rain washes out an event, especially a sports competition, there is so much rain that it cannot happen or continue ● *Heavy rain washed out the first day's play in New Zealand.*

   wash-out *n* [C] ● (usually singular) *Thunderstorms forced a wash-out in the second day of the tournament.*

wash out (sth) or **wash** (sth) **out**
   if a colour or dirty mark washes out of something, or if you wash it out, it can be removed by washing that thing ● *I've used a dark brown hair dye which washes out after two weeks.* ● *Red wine stains are hard to wash out.*

wash out *American informal*
   to fail to achieve or finish something, or to fail to reach the necessary standard in an activity ● *It was a tough training program but she was determined not to wash out.* ● *He was a big football star in college, but he washed out in the professional game.*

   wash-out *n* [C] ● *Scarcely anyone came to the festival – it was a complete wash-out.* (= failure)

wash over   washes, washing, washed

wash over sb
   if a feeling or emotion washes over you, you suddenly feel it strongly ● *A sense of despair washed over him.*

wash up   washes, washing, washed

wash up (sth) or **wash** (sth) **up** *British & Australian*

   to clean the plates, pans, and other things you have used for cooking and eating a meal ● *I like listening to the radio when I'm washing up.* ● *I'd better wash up the dishes before I go.*

   washing-up *n* [U] ● *Have you done the washing-up yet?* ● *There was a pile of washing-up* (= plates and pans which needed washing) *in the sink.* ● (used as *adj*) *We've run out of washing-up liquid.*

wash up *American*
   to clean your hands and face with soap and water ● *Go and wash up, kids, your dinner's ready.* ● *I went into the rest room to wash up.*

wash up sth or **wash** sth **up**
   if the sea or a river washes something up, it carries it onto the beach or land ● *His body was washed up on a remote beach.*

waste away   wastes, wasting, wasted

waste away
   to gradually get thinner and weaker, usually because of illness ● *It's terrible to watch someone you love waste away like that.*

watch out

Watch out! (always an order)
   something you say to tell someone to be careful so that they can avoid danger or an accident ● *Watch out – there's a car coming!*

watch out for   watches, watching, watched

watch out for sth
   to be careful to notice something, especially something that might cause you problems ● *Drivers were told to watch out for black ice on the road.* ● *Vegetarians should watch out for animal fat in biscuits.*

watch out for sb/sth

to be careful to notice someone or something interesting • *Watch out for his latest movie which comes out next month.* • *Tony Pritchard should be running in this race so watch out for him.*

watch over watches, watching, watched
watch over sb/sth

1 to protect or take care of a person or animal • *The princes' bodyguard was by the pool, watching over them as they played.*
2 to watch a person or activity carefully to make sure that the person behaves in the correct way or that the activity happens in the correct way • *Observers were sent from several countries to watch over the elections.*

water down waters, watering, watered
water down sth or **water** sth **down**

1 to add water to a drink, especially an alcoholic drink • *I suspect they water down the beer in that pub.* • *She'll drink a little white wine if it's been watered down.*
2 to make an idea or opinion less strong in order to make more people agree with it, or to make a plan or suggestion more acceptable • *The party has been criticized for watering down its more radical policies.* • *The bill has been watered down in response to pressure by farmers.*
watered-down adj • *The new law is a watered-down version of what the judges recommended.*

wave aside waves, waving, waved
wave aside sth or **wave** sth **aside**

to refuse to consider something that someone has said because you do not think it is important • *The referee waved aside Liverpool's protests and awarded a free kick to Arsenal.* • *Her objections to the plan were quickly waved aside by the committee.*

wave down waves, waving, waved
wave down sth/sb or **wave** sth/sb **down**

to make a vehicle stop by making a signal to the driver with your arms • *I waved down the first car that came along.*

wave off waves, waving, waved
wave off sb or **wave** sb **off**

to wave to someone as they leave a place in order to say goodbye • *We went to the station to wave him off.*

wave on waves, waving, waved
wave on sb or **wave** sb **on**

if someone waves on a person in a vehicle, they make a signal with their hands to show them that they can continue moving forwards • *Police officers at the scene of the accident were waving other drivers on.*

wean off weans, weaning, weaned
wean sb **off** sth

to make someone gradually stop using or wanting something that is bad for them • *I'm trying to wean myself off sugary food generally.*

wean on
be weaned on sb/sth (always passive)

to have learned about or experienced someone or something and to have been very influenced by them when you were young • *This is a generation that has been weaned on dance culture.* • *Modern classical music can be very difficult for people weaned on a diet of Mozart and Beethoven.*

wear down wears, wearing, wore, worn
wear down (sth) or **wear** (sth) **down**

to make something [e.g. rock, tyres] gradually thinner and smoother by rubbing the surface, or to become thinner and smoother in this way • *Wind and water have worn down the jagged rocks.* • *Your back tyre has worn right down – it needs replacing.*

wear down sb or **wear** sb **down**

to make someone feel tired and less able to deal with a situation • *The stress at work and all the extra travelling is starting to wear him down.* • *Extra troops were brought in to help the army wear down the guerillas.*

wear in wears, wearing, wore, worn
wear in sth or **wear** sth **in** British & Australian

to wear new shoes for short periods of time until they become comfortable • *Make sure you wear in your walking boots properly before the trip.*

wear off   wears, wearing, wore, worn

wear off

if a feeling or the effect of something [e.g. anaesthetic, alcohol] wears off, it gradually disappears • *The anaesthetic wears off after a couple of hours.* • *There was an initial excitement but it's started to wear off.* • *He used to spend all day playing with his computer games, but **the novelty soon wore off**.* (= the excitement of something new disappeared)

wear on   wears, wearing, wore, worn

wear on

if a period of time wears on, it seems to go past very slowly • *She became less confident about completing the course as the week wore on.* • *As the harsh winter wore on, supplies of coal became scarce.*

wear on sb

to make someone more and more tired or angry over a period of time • *The stress of the court case wore on me, and eventually my health began to suffer.*

wear out   wears, wearing, wore, worn

wear out (sth) or **wear** (sth) **out**

to use something so much that it becomes weak or damaged and cannot be used any more, or to become weak and damaged in this way • *I've already worn out two pairs of shoes this year.* • *The brake discs on the car have worn out and need to be replaced.*
worn-out adj • *It's dangerous to drive around with worn-out tyres.*

wear out sb or **wear** sb **out**

to make someone very tired • *Looking after six small children is enough to wear anyone out.*
worn out adj • *I was completely worn out by the end of term.*

weary of   wearies, wearying, wearied

weary of sth/sb

to start to feel that someone or something is boring • *Some people never seem to weary of eating the same food every day.* • *Hugh didn't share any of her interests, and Mira soon wearied of him.*

weasel out of   weasels, weaseling, weaseled

weasel out of sth *mainly American informal*

to avoid doing something that you have agreed to do, especially by being dishonest • *They'd promised to pay us for the work, but they tried to weasel out of it.*

wed to

be wedded to sth (always passive)

to believe strongly that an idea or system is right and to be very unwilling to change it • *The party is still wedded to the idea of high taxation.*

weed out   weeds, weeding, weeded

weed out sb/sth or **weed** sb/sth **out**

to get rid of people or things that you do not want from a group • *The first round of interviews will weed out the weakest applicants.* • *A simple computer program can easily weed out any duplicate records.*

weigh against   weighs, weighing, weighed

weigh sth **against** sth

1 to think carefully before doing or choosing something in order to judge whether the advantages are greater than the disadvantages • *Economic benefits have to be carefully weighed against the possible damage to the environment.*

2 to compare two facts or situations when you are making a decision in order to decide which is more important • *Our school has a limited budget, so requests for books have to be weighed against the need for more teachers.*

weigh against sth/sb *formal*

to make something less likely to happen, or to make someone less likely to be successful • *Political unrest weighed against their chances of achieving a lasting peace.*

weigh down   weighs, weighing, weighed

weigh down sb or **weigh** sb **down**

1 if you are weighed down with something, you are carrying too much of it • (usually passive + **with**) *You don't want to be weighed down with extra luggage.*

2 if you are weighed down by a problem or difficulty, you are worrying a lot about it • (usually passive + **by**) *I thought she looked older somehow, weighed down by all her responsibilities.*

weigh in   weighs, weighing, weighed

weigh in

1 to become involved in an argument or discussion in a forceful way • (often + **with**) *Several leading architects weighed in with attacks on the design for the new art gallery.*

2 to be officially weighed before competing in a sport, especially boxing or horse racing • (often + **at**) *The new rider weighs in at just over 150 pounds.* • *He weighed in five kilograms heavier than his opponent.*

weigh-in *n* [C] • *At the official weigh-in, Tyson promised to regain his title.*

weigh on/upon   weighs, weighing, weighed

weigh on/upon sb/sth

if a problem or responsibility weighs on you, it makes you worried or unhappy • *His failure to help his brother weighed on his mind.* • *I know I treated him badly and it weighs on my conscience.* • *He's having a few problems at work and I think they're **weighing heavily on** him.*

weigh out   weighs, weighing, weighed

weigh out sth or **weigh** sth **out**

to take a small amount of something from a larger amount and weigh it so that you have the amount you need • *I weighed out all the ingredients for the cake.*

weigh up   weighs, weighing, weighed

weigh up sth or **weigh** sth **up**

to think carefully about the advantages and disadvantages involved in a situation before making a decision • *I'm weighing up the options before I make a firm decision.* • (often + **against**) *You have to weigh up the pleasures of living in the country against the convenience of living in a town.*

weigh up sb or **weigh** sb **up**

to watch someone carefully in order to discover what they are like • *I could tell she was weighing me up as we spoke.*

weigh upon

see **weigh on/upon**

welch/welsh on   welches, welching, welched/welshes, welshing, welshed

welch/welsh on sth *informal*

to fail to do what you have promised to do • *They'd agreed to pay half the costs, but they welched on the deal at the last minute.*

well up   wells, welling, welled

well up

1 if tears well up, they appear in your eyes, and if water wells up, it comes up to the surface of the ground • *I felt tears welling up in my eyes.* • *He planned to build his house close to where the spring welled up.*

2 if an emotion or feeling wells up in someone, they experience it very strongly • (often + **inside**) *As I walked through the forest, a feeling of great joy welled up inside me.*

3 if a person wells up, tears come into their eyes • *Every time I hear that song I start to well up.*

welsh on

see **welch/welsh on**

whack off   whacks, whacking, whacked

whack off *British taboo*

if a man whacks off, he gives himself sexual pleasure by rubbing his penis

wheel around/round   wheels, wheeling, wheeled

wheel around/round *literary*

to quickly turn around • *She wheeled around to face her opponent.*

wheel out   wheels, wheeling, wheeled

wheel out sth/sb or **wheel** sth/sb **out**
mainly British & Australian informal

to use something or someone that you have used many times before in a way that is boring for other people • *You hear them wheeling out the same tired old clichés every time they speak.* • *Year after year they wheel out the same old celebrities to entertain us.*

wheel round

see **wheel around/round**

while/wile away

while/wile away whiles, whiling, whiled/wiles, wiling, wiled

while/wile away sth or **while/wile** sth **away** (never passive)
to spend time in a relaxed way because you are waiting for something or because you have nothing else to do • *I whiled away the days playing cards and reading.* • *She sat in the library, whiling away the hours before the meeting.*

whip out whips, whipping, whipped

whip out sth or **whip** sth **out**
to get something out quickly and suddenly • *He whipped out a knife.*

whip through whips, whipping, whipped

whip through sth *slightly informal*
to do something very quickly • *She whipped through the ironing in a matter of minutes.*

whip up whips, whipping, whipped

whip up sth or **whip** sth **up**
1 to mix a food or liquid [esp. eggs, cream] very fast until it becomes thick and full of air bubbles • *I'll whip up some cream to go with the strawberries.*
2 *informal* to make food or a meal very quickly and easily • *Within minutes he had whipped up a plate of spaghetti.*
3 if a strong wind whips up water or dust, it makes amounts of it rise from the surface • *Waves grew to gigantic heights, whipped up by the wind.*

whip up sth
to try to make people feel strongly about something • *He accused the media of whipping up hysteria.* • *See if you can whip up a bit of enthusiasm for Sunday's coach trip.* • *Both candidates are trying desperately to whip up some support.*

whip up sb or **whip** sb **up**
to try to make someone feel strong emotions • *She had whipped up the audience into a frenzy of excitement.* • *He whipped up the crowd with a highly controversial opening speech.*

whittle away whittles, whittling, whittled

whittle away sth or **whittle** sth **away**
to gradually reduce the size or importance of something until it does not exist

any more • *Her authority has been whittled away by quarrels within the group.*

whittle away at whittles, whittling, whittled

whittle away at sth
to gradually reduce the size or importance of something • *They have introduced new laws to whittle away at the power of the trade unions.*

whittle down whittles, whittling, whittled

whittle down sth/sb or **whittle** sth/sb **down**
to gradually reduce the size of something or the number of people in a group • (often + **to**) *We had eighty applicants for the job, but we've whittled them down to six.*

whoop up whoops, whooping, whooped

whoop it up *informal*
to enjoy yourself in a noisy and excited way • *It sounded like they were whooping it up next door.*

wile away
see **while/wile away**

wimp out wimps, wimping, wimped

wimp out *informal*
to decide not to do something because you are too frightened • *I was going to do a parachute jump but I wimped out at the last moment.* • (often + **of**) *He was supposed to be meeting my parents but he wimped out of it.*

win around/over/round wins, winning, won

win around/over/round sb or **win** sb **around/over/round**
to persuade someone to support you or to agree to do something, often when they did not agree with you before • *My mother didn't want me to marry Dave, but he won her around eventually.* • *He wasn't very keen on the idea to begin with but I managed to win him over in the end.*

win out wins, winning, won

win out
if a particular emotion or type of behaviour wins out, it is stronger than other emotions or types of behaviour • *In the*

movies *true love always wins out in the end.* • (often + **over**) *Unfortunately rage won out over common sense and I punched him on the nose.*

win over
see **win around/over/round**

win round
see **win around/over/round**

win through   wins, winning, won
win through
to finally succeed after trying hard to achieve something • *Most people are confident that the parents of the victims will win through in the end.*

wind down   winds, winding, wound
wind down (sth) or **wind** (sth) **down**
if a business, organization or activity winds down, or if someone winds it down, it gradually stops or is ended • *We had to wind down our Manchester office.* • *The market is usually busy all day but things start to wind down at about 5 o'clock.*

wind down
1 to gradually relax after doing something that has made you feel tired or worried • *I like to wind down with a cup of tea and a hot bath when I get home from work.*
2 if a machine [esp. clock, watch] winds down, it goes slower and slower until it stops completely • *My watch had wound down so I didn't know what time it was.*

wind on   winds, winding, wound
wind on sth or **wind** sth **on** *British & Australian*
to make the film in a camera move on to the next picture, or to make something that sounds or pictures are recorded onto [e.g. cassette, video] move forward to a later place • *Wind the tape on to the song I like.*

wind up   winds, winding, wound
wind up (always + *adv/prep/adj*) *slightly informal*
to finally be in a particular place, state, or situation, especially without having planned it • *If he carries on like this he's going to wind up in prison.* • *He'll wind up bankrupt if he's not careful.*

wind up doing sth *slightly informal*
to finally do something, especially with-

out having planned to • *I wound up having to start the course from the beginning again.*

wind up (sth) or **wind** (sth) **up**
to finish an activity • *We started to wind up the interview.* • *You need to wind up now, we've only got five minutes.*

wind up sth or **wind** sth **up**
1 to close a business or organization • *Lawyers were called in to wind up the company.* • *Rising prices have forced us to wind up our affairs in Germany.*
2 to make a clock, watch, or toy work by turning a small handle or part • *I forgot to wind my watch up and it's stopped.* • *It's a clockwork mouse – you wind it up and let it go.*
wind-up *adj* (always before noun) • *I've still got some old wind-up toys from my childhood.*

wind up sb or **wind** sb **up**
1 *British informal* to tell someone something that is not true in order to make a joke • *He said I'd missed the train, but he was just winding me up.*
wind-up *n* [C] *British informal* • (usually singular) *Are you being serious now or is this a wind-up?*
2 *British & Australian informal* to annoy someone • *It really winds me up when he says that teachers have an easy life.* • *That guy really winds me up.*

winkle out   winkles, winkling, winkled
winkle out sb/sth or **winkle** sb/sth **out**
to find or get someone or something when they are difficult to find or get • (often + **of**) *I managed to winkle the truth out of him eventually.*

wipe down   wipes, wiping, wiped
wipe down sth or **wipe** sth **down**
to clean the surface of something [e.g. floor, table] with a cloth • *Every evening they wiped the tables down before the restaurant closed.*

wipe off   wipes, wiping, wiped
wipe off sth or **wipe** sth **off** (sth) *British & Australian*
to reduce the value of something [e.g. shares, prices] by a particular amount • *The news has wiped nearly a third off*

the value of the company's shares.

wipe out   wipes, wiping, wiped

wipe out sth or **wipe** sth **out**
1 to destroy or get rid of something • *Two whole villages were wiped out in the flood.* • *The bank agreed to wipe out their debts.*
2 to remove information stored on part of a computer [esp. memory, hard disk] • *A sudden power cut wiped out my hard disk.*
3 to clean the inside of something • *Bowls like these I tend to wipe out with a clean cloth.*

wipe out sb or **wipe** sb **out**
1 *informal* to defeat someone easily in a sports competition • *He was wiped out in the first round of the Davis Cup.*
2 *mainly American & Australian informal* to make someone extremely tired • *The long plane journey had wiped her out.*
   wiped-out adj (always after verb) *informal* • *I'm always completely wiped-out by the end of the week.*
3 *American & Australian informal* to lose control, especially in a vehicle, and have an accident • *I was going too fast and I wiped out on the bend.*

wipe up   wipes, wiping, wiped

wipe up sth or **wipe** sth **up**
to remove a substance, usually a liquid, with a cloth • *Can you wipe up that mess on the kitchen floor?*

wipe up (sth) or **wipe** (sth) **up** *British & Australian*
to dry washed plates and dishes with a cloth • *If you wash, I'll wipe up.* • *Could you wipe up the dishes?*

wire up   wires, wiring, wired

wire up sth/sb or **wire** sth/sb **up**
to connect something or someone to a piece of electrical equipment by using electrical wires • *The area is wired up with instruments which detect the slightest movement in the earth's crust.* • (often + **to**) *They wired him up to a machine which measures brain activity.*

wise up   wises, wising, wised

wise up *mainly American informal*
to start to understand the truth about a situation • (often + **to**) *It's about time some employers wised up to the fact that staff who are happy work more efficiently.*

• *Those who think that it's a harmless recreational drug should wise up.*

wish away   wishes, wishing, wished

wish away sth or **wish** sth **away**
to want something unpleasant to disappear without doing anything to make it disappear • *You can't just wish the problem away, you're going to have to do something about it.*

wish on/upon   wishes, wishing, wished

wouldn't wish sth **on/upon** sb
if you say that you would not wish something unpleasant on someone, you mean that you would not like it to happen to them • *I don't really like Bernard, but I wouldn't wish a situation like that on anyone.* • *I wouldn't wish this illness on my worst enemy.*

witter on   witters, wittering, wittered

witter on *British informal*
to talk for a long time about unimportant things • *He kept wittering on about his neighbours, when he should have been working.*

wolf down   wolfs, wolfing, wolfed

wolf down sth or **wolf** sth **down**
informal
to eat something very quickly because you are very hungry • *I gave her a plate of soup and she wolfed it down.*

work against   works, working, worked

work against sb/sth
to cause problems for someone or something, especially by making it harder for them to achieve what they want to achieve • *Our image as a militant group has tended to work against us.* • *Inexperience can work against someone who's looking for a job.*

work around/round   works, working, worked

work around/round sth
to organize an activity so that things that could cause problems do not prevent you from doing what you want to do • *They knew how to work around the import restrictions.* • *I need to take the car into the garage some time today, but I'll work round it somehow.*

work at   works, working, worked
work at sth/doing sth

to try hard to achieve something or improve something • *You have to work at a marriage.* • *She needs to work at increasing her typing speed.*

work in   works, working, worked
work in sth or **work** sth **in**

1 to rub a soft substance onto a surface until it disappears, or to mix one substance, especially a type of food, into another • *Smear wax onto the leather and work it in with your fingers.*

2 to manage to include something in a piece of writing, speech, or activity • *He worked in several criticisms of the government in his report.*

work into   works, working, worked
work sth **into** sth

1 to rub a soft substance onto a surface until it disappears, or to mix one substance, especially a type of food, into another • *Work the remaining flour into the dough.*

2 to manage to include something in a piece of writing, speech, or activity • *Would it be possible to work a couple of meetings into your schedule?*

work yourself **into** sth (always reflexive) to make yourself become very angry or upset • *By the time we got back she had worked herself into a rage.*

work off   works, working, worked
work off sth or **work** sth **off**

1 to get rid of an unpleasant feeling [e.g. aggression, anger] by doing something energetic • *A game of tennis will help me work off my anger.*

2 to do something energetic to stop yourself becoming fat after eating a lot of food • *If you eat the occasional chocolate bar you can soon work it off in the gym.*

3 to reduce the size of a debt, either by earning money to pay for it or by working for the person you owe money to • *She took an evening job so that she could work off the loan as quickly as possible.*

work off sth

if a machine works off a supply of power [e.g. mains, electricity], or if it works off another machine, it uses that power or

machine to make it work • *The security system works off hidden sensors.*

work on/upon   works, working, worked
work on/upon sth

1 to spend time working in order to produce or repair something • *She's based in the lab, working full-time on a cure for AIDS.* • *Pete loves working on old cars.*

2 to try hard to improve something • *His dancing technique is good, but he needs to work on his fitness.*

3 to depend on something being true when you are making plans or calculating something • *We're working on the assumption that a third of the people we've invited won't come.*

work on/upon sb

to try to influence someone's opinions, or to try to persuade someone to do something • *Hannah's not very keen on the idea of a cycling holiday, but I'm working on her.* • (often + to do sth) *I'm working on my father to get him to take me to the airport.*

work out   works, working, worked
work out sth or **work** sth **out**

1 to do a calculation to get an answer to a mathematical question • *Can you work out the total cost of the trip?*

2 mainly British & Australian to understand something or to find the answer to something by thinking about it • (often + question word) *We couldn't work out why they looked so guilty.* • (often + that) *Eventually I worked out that the parcel had been sent to Paris by mistake.*

3 to think carefully about how you are going to do something and to make a plan or decision • (often + question word) *We need to work out how we can fix it to the wall.* • *Negotiators are trying to work out a peace settlement.*

4 to continue to do your job until the end of a fixed period of time • *He has a three month notice period to work out.*

work sb **out** British & Australian

to understand someone's character or the reasons for their behaviour • *Sometimes she seems friendly and sometimes she won't speak to me. I just can't work her out.*

work out

1 (always + adv/prep) to be the result of a mathematical calculation ● (often + **at**) *The cost of a minibus works out at £7 per person.* ● (often + **to**) *That works out to a 5.5% price decrease.* ● *Buying a new radio worked out cheaper than repairing the old one.*

2 to happen or develop in a particular way ● (usually + *adv/prep*) *The arrangement worked out rather badly for Leo.* ● *I got married later that year but it didn't work out.* (= the marriage was not successful)

3 to exercise in order to improve the strength or appearance of your body ● *I work out in the gym twice a week.*
workout *n* [C] ● *This 40 minute workout is designed to tone up your leg muscles.*

work itself **out** (always reflexive)
if a problem works itself out, it gradually becomes less until it is not a problem any more ● *Problems like these usually work themselves out – you'll see.*

work over   works, working, worked

work over sb or **work** sb **over** *slang*
to attack and injure someone ● *Do you want me to get some of the boys to work him over?*

work round
see **work around/round**

work through   works, working, worked

work through sth or **work** sth **through**
to deal with a problem or difficulty by talking about it in detail ● *Psychoanalysis has helped her work through years of trauma.*

work through (sth)
if the result of an action or decision works through, it becomes noticeable ● *It will take time for the effect of tax cuts to work through.* ● *Hospital staff will be affected as budget changes work through the healthcare system.*

work through
to work without stopping for a period of time ● *I often start at 7.30 and work through until midnight.*

work towards   works, working, worked

work towards sth
to try hard to achieve something ● *Both*

sides are working towards a comprehensive peace settlement. ● *I'm working towards a teaching qualification.*

work up   works, working, worked

work up sth or **work** sth **up**

1 to gradually produce something ● *I can't work up much enthusiasm for this trip.* ● *With the wind behind us we managed to work up some speed.* ● *Rub the shampoo in until you have worked up a good lather.* ● *Let's go for a walk to work up an appetite.* (= to make ourselves hungry)

2 to produce or improve a piece of writing ● *The commission has promised to work up proposals by the end of the year.* ● (often + **into**) *I'm hoping to work these notes up into a longer article.*

3 to develop an area of activity, especially part of a business ● *I'm hoping to work up the language teaching side of our business.*

work sb **up**
to make someone feel upset, worried, or excited ● (often reflexive; often + **about**) *He'd worked himself up about the interview until he was in quite a state.* ● (often + **into**) *She worked the crowd up into a frenzy.*
worked up *adj* (always after verb) ● *It's really not important – there's no need to get so worked up about it.*

work yourself **up** (always reflexive)
to try to make yourself feel confident and ready to do something well ● (usually + **to**) *I've been dreading this meeting, but now I've worked myself up to it I just want to get it over with.*

work up to   works, working, worked

work up to sth

1 to gradually do more of an activity until you reach a particular level ● *I started by practising for 10 minutes each morning and gradually worked up to an hour a day.*

2 to gradually prepare yourself for something that you will find difficult ● *He'd wanted to ask her out and he'd been working up to it all week.*

work upon
see **work on/upon**

worm out of   worms, worming, wormed

worm sth **out of** sb *informal*
to manage to get information from someone which they are trying to keep secret
• *He wasn't going to tell me but I managed to worm it out of him.*

wrap up   wraps, wrapping, wrapped

wrap up sth or **wrap** sth **up**
1 to cover something in paper, cloth, or other material, especially in order to give it to someone as a present or in order to protect it • *I haven't wrapped up her Christmas present yet.* • *Make sure you wrap that glass up carefully before you pack it.*
2 to complete an activity, especially successfully • *The two sides hope to wrap up an agreement by next month.* • *King hit two home runs to wrap up the game for his team.*

wrap-up *adj* (always before noun) American • *The author was asked a simple wrap-up question at the end of the TV interview.*

wrap-up *n* [C] American a short statement at the end of an event which gives the main details • *We'll be back later tonight with the post-game wrap-up.*

wrap up (sb) or **wrap** (sb) **up**
to dress in warm clothes, or to dress someone in warm clothes or cover them with material that protects them from the cold • *Make sure you wrap up well – it's cold outside.* • *Wrap him up in a blanket and give him a hot drink.*

be wrapped up in sth (always passive)
to give so much of your attention to something that you do not have time for anything else • *She's so wrapped up in her work that she hardly spends any time with her kids.*

wrestle with   wrestles, wrestling, wrestled

wrestle with sth
1 to try very hard to deal with a difficult problem or decision • *This government is wrestling with difficult economic problems.* • *I've wrestled with the decision for weeks and I still don't know what to do.*
2 to have difficulty holding or controlling something, usually because it is heavy or moves a lot • *She wrestled with the steering wheel as the car plunged out of control.*

wriggle out of   wriggles, wriggling, wriggled

wriggle out of sth *informal*
to avoid doing something that other people think you should do, often in a dishonest way • *He said he'd babysit for us last week and now he's trying to wriggle out of it.*

wring out   wrings, wringing, wrung

wring out sth or **wring** sth **out**
to remove liquid [esp. water] from a cloth or piece of clothing by twisting it with your hands • *She wrung out her swimming costume and hung it up to dry.*

wring out of   wrings, wringing, wrung

wring sth **out of** sb
to force or persuade someone to give you money or information • *It took several hours to wring a confession out of her.* • *They have wrung £40 million out of their accountants in compensation.*

write away   writes, writing, wrote, written

write away
to write a letter to an organization to order goods or ask for information • (often + **for**) *I've written away for details.*

write down   writes, writing, wrote, written

write down sth or **write** sth **down**

to write something on a piece of paper so that you do not forget it • *I wrote down his phone number on a scrap of paper.* • *He told me his address but I forgot to write it down.*

write in   writes, writing, wrote, written

write in

to write a letter to an organization • *The presenter invited students to write in with ideas for raising money.*

write in sth or **write** sth **in**

to write words or numbers in a space on a document • *Could you write in your name and age please?*

write in sb/sth or **write** sb/sth **in** *American*

to add someone's name to the official list for an election in order to show that you want to vote for them • *Many voters wrote her name in on the ballot.*

write-in *adj* (always before noun) • *They've organized a write-in campaign in support of their candidate.*

write in/into   writes, writing, wrote, written

write in sth/sb or **write** sth/sb **in**

write sth/sb **into** sth

to add a scene or character to a book, play, or film • *I wrote in the part of the mad bishop just to add a little humour.* • *The love scene was written into the script at the request of the film studio.*

write into   writes, writing, wrote, written

write sth **into** sth

to add a particular detail or rule to a document [esp. contract] • *She's obliged to produce a certain number of novels a year because it's written into her contract.*

write off   writes, writing, wrote, written

write off sth or **write** sth **off**

1 to accept that an amount of money [esp. debt, investment] has been lost or will never be paid • *The World Bank is being urged to write off debts from developing countries.*

2 to damage a vehicle so badly that it cannot be repaired • *That's the second car*

he's written off since he's been driving.

write-off *n* [C] • *She wasn't hurt, but the car was a write-off.*

write off sb/sth or **write** sb/sth **off**

to decide that someone or something will not be useful, important, or successful • *A lot of companies seem to write people off if they're over 50.* • (sometimes + **as**) *I'd written him off as a madman.*

write-off *n* [C] *informal*   a failure • (usually singular) *Last year was a complete write-off in financial terms.*

write off

to write a letter to an organization to order goods or ask for information • (often + **for**) *I've written off for a copy of the recipe.*

write out   writes, writing, wrote, written

write out sth or **write** sth **out**

1 to write something [e.g. report, list] on paper, often in order to write it in a better or more complete way • *He wrote out all the instructions for us.* • *It's just in note form but I'll write it out properly for you later.*

2 to write information on a document [e.g. cheque, prescription] so that it can be used • *He wrote out a prescription for painkillers.* • *I could write out a cheque if you preferred.*

write out sb or **write** sb **out**

to change the story of a regular television or radio programme so that a character is not in it any more • (usually passive; often + **of**) *Scandals about the actor's private life forced producers to have him written out of the series.*

write up   writes, writing, wrote, written

write up sth or **write** sth **up**

to write something on paper or on a computer in a complete or final form, often using notes you have made • *Have you written up that report yet?* • *He spent two years doing research for his thesis and a year writing it up.*

write-up *n* [C] a report or article in which someone gives their opinion about an event, performance, or new product • *I haven't seen the film myself but it's had really good write-ups.*

write up sb or **write** sb **up** *American*

if someone in authority writes you up,

they make an official record of something wrong that you have done • *The cop said he'd have to write me up for not stopping at the red light.*

x out xes, xing, xed

x out sth or **x** sth **out** *American & Australian*

to cover a word or words with x's in order to show that you do not want it or that it is a mistake ● *I've xed out the names of the people who've said they're not coming.*

its side effects.

yank out   yanks, yanking, yanked

yank out sb/sth or **yank** sb/sth **out**
mainly American & Australian informal
to suddenly remove someone or something from a place ● *He pulled the car door open and yanked him out.* ● (often + **of**) *Alarmed investors yanked their money out of the High Yield Fund.*

yank off   yanks, yanking, yanked

yank off sth or **yank** sth **off**
to quickly pull off a piece of clothing that you are wearing ● *He yanked off his shorts and dashed into the shower.*

yank sth **off** sth *mainly American informal*
to stop a radio or television programme from being broadcast, or to remove particular goods from shops because they might be dangerous ● *The show was yanked off television because of the political controversy surrounding it.* ● *The Food & Drug Administration yanked the medicine off the shelves after the report on*

yell out   yells, yelling, yelled

yell out (sth) or **yell** (sth) **out**
to suddenly shout something in a loud voice, especially to get someone's attention ● *'Get out of the way!' she yelled out.*

yield up   yields, yielding, yielded

yield up sth or **yield** sth **up**
1 *formal* to give something which you have or own to someone else ● *They were forced to yield up some of their land during the war.*

2 *formal.* to show something which was hidden ● *A rediscovered temple has yielded up some rare archeological treasures.*

Topic Pages

emotions

unhappy

- to make someone feel unhappy
*All the hassle over the house is starting to **get** me **down**.*
- to make someone very unhappy and upset
*Each time he became ill again, it **tore** her **apart**.*
- to remain in an unhappy mood and not try to get out of it
*He's not the sort of person to **wallow in** self-pity.*

annoyed

- to make someone feel angry or upset
*His constant criticism is starting to **get to** me.*
*The way she treats me is really **pissing** me **off**.*
*Don't let him **wind** you **up**.*
*She gets so **worked up** about silly little things.*
- annoyed because of something someone has said or done
*She was clearly **put out** that he hadn't called her back.*

happy

- to start to feel happier
*She'd **cheered up** a lot by the time I left.*
*Kate **perked up/brightened up** when I mentioned a trip to the beach.*
- to get a lot of pleasure from something
*He had a talent for engineering and **delighted in** constructing models.*
*She **revels in** the peacefulness of the countryside.*
*He was clearly **lapping up** all the attention.*

controlling emotions

- to stop feeling angry, upset or excited
***Calm down** and tell us what happened.*
*Come on, have a drink of water and try to **pull yourself together**.*
- to begin to feel better after an unhappy experience
*It took him a few days to **get over** the disappointment.*

losing control

- to be so excited that you do not control what you say or do
*He admits he got a bit **carried away**.*
- to feel suddenly extremely surprised or afraid
*We're all a bit **freaked out** by the attacks and don't like to go out alone.*
- to be unable to control your feelings and start to cry
*She **broke down** in tears when she saw the pictures.*

everyday life

waking and sleeping

- to become conscious after sleeping

*I **woke up** at six o'clock this morning.*

- to get out of bed

*What time do you usually **get up** in the morning?*

- to stay in bed later than usual

*He's had a busy week, why don't you just let him **sleep in**.*

*I usually **lie in** until about midday on a Sunday.*

- to go to bed later than usual

*Don't **stay up** too late watching TV.*

- to stay awake because you are waiting for someone to return

*I don't know what time I'll be back, so don't **wait up** for me.*

getting dressed and undressed

- to put a piece of clothing onto your body

*He **put on** his coat and walked towards the front door.*

- to put clothes on quickly and without being careful

*Furious, he **flung on** his dressing gown and stormed downstairs.*

- to fasten something

*She's put on so much weight she can't **do** her jeans **up** any more.*

- to remove a piece of clothing

*I can't wait to get home and **take** these boots **off**.*

- to remove all or most of your clothes

*It was such a hot day, the kids **stripped off** and jumped in the lake.*

jobs around the house

- to clean plates, pans etc. you have used for cooking or eating

*Leave those, I'll **wash** everything **up** later.*

- to quickly wash the inside of something with clean water

*She took her mug over to the sink and **rinsed** it **out**.*

- to dry washed plates and dishes using a cloth

*Can you come and **dry up/wipe up** for me?*

- to make a place clean and tidy

*I hope you're going to **clear up** this mess before you go out.*

- to make a place clean and tidy after someone else has made it dirty

*I seem to spend my whole time **clearing up after** my sons.*

- to put something in the place where it is usually kept

*He folded the clothes and **put** them **away** in the wardrobe.*

health and illness

getting ill

- to become ill

*I think I'm **coming down with** a cold.*
*Both brothers **went down with** a virus.*

- to get an infectious illness

*Many patients die of infections **picked up** in hospital.*

- to give a disease to someone

*Malaria is **passed on** by mosquitoes.*

- to suffer again from a disease which you have had before

*His eczema tends to **flare up** when he gets stressed.*

symptoms

- to become unconscious

*My father **passes out** at the sight of blood.*

*I **blacked out** and the next thing I remember is waking up in hospital.*

- to vomit

*He looked as if he might **throw up** at any moment.*

- (of part of your body) to become larger than normal

*Her face was **swollen up** and she had a black eye.*

- to injure part of your body by moving it out of its usual place

*Be careful, that's really heavy – don't **put your back out.***

medical treatment

- to take care of someone who is ill

*She was very well **cared for/looked after** while she was in hospital.*

- to give someone who is injured basic medical treatment

*We gave him a shot of morphine and **patched** him **up** as best we could.*

- to become conscious again or make someone become conscious

*When she **came round** from the anaesthetic she realised something was wrong.*
*It took the nurses a while to **bring** him **round/to** after his operation.*

recovering

- to get rid of an illness

*She'd been taking drugs to **fight off/shake off** a cold.*

- to feel better after an illness or injury

*He's only just **got over** a serious ankle injury.*

- (of an illness) to go away

*Most of the symptoms should **clear up** within a couple of days.*

- (of a cut or an injury) to repair itself and become healthy again

*If you keep it clean, it should **heal up** by itself.*

making and repairing

making things quickly

• to make something quickly, without much effort, especially using things that can be easily found
*Why don't we take a picnic? I could **throw** something **together**.*
*She could **knock up/run up** an outfit in a couple of hours.*
*We **cobbled together** a makeshift hospital to treat the wounded.*
*Ten people squeeze into a shack **patched together** with cardboard and a few bricks.*

• to quickly create something impressive
*She **conjured up** a delicious homemade stew.*

mass production

• to produce large amounts of something, often of low quality
*The studio **churned out** a string of low-budget movies.*
*The factory **cranks out** cheap exports for the European market.*
*They **turn out** some 1.3 million cars a year.*

new products

• to produce something to sell to the public
*Microsoft are expected to **bring out** a new version next year.*

• to become available for people to buy
*She's got a new album **coming out** in the autumn.*

repairing

• to repair something
*He was **fixing** his motorbike **up** in the back yard.*

• to repair something quickly and without much care
*Everything looked shabby and **patched up**.*

• to divide something into its separate parts/ to put the parts of something in the correct place
*He enjoys **taking** things **apart** and **putting** them back **together** again.*

• to spend time working to repair something
*He's out on in the garage **working on** the car.*

• to find ways of solving small problems
*The system is thoroughly tested to **iron out** any glitches.*

phrasal verbs in conversation

warnings and requests

● something you say or shout to tell someone to be careful or to warn them about danger
Look out!/Watch out!/Mind out! *The iron's hot!*
● something you say to tell someone to do something more quickly
Hurry up, *we're going to miss the train.*
Come along, *I've got to go out in a minute.*
● something you say to encourage someone to do something
Go on *Ali, it's your turn next.*
● used to ask someone to wait
Hang on *a moment, I'll just get a pen to write that down.*
Hold on, *I'll see if he's free on Wednesday.*

expressing surprise

● used to tell someone that what they are hoping for isn't possible
'They'll get to the finals no problem.'
'Dream on!'
● used to tell someone that you do not believe them
Go on!/Come off it!/Come on! *You've never even been to the States, have you?!*

on the phone

● to telephone someone who rang you earlier
She's in a meeting at the moment, can she **call** *you* **back** *later?*
I'll **ring** *you* **back** *as soon as I've got any news.*
I can't give you an answer now, can I **get back to** *you next week?*
● to connect a telephone caller to the person they want to speak to
I'll **put** *you* **through to** *our Customer Services department.*

talking more and less

● used to ask someone to speak more loudly
Sorry, can you **speak up**? *It's a really bad line.*
● used to tell someone to tell you something
Well, **spit it out**! *What did she say to you?*
● used to tell someone to be quiet
Can you **keep** *your voice* **down**, *please? People are trying to study.*
● an impolite way to tell someone to stop talking or stop making a noise
Just **shut up**, *will you? I don't need you to tell me what to do.*

phrasal verbs in formal writing

describing connections

● to be connected with something
*None of the above **appertain to** the taxi trade.*
*All the paperwork **pertaining to** the case was lost in a fire.*
*It is necessary to explore a number of theoretical issues which **bear on** practice.*

● to say or believe that something is caused by something else
*Several of the incidents can be **ascribed to** insufficient training.*

● to have something as a main part or quality
*The project **consists of** supplying and installing 350 units to government offices.*

discussions and negotiations

● to take part or become involved in something
*The company **entered into** negotiations for purchase of the site.*
*He is actively **engaged in** talks with the Chinese government.*

● to clearly state an opinion, idea, fact, etc.
*He **set forth** his reasons for opposing the deal.*

● to make people aware of a fact or a problem
*The report **points up** several areas which need improvement.*

● to give more details about something that has been said or written
*He was not prepared to **enlarge on** his earlier claims.*

rules and agreements

● to obey a rule or reach a necessary standard
*The design must **conform to** international standards.*
*All members must **adhere to** a national code of practice.*

● to be different from the usual or expected way of doing something
*A spokesman said that they would not be **departing from** the official policy.*

● to make plans to deal with a possible future event or problem
*The plan **provides for** an annual budget increase of 10 per cent.*
*Many insurance companies refuse to **provide against** natural disasters.*

politics

elections

• to compete in an election for an official position
*She first **stood for** Parliament in 2001.*

• to show you are interested in and want to understand someone
*We have to **engage with** younger voters.*

• to defend something you believe is important
*We need someone who will **stand up for** the rights of working people.*

• to elect someone to a position of power
*If you **vote** us **in**, we'll keep our promises.*

• to remove someone from power in an election
*The socialists were **voted out** at the last election.*

laws and policies

• to create a new rule, law, etc.
*The state **brought in** a law banning smoking in public buildings.*

• to make a decision about something by voting
*MPs will **vote on** the issue next week.*

• to make a plan or suggestion be officially accepted
*The government is trying to **push through** reforms to the tax system.*

• to do something to stop or limit an activity
*The government has vowed to **clamp down/crack down** on drugs.*

• to increase an activity
*The authorities are **stepping up** security ahead of the talks.*

problems and scandals

• to admit that you were wrong
*The Minister has had to **back down/climb down** over his claims.*

• to not do something that you promised to do
*Yet again, the Prime Minister has **gone back on** an election promise.*

• to give someone money so that they will not do something
*He alleged that officials had been **bought off/paid off**.*

• (of secret information) to become known by someone who should not know
*Details of the report **leaked out** ahead of its publication.*

• to stop people finding out the truth about something bad that has happened
*Top politicians tried to **hush the matter up**.*
*The full scale of the accident was **covered up** by the authorities.*

• to cause people in power to lose their positions
*This scandal could **bring down** the government.*

relationships

friends

• to like someone and become friendly immediately
*Nick and I **hit it off** as soon as we met.*
• to start a friendship with someone
*It wasn't long before she **struck up** a friendship with a colleague.*
• to like each other and be friendly
*In general they **got along/got on** well with their new neighbours.*
• to spend time with someone
*He got it from one of the lads he **hangs out with/hangs around with**.*
*She mostly **knocks around with** the other international students.*
• to stay friends with someone, especially because they can help you
*It's important to **keep in with** the members of the committee.*
*Those in the mining business **cosy up to** whichever regime is in power.*

ending a relationship

• to argue with someone and stop being friendly
*He **fell out** with his brother and they haven't spoken for years.*
• to gradually become less friendly, often because you do not have the same interests and opinions any more
*They just **grew apart/drifted apart** over the years.*
• a marriage or a relationship ends
*Did you know that Helen and Andy have **broken up/split up**?*
• to end a relationship with someone
*Kirsten's just **finished with** her boyfriend.*
• to suddenly leave your husband, wife or partner and end your relationship
*I don't blame her for **walking out on** him.*

starting a romance

• to talk to someone or behave in a way which shows you are attracted to them
*He had tried to **chat** her **up** at an office party.*
*I saw her joking and **flirting with** him.*
• to invite someone to go on a date, especially at the start of a relationship
*He was too shy to **ask** her **out**.*
• to start a romantic relationship
*We first **got together** after meeting on holiday in Italy.*
• to have a romantic relationship with someone
*How long have you been **going out together**?*
*She's **going out with** a much older man.*

sport and fitness

fitness and exercise

● to prepare for sport by doing gentle exercises
*Make sure you **warm up** properly before you go out for a run.*
*Do a few stretches to **loosen up/limber up**.*
● to exercise to improve your strength or fitness
*He's been **working out** at the gym lately.*
● to exercise to stop yourself getting fat after eating a lot
*I do aerobics twice a week to try and **work off/burn off** a few kilos.*
● to exercise hard
*He's been **sweating it out** on the training ground with his team mates.*

sporting competitions

● to play the last game in part of a competition to decide the winner
*Scotland will **play off** against Denmark for a place in the World Cup.*
● to win one part of a competition and progress to the next part
*The first two in each heat will **go through** to the final.*
● to defeat someone in a competition so that they leave the competition
*Gerard was **knocked out** in the second round.*
● to lose in a competition so that you have to leave the competition
*The team **went out/crashed out** in the semi finals.*
● to finish a race or competition in a particular time or position
*Barricello **came in** fifth behind his team mate.*

team sports

● to try to get a place in a sports team (*esp. AmE*)
*He **tried out for** the college basketball team.*
● to ask someone to play for a team, especially a national team
*He's been **called up** for the England squad to tour Pakistan.*
● (especially in football) a game starts
*The match **kicks off** at midday.*
● to order a player to leave the game because they have done something wrong
*The captain was **sent off** after getting two yellow cards.*
● to continue playing, especially after a game has stopped
*Jones appealed for a penalty, but the referee ordered him to **play on**.*

studying

reading

- to read something from beginning to end
*Can you **read through/look through** this for me?*
- to read something quickly without studying the details
*He began **skimming through** the reports on his desk.*
*She sat **flicking through** the magazine on her lap.*
- to study a book or a document carefully
*He spends his days **poring over** legal documents.*
- to look in a book or on a computer to find a piece of information
*It's sometimes difficult to **look** phrasal verbs **up** in a dictionary.*

writing

- to write something down on a piece of paper, especially so you remember it
*Did you **take down/note down/write down** the title of that book?*
- to write something down quickly on a piece of paper
*Can you **jot down** your e-mail address for me?*
- to write down the main parts of an idea without showing details
*You should have the outline for the project **roughed out** by next week.*
- to write something in its complete or final form, especially from notes
*You should **write up** your results and hand them in before Monday.*
- to write something on paper, especially in a clear or complete way
***Write out** a list of questions you would like to ask first.*

learning

- to learn something new by practising it rather than being taught it
*Martin quickly **picked up** the language.*
- to read about something in order to learn about it
*I've been **reading up on** Chinese history.*
- to practise a skill or knowledge you have forgotten
*We'll have to **brush up on** our Spanish before Jose arrives.*

exams

- to appear in an exam
*A question about the French Revolution **comes up/crops up** every year.*
- to manage to pass an exam
*She **got through/scraped through** her final exams.*
- to fail because of not being good enough in a particular area
*It's well written, but it **falls down on** the technical details.*

technology

starting and finishing

- to connect a piece of electrical equipment to the electricity supply
*Is the printer **plugged in**?*
- to put electricity into a piece of equipment which has batteries
*I need to **charge up** my mobile.*
- to touch a switch so that a piece of equipment starts working
*He **powered up** his laptop to check his e-mail.*
*She sat down at her desk and **switched on/turned on** her computer.*
- to type in your name, a password, etc to start using a computer system
*You'll need a user ID to **log in/log on** to the university network.*
*Once you've **signed in/signed on** you'll have access to the database.*
- to finish using a computer system
*Make sure you **log off/log out** so other users can't access your data.*
*Can you check that all the computers have been **shut down**?*
- to touch a switch so that a piece of equipment stops working
*He **switched off/turned off** the TV and went upstairs to bed.*

using a computer

- to put information into a computer using a keyboard
***Type in/Key in** the customer's name and address.*
- to make a copy of something you have written by typing it into a computer
*She went home to **type up** her handwritten notes.*
- to make a printed copy of something on a computer
*I've finished my assignment, I've just got to **print** it **out** and hand it in.*
- to make an image on a screen larger and more detailed or smaller and less detailed
*Click here to **zoom in** or **zoom out**.*
- to send someone a copy of an e-mail that you are sending to someone else
*Can you **copy** me **in on** all the arrangements?*

problems

- to suddenly stop working
*We couldn't do anything because the system had **gone down**.*
*My phone **cut out** and I couldn't get a signal.*
- to get into someone's computer system without permission
*He managed to **hack into** the Pentagon's computer system*
- to make a copy of computer information so that you do not lose it
*We **back up** data regularly in case of any problems.*

thinking

new ideas

- to think of a plan or an idea
*Who **came up with/thought up** the name for the band?*
*We looked through the slogans **dreamt up** by the marketing agency.*
- to produce or lead to new ideas
*A simple Internet search can **throw up** a range of possibilities.*
- to come to your mind
*It **occurred to** me that they might need somewhere to stay.*

making decisions

- to think carefully about something before making a decision
*Why don't you **think** it **over** and let me know next week?*
*It's an idea he's been **mulling over** for some time now.*
- to think carefully about a plan and its possible results or effects
*Don't rush into anything without stopping to **think** things **through**.*
- to think carefully about the advantages and disadvantages of something
*It's important to **weigh up** all the different courses of action.*
- to make a list of choices smaller by removing less important ones
*I went through the options and **narrowed** it **down** to three.*

planning

- to make plans for the future
*You can avoid many of these problems by **planning ahead**.*
*She was already **thinking ahead** to the winter.*
- to arrange or organize a future event or activity
*We've got a series of talks and seminars **lined up/set up** for next week.*
- to prepare for something you have to do
*The athletes are **gearing up** for the Olympics next summer.*
- to expect something to happen and prepare for it
*We didn't **reckon on/bargain for** quite so many people turning up.*

not thinking about

- to stop yourself thinking about something because it upsets you
*When I'm writing, I tend to **block/shut** everything else **out**.*
- to stop paying attention to something because you are not interested
*When she starts moaning about my grades, I just **tune out/switch off**.*

travel

starting a journey

● to leave a place in order to go somewhere
*What time do we need to **go out** in the morning?*
● to start a journey
*They planned to **set off/set out** at nine o'clock.*
*We're **heading off** to France on Saturday.*
● to go to an airport, station, etc to say goodbye to someone who is leaving
*The whole family came to the airport to **see** me **off**.*

by plane

● to show your ticket at an airport desk before a flight
*You need to **check in** at least an hour before your flight.*
● (of a plane) to leave the ground
*The plane was cleared to **take off**.*
● (of a plane) to land on the ground
*We expect to **touch down** in New York around 12.30 local time.*
● to stop somewhere for a short time during a long journey
*They **stopped over/laid over** in Singapore on the way to New Zealand.*

by train

● to go onto a bus, train, plane or boat
*The man **got on** the train at Kings Cross.*
● (of a train) to start to leave a station
*The train **pulled out** just as I arrived on the platform.*
● (of a train) to arrive in a station
*We're just **pulling into** Manchester now.*
● to leave a bus, train, plane or boat
*I'm **getting off** at the next station.*
● (of a train or plane) to arrive at a particular time
*I think the train's due to **get in** at around 11 o'clock.*

by car

● to drive onto a road from another road or from the side of the road
*A van suddenly **pulled out** of a side street in front of me.*
● to drive a car to the side of the road to stop
*I heard an ambulance coming up behind me so I **pulled over** to let it by.*
● to collect someone who is waiting for you by car
*The local rep will **pick** you **up** at the station and take you to your hotel.*
● to take someone to a place they want to go by car
*She **dropped** the kids **off** at school on her way to work.*

work

starting and finishing jobs

- to begin to employ someone
*The firm **took** him **on** as an apprentice at sixteen.*
- to start doing a job that someone else was doing before
*She **took over** as office manager last March.*
- to keep a job for a period of time
*Her health problems made it difficult for her to **hold down** a job.*
- to give someone else responsibility for something
*He **handed over** the day-to-day running of the business to his son.*
- to leave your job, especially an important position
*The chairman has announced he will **step down** at the end of the year.*
- to stop employing someone because you do not have work for them
*Last year the company **laid off** 20 per cent of its workforce.*

having lots of work

- to have too much work to deal with
*We're completely **snowed under** with work at the moment.*
- to not have done as much work as you should have done
*Several of the teachers are already **getting behind** with their marking.*
- to become more and more to be dealt with
*Requests are **piling up** and we don't have the staff to deal with them.*
- to be too busy to see or speak to someone
*He's **tied up** for the next couple of the days, but could probably see you on Friday.*
- to do something you did not have time to do earlier
*I sometimes go into the office on Saturday to **catch up on** paperwork.*
- to work very hard with little or no rest
*She's been **slaving away** to get the plans ready in time.*

dates in your diary

- to arrange something, such as a meeting
*Give my secretary a ring to **fix up** a date.*
*Have you got any more talks **lined up**?*
*Shall we **set up** a meeting for the end of next week?*
- to arrange something for a particular date, knowing it might be changed
*At the moment the tour is **pencilled in** for next September.*
- to manage to do something or see someone when you are very busy
*She might be able to **squeeze** you **in** at two o'clock.*
*Dr Warren could **fit** you **in** on Tuesday morning.*

Exercises

exercises

1. people

Match these phrasal verbs to the people:

1. call out   a. a soldier
2. stand in for   b. a footballer
3. send off   c. a criminal
4. send down   d. a colleague
5. call up   e. a doctor

2. children

Complete these sentences about children and childhood using the phrasal verbs from the box. You may need to change the form of the verb:

grow up	bring up	break up
take after		look after

1. Jamie really .... his dad – he's got the same bright blue eyes.

2. His parents went to the city to work and he was ....
by his grandmother.

3. She .... in a white middle-class suburb.

4. My mother .... the kids during the day while I'm at work.

5. When do the children .... from school for the summer?

3. weather

Complete these sentences about the weather with a word from the box:

rain	sky	storm
snow	sun	

1. The .... was beating down from a cloudless sky.

2. The garden was blanketed with thick ....

3. Outside, the .... was absolutely bucketing down.

4. By lunchtime the .... had clouded over.

5. We sheltered in a barn to wait for the .... to blow over.

4. gestures

Match the phrasal verbs and nouns which describe gestures:

1. stick out   a. your arms
2. flag down   b. a friend
3. burst into   c. your tongue
4. wave off   d. a taxi
5. throw up   e. tears

exercises

5. eating and drinking

Complete the sentences with the phrasal verbs from the box. You may need to change the form of the verb:

snack on	eat out	thaw out
top up		pour out

1. They both enjoy .... in fashionable restaurants.

2. Make sure you .... the fish thoroughly before you cook it.

3. Avoid .... sweets foods during the day.

4. She reached for the wine to .... her glass.

5. He .... another glass of orange juice.

6. moving

These phrasal verbs all mean to walk or move. Which ones mean to move quickly, and which ones to move slowly? Mark them Q or S.

1. We **plodded along** behind the others.
2. A young man with dark hair **sidled up** to her at the bar.
3. She had to **dash off** after the meeting to pick up her daughter.
4. He looked down on the people **milling around** in the square below.
5. Helen **wheeled round** and stared at her.

7. reading

Some of these phrasal verbs mean to read quickly, and some mean to read carefully. Mark them Q or C.

1. She sat in the waiting room *leafing through* a magazine.
2. Anyone who loves ships will find this new book a delight to *dip into*.
3. They are still *wading through* pages of detailed data.
4. He *thumbed through* the pages of his diary.
5. We spent long hours *poring over* maps of the region.

8. money 1

Choose the correct meaning for each phrasal verb on the left from the three possibilities on the right:

1. **take out**	lend	subtract	withdraw
2. **cut back**	reduce	repay	discount
3. **pay back**	withdraw	borrow	repay
4. **pick up**	total	buy	spend
5. **set aside**	borrow	save	increase

exercises

9. money 2

Use the phrasal verbs from *money 1* to complete these sentences. Use each phrasal verb only once:

1. Can I borrow some money? I'll .... you ....
next week.

2. Make sure you .... enough each month to cover
your bills.

3. We've had to .... on our travel budget this year.

4. I managed to .... a real bargain in the sales.

5. I need to stop at a cash machine to .... some money
....

10. information

Match the two parts of the sentences:

1. The minister put out   a. a secret if you promise not to
                               tell.

2. I've picked up   b. rumours about me leaving.

3. He sounded me out   c. about a plan to restructure the
                               project.

4. I'll let you into   d. a statement denying the
                               allegations.

5. Someone's putting   e. some information about
   around   courses.

11. maths

Complete these phrasal verbs describing maths tasks using verbs from the box:

work	take	add
go	come	

1. .... up the numbers in each column and write the total at the bottom.

2. How much does that .... to altogether?

3. Ten .... away four is six.

4. Three .... into twelve four times.

5. How do you .... out 15% of £400?

12. in the classroom 1

Choose the correct meaning for each phrasal verb on the left from the three possibilities on the right:

1. **hand out**	submit	distribute	correct
2. **rub out**	ignore	cancel	erase
3. **work out**	calculate	allocate	reply
4. **miss out**	return	cancel	omit
5. **hand in**	finish	submit	answer

exercises

13. in the classroom 2

Complete the sentences using the phrasal verbs from **in the classroom 1**. Use each phrasal verb only once.

1. If you don't know the answer, ... the question .... and go onto the next one.

2. We've got to .... our essays by Monday.

3. No talking now, I'm going to .... the test papers.

4. Write in pencil so you can .... it .... if you change your mind.

5. I can't .... the answer to number eight.

14. DIY metaphors

Choose a phrasal verb from the box to complete these sentences. You may need to change the form of the verb:

> nail down   dig up   hammer out
> paper over   chip away at

1. The exact number of people affected is difficult to ....

2. He's doing little more than .... the cracks in the party.

3. They're into the fifth day of negotiations to .... a deal.

4. Have you managed to .... anything interesting about his background?

5. Lots of little incidents .... her self-confidence.

15. orders

If someone say this, what do they want you to do?

1. Hurry up!   a. make space for them to sit down
2. Come in!   b. leave
3. Move over!   c. wait
4. Hang on!   d. walk more quickly
5. Get out!   e. enter a room

16. animals

Match these phrasal verbs containing the names of animals to the definitions:

1. monkey around   a. to talk a lot
2. rabbit on   b. to behave in a silly way
3. pig out   c. to work hard
4. weasel out of sth   d. to eat a lot
5. beaver away   e. to avoid doing sth

exercises

17. food

Match these phrasal verbs containing words for food to the definitions:

1. egg sb on
2. beef sth up
3. be sandwiched between
4. cream sth off

5. fish sth out

a. to make sth stronger
b. to encourage sb to do sth
c. to take money for yourself
d. to take sth out of a bag or pocket
e. to be in the middle of two things

18. nouns

The nouns in the box are make from phrasal verbs. Complete the sentences using these nouns. You may need to change the form of the noun:

> telling-off   falling-out   rip-off
> flashback   stopover

1. Three years after the accident, I'm still getting ....

2. The town makes a good .... before heading further north.

3. She gave both boys a .... and sent them to bed.

4. Many of the guided tours are a complete ....

5. He had a .... with his business partner.

19. adjectives

Match the two parts of the sentences:

1. We had to queue at the check-in	a. bed.
2. She's got two grown-up	b. name.
3. He signed in under a made-up	c. daughters.
4. In the guest room there's a fold-away	d. food.
5. We feed the birds on any leftover	e. desk.

20. which word?

Choose the correct noun or adjective to complete these sentences:

1. Several innocent standbys/bystanders were injured.
2. A new outbreak/breakout of the disease was reported in China.
3. She had some school friends to stay for a(n) sleepover/oversleep.
4. He took out a loan to cover his upstart/start-up costs.
5. There were rumours of a(n) overtake/takeover bid for the company.

exercises

21. verb forms

Put the verbs in brackets in the correct form:

1. Many shoppers end up (spend) .... more than they planned.

2. Opposition MPs have called on him (resign) ....

3. He's already signed up (learn) .... Spanish at evening classes.

4. She's been going around (tell) .... everyone we're getting married.

5. I'll look forward to (see) .... you in London next week.

22. prepositions

Complete these sentences using an appropriate preposition:

1. The trip didn't live up .... our expectations.

2. She would never miss out .... an opportunity to make some money.

3. All she kept on .... was going to live in Australia.

4. You have to have the courage to own up .... your mistakes.

5. The government says it will press on .... its reforms.

23. reflexives

Complete the sentences with a phrasal verb from the box.
You will need to use the correct form of the verb and the
correct reflexive pronoun – himself, herself, myself, etc.

pride yourself on	stand up for yourself
give yourself up	
put yourself out	fend for yourself

1. The gunman finally .... to the police.

2. She had always .... her cooking.

3. They need to have the confidence to .... and
their rights.

4. He really .... to make them feel at home.

5. While she was out at work, the children were left to
....

24. word order

Is the preposition in these sentences in the correct place?
Write a ✓ by correct sentences. Write a ✗ by incorrect
sentences and rewrite them so that they are correct.

1. Do you mind taking your shoes off?
2. I keep forgetting my PIN number, so I've written down it.
3. I'm looking after my neighbours' dog while they're away.
4. The referee stood his decision by and the player was sent off.
5. When you've finished with the tools, can you put away them?

exercises

25. key verbs: come

Complete the phrasal verbs with a preposition from the box so they match the definitions:

across	out	back
along		apart

1. come   find
2. come   separate into pieces
3. come   become known
4. come   arrive at a place
5. come   return

26. key verbs: get

Match the parts of the sentences:

1. We need to get across   a. a fight in the playground.
2. He's just getting over   b. on holiday in August.
3. We're hoping to get away   c. a throat infection.
4. George got into   d. the problem.
5. There are ways of   e. the message to young people.
getting round

27. key verbs: put

Complete these phrasal verbs with a preposition from the box:

about	down	forward
towards		through

1. put money
2. put a suggestion
3. put the phone
4. put rumours
5. put a caller

28. key verbs: give

Choose the correct preposition to complete these sentences:

1. When do we have to give to/off/in our assignments?
2. The fire gives across/off/away quite a bit of heat.
3. The tourist office gives out/to/off free maps of the city.
4. Don't give out/away/about the ending of the story.
5. Is she going to give over/up/down work when she has the baby?

answers

1. people
1.e 2.d 3.b 4.c 5.a

2. children
1.takes after 2.brought up 3.grew up 4.looks after 5.break up

3. weather
1.sun 2.snow 3.rain 4.sky 5.storm

4. gestures
1.c 2.d 3.e 4.b 5.a

5. eating and drinking
1.eating out 2.thaw out 3.snacking on 4.top up 5.poured out

6. moving
1.S 2.S 3.Q 4.S 5.Q

7. reading
1.Q 2.Q 3.C 4.Q 5.C

8. money 1
1.withdraw 2.reduce 3.repay 4.buy 5.save

9. money 2
1.pay back 2.set aside 3.cut back 4.pick up 5.take out

10. information
1.d 2.e 3.c 4.a 5.b

11. maths
1.add 2.come 3.take 4.goes 5.work

12. in the classroom 1
1.distribute 2.erase 3.calculate 4.omit 5.submit

13. in the classroom 2
1.miss out 2.hand in 3.hand out 4.rub out 5.work out

14. DIY metaphors
1.nail down 2.papering over 3.hammer out 4.dig up 5.chipped away at

15. orders
1.d 2.e 3.a 4.c 5.b

16. animals
1. b 2.a 3.d 4.e 5.c

17. food

1.b 2.a 3.e 4.c 5.d

18. nouns
1.flashbacks 2.stopover 3.telling-off 4.rip-off 5.falling-out

19. adjectives
1.e 2.c 3.b 4.a 5.d

20. which word?
1.bystanders 2.outbreak 3.sleepover 4.start-up 5.takeover

21. verb forms
1.spending 2.to resign 3.to learn 4.telling 5.seeing

22. prepositions
1.to 2.on 3.about 4.to 5.with

23. reflexives
1. gave himself up
2. prided herself on
3. stand up for themselves
4. put himself out
5. fend for themselves

24. word order
1. correct
2. incorrect. The correct sentence is: I keep forgetting my PIN number,
so I've written it down.
3. correct
4. incorrect. The correct sentence is:
The referee stood by his decision and the player was sent off.
5. incorrect. The correct sentence is: When you've finished with the tools, can you
put them away?

25. key verbs: come
1.across 2.apart 3.out 4.along 5.back

26. key verbs: get
1.e 2.c 3.b 4.a 5.d

27. key verbs: put
1.towards 2.forward 3.down 4.about 5.through

28. key verbs: give
1.in 2.off 3.out 4.away 5.up

Single verb
or
Phrasal verb?

Single verb or phrasal verb?

Sometimes learners of English use a single verb (often one which is similar to their own language) when a native speaker of English would be more likely to use a phrasal verb. Often the single verbs are more formal. Below is a list of rather formal verbs, along with a phrasal verb which would sound more natural in most situations. You can lose marks in exams for using very formal single verbs where they are not suitable.

Remember to look at the full entries in the dictionary for all the information you need to use these phrasal verbs correctly.

abandon/give up *He has given up all hope of becoming a journalist.*

accelerate/speed up *The government is trying to speed up new anti-terrorist laws.*

address/deal with *She'll never be happy if she doesn't deal with the problems at home.*

apply/put on *She put on her make-up very carefully.*

approach/come up *He came up to me and asked me for directions to the station.*

arise/come up *He was thrilled when a chance to work in Africa came up.*

arrive/get in *The train gets in at 8.57.*

assemble/put together *It took us hours to put the furniture together.*

attend/turn up *We had organised a whole series of talks, but only 3 people turned up.*

calculate/work out *I had to work out how much the food would cost altogether.*

cohabit/live together *We're not married, but we've lived together for years.*

confess/own up *Come on, own up! Who's eaten all the cheese?*

conform/fit in *I had a terrible time in the army – I just never fitted in.*

constitute/ make up *About half the work force is made up of local women.*

constitute/amount to *Her teaching experience amounted to six months in a kindergarten.*

continue/go on *He went on talking, even after the teacher had asked him to be quiet.*

decelerate/slow down *Make sure you slow down to go round the bend.*

decrease/go down or **come down** *I want to buy a DVD player, but I'm waiting for prices to go/come down.*

defend/stand up for or **stick up for** *My Mum said I was too young to go London on my own, but my sisters stood up for me, and eventually she gave in.*

deflate/let down *Someone has let down the tyres of my bike.*

delay/put off or **hold up** *We were held up by engineering works at Birmingham.*

delete/cross out *If you make a mistake, just cross it out and start again.*

deliver/drop off *I'm just stopping to drop of a book at Liam's house.*

demolish/knock down or **pull down** *Those houses were all pulled down in the sixties, to make room for a new road.*

detonate/set off *They caught him trying to set off a bomb near the police station.*

devise/work out *We worked out a way to cheat in our exams.*

disappoint/let down *I promised I'd visit my aunt, and I don't want to let her down.*

discard/throw away *He just throws his shirts away when they're dirty.*

discern/make out *We could just about make out the shape of a house through the fog.*

discover/find out *We need to find out what time the next train is.*

discuss/talk about *We didn't really talk about his illness at all.*

distinguish/make out *I could make out a black marking on the bird's head.*

distribute/hand out or **share out** *Oliver, would you hand out the books, please?*

eliminate/do away with *We have done away with all the old rules and regulations.*

emerge/come out *There was a lot of smoke coming out of the chimney.*

emit/give off or **send out** *The box sends out radio signals.*

encounter/come across *I came across some really strange people when I worked in Oxford.*

enter/come in or **go in** *My Dad came in and sat on the sofa.*

eradicate/stamp out *He tried to stamp out any sign of opposition to his regime.*

erase/rub out *The children use pencils, so they can rub out their mistakes.*

erect/put up *Our neighbours put up a large fence between our gardens.*

establish/set up *She set up a special school for bullied children.*

excuse/let off *We usually get homework, but as it was the last day, our teacher let us off.*

exhaust/tire out or **wear out** *All that walking has worn me out!*

experience/go through *They went through a period of great hardship during the war.*

extinguish/put out *We managed to put out the fire with a bucket of water.*

faint/pass out *My head started to swim, and I thought I was going to pass out.*

fasten/do up *Can you help me do up the buttons on this dress?*

increase/go up *Prices have gone up a lot since I was last here.*

indicate/point out *They pointed out the exact place where Kennedy was shot.*

inflate/blow up *We need a pump to blow up the rubber mattress.*

install/put in *They had a new kitchen put in last year.*

invent/make up *We liked to make up stories about the old lady who lived down the road.*

maintain/keep up *I read magazines to keep up my French.*

omit/leave out *His biography left out any mention of his first marriage.*

Single verb or phrasal verb?

participate/join in *All the children joined in the games.*

postpone/put off *We decided to put the wedding off until the next year.*

propose/put forward *They put forward a plan to cut costs.*

protrude/stick out *They made fun of me because my ears stuck out.*

raise/put up *Oil companies have put up their prices.*

rebuke/tell off *She told us off for leaving muddy footprints on the carpet.*

reduce/bring down *The government wants to bring down the number of people on hospital waiting lists.*

refuse or **reject/turn down** *She turned down our offer of help.*

replace/put back *Please make sure you put all the chairs back where you found them.*

reprimand/tell off *Dad will tell us off if we use his tools.*

request/ask for *He asked us for a glass of water.*

resemble/take after *Jude's so tall – she takes after her mother.*

return/go back *I left Ireland when I was twenty, and I've never been back.*

rise/go up *Prices have gone up a lot in the last year.*

sacrifice/give up *I wasn't willing to give up working when I had children.*

select/pick out *I picked out some green material for the curtains.*

separate/split up *My parents split up when I was five.*

socialize/go out *We don't go out much.*

subtract/take away *Even if you take away the cost of the materials, they're making a huge profit.*

summon/send for *They sent for a doctor to advise the king.*

support/hold up *Two wooden posts held up the net.*

survive/get through *He got through his ordeal by thinking of his family.*

tolerate/put up with *I won't put up with rudeness.*

yield/give in *Eventually he gave in and agreed to do the work again.*